FAMILY LAW

FOURTH EDITION

The West Paralegal Series

Your options keep growing with West Publishing.
Each year our list continues to offer you more options for every course, new or existing, and on-the-job reference materials. We now have over 140 titles from which to choose.

We are pleased to offer books in the following subject areas:

Administrative Law
Alternative Dispute Resolution
Bankruptcy
Business Organizations/Corporations
Civil Litigation and Procedure
CLA Exam Preparation
Client Accounting
Computer in the Law Office
Constitutional Law
Contract Law
Criminal Law and Procedure
Document Preparation
Environmental Law
Ethics

Family Law
Federal Taxation
Intellectual Property
Introduction to Law
Introduction to Paralegalism
Law Office Management
Law Office Procedures
Legal Research, Writing, and Analysis
Legal Terminology
Paralegal Employment
Real Estate Law
Reference Materials
Torts and Personal Injury Law
Will, Trusts, and Estate Administration

You will find unparalleled, practical teaching support.
Each text is enhanced by instructor and student supplements to ensure the best learning experience possible to prepare for this field. We also offer custom publishing and other benefits such as West's Student Achievement Award. In addition, our sales representatives are ready to provide you with needed and dependable service.

We want to hear from you.
The most important factor in improving the quality of our paralegal texts and teaching packages is active feedback from educators in the field. If you have a question, concern, or observation about any of our materials or you have written a proposal or manuscript, we want to hear from you. Please do not hesitate to contact your local representative or write us at the following address:

West Paralegal Series, 3 Columbia Circle, P.O. Box 15015, Albany, NY 12212-5015.

For additional information point your browser to
http://www.westpub.com/Educate and **http://www.delmar.com**

West Publishing — *Your Paralegal Publisher*
an imprint of Delmar Publishers

an International Thomson Publishing company I(T)P®

FAMILY LAW

FOURTH EDITION

William P. Statsky

WEST PUBLISHING

an International Thomson Publishing company I(T)P®

Albany • Bonn • Boston • Cincinnati • Detroit • London • Madrid
Melbourne • Mexico City • Minneapolis/St. Paul • New York • Pacific Grove
Paris • San Francisco • Singapore • Tokyo • Toronto • Washington

NOTICE TO THE READER

Copyediting:	Patricia Lewis
Text Design:	Roz Stendahl, Dapper Design
Cover Image:	*Lofting Model,* Bronze, 1991. Sculptor: Paul T. Granlund. Represented by Premier Gallery, Minneapolis. Sculpture photography: Stan Waldhauser.
Composition:	Parkwood Composition Services, Inc.

Photo Credits: 146—Photo courtesy of William P. Satsky   149—AP/Wide World Photos, Inc.   327—Georgia Office of Child Support 342—Library of Congress   343—Robert Eckert, EKM Nepenthe   469—AP/Wide World Photos, Inc.

British Library Cataloguing-in-Publication Data. A catalogue record for this book is available from the British Library.

COPYRIGHT © 1978, 1984, 1991, 1996
By West Publishing
an imprint of Delmar Publishers
a division of International Thomson Publishing

The ITP logo is a trademark under license.

Printed in the United States of America

For more information, contact:

Delmar Publishers
3 Columbia Circle, Box 15015
Albany, New York 12212-5015

International Thomson Publishing – Europe
Berkshire House
168–173 High Holborn
London, WC1V 7AA
England

Thomas Nelson Australia
102 Dodds Street
South Melbourne, 3205
Victoria, Austrialia

Nelson Canada
1120 Birchmount Road
Scarborough, Ontario
Canada M1K 5G4

International Thomson Editores
Campos Eliseos 385, Piso 7
Col Polanco
11560 Mexico D F Mexico

International Thomson Publishing GmbH
Königswinterer Strasse 418
53227 Bonn
Germany

International Thomson Publishing – Asia
221 Henderson Road
#05-10 Henderson Building
Singapore 0315

International Thomson Publishing – Japan
Hirakawacho Kyowa Building, 3F
2-2-1 Hirakawacho
Chiyoda-ku, Tokyo 102 Japan

    5 6 7 8 9 10   XXX   03 02 01 00 99 98

Library of Congress Cataloging-in-Publication Data

Statsky, William P.
    Family Law / William . Statsky—4th ed.
        p.   cm.
    Includes index.
    ISBN 0-314-06467-2 (hard : alk. paper)
    1. Domestic relations—United States.   I. Title.
    KF505.S83   1996
    346.7301'5—dc20   95–46551
    [347.30615]   CIP

For my own domestic relations: Pat, Jess, Gabe, Joe, Brenda, Rich, Clara, Bob, Matthew, Stan, Ann, Ann, Ann, et al.

SUMMARY TABLE OF CONTENTS

CONTENTS

APPENDIX □ **H**

Organizations and Resources

TABLE OF CASES

BY THE SAME AUTHOR:

Case Analysis and Fundamentals of Legal Writing, 4th ed. St. Paul: West Publishing Company, 1995 (with J. Wernet)

Essentials of Paralegalism, 2d ed. St. Paul: West Publishing Company, 1993

Essentials of Torts. St. Paul: West Publishing Company, 1994

Inmate Involvement in Prison Legal Services: Roles and Training Options for the Inmate as Paralegal. American Bar Association, Commission on Correctional Facilities and Services, 1974

Introduction to Paralegalism: Perspectives, Problems and Skills, 4th ed. St. Paul: West Publishing Company, 1992

Legal Desk Reference. St. Paul: West Publishing Company, 1990 (with B. Hussey, Michael Diamond, & R. Nakamura).

The Legal Paraprofessional as Advocate and Assistant: Roles, Training Concepts and Materials. Center on Social Welfare Policy and Law, 1971 (with P. Lang)

Legal Research and Writing: Some Starting Points, 4th ed. St. Paul: West Publishing Company, 1993

Legal Thesaurus/Dictionary: A Resource for the Writer and Computer Researcher. St. Paul: West Publishing Company, 1985

Legislative Analysis and Drafting, 2d ed. St. Paul: West Publishing Company, 1984

Paralegal Employment: Facts and Strategies for the 1990s, 2d ed. St. Paul: West Publishing Company, 1993

Paralegal Ethics and Regulation, 2d ed. St. Paul: West Publishing Company, 1993

Torts: Personal Injury Litigation, 3d ed. St. Paul: West Publishing Company, 1995

Rights of the Imprisoned: Cases, Materials and Directions. Indianapolis: Bobbs-Merrill Company, 1974 (with R. Singer)

What Have Paralegals Done? A Dictionary of Functions. National Paralegal Institute, 1973

A NOTE TO THE STUDENT: THE MEANING OF "YOUR STATE"

Throughout many of the assignments in this book, you will see the phrase, "your state," e.g., the state code of your state. The objective of many of these assignments is to help you relate the law outlined in the chapters of this book to the specific law of a particular state: "your state." The phrase, "your state" can have several meanings:

☐ The state where you intend to use your skills—where you hope to be employed.

☐ The state where you are studying (which may be different from the state where you will be employed).

☐ The state where you are now working (which may be different from the state where you hope to be employed).

Ask your teacher which meaning of "state" to use. If the choice is yours and you know the state where you will be employed, select this state as the focus of the assignments in this book.

The selection of a state may depend in part on the availability of certain law books. Chapter 2 (p. 38) lists the most important law books to which someone working in a family law practice should have access.

PREFACE

Say it isn't true. A recent *New York Times* story reported that a well-known divorce attorney was giving out pens to prospective clients that said, "Sue Someone You Love." This is not the image the legal profession wishes to project to the public. Yet newspapers, magazines, and talk shows do seem to give the impression that our society is in a litigation frenzy: "Son Sues to Divorce His Mother," "Wife Demands Half of Husband's Medical Practice in Divorce Settlement," "Surrogate Mother Refuses to Turn Over Baby," "Live-in Lover Seeks Palimony."

Our goal in this book is to sort through the headlines in order to find an accurate picture of the state of family law today and the role of the attorney-paralegal team within it. We are living in an era of great change in the practice of family law. The primary focus of the family law practitioner is no longer adultery and who gets the house. No-fault divorce has made marriage relatively easy to dissolve. The women's movement has helped bring about major shifts in determining what property can be split after a divorce and how to split it. The country has declared war on the "deadbeat" parent who fails to pay child support. Major new enforcement mechanisms have been designed to find these parents and make them pay. To the surprise of many, courts have come to the aid of unmarried fathers seeking to undo the adoption of their children. Science and technology have unleashed new concepts of motherhood and parentage. The law has not been able to keep pace with the scientific revolution taking place in the test tube and in the womb.

In short, there is a lot to talk about! It's a fascinating time to study family law.

CHAPTER FORMAT

Each chapter includes features designed to assist students in understanding the material:

☐ A chapter outline at the beginning of each chapter provides a preview of the major topics discussed in the chapter.

☐ Tables are used extensively to clarify concepts and present detailed information in an organized chart form.

☐ Assignments that ask students to apply concepts to particular fact situations are included in each chapter. These assignments cover critical skills such as analysis, investigation, interviewing, and drafting.

☐ A chapter summary at the end of each chapter provides a concise review of the main concepts discussed.

☐ Selected terms are defined in the margin next to the text to which the terms are relevant.

☐ Key terms are printed in boldface type the first time they appear in the text. A list of key terms also appears at the end of each chapter to help students review important terminology introduced in that chapter.

CHANGES TO THE FOURTH EDITION

☐ Selected court opinions have been added to the book. The opinions have been edited to highlight the family law issues covered in the chapters. Most of the opinions are followed by an assignment that will test the student's grasp of the principles in the opinion. The opinions cover important issues facing our courts today such as the legality of prenuptial and cohabitation agreements, squandering marital assets prior to a property division, and modifying child custody decisions when the custodial parent has a live-in boyfriend.

□ Coverage has been expanded for many topics including mediation, tools to enforce child support obligations, finality of adoptions, and resolving the conflict between genetic mothers and gestational mothers.

□ New and updated forms have been included such as a letter of authorization to obtain confidential information and a declaration of domestic partnership.

□ The focus of chapter 2 has been changed from legal research to the sources of family law and an introduction to the primary and secondary authorities on family law.

□ The interviewing material in chapter 5 has been redesigned to eliminate overlap and to give the chapter a greater checklist orientation.

□ Chapter 15 on the tax consequences of divorce has been restructured to provide greater emphasis on the laws affecting more recent divorces.

■■■■ SUPPLEMENTS

□ An **Instructor's Manual/Test Bank** contains competencies, answers to selected assignments, and teaching suggestions, as well as 30–40 multiple choice and essay questions per chapter.

□ **State Supplements** specific for Texas, California, New York, and Florida provide discussions of key differences in state law. These can be purchased at a discount shrinkwrapped with the text.

□ West's **Paralegal Video Library** includes *The Drama of the Law II* and *I Never Said I Was a Lawyer,* among other videos. Available to qualified adopters.

□ **WESTLAW®**, West's on-line computerized legal research system, offers students hands-on experience with a system commonly used in law offices. Ten hours are free to qualified adopters.

□ **WESTMATE® Tutorial** is an interactive software that introduces students to WESTLAW capabilities off-line.

□ **Strategies and Tips for Paralegal Educators,** a pamphlet by Anita Tebbe of Johnson County Community College, offers specific teaching ideas to instructors to aid students in reaching their educational goals.

■■■■ ACKNOWLEDGMENTS

I wish to thank the following people at West who were most helpful in the emergence of this book: Elizabeth Hannan, Patricia Bryant, and Matthew Thurber.

I also wish to thank users of the Third Edition who responded to a survey, giving us helpful feedback for this revision.

Finally, a word of thanks to the reviewers who made valuable suggestions:

□ Philip A. Augustino
Erie Community College, NY

□ John DeLeo
Central Pennsylvania Business School

□ Ann M. Dobmeyer
Bay Path College, MA

□ Patrick J. Faucheux
Gulf Coast Community College, FL

□ Merle B. Hamre
Southern College, FL

□ Kenneth Hill
Durham Technical Community
College, NC

□ Richard Hill
University of Houston—
Downtown, TX

□ Norman W. Holt II
Daytona Beach Community
College, FL

□ William L. Koleszar
Denver Business College, CO

□ Maryanne Manley
The American Institute, AZ

□ Robert E. Nowak
Queens College, NY

□ Jill H. O'Connor
Sacred Heart University, CT

□ Rebecca Parker
Arapahoe Community College, CO

William P. Statsky
San Diego, California

THE SCOPE AND SKILLS OF A FAMILY LAW PRACTICE

▰▰▰ THE SCOPE OF FAMILY LAW

A major theme of family law is the disintegration of the family. To work in an office where family law is practiced, you need compassion, flexibility, skill, and, above all, an ability to handle a wide diversity of problems. While some cases are straightforward and "simple," many are not. A veteran attorney recently observed that a family law practice required everyone "to become an expert in many fields of law and not just one."[1]

Assume that you are a paralegal working for Karen Smith, an attorney in your state. One of the clients of the office is Susan Miller who lives out of state. The attorney receives the following telegram from Ms. Miller:

2/7/96

Karen Smith:

I am leaving the state in a week to come live with my mother. She will help me move everything so that we can start a new life. I must see you as soon as I arrive. Yesterday my husband called from his business. He threatened me and the children. I will bring the twins with me. I don't know where my oldest boy is. He is probably with his father getting into more trouble.

Susan Miller

A checklist is provided below of many of the questions that are potentially relevant to the case of Susan Miller. As a paralegal, you might be asked to conduct preliminary interviews and field investigation on some of the questions. Others may require legal research in the law library. (For an overview of paralegal responsibilities in family law, see the job descriptions in Appendix A at the end of this book.) Many of the technical terms in this list will be defined

---

1. John Greenya, *Family Affairs: Seven Experts in Family Law Discuss Their Experiences . . .*, 9 The Washington Lawyer 23, 31 (November/December 1994).

later. Our goal here is simply to demonstrate that the scope of the law covered in a family law practice can be very broad.

Criminal Law

□ Has Mr. Miller committed a crime? What kind of threats did he make? Did he assault his wife and children?

□ Has he failed to support his family? If so, is the nonsupport serious enough to warrant criminal action against him?

□ Even if he has committed a crime, would it be wise for Ms. Miller to ask the district attorney to investigate and prosecute the case?

□ Is there any danger of further criminal acts by her husband? If so, what can be done, if anything, to prevent them? Can she obtain a restraining order to keep him away?

□ Is Ms. Miller subject to any penalties for taking the children out of state?

Divorce/Separation/Annulment Law

□ What does Ms. Miller want?

□ Does she know what her husband wants to do?

□ Does she have grounds for a divorce?

□ Does she have grounds for an annulment? (Were the Millers validly married?)

□ Does she have grounds for a judicial separation?

□ Does Mr. Miller have grounds for a divorce, annulment, or judicial separation against his wife?

Law of Custody

□ Does Ms. Miller want permanent custody of all three children? (Is she the natural mother of all three? Is he their natural father? Are there any paternity problems?) Will Mr. Miller want custody? What is the lifestyle of the parent or parents seeking custody? Is joint custody an option?

□ If she does not want a divorce, annulment, or judicial separation, how can she obtain legal custody of the children?

□ Does she want anyone else to be given temporary or permanent custody of any of the children (e.g., a relative)? Will such a person make a claim for custody *against* Ms. Miller?

□ If she wants custody, has she jeopardized her chances of being awarded custody by taking the children out of state?

Support Law

□ Is Mr. Miller adequately supporting his wife? Or, is she supporting him?

□ Is he adequately supporting the three children? Do they have any special medical or school needs? If so, are these needs being met?

□ Are the children now covered under Mr. Miller's health insurance policy? Is Ms. Miller covered? Is there a danger that the policy will be changed?

□ Can Ms. Miller obtain a court order forcing him to support them while she is deciding whether she wants to terminate the marital relationship?

□ If she files for divorce, annulment, or judicial separation, can she obtain a temporary support order while the case is in progress?

□ If she files for divorce, annulment, or judicial separation and loses, can she still obtain a support order against him?

☐ Does Mr. Miller have assets (personal property or real property) against which a support order can be enforced? Is there a danger he might try to hide or transfer these assets?

☐ If he cannot be relied upon for support and she cannot work, does she qualify for public assistance such as Aid to Families with Dependent Children (AFDC)?

☐ Would she be entitled to more support in the state she is coming from or in this state?

☐ Is Mr. Miller supporting any other children such as from a previous marriage? If so, how would this affect his duty to support the three he had with Ms. Miller?

Contract/Agency Law

☐ While she is living apart from her husband, can she enter into contracts with merchants for the purchase of food, clothing, furniture, medical care, prescriptions, transportation, and other necessaries and make *him* pay for them? Can she use his credit?

☐ Has she already entered into such contracts?

☐ Can he obligate her on any of his current debts?

☐ Has she ever worked for him or otherwise acted as his agent?

☐ Has he ever worked for her or otherwise acted as her agent?

☐ Have the children (particularly the oldest child) entered into any contracts under their own names? If so, who is liable for such contracts? Can they be canceled or disaffirmed?

Real and Personal Property Law

☐ Do either or both of them own any real property, e.g., land? If so, how is the real property owned? Individually? As tenants by the entirety? Who provided the funds for the purchase?

☐ What rights does she have in his property?

☐ What rights does he have in her property?

☐ What is his income? Can his wages be garnished? Is he in a profit-sharing plan at work? What pension or other retirement rights does he have?

☐ What other personal property exists—cars, bank accounts, stocks, bonds, furniture? Who owns this property?

Corporate Law/Business Law

☐ What kind of business does Mr. Miller have? Is it a corporation? A partnership? A sole proprietorship? If the parties separate and obtain a divorce, will Ms. Miller be entitled to a share of the business as part of the division of marital property?

☐ What are the assets and liabilities of the business?

☐ Is there a danger that Mr. Miller or his business might go into bankruptcy? If so, how would this affect her rights to support and to a share of the marital property?

Tort Law

☐ Has he committed any torts against her (e.g., assault, conversion)?

☐ Has she committed any torts against him?

☐ Can one spouse sue another in tort?

□ Have the children (particularly the oldest) damaged any property or committed any torts for which the parents might be liable?

Civil Procedure/Conflict of Law

□ If a court action is brought (e.g., divorce, custody, separate maintenance), what court would have jurisdiction? A court in this state? A court in the state where he resides?

□ How can service of process be made?

□ If she sues and obtains a judgment in this state, can it be enforced in another state?

Evidence Law

□ What factual claims will Ms. Miller be making, e.g., that Mr. Miller has money that could be used to support the family?

□ What testimonial evidence (oral statements of witnesses) exists to support her claims?

□ How much of this evidence is admissible in court?

□ How much of the admissible evidence is likely to be believed by a judge or jury?

□ What other relevant evidence should be pursued, e.g., documentary evidence such as marriage and birth certificates, records of purchases?

□ Whose depositions should be taken, if any?

□ What claims will Mr. Miller make against Ms. Miller? What evidence is he likely to use to support these claims? What objections can be made to this evidence?

Juvenile Law

□ Can a dependency or child neglect petition be brought against Mr. Miller? Against Ms. Miller?

□ Why is she upset about her eldest son? Has he committed any "acts of delinquency"?

□ Is he a Person in Need of Supervision (PINS) or a Child in Need of Supervision (CHINS)?

□ If he has damaged anyone else's property, can she be financially responsible for the damage?

Tax Law

□ Have Mr. Miller and his wife filed joint tax returns in the past?

□ Are there any refunds due (or money owed) on past returns?

□ In a property settlement following a divorce or separation, what would be the most advantageous settlement for Ms. Miller from a tax perspective?

□ What arrangement might Mr. Miller seek in order to obtain the best tax posture? What is negotiable? What will he be willing to give up in order to obtain his tax objectives? Will he, for example, cooperate in allowing her to have sole custody of the children in exchange for her cooperation in ensuring that his alimony payments are deductible?

Estate Law

□ Do they both have their own wills? If so, who are the beneficiaries? If there is no divorce, can he leave Ms. Miller out of his will entirely?

□ Who receives their property if they die without a will?

□ Are there any life insurance policies on Mr. Miller's life, with Ms. Miller or the children as beneficiaries? If so, is he allowed to change these beneficiaries?

Professional Responsibility/Ethics

□ Is Mr. Miller represented by counsel? If so, can we contact Mr. Miller directly, or must all communications to him be made through his attorney? If he is not yet represented, are there limitations on what we can and cannot say to him?

□ If Ms. Miller can find her eldest son, can she simply take him away from her husband when the latter is not around? Would this be illegal? What is the ethical obligation of an attorney whose client is about to do something illegal?

Miscellaneous

□ Can Mr. Miller be forced to pay her legal fees that grow out of present and future difficulties together?

□ Can she be forced to pay his legal fees?

The purpose of this book is to examine many of the above questions that could arise in a case such as *Miller v. Miller*. More specifically, the purpose is to equip you with the skills needed to be able to raise and to help answer such questions that could arise in your state.

■■■■■ THE SKILLS ASSIGNMENTS: GENERAL INSTRUCTIONS

INSTRUCTIONS FOR ASSIGNMENTS

The study of law should always have two components:

□ *Knowledge* of what the law is

□ *Skills* to use that knowledge on behalf of clients as part of a legal service delivery team

To help you develop such skills, this book provides various *assignments* that ask you to examine law books containing family law material such as:

codes	encyclopedias
digests	practice manuals
court rules	treatises

One of our objectives is to increase your ability to use such books. Indeed, they constitute the entire subject matter of chapter 2.

In the practice of family law, the attorney and the paralegal may need to:

□ Find a standard form in a practice book that they will adapt to the needs of a current client.

□ Check the court rules to determine how many days a client has to file a court document.

□ Check the state statutory code to determine the grounds for a divorce.

□ Find case law to determine whether your state courts have ever rendered a decision on a set of facts similar to the facts of a current client. Etc.

The assignments in this book are designed to train you to accomplish such tasks while you are studying the basic principles of family law.

Each law book (or set of law books) has its own peculiar features. Unfortunately, a common feature of many books is that the material in them is poorly organized. *If you are able to use the index of these books, however, 70 percent of the battle has been won.* The **CARTWHEEL** (Exhibit 1.1) is an index technique. Its objective can be simply stated: to help you develop the habit of phrasing every word involved in the client's problem *fifteen to twenty different ways!* When you go to the index of a law book, you naturally begin looking up the words and phrases that you think should lead you to the relevant material in the book. If you do not find anything on point, two conclusions are possible:

□ There is nothing on point in the law book.

□ You checked the wrong words in the index.

Too often we make the mistake of thinking that the first conclusion is accurate. Nine times out of ten, the second conclusion is more accurate. The solution is to be able to phrase a word in as many different ways and in as many different contexts as possible. Hence, the CARTWHEEL.

Suppose the problem of the client involved, among other things, a wedding. The structure of the CARTWHEEL for this example is illustrated in Exhibit 1.1.

The first step would be to look up the word "wedding" in the index of any law book. Assume that you are not successful with this word (either because the word is not in the index or because the page or section references after the word in the index do not lead you to relevant material in the body of the book). The next step is to think of as many different phrasings and contexts of the word "wedding" as possible. This is where the eighteen steps of the CART-WHEEL can be useful.

If you applied the steps of the CARTWHEEL to the word "wedding," here are some of the words and phrases that you would check:

1. *Broader words:* celebration, ceremony, rite, ritual, formality, festivity, etc.

2. *Narrower words:* civil wedding, church wedding, golden wedding, proxy wedding, sham wedding, shotgun marriage, etc.

3. *Synonyms:* marriage ceremony, nuptial, etc.

4. *Antonyms:* alienation, annulment, divorce, separation, legal separation, judicial separation, etc.

5. *Closely related words:* matrimony, marital, conjugal, domestic, husband, wife, bride, license, anniversary, custom, children, blood test, premarital, spouse, relationship, family, home, consummation, cohabitation, sexual relations, betrothal, minister, wedlock, oath, contract, community property, name change, domicile, residence, etc.

6. *Procedural terms:* action, suit, statute of limitations, complaint, discovery, defense, petition, jurisdiction, court, superior court, county court, etc.

7. *Agencies:* Bureau of Vital Statistics, County Clerk, Department of Social Services, License Bureau, Secretary of State, Justice of the Peace, etc.

8. *Long shots:* dowry, common law, single, blood relationship, fraud, religion, illegitimate, remarriage, antenuptial, alimony, bigamy, pregnancy, gifts, chastity, impotence, incest, virginity, support, custody, consent, paternity, etc.

If the CARTWHEEL can generate this many words and phrases from a starting point of just one word (wedding), potentially thousands more can be generated when you subject all of the important words from the client's case to the CARTWHEEL. Do you check them all in the index volume of every code, digest, encyclopedia, practice manual, and treatise? No. You can't spend your

□ **EXHIBIT 1.1 The CARTWHEEL: Using the Index of Law Books**

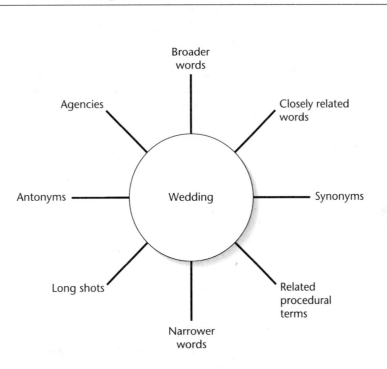

1. Identify all the *major words* from the facts of the client's problem, e.g., wedding (most of these facts can be obtained from the intake memorandum written following the initial interview with the client). Place each word or small set of words in the center of the CARTWHEEL.

2. In the index, look up all of these words.

3. Identify the *broader categories* of the major words.

4. In the index, look up all of these broader categories.

5. Identify the *narrower* categories of the major words.

6. In the index, look up all of these narrower categories.

7. Identify all *synonyms* of the major words.

8. In the index, look up all of these synonyms.

9. Identify all of the *antonyms* of the major words.

10. In the index, look up all of these antonyms.

11. Identify all words that are *closely related* to the major words.

12. In the index, look up all of these closely related words.

13. Identify all *procedural* terms related to the major words.

14. In the index, look up all of these procedural terms.

15. Identify all *agencies,* if any, that might have some connection to the major words.

16. In the index, look up all of these agencies.

17. Identify all *long shots.*

18. In the index, look up all of these long shots.

Note: The above categories are not mutually exclusive.

entire legal career in the law library working on one case! Common sense will tell you when you are on the right track and when you are needlessly duplicating your efforts. You may get lucky and find what you are after in a few minutes. For most important tasks in any line of work (or play), however, being comprehensive is usually time-consuming.

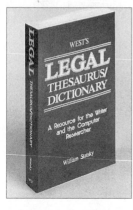

A legal thesaurus or a general thesaurus can often be helpful in generating word alternatives when using the CARTWHEEL technique. See, for example, West's *Legal Thesaurus/Dictionary* or *Roget's International Thesaurus*.

As indicated in the chart, the categories may overlap a bit; they are not mutually exclusive. Also, it is not significant whether you place a word in one category or another as long as the word comes to your mind as you comb through the index. The CARTWHEEL is, in effect, a *word association game* that should become second nature to you with practice. Perhaps some of the word selections in the above categories seem a bit far-fetched. You will not know for sure, however, whether a word will be fruitful until you try it. Be imaginative, and take some risks.

ASSIGNMENT 1.1

Cartwheel the following words:

a. cruelty

b. support

c. paternity

d. sex

ASSIGNMENT 1.2

a. The statutory code of your state probably has a number of different statutes that deal with "children." Use its indexes to help you find as many of these statutes as you can (up to a maximum of ten). Use the CARTWHEEL to help you think of many different phrasings and contexts for the word "children." Give a brief summary of what each statute says about children.

b. Repeat the above assignment for the word "woman."

Throughout the chapters of this book, you will find eleven major kinds of skill assignments:

On the pages where these assignments are found, you will be given *specific instructions*. In addition, a set of *general instructions* is available for each of the eleven categories of assignments. These general instructions are in chapter 1 and will be discussed next. Hence, throughout the remaining chapters of this book, you will be referred back to this chapter for *general instructions* for most of the assignments.

STATE-CODE ASSIGNMENT

A great deal of family law grows out of the state statutory law written by your state legislature. This law will be found within a multivolume state **statutory code.**

It is important that you become acquainted with the family law sections of your statutory code. Many of the assignments in this book ask you to examine this code on a particular family law topic.

The general instructions for all statutory code assignments are as follows:

▰▰▰ General Instructions for the State-Code Assignment

1. The first step is to make sure you know the name and location of the statutory code for your state. Some states have more than one code—each from a different publisher.

2. Be sure you are using the latest edition of the state code.

3. Use the CARTWHEEL technique to help you use the various indexes in the code. (There is often a general index at the end of the code volumes as well as smaller indexes after each volume or set of volumes covering the same topic area.)

4. Statutes can be changed or repealed, and new statutes can be added. Be sure that you are aware of such modifications by:

□ Checking the pocket part, if any, of every volume you use

□ Checking replacement volumes, if any

□ Checking supplement volumes or pamphlets, if any

□ Shepardizing the statute. To **shepardize** something means to use the volumes of *Shepard's Citations* to obtain specific information about a document. When you shepardize a statute, you go to the set of *Shepard's Citations* covering your state code and examine all of the references provided on your statute, e.g., amendments, repeals, opinions interpreting the statute. Find the citation of your statute in black bold print within each *Shephard's* pamphlet and bound volume. The references, if any, will be found in columns immediately beneath the citation of your statute.

5. It is also possible to find statutes electronically. If you have access to WESTLAW or LEXIS, you can locate the statutes of every state "on-line." To look for statutes on a family law topic, you go to the database that contains the statutes of your state legislature and formulate a "query," which is simply a question. The CARTWHEEL can help you decide what words or phrases to use in your query.

6. Give a complete **citation** to every statute that you think covers the assignment. (A citation is a reference to any material printed on paper or stored in a computer database. It is the "address" where you can locate and read the material.) Ask your teacher to explain the standard citation format used in your state. It will often include components such as:

□ The title or chapter number of the statute

□ The abbreviated name of the code

□ The section number of the statute

□ The date of the code. (Use the date you find on the spine of the volume, or the date you find on the title page, or the latest copyright year—in this order of preference.)

7. When you quote from a statute, use quotation marks around the language you are quoting.

8. If the assignment asks you to apply the statute to the facts of a problem in the assignment, follow the General Instructions for the Legal-Analysis Assignment, page 21.

9. When you need help in understanding a statute, use the following approaches:

□ See if there are definition statutes that define some of the words in the statute you are examining. (If such definition statutes exist, they will usually precede the statute you are examining at the beginning of the cluster of statutes on that topic.)

□ Examine cases that have interpreted the statute. You can obtain leads to these cases, if any exist, by checking the *Notes to Decisions,* which are summaries of cases and are found immediately after the text of the statute in annotated editions of the code. (**Annotated** simply means organized by subject matter with research references such as Notes to Decisions or other commentary.) You can also find cases interpreting the statute by shepardizing the statute.

—*Continued*

—*Continued*

10. If you cannot find what you are looking for in the statutory code, proceed as follows:

☐ Repeat step 3 above. Frequently, the difficulty is the failure to use the indexes creatively. Do the CART-WHEEL exercise again to try to come up with more words and phrases to be checked in the indexes of the statutory code.

☐ Check the court rules of your state courts to determine whether they treat the topic you are pursuing.

☐ Check the constitution of your state to determine whether it treats the topic you are pursuing.

☐ Find out if any court opinions have been written by your state courts on the topic you are pursuing. For techniques to find court opinions, see the General Instructions for the Court-Opinion Assignment, page 26.

ASSIGNMENT 1.3

a. What is the name of the statutory code of your state? (If more than one exists, list each one.)

b. Who publishes it?

c. How is it updated? By pocket parts? By supplemental pamphlets? Both?

d. Use the indexes of the code to find any statute on the grounds for divorce in your state. Give the citation of this statute. See instruction 6 in the General Instructions for the State-Code Assignment on the information to include in your citation. (See also Assignment 13.1 in Chapter 13.)

e. In addition to printing the text of the statute you have selected, what other information does the code provide about the statute, e.g., summary of cases interpreting the statute (Notes to Decisions), historical data about the statute? Give an overview of the kinds of information provided.

f. In question (c) you indicated how your code is updated. Use all of these updating features to determine whether there have been any changes in the statute you identified in question (d) since the date that the bound volume containing the statute was published. Summarize any changes.

g. What is the name of the set of *Shepard's Citations* that will enable you to shepardize the statutes of your state code?

h. Assume that your state legislature passed a statute on family law two weeks ago. Since the statute is so recent, it may not be mentioned anywhere in your state code. Later, it will be included in one of the code's updating features. Assume further, however, that you want to read this statute now. You could call the legislature and ask that a copy of the new statute be sent to you. Check with your librarian to find out if there are other ways to obtain recently enacted state statutes.

LEGAL-ANALYSIS ASSIGNMENT

Legal Analysis The application of rules to facts for the purpose of resolving a legal dispute or preventing one from arising.

Our concern here is to provide an introduction to legal reasoning or **legal analysis.** The process can be diagrammed as follows:

$$\boxed{\text{Facts}} \; + \; \boxed{\text{Rule}} \; = \; \boxed{\begin{array}{c} \text{Application} \\ \text{of Rule to Facts} \\ \text{Leading to a Conclusion} \end{array}}$$

Let's look at an example:

Facts: George and Helen are married. One day after a big argument, George walks out of the house and says, "Good-by. Find someone else to take care of you." As he walks out, he resolves to stay away forever.

Rule: One spouse abandons another by leaving without any intention of returning.

Application of rule to facts: When George walked out of the house resolving to stay away forever, he left "without any intention of returning." This is abandonment.

Most legal analysis, however, is not this simple. This can be due to a number of reasons, including:

☐ A word or phrase in the rule is ambiguous.

☐ You feel that you need more facts than you are given.

AMBIGUITY IN THE RULE *Facts:* George and Helen are married. One day after a big argument, George walks out of the apartment and says, "Good-by. Find someone else to take care of you." As he walks out, he resolves to stay away forever. He moves downstairs to a vacant, never-used room in the same building he and his wife jointly own. The room has its own exit to the street.

Rule: One spouse abandons another by leaving without any intention of returning.

There is an ambiguity in the rule. What does "leaving" mean? At least two interpretations are possible:

☐ Moving out of the entire dwelling.

☐ Moving out of whatever part of the dwelling in which both spouses normally live together.

Which is the correct definition of "leaving"? The difference in the definitions is critical. Depending on which definition is adopted, a different result is reached:

☐ According to the first definition, George has not abandoned Helen because he did not move out of the entire dwelling.

☐ According to the second definition, George did abandon Helen since he moved out of the rooms where they both normally lived. Under this definition, he can commit abandonment without moving out of the entire building.

Your task in legal analysis is to be sensitive to such ambiguity in the rules that you are trying to apply to facts. Unfortunately, most students are not. They do not like to search for ambiguity; they accept language at face value. To combat this tendency, you should look at every word in the rule you are applying and ask yourself: What is the definition of this word? Is more than one definition possible? If my initial answer is no, I need to think harder! Am I sure that both sides of the controversy would agree on the definition of the word I am examining?

When you are using legal analysis in an interoffice memorandum or in a school examination, one of the biggest mistakes you can make is to hit the reader over the head with one conclusion. Don't overlook ambiguity. When it exists, find it and write about it. Good legal analysis articulates both sides of the controversy. If you personally favor one side over the other, you may state your opinion, but only after you have placed yourself in the shoes of both sides and presented the best argument for each.

Once you have identified ambiguity in the rule being applied from the perspective of both sides, what do you do next? How do you *resolve* the ambiguity?

You would have to do legal research, e.g., find out whether any courts have interpreted any of the ambiguous words/phrases. Has a court ever defined the word "abandons" in our rule? If so, you need to find the opinion containing the definition. (For purposes of the legal-analysis assignments in this book, however, you will not do any legal research unless the instructions in the assignment, or your instructor, tell you otherwise.)

THE NEED FOR MORE FACTS   In the process of trying to connect rules to facts, you may sometimes feel that you need more facts to assess whether the rule applies. If so, state what additional facts you would like to have and *state why they may be helpful to your analysis.*

In the example involving George and Helen, suppose we are told that George said to Helen, "Good-by. Find someone else to take care of you," but we are not told whether he walked out. In your analysis, you would have to point out that the facts do not state what George did immediately after he made this statement to Helen. You need additional facts. You need to know whether he left the building or any part of the building after he made the statement. The rule refers to "leaving," and you do not know whether or how he left.

Also, if the facts do not clearly show that George left with the intent of never returning, you would need additional facts to help resolve the intent issue. For example:

- □ Did he take his clothes with him?
- □ Did he speak to anyone else after he left about what he was doing?
- □ How far away did he go when he left?
- □ Did he change his address officially, e.g., at the post office?
- □ Did he open any new bank accounts or change old ones?
- □ Did he call Helen or otherwise contact her after he left? If so, how long after he left, how often, and about what?

State why you need the additional facts. For example, if George took his clothes with him when he left, it would be some indication that his departure was permanent, i.e., that he had no intention of returning when he left. This should be stated as such in your legal analysis.

ANALYSIS OF ELEMENTS   One of the most important skills of legal analysis is the ability to break down any rule into its **elements.** An element of a rule is defined as follows:

□ **Element**

1. A *portion* of a rule that can conveniently be discussed separately from the other elements, and

2. A *precondition* of the applicability of the entire rule (if one of the elements of the rule does not apply, the entire rule does not apply).

To a very large extent, legal analysis proceeds by element analysis, as we shall see. In addition, we use element analysis as an aid in performing other tasks. For example:

- □ When drafting a complaint, the drafter often tries to allege enough facts to establish each element of the cause of action. (A cause of action is a legally acceptable reason for suing; it is simply a theory of recovery.)

Element   A portion of a rule that can conveniently be discussed separately from the rest and is a precondition to the applicability of the entire rule.

☐ When a trial judge gives instructions (the charge) to a jury, he or she must cover all of the elements of the cause of action and of the defenses. When counsel submits proposed instructions to the judge, the elements must likewise be covered.

☐ When an attorney is conducting a deposition, he or she will frequently organize the questions around the elements of the causes of action and defenses in the case.

☐ The organization of a memorandum of law will often follow the list of elements of the rules being discussed.

A major characteristic of *sloppy* legal analysis is that it does not clearly take the reader through the elements of a rule. Good analysis discusses every element, with an emphasis on the element(s) in contention. No element is passed over.

Suppose you are analyzing the following rule found in a statute:

§ 25–403   A pharmacist must not sell prescription drugs to a minor.

Note that the rule is not broken down into elements. You must identify the elements on your own:

Elements of §25–403

1. Pharmacist
2. Must not sell
3. Prescription drugs
4. To a minor

No violation exists unless all four elements of this statute are established. If a pharmacist sells simple aspirin (a nonprescription drug), he or she is not liable under the statute. The third element cannot be established. Hence no violation, since one of the elements (preconditions) cannot be met.

For a number of reasons, rules such as statutes and regulations can be difficult to break into elements. For example, the rule may be long or may contain:

☐ Lists
☐ Alternatives
☐ Exceptions or provisos

Nevertheless, the same process is used. You must take the time to dissect the rule into its component elements. Examine the following rule and its elements:

§ 5   While representing a client in connection with contemplated or pending litigation, a lawyer shall not advance or guarantee financial assistance to his client, except that a lawyer may advance or guarantee court costs, expenses of investigation, expenses of medical examination, and costs of obtaining and presenting evidence provided the client remains ultimately liable for such expenses.

Elements of § 5

1. A lawyer
2. Representing a client in connection with contemplated litigation or in connection with pending litigation.
3. Advance financial assistance to his client or guarantee financial assistance to his client, except that the following is proper:

a. lawyer advances or guarantees court costs, or

b. lawyer advances or guarantees expenses of investigation, or

c. lawyer advances or guarantees expenses of medical examination, or

d. lawyer advances or guarantees costs of obtaining and presenting evidence *provided the client remains ultimately liable for all expenses ("a"–"d").*

When an element is stated in the alternative, list all the alternatives within the same element. Alternatives related to one element should be kept within the phrasing of that element. The same is true of exception or proviso clauses. State them within the relevant element since they are intimately related to the applicability of that element.

In the above example, the most complicated element of § 5 is the third—(3). Within it there are lists, alternatives, an exception, and a proviso. But they all relate to the same point of the propriety of financial assistance. None of the subdivisions of the third element should be stated as a separate element. You sometimes must do some unraveling of a rule in order to identify its elements. This certainly had to be done with the third element of § 5. Do not be afraid to pick the rule apart in order to cluster its thoughts around unified themes that should stand alone as elements. Diagram the rule for yourself as you examine it.

If more than one rule is involved in a statute, regulation, constitutional provision, charter, ordinance, etc., treat one rule at a time. (Often each sentence can be treated as a separate rule.) Every rule should have its own elements, and, when appropriate, each element should be subdivided into its separate components, such as alternatives, exceptions, etc.

Once you have broken the rule into its elements, you have the structure of the analysis in front of you. Each element becomes a separate section of your analysis. You discuss one element at a time, concentrating on those that pose the greatest difficulties.

ASSIGNMENT 1.4

Break the following rules into their elements:

a. § 800. The parties can by mutual agreement elect to terminate their separation agreement.

b. § 52. A court of this State shall not exercise its jurisdiction under this Act if at the time of filing the petition a proceeding concerning the custody of the child was pending in a court of another state exercising jurisdiction substantially in conformity with this Act, unless the proceeding is stayed by the court of the other state because this State is a more appropriate forum or for other reasons.

c. § 10.2. With respect to a child who has no presumed father under Section 4, an action may be brought by the child, the mother or personal representative of the child, the appropriate state agency, the personal representative or a parent of the mother if the mother has died, a man alleged or alleging himself to be the father, or the personal representative or a parent of the alleged father if the alleged father has died or is a minor.

d. § 107(b). When the mental or physical condition (including the blood group) of a party, or a person in the custody or under the legal control of a party, is in controversy, the court in which the action is pending may order the party to submit to a physical or mental examination by a physician or to produce for examination the person in his custody or legal control. The order may be made only on motion for good cause shown and upon the notice to the person to be examined and to all parties and shall specify time, place, manner, conditions, and scope of the examination and the person or persons by whom it is to be made.

To do legal analysis, you must identify the **legal issue.** To fail to identify the issue would be like trying to steer a ship without a rudder or to drive a car without the steering wheel: your legal analysis would drift aimlessly.

A legal issue has two components:

☐ A brief quote from the element of the rule in contention

☐ The major facts to which you are applying that element

In formal legal analysis, both components should be present in your statement of the legal issue.

Every element of a rule is potentially the basis of a separate issue. A rule with five elements, for example, could lead to five separate issues, each structured around whether one of the elements applies. In practice, however, it is rare for every element to lead to a separate issue. This is because every element of a rule will probably not be an **element in contention.** To have such an element, you must be able to make a reasonable prediction that the parties to the dispute will probably disagree on whether the element applies. If it is clear that both parties will agree on the applicability or nonapplicability of a particular element, it would be a waste of time to construct an issue around that element and to spend time analyzing it.

At the time you write your memorandum, you may not know for certain what the other side will eventually say about the applicability of a rule. You must do your best to anticipate what your opponent *might* argue about the rule and any element within it.

There are two main kinds of disagreements that the parties can have about an element:

1. *Disagreement about the facts.* If you anticipate that the other side will disagree over whether the facts fit within an element, you should construct an issue around that element. In a child custody case, for example, each parent may present numerous conflicting facts on whether it would be in the "best interest" of the child to be placed with one parent or the other. An issue clearly exists on the element of "best interest."

Sometimes fact gaps will interfere with your ability to identify issues. (See the earlier discussion on the need for more facts.) If, for example, a tax deduction can be taken for alimony payments, but we are not told in the problem whether the alimony was in fact paid by the ex-husband, we have a fact gap. We will not know whether there is an alimony-tax issue until we close this gap by finding out.

2. *Disagreement about definitions.* If you anticipate that the other side will disagree over the definition of an element, you should construct an issue around that element. We saw an example of this earlier when we asked whether "leaving" in the abandonment rule meant moving out of the entire dwelling or moving out of that part of the dwelling in which both spouses normally live together.

Let's return to the pharmacy example:

§ 25–403 A pharmacist must not sell prescription drugs to a minor.

Suppose the following facts are involved:
Facts: Fred Jones owns a drugstore and is a licensed pharmacist. One day he sells tetracycline to Phil, a nineteen-year-old male.

Legal Issue A legal question; a question of whether a particular rule of law applies to a particular set of facts.

Element in Contention The portion of a rule (i.e., the element) that forms the basis of a legal issue because the parties disagree on the interpretation or application of that element to the facts of the case.

Has Fred violated § 25–403? Step one in answering this question is to break § 25–403 into its elements:

Elements of § 25–403

1. Pharmacist
2. Must not sell
3. Prescription drugs
4. To a minor

These elements become a checklist from which we begin to explore the presence of legal issues.

Elements 1 and 2 are not realistic candidates for legal issues. There is no reasonable doubt over whether Fred is a pharmacist and over whether he engaged in selling. The facts clearly tell us that he is a pharmacist who did make a sale.

What about element 3? Should it become the basis of a legal issue? Did Fred sell a "prescription drug"? Is tetracycline such a drug? There is a *factual* gap that hinders our ability to answer the question at this point. The facts do not tell us whether tetracycline is sold over-the-counter or whether Phil purchased it by prescription. Further interviewing or investigation is needed on this factual question. This is a "next step" that should be listed at the end of the memo.

Element 4 clearly poses some ambiguity. What is a minor? Is a nineteen-year-old a minor? It is not clear. This ambiguity should prompt the preliminary draft of a legal issue:

Is a nineteen-year-old a "minor" within the meaning of § 25–403?

An alternate (more formal) phrasing of the issue would be as follows:

When a pharmacist sells tetracycline to a nineteen-year-old, has the pharmacist violated § 25–403, which prohibits sales of "prescription drugs" to "a minor"?

Every element is part of a checklist that must be examined in the above manner. If one element is glossed over, a potential legal issue may be missed. Recall again the components of a legal issue:

□ A brief quote from the element in contention
□ The major facts to which you are applying that element

We have just explored how you go about determining whether an element is in contention. The next question is, how do you know which facts are major? Fortunately, the process of determining when an element is in contention will also tell you which facts are major. A fact is major, and therefore should be included in the phrasing of a legal issue, when that fact raises some doubt or ambiguity in your mind on whether the element is in contention. The fact that Phil is a nineteen-year-old is a major fact because this is the fact that prompted us to ask the question, what is a minor? Hence, the reason for the first phrasing of the above issue:

Is a nineteen-year-old a "minor" within the meaning of § 25–403?

Note that the fact that Phil is a male is left out of the statement of the issue. It does not appear to be relevant to the applicability of § 25–403 that the buyer is a male or female. Sex is not major, but age is.

Note also that we have used more facts in the alternative (more formal) phrasing of the same issue, e.g., pharmacist, selling, tetracycline. We phrased the issue in this way for two reasons. First, this phrasing raises the question of the applicability of the entire rule rather than simply one of the elements of the rule. Second, this phrasing contains facts that provide a context to an understanding of the issue even if all of the facts are not major to the element primarily in contention. Both reasons can justify a longer statement of a legal issue, provided the issue does not become so lengthy that it is too awkward to read, and provided the added facts will not detract from the focus on the element primarily in contention. Neither of these difficulties exists in the alternative (more formal) phrasing of our issue.

Examine the following statements of legal issues:

☐ Does § 504 apply?

☐ The issue is the admissibility of the confession.

☐ Does he have the burden of proof?

In general, you should avoid phrasing issues in this way. They are weak and incomplete because of the absence of facts. Legal disputes do not arise in the abstract. There must be a set of facts in order for a legal dispute to exist. You cannot comprehend the issue until you know the facts that give rise to that issue. This does not mean that the statement of the issue must contain a statement of all the facts; again, only the major ones need to be stated, along with perhaps a limited number of additional facts that help give context to the issue. Another reason these three statements of issues are incomplete is that they do not quote the pertinent language in the element of the rule that is in dispute (e.g., that is ambiguous) when applied to the major facts.

To summarize, the two guidelines that should govern the phrasing of issues are as follows:

1. The legal issue should contain a statement of the major facts from the problem that raise the ambiguity in the language of an element. A limited number of context facts may also be added.

2. The legal issue should also contain a brief quotation from the language of the element that is ambiguous in view of the major facts of the problem.

The components of the legal issue do not have to be stated in the above order—as long as both components are present in the legal issue.

ASSIGNMENT 1.5

In each of the following situations, you are given a fact situation plus a rule in the form of a statute. Phrase the legal issue involved in each situation.

a. *Facts:* Len is divorced from Mary, who is now deceased. His twenty-year-old son, Sam, has just graduated from Benton College. Len paid all of Sam's expenses at Benton. Sam has been accepted by the Benton College of Law to study to become an attorney. Len can afford to pay Sam's law school expenses, but refuses to do so. Sam says that his father is obligated to pay these expenses.

  Statute: § 49(g). Child support shall include payment of college expenses if the child has the ability to attend and the parent has the ability to pay.

b. *Facts:* Jane and her two children by a former marriage receive Aid to Families with Dependent Children (AFDC). Jane's friend, Jack, who is a traveling salesman, stays at Jane's apartment during his monthly business trips. This allows him to stay in town five to ten days at a time. He does not give Jane any money while he is with her.

  Statute: § 11351. Whenever an unrelated adult male resides with a family applying for or receiving AFDC, he shall be required to make a financial contribution to the family which shall not be less than it would cost him to provide himself with an independent living arrangement.

One format in which you present your legal analysis to your supervisor is the **interoffice memorandum.** Exhibit 1.2 presents an example.

☐ **EXHIBIT 1.2 Interoffice Memorandum**

INTEROFFICE MEMORANDUM

TO:	Mary Adams
FROM:	George Wilson
DATE:	March 26, 1995
NAME OF CASE:	Hagerty v. Hagerty
OFFICE FILE NO.:	95–49
COURT DOCKET NO.:	B–408–95
RE:	"Serious marital discord" and the refusal to seek alcoholism treatment under § 402(b)

Statement of Assignment

   You have asked me to determine whether our client, Linda Hagerty, can prevent her husband from dissolving the marriage on the ground of "irretrievable breakdown" under § 402(b).

Issue

   Is there "serious marital discord" constituting an "irretrievable breakdown" of a marriage under § 402(b) when one party believes that the marriage can be saved if the other party seeks treatment for alcoholism, which the latter refuses to seek?

Facts

   Paul Hagerty has filed for dissolution of the marriage on the ground of "irretrievable breakdown of the marriage." Linda and Paul Hagerty have been married for four years. They have two children. Paul has a serious drinking problem according to our client. While intoxicated, he breaks furniture and is abusive to the children and his wife. She has repeatedly asked him to seek rehabilitation treatment through AA or some other counseling service. Two months ago she told him that he must leave unless he seeks treatment. He did leave but has refused treatment. She now insists that he return and undergo treatment. He has filed for a dissolution of the marriage on the ground of an "irretrievable breakdown of the marriage." He feels that their marriage is hopeless. Our client wants to defend the action and prevent the dissolution.

Analysis

   Section 402(b) provides as follows:
   A court may make a finding that there has been an irretrievable breakdown of the marriage relationship if the finding is supported by evidence of serious marital discord adversely affecting the attitude of the parties toward the marriage.

Two elements must be present before a court will declare the existence of an "irretrievable breakdown of the marriage":
   (1) serious marital discord;
   (2) adversely affecting the attitude of the parties toward the marriage.

Section 402(b) has been in existence for less than a year. No case law exists defining the terms of § 402(b), and no other statutes exist providing these definitions.

(1) Serious Marital Discord

   Two definitions of the phrase are possible. Mr. Hagerty will argue that "serious marital discord" exists if either party to the marriage feels that there is no likelihood of reconciliation. Our client, on the other hand, should argue that both parties must agree that reconciliation is unlikely, or at least that evidence of marital collapse must exist in addition to the views of only one of the spouses. Under Mr. Hagerty's definition, there is "serious marital discord" because one party (himself in this case) feels that there is no likelihood of reconciliation. Our client feels that a reconciliation is likely if her husband will seek treatment for his alcoholism.

Continued

☐ **EXHIBIT 1.2   Interoffice Memorandum—*Continued***

Our client can argue that "marital discord" was meant to refer to the opinions of two people—the partners to the marriage. The agreement of both sides on the likelihood of reconciliation is critical to a determination of whether the marriage can survive. The lack of such a likelihood in the minds of both spouses amounts to an "irretrievable breakdown."

But our client is convinced that the marriage is retrievable. A court should not rule otherwise when one of the parties takes this position. In her view, Mr. Hagerty is sick and is in no position to judge whether a reconciliation is possible. His refusal to seek help for the treatable illness or sickness of alcoholism should disqualify him from making meaningful assessments as to whether the marriage can survive. The legislature could not have intended that a marriage would end simply at the whim of one of the parties, particularly when the party who wants out is too ill to make a considered judgment on the likelihood of reconciliation.

She can further argue that § 402(b) does not state that either party can obtain a dissolution of the marriage simply because one of the spouses says he or she wants it. The statute calls for "evidence" of "serious marital discord." There must be a showing of irreconcilability. This must mean that a court is required to look at the underlying evidence of whether there is hope. A mere statement by one of the parties that there is no hope is not enough "evidence." More is required. The court should examine Mr. Hagerty's condition and listen to whatever expert witnesses she may be able to call. She will want an opportunity to prove through such witnesses that hope does exist because of treatment. This opportunity is destroyed if the court accepts Mr. Hagerty's statement at face value that the marriage cannot be saved. Section 402(b) calls for a more thorough probe by a court.

Mr. Hagerty, on the other hand, will argue that our client is using the wrong definition of "serious marital discord" for purposes of establishing an "irretrievable breakdown." If either side feels that there is no likelihood of reconciliation, a court should find evidence of "serious marital discord" for purposes of establishing an "irretrievable breakdown." Otherwise, one of the parties could force a dead marriage to continue out of stubbornness, unreasonableness, or malice. The legislature could not have intended such a result.

Mr. Hagerty will argue that our client told him to leave and to enter treatment. We can probably assume from the facts that Mr. Hagerty does not want to enter treatment or that he thinks treatment will not be effective. In either event, Mrs. Hagerty has laid down a condition that Mr. Hagerty says cannot be met. He will argue that to force him into treatment would be as unproductive as to force him to continue his marriage.

He will further try to argue that our client's actions demonstrate that even she feels that "serious marital discord" exists. She threw him out, and she insisted on an unacceptable condition. She may say that she thinks the marriage is salvageable, but her actions point to the opposite conclusion.

(2) Adversely Affecting the Attitude of the Parties Toward the Marriage

It is unlikely that this element will be in contention. Both parties will probably argue that the difficulties have adversely affected their views of the marriage. The phrase "adversely affecting" is not defined in the statute or in any court opinions. An "attitude" that has been "adversely" affected means no more than negative feelings toward something—the marriage. Even Mrs. Hagerty cannot deny that she has negative feelings about the marriage as a result of the controversy surrounding alcoholism. She may not think the marriage is hopeless, but her feelings are certainly negative as evidenced by the fact that she told him to leave the house.

Continued

☐ **EXHIBIT 1.2   Interoffice Memorandum—*Continued***

It might be significant to note that the second element refers to "parties"—in the plural. The statute does not say "attitude of one of the parties." This point might bolster Mrs. Hagerty's argument on the first element that the legislature intended <u>both</u> parties to feel that reconciliation was not possible.

Conclusion

The only element in contention will be the first. I think that Mr. Hagerty has the stronger argument. If Mr. Hagerty feels that the treatment for his alcoholism will not help the marriage and if he refuses to undergo this treatment, it is difficult to avoid the conclusion that the parties to the marriage cannot be reconciled. The main argument favoring our client is that the legislature may not have intended a marriage to be terminated this easily.

NEXT STEPS

There are two things that I have not yet done on this case. Let me know if you want me to do either of them:

(1) I have not yet checked the legislative history of § 402(b) to determine whether it will provide any guidance on the meaning of § 402(b).

(2) I have not yet checked the statutes of other states to see if they have the same language as our § 402(b). If such statutes exist, then I need to check cases interpreting these statutes as potential persuasive authority for our case.

ASSIGNMENT 1.6

Bill and Pat were married in State A on March 13, 1973, where they continue to live. They have one child Brenda, age fifteen. Since 1990, Bill and Pat have been having marital difficulties. Bill is a traveling salesman who spends a good deal of time away from State A. From 1991 to 1994, he did not see his family at all. He returned on February 4, 1995. He and Pat attended marital counseling sessions for about three months. By the summer of 1995, problems again arose. Bill left home. On the day he left, he said to Pat, "If you can straighten yourself out, I'll consider coming back." He packed all of his clothes and books, but left behind the high school trophy he received for swimming. Although the departure was bitter, both sides agreed to maintain their joint checking account. Bill made deposits in the account. Pat wrote checks on the account to cover house expenses. In September of 1995, Bill contacted a real estate broker in State B about renting an apartment for six months in that state. The broker suggested tax advantages of buying a condominium in State B as opposed to renting. Bill was persuaded. He had been in State B only once or twice for his job, but wanted to explore the possibility of more extensive business opportunities there. On October 1, 1995, the broker called to inform Bill of a good condominium prospect in State B. On October 5, 1995 Bill was killed in an automobile accident on a highway in State B while on the way to examine the condominium for the first time.

State B wants Bill's estate to pay a state inheritance tax on the theory that at the time of death, Bill was domiciled in State B. The representative of Bill's estate disagrees and claims that Bill was domiciled in State A at the time of death.

In State B the following statute exists, which is the basis of State B's claim:

§ 14.   Inheritance taxes are owed by persons who die domiciled in this state, which exists when the decedent had a physical presence in the state with the intent of making the state a permanent home.

Prepare an interoffice memorandum of law on the question of State B's right to inheritance taxes. Do not do any legal research on the problem. Do the memo solely on the basis of the information provided above.

The office file number is 95–421. There is no court docket number since no court action has yet been initiated. The Tax Department of State B has taken the position that inheritance taxes are due under § 14.

The law office where you work has been retained by the representative of Bill's estate, who does not want to pay the inheritance tax to State B. Since the inheritance tax rate for State A is lower than for State B, it would be to the advantage of the estate to obtain a ruling that at the time of death, Bill was domiciled in State A.

For purposes of this assignment, you can assume following definitions apply:

□ *Physical presence:* actually being in a place

□ *Intent of making the state a permanent home:* the desire to live in the state indefinitely; the place to which one intends to return when away (a person can have only one permanent home)

General Instructions for the Legal-Analysis Assignments

1. The starting point in the legal-analysis exercise is a set of facts in the assignment. It is to this set of facts that you must apply the rule or rules.

2. How do you find the rule or rules to apply to the facts?

□ By examining the text of the chapter immediately preceding the assignment, or

□ By examining the state code of your state—if you are told to do so in the assignment.

3. Carefully examine each word/phrase in the rule being applied. Break the rule into its elements, and concentrate on those elements in contention.

4. Define each important word/phrase in each element.

5. Determine whether more than one definition exists for each important word/phrase.

6. If more than one definition is possible, state each definition and show what effect the different definitions would have on the result of the analysis. How would each side use the definition that is favorable to itself?

7. State the legal issue(s).

8. Carefully examine each of the facts given to you in the assignment.

9. Note any differences in the fact situation given in the assignment with comparable fact situations discussed in the text of the chapter immediately preceding the assignment. Assess whether such fact differences are significant.

10. If you determine that you need more facts to provide the analysis, state what facts you need and why you would like to have the additional facts. Specifically, how will the additional facts assist in completing the analysis?

11. Analyze the facts from the perspective of both sides. Do not be dogmatic in your analysis. Whenever possible, show how the facts might be interpreted differently by both sides.

12. Give your answers in the format of an interoffice memorandum of law as presented in Exhibit 1.2.

13. Do not do any legal research on the assignment unless you are specifically instructed to do so.

COMPLAINT-DRAFTING ASSIGNMENT

Court litigation begins when one party files a **complaint** against another party. This is the **pleading** that must state a **cause of action** such as negligence, breach of contract, or divorce on the ground of cruelty. (A cause of action is a theory of recovery—a legally acceptable reason for suing.) See Exhibit 1.3 for a sample divorce complaint. Later in chapter 14 we will examine complaints and other procedural matters in greater detail. Here our goal is simply to lay out some guidelines to use for the complaint-drafting assignments throughout the book.

Before you begin drafting the complaint (or any document) from scratch, find out if someone has already prepared a **standard form** that you can use. These are printed in a number of places, including formbooks, manuals, practice texts, some statutory codes, and some court rules. Many legal stationery stores print and sell them. Most are written by private attorneys. Occasionally, how-

Complaint A pretrial document filed in court by one party against another that states a grievance, called a cause of action.

Pleading A formal document that contains allegations and responses of the parties in litigation.

Cause of Action An allegation of facts that, if proved, would give a party a right to judicial relief.

Standard Form A frequently used format for a document such as a contract, complaint, or tax return.

☐ **EXHIBIT 1.3   The Basic Structure of a Complaint**

STATE OF _____ | Caption |

COUNTY OF _____

FAMILY COURT BRANCH

Mary Smith, Plaintiff

         v.   Civil Action No. _____

Fred Smith, Defendant

        COMPLAINT FOR ABSOLUTE DIVORCE | Commencement |

The plaintiff, through her attorney, alleges:

   (1) The jurisdiction of this court is based upon section _____ , title _____
of the State Code (1978).

   (2) The plaintiff is fifty years old.

   (3) The plaintiff is a resident of the State of _____ , County of _____ .
She has resided here for five years immediately preceding the filing of this complaint.

   (4) The parties were married on March 13, 1983 in the State of _____ ,
County of _____ .

   (5) There are no children born of this marriage. | Body |

   (6) The plaintiff and defendant lived and cohabitated together from the date of their
marriage until February 2, 1996 at which time they both agreed to separate because of
mutual incompatibility. This separation has continued voluntarily and without cohabitation for more than two years until the present time.

   (7) Since the separation, the plaintiff has resided at _____
_____ , and the defendant has resided at _____ .

   (8) There is no reasonable likelihood of reconciliation.

WHEREFORE, the plaintiff PRAYS: | Prayer |

(1) For an absolute divorce. | For |

(2) For alimony and a division of property. | Relief. |

(3) For restoration of her maiden name.

(4) For reasonable attorney's fees and costs.

(5) For such other relief as this Court may deem just and proper.

_____   _____

Linda Stout   Mary Smith, Plaintiff

Attorney for Plaintiff

234 Main St.

_____ , _____ 07237

STATE of _____ | Verification |

COUNTY of _____

   Mary Smith, being first duly sworn on oath according to law, deposes and says that
she has read the foregoing complaint by her subscribed and that the matters stated
therein are true to the best of her knowledge, information, and belief.

                                  _____

                                       Mary Smith

Subscribed and sworn to before me on this _____ day of _____ , 19 ____

                                  _____

                                       Notary Public

My commission expires _____

▰▰ General Instructions for the Complaint-Drafting Assignment

1. Your objective is to draft a complaint that would be acceptable to a trial court in your state.

2. Go to your state statutory code and read everything you can about complaints in general and about complaints involving divorce and other domestic relations matters in particular. To help you find material in the statutory code, use the CARTWHEEL technique.

3. Go to the court rules of the courts of your state and read everything you can about complaints in general and about complaints involving divorce and other domestic relations matters in particular. To help you find material in the court rules, use the CARTWHEEL technique.

4. Find out if your state has any standard form complaints written by the court or other official entity. Your state code or court rules will tell you if such forms exist and whether they are optional or required. Caution must be exercised in using standard forms, however. See How to Avoid Abusing a Standard Form, page 24.

5. Many states have practice manuals, formbooks, or other practice materials written by attorneys. On identifying such texts for your state, see the beginning of chapter 2. These materials often contain standard form complaints that may be helpful. See How to Avoid Abusing a Standard Form.

6. In the complaint-drafting assignments of this book, you will often need additional facts in order to write the complaint, e.g., the names of the parties, their addresses, the docket number of the case, some of the basic facts that prompted the plaintiff to file the complaint. You can make up the facts that you need so long as your facts are consistent with the limited facts that are provided in the assignment.

7. The heading or beginning of the complaint is called the *caption*. Normally, it contains:

☐ The name of the court

☐ The parties' names and their litigation status (plaintiff, defendant, etc.)

☐ The docket number assigned by the court

☐ The title of the pleading (complaint for . . .)

8. Each paragraph is usually numbered separately. The content of each paragraph should be limited to a single allegation or to a small number of allegations that are closely related.

9. The *commencement* goes after the caption. Find out what your state requires in the commencement of a complaint (see instructions 1–5 above). Some states require a citation to the statute that gives the court its subject-matter jurisdiction (its power to hear this kind of case—see chapter 14), a statement of basic facts that cover the residency of the plaintiff and the existence of a marriage, etc.

10. The *body* of the complaint contains a statement of the plaintiff's cause of action. In a divorce action, for example, this would consist of the facts constituting the grounds for the divorce.

11. The cause of action should be stated briefly and concisely. Avoid long recitations of the facts.

12. You cannot draft a complaint unless you know every component or element of the cause of action. For a divorce on the ground of separation, for example, there must be a voluntary living apart for a designated period of time, and the time apart must be consecutive. In most states, there should be allegations of fact in the complaint that cover each of these elements of the ground.

13. With the exception of the citation to the statute on subject-matter jurisdiction referred to above in instruction 9, you do not give citations to statutes, court rules, or opinions in the complaint. Limit yourself to the statement of facts—the essential facts.

14. If you are not sure of a fact, you can state it "on information and belief."

15. If the plaintiff has more than one cause of action or theory of recovery, you should state all of them. Each should be stated separately and numbered, I, II, III, etc. Each separate theory or cause of action is called a *Count*.

16. The *prayer for relief* should contain everything the plaintiff is asking the court to do.

17. The *verification* is a sworn statement that the contents of the document are true.

ever, a standard form will be written by the legislature or by the court as the suggested or required format to be used.

Considerable care must be exercised in the use of standard forms. They can be very deceptive in that they appear to require little more than a filling in of the blanks. Intelligent use of the forms, however, usually requires much more. The guidelines in the following list should be kept in mind:

How to Avoid Abusing a Standard Form

1. The cardinal rule is to *adapt* the form to the particulars of the client's case on which you are working.

2. Do not be afraid of changing the preprinted language of the form if you have a good reason for doing so. Whenever you make such a change, bring it to the attention of your supervisor for approval.

3. Never use a standard form unless and until you have satisfied yourself that you know the meaning of every word and phrase on it, especially **boilerplate.** The great temptation of most form users is to ignore what they do not understand because the form has been used so often in the past with no apparent difficulty. Do not give in to this temptation. Find out what everything means by:

- Asking your supervisor
- Asking more experienced paralegals or other knowledgeable people
- Doing other legal research
- Using a legal dictionary

4. You need to know whether the entire form or any part of it has ever been litigated in court. To find out, you must do legal research in the area of the law relevant to the form.

5. Once you have found a form that appears useful, look around for another form that covers the same topic. Analyze the different forms available. Which one is preferable? Why? The important point is to keep questioning the validity of the form. Be very skeptical about the utilization of any form.

6. Do not leave any blank spaces on the form. If a question does not apply to your case, write NA (not applicable) in the space for that question.

Boilerplate Language that is commonly used in a document; it is repetitive language that is often nonessential.

Looking for "model" documents in the closed case files.

7. If the form was written for another state, be sure it can be adapted and is adapted to the law of your state. Very often, out-of-state forms are unadaptable.

8. Occasionally, you may go to an old case file to find a document in that file that might be used as a model for a similar document that you need to draft on a current case. All of the above cautions apply equally to the adaptation of documents from closed case files.

Agreement-Drafting Assignment

Several times in this book you will be asked to draft an agreement, e.g., a separation agreement. Here are the general instructions for this assignment. You should keep a *documents file* that contains copies of agreements, complaints, and all the other documents you prepare for this and other courses. Such a file can be enormously beneficial in your job search later on. Prospective employers are often impressed by well-drafted documents, particularly from job applicants who have not had prior legal experience.

■■■ General Instructions for the Agreement-Drafting Assignment

1. You will need additional facts in order to draft the agreement, e.g., you may need the names of the parties, their addresses, the property they own, how they own it, other economic facts. You can obtain these facts in two ways:

□ Conduct a mock legal interview of fellow students according to the guidelines in the General Instructions for the Interview Assignment, page 30.

□ Make up any of these facts that you need, provided they are reasonable in the context of the circumstances of the assignment.

Your instructor will let you know which option to take.

2. It is often useful to obtain copies of similar agreements that were written in the past for other clients and/or to obtain copies of model agreements commonly found in formbooks, manuals, practice books, etc. Such material may provide effective starting points for your own drafting. Proceed with caution, however. See How to Avoid Abusing a Standard Form.

3. It is critical that you know the law of the area covered by the agreement. What can and cannot be accomplished by the agreement? What legal pitfalls must be avoided? Research in the area of the law, therefore, is an essential precondition of drafting.

4. For purposes of the agreement-drafting assignments in this book, however, you do not have to do any legal research unless your instructor tells you to do so. You will find all the law you need by reading the chapter text immediately preceding the drafting assignment you are doing.

5. When tax considerations are relevant, take them into consideration in drafting the agreement.

6. Know what the client wants to accomplish by the agreement. Know the *specific* client objectives. (If you don't know what they are, see instruction 1 above.) It is too general, for example, to say that the client wants to divide the property of the spouses in an equitable manner. A more specific and acceptable example of an objective would be to have the other spouse use the vacation home for ten years or until she remarries, whichever occurs earlier. Have all the specific objectives in mind when you draft. Each clause in the agreement should relate to one or more of the objectives. Your drafting guide is your statement of objectives.

7. At the beginning of the agreement, label the kind of agreement that it is, e.g., *Separation Agreement*. Also at the beginning, state the names and addresses of the parties entering the agreement.

8. Number each paragraph consecutively (1, 2, 3, etc.). Limit the subject matter of each paragraph to a single topic or to closely related topics. Be as narrow as possible in selecting the topic of a paragraph. For example, in a separation agreement dealing with the disposition of the property that the spouses accumulated during the marriage, each paragraph should cover a separate category of property. Similarly, there should be separately numbered paragraphs covering custody of the children, visitation rights, alimony, etc.

9. A mistake made by many drafters is to assume that everyone will be using the same definition of words. Major words should always be defined. A *major word* is any important word that could have more than one meaning. The word "property," for example, has several

—Continued

—Continued

meanings, e.g., real property, personal property, property in one's possession now, property to be received in the future, etc. What meaning did the parties intend for the word "property"? Such words should be carefully defined in the agreement.

10. One sign of an effective agreement is fairness. Avoid trying to take unfair advantage of the other side

in drafting the agreement. The result may be an unworkable agreement leading to considerable delay, animosity, and litigation expense. The cooperation of both sides is necessary to make the agreement work. An important incentive to such cooperation is a feeling by both parties that the agreement is fair.

COURT-OPINION ASSIGNMENT

You need to know how to locate court opinions on family law topics for two reasons:

☐ To help you find opinions that have interpreted statutes on family law topics.

☐ To help you find the **common law.** A considerable amount of family law is part of the common law, which is judge-made law in the absence of controlling statutory law. If the legislature passes a statute that covers a controversy in litigation, the statute controls even if there is also common law that covers the controversy. Suppose, however, there are no statutes governing the dispute. In such a case, the court is free to create new law to resolve the litigation. If it does so, the new law becomes part of the common law.

Common Law Judge-made law in the absence of controlling statutory law.

▬▬ General Instructions for the Court-Opinion Assignment

1. The objective of the assignment is to find opinions on a family law issue. The law library has a number of resources that can provide you with leads to such opinions. The major leads are:

☐ Notes to Decisions found within most annotated statutory codes

☐ The state digest or the regional digest covering opinions of your state, or the American Digest System

☐ *American Law Reports*

☐ Footnote references in formbooks, hornbooks, manuals, legal encyclopedias, legal periodical literature, etc.

☐ *Words and Phrases*

☐ WESTLAW and LEXIS

☐ Attorneys and paralegals experienced in family law

2. You may not be familiar with all the legal resources mentioned above. If that is the case, do not wait for a course in legal research before starting to learn how to use them. Start *now* by asking questions. Ask librarians, fellow students, teachers, practicing attorneys and paralegals, etc. Above all, browse through these resources on your own as often as you can. With a little practice and determination, you will soon be able to obtain basic information from them.

3. Notes to Decisions. To know how to use Notes to Decisions, you must first know how to use an annotated statutory code. (Review the General Instructions for the State-Code Assignments, page 9). The Notes contain summaries of opinions that have interpreted statutes. Hence in order to find these Notes, you must first find a statute that covers the topic under examination. If opinions exist interpreting this statute, they will be summarized in the Notes to Decisions following the statute. Be sure to check for more recent Notes in the pocket parts of the code.

4. Digests. Digests are volumes containing thousands of small paragraph summaries of court opinions. A digest is, in effect, a massive index to court opinions and consequently is often called a "case finder." There are three kinds of digests—all of which contain the same basic material and format:

☐ State Digest. Most states have their own digest, i.e., volumes of small paragraph summaries of all the opinions written by courts in a particular state.

☐ Regional Digest. There are a number of regional digests covering the opinions written by the state courts of several neighboring states.

—Continued

—Continued

☐ American Digest System. This is the most comprehensive digest of all, covering the opinions of almost every court in the country.

The main index in each of these digests is in separate volumes called the *Descriptive Word Index*. To use these indexes effectively, apply the CARTWHEEL technique.

5. *American Law Reports*. These volumes contain the full text of selected court opinions plus extensive research material following the opinions. This material is called an *annotation*. The annotations often include a state-by-state breakdown of the legal issues treated in the annotation. Hence, when you find an annotation on a family law topic, you can look for court opinions from your state on that topic. There are six units of the *American Law Reports* volumes: ALR, ALR2d, ALR3d, ALR4th, ALR5th, and ALR Fed. The main index to these volumes is called the *Index to Annotations*. The CARTWHEEL technique will help you use this index.

6. Footnote references in other books. Often the footnotes are the most valuable part of formbooks, hornbooks, manuals, legal encyclopedias, and legal periodical literature. These footnotes usually give citations to court opinions on the topics being discussed in the body of the text. In a set of books that has extensive footnotes, such as either of the major legal encyclope-

dias (*Corpus Juris Secundum* and *American Jurisprudence 2d*), the references to court opinions in the footnotes may be organized alphabetically by state, which will make it easier for you to determine if opinions of your state are provided.

7. *Words and Phrases*. This is a multivolume set of books containing thousands of definitions of legal terms. The definitions are quotations from court opinions. Try to find definitions of words from court opinions of your state on the family law topic under examination.

8. WESTLAW and LEXIS. It is also possible to find cases electronically. If you have access to WESTLAW or LEXIS, you can locate the court opinions of every state "online." To look for cases on a family law topic, you go to the database that contains the opinions of your state courts and formulate a "query," which is simply a question. The CARTWHEEL technique can help you decide what words or phrases to use in your query.

9. Experienced attorneys and paralegals. Never be reluctant to go to attorneys and paralegals in the field of family law to ask them for a lead to a court opinion of your state on a particular topic or to ask them for suggestions on how you might go about finding such an opinion. (For purposes of the assignments in this book, do not seek such suggestions until after you follow instructions 3–8 above on your own.)

Answer the following questions by going to the nearest large law library to which you have access (on locating libraries, see the beginning of chapter 2):

a. Give the name of every reporter in the library that will contain the full text of court opinions written by state courts of your state. Who publishes each reporter? What courts are covered in each?

b. Give the name of every digest that will provide small paragraph summaries of the court opinions of your state.

c. Go to one of the digests you mentioned in (b) above. Use the index features of this digest to locate a key topic and number for *any* five family law subjects. (Select five different family law subject areas.) What are the key topics and numbers? Give the cite of the first opinion summarized under each key topic and number you have selected.

ASSIGNMENT 1.7

CHECKLIST-FORMULATION ASSIGNMENT

It is important that you learn how to write checklists that could become part of a manual. Every rule that you are told about or that you read about can be "translated" into a checklist. Checklist formulation should eventually become second nature to you. The sooner you start thinking about and creating lists of do's, don'ts, tasks, etc., the better.

Suppose that you have before you the following statute of your state:

§ 1742 No marriage shall be solemnized without a license issued by the county clerk of any county of this state not more than thirty days prior to the date of the solemnization of the marriage.

One way to handle this statute is to create a checklist of questions that you would ask a client in order to determine whether the statute has been complied with or violated. Some of the questions would be:

1. Did you have a marriage license?

2. Where did you get the license? Did you obtain it from a county clerk in this state?

3. On what date did you obtain the license?

4. On what date did you go through the marriage ceremony ("solemnization")? (You want to determine if there were more than thirty days between the date the county issued the license and the date of the ceremony.)

These are some of the questions that must be asked as part of a large number of questions concerning the validity of a particular marriage. If you were creating a manual, the above four questions in your checklist for § 1742 could go under the manual topic of "Marriage Formation" or "Marriage License." Most laws can be translated into checklists in this way.

◼️ General Instructions for the Checklist-Formulation Assignment

1. The starting point in all the checklist-formulation assignments will be a rule. The rule usually will be found within a statute or a court opinion to which you will be referred.

2. Your objective is to make a list of questions that you would ask yourself, a client, or a witness for the purpose of determining whether the rule might apply.

3. Make sure you understand the rule. Closely analyze it. Make inquiries about what you do not understand in the rule. Consult a legal dictionary. Read closely related rules in order to see the rule you are examining in context. Read the rule again.

4. Break the rule down into elements as discussed earlier in this chapter.

5. For each element of the rule, design a question or a series of questions.

6. Every time the rule says that something must be done or that something must not be done, create a question or a series of questions designed to determine whether it was done.

7. Every time the rule imposes a precondition (i.e., *if* such and such occurs, *then* . . .), create a question or a series of questions designed to determine whether the precondition occurred.

8. Be alert to the word "and" in a rule. It usually refers to additional requirements. Create questions designed to determine whether all the additional requirements were met.

9. Be alert to the word "or" in a rule. It usually refers to alternative requirements. Create questions designed to determine which, if any, of the alternatives were met.

10. If you have been diligent in creating checklists, you will be taking major steps toward the creation of your own manual. Even if you do not create manuals, checklist creation is still valuable as a practical way of thinking about any law. (For other components of such a manual, see the General Instructions for the Systems Assignment later in this chapter.)

THE FACT-GATHERING ASSIGNMENTS

Fact Particularization
A fact-gathering technique designed to help you identify a large variety of questions you can try to answer through interviewing and investigation.

The next three categories of assignments cover various facets of the fact-gathering process in the area of family law. A cardinal principle in this process is the necessity of obtaining relevant factual detail. This is achieved through a technique called **fact particularization.** Once you identify the facts collected in the case thus far, you assume that these facts are woefully incomplete. For example, they fail to give more than one version of what happened. Then you identify a large number of basic who, what, where, why, when, and how questions that, if answered, will provide as complete a picture of what happened as is possible at this particular time.

Suppose you are working on a child custody case. To particularize this case, you ask a series of questions centered on the following interrelated and overlapping clusters: participant details, incident details, place details, time details, and verification details.

1. *Participant details.* Who is involved in the case? Obtain the names of children, parents, grandparents, other relatives, neighbors, government agency workers connected with the case, friends of the children and of the parents, teachers and ministers who know the family, employers of the parents, medical personnel who have treated the children, witnesses to specific events, etc. What does each participant know about current and past family living conditions? How do you know? What have they said? What is the age and the educational background of each participant? Etc.

2. *Place details.* Where do the children live? Where else have they lived? Where do they go for school, religious services, recreational activities, medical care, cultural events, etc? For each place, give the address, how far away from home it is, how the children get there, what costs are involved, who pays them, what happens there, what the feelings of the children are about the place, what they have said about it, what other participants think about the place, etc.

3. *Time details.* On an average day how much time do the children spend on their normal activities? When did any of the important events occur, e.g., abuse? How long did it last? Has it occurred more than once in the past? When?

4. *Incident details.* What happened? What events are relevant to the well-being of the children and the fitness of the parents to be guardians? Explain ordinary and extraordinary occurrences in their day-to-day lives.

5. *Verification details.* Every fact you have obtained has a source, e.g., the client, a record. Assume that you wanted to obtain an additional source to verify the original source of every important fact. Where would you go? Whom would you ask? What additional records would you try to obtain? How would you try to obtain them? Assess the believability of each source. Etc.

These categories of questions are interrelated. You will be simultaneously probing for details on people, incidents, dates, etc. There may be considerable overlap in your questions. This is not significant so long as you achieve comprehensiveness in factual detail, i.e., so long as you achieve factual particularity. Also, the above list of questions is just the tip of the iceberg. Scores and scores of additional questions in the same mold must be pursued. Given the complexity of human events and of human relationships, a great deal of factual detail is needed before you are able to achieve factual comprehensiveness. The objective of fact particularization is to get you into the habit of going beneath the surface in order to look at people and events from a variety of perspectives. Nothing is taken at face value.

INVESTIGATION-STRATEGY ASSIGNMENT

In many cases, an enormous number of facts must be gathered and verified. To keep from becoming overwhelmed, a plan of action must be developed. The investigation-strategy assignment is designed to help you construct such a plan in order to give the investigation some direction. The instructions for this assignment are as follows:

General Instructions for the Investigation-Strategy Assignment

1. The starting point in this assignment is a set of facts you are given in the assignment. Assume you have entered the case after these facts have been collected by someone else.

2. Assume further that these facts are inadequate because *many* more facts are needed. Review the material on *fact particularization* discussed earlier.

3. Closely examine the facts you have. Are they arranged chronologically? If not, rearrange them chronologically so that the facts tell a story with a beginning, middle, and end. Of course, there will be many gaps in the story. Your task will be to identify these gaps and to raise the questions that the investigator would need to ask to try to fill or close the gaps. These questions will become the investigator's strategy or plan for further investigation.

4. The focus of the questions will be on what you *don't* know about the facts that you have.

5. Isolate the facts you have into small clusters of facts, e.g., the child is unhappy, the husband left the house in a rage. For each small set of facts that you identify or isolate in this way, make a *large* list of questions that fall into two interrelated categories.

☐ Questions designed to obtain additional facts that will help you compile a much more detailed picture of what happened. To aid you in this list, ask the basic who, what, where, why, when, how questions about every fact. (See the material on fact particularization.)

☐ Questions designed to obtain facts that will help substantiate (or prove) the facts that you already have.

There is no rigid formula to follow in making these lists of questions. The goal is a comprehensive list of questions that, if answered, would provide a comprehensive picture of what happened.

6. Consider structuring questions to elicit details on participants, places, times, and incidents.

7. Be particularly scrupulous about dates. Ask questions about the dates that you have and also about the dates that are missing.

8. In your questions on participants, try to identify a diversity of *versions*. Make a list of every person who is involved or who could be involved in the facts. Assume that each person potentially has a different version of a critical incident or series of incidents. Structure questions that will elicit these different versions.

9. Preceding most of the assignments will be a discussion of some legal principles or rules of law governing family law topics. Include questions on the elements of any relevant rules of law. (On breaking rules into their elements, see the earlier discussion; see also General Instructions for the Checklist-Formulation Assignment.)

10. The list of questions in this assignment does not have to be written in any particular order. Select any format that is readable.

11. In some of the chapters, you will find lists of interviewing questions and investigation tasks. If these lists are relevant to the area of the assignment, expand on them. Use the lists as points of departure for further fact particularization.

INTERVIEW ASSIGNMENT

The interview assignment relies on some of the skills covered earlier, especially fact particularization and checklist formulation. Interviewing is deceptive in that many students feel that it is relatively easy to do. It isn't. The instructions for the interview assignment are as follows:

General Instructions for the Interview Assignment

1. In this assignment, you are asked to interview another person, e.g., a fellow student, someone at home.

2. Review the material on *fact particularization*. One of your objectives is to obtain substantial factual specificity.

As the interviewer, you should strive for a comprehensive picture of the people and events involved in the assignment.

3. In some of the chapters, you will find lists of inter-

—Continued

viewing questions. If the lists are relevant to the area of the assignment, expand on them. Use the lists as points of departure for further fact particularization.

4. After you complete the interview, prepare a report from your notes. For the heading of your report, see Exhibit 1.2 on the Interoffice Memorandum. (If you are interviewing a new client, label your report, "Intake Memorandum.") Indicate who wrote the report or memo (you), who will receive it (your teacher or supervisor), the name of the person interviewed (the interviewee), the date of the interview, and the date you turned in the report or memo. The first paragraph should state the assignment (e.g., "You have asked me to interview (name of the interviewee) in order to (state the purpose of the interview assignment).

5. In preparation for your interview, identify every rule of law that might be relevant to the fact situation (see the discussion in the text preceding the interview assignment). Break down each rule into its elements. Be

sure to ask questions that are relevant to the applicability of every element. (See also the General Instructions for the Checklist-Formulation Assignment.)

6. Try to arrange the facts in your intake memorandum in roughly chronological order so that the facts unfold as a story with a beginning, middle, and end.

7. *Instructions to Interviewee:* you can make up facts as you go along so long as the facts are reasonably consistent with the facts initially provided. Do not volunteer any information. Simply answer the questions asked.

8. Your teacher may decide to role-play the interview in front of the class. If so, the class may be asked to comment on how the interview was conducted, e.g., did the interview follow the assignment, was there adequate fact particularization, did the interview ramble, was the interviewee placed at ease, how could the interview have been improved?

INTERROGATORY ASSIGNMENT

The purpose of **interrogatories** is to obtain factual information about the other party's case in order to prepare for trial. The instructions for the interrogatory assignment are as follows:

Interrogatories A written set of factual questions sent by one party to another before the trial begins.

▇▇▇▇ General Instructions for the Interrogatories Assignment

1. Your objective in writing the questions, i.e., the interrogatories, is to obtain as much information as possible from the other side in order to assist you in preparing a case. See the material on *fact particularization.* The material on preparing investigation strategies should also be helpful in drafting interrogatories.

2. The interrogatories you draft should be acceptable in your state, which means that you should know whatever restrictions exist in statutes and in court rules of your state on the scope and format of interrogatories in family law cases. For example, is there a limited number of questions that can be sent?

3. The scope of questions you can ask is usually quite broad. The test is whether the question is reasonably calculated to lead to evidence that will be admissible in court. This is a much broader standard than whether the answer itself would constitute admissible evidence.

4. Avoid unduly long or oppressive interrogatories.

5. Avoid questions that improperly seek privileged information. For example:

a. Questions that violate the privilege against self-incrimination (e.g., "Did you burn your house on purpose?").

b. Questions that violate the attorney-client privilege (e.g., "What did you tell your attorney about the child?").

c. Questions that violate the doctor-patient privilege (e.g., "What did you tell your doctor about the pain?").

d. Questions that violate the husband-wife privilege (e.g., "What did you tell your wife about the pain?"). This privilege does not apply when spouses are suing each other.

e. Questions that violate the attorney work-product rule (e.g., "Does your attorney think my client has a valid claim?").

6. In many states it is permissible to ask a question that would involve the application of law to fact—some-

—Continued

—*Continued*

times called "contention interrogatories." For example, "Do you contend that Mr. _____ had no intent to marry you at the time of the wedding ceremony?" or, "Is it your position that Ms. _____ took the child out of the state in order to avoid complying with the custody decree?" If you ask such a question, be sure to follow it with a series of detailed questions that seek the factual reasons for the possible answers that could be given.

7. Be careful about the verb tense used in questions. Present tense (e.g., "is") is used to determine facts that are still current. Past tense (e.g., "was") is used to determine events that are over. If a question relates to past and present tense, break the question down into several questions.

8. It can be useful to try to find sample interrogatories in manuals, formbooks, and other practice materials. Such interrogatories, of course, would have to be adapted to the particular needs of the client's case on which you are currently working. On the dangers of using such forms, see How to Avoid Abusing a Standard Form. For a sample set of interrogatories designed to uncover the financial assets of a spouse, see page 197 in chapter 10. (As indicated earlier, a copy of all documents you prepare—such as interrogatories—should be placed in a personal documents file for possible later use as writing samples in your employment search.)

9. It can also be useful to go to the closed case file of another case that contains interrogatories in order to try to adapt them. Again, the use of such materials is only a point of departure. Great care must be used in determining what, if anything, can be borrowed from other interrogatories.

10. Before you draft your interrogatories, know the case (on which you are working) inside and out. Read all pleadings filed to date, e.g., complaint, answer, correspondences in the file, intake memorandum, etc. Many ideas for questions will come from this knowledge. For purposes of the assignments in this book, however, you will not have access to such data since the assignments will be based on hypothetical cases.

11. Litigation involves causes of action and defenses. Each of these causes of action and defenses can be bro-

ken down into elements. Each of these elements should become the basis of a checklist. Ask questions that seek facts that could potentially be used to support each of the elements. (See also the General Instructions for the Checklist-Formulation Assignment.)

12. Consider phrasing your questions in such a way that the "story" of the facts unfolds chronologically.

13. Be constantly concerned about dates, full names, addresses, exact amounts, etc.

14. Always ask what witnesses the other side intends to rely on to support its version of the facts at the trial. Ask for the names and addresses of such witnesses.

15. Ask what documentation, physical things, or exhibits the other side will rely on to support its version of the facts. You may want to ask that such items be sent along with the answers to the interrogatories (or that such items be brought to a later deposition).

16. Avoid questions that call for simple "yes" or "no" answers unless you immediately follow up such questions with other questions that ask for details.

17. Include a definition section at the beginning of the interrogatories to avoid confusion and undue repetition in the later questions. This section will define words and phrases you intend to use in more than one question. For example: "A 'medical practitioner' as used in these interrogatories is meant to include any medical doctor, osteopathic physician, podiatrist, doctor of chiropractic, naturopathic physician, nurse, or other person who performs any form of healing art."

18. Phrase the questions so that the person answering will have to indicate whether he or she is talking from first-hand knowledge, second-hand knowledge (hearsay), etc.

19. As to each fact, ask questions calculated to elicit the respondent's ability to comment on the fact, e.g., how far away was he or she, does he or she wear glasses, how long has he or she known the party, in what capacity, etc.

20. Avoid complicated and difficult-to-read questions. Be direct and concise.

FLOWCHART ASSIGNMENT

A flowchart is a step-by-step account of how something is done, e.g., a divorce; a particular kind of administrative proceeding such as a worker's compensation hearing. A number of assignments in this book ask you to prepare a flowchart on the legal process under discussion. The instructions for this assignment are as follows:

▮▮▮▮ General Instructions for the Flowchart Assignment

1. Design the flowchart based upon the law of your state. The chart will give an overview of how something is done in your state, e.g., how to adopt a child, how to change your name.

2. The two primary sources of information for the flowchart are your state statutory code and the court rules for the courts in your state. See General Instructions for the State-Code Assignment. See also the CART-WHEEL technique for using the index of statutory codes, court rules, or any reference materials.

3. You may be able to obtain information for the flowchart from manuals, formbooks, and other practice material. It is recommended, however, that you try to obtain the information directly from the statutory code and the court rules. The practice materials may be out of date. Furthermore, to use practice materials intelligently, you must know how to check the accuracy and timeliness of such materials by going to the primary sources, namely, the statutory code and the court rules (and occasionally, the state constitution).

4. The flowchart must be chronological, moving from the first step of the process to the last step.

5. The structure and graphics that present the steps in the flowchart can be varied:

☐ Use a series of boxes (one step per box) with all the boxes connected by arrows to show the progression of the process.

☐ Use a list of brief, numbered paragraphs with each paragraph stating one step.

☐ Use an outline with the major headings being the key phrases of the process, e.g., agency contact, pretrial, etc.

Use your imagination in designing the sequence of events outlined in the flowchart.

6. The information in the chart should pertain to **procedural law** rather than **substantive law**. Procedural law consists of the technical steps for bringing or defending actions in litigation before a court or an administrative agency. An example would be the number of days within which a party can request an extension of time to file an answer after the complaint has been filed. Substantive law consists of rights and obligations other than purely procedural matters. An example would be the right to a divorce on the ground of irreconcilable differences.

7. For each item of information in the flowchart, state your source, e.g., the citation to the statute or court rule that provided you with the procedural information you used in the flowchart.

8. Statutory codes and court rules may have sections that deal with litigation in general. Such sections are often listed in the index and table of contents of the codes and court rules under broad topics such as "Civil Procedure," "Actions," "Court Procedures," "Courts," etc. You should check these sections to see what, if anything, they say about the topic of your flowchart.

9. In addition, your state statutory code and court rules may have special sections that cover the procedural steps that are peculiar to the topic of your flowchart. Check these as well.

10. If you are flowcharting litigation of any kind, numerous steps are often involved at the pretrial, trial, appeal, and enforcement stages. These steps need to be incorporated into your flowchart. Here are some examples of questions you should ask yourself about most litigations. The answers to such questions must be outlined in your flowchart if they are relevant to whatever you are flowcharting.

☐ What agency, if any, has jurisdiction over the case?

☐ What is the application process at the agency?

☐ What court(s) have jurisdiction?

☐ How is service of process made?

☐ How is venue determined?

☐ Do you need to use any special format for the complaint?

☐ How is the complaint served and filed?

☐ Do you need to use any special format for the answer?

☐ How is the answer served and filed?

☐ Are there special rules for raising counterclaims?

☐ Are there any special motions that can be made, e.g., motion to dismiss?

☐ What rules govern pretrial discovery: deposition, interrogatories, request for production of documents and things, requests for admissions, and court-ordered examinations (physical and mental)?

☐ What sanctions can be imposed for violation of the pretrial discovery rules?

☐ What preliminary orders can be requested, and how must the request be made?

☐ What rules govern the issuing of the final judgment?

☐ How many days does a party have to appeal?

☐ What court has jurisdiction to hear the appeal?

☐ How can a judgment be enforced?

The above list is not exhaustive. If there are other steps or more detailed steps that apply to the process you are flowcharting for your state, include them.

SYSTEMS ASSIGNMENT

A **system** is a method of organizing people and resources to accomplish a task. Great skill is required to design and implement an effective system. A good way to start learning this skill is to identify and describe a system (or lack of a system) in the work lives of others. The systems assignment is designed to help you make such a start. The instructions for this assignment are as follows:

■■■■ General Instructions for the Systems Assignment

1. Your goal is to interview practicing attorneys, paralegals, and legal secretaries who handle family law cases in order to identify their system for providing legal services on a certain kind of case.

2. You are seeking the following kinds of information about the system for handling the kind of case involved in this assignment:

☐ Who does what on the case? What does the attorney do? The paralegal? The secretary?

☐ In what sequence is it all done?

☐ How long does the process take from beginning to end? Does the time involved differ from case to case? If so, what are the main factors causing the differences?

☐ What equipment is used, e.g., fax machines, computers?

☐ What computer software, if any, is used, e.g., word processing, spreadsheet?

☐ Are any standard forms used?

☐ Are any manuals particularly helpful? If so, were they written by the office or by someone else?

☐ Has the office changed its system for handling this kind of case? IF so, what were the changes and why were they made?

☐ Does anyone have any problems with how the present system now works? If so, what are they and what recommended improvements are contemplated?

3. If possible, try to interview someone from another firm that handles the same kind of case so that you can compare the systems used.

4. How do you find practicing attorneys, paralegals, and secretaries in the field of family law?

☐ You may have fellow classmates who are secretaries or paralegals.

☐ Check with your paralegal association.

☐ Check with the local association of legal secretaries.

☐ Ask your instructor for leads.

5. Another person who would have valuable information for this assignment is the law office manager or legal administrator of the larger firms.

6. Everyone is busy, particularly those working in a law office. You must not give the impression that you are going to take up a lot of the time of the people you interview. Have a checklist of questions ready. Be prepared. Guard against giving the impression that you are not sure what you want.

7. People you interview should never reveal any information about any particular clients in their offices, including the identity of the clients. This information is confidential. You are seeking generic information on systems for handling categories of cases. If by mistake you learn information about particular clients, be sure that you keep it confidential.

■■■■ SUMMARY

Family law encompasses a wide variety of legal problems. In addition to the obvious areas of divorce, custody, and support, the family law practitioner must know something about criminal law, contract law, corporate and business law, property law, tort law, civil procedure law, evidence law, juvenile law, tax law, estate law, etc. Our study of the law will have two dimensions: knowledge of what the law is, and skills to use that knowledge.

A number of these skills will take you into the law library, where the technique of *cartwheeling* will be very helpful. This technique is designed to generate numerous words and phrases that should be checked in the indexes of reference books.

A great deal of family law is contained in the state statutory code of your state. The *state-code assignments* will help you use the codes effectively. Once you find law in the codes, the next step is to apply it to concrete sets of facts. The *legal-analysis assignments* focus on this skill of application, primarily by asking you to identify and apply elements.

In the *complaint-drafting assignments,* you will spend a good deal of time with the critical pleading that initiates litigation by stating a cause of action. One way to avoid bitter litigation is to encourage the parties to agree on how to handle controversies that have arisen or that might arise. The *agreement-drafting assignments* will increase your appreciation of this aspect of family law.

Next to statutory law, the largest volume of law we will study comes from the courts in the form of common law. Many of the *court-opinion assignments* will ask you to find common law, although some of them will also ask you to find opinions that have interpreted statutory law. A practical method of handling statutory law and common law is to translate both into checklists. The *checklist-formulation assignments* will introduce you to this skill.

Three fact-gathering skills use the technique of fact particularization. First is the skill of formulating a plan of gathering new facts and substantiating ones you already have (the *investigation-strategy assignments*). Second is the skill of obtaining information in person from one individual (the *interview assignments*). Third is the skill of drafting written questions to be sent to the other side (the *interrogatory assignments*).

Finally, two assignments ask you to provide a step-by-step overview of how something is done. The first involves a legal proceeding in a court or in an administrative agency (the *flowchart assignments*); the second, a system of accomplishing a particular task in a law office (the *systems assignments*).

■■■■■ KEY CHAPTER TERMINOLOGY

CARTWHEEL	Legal Issue	Boilerplate
Statutory Code	Element in Contention	Common Law
Shepardize	Interoffice Memorandum	Fact Particularization
Citation	Complaint	Interrogatories
Annotated	Pleading	Procedural Law
Legal Analysis	Cause of Action	Substantive Law
Element	Standard Form	System

2 LAW BOOKS AND LEGAL INSTITUTIONS: A GUIDE TO THE FAMILY LAW OF YOUR STATE

FINDING A LAW LIBRARY

Law books are critical tools of a lawyer. The same should be true of the paralegal. Since there is so much law, and since a good deal of it is constantly changing, no one—including an experienced judge—can be expected to know all the family law of a particular state. In a child-support case, for example, the question is not so much, "What is the law of child support?" as it is "What is the law of child support *today*?" Understanding general principles is helpful as a starting point, but more is usually needed in the actual practice of law. And the ticket of admission to current law is the law library.

In this chapter, we will cover some of the fundamentals of the law library from the viewpoint of the family law practitioner. The chapter is not intended as a substitute for a full course in legal research, nor does it assume that you have already had such a course. Rather, we will highlight some of the basics in order to reinforce what you may have learned elsewhere, or to give you a headstart on what you will be learning for the first time elsewhere.

The first question is, where can you find a law library? To a large degree, the answer depends on the area where you live, study, or work. Rural areas will have fewer resources than larger cities and capitals. Eleven possibilities are listed below. Find out which are available to you in your area. You may need permission to use some of them.

☐ Law school library
☐ General university library (may have a law section)

□ Law library of a bar association

□ State law library (in the state capital and perhaps in branch offices in counties throughout the state)

□ Local public library (may have a law section)

□ Law library of a court

□ Law library of the legislature or city council

□ Law library of the county attorney, city solicitor, or corporation counsel

□ Law library of the state attorney, district attorney, or local prosecutor

□ Law library of the public defender

□ Law library of a federal, state, or local administrative agency (particularly in the general counsel's office of the agency)

Be sure to check whether any of these libraries is a **depository library.** This is a library that receives free law books from the federal government, e.g., *United States Code, Code of Federal Regulations*; in exchange, the library must allow the public access to those books. Some depository libraries are located in university libraries or law school libraries.

Depository Library A library that receives free law books from the federal government; in exchange, the library must allow the public access to those books.

There is one other law library you need to consider: your own. It is not too soon to start collecting your own law books, beginning with your course books on law. Proceed with caution, however. Never buy a practice book or manual on family law without checking with at least two lawyers or paralegals on the *practical* value of the book. Ask them how often they consult the book. Remember, it is not necessarily wise to purchase a book simply because it treats an area of the law you need to know something about. Also, be prepared for "sticker shock" when you find out what some of these practice books cost.

■■■■ LAW BOOKS ON FAMILY LAW: COMPILING A BIBLIOGRAPHY

Two kinds of law books are relevant to a family law practice: those books containing **primary authority** and those containing **secondary authority.** The former is more important by far. A court will want to know what primary authority is available to resolve a legal dispute in a family law case—or in any kind of case. Primary authority is any law that a court could rely on in reaching its conclusion, e.g., a statute, court opinion, court rule, constitutional provision, administrative regulation, or ordinance. Secondary authority is any nonlaw that a court could rely on in reaching its conclusion, e.g., a legal encyclopedia, legal treatise, or law review article. The main value of secondary authority is that it helps you locate and interpret primary authority.

Primary Authority Any law that a court could rely on in reaching its conclusion.

Secondary Authority Any nonlaw that a court could rely on in reaching its conclusion.

ESSENTIAL QUESTIONS TO ASK ABOUT LAW BOOKS

For every law book you use, determine the answers to the following questions:

1. What kind of primary authority does the book contain?

2. If the book contains secondary authority, who is the author and/or editor?

3. Who published the book?

4. Has there been more than one edition of the book? If so, what edition are you examining?

5. What is the latest date on the copyright page?

6. Is the book kept up to date? If so, how? Through pocket parts? Through supplemental volumes?

7. If the book is part of a set, how many volumes are in the set?

8. Is there a general index? If so, where is it located? Does the book contain narrower, topical indexes? If so, where are they located?

9. Same questions as in no. 8 with reference to tables of contents.

10. Are there any other tables in the book, e.g., abbreviation tables? Cross-reference tables? If so, locate and describe the purpose of each.

11. Does the book contain a preface or other introductory/explanatory features? If so, where are they located, and how useful are they?

MOST IMPORTANT PUBLICATIONS FOR FAMILY LAW PRACTITIONERS

The most important law books to which a family law practitioner should have access are as follows:

YOUR STATE STATUTORY CODE   The statutes of the legislature govern many aspects of family law. They will probably be found in three or four volumes of the **statutory code** for your state. (See page 9 for more about using statutory codes.)

COURT RULES   **Court rules** (also called rules of court) govern the mechanics of litigation before a particular court. They cover many of the procedural aspects of divorces, annulments, adoptions, etc. The rules often contain standard forms that are either required or recommended.

STATE COURT OPINIONS AND DIGESTS   A **court opinion** is a written explanation of the court's resolution of a legal issue. These opinions are printed in full in volumes called **reporters.** There are usually several sets of reporters containing the opinions of your state courts, particularly the highest state court. There may be an official reporter published by the state itself. In addition, there is a regional reporter published by a private company (West) containing the opinions of the highest state courts (and some lower courts) of a cluster of states in the same region of the country. You need to find out what region your state is in so that you can find your regional reporter. Court opinions are also available electronically on computer databases such as WESTLAW and LEXIS. (In addition, databases contain other kinds of law such as statutes and court rules.)

Almost every state has a **digest,** which is a set of volumes that contains small paragraph summaries of the court opinions of that state. Most of the regional reporters also have regional digests that give summaries of the opinions in their respective regional reporter. The largest digest covering every state is the *American Digest System.* You need to have access to your individual state digest, or to your regional digest (if one exists for your region), or to the *American Digest System.*

PRACTICE MANUAL   Many states have a **practice manual** covering a variety of topics such as Family Law, Probate Law, Corporate Law, etc. In addition to summaries of the law, the manuals usually contain practical information, e.g., standard forms, checklists.

LEGAL NEWSPAPERS   The **legal newspaper** gives current cases, docket calendars for local courts, news on what the legislature and bar association are doing, etc.

▰▰▰ SAMPLE PROBLEM: FINDING LAW ON SURROGATE MOTHERS

Let us assume that you work in a law office whose client signed a surrogate motherhood contract. She agreed to be artificially inseminated with the semen of a man who is not her husband and, upon birth, to allow the child to be adopted by this man and his wife. Problems have arisen in this arrangement. Your supervisor asks you to do some legal research on the legality of surrogacy contracts. Later in chapter 20 we will study such contracts in greater detail. For now our goal is simply to give you an overview of some of the law books you might consult when researching a family law case such as this.

Where would you start? This question has no absolute answer. If you or your supervisor has had prior experience with surrogacy or adoption cases, you would begin by examining the citation to any laws you already know about. Suppose, however, this is the first time anyone in your office has worked on this kind of case.

Example of a statutory code volume.

STARTING WITH PRIMARY AUTHORITY

One possible starting point would be to go directly to law books containing or indexing primary authority.

STATUTES   To find out if there are any statutes on surrogacy, check the index of your state statutory code. It might lead you to such statutes. See Exhibit 2.1 for an example. For a summary of techniques to use when trying to find statutory law, see page 9 in chapter 1.

COURT OPINIONS   Exhibit 2.2 gives an example of a page from a regional reporter volume containing *Doe v. Attorney General,* a court opinion on the legality of surrogate motherhood contracts. One of the major ways to find such opinions is through the digests, which, as indicated, are volumes of small paragraph summaries of court opinions. Another way is to use computer databases such as WESTLAW and LEXIS. In Exhibit 2.3 you will find the beginning of a WESTLAW page containing *Doe v. Attorney General,* the same case we looked at in a reporter volume in Exhibit 2.2. For a summary of techniques to use when trying to find court opinions, see page 26 in chapter 1.

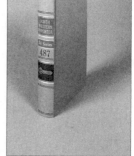

Example of a regional reporter volume.

772.851.   Short title

This act shall be known and may be cited as the "surrogate parenting act". P.A.1988, No. 199, § 1, Eff. Sept.1, 1988.

722.855.   Contracts; void and unenforceable

A surrogate parentage contract is void and unenforceable as contrary to public policy. P.A.1988, No. 199, § 5, Eff. Sept. 1, 1988.

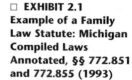

☐ **EXHIBIT 2.1**
Example of a Family Law Statute: Michigan Compiled Laws Annotated, §§ 772.851 and 772.855 (1993)

☐ **EXHIBIT 2.2   Example of a Page from a Regional Reporter Volume Containing a Family Law Court Opinion:** *Doe v. Attorney General*, 487 N.W.2d 484 (Mich. Ct. App. 1992)

DOE v. ATTORNEY GENERAL   Mich.   **484**
Cite as 487 N.W.2d 484 (Mich.App. 1992)

Caption (parties, their litigation status, docket number, dates, etc.)

194 Mich.App. 432

Jane DOE, John Doe, Rena Roe, Richard Roe, Carol Coe, Carl Coe, Paula Poe, and Nancy Noe, Plaintiffs-Appellants,

v.

ATTORNEY GENERAL, Defendant-Appellee.

Docket No. 113775.

Court of Appeals of Michigan.

Submitted March 20, 1990, at Detroit.

Decided June 1, 1992, at 9:10 a.m.

Released for Publication August 28, 1992.

Syllabus (summary of the entire opinion)

Infertile couples and prospective surrogate mothers brought action for declaratory judgment against state Attorney General regarding constitutionality of Surrogate Parenting Act. The Circuit Court, Wayne County, John H. Gillis, Jr., J., granted summary disposition for the Attorney General, and plaintiffs appealed. The Court of Appeals, Holbrook, P.J., held that: (1) case or controversy existed concerning constituionality of statute, giving court jurisdiction for declaratory judgment; (2) state had compelling interests sufficient to warrant governmental intrusion into protected area of privacy in matter of procreation; and (3) surrogate parentage contract involving voluntary relinquishment after conception of female's parental rights to child, is void and unenforceable.

Affirmed in part and reversed in part.

Murphy, J., concurred and filed opinion.

Headnote (summary of a portion of the opinion) At the top, you find Key Topic and Number "Declaratory Judgment 124." You can take this key topic and number to any West digest to try to find additional cases.

1. Declaratory Judgment ⚷124

"Case or controversy" existed, for purposes of declaratory judgment, despite agreement as to interpretation of statute, where attorney for infertile couples and prospective surrogate mothers later informed trial court that he misunderstood agreement with state concerning constitutionality of interpretation of Surrogate Parenting Act. M.C.L.A. § 722.851 et seq.; U.S.C.A. Const.Amends. 5, 14; MCR 2.605(A).

Headnote (summary of a portion of the opinion) At the top, you find Key Topic and Numbers "Constitutional Law 82(10)" and "274(5)". You can take them to any West digest to try to find additional cases.

2. Constitutional Law ⚷ **82(10), 274(5)**

Due process clauses of State and Federal Constitutions, together with penumbral rights emanating from specific guarantees of the Bill of Rights, protect individual decisions in matters of childbearing from unjustified intrusion by the state. U.S.C.A. Const. Amends. 5, 14.

American Civil Liberties Union Fund of Michigan by Robert A. Sedler, Elizabeth L. Gleicher and Paul J. Denenfeld, Detroit, for plaintiffs-appellants.

Frank J. Kelley, Atty. Gen., Gay Secor Hardy, Sol. Gen., and A. Michael Leffler and Vincent J. Leone, Asst. Attys. Gen., for defendant-appellee.

Attorneys who litigated the case

Before HOLBROOK, P.J., and MURPHY and JANSEN, JJ.

HOLBROOK, Presiding Judge. ◄ *Name of judge who wrote the opinion*

In this action for a declaratory interpretation of the Surrogate Parenting Act, M.C.L. § 722.851 *et seq.;* M.S.A. § 25.-248(151) *et seq.,* plaintiffs appeal as of right from an order of the Wayne Circuit Court granting defendant's motion for summary disposition for failure to state a claim. We affirm in part and reverse in part.

The body of the opinion begins.

Plaintiffs are infertile couples and prospective surrogate mothers. In their suit, filed on August 4, 1988, plaintiffs assert that if the Surrogate Parenting Act were interpreted as being an outright ban on surrogacy contracts for pay, the statute would deny them their constitutionally protected privacy rights and would offend the Due Process and Equal Protection Clauses of the state and federal constitutions. . . .

☐ **EXHIBIT 2.3   Example of a Page from WESTLAW Containing a Family Law Court Opinion:** *Doe v. Attorney General,* **487 N.W.2d 484 (Mich. Ct. App. 1992)**

START*START*START*START*START*START*START*START*START*START*START*START*START

Copr. (C) West 1995 No claim to orig. U.S. govt. works

(Cite as: 194 Mich.App. 432, 487 N.W.2d 484)

Jane DOE, John Doe, Rena Roe, Richard Roe, Carol Coe,
Carl Coe, Paula Poe, and Nancy Noe, Plaintiffs-Appellants,

v.

ATTORNEY GENERAL, Defendant-Appellee.

Docket No. 113775.

Court of Appeals of Michigan.

Submitted March 20, 1990, at Detroit.

Decided June 1, 1992, at 9:10 a.m.

Released for Publication August 28, 1992.

Infertile couples and prospective surrogate mothers brought action for declaratory judgment against state Attorney General regarding constitutionality of Surrogate Parenting Act. The Circuit Court, Wayne County, John H. Gillis, Jr., J., granted summary disposition for the Attorney General, and plaintiffs appealed. The Court of Appeals, Holbrook, P.J., held that: (1) case or controversy existed concerning constitutionality of statute, giving court jurisdiction for declaratory judgment; (2) state had compelling interests sufficient to warrant governmental intrusion into protected area of privacy in matter of procreation; and (3) surrogate parentage contract involving voluntary relinquishment after conception of female's parental rights to child, is void and unenforceable.

Affirmed in part and reversed in part.

Murphy, J., concurred and filed opinion. . . .

STARTING WITH SECONDARY AUTHORITY

Another option is to start with secondary authority. This approach is often valuable when you are doing research in an area of the law that is new to you. Secondary authority will not only give you leads to primary authority, but will also often give you background information about the law. This background can be tremendously helpful in providing basic terminology and general understanding. Here are some of the main secondary authorities:

LEGAL ENCYCLOPEDIAS   A **legal encyclopedia** is a multivolume set of books that summarizes almost every major legal topic. The two most important national legal encyclopedias are:

Example of an *Am. Jur. 2d* volume.

☐ *American Jurisprudence, 2d* (Lawyers Co-op) *(Am. Jur. 2d)*

☐ *Corpus Juris Secundum* (West) *(C.J.S.)*

Exhibit 2.4 contains a page from a volume of *American Jurisprudence, 2d* on surrogate motherhood. Exhibit 2.5 contains a page from a volume of *Corpus Juris Secundum* on the same topic. In addition to these national encyclopedias, some states have their own encyclopedia covering the law of one state, e.g., *Florida Jurisprudence, 2d, Michigan Law and Practice.*

LEGAL TREATISES   A **legal treatise** is a book written by a private individual (or a public official writing as a private citizen) that provides an overview, summary, or commentary on a legal topic. Exhibit 2.6 contains a page from a widely used legal treatise on Family Law, Homer H. Clark, *The Law of Domestic Relations in the United States* (2d ed. 1987). If the legal treatise contains very practical material such as litigation techniques and standard forms, it is often also called a formbook or a practice manual.

Example of a *C.J.S.* volume.

□ **EXHIBIT 2.4**
Example of a Discussion of a Family Law Topic from a Volume of *American Jurisprudence, 2d:* **59 Am. Jur. 2d § 3 (1987)**

---

59 Am Jur 2d   PARENT AND CHILD   § 4

§ 3. —"Surrogate mother"

   The surrogate mother arrangement is an arrangement between a surrogate mother and a husband and wife, whereby the surrogate mother agrees to be artificially inseminated with the husband's semen, bear a child, and relinquish all rights regarding that child to the husband and wife. They agree to pay the costs of the surrogate mother's pregnancy and to accept the child at birth. In addition, they may agree to pay the surrogate mother a fee in excess of the costs of bearing a child.[22] The legality and enforceability of a surrogate mother arrangement is questionable.[23]

LEGAL PERIODICALS   A **legal periodical** is an ongoing publication (e.g., published quarterly) that contains articles, studies, reports, or other information on legal topics. Many legal periodicals are published by law schools such as the one in Exhibit 2.7 from the *Marquette Law Review*.

ANNOTATIONS   An **annotation** is a set of notes or commentaries on something. The most widely used annotations are those printed in:

- □ *American Law Reports* (A.L.R.)
- □ *American Law Reports, Second Series (A.L.R.2d)*
- □ *American Law Reports, Third Series (A.L.R.3d)*
- □ *American Law Reports, Fourth Series (A.L.R.4th)*
- □ *American Law Reports, Fifth Series (A.L.R.5th)*
- □ *American Law Reports, Federal Series (A.L.R. Fed)*

All six sets are sometimes referred to collectively as *American Law Reports* or *ALRs*. Exhibit 2.8 contains an example of an annotation on surrogacy from *A.L.R.4th*.

MARTINDALE-HUBBELL   The *Martindale-Hubbell Law Directory* contains a listing of the names and addresses of many of the practicing attorneys in the

Example of a legal treatise.

Example of a legal periodical.

Example of an *A.L.R.4th* volume.

Example of *Martindale-Hubbell Law Digest* volume.

□ **EXHIBIT 2.5 Example of a Discussion of a Family Law Topic from a Volume of** *Corpus Juris Secundum:* **2 C.J.S. § 25 (1972), (Supp. 1994)**

---

2 C.J.S.   **ADOPTION OF PERSONS**   §§ 24–25

§ 25. In General

While an adoption relationship cannot ordinarily be created by private contract, contracts for the adoption of persons are usually not considered as opposed to public policy and in some circumstances such a contract may be treated as an adoption and enforced with consequences equivalent to a formal adoption. . . .

While surrogate parenting agreements in which the surrogate mother receives payment for bearing and surrendering the baby to the natural father and his wife for adoption have been prohibited,[29.5] such surrogate parenting agreements which compensate the surrogate mother have been given legal effect.[29.10]

A contractual provision in a surrogate parenting agreement purporting to terminate the parental rights of the surrogate mother does not conform to statutory prerequisites for termination and is invalid and unenforceable.[29.15]

---

§ 21.9   Adoption—The Surrogate Mother Contract

If the soundness of the solutions to legal problems varied directly with the number of words devoted to the problems and with the number of persons engaged in producing the words, we would need to have no fears about being able to cope with the difficulties created by surrogate mother contracts.[1] The legal and nonlegal output on the subject has been enormous[2] and will doubtless continue at the same rate until some other fascinating and unanswerable question appears. Unfortunately, however, the ability to solve legal problems probably varies inversely with the number of words expended. Generally acceptable methods of dealing with these contracts therefore do not seem likely to be devised.

□ **EXHIBIT 2.6**
Example of a Page from a Legal Treatise on Family Law: Homer H. Clark, *The Law of Domestic Relations in the United States,* **§ 21.9, pp. 669–670 (2d ed. 1987)**

Example of a *Words and Phrases* volume.

country. It also has a feature called the **Martindale-Hubbell Law Digest.** It contains brief summaries of the law of every sate. Exhibit 2.9 contains an example of a page from the summary for New York on surrogacy parenting.

WORDS AND PHRASES   *Words and Phrases* is a multivolume legal dictionary published by West. Most of its definitions come from court opinions. Exhibit 2.10 presents an excerpt from the "S" volume of the dictionary where the phrase "surrogate parentage contract" is defined. Note that the case defining this phrase is the same case we examined earlier in Exhibits 2.2 and 2.3, *Doe v. Attorney General.* One of the common features of different secondary authorities is that they often refer you to the same laws.

SURROGATE GESTATOR: A NEW AND HONORABLE PROFESSION

JOHN DWIGHT INGRAM

☐ **EXHIBIT 2.7**
Example of a Page from a Legal Periodical Article on Family Law: 76 Marquette Law Review 675 (1993)

I. INTRODUCTION

In recent decades, sex without reproduction has become common and widely accepted, and more recently medical science has made it increasingly possible to have reproduction without sex. The former is much more enjoyable than the latter for most of us and, while it does entail some moral and legal issues, is a great deal less complex than the latter.[1] A major cause of the complexity of the issues associated with noncoital reproduction is that, while ''science [tends to] look ... forward to anticipate new and unforeseen possibilities, the law looks backward, drawing its support from precedent.''[2] Our society seems to first develop and perfect medical and scientific techniques, and only later consult experts in ethics and law to determine if we *should* be doing that which in fact we already *are* doing. Meanwhile, we try to resolve disputes arising from new reproductive technologies by using ''old legal codes of paternity, maternity, baby-selling, adoption, and contracts.''[3]

☐ **EXHIBIT 2.8   Example of a Page from an Annotation on Family Law: 77 A.L.R.4th 70 (1990)**

ANNOTATION

VALIDITY AND CONSTRUCTION OF SURROGATE PARENTING AGREEMENT

by

Danny R. Veilleux, J.D.

I. Preliminary Matters

§ 1. Introduction

[a] Scope

This annotation collects and analyzes the reported cases in which the courts have construed or considered the validity of a surrogate parenting agreement. For the purposes of this annotation, the ''surrogate parenting'' or ''surrogacy'' agreement refers to a contract in which the natural or ''surrogate'' mother, for a fee, agrees to conceive a child through artificial insemination with the sperm of the natural father, to bear and deliver the child to the natural father, and to terminate all of her parental rights subsequent to the child's birth. Although the parties to a surrogacy agreement generally anticipate the eventual adoption of the child by the natural father's wife, this annotation will discuss all surrogacy agreements, regardless of whether they contain any provisions concerning such adoption. Moreover, the surrogate mother's husband, or the natural father's wife, assuming either parent is married, may be a party to the surrogacy agreements included within the scope of this annotation.

MARTINDALE-HUBBELL LAW DIGEST - 1994

Effect of Adoption.—Adopted child after Mar. 1, 1964 does not retain right to inherit from natural family upon making of order of adoption but will inherit from his adoptive parents and their kindred. All inheritance rights by adopted child from his natural parents is terminated, except where natural parent remarries and consents to adoption of child in which case, adopted child only inherits through natural parent who has remarried and consented to adoption and not from other natural parent. Where adoptive parent is married to natural parent, or is natural grandparent or descendant of natural grandparent, adopted child can inherit through natural grandparents or descendants of natural grandparents dying after Aug. 31, 1987. Adopted and natural children have all rights of fraternal relationship, including inheritance from each other. Right of inheritance of adoptive child extends to distributees of such child. (D. R. L. §117).

Wills of persons dying after Mar. 1, 1964 or inter vivos instruments theretofore executed which are subject to being revoked or amended shall be affected by this law, otherwise provisions of this section in effect prior to that date shall be applicable. (D. R. L. §117).

Setting Aside Adoption.—See supra, subhead Order.

Surrogate parenting contracts void. (D. R. L. §124). Payments or receipts of payments of compensation in connection with surrogate parenting prohibited. (D. R. L. §123).

☐ **EXHIBIT 2.9**
Example of a Family Law Topic Discussed in the "Martindale-Hubbell Law Digest" volume of *Martindale-Hubbell Law Directory* **(1994)**

SURROGATE PARENTAGE CONTRACT
"Surrogate parentage contract," which is void and unenforceable under Surrogate Parenting Act, consists of (1) conception, through either natural or artificial insemination, of, or surrogate gestation by female and (2) voluntary relinquishment of her parental rights to the child; but contract that does not contain both such elements is not void or unenforceable under the Act even when entered into for compensation. Doe v. Attorney General, 487 N.W.2d 484, 488, 194 Mich.App. 432.

SURROGATE TEST
Supplier of blood bank cannot be held liable for transmission of AIDS virus on the basis of having failed to employ a "surrogate test" for identifying donors who were at a high risk for transmitting AIDS (acquired immune deficiency syndrome), even though recipient asserted that blood supplier should have used the test for hepatitis B core antibody. Doe v. American Red Cross Blood Services, S.C. Region, D.S.C., 125 F.R.D. 637, 640.

☐ **EXHIBIT 2.10**
Example of a Page from *Words and Phrases* **(1994) that Defines a Family Law Term**

ASSIGNMENT 2.1

a. What is the name of the statutory code containing the statutes of your legislature? If more than one exists, list each one. (See also Assignment 1.3 in chapter 1.)

b. In this code, find any statute on divorce. Quote and cite the first line from this statute.

c. Find the court rules of any court in your state that can hear family law cases. Select any court rule on any family law topic. Quote and cite the first sentence of this rule.

d. What is the name of the regional reporter that contains the court opinions of the highest state court in your state? (See also Assignment 1.7 in chapter 1.)

e. How many West digests contain small paragraph summaries of the opinions of your state courts? Name each one.

f. Go to the "Descriptive Word Index" of any digest covering your state courts. List any three key topics and numbers on divorce.

g. Go to one of the three key topics and numbers in the main volumes of your digest. Under that key topic and number, find one case written within the last ten years by a state court of your state. What is the citation of this case? What key topics and numbers did you find it digested under?

h. Go to the reporter volume that contains the case you identified in question (g). What is the name of the court that wrote this opinion? Quote and cite the first line of the opinion.

i. What is the name of the legal newspaper most practitioners rely on in your state? In a recent issue of this newspaper, find any reference to a family law topic or case. Quote from and cite the reference.

j. Go to *American Jurisprudence, 2d.* Use the index volumes to find any topic on divorce. What topic did you select? Find that topic in the main volumes of *Am. Jur. 2d.* Quote and cite the first line of that topic in the encyclopedia.

k. In the footnotes for the topic you selected in *Am. Jur. 2d,* find a citation to an opinion written by a state court of your state. (Be sure to check the pocket part for the volume you are using.) If you can't find such an opinion, pick another divorce topic until you can. What is the citation of the opinion?

l. Go to *Corpus Juris Secundum.* Use the index volumes to find any topic on divorce. What topic did you select? Find that topic in the main volumes of *C.J.S.* Quote and cite the first line of that topic in the encyclopedia.

m. In the footnotes for the topic you selected in *C.J.S.,* find a citation to a court opinion written by a state court of your state. (Be sure to check the pocket part for the volume you are using.) If you can't find such an opinion, pick another divorce topic until you can. What is the citation of the opinion?

n. Use the card catalog to find any legal treatise that covers the law of your state alone. Go to the index in that treatise to find a discussion of any family law topic of your state. Quote and cite the first sentence of this discussion. If the legal treatise you selected does not cover the family law of your state, pick another treatise.

o. Find a legal periodical article or story that meets the following criteria: it covers a family law topic, and the name of your state appears in the title of the article. Quote and cite the first sentence of this article. (To find such an article, use whatever legal periodical index system is available in your library, e.g., *LegalTrac, Legal Resource Index, Index to Legal Periodicals.*

p. Go to the *Index to Annotations.* Use it to find any annotation on any family law topic in *A.L.R., A.L.R.2d, A.L.R.3d, A.L.R.4th, A.L.R.5th,* or *A.L.R. Fed.* Go to this annotation. Find a reference in the annotation to any court opinion written by a court of your state. What is the citation of the annotation? What is the citation of the court opinion you found in the annotation? If the annotation you select does not cite an opinion from your state, pick another annotation from the *Index to Annotations.*

q. Go to the "Martindale-Hubbell Law Digest" volume of *Martindale-Hubbell Law Directory.* Find the summary for your state. Find a discussion of any family law topic. Quote and cite the first sentence of this discussion.

r. Go to the legal dictionary, *Words and Phrases.* Look up the definitions of any of the following words: adultery, antenuptial, domicile, joint custody, or alimony. Find a definition written by a state court of your state. What word did you select? What is the definition? What is the citation of the opinion from which this definition is taken?

▬▬▬ LEGAL INSTITUTIONS THAT APPLY FAMILY LAW

COURTS

Here our concern is as follows: what courts in your state have jurisdiction (sometimes called **subject-matter jurisdiction**) over family law problems? These courts may have different names in different states, e.g., Family Court, Domestic Relations Court, Juvenile Court, Superior Court, District Court, Circuit Court, etc. If a court has *concurrent jurisdiction* over a matter, it means that more than one category of court in the state can hear the case. *Exclusive juris-*

diction, on the other hand, means that only one category of court can hear the particular kind of case.

How can you determine which courts in your state have jurisdiction over family law problems and what the limitations are, if any, on that jurisdiction? Several ways exist:

1. Examine all state statutes in the statutory code on the judicial system of your state.

2. Examine all constitutional provisions in the state constitution on the judicial system of your state.

3. Examine the court rules of each court in your state.

4. Ask court clerks, experienced lawyers, and experienced paralegals.

5. Examine practice manuals or other legal treatises.

While the latter two sources of information (4 and 5) can be quite reliable, it is highly recommended that you learn to consult the primary sources of information: statutes, constitutions, and court rules.

Check your state statutory code to determine what courts in your state have subject matter jurisdiction over family law problems. For each court, make a list of the kinds of family law problems it can hear. (See General Instructions for the State-Code Assignment in chapter 1.)

ASSIGNMENT 2.2

ADMINISTRATIVE AGENCIES

Unlike other areas of the law, administrative agencies are minimally involved in family law. The courts are the primary institutions that resolve family law conflicts. Some of the agencies that do play a role are the Bureau of Vital Statistics, Adoption Department, Department of Social Services, Probation Department, Child Welfare Agency, Marriage Conciliation Bureau, etc.

Make a list of every state agency in your state that handles children in trouble, husband-wife difficulties, or any other family law problem. Select two of these agencies. Write, call, or visit these two agencies and ask for copies of the following:

□ Program literature describing the services of the agency

□ Sample application forms that the public uses to obtain the benefits and services of the agency

□ Examples of the agency's regulations

Be prepared to give a class presentation on the workings of one of the agencies you selected.

ASSIGNMENT 2.3

◼◼◼◼ SUMMARY

Since family law is constantly changing, anyone who works in this area must know how to keep current. The main resource for doing so is the law library. This is where you use secondary authority to help you find and understand primary authority. The six most important legal publications for

the family law practitioner are the statutory code, court rules, court opinions, digests, practice manuals, and legal newspapers. There are two main ways to begin your research task. First, you could go directly to the primary sources such as the statutory codes (through their indexes) and the reporter volumes (through digests or computer databases). Second you could start with some of the main secondary authorities such as legal encyclopedias, legal treatises, legal periodicals, and annotations. You also need to know which courts have subject matter jurisdiction over family law cases and which administrative agencies handle aspects of such cases.

■■■■ KEY CHAPTER TERMINOLOGY

Depository Library
Primary Authority
Secondary Authority
Statutory Code
Court Rules
Court Opinion
Reporters
Digest

Practice Manual
Legal Newspaper
Syllabus
Headnote
Legal Encyclopedia
American Jurisprudence, 2d
Corpus Juris Secundum
Legal Treatise

Legal Periodical
Annotation
American Law Reports
Martindale-Hubbell Law Directory
Martindale-Hubbell Law Digest
Words and Phrases
Subject Matter Jurisdiction

THE DYNAMICS OF WORKING IN A FAMILY LAW OFFICE

▰▰▰ INTRODUCTION

"One of the worst kept secrets in legal practice is the toll that domestic relations work can take on a lawyer's staff, resources, and psyche."[1] There is nothing dull about working in a family law office. One attorney called it "endlessly fascinating." But it's not for the faint of heart. Attorneys and paralegals often work on many cases simultaneously. Keeping track of the documents and deadlines for all these cases can be a daunting task. Furthermore the case stories of the clients are often emotionally draining. To respond appropriately, workers must be professionals in the truest sense of this word. The client's world may be falling apart in a volcano of pain, anger, and confusion. To be of help in this environment, the attorney and paralegal must demonstrate empathy, stability, and expertise.

Our goal in this chapter is twofold: to introduce you to some of the human dimensions faced by workers in a family law practice and to suggest techniques for maintaining sanity and competence within it.

▰▰▰ HOW TO BE SUPERVISED

Assume that you have just joined a busy family law practice. The first rule of survival is to have a realistic understanding of what you could find during your first month on the job. The following list outlines possible problems:

☐ The family law you learned in school is not enough to enable you to handle every assignment you are given on the job.

---

1. Jennifer J. Rose, *The Ten Commandments of Family Law Economics*, 39 The Practical Lawyer 85 (Jan. 1993).

☐ Your supervisors give you numerous, hard-to-follow instructions; they assume you know a lot more than you do.

☐ When you receive your first few assignments, you have the strange feeling that you don't remember anything you learned, and you panic momentarily.

☐ Your supervisor tells you to forget everything you learned because "we do things differently here."

☐ Some of the attorneys are suspicious of paralegals—they are not quite sure what you are trained to do; you've got to prove yourself.

☐ One or more of the secretaries, who have been at the firm some time, are suspicious and perhaps resentful of your presence—they think that they should have been upgraded into the job you were given.

☐ The office moves at a frantic pace with seemingly no time for you to think.

What should you do when confronted with such situations? One solution is to learn *how to be supervised.*

Supervision—whether given or received—does not come naturally to most of us. Unfortunately, very few people know how to supervise effectively.[2] This includes attorneys and paralegals, who are sometimes required to supervise secretaries, clerks, and other paralegals. The skill of *being* supervised is no easier to acquire, even though most of us have more experience at it. This skill requires:

1. Carrying out an assigned responsibility according to the instructions of the supervisor

2. Taking maximum advantage of each assignment to develop knowledge and skills.

Both of these objectives may sound relatively easy to accomplish. You may feel that you are already an expert at carrying out assigned tasks and at learning while doing. Are you?

If you asked a supervisor to assess the quality of the people he or she has supervised, you might be told that one in twenty is a "good worker." Are you the one in twenty? Possibly 99 out of 100 of us *do not know what our supervisors really think of us* in spite of what they have told us about our work.

ASSIGNMENT 3.1

Think of the last five people who have supervised you in an employment setting. (If you have not yet worked enough to have had five work supervisors, select other settings in which others had to supervise you, e.g., school/church projects, other volunteer activity.) For each supervisor, answer the following questions:

a. What is that person's general impression of you as a worker?

b. What negative comments would he or she make about you as a worker?

c. If any of the supervisors could have replaced you before you left, would they have done so? Why or why not?

Most of us would have great difficulty answering the questions of Assignment 3.1 objectively. When we think about our prior work settings that have been less than satisfactory, our inclination is to blame someone else for what went wrong. While it may be true that others deserve some blame, we need to look

---

2. See William P. Statsky, *Techniques for Supervising Paralegals,* 22 The Practical Lawyer 81 (June 1976).

at our own participation, our own shortcomings, our own responsibility for what happened.

Step one, therefore, in the process of learning how to be supervised is to try to answer the questions, "Who am I as a worker?" "What are my strengths and weaknesses?" "Would I hire myself?" "Where do I need improvement?" "Does my ego interfere with my performance?" "Am I afraid to say, 'I don't understand'?" "Do I know how to ask for help?" Your ability to give honest and positive answers to questions such as these will be much more important in determining your success as a paralegal than the amount of family law you learn in this course.

We now turn to a number of concrete suggestions to maintain a healthy supervisor-supervisee relationship.

KING'S CLOTHES

Don't play **king's clothes** with the instructions you receive. Recall the story in which the king was naked, but everybody kept admiring his beautiful wardrobe. As new people arrived, they saw that he had no clothes, but they heard everyone talking as if he were fully dressed. Not wanting to appear stupid, they, too, began admiring the king's wardrobe. Paralegals play king's clothes when they pretend they understand all the instructions they are receiving when in fact they do not. For obvious reasons, this is a serious mistake.

Whenever you are given an assignment in a new area, there should be a great deal that you do not understand. This is particularly true during your first few months on the job when everything is new! Suppose an attorney says to you, "Get the show cause order from the Kingston file and prepare a draft of a 302 motion in response." Do you know what a show cause order is? Do you know what a 302 motion is? Have you ever drafted one? Do you know where the Kingston file is? If you have any doubts, don't play king's clothes. Don't pretend to have knowledge and skills that you do not yet have. Constantly ask questions about new things. Don't be reluctant to ask for explanations. Learn how to ask for help. *It will not be a sign of weakness.* Quite the contrary. People who want to make sure that they fully understand all their instructions soon gain a reputation for responsibility and conscientiousness.

REPETITION OF INSTRUCTIONS

Repeat the instructions to your supervisor before you leave the room. Once your supervisor has told you what he or she wants you to do, do not leave the room in silence or with the general observation, "I'll get on that right away." First make sure you are on the same wavelength by repeating the instructions back to the supervisor *as you understand them.* This will be an excellent opportunity for the supervisor to determine what you did and did not understand and to provide you with clarifications where needed.

Supervisors are not always sure what they want. Discussing instructions with you provides the supervisor with the opportunity to think through, and possibly even change, what he or she wants done.

WRITTEN INSTRUCTIONS

Write your instructions down. Never go to your supervisor without pen and paper. Preferably, keep an Instructions Notebook in which you record the following information:

☐ Notes on what you are supposed to do

☐ The date you are given the assignment

☐ The date the supervisor expects you to complete all or part of the assignment; seek clarification of vague due dates

☐ Later changes made by your supervisor on your assignment

☐ Dates you actually complete the assignment

The notes will serve as your memory bank. If questions arise about what you were supposed to do, you have something concrete to which to refer.

SEPARATION OF TASKS

If the instructions appear to be complicated, ask your supervisor to segment them into separate tasks and to assign priorities to each one. Many supervisors do not give instructions in clear, logical patterns. They may talk in a rambling, stream-of-consciousness fashion. When you feel overwhelmed by the instructions, simply say: "OK, but can you break that down for me a little more in terms of what you want me to do first? I'll be able to do the entire assignment, but it would help if I approach it one step at a time. Where do you want me to start?"

YOUR OWN CHECKLISTS

As often as possible, write your instructions and what you do in the form of **checklists.** A methodical mind views a project in "do-able" steps that can be tackled one at a time. You need a methodical mind in order to function in a busy law office. One of the best ways to develop such a mind is to think in terms of checklists. A checklist is simply a chronological sequencing of tasks that must be performed in order to complete a project. We have already seen how to translate a rule into a checklist (page 27). This same process can be used to convert the instructions from your supervisor into a detailed checklist.

To be sure, it can be time-consuming to draft checklists. Keep in mind, however, that:

☐ The checklists will be a benefit to you in organizing your time and in assuring completeness.

☐ The checklists can be invaluable for other employees who are given similar assignments in the future.

You will not be able to draft checklists for everything you do. Perhaps you will not be able to write more than one checklist a week. Perhaps you will have to use some of your own time to write the checklists. Whatever time you can devote to checklists will be profitably spent so long as you are serious about using them. They may have to be rewritten or modified later. This should not deter you from the task, since most things that are worth doing require testing and reassessment.

Once you have a number of checklists, you have the makings of a how-to-do-it manual that you have written yourself. If you want to see the face of your supervisor light up, watch his or her reaction upon discovering that you are this organized!

OFFICE MANUALS AND CHECKLISTS

Don't reinvent the wheel. If manuals and checklists already exist in your office on the topic of your assignments, you should find and use them, adapting what you find to the particular assignment on which you are working. Unfortunately, the how-to-do-it information is usually buried in the heads of the attorneys, paralegals, and secretaries of the office. No one has taken the time to write it all down. This is particularly true in small offices.

MODELS

One of the best ways of making sure you know what the supervisor wants is by asking whether any models exist that you could use as a guide for what you are being asked to do. Such models may be found in closed case files, manuals, formbooks, practice texts, etc. As pointed out in Chapter 1, however, great care is needed in using such material. Every new legal problem is potentially unique. What will work in one case may not work in another. A model is a guide, a starting point, and nothing more.

LEGAL RESEARCH

Do some independent legal research on your own on the instructions you are given. Often you will be told what to do without being given more than a cursory explanation of why it needs to be done that way. However, all of the instructions you are given have a basis in the law. A complaint, for example, is served on an opposing party in a designated way because the law has imposed rules on how such service is to be made. You will be asked to serve a complaint in a certain way without being told what section of the state code (or of your court rules) *requires* it to be served in that way. It would be highly impractical for you to read all the law that is the foundation for the instructions you are given. It is not necessary, and you would not have time to do so.

What you *can* do, however, is select certain instructions on certain assignments and do some background legal research in order to gain a greater appreciation for why the instructions were necessary to accomplish the task. You will probably have to do such legal research on your own time unless the assignment you are given includes some legal research. The research can be time-consuming, but you will find it enormously educational. It can give you a totally new perspective on the assignment and, indeed, on your entire job.

SECRETARIES AND PARALEGALS

Secretaries and other paralegals who have worked in the office for a long time can be very helpful to you if you approach them properly. Everybody wants to feel important. Everybody wants to be respected. Avoid asking for something in a way that gives the impression that you are *entitled* to what is being sought—even if you are. Think of how you would like to be approached if you were in the position of the secretary or other paralegal. What approach would disturb you? What would make you want to go out of your way to cooperate with and assist a new paralegal employee who needs help? Your answers (and sensitivity) to questions such as these will go a long way toward enabling you to draw on the experience of others in the office.

FEEDBACK BEFORE DUE DATE

Unless the assignment you are given is very simple, do not wait until the due date to communicate with, and obtain feedback from, your supervisor. Of course, if you are having trouble with the assignment, you will want to check with your supervisor as soon as possible and as often as necessary. It would be a mistake, however, to contact the supervisor only when trouble arises. To be sure, you should limit your contacts with any busy supervisor to essential matters. You could take the following approach in your discussions: "Everything seems to be going fine on the project you gave me. I expect to have it in to you on time. I'm wondering, however, if you could give me a few moments of your time so that I can bring you up to date on where I am so that you can let me know if I am on the right track."

Perhaps this "perception check" could take place on the phone or during a brief office visit. Suppose you have gone astray on the assignment without knowing it? It is obviously better to discover this before the assignment is due. The more communication you have with your supervisor, the more likely it is that you will catch such errors before much time is wasted.

ONGOING EDUCATION

Sometimes a law firm conducts training sessions for its new attorneys. You should ask that you be included in some or all of them. Bar associations and paralegal associations often conduct all-day seminars on legal topics relevant to your work. Seek permission to attend them if they are held during work hours.

REGULAR EVALUATIONS

Ask for a critique of your work on a regular basis. For a number of reasons, evaluations are either not given or are unhelpful when they are given:

- ☐ Evaluations can be time-consuming.
- ☐ Evaluators are reluctant to say anything negative, especially in writing.
- ☐ Most people don't like to be evaluated; it's too threatening to their egos.

The major antidote is to let your supervisor know that you want to be evaluated and that you can handle criticism. If you are defensive when you are criticized, you will find that the evaluations of your performance will take place behind your back. Such a work environment is obviously very unhealthy.

Consider this approach that a paralegal might take with a supervisor: "I want to know what you think of my work. I want to know where you think I need improvement. That's the only way I'm going to learn. I also want to know when I'm doing things correctly, but I'm mainly interested in your suggestions on what I can do to increase my skills." If you take this approach *and mean it,* the chances are good that you will receive some very constructive criticism. Furthermore you demonstrate your responsibility and maturity when you take the initiative in obtaining evaluations of your performance.

In addition to the occasional oral evaluations that you might ask for, you may want to use an evaluation form that could be filled out in a short time by each of your supervisors. A sample of such a form is shown in Exhibit 3.1. You will note that the form is centered around basic legal skills.

The advantage of this form is that it takes only moments to fill in. All it requires is the circling of a small number of words. The disadvantage is that the evaluation does not provide much detail. Most supervisors, however, are not going to have time to provide you with lengthy, narrative evaluations. During conversations with your supervisor, you should be able to receive more

☐ **EXHIBIT 3.1** **Performance Evaluation Form**

PERFORMANCE EVALUATION

Employee:
Supervisor completing this evaluation:
Date this evaluation was completed:
Period covered by this evaluation:
Instructions: For each item in column one, circle the appropriate word in each of three corresponding columns.

Areas Being Evaluated	To What Extent Has Paralegal Been Given Tasks in This Area	Complexity of Paralegal Tasks in Area	Evaluation of Paralegal's Performance in Area
1. Fact Analysis; Fact Organization	Extensive Minimal None	Very Complex Average Complexity Simple	Excellent Good Fair Needs Improvement
2. Writing Ability, e.g., memos, divorce complaint or other pleadings	Extensive Minimal None	Very Complex Average Complexity Simple	Excellent Good Fair Needs Improvement
3. Outside Contact, e.g., clients, witnesses, agencies, vendors	Extensive Minimal None	Very Complex Average Complexity Simple	Excellent Good Fair Needs Improvement
4. Field Investigation	Extensive Minimal None	Very Complex Average Complexity Simple	Excellent Good Fair Needs Improvement
5. Using the Law Library	Extensive Minimal None	Very Complex Average Complexity Simple	Excellent Good Fair Needs Improvement
6. Tasks requiring an ability to Work Independently	Extensive Minimal None	Very Complex Average Complexity Simple	Excellent Good Fair Needs Improvement
7. Working with Others in the Office	Extensive Minimal None	Very Complex Average Complexity Simple	Excellent Good Fair Needs Improvement
8. Time Management/ Working under Pressure	Extensive Minimal None	Very Complex Average Complexity Simple	Excellent Good Fair Needs Improvement
9. Following Instructions	Extensive Minimal None	Very Complex Average Complexity Simple	Excellent Good Fair Needs Improvement
10. Showing Initiative	Extensive Minimal None	Very Complex Average Complexity Simple	Excellent Good Fair Needs Improvement
11. Motivation			Excellent Good Fair Needs Improvement
12. Overall Abilities			Excellent Good Fair Needs Improvement

comprehensive assessments of strengths and weaknesses. The form might be a catalyst for such conversations.

The form lists a number of "areas being evaluated." Other areas could be added, and some of the areas listed can be broken down into narrower areas. Adapt the form to the particular needs of the law office setting in which you find yourself. The objective is to devise an evaluation instrument that is not burdensome to supervisors, that helps them organize their thoughts about what you have been doing, and that provides you with some useful information about your current standing.

■■■■ ASSESSING YOUR OWN BIASES

Your involvement in a domestic relations case may come at a number of stages:

☐ You might do the comprehensive client interview after the attorney has decided to take the case and has established the attorney-client relationship.

☐ You might do field investigation in order to uncover and verify facts relevant to the case.

☐ You might handle intermediate client contact in order to obtain and exchange needed information.

☐ You might be asked to undertake legal research on the case and prepare drafts of certain documents, e.g., the divorce complaint.

☐ You might schedule client appointments, conduct witness interviews, and make a variety of arrangements centered around court dates.

No matter what stage of a case you are working on, you need to be aware of how your personal feelings might affect your work on the case. Such feelings are the foundation of **bias,** which is a predisposition to act in a certain way. How would you answer the following question: "Am I objective enough that I can assist a person even though I have a personal distaste for what that person wants to do or what that person has done?" Many of us would quickly answer "yes" to this question. We all like to feel that we are levelheaded and not susceptible to letting our prejudices interfere with the job we are asked to accomplish. Most of us, however, have difficulty ignoring our personal likes and dislikes.

ASSIGNMENT 3.2

The following fact situations involve aspects of domestic relations cases. To what extent might an individual be hampered in delivering legal services because of personal reactions toward the client? Identify potential bias.

a. Mr. Smith, the client of your office, is being sued by his estranged wife for custody of their two small children. Mr. and Mrs. Smith live separately, but Mr. Smith has had custody of the children during most of their lives while Mrs. Smith has been in the hospital. Mrs. Smith has charged that Mr. Smith often yells at the children, leaves them with neighbors and day care centers for most of the day, and is an alcoholic. Your investigation reveals that Mrs. Smith will probably be able to prove all these allegations in court.

b. Mrs. Jones is being sued by Mr. Jones for divorce on the ground of adultery. Mrs. Jones is the client of your office. Thus far your investigation has revealed that there is considerable doubt over whether Mrs. Jones did in fact commit adultery. During a recent conversation with Mrs. Jones, however, she tells you that she is a prostitute.

c. Jane Anderson is seeking an abortion. She is not married. The father of the child wants to prevent her from having the abortion. Jane comes to your office for legal help. She wants to know what her rights are. You belong to a church that believes abortion is murder. You are assigned to work on the case.

d. Tom Donaldson is a client of your office. His former wife claims that he has failed to pay court-ordered alimony payments and that the payments should be increased substantially because of her needs and his recently improved financial status. Your job is to help Tom collect a large volume of records concerning his past alimony payments and his present financial worth. You are the only person in the office who is available to do this record gathering. It is clear, however, that Tom does not like you. On a number of occasions, he has indirectly questioned your ability.

Having analyzed the fact situations in Assignment 3.2, do you still feel the same about your assessment of your own **objectivity?** Clearly, we cannot simply wish our personal feelings away or pretend that they do not exist. Nor are there any absolute rules or techniques that apply to every situation you will be asked to handle. Nor are the following admonitions very helpful: "Be objective," "be dispassionate," "don't get personally involved," "control your feelings." Such admonitions are too general, and when viewed in the abstract, they may appear not to be needed, since we want to believe that we are always objective, dispassionate, detached, and in control.

We must recognize that there are facts and circumstances that arouse our emotions and tempt us to impose our own value judgments. Perhaps if we know where we are vulnerable, we will be in a better position to prevent our reactions from interfering with our work. It is not desirable for you to be totally dispassionate and removed. A paralegal who is cold, unfeeling, and incapable of empathy is not much better than a paralegal who self-righteously scolds a client. It is clearly not improper for a paralegal to express sympathy, surprise, and perhaps even shock at what unfolds from the client's life story. If these feelings are genuine and if they would be normal reactions to the situation at a given moment, then they should be expressed. The problem is *how to draw the line* between expressing these feelings and reacting so judgmentally that you interfere with your ability to communicate with the client now and in the future. Again, there are no absolute guidelines. As you gain experience in the art of dealing with people, you will hopefully develop styles and techniques that will enable you to avoid going over that line. The starting point in this development is to recognize how easy it is to go over the line.

Some paralegals apply what is called the "stomach test." If your gut tells you that your personal feelings about the case are so intense that you may not be able to do a quality job for the client, you need to take action.[3] Talk with your supervisor. You may have some misunderstandings about the case that your supervisor can clear up. You may be able to limit your role in the case or be reassigned to other cases. Without breaching client confidentiality, contact your local paralegal association to try to talk with other paralegals who have handled similar situations. They may be able to give you some guidance.

Attorneys often take unpopular cases involving clients who have said or done things that run the gamut from being politically incorrect to being socially reprehensible. As professionals, attorneys are committed to the principle that

3. Shari Caudron, *Crisis of Conscience*, 12 Legal Assistant Today 73, 75 (September/October 1994).

everyone is entitled to representation. Paralegals need to have this same commitment. But attorneys and paralegals are human beings. No one can treat every case identically. In the final analysis, you need to ask yourself whether your bias is so strong that it might interfere with your ability to give the needs of the client 100% of your energy and skill. If so, you have an obligation not to work on the case.

ASSIGNMENT 3.3	**a.** Think about your past and present contacts with people who have irritated you the most. Make a specific list of what bothered you about these people. Suppose that you are working in a law office where a client did one of the things on your list. Could you handle such a case?

b. In the relationship among husband, wife, and child, many things can be done that would be wrong (i.e., illegal, immoral, improper) according to your personal system of values. Make a list of the ten things that could be done by husband, wife, or child to another family member (e.g., husband to wife, child to parent) that would be most offensive to your sense of values. Assume that a client in the office where you work has done one of these ten things and is being challenged in court by someone because of it. Your office is defending the client against this challenge. What difficulties do you see for yourself in being able to assist this client?

■■■■■ WHAT DOES THE CLIENT WANT?

A number of assumptions can be made about many clients with family law problems:

☐ The client is not sure what he or she wants in spite of what he or she says.

☐ The client keeps changing his or her mind about what he or she wants.

☐ The client is not aware of his or her legal and nonlegal options.

☐ The family law problem involves other legal problems about which the client is unaware and about which even you may be unaware at the outset.

Suppose that a client walks into the office and tells the attorney, "I want a divorce." The following observations *might* be possible about the client:

1. The client has an incorrect understanding of what a divorce is.

2. The client says she wants a divorce because she thinks this is the only legal remedy available to solve her problem.

3. If the client knew that other remedies existed (e.g., annulment, judicial separation, a support order), she would consider these options.

4. What really troubles the client is that her husband beats the kids; a divorce is the only way she thinks she can stop it.

5. The client does not want a divorce. She is being pressured by her husband to institute divorce proceedings. He has threatened her with violence if she refuses.

6. The client consciously or unconsciously wants and needs an opportunity to tell someone how badly the world is treating her, and if given this opportunity, she may not want to terminate the marriage.

7. If the client knew that marriage or family counseling was available in the community, she would consider using it before taking the drastic step of going to a law office for a divorce.

If any of these observations is correct, think of how damaging it would be for someone in the law office to take out the standard divorce forms and quickly fill them out immediately after the client says, "I want a divorce." This response would not be appropriate without first probing beneath the statement to determine what in fact is on the client's mind. Some clients who speak only of divorces and separation agreements would be receptive to and even anxious for reconciliation. The danger exists that the client might be steered in the direction of a divorce because no other options are presented to her, because no one takes the time to help her express the ideas, intentions, and desires that are lurking beneath the seemingly clear statement, "I want a divorce."

This is not to say that you must be prepared to psychoanalyze every client or that you must always distrust what the client initially tells you. It is rather a recognition of the fact that *most people are confused about the law and make requests based upon misinformation as to what courses of action are available to solve problems.* Common sense tells us to avoid taking all statements at face value. People under emotional distress, particularly in situations of family conflict, need to be treated with sensitivity. We should not expect them to be able to express their intentions with clarity all the time in view of the emotions involved and the sometimes complicated nature of the law.

ASSIGNMENT 3.4

For each of the following statements made by a client, what areas do you think would be reasonable to probe in order to determine if the statement is an accurate reflection of what the client wants? What misunderstandings do you think the client might have? What further questions would you want to ask in order to be sure that you have identified what the client wants?

a. "I want to commit my husband to a mental institution."
b. "I can't control my teenage son anymore. I want him placed in a juvenile home."
c. "I want to put my baby daughter up for adoption."

■■■■■ THE PIGEONHOLE MENTALITY

A great deal of **specialization** exists in the practice of law. Lawyers often concentrate on certain kinds of cases, e.g., bankruptcy, criminal law, tax law, and, of course, family law. Many paralegals do the same if they happen to work for specialists. The danger of specialization is "pigeonholing": seeing everything in terms of the specialty and blocking out what does not fall within it. A bankruptcy lawyer may overlook a tax problem, and a tax lawyer may overlook a bankruptcy problem. The following article by Marc Ullom examines this problem from the perspective of the paralegal.

WHAT YOU HEAR IS WHAT YOU GET
By Mark Ullom, Esq. The Paralegal Forum 5,
Philadelphia Association of Paralegals (March 1988).

Scenario A

It was a typically successful day. Two clients came to the door with divorce agreements amicably outlined. Another brought in bankruptcy creditor lists that were complete to the last name and address. Another came in with perfect liability in a personal injury case, carrying stacks of medical bills neatly catalogued for each doctor who treated the injuries. Each consultation took fifteen minutes. The first three paid their fees in full. My paralegal took the paperwork, transferred it into the pleadings, and we had time left over for the staff to take a long lunch at our favorite restaurant.

Scenario B

Then I woke up. The alarm hadn't gone off. I almost missed my nine o'clock appointment with a divorce cli-

ent who then said she couldn't afford to start the case. Then I had to rush down to a bankruptcy hearing for a guy who got hurt at work, fell behind on his bills, and then was laid off from his job because he couldn't afford to get his car fixed.

So much for the textbook cases with neatly packaged issues. Hope as we might for the "Scenario A" days of our dreams, the "Scenario B" days are as common as calendar pads.

Attractive as the first scenario might seem, the practice of law would become dull indeed if everything were so convenient. More importantly, if my days ever begin to seem simple, I'll know I'm not listening to my clients as well as I should.

In these times of specialization, we do oversimplify things. We tend to shoehorn the client's needs into the skills we have to fit them. Bankruptcy specialists notice only bankruptcy problems. Divorce people see only the domestic issues. If that is the skill we have, that is the service we will provide. But in so doing, both we and the client stand to lose. The client loses when the real problems are only partly solved. The law firm loses when we overlook an opportunity to serve effectively, be properly paid for it, and win a client who will have the confidence to return with legal needs in the future.

Consider the number of client contacts that are handled by the paralegal rather than the attorney. Clients mention facts to a paralegal in brief conversation that they do not think are important enough to "bother" the lawyer. If you are well attuned to the client's words, you will be alerting the attorney to issues even if they are not in your area of specialty.

How well are you attuned to the client? Take a moment to reread "Scenario B." How many cases are really there? Nobody knows until the lawyer asks a few more questions, but try these: divorce, financial problems due to accumulated debt of a separated spouse, financial problems due to child support arrearages, money problems due to illness, injury or job layoffs, bankruptcy, worker's compensation injury, other personal injury claims, unemployment compensation. There may even be more, but the most important fact is that nobody knows until the appropriate follow-up questions are asked.

As a paralegal, there is much you can do to help your attorney spot all the needs of the client:

1. Listen to the casual comments of the client, such as: "can't make it in today—got hurt," or "looking for a house."

2. Notice changes in the client's mood, in comments like: "why does it take so long," "my friend's case went smoother," "money getting tight," and "my spouse doesn't agree with you" (when it's not a divorce case!).

3. Alert the attorney first, so the attorney can decide what action is appropriate, if any.

4. Document your contact in the case file, too, so that the attorney will remember your contact when reviewing the file.

5. Defer any comment to the client until the attorney makes a decision how to proceed.

6. Brush up on other areas of procedure, too, especially those areas that most often touch the edges of your practice.

Properly handled, your communications with the client—which are usually more frequent than those of the attorney—will tell the client that you are interested in *all* the client's legal needs, and stand ready to serve.

■ VIOLENCE DIRECTED AT ATTORNEYS

As the following article indicates, attorneys practicing family law can be the targets of physical violence from emotionally distraught people.

ON THE FIRING LINE
By D. Weikel
Calif. Lawyer 22 (November 1988).

When divorce and romantic discord turn to war, lawyers are sometimes the first casualties. Orange County attorney William M. Swain, for example, will never use his left hand again—a grim reminder of the heights to which violence can rise during a divorce case.

While taking a court-ordered inventory of a Fullerton pawn shop, . . . Swain was shot twice by Victor Pahl, the estranged husband of Swain's client. Swain lost his spleen and part of his pancreas. He also suffered a punctured stomach and lung as well as permanent damage to his hand.

Pahl admitted pulling the trigger, but was acquitted . . . of attempted murder, assault and attempted manslaughter charges. Jurors said they believed the defense contention that Pahl, depressed by his pending divorce, was in a "zombielike" state and did not know what he was doing.

Swain's experience may be extreme, yet the risks he faced are not uncommon for attorneys handling dissolutions, palimony cases and restraining orders. No statistics reveal the number of times family lawyers have been threatened or assaulted. But the frequency of family-related violence means that family law attorneys often get caught on the firing line. Roughly a third of all female homicide victims are killed by husbands or boyfriends, according to the FBI and the state attorney general's office. And crime figures show that 20 percent of all murders involve some kind of family relationship.

"It really doesn't matter if the violence happens in 1 percent or 100 percent of your cases," says Margaret Anderson of Santa Rosa, chair of the State Bar's Family Law Section. "One percent can do a lot of damage."

Although the problem has been discussed by local and state bar associations, attorneys and judges say there are few solutions except restraining orders, training for lawyers, and beefed-up security.

Some courthouses across the state have increased the number of bailiffs in domestic law courts, and a few have installed metal detectors to screen everyone, lawyers included.

Santa Clara County Superior Court installed its metal detector after a bailiff found a gun in a lunch box brought into court by an estranged husband. "The sheriff and the judges have finally realized how dangerous family law can be," says San Jose attorney Lynne Yates-Carter, who sits on the executive committee of the State Bar's Family Law Section. In some counties, lawyers and clients threatened by ex-spouses can request bailiffs to escort the threatened ones around the courthouse or to their cars.

To help attorneys cope with potentially violent situations, some bar associations sponsor seminars on how to keep client emotions under control. Divorce lawyers say they regularly consult therapists. With experience, attorneys can become adept at identifying potential problems and avoiding catastrophes.

When that can't be done, some attorneys have old-fashioned ways to deal with the situation.

Lisa Hughes, a petite family law practitioner in Santa Ana, keeps a loaded .38-caliber pistol in her office. The door to her firm has a peephole.

"I have had hundreds of clients beaten and threatened, and I have had at least six death threats," Hughes says. "On two occasions I have had a coroner call and say they had someone in the morgue with my card in their pocket. They were not my clients. Perhaps they would have been."

▐▌ SUMMARY

A law office can be a hectic environment in which to work. Survival may depend on the new employee's ability to take advantage of numerous on-the-job learning opportunities. A wealth of information and technique can be acquired and developed this way.

First, ask lots of questions about the instructions you are given. Repeat the instructions back to your supervisor, and write them down in a notebook. Whenever possible, segment the instructions into separate tasks, and make a checklist of all the steps needed to perform each task. Find out if there are other relevant checklists and manuals already in the office. Look for a model of what you have been asked to prepare. Do some independent research in the law library on several of the instructions you have been given. Solicit the assistance of experienced secretaries and paralegals. If possible, find out from your supervisor if you are proceeding properly before the due date of the assignment. Participate in training programs conducted in the office and by outside associations. Seek regular evaluations of your work.

Effective communication between a client and a law office is subject to three potential interferences. The first is the personal bias of office workers. Since the cases handled in a family law practice can be emotionally charged, the need for professionalism is clear, particularly if the office is defending a client who has done something that clashes with a worker's personal values. A second interference is the inarticulateness of some clients. Clients are not always sure what they want until options are presented to them. A third interference is the pigeon-holing that results from legal workers letting their specialized training and experience block out client problems that fall outside the training and experience they have acquired.

Violence is another potential issue in family law. Perhaps more than in any other area of law practice, there is a potential for violence between spouse and spouse, and sometimes between defendant and opposing counsel.

▰▰▰ KEY CHAPTER TERMINOLOGY

Supervision	Checklists	Objectivity
King's Clothes	Bias	Specialization

ETHICS AND MALPRACTICE

4

▄▄▄▄ ETHICS

INTRODUCTION

A recent **ethics** study in a state revealed that 25 percent of all grievances filed against lawyers involved family law cases.[1] This was almost double the percentage for every other area of practice. An uncomfortably large number of family law clients eventually turn on their own lawyer with a charge of unethical conduct. "Emotions tend to run high among the clients of divorce lawyers and it's not unusual for clients to 'blame' their lawyers for their misery, deservedly or not."[2] Needless to say, everyone working in a family law practice must be scrupulous about ethical matters. A family law paralegal cannot know too much about ethics.

There are two main kinds of ethics: those that could lead to **sanctions** when violated and those that are not enforced by sanctions. All lawyers are subject to ethical rules that are backed by sanctions. These rules are called canons of ethics, codes of ethics, or rules of professional responsibility. They are issued and enforced by the courts, usually through the state bar association. The sanctions courts can impose on lawyers for unethical conduct include a reprimand, suspension, or disbarment.

What happens when *paralegals* violate the canons of ethics? They could face immediate dismissal, but since they cannot be full members of the bar, they cannot be reprimanded, suspended, or "disbarred" by the courts for unethical behavior. Some paralegal associations have written their own code of paralegal ethics. To a large extent, these codes are based on the ethical rules governing lawyers. The paralegal codes, however, are not backed by sanctions. There is almost no enforcement mechanism to ensure compliance with the paralegal codes.

Ethics Standards or rules of behavior to which members of an occupation, profession, or other organization are expected to conform.

Sanctions Penalties or punishments of some kind.

---

1. *Report: Lawyer Discipline,* Washington State Bar News 37 (August 1993).
2. *All Lawyers May Have It Bad with the Public, But Family Lawyers . . . ,* 11 The Compleat Lawyer 6 (Winter 1994). (Source: New York Times, 9/5/93).

ASSIGNMENT 4.1

a. Give the full citation to the ethical rules that govern the conduct of lawyers in your state.

b. What is the name of the bar association committee in your state that has jurisdiction over the ethical standards of lawyers? What disciplinary powers does this committee have over lawyers?

c. If a lawyer is dissatisfied with the ruling of the above committee concerning his or her ethical conduct, to what court can the lawyer appeal? (To find answers to the above questions, check your state statutory code and your state constitution. See General Instructions for the State Code Assignment in chapter 1. In addition, you may want to contact your state bar association. Ask it to send you any descriptive literature available on the system for disciplining lawyers.)

d. Draft a flowchart of all the procedural steps that must be taken to discipline a lawyer for unethical conduct. (See General Instructions for the Flowchart Assignment in chapter 1.)

The American Bar Association (ABA) is a voluntary national bar association; lawyers are not required to belong to it. Although the ABA publishes ethical rules, it does not discipline lawyers for unethical conduct. Such conduct is regulated by the state court and the state bar association. The role of the ABA is merely to *propose* ethical rules for consideration by the various states. A state is free to adopt, modify, or reject the ethical rules recommended by the ABA. In view of the prestige of the ABA, many states have adopted its proposals with very little change. The most recent proposals of the ABA are found within the very influential *Model Rules of Professional Conduct.* The following overview is based on these rules.

Ethical issues for the family law practitioner arise in the following major areas:

- □ **Competence**
- □ **Fees**
- □ **Confidentiality of information**
- □ **Conflict of interest**
- □ **Safekeeping property**
- □ **Withdrawal**
- □ **False statements/failure to disclose**
- □ **Communication with the other side**
- □ **Nonlawyer assistants**
- □ **Solicitation**
- □ **Advertising**
- □ **Unauthorized practice of law**

COMPETENCE

Rule 1.1 A lawyer shall provide competent representation to a client.

A classic example of an incompetent lawyer is one who accepts more cases than his or her office can handle. As a consequence, court dates and other filing deadlines are missed, documents are lost, and the lawyer fails to determine what law governs each case. Such a lawyer is practicing law "from the hip"— unethically.

Lawyers must be **competent.** The amount of knowledge and skill they need depends on the complexity of the case. A great deal may be needed when

Competent Using the knowledge, skill, thoroughness, and preparation reasonably needed to represent a particular client.

representing a wife in a divorce case where the issue is the present value of the husband's partially vested pension or his partnership interest in a foreign business. Less may be required for a garden-variety, **uncontested** divorce case in which the parties have no children and no assets.

Uncontested Not disputed; not challenged.

How do ethical lawyers become competent? They draw on the general principles of analysis learned in law school. They take the time needed to *prepare* themselves. They spend time in the law library. They talk with their colleagues. In some instances, they formally associate themselves with more experienced lawyers in the area. A lawyer who fails to take these steps is acting unethically if his or her knowledge and skill are not what is deemed reasonably necessary to represent a particular client.

FEES

Rule 1.5(a)   A lawyer's fee shall be reasonable.

Rule 1.5(d)   A contingent fee in a domestic relations case is prohibited if the payment or amount of the fee is dependent on securing a divorce, on the amount of alimony obtained, on the amount of support obtained, or on the amount of a property settlement in lieu of alimony or support.

There is no absolute rule on when a fee is excessive and therefore unreasonable. A number of factors must be considered: the amount of time and labor involved, the complexity of the matter, the experience and reputation of the lawyer, the customary fee in the locality for the same kind of case, etc. The basis or rate of the fee should be communicated to the client before or soon after the lawyer starts to work on the case. This is often done in the contract of employment called the **retainer.** (Two other meanings of retainer are the money paid by a client to ensure that a lawyer will be available to work for the client and the deposit against future fees and costs of representation.)

Retainer The contract of employment between lawyer and client.

There are two main kinds of fees: fixed or contingent. A **fixed fee** is one that is paid regardless of who wins the case. It may be a flat sum, an hourly rate, or a combination. A **contingent fee** is dependent on the outcome of the case, e.g., a lawyer receives 30 percent of a jury award in a negligence case, but nothing if the client loses the case.

Fixed Fee A fee that is paid regardless of the outcome of the case.

Contingent Fee A fee that is dependent on the outcome of the case.

In most states, contingent fees are unethical if they are directly tied to obtaining a divorce or to the amount of alimony, support, or property settlement. A main argument against contingent fees in such cases is that the lawyer might be so anxious to obtain the divorce or a certain amount from the other side that he or she will interfere with possibilities of reconciliation between the parties—since the contingent fee is not paid if the parties get back together again. Suppose, however, the parties are already divorced and the dispute is over unpaid alimony or child support—**arrearages.** Some states allow lawyers to charge a contingent fee in such cases. Since the marriage has already been dissolved, there is little likelihood that the lawyer's personal interest in collecting this kind of contingent fee will hinder a reconciliation.

Arrearages Money overdue and unpaid.

Dan and Elaine were divorced in 1995. The divorce decree ordered Dan to pay $350 a month in child support for their daughter, which he has faithfully paid. A year later, Elaine goes to a lawyer to seek help in obtaining an increase in child support to $500 a month. Is there any policy reason against the lawyer taking this case for a fee of 20 percent of everything a court orders Dan to pay above $350 a month? (See General Instructions for the Legal Analysis Assignment in chapter 1.)

ASSIGNMENT 4.2

Fee Splitting (1) One bill to a client covering the fee of two or more lawyers not in the same firm. (2) Giving a nonlawyer part of the fee of a particular client.

Finally, we examine the problem of **fee splitting.** This can occur in different situations. First, two lawyers from different firms might split a fee. For example:

> Ed Jones, Esq., and Mary Smith, Esq., both work on behalf of a husband seeking custody of his children. The husband receives one bill for the work of both lawyers even though they work for different law firms.

The lawyers, in effect, are splitting or dividing the fee between them. This arrangement is proper under certain conditions, e.g., the total fee is reasonable, the client does not object to the participation of all the lawyers involved.

Second, a lawyer might give part of a fee to a nonlawyer. For example:

> Bob Davis, Esq., has a large divorce practice. He has an arrangement with Alice Grover, an independent paralegal, under which Davis will pay Grover 40 percent of the fees he collects from every client she refers to him.

This kind of fee splitting between lawyer and nonlawyer involving a particular client is unethical even if the total amount of the fee is reasonable and the client consents to the split.

CONFIDENTIALITY OF INFORMATION

Rule 1.6 A lawyer must not reveal information relating to the representation of a client unless (a) the client consents to the disclosure, or (b) the lawyer reasonably believes the disclosure is necessary to prevent a client from committing a criminal act that is likely to result in imminent death or substantial bodily harm.

Rule 5.3 (Comment) Lawyers must instruct and supervise their paralegals and other nonlawyer assistants on the obligation not to disclose information relating to the representation of a client.

The confidentiality rule applies to *all* information relating to the representation of a client, whatever its source. The prohibition is not limited to so-called secrets or matters explicitly communicated in confidence. Here are some examples of unethical breaches of confidentiality:

> ☐ At home, a paralegal tells her husband that J. K. Thompson is one of the new divorce clients in the office where the paralegal works.

> ☐ In an elevator crowded with strangers, a paralegal tells her supervisor that the adoption notice in the Smith case came in today's mail.

> ☐ In a paralegal's office, a client file is left open on the desk, visible to an electrician in the office repairing a light fixture.

The confidentiality rule is designed to encourage clients to discuss their cases fully and frankly with the law office they have hired, including embarrassing or legally damaging information. Arguably, clients would be reluctant to tell the office everything if they had to worry about whether a lawyer, paralegal, or anyone else in the office might reveal the information to others.

In some situations, however, it is proper for a lawyer to breach confidentiality. For example:

> A lawyer represents a husband in a bitter divorce case against his wife. During a meeting at the law firm, the husband shows the lawyer a gun and says he is going to use it to kill his wife later the same day.

Can the lawyer tell the police what the husband said? Yes. It is not unethical for a lawyer to reveal information about a client if the lawyer reasonably believes the disclosure is necessary to prevent the client from committing a criminal act that could lead to someone's imminent death or substantial bodily harm.

CONFLICT OF INTEREST

Rule 1.7   A lawyer should avoid a conflict of interest with his or her client.

A **conflict of interest** can exist in many settings. For example, assume that a salesman does part-time work selling the same kind of products of two competing companies. The salesman has a conflict of interest. How can he serve two masters with the same loyalty? How does he divide his customers between the two companies? There is an obvious danger that he will favor one over the other. The fact that he may try to be fair in his treatment of both companies does not eliminate the conflict of interest. The potential exists for one of the companies to be disadvantaged. It may be that the two companies are aware of the problem and are not worried. This does not mean that there is no conflict of interest; it simply means that the affected parties are willing to take the risks involved in the conflict. As we shall see, consent is usually a valid defense to a conflict-of-interest charge.

> **Conflict of Interest**
> Divided loyalty that actually or potentially places a person at a disadvantage even though he or she is owed undivided loyalty.

In a law office, a number of conflict-of-interest issues can arise:

- ☐ Multiple representation
- ☐ Former client/present adversary
- ☐ Law firm disqualification
- ☐ Business transactions with a client
- ☐ Gifts from a client
- ☐ Loaning money to a client
- ☐ Sex with a client

We will explore these issues through a series of fact situations involving a family law practice.

MULTIPLE REPRESENTATION

Bob and Patricia Fannan are separated, and they both want a divorce. They disagree over who should have sole custody of the children and how the marital property should be divided. Mary Franklin, Esq., is a lawyer that Jim and Mary know and trust. They decide to ask Franklin to represent both of them in the divorce.

In this case, Franklin has a conflict of interest due to **multiple representation.** How can she give her undivided loyalty to both sides? On the custody question, for example, how can Franklin vigorously argue that Bob should have sole custody, and at the same time vigorously argue that Patricia should have sole custody? A client is entitled to the *independent professional judgment* of a lawyer. How can Franklin act independently for two different people who are at odds with each other? Franklin's commitment to be fair and objective in giving her advice to the parties will not solve the difficulty. Her role as lawyer is to be a *partisan advocate* for the client. It is impossible for Franklin to play this role for two clients engaged in such a dispute. A clear conflict of interest exists. In every state, it would be unethical for Franklin to represent both Jim and Mary in this case.

> **Multiple Representation**
> Representing more than one side in a legal matter or controversy. Also called joint representation and common representation.

Suppose, however, that the divorce case involved different facts:

Jim and Mary Smith are separated, and they both want a divorce. They have been married only a few months. There are no children and no marital assets to divide. George Davidson, Esq., is a lawyer that Jim and Mary know and trust. They decide to ask Davidson to represent both of them in the divorce.

Can Davidson ethically represent both sides here? Some states *will* allow him to do so on the theory that there isn't much of a conflict between the parties. Hence the potential for harm in multiple representation is almost nonexistent. Other states, however, disagree. They frown on multiple representation even in so-called friendly divorces of this kind.

The ABA *Model Rules of Professional Responsibility* do not impose an absolute ban on all multiple representation, although they certainly discourage it. The rule is as follows:

> **Rule 1.7**   A lawyer shall not represent a client if the representation of that client will be directly adverse to another client, *unless:*
>
> **1.** the lawyer reasonably believes the representation will not adversely affect the relationship with the other client, *and*
>
> **2.** both of the clients consent after consultation about the risks of the multiple representation.

In the Smith divorce, both conditions can probably be met. Such a divorce is little more than a paper procedure since there is no real dispute between the parties. Hence Davidson *would* be reasonable in believing that his representation of Jim would not adversely affect Mary, and vice versa. Davidson can represent both sides so long as Jim and Mary consent to the multiple representation after Davidson clearly explains to both of them whatever risks might be involved in doing so.

Nevertheless, lawyers are urged to avoid multiple representation even when ethically proper. The divorce may have been "friendly" when granted, but years later, one of the ex-spouses may attack the lawyer for having had a conflict of interest. When reminded that both parties consented to the multiple representation, the ex-spouse will inevitably respond by saying, "I didn't understand what I was being asked to consent to."

The coming of no-fault divorce (discussed in chapter 13) has in part been due to a desire to take some of the animosity out of the divorce process. A full **adversary** confrontation is not needed in every case, particularly where there is no custody dispute and few assets to divide. Hence there are pressures on the bar associations and the courts to relax the conflict-of-interest rules in divorce cases where the actual disputes between the parties are minimal or nonexistent. The legal profession is sensitive to the criticism that a too-strict application of the rules in such cases simply results in more business for more lawyers. Yet the cautious lawyer remains understandably reluctant to take chances.

Adversary   (1) Involving a dispute between opposing sides who argue their case before a neutral official such as a judge. (2) An opponent.

FORMER CLIENT/PRESENT ADVERSARY

Jessica Winters, Esq., represented Gregory Noonan in his divorce action against his former wife, Eileen Noonan. In this action, Eileen received custody and alimony. Five years later, Eileen wants to reopen the case in order to obtain more alimony. Winters no longer represents Gregory who now has a different lawyer. Eileen hires Winters in her action for increased alimony.

A former client is now an adversary. Winters once represented Gregory; she is now suing him. Without the consent of the former client (Gregory), it is unethical for Winters to "switch sides" and represent Eileen against him. Consent is needed whenever the second case is the same as the first one, or when the two are substantially related. It is not necessary that the two cases involve the same set of parties. Without Gregory's consent, it would be equally unethical for Winters to represent one of his children who later sues the father for support to force him to pay college expenses. Such an action would be substantially related to the original divorce action.

Why is this so? If the cases are the same or are substantially related, the likelihood is strong that the lawyer will use information learned in the first case to the detriment of the former client in the second case. Winters undoubtedly found out a good deal about Gregory when she represented him in the divorce case. She might now be able to use this information *against* him in Eileen's attempt to increase her alimony or in the child's attempt to force him to pay college expenses.

Winters had a duty of loyalty when she represented Gregory. This duty does not end once the lawyer's fees are paid. The duty continues if the same case arises again or if a substantially related case arises later—even if the lawyer no longer represents the client. A conflict of interest would exist if Winters subsequently acquires a new client who goes against Gregory in the same case or in a substantially related case. Her new duty of loyalty to the second client would clash with her *continuing* duty to the former client in such a case.

Suppose, however, that the second case against a former client is totally unrelated to the first. The lawyer still has an ethical obligation to refrain from using any information relating to the representation in the first case to the disadvantage of the former client in the second case. There is no ban on taking the case, but if the office has any information relating to the first case, that information cannot be used against the former client in the second case.

LAW FIRM DISQUALIFICATION

Two years ago, John Farrell, Esq., represented the father in a custody dispute with the child's maternal grandparent. The father won the case, but the grandmother was awarded limited visitation rights. The grandmother now wants to sue the father for failure to abide by the visitation order. She asks John Farrell to represent her. (The father is now using a different law firm.) John declines because of a conflict of interest, but he sends her to his law partner down the corridor.

If a lawyer is disqualified from representing a client because of a conflict of interest, every lawyer in the *same law firm* is also disqualified unless the client being protected by this rule consents to the representation. In the above example, the *father* would have to consent to the representation of the grandmother by the partner or, indeed, by John Farrell himself. The disqualification of the partner and the entire law firm is called an **imputed disqualification**. It occurs when a lawyer causes another lawyer or law firm to be disqualified. In effect, John Farrell's knowledge about the father is imputed to the partner and everyone else in the firm.

A paralegal can also cause the imputed disqualification of a law firm. This situation most commonly arises when the paralegal switches jobs. For example:

Claire Anderson is a paralegal at the firm of Lawrence Burton, Esq. Her sole assignment is to work on the Vickers divorce case. The firm represents Sam Vickers. One of Anderson's tasks is to make an inventory of all the assets of Sam Vickers. His wife, Karen Vickers, is represented by Edward Walsh, Esq. Before this case comes to trial, Anderson quits her job with Burton in order to become a paralegal with Walsh, who immediately assigns her to the Vick-

Imputed Disqualification
Something is *imputed* when it is forced upon or attributed to someone or something else.

ers case. When Burton finds out that Anderson has performed substantial work on the Vickers case, he makes a motion in court to disqualify Walsh from continuing to represent Karen Vickers.

This motion will probably be granted. A conflict of interest exists that will cause the imputed disqualification of Edward Walsh from any further involvement in the Vickers case. Claire Anderson once worked as a paralegal on behalf of Sam Vickers and acquired information about him in the process. She is now in a position to use this knowledge against him. Her knowledge is imputed to her new employer, Edward Walsh, who is therefore now disqualified and must withdraw from the case. Karen Vickers must find someone else to represent her.

Suppose, however, that Claire Anderson had *not* done any substantial paralegal work on the Vickers case before she arrived at the new firm. Is her new employer still disqualified? In many states, the answer is *no*, if the new employer places a **Chinese Wall** around the paralegal. This involves isolating the **tainted** paralegal from the case through specific steps such as ordering the paralegal to say nothing about the case and have no involvement with it, instructing all other employees in the firm to refrain from discussing the case with the paralegal, and physically storing the file on the case in a section of the office away from the paralegal. If a paralegal with a conflict of interest is effectively screened from the case in this manner, most states will *not* impose an imputed disqualification on the paralegal's new employer.

Chinese Wall Steps taken in an office to prevent a tainted employee from having any contact with a particular case in order to avoid the disqualification of the office from the case.

Tainted Having a conflict of interest in a case.

CASE ──────────────────────────────

Proposed Opinion RPC 176

April 14, 1994
Ethics Committee of the North Carolina State Bar Association
19 North Carolina State Bar Newsletter 16 (1994).

Background: In most states, attorneys can submit ethical questions to the ethics committee of their state bar association. Names of specific clients are not mentioned. The question or inquiry is presented in a generic form to preserve the confidentiality of the clients involved.

Inquiry

Attorney A had two full-time staff members: a receptionist/secretary and a paralegal/secretary ("Paralegal"). Paralegal's normal duties included working on personal injury actions and real estate matters. On occasion, Paralegal helped with domestic actions. While Paralegal was employed by Attorney A, Attorney A represented Client A in a domestic matter. Paralegal denies working on the case on a regular basis while she was employed by Attorney A. Paralegal also denies having any knowledge of the specific facts of the case. Attorney A contends that Paralegal was substantially involved in assisting in the representation of Client A and was privy to confidential information regarding Client A. It is clear that Paralegal had some exposure to the case while employed by Attorney A.

After the employment of Paralegal was terminated by Attorney A, Paralegal went to work for Attorney B in another law firm. Attorney B represents Client B in same domestic action in which Attorney A represents Client A.

Attorney A has requested that Attorney B withdraw from the representation of Client B because of Paralegal's prior involvement in the action. Should Attorney B withdraw from the representation of Client B?

Opinion

No, Attorney B may continue to represent Client B in the case and may continue to employ Paralegal. . . . However, Attorney B must take extreme care to ensure that Paralegal is totally screened from participation in the case even if Paralegal's involvement in the case while employed by Attorney A was negligible. See RPC 74. This requirement is consistent with a lawyer's duty, pursuant to Rule 3.3(B), to make reasonable efforts to ensure that the conduct of a nonlawyer over whom the lawyer has direct supervisory authority is compatible with the professional obligations of the lawyer including the obligation to avoid conflicts of interest and to preserve the confidentiality of client information.

a. Opinion RPC 176 says that "extreme care" must be used to ensure that the tainted paralegal is "totally screened" from the family law ("domestic") case. Make a list of the steps Attorney B can take to accomplish this.

b. Assume that the Paralegal makes a mistake and discloses something relatively unimportant about the case to Attorney B. For example, the Paralegal tells Attorney B that the client in the case was once late for an appointment at the law office of Attorney A. Do you think the North Carolina Ethics Committee would conclude that Opinion RPC 176 had been violated?

BUSINESS TRANSACTIONS WITH A CLIENT

Paul Kelly, Esq., is Ed Johnson's lawyer in a divorce case. Johnson owns a cleaning business for which Kelly does some of the legal work. Johnson offers to allow Kelly to buy a 30 percent interest in the business. Kelly would continue as Johnson's lawyer.

Assume that the business runs into difficulties and Johnson considers bankruptcy. He goes to Kelly for advice on bankruptcy law. Kelly has dual concerns: to give Johnson competent legal advice, and to protect his own 30 percent interest in the business. Bankruptcy may be good for Johnson, but disastrous for Kelly's investment. How can he give Johnson independent professional advice when the advice may go against Kelly's own interest?

This is not to say, however, that it is always unethical for a lawyer to enter a business transaction with a client. If certain strict conditions are met, it can be proper. The rule is as follows:

Rule 1.8(a) A lawyer shall not enter a business transaction with a client, *unless*

1. the terms of the business transaction are fair and reasonable to the client and are fully disclosed to the client in understandable language in writing, *and*

2. the client is given reasonable opportunity to seek advice on the transaction from another lawyer who is not involved with the transaction or the parties, *and*

3. the client consents to the business transaction in writing.

In our example, Johnson must be given the chance to consult with an attorney other than Kelly on the prospect of letting Kelly buy a 30 percent interest in the business. Kelly would have to give Johnson a clear, written explanation of their business relationship. And the relationship must be fair and reasonable to Johnson.

GIFTS FROM A CLIENT

William Stanton, Esq., has been the family attorney of the Tarkinton family for years. At Christmas, Mrs. Tarkinton gave Stanton a television set and told Stanton to change her will so that Stanton's daughter would receive funds to cover her college education.

Generally, attorneys are allowed to accept a gift from a client. If, however, a document must be prepared in order to carry out the gift, it is unethical for the lawyer to prepare that document. A conflict of interest would exist. In our example, it would probably be in Mrs. Tarkinton's interest to have the will written so that she could retain maximum flexibility on how much she would pay for the college education and so that she could change her mind if she wanted to. Yet it would be in Stanton's interest to try to write the will so that it would be difficult for her to back out of her commitment.

Thus, a lawyer cannot prepare a document such as a will, a trust fund, a contract, etc., that results in any substantial gift from a client to the lawyer, or to the lawyer's children, spouse, parents, brothers, or sisters. If a client wants to make such a gift, another lawyer must prepare the document. There is, however, one exception. If the client is *related* to the person receiving the gift, the lawyer can prepare the document.

There does not appear to be any ethical problem in taking the gift of the television set. No documents are involved.

LOANING MONEY TO A CLIENT

Henry Harris, Esq., is Barbara Atkinson's attorney in a divorce action against her husband. While the case is pending, Harris agrees to lend Atkinson living expenses and court filing fees.

It can be a conflict of interest for a lawyer to give financial assistance to a client in connection with current or planned litigation. A loan covering litigation expenses, however, is an exception to this rule. In our example, the main difficulty is the loan to cover the client's living expenses. Suppose that the husband makes an offer to settle the case with Barbara. There is a danger that Harris's advice will be colored by the fact that he has a financial interest in Barbara—he wants to have his loan for living expenses repaid. The offer to settle from the husband may not be enough to cover the loan. Should he advise Barbara to accept the offer? It may be in Barbara's interest to accept the offer, but not in his own interest. Such divided loyalty is the essence of a conflict of interest.

As indicated, a major exception concerns the expenses of litigation such as filing fees and other court costs. It is not unethical for a lawyer to lend the client money to cover such expenses.

SEX WITH A CLIENT   One of the more dramatic examples of a conflict of interest is the lawyer who develops a romantic relationship with a current client, particularly a sexual relationship. Family law clients often come to lawyers when they are most vulnerable. Under such circumstances, it is unconscionable for the lawyer to take advantage of this vulnerability. A lawyer with a physical or emotional interest in a client will be looking for ways to increase that interest and to inspire a reciprocal interest from the client. Needless to say, this may not be what the client needs. But the lawyer's own need could well cloud his or her ability to put the client's welfare first. The only way to maintain professional independence is for lawyers—as well as their paralegals and other employees—to avoid these kinds of relationships with current clients. When the cases are over, however, and they cease being clients, such relationships are less likely to constitute a conflict of interest.

SAFEKEEPING PROPERTY

Rule 1.15 A lawyer shall hold client property separate from the lawyer's own property.

Commingling of Funds Mixing general law firm funds with client funds in a single account. More broadly, it means combining one's own funds with those to whom a fiduciary duty is owed.

Client funds—or the funds of others connected with a client's case—should be kept in a separate account, and complete records should be kept on the funds. The **commingling of funds** is unethical no matter how good the records are on who owns the amounts in the account. In a commingled account, the danger is simply too great that client funds will be used for nonclient purposes. This is extremely important for paralegals to know since they are often placed in charge of bookkeeping records in a law firm. Their supervising attorney may tell them that "it's OK to put everything in a single account." Doing something unethical, however, is never OK.

WITHDRAWAL

Rule 1.16(a) A lawyer must withdraw from a case if continuing would result in a violation of the law or of these ethical rules. The lawyer must also withdraw if discharged by the client, and if the lawyer's physical or mental condition materially impairs his or her ability to represent the client.

Lawyers are not required to take every case. Furthermore, once lawyers begin a case, they are not obligated to stay with a client until the case is over. If, however, the lawyer has been appointed to the case, or if the case has already begun in court, the permission of the court must usually be obtained before withdrawal is ethical.

There are circumstances in which a lawyer must not accept a case or must withdraw from a case:

☐ The representation of the client would violate the law, e.g., the lawyer is asked for advice on how to defraud the Internal Revenue Service.

☐ The representation of the client would violate ethical rules, e.g., the lawyer discovers he or she has a conflict of interest with the client that cannot be cured by consent.

☐ The client fires the lawyer.

☐ The lawyer's physical or mental condition has deteriorated (e.g., alcohol problems, depression due to grief) to the point where the lawyer's ability to represent the client has been materially impaired.

A lawyer has the option of withdrawing if the client insists on an objective that the lawyer considers "repugnant" (e.g., the client wants to pursue litigation solely to harass someone) or "imprudent" (e.g., the client insists that a motion be refiled that the lawyer feels is an obvious waste of time and is likely to incur the anger of the court).

FALSE STATEMENTS/FAILURE TO DISCLOSE

Rule 3.3(a) A lawyer shall not knowingly: (1) make a false statement of material fact or law to a tribunal, (2) fail to disclose a material fact to a tribunal when disclosure is necessary to avoid helping a client commit a criminal or fraudulent act, (3) fail to tell a tribunal about laws or other authority that go directly against the position of the lawyer's client if this law or authority is not disclosed by opposing counsel, or (4) offer evidence that the lawyer knows is false.

One of the reasons the legal profession is held in low esteem by the general public is the perception that lawyers do not always comply with Rule 3.3(a). The implications of subsection 3 of the rule are particularly startling.

Karen Singer and Bill Carew are attorneys opposing each other in a bitter divorce case involving a large sum of money. Singer is smarter than Carew. Singer knows about a very damaging but obscure case that goes against her client. But because of sloppy research, Carew does not know about it. Singer never mentions the case and it never comes up during the litigation.

Singer may pay a price for her silence. She is subject to sanctions for a violation of her ethical obligation of disclosure under Rule 3.3(a)(3).

COMMUNICATION WITH THE OTHER SIDE

> **Rule 4.2** In representing a client, a lawyer shall not communicate with a party on the other side about the subject of the case if the lawyer knows that the party is represented by another lawyer. The latter lawyer must consent to such a communication.

> **Rule 4.3** If the other side is not represented, a lawyer must not give him or her the impression that the lawyer is uninvolved. The lawyer should not give this person advice other than the advice to obtain his or her own lawyer.

The great fear is that a lawyer will take advantage of the other side.

Dan and Theresa Kline have just separated and are thinking about a divorce. Each claims the marital home. Theresa hires Thomas Darby, Esq., to represent her. Darby calls Dan to ask him if he is interested in settling the case.

It is unethical for Darby to contact Dan about the case if Darby knows that Dan has his own lawyer. (The same would be true of efforts to contact Dan made by paralegals or other employees of Darby.) The communication must be with Dan's lawyer. Only the latter can give Darby permission to communicate with Dan. If Dan does not have a lawyer, Darby can talk with Dan, but he must not allow Dan to be misled about Darby's role. Dan must be made to understand that Darby works for the other side. It would be unethical for Darby to suggest that he is **disinterested.** The only advice Darby can ethically give Dan in such a situation is to obtain his own lawyer.

Disinterested Impartial; having no desire or interest in either side winning.

NONLAWYER ASSISTANTS

> **Rule 5.3** A lawyer must make reasonable efforts to ensure that paralegals, secretaries, and other nonlawyers working in the office are aware of and act in accordance with the lawyer's ethical responsibilities.

Lawyers act unethically if they do not properly supervise nonlawyers working in the office. Such supervision must include "appropriate instruction" on the ethical rules governing a lawyer's conduct.

Let's look at an example:

Thomas Monroe, Esq., has a busy family law practice consisting of himself and a part-time secretary. He decides to hire Alex Ogden, a paralegal who recently graduated from a paralegal program. Ogden did not take a family law course in school and has never worked in this area of the law. Monroe gives him the files of all current divorce cases and asks him to "read through them to get an idea of the kind of cases we handle in this office." Since Ogden arrived, Monroe has spent a great deal of time in court. Ogden is often alone in the office. During these times, divorce clients call with questions about their cases. Ogden takes these calls and answers the questions as best he can based on whatever information he finds in the files and on his general understanding of the law. Here are examples of questions he has answered: "When is the date of my next hearing?" "Have you received the appraisal from my husband's lawyer?" "Can I sue my ex-husband for the slanderous things he has been saying about me to our daughter?"

Monroe is unethically failing to supervise his paralegal. Indeed, there seems to be almost no supervision at all. A lawyer cannot hire a paralegal and disappear. Employees must be given needed on-the-job training and supervision. One of the dangers of having unsupervised employees is that they might give clients

legal advice, which is unethical even if the advice is correct. The first two examples of questions Ogden answered (on the date of a hearing and the receipt of an appraisal) do not call for legal advice. The opposite is true of the last example. Ogden would be providing legal advice if he tells a client whether her husband can be sued for slander.

Legal Advice Telling a specific person how the law applies to the facts of that person's legal problem or concern.

SOLICITATION

> **Rule 7.3** A lawyer may not solicit employment from a prospective client with whom the lawyer has no family or prior professional relationship when a significant motive for doing so is the lawyer's monetary gain.

Frank Ellis, Esq., stands outside the office of a marriage counselor and gives a business card to any depressed, angry, or otherwise distraught husband or wife coming out of the office after a therapy session. The card says that Ellis is a lawyer specializing in divorce cases.

Ellis's way of looking for prospective divorce clients is pejoratively referred to as "ambulance chasing." There is no indication that Ellis is related to any of the people coming out of the therapy sessions, nor that he has any prior professional relationship with them, e.g., as former clients. Ellis appears to have one goal: finding a source of fees. His conduct is therefore unethical under Rule 7.3. This kind of solicitation would also be improper for the lawyer's paralegals or other employees whom he sends out to try to "drum up business." It makes no difference if the solicitation is made on the phone, through the mail, or in person so long as the target is a specific person who is known to need legal services. Direct, one-on-one solicitation of clients in this way is not allowed. The concern is that a lawyer who approaches a stranger in trouble may exert undue influence on him or her. Citizens should not be pressured into using the legal system or into using any particular lawyer at a time when they may be vulnerable to such pressure.

A different result would follow if Ellis engaged in proper *advertising,* a topic to which we now turn.

ADVERTISING

> **Rule 7.2** A lawyer may advertise services on radio, on TV, in the newspaper, or through other public media so long as the ad is neither false nor misleading and does not constitute improper solicitation under Rule 7.3.

At one time, almost all forms of advertising by lawyers were disallowed. In 1977, however, the United States Supreme Court stunned the legal profession by holding that truthful advertising cannot be completely prohibited. *Bates v. State Bar of Arizona,* 433 U.S. 350 (1977). The first amendment protects such advertising. Furthermore, truthful and nonmisleading advertising to the general public does not pose the same danger of undue pressure on specific persons from lawyers primarily interested in money.

The *Bates* opinion has had a dramatic impact on the legal profession. Prior to the opinion, traditional lawyers considered any form of advertising to be highly offensive to the dignity of the profession. Many still do. While *Bates* forced the profession to change, the scope of this change is still the subject of debate, since the Supreme Court did not prohibit all regulation of lawyer advertising. Consequently, states differ on what regulations should be imposed.

UNAUTHORIZED PRACTICE OF LAW

Rule 5.5(b) A lawyer shall not assist someone who is not a member of the bar in the unauthorized practice of law.

Lay people can represent themselves. Thus, a lawyer who gives assistance to such people in their endeavor is not engaging in the unauthorized practice of law. Suppose, however, that a lawyer assists a nonlaywer in helping *others* with their legal problems:

Sam Grondon is a nonlawyer who sells Do-It-Yourself Divorce Kits. A kit contains all the forms for a divorce in the state, plus written instructions on how to use the forms. Paulene Unger, Esq., writes the kits and obtains a royalty from Sam on every sale. She never talks to any buyers of the kits. Most customers make their purchase by mail without talking to Sam. A few customers go to Sam's house to buy the kits. Occasionally, Sam will answer questions to help these buyers decide which forms they need to file and how to fill them out.

Has Paulene assisted a nonlawyer in the unauthorized practice of law? Yes, but only with respect to the customers who come to Sam's home and receive in-person instruction on selecting and filling out the forms. Such activity is the unauthorized practice of law, and a lawyer must not assist someone to engage in it. It is proper for a nonlawyer to sell (and indeed, to write) how-to-do-it texts and to give written instructions on using the material in the texts—so long as the instructions are not directed at a particular person. Giving generalized legal instructions to the public at large is not the practice of law. Kits on divorcing yourself, suing your landlord, incorporating, etc., are illegal only when personal legal advice is provided along with the kits—as when Sam helped particular buyers select and fill out the forms. An attorney acts unethically to the extent that he or she is associated with a nonlawyer engaged in such activity.

ASSIGNMENT 4.4

Smith is a lawyer who works at the firm of Johnson & Johnson. He represents Ralph Grant, who is seeking a divorce against his wife, Alice Grant. In their first meeting, Smith learns that Ralph is an experienced carpenter who is out of work and has very little money. Smith's fee is $150 an hour. Since Ralph has no money and has been having trouble finding work, Smith tells Ralph that he won't have to pay the fee if the court does not grant him the divorce. One day while Smith is working on another case involving Helen Oberlin, he learns that Helen is looking for a carpenter. Smith recommends Ralph to Helen, and she hires him for a small job.

Six months pass. The divorce case is dropped when the Grants reconcile. In the meantime, Helen Oberlin is very dissatisfied with Ralph's carpentry work for her; she claims he didn't do the work he contracted to do. She wants to know what she can do about it. She tries to call Smith at Johnson & Johnson, but is told that Smith does not work there anymore. Another lawyer at the firm, Georgia Quinton, Esq., helps Helen.

Have any ethical violations occurred in this situation? See the General Instructions for the Legal-Analysis Assignment in chapter 1.

■■■■■ OTHER WRONGDOING[3]

The following list provides an overview of the major ways lawyers can be sanctioned. These sanctions are in addition to bar discipline if unethical conduct

---

3. See W. Statsky, *Torts: Personal Injury Litigation* (3d ed. 1995).

is also committed. The phrase "legal malpractice" usually refers to the last item on the list—negligence.

- ☐ Contempt of court
- ☐ Criminal action
- ☐ Malicious prosecution
- ☐ Abuse of process
- ☐ Defamation
- ☐ Negligence

While our primary emphasis in this section will be the last sanction, a civil negligence action (see Exhibit 4.1), a brief mention of the others is appropriate.

CONTEMPT OF COURT

A lawyer can be cited for contempt of court for conduct such as insulting a judge in open court and flagrantly disobeying a court order. The punishment for such conduct can be a fine or imprisonment.

CRIMINAL CONDUCT

A lawyer, like any citizen, can be convicted of a crime. Stealing a client's funds, for example, can lead to a larceny conviction. Obstruction of justice and certain kinds of income tax evasion are also crimes.

MALICIOUS PROSECUTION

Malicious prosecution is a tort brought against someone for maliciously instituting legal proceedings. Here is an example of how a lawyer could become a defendant in a malicious prosecution action:

> After a bitter divorce proceeding, Diana is awarded custody of the only child of the marriage. George, her ex-husband, asks his lawyer to institute proceedings against Diana to remove custody of the child from her because she is a prostitute. It is clear to the lawyer, however, that Diana is not a prostitute and that George wants to bring the action solely to "get even" with her. Nevertheless, the lawyer agrees to go ahead. The strategy they decide to take is to file a criminal neglect case against Diana because of the

☐ **EXHIBIT 4.1 Predominant Errors in Family Law**

14.2%	Failure to obtain client's consent
11.2%	Failure to know the law
10.8%	Inadequate investigation
10.3%	Failure to follow client's instructions
8.8%	Planning error

SOURCE: American Bar Association, Standing Committee on Lawyers' Professional Liability, National Legal Malpractice Center, *History of Statistical Analysis* (1985).

prostitution. They ask a court to take the child away from her. George is the complaining witness against Diana in the criminal neglect proceeding.

The prosecutor loses the criminal case; Diana is acquitted of criminal neglect.

Diana now brings a malicious prosecution civil suit against *both* George and his lawyer. She will win if she can prove malice—that George and his lawyer knew that the criminal case was without any foundation. She must show that it was not brought in the good faith belief that it could be won.

ABUSE OF PROCESS

Suppose an attorney advises a client to institute an otherwise valid criminal action against an individual solely for the purpose of pressuring that individual to settle a pending civil action on favorable terms. The lawyer and the person initiating the criminal action may both be liable for the separate tort called *abuse of process*. They both misused the criminal court process: forcing someone to settle a civil suit is not one of the purposes of the criminal law.

DEFAMATION

In the course of heated litigation, it would not be uncommon for a lawyer to defame one of the parties, a nonparty witness, or the other attorney. If, however, the defamation occurs in connection with a court proceeding, the defaming lawyer enjoys the defense of absolute privilege.

NEGLIGENCE

Negligence
Unreasonable conduct that causes injury or damage to someone to whom you owe a duty of reasonable care.

One in every seventeen lawyers will be sued for **negligence.** This is a dramatic increase from only a short time ago. In a negligence suit against a lawyer, the standard of care against which the lawyer's conduct will be measured is the *reasonable person*, with the qualification that since the lawyer holds him or herself out as a person with special skills, the standard of care will be a reasonable person possessing such skills. The lawyer will not be liable simply because he or she made a mistake or lost a case. Unless the lawyer specifically guarantees a result, the standard of care will be reasonableness, not warranty. Expressed in greater detail, the standard is as follows:[4]

> An attorney who acts in good faith and in an honest belief that his advice and acts are well founded and in the best interest of his client is not answerable for a mere error of judgment or for a mistake in a point of law which has not been settled by the court of last resort in his State and on which reasonable doubt may be entertained by well-informed lawyers.
>
> Conversely, he is answerable in damages for any loss to his client which proximately results from a want of that degree of knowledge and skill ordinarily possessed by others of his profession similarly situated, or from the omission to use reasonable care and diligence, or from the failure to exercise in good faith his best judgment in attending to the litigation committed to his care.

A distinction should be made between:

□ A mistake that could have been made by any lawyer in good standing using the skill and knowledge normally possessed by lawyers, and

---

4. *Hodges v. Carter,* 239 N.C. 517, 519–20, 80 S.E.2d 144, 145–46 (1954).

☐ A mistake that would not have been made by a lawyer in good standing using the skill and knowledge normally possessed by lawyers.

Only the latter category of mistake is considered unreasonable and hence will lead to liability for negligence. The test is not whether the *average* lawyer would have made the mistake. The focus is on the lawyer *in good standing* using the knowledge and skills *ordinarily* or *normally* found in lawyers.

It is important to keep in mind that the lawyer is the *agent* of the client. While the lawyer is representing the client (within the scope of the lawyer's "employment"), the client is bound by what the lawyer does. This includes both successes and mistakes. Therefore, if the lawyer makes a mistake and the client loses the case as a result, the client's recourse is to sue the lawyer and try to establish that an unreasonable mistake was made that would not have been made by a lawyer in good standing using the skill and knowledge normally possessed by lawyers.[5]

AVOIDING MALPRACTICE: PRACTICE GUIDE

Reprinted with permission from ABA/BNA's Lawyer's Manual on Professional Conduct (Trial Practice Series), p. 301:1001. Copyright 1989 by The Bureau of National Affairs, Inc., jointly with the American Bar Association.

With the dramatic increase in the number of malpractice claims that are being asserted against lawyers, the need for methods of reducing a lawyer's potential exposure to liability is obvious. There are a variety of practices lawyers can institute to improve their chances of avoiding malpractice:

☐ Decline representation of prospective clients whose legal matter, expectation about the legal system, or personality gives a strong impression of trouble.

☐ Use a system to screen prospective clients' cases for actual and potential conflicts of interest.

☐ If a prospective client's business is declined, put that decision in writing and send a non-engagement letter to the would-be client. [The letter should explicitly state that the lawyer is not accepting the case.]

☐ Establish what services the client wants and shape the client's expectations to encourage an understanding of what the lawyer and legal system can and cannot accomplish, and how long it may take to resolve the matter.

☐ Do not make promises or guarantees of results unless they can be fulfilled.

☐ Always use a written representation agreement that sets out both the objects of the retainer and the details of the fee arrangement.

☐ Maintain rapport with the client and keep him or her informed of all the significant occurrences in the case.

☐ Bill the client regularly and detail the services rendered.

☐ Research both the facts and law of the client's case before commencing legal action on his or her behalf.

☐ Have an effective time and docket control system.

☐ Refer cases to, or associate with, more experienced counsel when necessary, but check the other lawyer's qualifications first to assure his or her good standing and expertise.

☐ Do not withhold legal services on the sole basis that the client has not paid your fee. [If you must withdraw from a case, do so properly. If the case has already begun in court, you may need the court's permission to withdraw.]

☐ Stay out of business deals with clients.

☐ Think twice before suing a client to recover payment of your fee.

☐ Be aware of situations in which liability to non-client third parties could arise.

---

5. Depending upon the kind of mistake the lawyer made, some courts might permit the client to "undo" the error by correcting it, e.g., permit a client to file a document even though the client's lawyer had negligently allowed the deadline for its filing to pass. It is rare, however, that the courts will be this accommodating. A client will have to live with the mistakes of his or her lawyer and seek relief solely by suing the lawyer for negligence. See R. Mallen and V. Levit, *Legal Malpractice*, 45ff (1977).

■■■ PARALEGALS

Our concern is twofold: when is a paralegal liable for his or her wrongdoing, and when is the employing lawyer liable for the wrongdoing of the paralegal? The governing principle of employer liability is **respondeat superior.** Assume that George Rothwell is a paralegal working for Helen Farrell, Esq. In the course of George's job, he does some negligent work that harms a client. Helen Farrell, Esq., is liable to the client for this negligence even if she did nothing wrong or negligently herself. She is **vicariously liable** because she stands in the place of someone else who actually committed the wrong.

It is important to keep in mind, however, that employees are *also* responsible for their own torts. The client in the above example could elect to bring a direct action against the paralegal, George Rothwell, for negligence.

Respondeat superior is simply a basis upon which liability can be imposed on the employer in the event that the client decides not to sue the employee directly or decides to sue both the employer and employee. Of course, the client cannot obtain double damages by suing the master (employer) and the servant (employee). There can be only one recovery. The choice is usually to pursue the **deep pocket.** Most often, of course, this is the employer.

INTENTIONAL TORTS AND CRIMINAL ACTIVITY

If a paralegal commits an intentional tort, e.g., deceit, battery, malicious prosecution, the paralegal is personally liable to the injured party. If the paralegal commits a crime, the criminal act may also be the basis for a civil action against the paralegal. What about the employing attorney? Is he or she also liable for the employee's intentional torts or for the civil wrong growing out of the paralegal's criminal act?

The answer depends, in part, on whether the paralegal was attempting to further the "business" of his or her employing lawyer at the time. If so, the lawyer is liable to the client under the doctrine of respondeat superior. The tortious activity in such cases will be considered within the scope of employment. For example, suppose that while trying to collect an unpaid law firm bill, the paralegal assaults or slanders the client. Such activity would probably be considered within the scope of employment since the incident centered on a law firm matter—the client's bill. Quite a different result, however, might be reached if the paralegal happens to meet a law firm client at a bar and assaults or falsely imprisons the client following an argument over a football game.

NEGLIGENCE

It is often much easier to establish that the paralegal's negligence was within the scope of employment (making the employer vicariously liable under respondeat superior) than it is to prove that intentional torts fall within this scope.

When the paralegal allegedly makes a negligent mistake, what is the standard of care? Is the paralegal held to the standard of care of a lawyer or of a paralegal? The basic standard of care is reasonableness under the circumstances. If the person is engaged in a trade or profession and thereby possesses greater skills than the average citizen, then the standard of care will be the reasonable person possessing such skills. According to the *Restatement of Torts:*[6]

Respondeat Superior An employer is responsible for the conduct of employees while they are acting within the *scope of employment.*

Vicariously Liable Being liable because of what someone else has done.

Deep Pocket The person who probably has sufficient resources to pay damages if a judgment is awarded by a court.

---

6. American Law Institute, *Restatement (Second) of Torts,* § 299A (1965).

§ 299A Undertaking in Profession or Trade Unless he represents that he has greater or less skill or knowledge, one who undertakes to render services in the practice of a profession or trade is required to exercise the skill and knowledge normally possessed by members of that profession or trade in good standing in similar communities.

The implication of § 299A is that if the paralegal "represents" him or herself as having more skill than most paralegals, he or she will be held to the higher skill standard. Suppose, for example, that the paralegal (or secretary or law clerk) deals directly with a client and does not make clear to the client that he or she is *not* a lawyer. Assume that by the manner in which the paralegal acts, the client justifiably is under the impression that the paralegal is the lawyer. The paralegal then makes a negligent mistake. If the client brings a negligence action against the paralegal, the standard of care against which the paralegal's conduct will be measured will be that of a lawyer since the paralegal, in effect, represented him or herself (held him or herself out) to the client as a lawyer. If, on the other hand, the paralegal makes clear to the client that he or she is not a lawyer and that he or she has less training and skill than a lawyer, then the standard of care, under § 299A, is "the skill and knowledge normally possessed" by paralegals.

Suppose, however, that the paralegal never deals directly with the client. The entire work product of the paralegal in such situations blends into the work product of the lawyer. Therefore, the legal services are represented to the client as the work product of the lawyer. Hence, even though the negligent act about which the client is complaining was committed by the paralegal, that standard of care will be the reasonable *lawyer* under the circumstances, since the client had every right to believe he or she was receiving the services of a lawyer.

CASE

IN THE MATTER OF ELOY F. MARTINEZ

107 N.M. 171, 754 P.2d 842 (1988)
Supreme Court of New Mexico.

Background: John Felix is the paralegal of Eloy F. Martinez, Esq., a New Mexico attorney. The paralegal committed a number of improprieties, e.g., he failed to inform clients that he was not an attorney and he gave legal advice to a client. A grievance was filed against Martinez before the Disciplinary Board governing attorneys in the state. The Board found that Martinez acted unethically in the way he ran his practice. He now appeals to the Supreme Court of New Mexico. (The portion of the opinion reprinted below pertains to the family law case on which the paralegal worked.)

Decision on Appeal: The conclusion of the Disciplinary Board is affirmed.

Opinion of Court:
PER CURIAM . . . .

Martinez employed the services of [a] legal assistant named John Felix, who is not a licensed attorney. Felix maintained his own office separate from the offices of Martinez. . . . In early February 1987, Martinez accepted a $1000 retainer from Nina Martinez (no relation to him) to obtain for her a divorce and a re-

straining order against her husband. She told [Martinez] that the matter was of some urgency. Martinez never filed a divorce petition or sought a restraining order, although his legal assistant Felix represented to Nina Martinez that this had been done. In early April, Nina Martinez became the respondent in a divorce action filed by her husband and was forced to leave the family home with her children. Martinez filed a brief response to the petition on behalf of his client, but took no steps to preserve for her any share of the community assets, which were subsequently disposed of by her husband.

Nina Martinez wrote to Martinez in mid-May discharging him as her attorney and requesting a refund. When Martinez did not respond to her letter, she retained the services of another attorney who also wrote to Martinez requesting the file, an accounting, and a refund of any unused portion of the fee advanced to him by Nina Martinez. Martinez signed and returned a Substitution of Attorney, but otherwise ignored the attorney's requests.

In this instance, Martinez violated SCRA 1986, 16-103[1] by his lack of diligence in representing a cli-

---

1. RULE 16-103. A lawyer shall act with reasonable diligence and promptness in representing a client.

ent. His failure to provide his client with an accounting of her money and an appropriate refund as requested or to produce any records to even indicate the money had been placed in trust and appropriate records maintained violated SCRA 1986, 16-115(A) and (B).[2] A fee of $1000 constitutes a clearly excessive fee under the facts presented and is violative of SCRA 1986, 16-105(A).[3] The failure of Martinez to protect his client's interests upon withdrawal by promptly forwarding the file to her new attorney and refunding any fee that was advanced but not earned, violated SCRA 1986, 16-116(D).[4] . . . [T]he misconduct of a legal

_____

2. RULE 16-115. Safekeeping property.
   A. Holding another's property separately. A lawyer shall hold property of clients or third persons that is in a lawyer's possession in connection with a representation separate from the lawyer's own property. Funds shall be kept in a separate account. . . . Complete records of such account funds and other property shall be kept by the lawyer . . . and shall be preserved for a period of five (5) years after termination of the representation of the client in the matter or the termination of the fiduciary or trust relationship.
   B. Notification of receipt of funds or property. Upon receiving funds or other property in which a client or third person has an interest, a lawyer shall promptly notify the client or third person. . . .
3. RULE 16-105. Fees. A. Determination of reasonableness. A lawyer's fee shall be reasonable. The factors to be considered in determining the reasonableness of a fee include the following:
   (1) the time and labor required, the novelty and difficulty of the questions involved, and the skill requisite to perform the legal service properly; . . . .
4. RULE 16-116. Declining or terminating representation. . . .
   D. Orderly termination. Upon termination of representation, a lawyer shall take steps to the extent reasonably practicable to protect a client's interests, such as giving reasonable notice to the client, allowing time for employment of other counsel, surrendering papers and property to which the client is entitled and refunding any advance payment of fee that has not been earned. The lawyer may retain papers relating to the client to the extent permitted by law, or the Rules of Professional Conduct.

assistant is imputed to an attorney under SCRA 1986, 16-503(C).[5] Martinez thus bears responsibility for the misrepresentations of Felix to Nina Martinez about the status of her divorce and has again violated SCRA 1986, 16-804(C).[6] The entire course of conduct by Martinez in this instance was prejudicial to the administration of justice. . . .

IT IS THEREFORE ORDERED that Eloy F. Martinez be and hereby is suspended indefinitely from the practice of law . . . effective May 9, 1988. His reinstatement will not be automatic, but shall occur only after a reinstatement proceeding . . . where Martinez will have the burden of demonstrating by clear and convincing evidence that he has the requisite moral qualifications and is once again fit to resume the practice of law. . . .

IT IS FURTHER ORDERED that the Clerk of the Supreme Court strike the name of Eloy F. Martinez from the roll of those persons permitted to practice law in New Mexico and that this Opinion be published in the State Bar of New Mexico News and Views and in the New Mexico Reports. . . .

_____

5. RULE 16-503. With respect to a nonlawyer employed or retained by or associated with a lawyer: . . .
   C. a lawyer shall be responsible for conduct of such a person that would be a violation of the Rules of Professional Conduct if engaged in by a lawyer if:
   (1) the lawyer orders or, with the knowledge of the specific conduct, ratifies the conduct involved; or
   (2) the lawyer is a partner in the law firm in which the person is employed, or has direct supervisory authority over the person, and knows of the conduct at a time when its consequences can be avoided or mitigated but fails to take reasonable remedial action.
6. RULE 16-804. It is professional misconduct for a lawyer to: . . .
   C. engage in conduct involving dishonesty, fraud, deceit or misrepresentation; . . .

_____

ASSIGNMENT 4.5   What specific conduct of the paralegal was unethical? Make a list of what Martinez should have done when he hired the paralegal to have avoided such conduct.

■■■■ SUMMARY

Two of the worst things that can happen to a lawyer are (1) to be disciplined by the bar association for unethical conduct; (2) to be sued in court by a client for malpractice.

Ethical rules govern the conduct of lawyers. The violation of these rules can lead to the ultimate sanction of disbarment. There are, however, no ethical rules governing paralegals that are backed by sanctions. Yet lawyers can be sanctioned for what paralegals do in the law office. A lawyer has an

ethical obligation to give proper supervision to paralegals.

There are twelve major categories of ethical violations. It is unethical for a lawyer to fail to have the knowledge and skill that is reasonably necessary to represent a particular client; to charge an unreasonable fee, or to charge most forms of contingent fees in a family law case; to reveal information relating to the representation of a client; to represent a client to whom the lawyer cannot give undivided loyalty; to commingle general law firm funds with client funds in the same account; to withdraw from a case improperly; to make false statements to a tribunal or to fail to disclose certain information to the tribunal; to communicate with the other side without the permission of the latter's lawyer; to fail to inform paralegals and other employees of the lawyer's ethical responsibilities; to solicit prospective clients improperly; to advertise in a false or misleading manner; and to assist a nonlawyer engage in the unauthorized practice of law.

Closely related to (and often overlapping) these ethical violations are other kinds of wrongdoing by lawyers. For example, a lawyer can be sued for malicious prosecution and, most importantly, negligence. In addition, the lawyer is liable, under the doctrine of respondeat superior, for similar wrongdoing committed by a paralegal within the office. The paralegal is also individually liable for such wrongdoing. The client can sue the paralegal, the supervising lawyer, or both until the client's damages have been paid.

■■■■ KEY CHAPTER TERMINOLOGY

Ethics	Fee Splitting	Disinterested
Sanctions	Conflict of Interest	Legal Advice
Competent	Multiple Representation	Negligence
Uncontested	Adversary	Respondeat Superior
Retainer	Imputed Disqualification	Vicariously Liable
Fixed Fee	Chinese Wall	Deep Pocket
Contingent Fee	Tainted	
Arrearages	Commingling of Funds	

5 PRELIMINARY LEGAL INTERVIEW

INTRODUCTION

When a lawyer first meets with a prospective client, one of the first concerns is whether to accept the case. If the decision is not to accept the case, the office should send out a **letter of nonengagement** in order to refute a later claim by the prospective client who says he or she thought the office was going to provide representation (see chapter 4). A client may be rejected for a number of reasons such as the lawyer's belief that the prospective client does not have a **meritorious** case, the presence of a conflict of interest (see chapter 4), the likelihood that the office would not be able to collect its fees and costs of representation, etc. If the decision is to accept the case, the lawyer explains the scope of the representation, the fees, and the costs involved. If the client agrees, the arrangement is formalized in the **retainer** (see Exhibit 5.1). The client is also asked to sign a **letter of authorization,** which will help the office obtain needed facts about the client from outside organizations. The example in Exhibit 5.2 presents a general letter of authorization that can be used with many different kinds of organizations. An alternative is to have the client sign more than one letter of authorization that will be addressed to individual organizations such as the Internal Revenue Service (for tax records), an accounting firm once used by the client's business (for financial records), a doctor or hospital (for health records), etc.

Letter of Nonengagement A letter sent by a lawyer to a prospective client explicitly stating that the lawyer will not be representing this person.

Meritorious Having a reasonable basis to believe that a person's claim or defense will succeed.

Retainer The contract of employment between lawyer and client.

Letter of Authorization A letter that tells the recipient that the office represents the client and that the client consents to the release of any information about the client to the office.

INTERVIEWING GUIDELINES

1. Set aside an adequate amount of time to conduct the interview. You do not want to be rushed. Try to avoid taking calls during the interview.

2. Dress conservatively and professionally.

3. Clear away open files and papers of other clients. You do not want to violate their confidentiality by allowing the client to see anything in their

☐ **EXHIBIT 5.1   Example of a Retainer**

ATTORNEY-CLIENT CONTRACT

DISSOLUTION OF MARRIAGE

IT IS AGREED between _____ as Client, and Honohan, Epley, Haymond, Braddock & Brenneman, Attorney, as follows:

1. EMPLOYMENT. Client employs Attorney to represent Client in connection with an action involving a dissolution of the marriage of the client.

Attorneys agree to represent the client in this matter and to pursue the matter on client's behalf with reasonable diligence, to inform the client as to the progress of the matter and make such recommendations as may be needed. Attorney agrees to report all settlement offers promptly to client. If it is necessary, attorneys shall represent the client in trial or on appeal. Attorneys agree to keep confidential all client matters unless authorized by client to release information as requested by attorney. Client understands and agrees that the attorney may release confidential information to other attorneys in the firm and to law clerks and paralegals employed by the firm. Client understands that during the handling of the matters involved in the dissolution of marriage that attorney may be required pursuant to Court order or rule to release information material to the dissolution of marriage and client authorizes the attorney to disclose such information as is required under order of Court or pursuant to Court rules.

As a part of said employment, the firm of Honohan, Epley, Haymond, Braddock & Brenneman is hereby authorized to investigate all matters involving the dissolution of marriage on client's behalf and to represent client in negotiations with attorneys and representatives of client's spouse and to appear on behalf of client in the District Court and to file appropriate pleadings in the matter of client's dissolution of marriage.

It is understood that the client makes all final determinations as to the type of action to be taken in the matter and the attorney will advise the client of the action needed to be taken. This final determination includes the right of the client to dismiss the dissolution of marriage action. It is understood that the decision of the client is limited to the decisions as to types of actions to be taken and dismissal and settlement offers. The attorney shall make all decisions regarding the procedures to be taken and the handling of the matter.

Client agrees that this employment is between the client and the firm of Honohan, Epley, Haymond, Braddock & Brenneman and includes all attorneys in the firm, including partners and associates and that different attorneys may work on client's matter. Honohan, Epley, Haymond, Braddock & Brenneman employs paralegals and law clerks to assist them in their practice and may use said paralegals and law clerks to assist in the conduct of client's dissolution of marriage under the supervision of an attorney and client agrees to the use of paralegals and law clerks. Paralegals or law clerks may contact the client to obtain information or to report to the client on behalf of the attorneys. Client agrees to cooperate with the paralegals and law clerks.

2. HOURLY RATE. Client shall pay a fee per hour for attorney work and a fee per hour for the work of law clerks and paralegals in the performance of this contract. Said hourly rates being set by the firm of Honohan, Epley, Haymond, Braddock & Brenneman from time to time. Client understands that the hourly rates for various tasks performed in the office vary by the individual who performs the task and the task undertaken and has had the current hourly rate schedule explained to client. Client further understands that from time to time these rates change and agrees to pay the future rates. Attorney agrees to send client a bill approximately every thirty (30) days, which shall specify the work done since the previous bill and the fee due. All fees shall be due and payable at the time of billing. Attorney agrees to accept and client agrees to pay $ _____ per (week, month) to be applied toward attorney fees. Any unused portion of such installments shall be refunded to client when the case is completed. Unpaid bills will draw interest at a rate of _____ % per annum.

Notwithstanding attorney's agreement to accept an installment payment in lieu of payment in full each month, client agrees to pay his or her outstanding account in full by one month prior to a trial date or one week prior to taking a default judgment unless a different arrangement is made in writing. Client agrees also to pay money in addition to the monthly fees from time to time as requested by attorney to avoid accumulating an outstanding account with attorney in excess of $500.

3. ADVANCE FEE. Client shall advance a fee of $ _____ to be applied toward attorney fees as incurred prior to the commencement of work by the attorneys. Any unused portion of the retainer shall be refunded to client.

4. EXPENSES. Client shall pay all expense for long distance telephone calls, travel expenses, photocopies, photographs, securing records or documents, hospital records, medical reports, medical examination, court costs, depositions, expert witness fees, and all other expenses incurred on behalf of client. Client shall advance the sum of $ _____ for filing fees and service fees before the Petition shall be filed, and shall advance additional expense money from time to time as requested by attorney to pay anticipated expenses. Any unpaid expense may be billed periodically by attorney and shall be paid by client upon receipt of the bill.

Continued

□ **EXHIBIT 5.1   Example of a Retainer—*Continued***

Client and Attorney agree that no deposition will be taken or expert witness employed without prior agreement by client, except for depositions taken by the other side. Client further agrees that if he or she has agreed to a deposition or the hiring of an expert, that he or she shall pay $ _____ (per week, month) as an advance against expenses for depositions and expert witnesses if requested by attorney. Client agrees to pay other expenses determined reasonable and necessary by attorney. Any unused expense money advanced to attorney by client shall be refunded to client or credited to any unpaid balance of attorney fees.

5. WITHDRAWAL. Non-payment of expenses, fees, or installment payment as agreed upon herein shall be a basis for attorney's withdrawal from representation of client. Attorney shall give client reasonable notice before withdrawing so that client may have adequate time to find other counsel. In the event that any rule of Court in which this matter is filed requires Court approval prior to withdrawal, the attorney will obtain such approval prior to withdrawal.

6. RESPONSIBILITY FOR PAYMENT. Client accepts the responsibility of making the above payments. Attorney cannot accept payments from opposing clients. If the opposing party agrees or is ordered to pay all attorney fees, these payments must be made through the Clerk of Court and will be credited to client's account upon receipt. However, if the opposing party fails to make payments for attorney fees the primary obligation for payment is with client.

7. TOTAL FEES. Client understands that attorney makes no representation as to the total attorney fees and costs for the prosecution of this case. Client understands and agrees that fees and costs depend upon the circumstances of the case. An estimate has been given to client initially but both parties understand this to be an estimate only and not the expected cost of the prosecution of the case.

Client further understands that the client may elect at any time to drop the prosecution of the case or to change attorney. These elections are personal to the client and solely the client's choice. In the event that the client terminates the employment of Honohan, Epley, Haymond, Braddock & Brenneman the client shall be liable for the fees accrued to date and shall pay said fees upon termination.

8. PLACE OF PAYMENT. All sums due herein shall be paid at attorney's office at the address stated below.

9. NO GUARANTEE. Attorney makes no guarantee as to the outcome of the case.

10. ADDITIONAL TERMS. Any additional terms agreed to between the parties shall be set out in an exhibit attached to this agreement and by this reference incorporated into this agreement. If there is no exhibit, this agreement shall constitute the entire agreement and the client understands that no representations not set out in this agreement are a part hereof.

11. BINDING AGREEMENT. Client acknowledges that client has read this agreement and understands the provisions of this agreement and that this agreement is binding upon the parties and client agrees to abide by the terms of this agreement.

Dated this _____ day of _____ , 19 _____ .

_____   HONOHAN, EPLEY, HAYMOND, BRADDOCK
                                    (Client)   & Brenneman
                                                         330 E. Court St.
                                                         P.O. Box 3010
                                                         Iowa City, Iowa   52244

                                                         By: _____

dom/domcont3

files. Confidentiality is another reason to avoid taking calls during the interview. A client in the office should not be able to hear you discuss the cases of other clients on the phone.

4. Make sure the client is comfortable. Offer coffee or water. Have a supply of tissues available.

5. At the beginning of the interview, give the client your business card that states your name, title, address, and phone number.

6. Make sure the client knows you are not an attorney. It is usually not enough to tell the client that you are a "paralegal" or a "legal assistant." In addition to stating your title, use the word "nonlawyer" or the phrase "I am not a lawyer," so that there will be no misunderstanding. You can also say that you will be working closely with the lawyer handling the case.

☐ **EXHIBIT 5.2 Example of a Letter of Authorization**

HONOHAN, EPLEY, HAYMOND, BRADDOCK & BRENNEMAN
330 E. Court St.
P.O. Box 3010
Iowa City, Iowa 52244

_____ — , 19 _____

To Whom It May Concern:

_____ is a client of this office. The client requests that you cooperate in revealing to our office any and all facts pertaining to the client. We will be contacting you to make specific requests for information in this regard. The client's authorization and waiver of confidentiality is printed below.

Sincerely,

_____

Attorney for

_____

Authorization

Honohan, Epley, Haymond, Braddock & Brenneman is my legal counsel. I authorize you to release any information pertaining to me that is requested by Honohan, Epley, Haymond, Braddock & Brenneman or by anyone designated in writing by this law firm. I hereby waive confidentiality as to such information. You are further authorized to discuss any aspect of this information with this law firm or its agents.

_____ — , 19 _____

_____
(signature of client)

dom/authoriz.ltr

---

7. Prepare the client for what will happen during the interview. Explain that you may need to meet with the client more than once. Let the client know you will be taking detailed notes in order to obtain an accurate picture of the case.

8. Maintain eye contact as much as possible even though you are taking notes.

9. Use great sensitivity in obtaining facts from the client. You are about to learn a large number of highly personal facts about the client's life. Think of how you would feel if you were revealing such facts about yourself to a stranger. Think of how you would want this other person to react to what you are revealing. At such a vulnerable time, clients need understanding and compassion. (See also What Does the Client Want? in chapter 3.)

10. Listen carefully. The best way to build rapport with a client is to demonstrate that you are listening to everything the client has been saying. A useful technique is to repeat back a portion of what the client has told you. Not only does this tend to assure the client that you have been listening, but it also often triggers the client's memory to provide more detail or explanation. Another technique is to refer back to something the client said as the basis of a new question (e.g., "Earlier you said that you rarely used the vacation home. Could you tell me more about the vacation home?").

11. Encourage the client to do almost all of the talking. If you receive a one- or two-word answer, ask the client to explain the answer in greater detail.

12. Encourage the client to express his or her feelings when this is helpful in obtaining underlying facts (e.g., "How did you feel when your husband told you that your daughter wanted to live with him?").

13. Take your notes in the language of the client. Use quotation marks as often as possible (e.g., client said she is "certain the father is unable to raise the children on his own"). Avoid extensive paraphrasing in which you re-state what the client said in your own words.

14. Never talk down to or criticize a client.

15. Avoid disparaging comments about the opposing lawyer or about the client's spouse.

16. Do not give legal advice. If the client asks you a legal question, say that you are not permitted to give legal advice but that you would be glad to bring the question to the lawyer's attention.

17. Clients will often ask you what their chances of success are. The only appropriate answer you can give is that the office will do the best it can. Never give a client any reason to believe you think the client will win.

18. Let the client know how to reach you if he or she thinks of other relevant information after the interview is over.

19. Make mental notes of the client's personality. Here is how one lawyer described this aspect of the interview: "Assess the client's personality" and whether the office "can work with this person. Watch for red flags or danger signals, including the client who is emotionally distraught or vengeful; is inconsistent with the story or avoids answering questions; has unrealistic objectives; suggests use of improper influence or other unethical or illegal conduct; rambles, wanders off the subject, or constantly interrupts you;" tells the office "how to run the case; has already discharged or filed disciplinary complaints against other lawyers; has a personality disorder; or is flirtatious."[1] In your report or memorandum to your supervisor on the interview, be sure to include your observations and assessments relevant to concerns such as these.

■ INTERVIEWING CHECKLIST

The office will need a great deal of factual detail from the client in order to represent him or her properly. One interview technique that can help you achieve this kind of detail is fact particularization, discussed in chapter 1 (page 28). Another technique is to use a checklist to remind you of what needs to be covered. Exhibit 5.3 presents a checklist of questions and tasks for a comprehensive client interview.[2] The questions will not necessarily be asked in the order listed in this checklist. Indeed, some of the items (e.g., information on a possible conflict of interest) might be covered before this interview takes place.

(*text continues on page 100*)

1. *The Initial Interview,* 12 Family Advocate 6 (Winter 1990).
2. Many of the questions are adapted from L. Brown, *A Family Legal Information Check List,* 3 The Practical Lawyer 60, no. 6 (October 1957), and L. Barrett, *The Initial Interview with a Divorce Client,* 23 The Practical Lawyer 75, no. 4 (June 1977). Copyright by the American Law Institute. Reprinted with the Permission of *The Practical Lawyer.* See also L. Brown, Manual for Periodic Checkup (1983).

☐ **EXHIBIT 5.3 Interviewing Checklist**

FROM: (name of interviewer)   NAME OF CLIENT _____

TO: (name of supervisor)   CASE FILE NUMBER _____

DATE OF INTERVIEW: _____

RE: Client interview to obtain comprehensive financial and related information about the case.

I. DOCUMENTS WE HAVE ASKED THE CLIENT TO BRING TO THE INTERVIEW

☐ Prior divorce decree or decrees.

☐ Antenuptial agreement.

☐ Powers of attorney the client and spouse gave each other.

☐ Other written agreements between client and spouse entered prior to and during the marriage.

☐ Recent tax returns (three years, if available).

☐ Tax assessments.

☐ Deeds of property purchased during the marriage.

☐ Deeds of property the client purchased before the marriage.

☐ Several recent pay stubs of client and spouse.

☐ Business records such as copies of articles of incorporation and partnership agreements, if either or both of the parties operated a business during the marriage.

☐ Net worth statements.

☐ Recent bank statements for all personal and business accounts of client and spouse.

☐ Recent statement from pension fund.

☐ Copies of loan or refinancing applications made by client or spouse.

☐ Copies of major bills, e.g., mortgage payment, tuition bill, hospital bill.

☐ Credit reports on client, spouse, or family business.

☐ Wills.

☐ Marital trust agreements.

☐ Client's résumé.

☐ Spouse's résumé.

☐ Medical and police records, particularly if the case involves violence.

II. CONFLICT OF INTEREST INFORMATION (needed to make sure the office will not have a conflict of interest in representing this client)

☐ Client's full name.

☐ Maiden name (if a woman).

☐ Other names used by client.

☐ Has this office ever represented the client before?

☐ Has this office ever represented any relatives of the client?

☐ Has this office ever represented any business associates of the client?

☐ Names of other attorneys the client has contacted about this case.

☐ Names of attorneys who have represented the client on any other matter in the past.

☐ Spouse's full name.

☐ Maiden name (if a woman).

☐ Other names used by spouse.

☐ Has this office ever represented the spouse before?

☐ Has this office ever represented any relatives of the spouse?

☐ Has this office ever represented any business associates of the spouse?

☐ Names of other attorneys who have represented the spouse on any matter in the past.

Continued

□ **EXHIBIT 5.3   Interviewing Checklist—*Continued***

III. EMERGENCY CONCERNS

□ Does the client think there is a danger the spouse will remove the children out of state? (Protective order needed?)

□ Is the spouse abusing the client or the children? (Restraining order needed?)

□ Does the client think there is a danger the spouse will give away marital assets? (Protective order needed?)

□ Does the client think there is a danger the spouse will conceal marital assets? (Protective order needed?)

□ While waiting for a court date on the divorce case, do client and children have immediate support needs? (Motion for support pending the case? Application for public assistance?)

□ Is the client suffering emotional trauma? (Provide recommended list of psychologists, other counselors, or support agencies.)

□ Did the parties have joint credit cards or joint charge cards? (Cancel as soon as possible?)

□ Did the client cosign or guarantee a loan secured by the spouse? (Contact the lender to cancel client's backing of any future indebtedness incurred by spouse?)

IV. BACKGROUND

□ How client was referred to this office.

□ Current address of client; phone numbers.

□ Length of time lived at this address.

□ Mailing address (if different from above).

□ Other residences (if any) and the amount of time lived at each.

□ Length of time (number of consecutive months) client has been a resident of this state.

□ Date of birth.

□ Place of birth.

□ Occupation.

□ Social Security number.

□ Business address; phone numbers.

□ Educational background.

□ Religious affiliation and extent of involvement.

□ Race.

□ Current address of spouse; phone numbers.

□ Length of time lived at this address.

□ Mailing address (if different from above).

□ Other residences (if any) and the amount of time lived at each.

□ Length of time (number of consecutive months) spouse has been a resident of this state.

□ Date of birth.

□ Place of birth.

□ Occupation.

□ Social Security number.

□ Business address; phone numbers.

□ Educational background.

□ Religious affiliation and extent of involvement.

□ Race.

□ Name and address of spouse's lawyer.

V. MARITAL FACTS

□ Date of current marriage.

□ Place of current marriage.

□ Date on marriage license.

□ Place where marriage license is now kept.

□ Name and address of person who performed marriage ceremony.

Continued

☐ **EXHIBIT 5.3 Interviewing Checklist—*Continued***

☐ Date on marriage certificate.

☐ Place where marriage certificate is now kept.

☐ Names and addresses of witnesses to the marriage ceremony.

☐ Facts that would lead others to believe the parties were married, e.g., whether they used the same last name, whether they introduced each other to others as "my husband" and "my wife" (relevant if there was no ceremonial marriage and the parties may have entered a common law marriage).

☐ For each child born to the marriage, state his or her full name, date of birth, place of birth, current address, prior addresses, adults with whom the child has lived since birth, past sources of support, and current sources of support.

☐ Is client or spouse now pregnant? Expected date of delivery?

☐ For each child to whom the client or the spouse was an adoptive parent, guardian, or stepparent, state his or her full name, date of birth, place of birth, current address, prior addresses, adults with whom the child has lived since birth, past sources of support, and current sources of support. Also state the circumstances of how the child came into the family.

☐ If client was ever married before, state the name of each former spouse, his or her current address (if still alive), the date, place, and circumstances of each marriage, how each marriage was terminated, the names of all children born or adopted in this marriage, and how these children are (or were) supported.

☐ If the spouse of the client was ever married before, state the name of each former spouse, his or her current address (if still alive), the date, place, and circumstances of each marriage, how each marriage was terminated, the names of all children born or adopted in this marriage, and how these children are (or were) supported.

☐ State all outstanding debts or obligations owed to or by former spouses, e.g., alimony, child support, property division. Was a court order used?

VI. DETERIORATION OF MARRIAGE

☐ Does the client want the divorce? Why or why not?

☐ Does the spouse want the divorce? Why or why not?

☐ When did the marriage start to deteriorate? State the circumstances.

☐ Length of time the parties have had marital difficulties.

☐ Nature of past and current sexual relationship between client and spouse.

☐ Date and circumstances of the last sexual intercourse.

☐ Are the parties now separated?

☐ If so, state the date the separation began, who initiated it, the reason the client thinks the separation occurred, the reason the spouse thinks the separation occurred, where each party and the children have lived since the separation, and how each party and the children have been supported since the separation.

☐ Have the parties ever separated in the past?

☐ If so, for each separation, state the dates involved, who initiated the separation, the reason the client thinks the separation occurred, the reason the spouse thinks the separation occurred, where each party and the children lived during the separation, how each party and the children were supported during the separation, and the circumstances of the end of the separation leading to a resumption of the marital relationship.

☐ Does the client think there is a realistic chance of reconciliation? Why or why not?

☐ Does the spouse think there is a realistic chance of reconciliation? Why or why not?

☐ Have the parties ever attempted marital counseling? If so, who initiated each effort and to what extent was the effort successful? Who was the counselor? How was he or she paid?

☐ Does either party now want to try marital counseling? Why or why not?

VII. PRIOR CONTRACTS

☐ Did the parties have an antenuptial agreement?

☐ Date it was signed.

☐ Names and addresses of the attorneys, if any, who represented either party during the negotiation and drafting of the antenuptial agreement.

Continued

☐ **EXHIBIT 5.3 Interviewing Checklist—*Continued***

☐ Location of the original agreement.

☐ Describe the nature of the disclosure the spouse gave the client concerning the spouse's financial assets and worth before the client signed the agreement.

☐ Describe the nature of the disclosure the client gave the spouse concerning the client's financial assets and worth before the spouse signed the agreement.

☐ What rights did each side waive in the agreement, e.g., dower and curtesy?

☐ Describe the provisions in the agreement for the client and for the spouse in the event of a divorce.

☐ Describe the provisions in the agreement for the client and for the spouse upon the death of either during the marriage.

☐ Have the parties discussed or entered a separation agreement?

☐ Date it was signed.

☐ Were the parties already separated when it was signed?

☐ Names and addresses of the attorneys, if any, who represented either party during the negotiation and drafting of the separation agreement.

☐ Location of the original agreement.

☐ Summarize the major provisions in the agreement on support, custody, and property division.

☐ Has the client or spouse entered employment agreements with each other? Have they entered such agreements with a business owned by either?

☐ Summarize the major provisions in the agreement.

☐ Has the client or spouse ever lent the other money?

☐ If so, describe the major terms of the agreement, e.g., interest charged. What is the present status of the loan? What amounts have been repaid?

☐ Where are these loan documents kept?

☐ Names and addresses of the attorneys, if any, who represented either party during the negotiation and drafting of the loan agreement.

☐ Has a relative of the client ever lent the spouse any money? Describe the circumstances and present status of the loan.

☐ Has a relative of the spouse ever lent the client any money? Describe the circumstances and present status of the loan.

VIII. ITEMIZED EXPENSES (where relevant, state whether the expense is for client only or for children only; use monthly figures where appropriate; to obtain a monthly figure for an expense that is incurred less frequently than monthly, add the total spent for that item for the year and divide by 12)

☐ Mortgage (state whether mortgage payments include taxes and insurance).

☐ Rent.

☐ Real property taxes.

☐ Homeowner association fees.

☐ Utilities: gas/oil.

☐ Utilities: electric.

☐ Utilities: water and sewer.

☐ Water softener.

☐ Telephones.

☐ Maintenance of house.

☐ Maintenance of swimming pool.

☐ Gardener.

☐ Groceries.

☐ Restaurants.

☐ Clothes: purchase.

☐ Clothes: maintenance (tailor, laundry, etc.).

Continued

☐ **EXHIBIT 5.3   Interviewing Checklist—*Continued***

☐ Shoes.
☐ Maid.
☐ Baby-sitter.
☐ Day care center.
☐ School expenses: tuition.
☐ School expenses: books and supplies.
☐ School expenses: tutoring.
☐ School expenses: transportation.
☐ School expenses: after-school programs.
☐ School expenses: miscellaneous.
☐ Lessons: music, dance, sports, theater, etc.
☐ Equipment maintenance: music, sports, etc.
☐ Summer camp.
☐ Visitation expenses when child visits noncustodial parent (transportation, phone calls, meals, etc.).
☐ Car: payments.
☐ Car: gas.
☐ Car: maintenance.
☐ Car: registration.
☐ Car: tolls.
☐ Car: automobile club dues.
☐ Insurance premium: house.
☐ Insurance premium: car.
☐ Insurance premium: life.
☐ Insurance premium: dental.
☐ Insurance premium: health.
☐ Insurance premium: disability.
☐ Uninsured costs for medical doctors, dentists, orthodontists, prescription and nonprescription drugs, glasses and eye care, etc.
☐ Hairdresser.
☐ Haircuts.
☐ Toiletries and cosmetics.
☐ Pets: veterinarian.
☐ Pets: food and supplies.
☐ Entertainment.
☐ Cable TV access.
☐ Vacation.
☐ Film and camera supplies.
☐ Contribution: church/synagogue.
☐ Contribution: other charity.
☐ Newspaper/magazine subscriptions.
☐ Allowances for child.
☐ Membership: country club.
☐ Membership: WMCA/YWCA.
☐ Cost of gifts (birthdays, holidays, etc.).
☐ Payments to IRA or other retirement fund.
☐ Accountant/tax preparer fees.
☐ Court-ordered payments of child support or alimony from a prior marriage.
☐ Miscellaneous expenses.

Continued

☐ **EXHIBIT 5.3 Interviewing Checklist—*Continued***

IX. HEALTH INFORMATION

☐ Physical and emotional health history of client (condition before marriage, during marriage, since separation, major problems, names and addresses of treating physicians or counselors, dates of hospitalizations or other major treatments, diagnosis for future, etc.).

☐ Physical and emotional health history of spouse (condition before marriage, during marriage, since separation, major problems, names and addresses of treating physicians or counselors, dates of hospitalizations or other major treatments, diagnosis for future, etc.).

☐ Physical and emotional health history of each child (condition while parents were together, since separation, major problems, names and addresses of treating physicians or counselors, dates of hospitalizations or other major treatments, diagnosis for future, etc.).

X. WILLS AND TRUSTS

☐ Kinds of wills in existence (client's separate will? spouse's separate will? joint will?). Address the following topics for each will.

☐ Date signed/executed.

☐ Name and address of attorney who prepared the will.

☐ Location of original.

☐ Name and address of initial executor; name and address of alternate/successor executor.

☐ Guardian for minor children.

☐ Primary beneficiaries (who receives what).

☐ Remainder beneficiaries.

☐ Codicils or amendments (reasons for changes, dates executed, summary of changes).

☐ Kinds of trusts in existence (testamentary trust? inter vivos trust? other?). Address the following topics for each trust.

☐ Date signed/executed.

☐ Name and address of attorney who prepared the trust.

☐ Location of original.

☐ Name and address of initial trustee; name and address of alternate/successor trustee.

☐ Description of assets/property to go in the trust.

☐ Lifetime beneficiaries.

☐ Remainder beneficiaries.

☐ Amendments (reasons for changes, dates executed, summary of changes).

XI. REARING AND CUSTODY OF CHILDREN

☐ Names and dates of birth of natural (birth) children, adopted children, and stepchildren. Address the following topics for each child.

☐ Place of birth. Location of birth certificate.

☐ Names and addresses of natural parents (Does birth certificate accurately state this information?).

☐ Reasons client wants custody.

☐ Reasons spouse wants custody.

☐ Client's feelings about joint custody.

☐ Spouse's feelings about joint custody.

☐ Strengths and weaknesses of client as a parent.

☐ Strengths and weaknesses of spouse as a parent.

☐ Career responsibilities and goals of client and how they affect availability of client to care for the child.

☐ Career responsibilities and goals of spouse and how they affect availability of spouse to care for the child.

☐ Relatives of client in the area who are available to help client with child care.

☐ Relatives of spouse in the area who are available to help spouse with child care.

☐ Child's relationship with other children in the home.

Continued

☐ **EXHIBIT 5.3   Interviewing Checklist—*Continued***

☐ Court actions, e.g., paternity petition, child support, guardianship, adoption, juvenile delinquency (cover dates; names and addresses of courts and agencies involved, attorneys, and parties; reasons court action was initiated; name of person who initiated proceeding; outcome/decision of court; major events since, etc.).

☐ Names and addresses of all adults with whom child has lived. Dates involved.

☐ Sources of child support since birth.

☐ Police involvement, e.g., misconduct by child, abuse of child by others (cover dates, names and addresses of enforcement agencies involved; reasons police became involved; name of person who called police; action taken by police; major events since, etc.).

☐ Religious activities of child: describe role of each parent.

☐ Major school functions: describe role of each parent.

☐ Homework: describe role of each parent.

☐ After-school activities at home, at friend's house, at playground: describe role of each parent.

☐ Sports: describe role of each parent.

☐ Medical and dental appointments: describe role of each parent.

☐ Birthdays: describe role of each parent.

☐ Vacations: describe role of each parent.

☐ Discipline at home: describe role of each parent.

☐ Church/synagogue activities: describe role of each parent.

☐ Other major events in child's life: describe role of each parent.

☐ Attitude of child toward each parent. Where would child like to live (if old enough to express a preference)?

☐ Client's efforts to encourage child to have positive attitude about spouse.

☐ Spouse's efforts to encourage child to have positive attitude about client.

☐ Child's awareness of client's sexual relationships with others since the separation from the spouse. Impact on the child.

☐ Child's awareness of spouse's sexual relationships with others since the separation from the client. Impact on the child.

☐ Third parties who might be witnesses to the home environment, e.g., neighbors, relatives, teachers, day care providers, clergy, counselors, friends.

XII. BUSINESSES

☐ Ownership (solely owned by client? solely owned by spouse? jointly owned?). Address the following topics for each business.

☐ Name of business. Description of its products or services.

☐ Legal category of business (partnership? corporation? limited liability company? sole proprietorship?).

☐ Address of headquarters and all major branches or entities.

☐ Names and addresses of accountants or others responsible for compiling and storing financial records of the business.

☐ Date the business was created or entered.

☐ Source of funds used to start the business.

☐ Source of funds used to develop the business.

☐ Distribution of profits.

☐ Location of accounts in which profits were deposited. Ownership of these accounts.

☐ Allocation of losses and liabilities suffered by the business.

☐ Partnership: kind (limited, general, etc.).

☐ Partnership: profit and loss history.

☐ Partnership: percentage interest of client and of spouse.

☐ Partnership: names of other partners.

☐ Partnership: provisions for sale of a partner's interest.

☐ Partnership: provisions for termination.

☐ Corporation: kind (public, closely held, etc.).

Continued

☐ **EXHIBIT 5.3 Interviewing Checklist—*Continued***

☐ Corporation: state of incorporation.

☐ Corporation: names and addresses of incorporators.

☐ Corporation: total issued shares. Kinds of shares.

☐ Corporation: profit and loss history.

☐ Corporation: number and kind of shares owned by client or spouse.

☐ Corporation: names of officers of corporation.

☐ Corporation: names of officers of board of directors.

☐ Corporation: provisions for sale of stock.

☐ Corporation: provisions for dissolution.

XIII. EMPLOYMENT HISTORY (answer separately for client and for spouse)

☐ Name and address of employer. Address the following topics for the current employer and for each prior employer.

☐ Date began.

☐ Title and responsibilities.

☐ Name of supervisor.

☐ Compensation history. Methods of payment (periodic salary? commission? deferred compensation? dividends?).

☐ Deductions from salary.

☐ Bonus availability. Other incentive plans. History.

☐ Cost of living adjustments.

☐ Benefits: pension (defined-benefit plan? defined-contribution plan?).

☐ Benefits: deferred savings plan, profit sharing plan.

☐ Benefits: life insurance.

☐ Benefits: health insurance.

☐ Benefits: dental insurance.

☐ Benefits: disability insurance.

☐ Benefits: vacation.

☐ Benefits: sick leave.

☐ Benefits: severance pay.

☐ Benefits: union.

☐ Benefits: perks (payment of membership fees at clubs or professional associations, company car, company yacht, recreational facilities, entertainment allowance, sports tickets).

XIV. REAL PROPERTY

☐ Ownership (solely owned by client? solely owned by spouse? jointly owned?). Address the following topics for each.

☐ Legal category (joint tenancy? tenancy by the entirety? tenancy in common? fee simple? landlord-tenant interest? other?).

☐ Nature of the property (residence? vacation? time-share? business? rental property? vacant land?).

☐ Location/address.

☐ Persons currently using/benefiting from property.

☐ Original cost. Date of purchase.

☐ Name and address of seller.

☐ Source of funds used to purchase.

☐ Amount owed on the property. Name and address of creditor/mortgagee.

☐ Source of funds used to pay ongoing debt.

☐ Current fair market value of property (written appraisal available?).

☐ If acquired by gift, name and address of the donor. Circumstances of the gift.

☐ Improvements made to property. Dates and sources of funds used.

☐ Sources of funds used to pay insurance covering the property.

☐ Sources of funds used to pay taxes on the property.

Continued

☐ **EXHIBIT 5.3 Interviewing Checklist—*Continued***

XV. STOCKS, BONDS, ACCOUNTS, SAFE DEPOSIT BOXES (Address the following topics for each separately owned item.)

☐ Stocks: name of corporation.
☐ Stocks: name of owner as shown on stock certificate.
☐ Stocks: number of shares.
☐ Stocks: certificate numbers.
☐ Stocks: dates acquired.
☐ Stocks: cost of shares.
☐ Stocks: source of funds used to purchase.
☐ Bonds: name of corporation or obligor.
☐ Bonds: name of owner as shown on bond certificate.
☐ Bonds: dates acquired.
☐ Bonds: bond numbers.
☐ Bonds: face amount at maturity. Maturity date.
☐ Bonds: interest rate.
☐ Bonds: coupons attached.
☐ Bonds: cost of bond.
☐ Bonds: source of funds used to purchase.
☐ Certificates of deposits (kinds, name of owners, amounts, banks or institutions issuing, dates opened and renewed, maturity dates, interest earned, penalties, source of funds used to open).
☐ Money market accounts (kinds, name of owners, amounts, banks or institutions issuing, dates opened and renewed, maturity dates, interest earned, penalties, source of funds used to open).
☐ IRA accounts (kinds, amounts, name of owners, banks or institutions issuing, dates opened and renewed, maturity dates, interest earned, penalties, source of funds used to open).
☐ 401K account (kinds, amounts, name of owners, banks or institutions issuing, dates opened and renewed, features, interest earned, penalties, source of funds used to open).
☐ Keogh plan (kinds, amounts, name of owners, banks or institutions issuing, dates opened and renewed, features, interest earned, penalties, source of funds used to open).
☐ Checking accounts (kinds, amounts, name of owners, dates opened, banks or institutions issuing, features, interest earned, penalties, source of funds used to open).
☐ Savings accounts (kinds, amounts, name of owners, dates opened, banks or institutions issuing, features, interest earned, penalties, source of funds used to open).
☐ Christmas club accounts (kinds, amounts, name of owners, dates opened, banks or institutions issuing, features, interest earned, penalties, source of funds used to open).
☐ Safe deposit box (banks or institutions holding, dates opened, number of box, persons authorized to enter, contents).

XVI. OTHER PERSONAL PROPERTY (Address the following topics for each item of personal property with a value over $100.)

☐ Ownership (solely owned by client? solely owned by spouse? jointly owned?).
☐ Nature of the property, e.g., furniture, jewelry, precious metals, antiques, art, china, furs, cars, boats, sporting equipment, coin collection, stamp collection, planes, pets, other.
☐ Location/address.
☐ Persons currently using/benefiting from property.
☐ Original cost. Date of purchase.
☐ Name and address of seller.
☐ Source of funds used to purchase.
☐ Amount owed on the property. Name and address of creditor/mortgagee.

Continued

☐ **EXHIBIT 5.3 Interviewing Checklist—*Continued***

☐ Source of funds used to pay ongoing debt.

☐ Current fair market value of property (written appraisal available?).

☐ If acquired by gift, name and address of the donor. Circumstances of gift.

☐ Improvements made to property. Dates and sources of funds used.

☐ Sources of funds to pay insurance covering the property.

XVII. INSURANCE

☐ Life insurance: name and address of insurance company, policy number, beneficiaries (state whether beneficiaries can be changed), face amount, amount of premium, source of funds used to pay premiums, date premiums are due, assignability of policy, loans against policy, other benefits.

☐ Health insurance: name and address of insurance company, policy number, benefits provided, insured parties, amount of coverage, amount of premium, source of funds used to pay premiums, date premiums are due.

☐ Fire/homeowner insurance on residence or vacation home: name and address of insurance company, policy number, insured parties, premises insured, face amount, amount of premium, source of funds used to pay premiums, date premiums are due, assignability of policy, other benefits.

☐ Car or truck insurance: name and address of insurance company, policy number, insured parties, vehicle insured, face amount, amount of premium, source of funds used to pay premiums, date premiums are due, assignability of policy, other benefits.

☐ Boat insurance: name and address of insurance company, policy number, insured parties, vehicle insured, face amount, amount of premium, source of funds used to pay premiums, date premiums are due, assignability of policy, other benefits.

☐ Disability insurance: name and address of insurance company, policy number, benefits provided, insured parties, beneficiaries (state whether beneficiaries can be changed), face amount, amount of premiums, source of funds used to pay premiums, date premiums are due, assignability of policy.

XVIII. MISCELLANEOUS INCOME (Address the following topics for each source of income listed: name and address of payor, dates of receipt, source of the funds, and reason payments are made.)

☐ Social Security income (client? spouse?).

☐ Unemployment compensation income (client? spouse?).

☐ Worker's compensation income (client? spouse?).

☐ Income from veterans benefits (client? spouse?).

☐ Public assistance, e.g., AFDC (client? spouse?).

☐ Anticipated tax refund (client? spouse?).

☐ Income from annuity (client? spouse?).

☐ Income from trusts (client? spouse?).

☐ Income from alimony/maintenance obligation (client? spouse?).

☐ Income from book or patent royalties (client? spouse?).

☐ Income from rental property (client? spouse?).

☐ Income from personal loans (client? spouse?).

☐ Gift from client to spouse.

☐ Gift from spouse to client.

☐ Other income (client? spouse?).

☐ Separate income of the children, e.g., trust fund established by a grandparent or other relative.

XIX. LIABILITIES (Address the following topics for each liability listed: nature of debt or other kind of liability, name and address of creditors, name and address of debtors, loan number, date liability was incurred, source of funds in the past and currently used to pay it, reason debt was incurred, original amount of the debt, amount outstanding, date and amount of next payment, whether the client or spouse can increase the amount of the debt on his or her own.)

☐ Mortgage on primary residence.

☐ Mortgage on second home or vacation home.

Continued

☐ **EXHIBIT 5.3   Interviewing Checklist—*Continued***

☐ Mortgage on business property.

☐ Mechanic's lien.

☐ Credit cards.

☐ Charge cards.

☐ Car loan.

☐ Boat loan.

☐ Education loan.

☐ Loan against cash value of life insurance policy.

☐ Loan from a friend.

☐ Other notes.

☐ Court judgment for money.

☐ Bankruptcy payments (e.g., Chapter 13).

XX. TAX RETURNS (Address the following topics for the last three years in which returns were filed: gross income, taxable income, amount due, source of funds used to pay the amount due, accountant or attorney who helped prepare the return, extent to which the client or spouse was involved in the preparation of the return, location of a copy of the return.)

☐ Federal income tax return.

☐ Federal corporate (or other business) tax return.

☐ State income tax return.

☐ State corporate (or other business) tax return.

☐ City or other local tax return.

☐ City or other local corporate (or other business) tax return.

☐ Gift tax return.

☐ Estate tax return.

XXI. OTHER FINANCIAL DATA

☐ Right of spouse or client to bring a cause of action against a third party for damages, e.g., spouse or client was recently injured in an automobile accident.

☐ Payment of insurance premiums, education costs, or other expenses made by a third party (e.g., a relative) on behalf of spouse or client.

☐ Record of charitable contributions (cash and in-kind) made by spouse or client.

☐ Evidence of loans made by spouse or client that are not being collected.

☐ Written family budgets.

☐ Newspaper or other media stories on spouse or client.

☐ Family or business photographs of spouse or client in settings of wealth.

XXII. PERSONS FAMILIAR WITH CLIENT'S AFFAIRS AND SPOUSE'S AFFAIRS (Address the following topics for each person listed: name and address, dates hired or consulted, whether hired by client or spouse, fees paid, kinds of financial or other records he or she now possesses, etc.)

☐ Attorneys.

☐ Accountants.

☐ Real estate agents or brokers.

☐ Insurance agents.

☐ Bankers.

☐ Stockbrokers.

☐ Relatives.

☐ Friends.

☐ Clergy.

☐ Doctors.

☐ Others.

(text continued from page 88)

Also, the questions overlap somewhat since topics such as child care must be covered in more than one category. In later chapters of this book, we will present more specific interviewing checklists on the specific grounds for divorce, the preparation of a separation agreement, and other topics. Later when we examine interrogatories, we will see how similar information, particularly financial information, is sought from an opposing party.

Occasionally, a lawyer will ask the client to fill out a detailed questionnaire at home before the comprehensive interview is held. The lawyer might also ask the client to write a detailed narrative or biography that describes major events of the marriage, wrongs or improprieties committed by both spouses, strengths and weaknesses of each as a spouse and parent, changes in the standard of living of each spouse before and during the marriage, contributions each spouse made to raising the children, contributions each made to the financial stability of the family (who bought what property, when, and with what funds?), circumstances of separations, and objectives the client has in seeking or resisting the divorce. If the client has the stamina and ability to write such a document, it can be very helpful.

Intake Memorandum A written report that summarizes an interview with a new client of the office. It normally contains basic facts on the client and on his or her legal problems.

After the client interview, the interviewer prepares an **intake memorandum** based on an extensive set of notes taken during the interview. For the heading and organization of the intake memorandum, see instructions 4 and 6 in the General Instructions for the Interview Assignment in chapter 1.

ASSIGNMENT 5.1

Interview a married person. Cover the questions outlined in this chapter as well as any additional questions you think should be included. Tell the person you interview:

a. To assume he or she is about to file for divorce and has hired the law firm where you work as a paralegal.

b. To assume the spouses acquired considerable wealth during the marriage.

c. To make up answers to all the questions you ask.

(See General Instructions for the Interview Assignment in chapter 1. Instructions 5 and 6 in these General Instructions do not apply to Assignment 5.1).

■■■■ SUMMARY

After the office has accepted a new client and the retainer is signed, one of the first major steps is to conduct a comprehensive interview of the client. During this interview, the office determines whether there are any immediate needs that must be taken care of, such as obtaining a protective order to prevent a spouse from giving away or hiding marital assets. Information is collected to ensure that the office does not have a conflict of interest (unless this information was obtained earlier). Numerous questions are asked about the background of the client; spouse; children; prior marriages; circumstances surround the deterioration of the marriage; prior contracts between the spouses; itemized current expenses; physical and emotional health of the spouses and children; wills and trusts prepared during the marriage; standard of living of the children and the roles of the spouses in maintaining this standard; businesses owned by the spouses; employment history; real and personal property owned; insurance policies; other sources of income; liabilities incurred; tax returns; and the names and addresses of individuals familiar with the personal, business, and family affairs of the parties.

■■■■ KEY CHAPTER TERMINOLOGY

Letter of Nonengagement	Retainer	Intake Memorandum
Meritorious	Letter of Authorization	

BREACH OF PROMISE TO MARRY, THE HEART BALM STATUTE, AND CONTRACTS RESTRAINING MARRIAGE

6

▬▬▬ BREACH OF PROMISE TO MARRY

Over 100,000 engagements are broken each year. This can be a costly experience. In some cities "traditional weddings can cost as much as $50,000 or $100,000, and as the wedding day approaches, less and less of the expense of the event can be recovered if the event is canceled." In New York City, for example, a caterer and hotel may be allowed to charge for services and rooms that cannot be rebooked when canceled with less than six months notice.[1] When faced with such costs, some victims of broken engagements look for a way to sue. Can they sue for breach of **contract,** or more specifically, breach of promise to marry?

Contract An agreement that a court will enforce.

For centuries, one of the sacred principles in law has been the stability of contracts. An organized society depends on the faithful performance of contractual commitments. Hence courts are available to force parties to abide by their contracts. In the business world, thousands of contracts are made every hour. Merchants invest large amounts of money and other resources in reliance on these contracts. Consequently, the law will not allow a merchant to avoid performing its contract simply because it is now having second thoughts about the agreement reached or because it can now obtain a better deal elsewhere. But does the sacred principle of contractual stability apply to broken promises

---

1. Keith Bradsher, *Modern Tale of Woe: Being Left at the Altar,* New York Times, March 7, 1990, at B8.

to marry? Should courts be used to force parties to honor such contracts? Before answering these questions, let's review the major components or elements of a contract:

Elements of a Contract

☐ There must be an offer.

☐ There must be an acceptance of the offer.

☐ There must be **consideration.** (Consideration is something of value that is given or exchanged, e.g., an exchange of money for services, an exchange of promises to do something or to refrain from doing something.)

☐ The parties must have the **capacity** to enter a contract.

☐ Some contracts must comply with the **Statute of Frauds.**

EXAMPLE John, age thirty-four, has been dating Mary, an independently wealthy woman of thirty-three. She proposes, John accepts, and they both agree on a wedding date. The next day Mary changes her mind and tells John that she no longer wants to marry him. Does a contract exist that is enforceable by John against Mary? Each of the elements needs to be examined:

1. *Offer.* Mary offered to marry John.

2. *Acceptance.* John agreed to marry her (he accepted her offer).

3. *Consideration.* Something of value was exchanged by both parties; they both exchanged *promises* to marry each other. This mutual *exchange of promises* was the consideration for the contract.

4. *Capacity.* There was no indication that either John or Mary lacked the capacity to enter the contract. For example, when the offer was accepted, neither was a minor, and neither appeared to be mentally incapable of understanding the nature of the agreement.

5. *Writing.* Mutual promises to marry do *not* have to be in writing to be enforceable; the Statute of Frauds does not apply to this kind of contract.

All of the requirements for a contract, therefore, appear to have been met. Does John have a **cause of action** against Mary? Years ago, the answer was yes. The suit for breach of promise to marry was referred to as a **heart balm action.**

The tide has begun to turn against heart balm actions in many states, however. These states have passed **heart balm statutes** such as the following:

§ 100 Breach of contract to marry shall not constitute an injury or wrong recognized by law, and no action, suit or proceeding shall be maintained therefor.

These statutes were enacted for a number of reasons. The emotions involving a refusal to marry are usually so personal, intense, and possibly bitter that a court did not appear to be a proper setting to handle them. Furthermore, many feel that engaged persons should be allowed to correct their mistakes without fear of a lawsuit. As one judge said, the "courtroom scene" should not be "transposed into a grotesque marketplace whose wares would be the exposure of heart-rending episodes of wounded pride, which should be best kept private rather than public." Courts were also afraid of being flooded with breach-of-promise lawsuits, particularly by unscrupulous "gold diggers and blackmailers" who use the threat of publicity to force a settlement.[2]

Another criticism of heart balm actions is the difficulty of designing an appropriate **remedy** for the aggrieved party. In the business world, one of the possible remedies for a breach of contract is **specific performance.** For the mar-

---

Consideration
Something of value that is exchanged between the parties.

Capacity The legal power to do something. Minors, for example, do not have the capacity to enter a contract that can be enforced against them if they wish to walk away from it.

Statute of Frauds The requirement that certain kinds of contracts be in writing in order to be enforceable.

Cause of Action An allegation of facts that gives a party a right to judicial relief.

Heart Balm Action An action based on a broken heart, e.g., breach of promise to marry, alienation of affections.

Heart Balm Statute A statute (sometimes called an anti–heart balm statute) that abolishes heart balm actions.

Remedy The method or means by which a court or other body will enforce a right or compensate someone for a violation of a right.

Specific Performance A remedy for breach of contract that forces the wrongdoing party to complete the contract as promised.

---

2. *Prosser & Keeton on Torts,* 929 (5th ed. 1984).

riage contract that is breached, the remedy of specific performance would mean that the court would force the reluctant party to go through with the marriage contract. The obviously unacceptable concept of a compulsory marriage under these circumstances led many states to abolish the cause of action altogether. Another possible remedy is the payment of **damages** caused by the breach. But what should the damages be, and are the problems involved in calculating them so great that we should abolish heart balm actions altogether? These are some of the concerns addressed in the *Stanard* opinion.

Damages Money paid because of a wrongful injury or loss to person or property.

CASE

STANARD V. BOLIN

88 Wash. 2d 614, 565 P.2d 94 (1977)
Supreme Court of Washington.

Background: *During their courtship, defendant assured plaintiff that he was worth in excess of $2 million, that he was planning to retire in two years, and that the two of them would then travel. He promised plaintiff that she would never have to work again and that he would see to the support of her two teenage boys. He also promised to see that the plaintiff's mother would never be in need. After he proposed, the parties found a suitable home for their residence and signed the purchase agreement as husband and wife. At the insistence of defendant, plaintiff placed her home on the market for sale and sold most of her furniture at a public auction. The parties set the wedding date, reserved a church, and hired a minister to perform the service. Dresses for plaintiff, her mother, and the matron of honor were ordered, and a reception was arranged at a local establishment. The parties began informally announcing their plans to a wide circle of friends. After the wedding date was set, plaintiff's employer hired another person and asked plaintiff to assist in teaching the new employee the duties of her job. A month before the wedding, defendant informed plaintiff that he would not marry her. This came as a great shock to plaintiff and caused her to become ill and lose sleep and weight. She sought medical advice and was treated by her physician. Plaintiff also had to take her home off the market and repurchase furniture at a cost in excess of what she received for her older furniture. In addition, plaintiff was forced to cancel all wedding plans and reservations; return wedding gifts; and explain to her friends, family, and neighbors what had happened.*

Plaintiff sued the defendant for breach of promise to marry. In her first claim for relief, she sought damages to compensate her for her pain, impairment to health, humiliation, and embarrassment. Her second claim sought damages to compensate her for her loss of expected financial security. Washington state does not have a heart balm statute. Yet the trial court concluded on its own that such a lawsuit would be against public policy and dismissed the case. Plaintiff is now appealing before the Supreme Court of Washington.

Decision on Appeal: *The trial court is reversed. The plaintiff should be allowed to sue for breach of promise, although there are limitations on the kind of damages that can be awarded.*

Opinion of the Court:

Justice HAMILTON delivered the opinion of the court.

This appeal presents the question of whether the ... action for breach of promise to marry should be abolished. ... Although the action is treated as arising from the breach of a contract (the contract being the mutual promises to marry), the damages allowable more closely resemble a tort action. [If the action is allowed,] the plaintiff may recover for loss to reputation, mental anguish, and injury to health, in addition to recovering for expenditures made in preparation for the marriage and loss of the pecuniary and social advantages which the promised marriage offered. In addition, some states allow aggravated damages for seduction under promise to marry and for attacks by the defendant on the plaintiff's character. Furthermore, some states allow punitive damages when the defendant's acts were malicious or fraudulent. ...

When two persons agree to marry, they should realize that certain actions will be taken during the engagement period in reliance on the mutual promises to marry. Rings will be purchased, wedding dresses and other formal attire will be ordered or reserved, and honeymoon plans with their attendant expenses will be made. Wedding plans such as the rental of a church, the engagement of a minister, the printing of wedding invitations, and so on, will commence. It is also likely that the parties will make plans for their future residence, such as purchasing a house, buying furniture, and the like. Further, at the time the parties decide to marry, they should realize that their plans and visions of future happiness will be communicated to friends and relatives and that wedding gifts soon will be arriving. When the plans to marry are abruptly ended, it is certainly foreseeable that the party who was unaware that the future marriage would not take place will have expended some sums of money and will suffer some forms of mental anguish, loss to reputation, and injury to health. We do not feel these injuries should go unanswered merely because the breach-of-promise-to-marry action may be subject to abuses; rather, an attempt should be made to eradicate the abuses from the action.

One major abuse of the action is allowing the plaintiff to bring in evidence of the defendant's wealth and social position. This evidence is admissible under the theory that the plaintiff should be compensated for what she or he has lost by not marrying the defendant. See, e.g., *Bundy v. Dickinson*, 108 Wash. 52, 182 P. 947 (1919).

Although damages for loss of expected financial and social position more closely resemble the contract theory of recovery than the other elements of damages for breach of promise to marry, we do not believe these damages are justified in light of modern society's concept of marriage. Although it may have been that marriages were contracted for material reasons in 17th Century England, marriages today generally are not considered property transactions, but are, in the words of Professor Clark, "the result of that complex experience called being in love." H. Clark, *The Law of Domestic Relations in the United States* 2 (1968) (hereafter cited as Clark). A person generally does not choose a marriage partner on the basis of financial and social gain; hence, the plaintiff should not be compensated for losing an expectation which he or she did not have in the first place. Further, the breach-of-promise-to-marry action is based on injuries to the plaintiff, and evidence of the defendant's wealth tends to misdirect the jury's attention when assessing the plaintiff's damages towards an examination of the defendant's wealth rather than the plaintiff's injuries.... We conclude that damages for loss of expected financial and social position should no longer be recoverable under the breach-of-promise-to-marry actions. This means that evidence of the defendant's wealth and social position becomes immaterial in assessing the plaintiff's damages.

Other damages subject to criticism are those damages given for mental anguish, loss to reputation, and injury to health. It is argued that these injuries are "so vague and so little capable of measurement in dollars that they give free rein to the jury's passions, prejudices and sympathies." See Clark, supra at 12. This argument has little merit, for it places no faith in the jury's ability to evaluate objectively the evidence regarding plaintiff's injuries and render a just verdict. If a jury's verdict is tainted by passion or prejudice, or is otherwise excessive, the trial court and the appellate court have the power to reduce the award or order a new trial. See *Hogenson v. Service Armament Co.*, 77 Wash. 2d 209, 461 P.2d 311 (1969). Lack of ability to quantify damages in exact dollar amounts does not justify abolishing the breach-of-promise-to-marry action. In her complaint plaintiff alleged that she had suffered pain, impairment to health, humiliation, and embarrassment as a result of the defendant's breach of his promise to marry. If this is true . . ., then she is entitled to compensation for these injuries.

As for retaining aggravated damages for seduction under a promise to marry, and the like, since plaintiff here was not seeking aggravated damages, we leave a decision on aggravated damages for a future case in which the issue for these damages arises. Also, we note that although other states allow punitive damages, these damages are not allowed in this state because they are not authorized by statute. See *Steele v. Johnson*, 76 Wash. 2d 750, 458 P.2d 889 (1969).

We also do not believe the action should be abolished so that engaged persons are free from compulsion to choose whether to end an engagement. Although the policy of the state should not be to encourage a person to marry when he or she has begun to have second thoughts about a prospective mate, it is also the policy of the state to afford an avenue of redress for injuries suffered due to the actions of another. . . .

The judgment of the trial court is reversed on plaintiff's first claim for relief, and remanded for further proceedings consistent with this opinion. The judgment is affirmed on plaintiff's second claim for relief, which sought damages for loss of prospective economical and social advantage.

ASSIGNMENT 6.1

a. Do you agree with the result reached by the court in *Stanard*? Why or why not? Is marriage a property transaction today?

b. Give (i) specific examples of evidence of damages you think the plaintiff will try to introduce at the new trial, and (ii) specific examples of evidence of damages she will be forbidden to introduce.

a. Does your state code contain a heart balm statute for breach of contract to marry? If so, give its citation and summarize what it says. (See General Instructions for the State-Code Assignment in chapter 1.)

b. Find a court opinion written by one of your state courts that tells whether a heart balm action for breach of contract to marry can be brought. Briefly state the facts and conclusion of this opinion. (See General Instructions for the Court-Opinion Assignment in chapter 1.)

c. If your state allows heart balm actions for breach of contract to marry, draft a complaint alleging such a breach. In the hypothetical situation involving John and Mary (page 102), assume that John is bringing the complaint against Mary for breach of contract to marry in your state. (See General Instructions for the Complaint-Drafting Assignment in chapter 1.)

d. If your state allows heart balm actions for breach of contract to marry, prepare a flowchart of the procedural steps necessary to bring such an action. (See General Instructions for the Flowchart Assignment in chapter 1.)

ASSIGNMENT 6.2

Assume that you live in a state where heart balm actions can be brought. Dan asks Carol to marry him. Carol says yes. The date is set for the wedding. Two weeks before the wedding, Carol learns that Dan has just married Linda. At the time Dan was engaged to Carol, Carol was already married to Bill, but Dan did not know this. Carol was in the process of divorcing Bill and hoped to have had the divorce finalized before her marriage to Dan. Carol wanted to wait until the divorce was final before telling Dan about the prior marriage and divorce. Dan did not learn about any of this until after his marriage to Linda. When Carol's divorce to Bill became final, she sued Dan. The cause of action stated in Carol's complaint against Dan is breach of promise to marry. Should Carol be allowed to bring this action? Why or why not? (See General Instructions for the Legal-Analysis Assignment in chapter 1.)

ASSIGNMENT 6.3

Assume that a woman lives in a state where it is still possible to sue for breach of promise to marry. Today even these states would not grant her the remedy of specific performance if she won. No court will order a marriage to occur. What then does a court victory mean? What can she recover? What are her damages? Four aspects of damages are possible:

1. **Compensatory damages.** For example:
   - Out-of-pocket expenses. Money spent by plaintiff in purchasing a trousseau, a hall, rings, etc.
   - Loss of income. The plaintiff may have lost income by leaving a job in order to marry the defendant.
   - Physical and mental health deterioration due to worry, publicity, and humiliation.
   - Injury to the plaintiff's reputation and chances of obtaining a new marriage proposal.
   - Destroyed financial expectations. If the defendant was wealthy and the plaintiff was poor, the plaintiff has obviously lost a great deal in terms of potential standard of living. Note, however, that most states would agree with the *Stanard* opinion in *not* allowing damages for this kind of loss.

2. **Aggravated damages.** For example:
   - Sexual intercourse due to seduction.

Compensatory Damages Money to restore the injured party to the position he or she was in before the injury or loss; money to make the aggrieved party whole.

Aggravated Damages Money paid to cover special circumstances that justify an increase in the amount paid.

- Pregnancy, miscarriage.
- An unusual degree of publicity and resulting humiliation.

3. **Punitive damages.** For example:

- Deceit. The defendant never intended to marry the plaintiff in spite of the promise made.
- Malice. The defendant wanted to hurt and humiliate the plaintiff, or the defendant recklessly disregarded the impact of the breach of promise.

4. **Mitigating circumstances.** For example:

- Plaintiff never loved the defendant. Plaintiff was trying to marry for money only.
- Plaintiff was unchaste before meeting the defendant.
- Defendant broke the promise to marry, but with some sensitivity to the feelings of the plaintiff.

Punitive Damages (also called Exemplary Damages) Money paid to punish the wrongdoer and to deter others from similar wrongdoing.

Mitigating Circumstances Facts that in fairness justify a reduction in damages because of the conduct of the aggrieved party.

At one time, juries returned very high verdicts against defendants in breach-of-promise actions, e.g., $250,000. More recently, however, the trend has been toward smaller verdicts. Some states will limit damage awards to out-of-pocket losses, e.g., the cost of wedding preparation, and will not compensate the victim for more speculative harm such as that caused by humiliation.

▮▮▮▮ Interviewing and Investigation Checklist

Factors Relevant to the Promise to Marry (C = client; D = Defendant)

Legal Interviewing Questions

1. On what date did you and D first agree to be married?

2. Where were you at the time of this agreement? Were you in this state? If not, what state?

3. How old were you at the time? How old was D?

4. What specific language did D use when he or she promised to marry you? What specific language did you use when you accepted? (Try to obtain exact quotations.)

5. Who were the first people you told? Did you and D tell them together?

6. Was a date set for a wedding? If so, what date? If not, why not?

7. Were any preparations made, e.g., church selected or caterer ordered?

8. Did D send you any letters ("love letters") about the engagement? Did you send D any?

9. Did D ever repeat his or her promise to marry you? If so, under what circumstances?

10. What other actions did D take to indicate to you that D wanted to marry you? How much time did you spend together? Did you live together? (Where? How long?) Did you talk about children? Did you meet each other's parents?

11. When did you first learn that D no longer wished to marry you? What specifically was said and done?

12. What reason did D give?

13. What did you say or do when you learned about this? Did you give any indication to D that you did not want to marry D? Were you angry? How were your feelings expressed?

14. Was there anything about *your* life prior to the time that D promised to marry you that D did not know but which D now feels you should have revealed, e.g., information about a prior marriage, your age, your prior sex life?

15. What expenses did you incur to prepare for the wedding (clothes, church, rings, etc.)?

16. Were you employed before the engagement? Did you leave your job? How did the cancellation of the marriage affect your job, if at all?

17. Describe your standard of living before the cancellation, e.g., kind of dwelling, car, travel, entertainment interests, etc.

18. Describe D's standard of living.

19. If D had married you, describe what you think your financial standing and standard of living would have been.

20. Describe the effect of D's breach of promise on your physical and mental health, e.g., did you lose any sleep, were there any special mental problems?

—Continued

—Continued

21. When D broke the promise to marry you, who knew about it? Was there any publicity?

22. Were you humiliated? Describe the reasons why.

23. Since D broke the engagement, have you dated others? When they find out about the broken engagement, what is their reaction? Do you think your chances of marrying in the future are diminished because of D's breach of promise? Why?

24. Did you have sexual relations with D? Were you seduced by D? Did D impregnate you? (If so, inquire into pregnancy problems, abortion, miscarriage, delivery.)

25. Do you have any reason to believe that at the time D promised to marry you, D never intended to fulfill this promise? Explain.

26. Do you have any reason to believe D wanted to hurt you? Explain.

27. Could D say that you never loved D?

28. Did D ever give you any gifts?

29. On what date did you receive each gift? Was it before or after the engagement?

30. What were D's exact words when D gave you each gift? What did you say to D?

31. When did each gift come into your possession?

32. Answer questions 28–31 for any gifts you gave D.

33. Did you or D receive any shower gifts or wedding gifts from others before the engagement was broken? Explain.

Possible Investigation Tasks

☐ Try to contact people who may have heard about D's promise to marry C. Obtain witness statements.

☐ Contact church, caterer, etc., to determine if wedding preparations were made. Obtain witness statements.

☐ Help C locate all letters from D.

☐ Locate all receipts of expenses due to wedding preparation. If not available, contact merchants and others to whom money was paid in order to obtain new receipts or copies.

☐ Obtain financial records, e.g., bank statements, to show C's financial worth and standard of living before the engagement was broken. Try to obtain the same kind of records for D.

☐ Obtain medical records to document the physical and mental strain caused C when D broke the promise to marry, e.g., hospital records, doctor bills.

☐ Determine what kind of publicity, if any, accompanied the news that D broke the engagement, e.g., newspaper clippings.

☐ Attempt to determine whether D had broken any other marriage engagements.

☐ Draft an inventory of every gift in any way connected with D's relationship with C. For each gift, identify the donor, donee, date of gift, kind and value of gift, circumstances surrounding the gift, present location of the gift, etc.

FRAUD

Where a heart balm statute exists, some plaintiffs have tried to get around it by bringing a *tort* cause of action for **fraud** rather than the breach-of-contract cause of action.

Elements of the Tort of Fraud

(Sometimes called misrepresentation or deceit)

☐ There must be a *false* statement of present fact by the defendant (D).

☐ The D must *know* that it is false.

☐ The D must *intend* that the plaintiff (P) rely upon the statement.

☐ The P must *rely* on the statement of the D and be reasonable in so relying.

☐ The P must suffer *harm* due to the reliance.

Fraud Knowingly making a false statement of present fact with the intention that the plaintiff rely on the statement. The plaintiff's reasonable reliance on the statement harms him or her.

In a case of a broken engagement, an example of a fraud cause of action, if allowed, would be as follows: D told P that he wanted to marry P. At the time D made this *statement*, it was *false* because D never wanted to marry P. D *knew* that the statement was a lie and *intended* to use the statement to get P to do something (e.g., lend D money, have sexual relations with D). P believed that D wanted to marry her and *relied* on D's statement (e.g., by giving D money, by having sex with D). P suffered *harm* because of this reliance (e.g., lost funds, humiliation, unwanted pregnancy).

Can such a fraud cause of action be brought in a state that has abolished the breach-of-contract cause of action? The question is whether the legislature intended the heart balm statute to eliminate both causes of action even though the act may specifically mention only the contract action. Some states allow the fraud action. Others have said that the heart balm statute eliminates both the contract *and* the tort action.

ASSIGNMENT 6.4

On July 4, 1987, in your state, Jim Smith asked Linda Jones to marry him. Jim has a middle-class background, while Linda is independently wealthy. Linda told Jim she had never loved any other man in her life. This was not true, but she felt that unless she told this to Jim, he would never have proposed to her. On July 25, 1987, Linda told Jim that she would marry him, but on August 19, 1987, she informed him that she had changed her mind. Jim is very upset. On October 4, 1989, he filed suit against her in your state.

a. On behalf of Jim, draft a complaint against Linda for breach of promise to marry. If you live in a state that has abolished breach-of-promise actions, draft the complaint on a fraud cause of action. Assume that fraud causes of action have not been abolished in such situations even though the breach-of-promise causes of action have been. (See General Instructions for the Complaint-Drafting Assignment in chapter 1.)

b. Every state has statutes of limitations, which specify the time limits within which suits must be brought. If they are not brought within the statutory time period, they will be barred forever. In assignment (a), you drafted Jim's complaint. In answer to that complaint, would Linda be able to raise the defense that Jim's suit is barred by the statute of limitations? Check your state code to find out what the statute of limitations would be for this cause of action. (See General Instructions for the State-Code Assignment in chapter 1.)

c. Draft a set of interrogatories to be sent to Jim. Concentrate on questions calculated to uncover facts that might be used to assess damages. (See General Instructions for the Interrogatories Assignment in chapter 1.)

INTENTIONAL INFLICTION OF EMOTIONAL DISTRESS

Intentional Infliction of Emotional Distress Intentionally causing severe emotional distress by extreme or outrageous conduct.

Another tort action some plaintiffs have tried to bring is **intentional infliction of emotional distress.** The plaintiff must overcome the burden of establishing that the heart balm statute does not bar this action as well. If this can be done, the next step is to prove that he or she was the victim of particularly shocking conduct by the defendant. For example, a man knows his fiancée is emotionally unstable because she is a former mental patient. He proposes marriage for the sole purpose of humiliating her by changing his mind just after she makes elaborate, public, and expensive wedding plans. A state might conclude that this is sufficiently outrageous and shocking conduct. A more common change-of-mind case, on the other hand, would probably not be enough for this tort.

ASSIGNMENT 6.5

Review the facts of Assignment 6.4. Could Jim sue Linda for intentional infliction of emotional distress? (See General Instructions for the Legal-Analysis Assignment in chapter 1.)

Irrevocable That which cannot be revoked or recalled.

■ THE PROBLEM OF GIFTS

Donor The person who gives a gift. The *donee* receives it.

It is not commonly known that once a gift is made, it is **irrevocable**—the **donor** cannot reclaim the gift from the *donee*. For a gift to be irrevocable in this way, all of the elements of a gift must be present:

Elements of an Irrevocable Gift

☐ There must be a *delivery* of the property.[3]

☐ The transfer must be *voluntary*.

☐ The donor must intend to relinquish *title* and *control* of what is given.

☐ There must be *no consideration* (e.g., payment by the donee).

☐ The donor must intend that the gift take effect *immediately;* there must be a *present* intention to give an *unconditional* gift.

☐ The donee must *accept* the gift.

If Pat says to Bill, "I'll give you my car next year," no gift has been given. There was no intent that an immediate transfer occur; hence, there was no delivery. If Pat says to Bill, "You have borrowed my pen; maybe I'll give it to you tomorrow," again there is no gift since there was no intent by Pat to relinquish her title and dominion over the pen now. This is so even though Bill already had possession of the pen.

Suppose that Pat says to Bill, "I'll give you this desk if it rains tomorrow." No gift has occurred because a condition exists that must be fulfilled before the gift becomes effective, i.e., it must rain tomorrow. There is no present intention to relinquish title and dominion. Suppose that Frank and Judy exchange engagement rings after they both agree to be married. One or both of them then change their minds. Did a legally binding gift occur? It appears that all of the elements of a binding gift existed, so either Frank or Judy can refuse to return the ring. Yet, should we not *infer* a condition that the parties intended the gift to be binding only if the marriage took place? They never explicitly said this to each other, but it is reasonable to infer that this is what they had in mind. This is what they would have intended if they had thought about it. Courts often find that such an *implied intention* exists, thereby forcing a return of premarital gifts.

Examine the following sequence of events:

January 1, 1995:	Mary and Bob meet.
January 2, 1995:	On a date at a restaurant, Bob gives Mary a bracelet.
March 13, 1995:	Mary and Bob become engaged; they exchange rings. The marriage date will be November 7, 1995.
March 26, 1995:	This is Mary's birthday; Bob gives Mary a new car.
June 5, 1995:	Bob and Mary change their minds about marriage.

Bob wants the bracelet, ring, and car back. When Mary refuses, Bob sues her, contending in court that the elements of a gift were not present when he gave Mary the items, because he intended her to keep them only if they married. Should the court infer this condition of marriage? The answer depends on Bob's intention *at the time* he gave each of the items to Mary.

The exchange of rings poses the least problem. Most courts would agree that a condition of marriage was implied and force their return. At the time the bracelet was given, however, the parties were not engaged. A jury might conclude that Bob's intent was to please Mary, but not necessarily to win her hand in marriage. The bracelet was given the day after they met when it is unlikely that marriage was on anyone's mind. It would be rare, therefore, for a court to rule that the gift of the bracelet was conditional and force Mary to return it.[4]

---

3. The delivery of the gift of a house or of the contents of a safe deposit box can be accomplished by a symbolic act such as giving the donee the key to the house or box.

4. On the other hand, the facts show that two months after the bracelet was given, the parties became engaged. This short time period does raise the possibility, however slight, that marriage *was* on Bob's mind when he gave Mary the bracelet, i.e., that the gift was conditional. More facts would be needed in order to determine whether this argument has merit.

The birthday gift of the car is the most troublesome item. Again the central question is, what was Bob's intent at the time he gave her the car? Mary would argue that no condition of marriage was attached to the gift. She would say that a birthday gift would have been given whether or not they were engaged. Bob, on the other hand, would argue that the extraordinary cost of a new car is strong evidence that it would not have been given as a birthday gift unconnected with the impending marriage. His argument is probably correct. Do you agree?

ASSIGNMENT 6.6   What further facts would you seek in order to assess whether the car was a gift in the case of Bob and Mary above? (See General Instructions for the Investigation-Strategy Assignment in chapter 1.)

Suppose that Bob unilaterally broke the engagement without any plausible reason or justification. In such a situation, many courts would consider Bob a wrongdoer who should not be able to profit from his wrong by reclaiming any of the gifts. In such courts, the donor can have the conditional gifts returned only if the engagement ended by mutual agreement or if the *donee* broke the engagement without justification.

Third parties, e.g., relatives and friends, often send gifts in contemplation of the coming marriage. When the marriage does not take place, these parties can force a return of the gifts since courts almost always will conclude that such gifts were conditional.

Earlier we saw that some states passed heart balm statutes that abolished the cause of action for breach of promise to marry. Some of these statutes are worded so broadly that courts might interpret them to mean that *any* cause of action growing out of a broken engagement will not be allowed, including a cause of action to obtain the return of conditional gifts.

ASSIGNMENT 6.7   Examine the following sequence of events:

February 13, 1995:	Jim says to Bob, "Please introduce me to Joan. I want to meet her because I know that she is the girl I want to spend the rest of my life with." Bob does so. Jim is so happy that he gives Bob a gold wristwatch and says to him, "I want you to have this. Thanks for being my friend. I want you to wear this watch to my wedding some day."
March 1, 1995:	Joan brings Jim home to meet her mother. When the evening is over, Jim gives Joan's mother an expensive family Bible.
June 23, 1995:	Jim loans Joan $1,000 to pay a medical bill of Joan's youngest brother, giving her one year to pay back the loan without interest.
July 23, 1995:	Joan pays back the $1,000.
September 5, 1995:	They agree to marry. The wedding date is to be February 18, 1996. On the day that they agree to marry, Jim gives Joan a diamond bracelet, saying, "I want you to have this no matter what happens."
December 14, 1995:	They both agree to break the engagement.

Jim asks Bob for the wristwatch back. Bob refuses. Jim asks Joan's mother for the Bible back. The mother refuses. Jim asks Joan for one month's interest at 10 percent on the $1,000 loan and also asks for the bracelet back. Joan refuses both requests.

a. Assume that the law office where you work represents Jim. Conduct a legal interview of Jim. (See General Instructions for the Interview Assignment in chapter 1.)

b. Can Jim obtain any of these items from Bob, the mother, or Joan? (See General Instructions for the Legal-Analysis Assignment in chapter 1.)

c. Draft a complaint against Joan in which Jim seeks the return of the bracelet and one month's interest. (See General Instructions for the Complaint-Drafting Assignment in chapter 1.)

d. Prepare a flowchart of the steps necessary to litigate the matter raised in the complaint that you drafted in (c) above. (See General Instructions for the Flowchart Assignment in chapter 1.)

■■■■■ Contracts Restraining Marriage

In this section we consider contracts of private parties that have the effect of restraining marriage. The state, of course, also restrains the formation of marriages through regulations on obtaining licenses, blood tests, etc. The legality of these regulations will be considered later.

The law looks with disfavor on attempts to limit the right to marry, even with the consent of the person subject to the limitation. Not all restrictions, however, are invalid. A distinction must be made between a *general restraint* on marriage and a *reasonable limitation* on marriage.

GENERAL RESTRAINT

Consider the following situations:

□ In exchange for a large sum of money to be given to her by her father, Mary agrees never to marry.

□ As John goes off to war, Jane says, "It is you that I want to marry, and even if you don't want to marry me, even if you marry someone else, even if you die, I promise you that I will never marry anyone else as long as I live." John leaves without promising to marry Jane.

A **general restraint on marriage** is a total or near total prohibition against marriage and is unenforceable. Mary's father cannot sue her to hold her to her agreement never to marry, nor can Jane be sued by John for breach of her promise should she marry someone other than him. People may decide on their own never to marry, but no court will force them to abide by that decision.

The John/Jane agreement is unenforceable for another reason. You will recall that for a contract to exist, there must be consideration. Jane's consideration was her promise never to marry anyone but John. John, however, gave no consideration in exchange. Hence, Jane's promise is unenforceable because she received no consideration; there was no contract to breach.

REASONABLE LIMITATION

A **reasonable limitation on marriage** is one that (1) is a partial rather than a general prohibition, (2) serves what the court feels is a useful purpose, and (3) is not otherwise illegal. Consider the following situations:

☐ John enters a contract in which he promises that he will never marry a woman who is not of his religious faith.

☐ Mary enters a contract in which she promises never to marry anyone who has a criminal record.

☐ Jane enters a contract in which she promises that she will not marry before she turns eighteen, and that she will obtain the permission of her parent if she decides to marry between the ages of eighteen and twenty-one.

☐ Linda enters a contract in which she promises that she will not marry until she completes her college education.

Assume that John, Mary, Jane, and Linda received consideration (e.g., cash) in exchange for their promises. Are the promises enforceable? If John, Mary, Jane, and Linda later decide to marry contrary to their promises, can they be forced through litigation to abide by those promises? Not all states will answer this question in the same way, but generally the answer is yes. The restraints on marriage to which they agreed are enforceable. All of the restraints are *partial:* they do not totally prohibit marriage or come near such a total prohibition. All of the restraints arguably serve a *useful purpose:* to protect a person or a valuable tradition. Do you agree? There is no *illegality* evident in any of the restraints, e.g., no one is being asked to refrain from marriage in order to engage in adultery or fornication (which are crimes in some states). Hence, all of the restraints could be considered reasonable limitations on one's right to marry and are enforceable in most states.

Suppose schoolteachers sign a contract containing a clause that they will quit if they marry. This is not a general restraint on marriage, but is it enforceable as a reasonable limitation? Is there a useful or beneficial purpose to the restriction? Many courts have said yes, although this conclusion has been criticized. Can you see any useful purpose in forcing a teacher to resign under these circumstances? Do not answer this question by saying that people should be forced to do what they have agreed to do. Answer it on the basis of whether you think any person, tradition, value, etc., is being protected by holding the teacher to his or her contract.

Thus far we have been examining *contracts* that restrain marriage. Suppose, however, that the attempted restriction on marriage came as a condition attached to a *gift* rather than through a contract. For example:

Bequest A gift of personal property in a will.

☐ In Bob's will, he promises to give $100,000 to Fran so long as she remains unmarried. When Bob dies, Fran is not married. She is given the **bequest** of $100,000. One year later, Fran marries. Bob's estate brings a suit against Fran to have the money returned.

☐ John has a deed drafted that states, "I convey all my property to my widowed sister, Joan, to be owned and used by her until she remarries, at which time all remaining property shall go to the Red Cross."

The same rules on marriage restrictions should apply to such gifts as apply to contracts. If a person is going to lose a substantial gift upon marriage, the gift obviously operates to restrain marriage. In theory, the same rules do apply. In fact, however, some courts are more inclined to find the restrictions to be reasonable (and hence enforceable) when gifts are involved than when the restraint is embodied in a contract.

Closely examine each of the following situations. Determine which restraints on marriage, if any, are enforceable. Give specific reasons you think the restraint is or is not enforceable. (See General Instructions for the Legal-Analysis Assignment in chapter 1.)

a. John is married to Brenda. John enters a contract with Brenda's father stating that if children are born from the marriage and if Brenda dies before John, John will never remarry. In exchange, John is given the father's large farm to live on for life rent-free. Children are born, and Brenda does die first. John marries Patricia. Brenda's father then sues to evict John from the farm. Does John have a defense to this suit?

b. Joan enters a contract with her aunt stating that she will not have children before she turns twenty-one. In exchange, Joan is given a sum of money. Before she turns twenty-one, Joan has a baby (out of wedlock). The aunt sues Joan for breach of contract. Does Joan have a defense?

c. Fred enters a contract with his father in which the father agrees to pay for Fred's entire medical education if Fred agrees to marry a doctor or a medical student if he decides to marry. When Fred becomes a doctor, he marries Sue, an electrician. The father sues Fred for the cost of the medical education. Does Fred have a defense?

d. Bill and Jean are not married. They live together, sharing bed and board. They enter a contract by which Jean promises to continue to live with Bill and to care for him. Bill agrees to place $500 per month in a bank account for Jean so long as she carries out her promise. Jean cannot receive the money until Bill dies. Also, if she marries before Bill dies, she forfeits the right to all the money in the account. After living with Bill for twenty years, Jean leaves him to marry Tom. Can Jean sue Bill to recover $120,000, (plus interest), the amount in the account at the time she married Tom?

▰▰▰ SUMMARY

When two people promise to marry each other, a contract is created so long as the parties have the legal capacity to enter a contract, and the elements of a valid contract exist—offer, acceptance, and consideration. Years ago, if one of the parties refused to enter the marriage, and thereby breached the contract, the other party could bring a heart balm cause of action for breach of promise to marry. Some states, however, have enacted heart balm statutes that abolish this contract action because of the difficulty of assessing damages, the danger of blackmail, and the inappropriateness of trying to force someone to enter a marriage he or she no longer wants.

Fraud is an alternative cause of action a plaintiff might try to bring against a defendant who reneges on a promise to marry. The elements of fraud are a deliberately false statement of present fact by the defendant, intent to have the plaintiff rely on the statement, actual reliance by the plaintiff on the statement, and resulting harm. Not all states, however, allow a fraud suit. They have interpreted the heart balm statute as abolishing both the contract action and the fraud action. Another possibility is

the tort of intentional infliction of emotional distress, but it, too, may not be permitted in a state with a heart balm statute.

In states where a suit is possible, the usual remedy is for the plaintiff to seek compensatory damages. The damage award may be increased by aggravated damages for special circumstances, or by punitive or exemplary damages intended to punish the defendant and deter others from similar conduct. Mitigating circumstances, on the other hand, will decrease the award.

When a planned marriage does not occur, any gifts that have already been exchanged are irrevocable, provided all the elements of a gift exist: delivery, voluntary transfer, intent to relinquish title and control, no consideration, intent to have the gift take effect immediately, and acceptance by the donee. If, however, a court concludes that the donor would not have made the gift except for the anticipation of marriage, the gift is considered conditional and thus must be returned. Some states, however, will reach this result only if the engagement was broken by the donee without justification.

A contract that imposes a total or a near total prohibition on marriage is an unenforceable, general restraint on marriage. On the other hand, contracts that impose reasonable limitations on one's right to marry can be enforceable.

■■■■■ KEY CHAPTER TERMINOLOGY

Contract
Consideration
Capacity
Statute of Frauds
Cause of Action
Heart Balm Action
Heart Balm Statute
Remedy
Specific Performance

Damages
Compensatory Damages
Aggravated Damages
Punitive Damages
Mitigating Circumstances
Fraud
Intentional Infliction of
  Emotional Distress

Irrevocable
Donor
Donee
General Restraint on Marriage
Reasonable Limitation on
  Marriage
Bequest

ANTENUPTIAL AGREEMENTS AND COHABITATION AGREEMENTS

■ KINDS OF AGREEMENTS

We need to distinguish between different kinds of agreements that can be entered by adult parties living together. They are summarized in Exhibit 7.1. Our main concerns in this chapter are the antenuptial agreement and the cohabitation agreement. We will consider the others later in the book.

■ ANTENUPTIAL AGREEMENTS

A major function of an antenuptial agreement is to define rights and obligations during the contemplated marriage as well as upon the termination of the marriage by divorce or death. Why, you might ask, would two individuals about to enter the blissful state of marriage discuss such matters as "who gets what" if there is a divorce? The kinds of people who tend to make antenuptial agreements:

☐ are older
☐ have substantial property of their own
☐ have an interest in a family-run business
☐ have children and perhaps grandchildren from prior marriages

Such individuals may want to make clear that the new spouse is not to have any claim on designated property, or that the children of the former marriage have first claim to property acquired before the second marriage.

An awareness of the large number of marriages that end in divorce causes some people to seek a measure of advance protection through an antenuptial agreement, particularly men and women who have separate careers and have lived together before marriage.

☐ **EXHIBIT 7.1   Kinds of Agreements**

KIND	DEFINITION	EXAMPLE
Cohabitation Agreement	A contract made by two individuals who intend to stay unmarried indefinitely that covers financial and related matters while living together, upon separation, or upon death.	Ed and Claire meet at a bank where they work. After dating several years, they decide to live together. Although they give birth to a child, they do not want to be married. They enter an agreement that specifies what property is separately owned and how they will divide property purchased with joint funds in the event of a separation.
Antenuptial Agreement (also called prenuptial or premarital agreement)	A contract made by two individuals who are about to be married that covers support, property division, and related matters in the event of the death of one of the parties or the dissolution of the marriage by divorce or death.	Jim and Mary want to marry. Each has a child from a prior marriage. Before the wedding, they enter an agreement that specifies what property each brings to the marriage is separate property. The agreement also states that neither will have any rights in this property; it will go to the children from their prior marriages.
Post-nuptial Agreement	A contract made by two individuals while they are married that covers financial and related matters. The parties may have no intention of separating. If they have this intention, the agreement is called a separation agreement.	While happily married, George and Helen enter an agreement whereby George lends Helen $5,000 at 5% interest. She is to make monthly payments of $300. (To make this loan, George uses money he recently inherited from his mother.)
Separation Agreement	A contract made by two married individuals who have separated or are about to separate that covers support, custody, property division, and other terms of their separation.	Sam and Jessica have separated. In anticipation of their divorce, they enter an agreement that specifies how their marital property will be divided, who will have custody of their children, and what their support obligations will be. Later they will ask the divorce court to approve this agreement.

Changing lifestyles, skyrocketing divorce rates and increased awareness about prenuptial agreements have prompted more middle-aged, middle income and young professionals to clamor for such protection from their soon-to-be-spouses. Matrimonial lawyers across the country say they are doing double or triple the number of prenuptial agreements compared to the volume during the previous five to ten years.[1]

Parties, however, cannot completely reshape the nature of their marital status through a contract. While antenuptial agreements are favored by the courts, there are limitations and requirements we need to explore.

VALID CONTRACT

States differ on the requirements for a valid antenuptial contract. (For a general overview of the elements of a contract, see the beginning of chapter 6.) In most states the Statute of Frauds requires the contract to be in writing. The

---

1. Nance, *Prenuptial Pacts: "Till Some Breach Doth Them Part,"* 1 National Law Journal at 26 (November 7, 1988).

"It's a prenuptial agreement silly! I'm asking you to *marry* me!"

SOURCE: Mark Hannabury, 90 CASE AND COMMENT 34 (March-April 1985).

parties must have legal capacity to enter a binding contract and must sign voluntarily. Fraud or duress will invalidate the agreement. An additional requirement in a few states is that the contract be notarized.[2]

What are the requirements for entering a valid antenuptial agreement in your state? (See General Instructions for the State-Code Assignment in chapter 1.)

ASSIGNMENT 7.1

DISCLOSURE OF ASSETS

One of the main objectives of an antenuptial agreement is to take away rights that spouses would otherwise have in each other's assets. This is done by a **waiver** of such rights. For a waiver to make sense, you must have knowledge of the other person's assets. This raises a number of questions:

□ Do the parties have a duty to make a disclosure of their assets to each other before signing the antenuptial agreement?

□ If so, how detailed must this disclosure be?

□ Can the parties waive their right to have this disclosure?

Most states require disclosure, but allow parties to waive their right to receive it. Of course, a party is not entitled to disclosure if he or she already has knowl-

Waiver Giving up a right or privilege by explicitly rejecting it or by failing to take appropriate steps to claim it at the proper time.

---

2. In most states, the consideration for the contract is the marriage itself. Section 2 of the Uniform Premarital Agreement Act, however, provides that the agreement "is enforceable without consideration." 9B *Uniform Laws Annotated* § 2 (1987).

edge of the other party's wealth. When disclosure is required, states differ on how much disclosure is necessary. Some insist on a full and frank disclosure. In other states, it is enough to provide a general picture of one's financial worth. (We will see this diversity when we study the *DeLorean* case below.) Careful attorneys will always try to provide maximum disclosure in order to rebut a later claim by a spouse that he or she did not know the scope of the other spouse's wealth when the antenuptial agreement was signed. Furthermore, such attorneys will make sure the assets that are disclosed are not undervalued. Often the agreement includes a clause that says full disclosure has been made. This clause, however, is not always controlling, particularly if it can be shown that the party was tricked or forced into signing the entire agreement.

FAIRNESS AND UNCONSCIONABILITY

A few states require the agreement to be fair to both parties. There was a time when society viewed women as vulnerable and in need of special protection. There was almost a presumption that a woman's prospective husband would try to take advantage of her through the antenuptial agreement. Courts that took this view of the status of women tended to scrutinize such agreements to make sure they were fair to the prospective spouse.

The women's movement has helped change this perspective. There is a greater degree of equality between the sexes. Consequently, if a woman makes a bad bargain in an antenuptial agreement, most courts are inclined to force her to live with it so long as:

☐ there was adequate disclosure of the other's assets,

☐ there was no fraud or duress,

☐ there was an opportunity to seek advice from independent counsel or financial advisers, and,

☐ there is no danger of her becoming a public charge and going on welfare because of how little the antenuptial agreement provided.

Of course, the same is true of males of modest means who later regret signing antenuptial agreements with relatively wealthy women.

Unconscionable
Shocking to the conscience; substantially unfair.

Courts do not want to see spouses become destitute as a result of what they gave up in an antenuptial agreement. The agreement is **unconscionable** and therefore unenforceable to the extent that it has this consequence. The agreement may have been fair and reasonable at the time the parties signed it before the marriage. But circumstances may substantially change by the time the parties separate or divorce.

EXAMPLE Norm and Irene enter an antenuptial agreement in which they waive all rights they have in each other's separate property. In the event of a divorce, the agreement provides that Norm will pay Irene support of $2,000 a month for two years. A year before the parties divorce, Irene is diagnosed with cancer. She will need substantially more than $2,000 a month for support. Norm has resources to pay her more than what the antenuptial agreement provides. If he doesn't do so, Irene will need public assistance.

To avoid this unconscionable result, a court will be inclined to disregard the antenuptial agreement and order Norm to pay Irene additional support. The enforceability of this part of the agreement will be judged as of the date of the separation or divorce, not the date the agreement was signed.

ASSIGNMENT 7.2

Do you think that women should be treated differently than men on the issue of whether an antenuptial agreement should be enforced? Do women have enough equality in today's society to require them to live with agreements that, in hindsight, they shouldn't have made? Why or why not?

Careful attorneys advise their clients to give their prospective spouses sufficient time to study and think about the antenuptial agreement before signing. Waiting until the morning of the wedding to bring up the idea of an antenuptial agreement is not wise. This late notice does not necessarily prove that the surprised spouse acted involuntarily when he or she signed. Nevertheless, an attorney recently warned that "Eve-of-wedding prenups give rise to cries of foul later."[3]

PUBLIC POLICY

Care must be taken to avoid provisions in an antenuptial agreement that are illegal because they are against **public policy.** For example, the parties cannot agree in advance that neither will ever make a claim on the other for the support of any children they might have together. The livelihood of children cannot be contracted away by such a clause. So, too, it would be improper to agree never to bring a future divorce action or other suit against the other side. It is against public policy to discourage the use of the courts in this way, since legitimate grievances might go unheard.

Public Policy The principles inherent in the customs, morals, and notions of justice that prevail in a state. The foundation of public laws. The principles that are naturally and inherently right and just.

ASSIGNMENT 7.3

Would the following provisions in an antenuptial agreement be legal in your state? Explain why. (See General Instructions for the Court-Opinion Assignment in chapter 1.)

a. A clause designating how much support one spouse will receive from the other during the marriage.

b. A clause stating that the husband will never have to wash the dishes.

c. A clause stating that the children from a prior marriage will not live with the parties.

d. A clause stating that any children born to the couple will not attend formal services of any religion.

e. A clause stating a minimum number of times that the parties will engage in sexual intercourse per month.

Very often the antenuptial agreement will specify alimony and other property rights in the event of a divorce. Many courts once considered such provisions to be against public policy because they *facilitate* (or encourage) *divorce*. The theory is that a party will be more inclined to seek a divorce if he or she knows what funds or other property will be available upon divorce, particularly, of course, if the financial terms upon divorce are favorable. Most courts, however, are moving away from this position. Divorces are no longer difficult to obtain in view of the coming of no-fault divorce laws. There is less pressure from society to keep marriages together at all costs. A spouse who wants a divorce can obtain one with relative ease and probably does not need the inducement of a favorable antenuptial agreement to end the marriage. Hence most (but by no means all) courts uphold provisions in antenuptial agreements

---

3. Harriet Cohen, *The "Do's and Don'ts" of Family Law Practice,* 40 The Practical Lawyer 25, 26 (April 1994).

that provide a designated amount of alimony, or indeed that provide no alimony in the event of a divorce.

As indicated, however, this approach is not taken in all states. Some courts refuse to enforce *any* antenuptial agreement that tries to define rights in the event of a divorce. They will enforce only non-divorce clauses such as one covering the disposition of property upon death. Other courts distinguish between an alimony-support clause and a property-division clause in an antenuptial agreement. When the parties eventually divorce and one of them tries to enforce the antenuptial agreement, such courts are more likely to enforce the property-division clause than the alimony-support clause.

ASSIGNMENT 7.4

a. The property division clause in the antenuptial agreement of George and Jane provides that in the event of a divorce George will receive $750,000 and Jane will receive all other property acquired during the marriage. Is this clause legal? (See the General Instructions for the Legal-Analysis Assignment in chapter 1.)

b. Assume that George and Jane live in a community property state where it is legal for the parties to agree to treat community property as separate property so that each is no longer entitled to 50 percent of that property. The property division clause in their antenuptial agreement provides that in the event of a divorce, all community property will be treated as separate property and will go to the party who has title to the property at the time of the divorce. Is this clause legal? (See General Instructions for the Legal-Analysis Assignment in chapter 1.)

Death clauses in antenuptial agreements are less controversial. Parties often agree to give up the rights they may have (e.g., dower, page 145) in the estate of their deceased spouse. If the antenuptial agreement is not otherwise invalid, such terms are usually upheld by the courts.

The **Uniform Premarital Agreement Act,** which has been adopted in about a fourth of the states, has a very liberal view of what the parties can cover in an antenuptial agreement:

Uniform Premarital Agreement Act, 9B Uniform Laws Annotated § 3 (1987)

(a) Parties to a premarital agreement may contract with respect to:

    (1) the rights and obligations of each of the parties in any of the property of either or both of them whenever and wherever acquired or located;

    (2) the right to buy, sell, use, transfer, exchange, abandon, lease, consume, expend, assign, create a security interest in, mortgage, encumber, dispose of, or otherwise manage and control property;

    (3) the disposition of property upon separation, marital dissolution, death, or the occurrence or nonoccurrence of any other event;

    (4) the modification or elimination of spousal support;

    (5) the making of a will, trust, or other arrangement to carry out the provisions of the agreement;

    (6) the ownership rights in and disposition of the death benefit from a life insurance policy;

    (7) the choice of law governing the construction of the agreement; and

    (8) any other matter, including their personal rights and obligations, not in violation of public policy or a statute imposing a criminal penalty.

(b) The right of a child to support may not be adversely affected by a premarital agreement.

▰ Interviewing and Investigation Checklist

Factors Relevant to the Validity of the Antenuptial Agreement

(C = client; D = defendant/spouse)

Legal Interviewing Questions

1. On what date did you begin discussing the antenuptial agreement?

2. Whose idea was it to have an agreement?

3. On what date did you first see the agreement?

4. Who actually wrote the agreement?

5. Did you read the agreement? If so, how carefully?

6. Did you understand everything in the agreement?

7. Describe in detail what you thought was in the agreement.

8. Did you sign the agreement? If so, why?

9. Were any changes made in the agreement? If so, describe the circumstances, the nature of the change, who proposed it, etc.

10. Do you recall anything said during the discussions on the agreement that was different from what was eventually written down?

11. Was anyone present at the time you discussed or signed the agreement?

12. Where is the agreement kept? Were you given a copy at the time you signed?

13. Before you signed the agreement, did you consult with anyone, e.g., attorney, accountant, relative?

14. If you did consult with anyone, describe that person's relationship, if any, with D.

15. What were you told by the individuals with whom you consulted? Did they think it was wise for you to sign the agreement? Why or why not?

16. How old were you when you signed the agreement? How old was D?

17. How much did you know about D's background before you agreed to marry? What generally did you think D's wealth and standard of living were?

18. How did you obtain this knowledge?

19. While you were considering the antenuptial agreement, describe what you specifically knew about the following: D's bank accounts (savings, checking, trust), insurance policies, home ownership, business property, salary, investments (e.g., stocks, bonds), rental income, royalty income, inheritances (recent or expected), cars, planes, boats, etc. Also, what did you know about D's debts and other liabilities? For each of the above items about which you had knowledge, state how you obtained the knowledge.

20. When did you first learn that D owned (_____) at the time you signed the agreement? (Insert items in parentheses that C learned about only after the agreement was signed.)

21. Do you think you were given an honest accounting of all D's assets at the time you signed? Why or why not?

22. Do you think the agreement you signed was fair to you and to the children you and D eventually had? Why or why not?

Possible Investigation Tasks

☐ Obtain copies of the antenuptial agreement and of drafts of the agreement, if any, reflecting changes.

☐ Contact and interview anyone who has knowledge of or was present during the discussions and/or signing of the agreement.

☐ Try to obtain bank records, tax records, etc., that would give some indication of the wealth and standard of living of D and of C at the time they signed the antenuptial agreement.

☐ Prepare an inventory of every asset that C *thought* D owned at the time the agreement was signed, and an inventory of every asset your investigation has revealed D *in fact* owned at the time of the signing.

▰ CASE

DELOREAN V. DELOREAN

211 N.J. Super. 432, 511 A.2d 1257 (1986)
Superior Court of New Jersey, Chancery Division

Background: John DeLorean is a General Motors automobile magnate worth over $20 million. (He later became the designer and manufacturer of the DeLorean car.) Hours before his marriage to Christina DeLorean in California, he presented her with a proposed antenuptial agreement. It provided that all property acquired by each before and during the marriage should be the separate property of the person acquiring it. With some reluctance, she signed. When the marriage ended thirteen years later, Christina asked the Superior Court of New Jersey to rule that the *antenuptial agreement should not be enforced because John used undue influence and did not fully disclose his financial assets before she signed.*

Decision of the Court: The antenuptial agreement is valid and enforceable.

Opinion of the Court:

Justice IMBRIANI delivered the opinion of the court. . . .

The intent of most marriages is to create an "indivisible union of one" in which both spouses generally contribute whatever they own prior to the marriage or acquire thereafter into a common marital fund. Upon death the survivor usually receives whatever has been accumulated but, if a divorce ensues, in the usual case they share all marital assets equally. However, when parties enter into an antenuptial agreement their purpose is to alter that usual arrangement and enter into an economic partnership whereby many or all of the assets owned prior to the marriage or acquired thereafter are not contributed into a common marital fund but are kept segregated and, when the marriage ceases, whether by death or divorce, they are not shared equally but pursuant to a plan conceived and agreed upon before the marriage was consummated. It is important that we understand that normally the intent of most antenuptial agreements is to deny a spouse an interest in assets held in the sole name of the other which the former would ordinarily receive by operation of law when the marriage ceased. . . .

In determining whether to enforce an antenuptial agreement there are at least three requirements that have to be met.

First, that there was no fraud or duress in the execution of the agreement or, to put it another way, that both parties signed voluntarily. The wife alleges she did not sign voluntarily because her husband presented the agreement to her only a few hours before the marriage ceremony was performed and threatened to cancel the marriage if she did not sign. In essence she asserts that she had no choice but to sign. While she did not have independent counsel of her own choosing, she did acknowledge that before she signed she did privately consult with an attorney selected by her husband who advised her not to sign the agreement. Yet, for whatever reasons, she rejected the attorney's advice and signed.

While her decision may not have been wise, it appears that she had sufficient time to consider the consequences of signing the agreement and, indeed, although she initially refused to sign it, after conferring with her intended spouse and an attorney, she reconsidered and decided to sign it. Concededly, the husband was 25-years older and a high powered senior executive with General Motors Corporation, but she was not a "babe in the woods." She was 23-years old with some business experience in the modeling and entertainment industry; she had experienced an earlier marriage and the problems wrought by a divorce; and she had advice from an attorney who, although not of her own choosing, did apparently give her competent advice and recommended that she not sign. While it may have been embarrassing to cancel the wedding only a few hours before it was to take place, she certainly was not compelled to go through with the ceremony. There was no fraud or misrepresentation committed by the husband. He made it perfectly clear that he did not want her to receive any portion of the marital assets that were in his name. At no time did she ever make an effort to void the agreement and, of course, it was never voided. Under these circumstances the court is satisfied that the wife entered into the agreement voluntarily and without any fraud or duress being exerted upon her.

Second, the agreement must not be "unconscionable." This is not to say that the agreement should be what a court would determine to be "fair and equitable." The fact that what a spouse receives under an antenuptial agreement is small, inadequate or disproportionate does not in itself render the agreement voidable if the spouse was not overreached and entered into the agreement voluntarily with full knowledge of the financial worth of the other person. See 41 *Am. Jur. 2d* § 298. So long as a spouse is not left destitute or as a public charge the parties can agree to divide marital assets in any manner they wish. *Marschall v. Marschall*, 195 N.J. Super. 16, 30–31, 477 A.2d 833 (Ch. Div. 1984). Mrs. DeLorean presently enjoys substantial income from her employment as a talk-show television hostess and was given a life interest in a trust of unknown amount created by Mr. DeLorean, which he testified had assets of between $2 and $5 million dollars. She will not be left destitute. The court is unaware of any public policy which requires that the division of marital assets be made in what the court believes to be fair and equitable if the parties freely and voluntarily agree otherwise. In the final analysis it is for the parties to decide for themselves what is fair and equitable, not the court. So long as a spouse had sufficient opportunity to reflect on her actions, was competent, informed, and had access to legal advice and that of any relevant experts, a court should not, except in the most unusual case, interject its own opinion of what is fair and equitable and reject the wishes of the parties. Since the wife voluntarily agreed to this division of the marital assets and she will not become destitute or a public charge, the agreement is not unconscionable.

Third, the spouse seeking to enforce the agreement made a full and complete disclosure of his or her financial wealth before the agreement was signed. Obviously, one cannot make a knowing and intelligent

waiver of legal and financial rights unless fully informed of all of the facts; otherwise one cannot know what is being waived. The husband asserts that the wife acknowledged that she received a full and complete disclosure of his financial wealth because the agreement states: "Husband is the owner of substantial real and personal property and he has reasonable prospects of earning large sums of monies; these facts have been fully disclosed to Wife." However, that statement is not very meaningful and is insufficient to satisfy his obligation to make a full and complete disclosure of his financial wealth. While several states hold that a full and complete disclosure is not synonymous with a detailed disclosure, see e.g., *Lopata v. Metzel*, 641 P.2d 952 (Sup. Ct. Colo. 1982), those cases can be distinguished because they impose upon each spouse a duty to inquire and investigate into the financial condition of the other. However, as far as this court can ascertain, New Jersey imposes no such duty.
. . .

While the wife was aware that Mr. DeLorean was a person of substantial wealth, there was no way that she could have known with any substantial degree of certainty the extent of his wealth. This is important because one can appreciate that while a wife might waive her legal rights to share in marital assets of $1 million, she might not be willing to do so if she knew the marital assets were worth $20 million. And the suggestion that Mrs. DeLorean had a duty to investigate to ascertain the full nature and extent of his financial wealth is both unfair and unrealistic. How many people when about to marry would consider investigating the financial affairs of their intended spouse? How many people would appreciate or tolerate being investigated by an intended spouse? And how many marriages would be canceled when one of the parties is informed of an investigation being conducted by the other? Such a requirement would cause embarrassment and impose a difficult burden. The better rule is that the . . . burden is not on either party to inquire, but on each to inform, for it is only by requiring full disclosure of the amount, character, and value of the parties' respective assets that courts can ensure intelligent waiver of the statutory [and other] rights involved. When a spouse has a duty to fully and completely disclose his financial wealth we would eviscerate and render meaningless that duty if we imposed upon the other spouse a duty to investigate.

The only way that Mrs. DeLorean could knowingly and intelligently waive her legal rights in Mr. DeLorean's assets was if she was fully and completely informed what they were. And for Mr. DeLorean to merely state that he had an interest in a farm in California, a large tract of land in Montana, and a share

in a major league baseball club fell far short of a full and complete disclosure. If this issue were decided under New Jersey law the court would conclude that Mr. DeLorean did not make a full and complete disclosure of his financial wealth before his spouse signed the antenuptial agreement and, therefore, it would not be valid and enforceable.

However, it is argued that California, not New Jersey, law should be applied. The parties married and executed the agreement in California. It is hornbook law that when an agreement is silent as to which law should be applied, the validity and construction of a contract shall be determined by the law of the place of contracting. *Colozzi v. Bevko, Inc.*, 17 N.J. 194, 110 A.2d 545 (1955). But this agreement is not silent and expressly provides that it shall be construed under the laws of the State of California and enforceable in the proper courts of jurisdiction of the State of California. When the agreement was executed the parties had substantial contacts with California and reasonably expected to retain many of them which, indeed, has been the case. For these reasons the law of California must be applied in this case.

That being so, what duty does California law impose upon a party to an antenuptial agreement with regard to the disclosure of one's financial wealth? In both California and New Jersey fiduciaries are required to exercise a high degree of trust, good faith and candor in their dealings with each other. [T]he person occupying a position of trust, has the burden of showing affirmatively that no deception was practiced . . ., that no undue influence was used, and that all was fair, open and voluntary *as well as understood.* [*Petruccio v. Petruccio*, 205 N.J. Super. 577, 580, 501 A.2d 593 (App. Div. 1985); emphasis supplied] Where California and New Jersey law part is in their determination of what constitutes a fiduciary because, unlike New Jersey, California does not treat a party to an antenuptial agreement as a fiduciary on the theory that "parties who are not yet married are not presumed to share a confidential relationship." *Marriage of Dawley*, 17 Cal. 3d 342, 355, 131 Cal. Rptr. 3, 551 P.2d 323 (1976). So long as the spouse seeking to set aside such an agreement has a general idea of the character and extent of the financial assets and income of the other, that apparently is sufficient in California. Indeed, absent fraud or misrepresentation, there appears to be a duty to make some inquiry to ascertain the full nature and extent of the financial resources of the other. See *Boeseke v. Boeseke*, 255 Cal. App. 2d 848, 63 Cal. Rptr. 651 (1967). As this court reads California law, the disclosures made by John DeLorean appear to be sufficient for purposes of enforcing this agreement. . . .

[Therefore the DeLorean antenuptial agreement] is valid and enforceable in New Jersey.

ASSIGNMENT 7.5

a. *DeLorean* is a New Jersey case, but it applies California law. Explain why. Christina would have won the case if the New Jersey court had applied New Jersey law. Explain why. In what sense is the law of these two states different?

b. Explain whether you agree or disagree with the following statement based on your understanding of the *DeLorean* case: In New Jersey a spouse will be forced to live with an unwise and unfair antenuptial agreement so long as this spouse was dumb enough to sign it voluntarily and will not end up on welfare.

c. The court says Christina was not a "babe in the woods." Do you think it would have reached a different result if she did fall into this category?

d. Christina consulted with an attorney who advised her not to sign the antenuptial agreement. Did this attorney act unethically in giving her this advice?

e. Assume that Christina now appeals this decision to a higher New Jersey court. Conduct a mock oral argument in class. Prepare the argument for John. Prepare the argument for Christina. (Assume that Christina agrees that California law applies to the disclosure issue.) Those students who represent John will point to every fact in the case that supports the conclusion that the antenuptial agreement should be enforced. Those students who represent Christina will point to every fact in the case that supports the conclusion that the antenuptial agreement should not be enforced. Do not do any legal research; just use the law and facts presented in the opinion.

ASSIGNMENT 7.6

a. Find an opinion written by a court in your state that discusses the fairness or reasonableness of an antenuptial agreement. Give the facts and result of the opinion. If no such opinion exists in your state, try to find one written by a court in a neighboring state. According to the opinion, what standards are used in the state to assess the enforceability of the antenuptial agreement? (See General Instructions for the Court-Opinion Assignment in chapter 1.)

b. Pretend you are about to be married. Draft an antenuptial agreement for you and your future spouse. You can assume anything you want (within reason) about the financial affairs and interests of your spouse-to-be and yourself. Number each clause of the agreement separately and consecutively. Try to anticipate as many difficulties as possible that could arise during the marriage and state in the agreement how you want them resolved. (See General Instructions for the Agreement-Drafting Assignment in chapter 1.)

c. After your instructor makes note of the fact that you have drafted an agreement, you will be asked to exchange agreements with another member of the class. You are to analyze the agreement written by your classmate. Go through each numbered clause in the agreement and determine whether it is valid or invalid according to the standards identified in this chapter and/or according to the law governing antenuptial agreements in your state. When you cannot apply a standard, in whole or in part, because you need more facts, simply list the factual questions to which you would like answers in order to be able to assess the validity of the clause in question. (See General Instructions for the Legal-Analysis Assignment in chapter 1.)

■ SAMPLE ANTENUPTIAL AGREEMENT CLAUSES

Sample Antenuptial Agreement Clauses
B. Stone, Modern Legal Forms
§§ 4493ff., p. 220ff. (West Publishing Co., 1977).

I
Release of Husband's Rights in Wife's Property

Agreement made this _____ day of _____ , 19 ____ , between John Day, of _____ , and Jane Kent of _____ .

Whereas a marriage is shortly to be solemnized between the parties hereto;

Whereas Jane Kent now owns a large amount of property and expects to acquire from time to time additional property under a trust established for her by her father, _____ ;

Whereas John Day has agreed that all of the property now or in the future owned by Jane Kent, or her estate, shall be free of all rights that he might acquire by reason of his marriage to her;

Whereas both parties have made a full and complete disclosure of all their assets and liabilities and have attached a detailed schedule of these assets and liabilities to this agreement as Attachments A and B.

It is agreed as follows:

Wife Retains Full Control of Property

1. Jane Kent shall have full right and authority, in all respects the same as she would have if unmarried, to use, enjoy, manage, convey, mortgage, and dispose of all of her present and future property and estate, of every kind and character, including the right and power to dispose of same by last will and testament.

Husband Releases All Right in His Wife's Property

2. John Day releases to Jane Kent, her heirs, legal representatives and assigns, every right, claim, and estate, actual, inchoate, or contingent, that he might have in respect to said property by reason of his marriage to Jane Kent.

Deceased Minor Child's Property

3. In the event any child of said marriage shall survive Jane Kent and shall then die a minor, John Day releases every right, claim, and estate he might inherit by reason of death of such minor child, and agrees that the property of such minor child shall be subject to any bequest or devise thereof made by Jane Kent.

Additional Instruments

4. John Day further agrees that upon the request of Jane Kent he will execute, acknowledge and deliver any additional instruments that may reasonably be necessary to carry out more effectually the purpose of this agreement.

Representatives Bound

This agreement shall bind the parties and their heirs, legal representatives and assigns. In Witness Whereof, etc.

II
Clause Releasing Husband's Interest in Wife's
Property for a Lump Sum Payable on Wife's Death

Now, therefore [*Wife*] agrees that she will, upon her death, cause to be paid to [*Husband,*] if he is then living, $ _____ , within one year after her death; and [*Husband*] agrees that he will, upon the death of [*Wife,*] take the said $ _____ in full of all rights of curtesy, homestead, survivorship, inheritance, separate maintenance, widower's award,

—Continued

Sample Antenuptial Agreement Clauses—*Continued*

or otherwise in or to her estate, and in full of all other rights, interests, claims or allowances which he might be entitled to but for this agreement, and that on payment to him of the $ _____ he will release, quitclaim and discharge to her representatives or heirs all rights of curtesy, homestead, survivorship, inheritance, separate maintenance, widower's award, and all other rights, claims or interests which he might have in her estate but for this agreement.

III
Release of Wife's Interest in
Husband's Property—Present Payment of a Lump Sum

Agreement made this day _____ day of _____ , 19 ____ , between Alex Fin, of _____ , and Mary Sims, of _____ , witnesseth:

Whereas the parties contemplate entering into marriage relations:

Whereas Alex Fin is the owner of property listed on the memorandum attached hereto; and

Whereas Alex Fin desires to make suitable provision for Mary Sims in lieu of dower or other interest in his property which she otherwise might have.

Now, therefore, the parties agree as follows:

Payment of Lump Sum

1. Alex Fin agrees to pay to Mary Sims, immediately after the solemnization of said marriage, the sum of _____ dollars, the said sum to be her sole and separate property.

Wife Releases Rights in Husband's Property

2. Mary Sims agrees that she will accept the said sum in lieu of any and all claims of dower, inheritance and descent in and to the property of Alex Fin, now owned or that may hereafter be acquired by him, and in lieu of any and all other claims which might otherwise arise or accrue to her by reason of said marriage.

Management of Lump Sum

3. In view of the nature of the property set forth in the memorandum attached hereto, the nature and extent of which property is fully understood by Mary Sims, it is the desire of Mary Sims, and it is therefore agreed, that Alex Fin shall take over the management of the _____ dollars this day given by him to the end that its value may be preserved and made productive.

Wife to Join in Conveyances

4. Mary Sims agrees that upon the request of Alex Fin, she will execute all and any proper instruments of conveyance in order to enable Alex Fin to sell or convey real estate now owned or afterward acquired by him.

In Witness Whereof, *etc.*

IV
Release of Marital Rights in Husband's Estate—
Payment of Lump Sum Out of Husband's Estate

This agreement, made this _____ day of _____ , 19 ____ , between Albert Smith, of _____ , and Joan May, of _____ .

Whereas, a marriage is about to be solemnized between the parties to this agreement, who have made a full disclosure to each other as to their property, and are desirous that Joan May should have a cash payment instead of an interest in the estate of Albert Smith.

Now, therefore, if Joan May survives Albert Smith, Joan May agrees to accept from the estate of Albert Smith the sum of _____ dollars in lieu of dower and her distributive share of the personal property, and Albert Smith shall hold all the real estate which he now

—Continued

Sample Antenuptial Agreement Clauses—*Continued*

owns or may hereafter acquire free from any claim of dower, inchoate or otherwise; in consideration whereof Albert Smith agrees that Joan May shall be paid said sum of _____ dollars as soon after his decease as may be practicable.

In Witness Whereof, *etc.*

V
Clause Providing for Monthly
Payment to Wife After Husband's Death

Now, therefore, the Husband agrees that the representative of his estate shall pay to the Wife the sum of _____ dollars ($ _____), payable as follows: _____ dollars ($ _____) _____days after the decease of the Husband and a like amount each _____days thereafter, until the full sum is paid in full, which cash payment shall be a lien on any real estate owned by the husband at the time of his decease, provided, however, that at his option the Husband, during his life, may purchase an annuity for a like sum payable in monthly installments in any good and solvent insurance company, which annuity shall be received by the Wife as a substitute for said cash payment. Provided also that if the Wife shall predecease the Husband, this agreement shall terminate upon her death.

VI
Release of Husband's Interest in Wife's Estate and
Limiting Wife's Interest in Husband's Estate

Whereas, _____ , of _____ , herein called the Husband, and _____ , of _____ , herein called the Wife, contemplate entering into marriage relations; and whereas, the Husband has a large estate and has children by a former marriage; and whereas, the Wife is possessed of property in her own right and has a child by a former marriage; and whereas, the said parties desire to prescribe, limit, and determine the interest and control which each of them may have in the estate of the other party; therefore the following agreement is entered into:

Know all men by these presents: That we, _____ and _____ , being about to enter into the marriage relations, do hereby agree:

Husband Releases His Rights in Wife's Estate

1. In the event of the death of the Wife during the continuance of said marriage relations, the Husband surviving her, then the Husband shall receive from the estate of the Wife the sum of five dollars; such sum when paid by the executors or administrators of the estate of the Wife to be in full for all claims and demands of every kind and character which the Husband shall have against the estate of the wife.

Wife Limits Her Rights in Husband's Estate

2. In the event of the death of the Husband during the said marriage relations, the Wife agrees that her claim upon the estate of the Husband shall be limited to $ _____ , and a payment by the executors or the administrators of the estate of the Husband to the Wife, her heirs or legal representatives, of the sum of $ _____ shall be in full for all claims and demands of every kind and character which the Wife shall have against the estate of the Husband.

During Marriage Each to Have Full Control of Own Property

3. During the continuance of said marriage relations, each of the parties is to have full right to own, control, and dispose of his or her separate property same as if the marriage relations did not exist, and each of the parties is to have full right to dispose of and sell any and all real or personal property now or hereafter owned by each of them without the other party joining, and said transfer by either of the parties to this contract shall convey the same

—Continued

Sample Antenuptial Agreement Clauses—*Continued*

title that said transfer would convey had the marriage relations not existed. This contract limits the right of either party to participate in the estate of the other, whether the marriage relation is terminated by death or legal proceedings.

Purpose of Contract to Limit Rights

4. The purpose of this agreement is to define and limit the claims and demands which each of the parties shall have against the estate of the other. Should either party die during the pendency of this contract, or should the contract be terminated by legal proceedings, the claims herein stipulated and defined shall be the limit which either party may have against the other party or his or her estate.

Contract Made with Full Knowledge

5. This agreement is entered into with full knowledge that each of the parties has a separate estate, and no claim or demand can be predicated upon the fact that there has been any misrepresentation or concealment as to the amount and condition of said separate estate, it being expressly agreed that each of the parties considers the amount hereinabove fixed to be sufficient participation in the estate of the other, and it being expressly stated that each of the parties has sufficient general knowledge of the condition of the estate of the other to justify making and entering into this agreement.

In Witness Whereof, *etc.*

VII
Each Relinquishing Interest in Other's Property

Agreement made the _____ day of _____ , 19 _____ , between Ed Gray, of _____ , and Grace Kay, of _____ .

Whereas, the parties contemplate entering into the marriage relation with each other, and both are severally possessed of real and personal property in his and her own right, and each have children by former marriages, all of said children being of age and possessed of means of support independent of their parents, and it is desired by the parties that their marriage shall not in any way change their legal right, or that of their children and heirs, in the property of each of them.

Therefore it is agreed:

Home

1. Ed Gray agrees that he will provide during the continuance of the marriage a home for Grace Kay, and that the two children of Grace Kay may reside in such home with their mother so long as said children remain unmarried.

Husband Releases Rights in Wife's Property

2. Ed Gray agrees, in case he survives Grace Kay, that he will make no claim to any part of her estate as surviving husband; that in consideration of said marriage he waives and relinquishes all right or curtesy or other right in and to the property, real or personal, which Grace Kay now owns or may hereafter acquire.

Wife Releases Rights in Husband's Property

3. Grace Kay agrees, in case she survives Ed Gray, that she will make no claim to any part of his estate as surviving wife; that in consideration of said marriage she waives and relinquishes all claims to dower, homestead, widow's award, or other right in and to the property, real or personal, which Ed Gray now owns or may hereafter acquire.

Intent That Marriage Shall Not Affect Property

4. It is declared that by virtue of said marriage neither one shall have or acquire any right, title, or claim in and to the real or personal estate of the other, but that the estate of

—Continued

Sample Antenuptial Agreement Clauses—*Continued*

each shall descend to his or her heirs at law, legatees, or devisees, as may be prescribed by his or her last will and testament or by the law of the state in force, as though no marriage had taken place between them.

Agreement to Join in Conveyances

5. It is agreed that in case either of the parties desires to mortgage, sell or convey his or her real or personal estate, each one will join in the deed of conveyance or mortgage, as may be necessary to make the same effectual.

Full Disclosure between the Parties

6. It is further agreed that this agreement is entered into with a full knowledge on the part of each party as to the extent and probable value of the estate of the other and of all the rights conferred by law upon each in the estate of the other by virtue of said proposed marriage, but it is their desire that their respective rights to each other's estate shall be fixed by this agreement, which shall be binding upon their respective heirs and legal representatives.

In Witness Whereof, *etc.*

VIII
Each Relinquishing Interest in Other's Property

This Agreement made the _____ day of _____ , 19 _____ , between Paul Oran, of _____ , and Diane Leno of _____ .

Whereas the parties contemplate legal marriage under the laws of the State of _____ ; and

Whereas, it is their mutual desire to enter into this agreement whereby they will regulate their relationships toward each other with respect to the property each of them owns and in which each of them has an interest.

Now, therefore, it is agreed as follows:

1. That all properties of any kind or nature, real, personal or mixed, wherever the same may be found, which belong to each party, shall be and forever remain the personal estate of said party, including all interest, rents and profits which may accrue therefrom.

2. That each party shall have at all times the full right and authority, in all respects the same as each would have if not married, to use, enjoy, manage, convey and encumber such property as may belong to him or her.

3. That each party may make such disposition of his or her property as the case may be, by gift or will during his or her lifetime, as each sees fit; and in the event of the death of one of the parties, the survivor shall have no interest in the property of the estate of the other, either by way of inheritance, succession, family allowance or homestead.

4. That each party, in the event of a separation, shall have no right as against the other by way of claims for support, alimony, attorney fees, costs, or division of property.

In Witness Whereof, *etc.*

IX
Each Relinquishing Interest in Other's Property

This agreement is made the _____ day of _____ , 19 _____ , between _____ , of _____ , and _____ , of _____ .

Whereas, a marriage is intended to be shortly after the date hereof solemnized between the said _____ and _____ ; and

Whereas, each of the parties is possessed of considerable property, and has made a full and frank disclosure to the other in relation to its character and amount, and they have been advised as to their respective rights therein in the event of their marriage and in the absence of any agreement between them:

Now, therefore, the [bridegroom] and [bride], hereby declare it to be their intention that during their marriage each of them shall be and continue completely independent of the other as regards the enjoyment and disposal of all property, whether owned by either of

—Continued

Sample Antenuptial Agreement Clauses—*Continued*

them at the commencement of the marriage or coming to them or either of them during the marriage. Accordingly, they agree that all property belonging to either of them at the commencement of the marriage or coming to either of them during the marriage shall be enjoyed by him or her, and be subject to the dispositions of him or her, as his or her separate property, and after the death of either it shall be free from any claim by the other on account of dower, curtesy, or other statutory right, in the same manner as if the marriage had never been celebrated.

In Witness Whereof, *etc.*

X
Pooling of Property

This agreement made this the _____ day of _____ , 19 ____ , between _____ , of _____ , and _____ , of _____ .

Whereas, the parties are contemplating marriage and establishing a home together; and

Whereas, the parties upon their marriage desire to pool their resources for the benefit of each other; and

Whereas, this agreement is made in order to avoid any future conflict as to their rights and interests in said property.

Now, therefore, the parties agree as follows:

1. The parties shall enter into the marriage relation and live together as husband and wife.

2. On or before the date of marriage all property belonging to the parties, including bonds, bank accounts and realty, shall be reissued, redeposited and deeds drawn so that each party shall be the joint owner, with right of survivorship, of all of the property at present owned and held by the parties individually.

3. Each party obligates himself or herself to purchase and hold all property, present and future, jointly with the other party and agrees to execute any instrument necessary to convey, sell, or encumber any property, real or personal, when it is to the best interest of both parties that same be conveyed, sold, or encumbered.

4. At the death of either party the property belonging to both shall become the absolute property of the other, free from claims of all other persons. To make effective this section of the agreement a joint will of the parties is made and is placed in their safe deposit box in the _____ Bank in the City of _____ , _____ .

5. Should either party file a divorce against the other, then the party so filing shall by such filing forfeit to the other all right, title, and interest in all the property, real, personal or mixed, jointly held and owned by them.

6. The parties agree that the original of this instrument shall be deposited in escrow with _____ to be held by him.

7. This agreement cannot be revoked except by written consent of both parties and the holder in escrow shall not deliver the original to anyone except a court of competent jurisdiction or to the parties to this instrument upon their mutual demand for the surrender thereof.

8. This agreement is made in triplicate with each party hereto retaining a copy thereof, but the copy shall not be used in evidence or serve any legal purpose whatsoever if the original is available.

In Witness Whereof, *etc.*

▬▬ COHABITATION AGREEMENTS

Compare the following two situations:

Jim hires Mary as a maid in his house. She receives weekly compensation plus room and board. For a three-month period Jim fails to pay Mary's wages, even though she faithfully performs all of her duties. During this period, Jim seduces Mary. Mary sues Jim for *breach of contract* due to non-payment of wages.

Bob is a prostitute. Linda hires Bob for an evening but refuses to pay him his fee. Bob sues Linda for *breach of contract* due to nonpayment of the fee.

The result in the second situation is clear. Bob cannot sue Linda for breach of contract. A contract for sex is not enforceable in court. Linda promised to pay money for sex. Bob promised and provided sexual services. This was the consideration he gave in the bargain. But sex for hire is illegal in most states. In fact, **fornication** and **adultery** are crimes in some states even if no payment is involved. Bob's consideration was **meretricious** sexual services and, as such, cannot be the basis of a valid contract.

The result in the first situation above should also be clear. Mary has a valid claim for breach of contract. Her agreement to have a sexual relationship with Jim is incidental and, therefore, irrelevant to her right to collect compensation due her as a maid. She did not sell sexual services to Jim. There is no indication in the facts that the parties bargained for sexual services or that she engaged in sex in exchange for anything from Jim, e.g., continued employment, a raise in pay, lighter work duties. Their sexual involvement with each other is a **severable** part of their relationship and should not affect her main claim. Something is severable when what remains after it is removed can survive without it. (The opposite of severable is essential or indispensable.)

Now we come to a more difficult case:

Dan and Helen meet in college. They soon start living together. They move into an apartment, pool their resources, have children, etc. Twenty years after they entered this relationship, they decide to separate. Helen now sues Dan for a share of the property acquired during the time they lived together. At no time did they ever marry.

The fact that Dan and Helen never married does not affect their obligation to support their children, as we shall see in chapter 12. But what about Dan and Helen themselves? They **cohabited** and never married. They built a relationship, acquired property together, and helped each other over a long period of time. Do they have any support or property rights in each other now that they have separated?

This is not an academic question. The Bureau of the Census says that between 1970 and 1993 the number of "unmarried-couple households" in America increased by 600 percent—from 523,000 to 3.5 million. This category consists of two unrelated adults of the opposite sex who share a housing unit (see Exhibit 7.2). Furthermore, an additional 1.5 million households consist of two unrelated adults of the same sex.[4]

For years, the law has denied any rights to an unmarried person who makes financial claims based upon a period of cohabitation. The main reasons for this denial are as follows:

□ To grant financial or property rights to unmarried persons would treat them as if they were married. Our laws favor the institution of marriage. To

Fornication Sexual relations between unmarried persons or between persons who are not married to each other.

Adultery Sexual relations between a married person and someone other than his or her spouse.

Meretricious Pertaining to unlawful sexual relations; vulgar or tawdry.

Severable Removable without destroying what remains.

Cohabited Lived together as husband and wife whether or not they were married.

---

4. These are not all homosexual-couple households. The count includes some couples who are not cohabiting, e.g., those that include a roommate, a boarder, or a paid employee. In the future, the Bureau will use a new category of "unmarried partner," which is a person who is not related to the householder, who shares living quarters, and who has a close personal relationship with the householder.

□ **EXHIBIT 7.2**
Unmarried-Couple
Households

YEAR	TOTAL NUMBER OF MARRIED COUPLES	TOTAL NUMBER OF UNMARRIED COUPLES	NUMBER OF THESE UNMARRIED COUPLES WITH CHILDREN UNDER 15 YEARS OF AGE	RATIO OF UNMARRIED COUPLES PER 100 MARRIED COUPLES
1993	54,199,000	3,510,000	1,236,000	6
1990	56,112,000	2,856,000	891,000	5
1985	51,114,000	1,983,000	603,000	4
1980	49,714,000	1,589,000	431,000	3
1970	44,593,000	523,000	196,000	1

SOURCE: Arlene Saluter, *Marital Status and Living Arrangements,* Table D, Current Population Reports, P20-478, U.S. Bureau of the Census (May 1994).

recognize unmarried relationships would denigrate marriage and discourage people from entering it.

□ Sexual relations are legal and morally acceptable within marriage. If the law recognizes unmarried cohabitation, then illicit sex is being condoned. The relationship is not much different from prostitution.

These two arguments are still dominant forces in many states. In 1976, however, a major decision came from California: *Marvin v. Marvin* 18 Cal. 3d 660, 134 Cal. Rptr. 815, 557 P.2d 106 (1976). This case held that parties living together would not be denied a remedy in court upon their separation solely because they never married. Although all states have not followed *Marvin,* the decision has had a major impact in this still-developing area of the law.

The parties in *Marvin* lived together for seven years without marrying.[5] The plaintiff alleged that she entered an oral agreement with the defendant that provided (1) that he would support her, and (2) that while "the parties lived together they would combine their efforts and earnings and would share equally any and all property accumulated as a result of their efforts whether individual or combined." She further alleged that she agreed to give up her career as a singer in order to devote full time to the defendant as a companion, homemaker, housekeeper, and cook. During the seven years that they were together, the defendant accumulated in his name over $1 million in property. When they separated, she sued for her share of this property.

The media viewed her case as an alimony action between two unmarried "ex-pals" and dubbed it a **palimony** suit. Palimony, however, is not a legal term. The word *alimony* should not be associated with this kind of case. Alimony is a court-imposed obligation of support that grows out of a failed marital relationship. There was no marital relationship in the *Marvin* case.

One of the first hurdles for the plaintiff in *Marvin* was the problem of "meretricious sexual services." The defendant argued that even if a contract did exist (which he denied), it was unenforceable because it involved an illicit relation-

Palimony A nonlegal term for payments made by one nonmarried party to another after they cease living together, usually because they entered an express or implied contract to do so while they were cohabiting.

5. The parties were Michelle Marvin and the famous actor, Lee Marvin. Although they never married, Michelle changed her last name to Marvin.

ship. The parties were not married but were engaging in sexual relations. The court, however, ruled that

> "[A] contract is unenforceable only *to the extent* that it *explicitly* rests upon the immoral and illicit consideration of meretricious sexual services. . . . The fact that a man and woman live together without marriage, and engage in a sexual relationship, does not in itself invalidate agreements between them relating to their earnings, property, or expenses."

The agreement will be invalidated only if sex is an express condition of the relationship. If the sexual aspect of their relationship is severable from their agreements or understandings on earnings, property, and expenses, the agreements or understandings will be enforced. An example of an *un*enforceable agreement would be a promise by a man to provide for a woman in his will in exchange for her agreeing to live with him and bear his children. This agreement is *explicitly* based on a sexual relationship. Thus sex in such a case cannot be separated from the agreement and is *not* severable.

The next problem faced by the plaintiff in *Marvin* was the theory of *recovery.* The main reason married parties have financial rights in each other is their *marital status,* which gives rise to duties imposed by law. What about unmarried parties? The *Marvin* court suggested several theories of recovery for such individuals:

- ☐ Express contract
- ☐ Implied contract
- ☐ Quasi contract
- ☐ Trust
- ☐ Partnership
- ☐ Joint venture
- ☐ Putative spouse doctrine

Before we examine these theories, several points need to be emphasized. First, as indicated earlier, not all states agree with the *Marvin* doctrine that there are circumstances when unmarried cohabiting parties should be given a remedy upon separation. Second, the above list of seven remedies is not exhaustive. The *Marvin* court recognized that new theories may have to be developed to achieve justice in particular situations. Third, all of the theories will be to no avail, even in states that follow *Marvin,* if it can be shown that "meretricious sexual services" were at the heart of the relationship and cannot be separated (are not severable) from the other aspects of the relationship.

EXPRESS CONTRACT

In an express cohabitation agreement or contract, the parties expressly tell each other what is being "bargained" for, e.g., household services in exchange for a one-half interest in a house to be purchased, or companion services (nonsexual) in exchange for support during the time they live together. There must be an offer, acceptance, and legal consideration. The latter is the exchange of promises. While this is the cleanest theory of recovery, it is often difficult to prove. Rarely will the parties have the foresight to commit their agreement to writing, and it is equally rare for witnesses to be present when the parties make their express agreement. Ultimately the case will turn on which party the court believes.

IMPLIED CONTRACT

Implied Contract A contract that is not created by an express agreement between the parties but is inferred as a matter of reason and justice from their conduct and the surrounding circumstances.

Another remedy is to sue under a theory of **implied contract,** also called an *implied in fact contract.* This kind of contract exists when a reasonable person would conclude that the parties had a tacit understanding that they had a contractual relationship even though its terms were never expressly discussed. Consider the following example:

Someone delivers bottled milk to your door daily, which you never ordered. You consume the milk every day, place the empty bottles at the front door, exchange greetings with the delivery person, never demand that the deliveries stop, etc.

At the end of the month when you receive the bill for the milk, you will not be able to hide behind the fact that you never expressly ordered the milk. Under traditional contract principles, you have entered an "implied contract" to buy the milk, which is as binding as an express contract. Unless the state has enacted special laws to change these principles, you must pay for the milk.

In the case of unmarried individuals living together, we must similarly determine whether an implied contract existed. Was it clear by the conduct of the parties that they were entering an agreement? Was it obvious under the circumstances that they were exchanging something? Did both sides expect "compensation" in some form for what they were doing? If so, an implied contract existed, which can be as enforceable as an express contract.

QUASI CONTRACT

Quasi Contract A contract created by law to avoid unjust enrichment.

A **quasi contract** is also called an *implied in law contract.* Although called a contract, it is a legal fiction since it does not involve an express agreement and we cannot reasonably infer that the parties had an agreement in mind. The doctrine of quasi contract is simply a device designed by the courts to prevent **unjust enrichment.**[6] An example might be a doctor who provides medical care to an unconscious motorist on the road. The doctor can recover the reasonable cost of medical services under a quasi contract theory even though the motorist never expressly or impliedly asked for such services. Another example might be a man who arranges for a foreign woman to come to this country to live in his home and provide domestic services. If she came with the expectation of being paid and if what she provided was not meretricious, the law might obligate him to pay the reasonable value of her services, less the value of any support she received from him during the time they were together. The court's objective would be to avoid unjust enrichment. A court might reach a similar result when unmarried cohabitants separate.

Unjust Enrichment Receiving property or benefit from another when in fairness and equity the recipient should make restitution of the property or provide compensation for the benefit even though there was no express or implied promise to do so.

TRUST

Trust A legal entity that exists when one person holds property for the benefit of another.

A **trust** is another option to consider. At times, the law will hold that a trust is implied. Assume that Tim and Sandra, an unmarried couple, decide to buy a house. They use the funds in a joint account to which both contribute equally. The deed to the house is taken in Tim's name so that he has legal title. On such facts, a court will impose an implied trust for Sandra's benefit. She will be entitled to a half-interest in the house through the trust. A theory of implied

---

6. The amount of recovery is measured by what is called *quantum meruit,* which means "as much as he deserves."

trust might also be possible if Sandra contributed services rather than money toward the purchase of the property. A court would have to decide what her interest in the property should be in light of the nature and value of these services.

Another example of a trust that is imposed by law is called a **constructive trust.** Assume that a party obtains title to property through fraud or an abuse of confidence. The funds used to purchase the property come from the other party. A court will impose a constructive trust on the property if this is necessary to avoid the unjust enrichment of the person who obtained title in this way. This person will be deemed to be holding the property for the benefit of the party defrauded or otherwise taken advantage of.

Constructive Trust A trust created by operation of law against one who has obtained legal possession of property (or legal rights to property) through fraud, duress, abuse of confidence, or other unconscionable conduct.

PARTNERSHIP

A court might find that an unmarried couple entered the equivalent of a **partnership** and thereby acquired rights and obligations in the property involved in the partnership.

Partnership A voluntary contract between two (or more) persons to use their resources in a business or other venture, with the understanding that they will proportionately share losses and profits.

JOINT VENTURE

A **joint venture** is like a partnership, but on a more limited scale. A court might use the joint venture theory to cover some of the common enterprises entered into by two unmarried individuals while living together, e.g., the purchase of a home. Once a joint venture is established, the parties have legally enforceable rights in the fruits of their endeavors.

Joint Venture An express or implied agreement to participate in a common enterprise in which the parties have a mutual right of control.

PUTATIVE SPOUSE DOCTRINE

In limited circumstances, a party might have the rights of a **putative spouse.** This occurs when the parties attempt to enter a marital relationship, but a legal *impediment* to the formation of the marriage exists, e.g., one of the parties is under age or is married to someone else. If at least one of the parties is ignorant of this impediment, the law will treat the "marriage" as otherwise valid. Upon separation, the innocent party might be entitled to the reasonable value of the services rendered while together, or a share of the property accumulated by their joint efforts.

Putative Spouse A person who reasonably believed he or she entered a valid marriage even though there was a legal impediment that made the marriage unlawful.

CASE

HEWITT V. HEWITT

77 Ill. 2d 49, 394 N.E.2d 1204, 3 A.L.R. 4th 1 (1979)
Supreme Court of Illinois

Background: *Victoria Hewitt met Robert Hewitt in college. When she became pregnant, he told her they were husband and wife and that no formal ceremony was necessary. He said he would "share his life, his future, his earnings and his property" with her. They announced to their parents that they were married and held themselves out as husband and wife. She helped him in his education and business. During fifteen years together, they had three children. They never entered a ceremonial marriage. (Since 1905 Illinois has not allowed common law marriages.*) Upon their separation, she sued him for "an equal share of*

the profits and properties accumulated" while together. The circuit court dismissed her complaint. She appealed. The lower appellate court reversed and ruled that she could sue him for violating an express oral contract. Robert then appealed. The case is now on appeal before the Supreme Court of Illinois.

Decision on Appeal: *Judgment for Robert. It is against public policy in Illinois to enforce property rights of unmarried cohabitants.*

Opinion of the Court:

---

*A common law marriage is a marriage of two people who agree to be married, cohabit, and hold themselves out as husband and wife even though they do not go through a traditional ceremonial marriage.

Justice UNDERWOOD delivered the opinion of the court. . . .

In finding that plaintiff's complaint stated a cause of action on an express oral contract, the appellate court adopted the reasoning of the California Supreme Court in the widely publicized case of *Marvin v. Marvin* (1976), 18 Cal. 3d 660, 134 Cal. Rptr. 815, 557 P.2d 106, . . . The issue of unmarried cohabitants' mutual property rights, however, . . . cannot appropriately be characterized solely in terms of contract law, nor is it limited to considerations of equity or fairness as between the parties to such relationships. There are major public policy questions involved in determining whether, under what circumstances, and to what extent it is desirable to accord some type of legal status to claims arising from such relationships. Of substantially greater importance than the rights of the immediate parties is the impact of such recognition upon our society and the institution of marriage. Will the fact that legal rights closely resembling those arising from conventional marriages can be acquired by those who deliberately choose to enter into what have heretofore been commonly referred to as "illicit" or "meretricious" relationships encourage formation of such relationships and weaken marriage as the foundation of our family-based society? In the event of death shall the survivor have the status of a surviving spouse for purposes of inheritance, wrongful death actions, workmen's compensation, etc.? And still more importantly: what of the children born of such relationships? What are their support and inheritance rights and by what standards are custody questions resolved? What of the sociological and psychological effects upon them of that type of environment? Does not the recognition of legally enforceable property and custody rights emanating from nonmarital cohabitation in practical effect equate with the legalization of common law marriage at least in the circumstances of this case? And, in summary, have the increasing numbers of unmarried cohabitants and changing mores of our society reached the point at which the general welfare of the citizens of this State is best served by a return to something resembling the judicially created common law marriage our legislature outlawed in 1905?

Illinois' public policy regarding agreements such as the one alleged here was implemented long ago in *Wallace v. Rappleye* (1882), 103 Ill. 229, 249, where this court said: "An agreement in consideration of future illicit cohabitation between the plaintiffs is void." . . .

It is true, of course, that cohabitation by the parties may not prevent them from forming valid contracts about independent matters, for which it is said the sexual relations do not form part of the consideration. (*Restatement of Contracts* secs. 589, 597 (1932). . . .

The real thrust of plaintiff's argument here is that we should abandon the rule of illegality because of certain changes in societal norms and attitudes. It is urged that social mores have changed radically in recent years, rendering this principle of law archaic. It is said that because there are so many unmarried cohabitants today the courts must confer a legal status on such relationships. . . . If this is to be the result, however, it would seem more candid to acknowledge the return of varying forms of common law marriage than to continue displaying the naivete we believe involved in the assertion that there are involved in these relationships contracts separate and independent from the sexual activity, and the assumption that those contracts would have been entered into or would continue without that activity. . . .

[J]udicial recognition of mutual property rights between unmarried cohabitants would, in our opinion, clearly violate the policy of our recently enacted Illinois Marriage and Dissolution of Marriage Act . . . "[to] strengthen and preserve the integrity of marriage and safeguard family relationships." (Ill. Rev. Stat. 1977, ch. 40, par. 102.) We cannot confidently say that judicial recognition of property rights between unmarried cohabitants will not make that alternative to marriage more attractive by allowing the parties to engage in such relationships with greater security. . . .

The policy of the Act gives the State a strong continuing interest in the institution of marriage and prevents the marriage relation from becoming in effect a private contract terminable at will. This seems to us another indication that public policy disfavors private contractual alternatives to marriage. . . .

[W]e believe that these questions are appropriately within the province of the legislature, and that, if there is to be a change in the law of this State on this matter, it is for the legislature and not the courts to bring about that change. We accordingly hold that plaintiff's claims are unenforceable for the reason that they contravene the public policy, implicit in the statutory scheme of the Illinois Marriage and Dissolution of Marriage Act, disfavoring the grant of mutually enforceable property rights to knowingly unmarried cohabitants.

Appellate court reversed; circuit court affirmed.

CASE

WATTS V. WATTS

137 Wis. 2d, 506, 405 N.W.2d 303 (1987)
Supreme Court of Wisconsin

Background: Sue Watts alleges that she quit her job and abandoned her career in exchange for James Watts's promise to take care of her. For twelve years, they raised a family and worked in a family business together. They never married. (Common law marriages are not allowed in Wisconsin.) When the relationship deteriorated, she sued him in circuit court for her share of the property they had accumulated. Among her legal theories were breach of contract, constructive trust, and unjust enrichment. The circuit court dismissed the case, arguing that the legislature, not the court, should provide relief to parties who have accumulated property in nonmarital cohabitation relationships. The case is now on appeal before the Supreme Court of Wisconsin.

Decision on Appeal: *Reversed. Sue Watts should be allowed to bring her claims against James.*

Opinion of the Court:

Justice ABRAHAMSON delivered the opinion of the court. . . .

Nonmarital cohabitation does not render every agreement between the cohabiting parties illegal. . . . The plaintiff alleges that during the parties' relationship, and because of her domestic and business contributions, the business and personal wealth of the couple increased. Furthermore, the plaintiff alleges that she never received any compensation for these contributions to the relationship and that the defendant indicated to the plaintiff both orally and through his conduct that he considered her to be his wife and that she would share equally in the increased wealth.

The plaintiff asserts that since the breakdown of the relationship the defendant has refused to share equally with her the wealth accumulated through their joint efforts or to compensate her in any way for her contributions to the relationship. . . . [H]er claim . . . is that she and the defendant had a contract to share equally the property accumulated during their relationship. The essence of the complaint is that the parties had a contract, either an express or implied in fact contract, which the defendant breached.

Wisconsin courts have long recognized the importance of freedom of contract and have endeavored to protect the right to contract. A contract will not be enforced, however, if it violates public policy. A declaration that the contract is against public policy should be made only after a careful balancing, in the light of all the circumstances, of the interest in enforcing a particular promise against the policy against enforcement. Courts should be reluctant to frustrate a party's reasonable expectations without a corresponding benefit to be gained in deterring "misconduct" or avoiding inappropriate use of the judicial system. *Merten v. Nathan*, 108 Wis. 2d 205, 211, 321 N.W.2d 173, 177 (1982); *Restatement (Second) of Contracts*, Section 178 comments b and e (1981).

The defendant appears to attack the plaintiff's contract theory on three grounds. First, the defendant apparently asserts that the court's recognition of plaintiff's contract claim for a share of the parties' property contravenes the Wisconsin Family Code. Second, the defendant asserts that the legislature, not the courts, should determine the property and contract rights of unmarried cohabiting parties. Third, the defendant intimates that the parties' relationship was immoral and illegal and that any recognition of a contract between the parties or plaintiff's claim for a share of the property accumulated during the cohabitation contravenes public policy.

The defendant rests his argument that judicial recognition of a contract between unmarried cohabitants for property division violates the Wisconsin Family Code on *Hewitt v. Hewitt*, 77 Ill. 2d 49, 394 N.E.2d 1204, 3 A.L.R. 4th 1 (1979). In *Hewitt* The Illinois Supreme Court concluded that judicial recognition of mutual property rights between unmarried cohabitants would violate the policy of the Illinois Marriage and Dissolution Act because enhancing the attractiveness of a private arrangement contravenes the Act's policy of strengthening and preserving the integrity of marriage. The Illinois court concluded that allowing such a contract claim would weaken the sanctity of marriage, put in doubt the rights of inheritance, and open the door to false pretenses of marriage. . . .

The defendant has failed to persuade this court that enforcing an express or implied in fact contract between these parties would in fact violate the Wisconsin Family Code. The Family Code, chs. 765–68, Stats. 1985–86, is intended to promote the institution of marriage and the family. We find no indication, however, that the Wisconsin legislature intended the Family Code to restrict in any way a court's resolution of property or contract disputes between unmarried cohabitants.

The defendant also urges that if the court is not willing to say that the Family Code proscribes contracts between unmarried cohabiting parties, then the court should refuse to resolve the contract and property rights of unmarried cohabitants without legislative guidance. The defendant asserts that this court should conclude, as the *Hewitt* court did, that the task of determining the rights of cohabiting parties is too complex and difficult for the court and should be left to the legislature. We are not persuaded by the defendant's argument. Courts have traditionally developed principles of contract and property law through the case-by-case method of the common law. While ultimately the legislature may resolve the problems raised by unmarried cohabiting parties, we are not persuaded that the court should refrain from resolving such disputes until the legislature gives us direction. . . .

We turn to the defendant's third point, namely, that any contract between the parties regarding property division contravenes public policy because the contract is based on immoral or illegal sexual activity. . . . Courts have generally refused to enforce contracts for which the sole consideration is sexual relations, sometimes referred to as "meretricious" relationships.

See *In Matter of Estate of Steffes*, 95 Wis. 2d 490, 514, 290 N.W.2d 697 (1980), citing *Restatement of Contracts*, Section 589 (1932). Courts distinguish, however, between contracts that are explicitly and inseparably founded on sexual services and those that are not. This court, and numerous other courts, have concluded that "a bargain between two people is not illegal merely because there is an illicit relationship between the two so long as the bargain is independent of the illicit relationship and the illicit relationship does not constitute any part of the consideration bargained for and is not a condition of the bargain." *Steffes*, supra, 95 Wis. 2d at 514, 290 N.W.2d 697.

While not condoning the illicit sexual relationship of the parties, many courts have recognized that the result of a court's refusal to enforce contract and property rights between unmarried cohabitants is that one party keeps all or most of the assets accumulated during the relationship, while the other party, no more or less "guilty," is deprived of property which he or she has helped to accumulate. See e.g., *Marvin v. Marvin*, 18 Cal. 3d 660, 682, 134 Cal. Rptr. 815, 830, 557 P.2d 106, 121 (1976).

The *Hewitt* decision, which leaves one party to the relationship enriched at the expense of the other party who had contributed to the acquisition of the property, has often been criticized by courts and commentators as being unduly harsh. Moreover, courts recognize that their refusal to enforce what are in other contexts clearly lawful promises will not undo the parties' relationship and may not discourage others from entering into such relationships. *Tyranski v. Piggins*, 44 Mich. App. 570, 577, 205 N.W.2d 595 (1973). A harsh, per se rule that the contract and property rights of unmarried cohabiting parties will not be recognized might actually encourage a partner with greater income potential to avoid marriage in order to retain all accumulated assets, leaving the other party with nothing.

In this case, the plaintiff has alleged many facts independent from the parties' physical relationship which, if proven, would establish an express contract or an implied in fact contract that the parties agreed to share the property accumulated during the relationship. The plaintiff has alleged that she quit her job and abandoned her career training upon the defendant's promise to take care of her. A change in one party's circumstances in performance of the agreement may imply an agreement between the parties. *Steffes*, supra, 95 Wis. 2d at 504, 290 N.W.2d 697; *Tyranski*, supra, 44 Mich. App. at 574, 205 N.W.2d at 597. In addition, the plaintiff alleges that she performed housekeeping, childbearing, childrearing, and other services related to the maintenance of the parties' home, in addition to various services for the defendant's business and her own business, for which

she received no compensation. Courts have recognized that money, property, or services (including housekeeping or childrearing) may constitute adequate consideration independent of the parties' sexual relationship to support an agreement to share or transfer property. See *Tyranski*, supra, 44 Mich. App. at 574, 205 N.W.2d at 597; *Steffes*, supra 95 Wis. 2d at 501, 290 N.W.2d 697.*

According to the plaintiff's complaint, the parties cohabited for more than twelve years, held joint bank accounts, made joint purchases, filed joint income tax returns, and were listed as husband and wife on other legal documents. Courts have held that such a relationship and "joint acts of a financial nature can give rise to an inference that the parties intended to share equally." *Beal v. Beal*, 282 Or. 115, 122, 577 P.2d 507, 510 (1978). The joint ownership of property and the filing of joint income tax returns strongly implies that the parties intended their relationship to be in the nature of a joint enterprise, financially as well as personally.

Having reviewed the complaint and surveyed the law in this and other jurisdictions, we hold that the Family Code does not preclude an unmarried cohabitant from asserting contract and property claims against the other party to the cohabitation. We further conclude that public policy does not necessarily preclude an unmarried cohabitant from asserting a contract claim against the other party to the cohabitation so long as the claim exists independently of the sexual relationship and is supported by separate consideration. Accordingly, we conclude that the plaintiff in this case has pleaded the facts necessary to state a claim for damages resulting from the defendant's breach of an express or an implied in fact contract to share with the plaintiff the property accumulated through the efforts of both parties during their relationship. . . . [W]e do not judge the merits of the plaintiff's claim; we merely hold that she be given her day in court to prove her claim. . . .

The plaintiff's [next] theory of recovery involves unjust enrichment. Essentially, she alleges that the defendant accepted and retained the benefit of services she provided knowing that she expected to share equally in the wealth accumulated during their rela-

*Until recently, the prevailing view was that services performed in the context of a "family or marriage relationship" were presumed gratuitous. However, that presumption was rebuttable. In *Steffes*, we held the presumption to be irrelevant where the plaintiff can show either an express or implied agreement to pay for those services, even where the plaintiff has rendered them "with a sense of affection, devotion and duty." Id. 95 Wis. 2d at 503, 290 N.W.2d at 703–704. For a discussion of the evolution of thought regarding the economic value of homemaking services by cohabitants, see Bruch, *Property Rights of De Facto Spouses Including Thoughts on the Value of Homemakers' Services*, 10 Family Law Quarterly 101, 110–14 (Summer 1976).

tionship. She argues that it is unfair for the defendant to retain all the assets they accumulated under these circumstances and that a constructive trust should be imposed on the property as a result of the defendant's unjust enrichment. . . .

Unlike claims for breach of an express or implied in fact contract, a claim of unjust enrichment does not arise out of an agreement entered into by the parties. Rather, an action for recovery based upon unjust enrichment is grounded on the moral principle that one who has received a benefit has a duty to make restitution where retaining such a benefit would be unjust. *Puttkammer v. Minth,* 83 Wis. 2d 686, 689, 266 N.W.2d 361, 363 (1978).

Because no express or implied in fact agreement exists between the parties, recovery based upon unjust enrichment is sometimes referred to as "quasi contract," or contract "implied in law" rather than "implied in fact." Quasi contracts are obligations created by law to prevent injustice. *Shulse v. City of Mayville,* 223 Wis. 624, 632, 271 N.W. 643 (1937).

In Wisconsin, an action for unjust enrichment, or quasi contract, is based upon proof of three elements: (1) a benefit conferred on the defendant by the plaintiff, (2) appreciation or knowledge by the defendant of the benefit, and (3) acceptance or retention of the benefit by the defendant under circumstances making it inequitable for the defendant to retain the benefit. . . .

As part of his general argument, the defendant claims that the court should leave the parties to an illicit relationship such as the one in this case essentially as they are found, providing no relief at all to either party. For support, the defendant relies heavily on *Hewitt v. Hewitt,* supra, to argue that courts should provide no relief whatsoever to unmarried cohabitants until the legislature provides specifically for it.

As we have discussed previously, allowing no relief at all to one party in a so-called "illicit" relationship effectively provides total relief to the other, by leaving that party owner of all the assets acquired through the efforts of both. Yet it cannot seriously be argued that the party retaining all the assets is less "guilty" than the other. Such a result is contrary to the principles of equity. Many courts have held, and

we now so hold, that unmarried cohabitants may raise claims based upon unjust enrichment following the termination of their relationships where one of the parties attempts to retain an unreasonable amount of the property acquired through the efforts of both.

In this case, the plaintiff alleges that she contributed both property and services to the parties' relationship. She claims that because of these contributions the parties' assets increased, but that she was never compensated for her contributions. She further alleges that the defendant, knowing that the plaintiff expected to share in the property accumulated, "accepted the services rendered to him by the plaintiff" and that it would be unfair under the circumstances to allow him to retain everything while she receives nothing. We conclude that the facts alleged are sufficient to state a claim for recovery based upon unjust enrichment.

As part of the plaintiff's unjust enrichment claim, she has asked that a constructive trust be imposed on the assets that the defendant acquired during their relationship. A constructive trust is an equitable device created by law to prevent unjust enrichment. *Wilharms v. Wilharms,* 93 Wis. 2d 671, 678, 287 N.W.2d 779, 783 (1980). To state a claim on the theory of constructive trust the complaint must state facts sufficient to show (1) unjust enrichment and (2) abuse of a confidential relationship or some other form of unconscionable conduct. The latter element can be inferred from allegations in the complaint which show, for example, a family relationship, a close personal relationship, or the parties' mutual trust. These facts are alleged in this complaint or may be inferred. *Gorski v. Gorski,* 82 Wis. 2d 248, 254–55, 262 N.W.2d 120 (1978). Therefore, we hold that if the plaintiff can prove the elements of unjust enrichment to the satisfaction of the circuit court, she will be entitled to demonstrate further that a constructive trust should be imposed as a remedy. . . .

In summary, we hold that the plaintiff's complaint has stated a claim upon which relief may be granted. . . . Accordingly, we reverse the judgment of the circuit court, and remand the cause to the circuit court for further proceedings consistent with this opinion.

---

a. Why did the *Hewitt* court rule that cohabitation agreements were illegal? Why did the *Watts* court rule that they can be legal?

b. Which opinion was correctly decided, *Hewitt* or *Watts?*

c. Assume that James Watts died without leaving a will while he still had a good relationship with Sue Watts. Would she be able to claim a share of his estate as one of his heirs?

d. How would the facts of *Hewitt* be resolved in your state? How would the facts of *Watts* be resolved in your state? (See General Instructions for the Court-Opinion Assignment in chapter 1.)

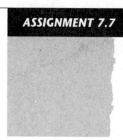

ASSIGNMENT 7.7

ASSIGNMENT 7.8

a. Helen Smith and Sam Jones live together in your state. They are not married and do not intend to become married. They would like to enter a contract that spells out their rights and responsibilities. Specifically, they want to make clear that the house in which they both live belongs to Helen even though Sam has done extensive remodeling work on it. They each have separate bank accounts and one joint account. They want to make clear that only the funds in the joint account belong to both of them equally. Next year they hope to have or adopt a child. In either event, they want the contract to specify that the child will be given the surname, "Smith-Jones," a combination of their own last names. Draft a contract for them. Include any other clauses you think appropriate, e.g., on making wills, the duration of the contract, on the education and religion of children. (See General Instructions for the Agreement-Drafting Assignment in chapter 1.)

b. Tom and George are gay. They live together. George agrees to support Tom while the latter completes engineering school, at which time Tom will support George while the latter completes law school. After Tom obtains his engineering degree, he leaves George. George now sues Tom for the amount of money that would have been provided as support while George attended law school. What result? (See General Instructions for the Legal-Analysis Assignment in chapter 1.)

c. Richard and Lea have lived together for ten years without being married. This month, they separated. They never entered a formal contract, but Lea says that they had an informal understanding that they would equally divide everything acquired during their relationship together. Lea sues Richard for one-half of all property so acquired. You work for the law firm that represents Lea. Draft a set of interrogatories for Lea that will be sent to Richard in which you seek information that would be relevant to Lea's action. (See General Instructions for the Interrogatories Assignment in chapter 1.)

▆▆▆ Interviewing and Investigation Checklist

Factors Relevant to the Property Rights of Unmarried Couples

Legal Interviewing Questions

1. When and how did the two of you meet?

2. When did you begin living together?

3. Why did the two of you decide to do this? What exactly did you say to each other about your relationship at the time?

4. Did you discuss the living arrangement together? If so, what was said?

5. What was said or implied about the sexual relationship between you? Describe this relationship.

6. What was your understanding about the following matters: rent, house purchase, house payments, furniture payments, food, clothing, medical bills?

7. Did you agree to keep separate or joint bank accounts? Why?

8. What other commitments were made, if any? For example, was there any agreement on providing support, making a will, having children, giving each other property or shares in property? Were any of these commitments put in writing?

9. Did you ever discuss marriage? If so, what was said by both of you on the topic?

10. What did you give up in order to live with him or her? Did he or she understand this? How do you know?

11. What did he or she give up in order to live with you?

12. What other promises were made or implied between you? Why were they made?

13. How did you introduce each other to others?

14. Did you help each other in your businesses? If so, how?

15. What were your roles in the house? How were these roles decided upon? Through agreement? Explain.

16. Did he or she ever pay you for anything you did? Did you ever pay him or her? Explain the circumstances.

17. If no payment was ever made, was payment expected in the future? Explain.

18. Were the two of you "faithful" to each other? Did either of you ever date others? Explain.

19. Did you use each other's money for any purpose? If so, explain the circumstances. If not, why not?

Possible Investigation Tasks

☐ Obtain copies of bank statements, deeds for property acquired while the parties were together, loan applications, tax returns, etc.

☐ Interview persons who knew the parties.

☐ Contact professional housekeeping companies to determine the going rate for housekeeping services.

▰▰▰ Sample Cohabitation Agreement

Cohabitation Agreement
W. Mulloy, West's Legal Forms, 2d
§ 3.54, pp. 225–229 (1983).

I
Intention of the Parties

_____and _____declare that they are not married to each other, but they are living together under the same roof, and by this agreement intend to protect and define each other's rights pertaining to future services rendered, earnings, accumulated property and furnishings and other matters that may be contained herein. It is expressly set forth herein that the consent of either party to cohabit sexually with the other is not a consideration, either in whole or in part, for the making of this agreement. It is further expressly set forth herein that the general purpose of this agreement is that the earnings, accumulations and property of each party herein shall be the separate property of the person who earns or acquires said property, and shall not be deemed community property, joint property, common law property or otherwise giving the non-earning or non-acquiring party an interest in same.

II
Representations to the Public

It is agreed that should either or both of the parties to this agreement represent to the public, in whatever manner, that they are husband and wife, that said representation shall be for social convenience only, and shall in no way imply that sexual services are a consideration for any party of this agreement, nor shall it imply that sexual cohabitation is taking place.

III
Property, Earnings, and Accumulations

It is agreed that all property of any nature or in any place, including but not limited to the earnings and income resulting from the personal services, skill, effort, and work of either party to this agreement, whether acquired before or during the term of this agreement, or acquired by either one of them by purchase, gift or inheritance during the said term, shall be the separate property of the respective party, and that neither party shall have any interest in, and both parties hereby waive any right or interest he or she may have in the property of the other.

IV
Services Rendered

It is agreed that whatever household, homemaking, or other domestic work and services that either party may contribute to the other or to their common domicile shall be voluntary, free, and without compensation, and each party agrees that work of this nature is done without expectation of monetary or other reward from the other party.

V
Debts and Obligations

It is agreed that all debts and obligations acquired by either party which is to the benefit of that party shall be the debt or obligation of that party only, and that the other shall not be liable for same. Should one party be forced to pay a debt rightfully belonging to and benefitting the other, the other promises to reimburse, indemnify and hold harmless the one who has paid said debt or obligation.

Those debts and obligations which are to the benefit of both parties, such as utilities, garbage, local telephone service, rent, and renter's insurance shall be paid in such sums and in such proportion by each party as shall be mutually agreeable.

—Continued

Cohabitation Agreement—*Continued*

VI
Money Loaned

All money, with the exception of mortgage or rent payments, transferred by one party to the other, either directly or to an account, obligation, or purchase of the other, shall be deemed a loan to the other, unless otherwise stated in writing. This shall include such things as downpayments on a home or vehicle, and deposits in either party's separate bank account.

VII
Rented Premises

It is agreed that should the parties share rented premises, said rented premises shall "belong" to the person who first rented the same, and should the parties separate, the second one shall leave taking only such belongings as he or she owned prior to moving in or purchased while living together.

If the parties both rent the premises from the beginning, then it is agreed that they will have a third person flip a coin to see who "owns" the premises, and the winner will have the option to remain while the loser leaves.

VIII
Rent or Mortgage

It is agreed that the parties may split the rent or mortgage payments in whatever proportion they choose, each contributing such sum as is mutually agreeable. It is also agreed that if one party contributes to the mortgage payment of a premises belonging to or being purchased in the name of the other party, that such contribution shall be deemed rent only, and shall be non-refundable and shall not create in the person who is living in the premises owned or being purchased by the other, any interest in said property or in the equity therein.

IX
Business Arrangements

A. It is agreed that should one party hereto contribute services, labor, or effort to a business enterprise belonging to the other, that the party contributing said services, labor or effort shall not acquire by reason thereof any interest in, ownership of, or claim to said business enterprise, nor shall said person be compensated in any way for said services, labor, or effort, unless the terms of said compensation are expressly agreed to by both parties.

B. Should the parties share services, labor or effort in a jointly owned business enterprise the relative interests of each party shall be apportioned according to a separate partnership agreement, or, if there is no express agreement, then in proportion that each contributed thereto.

C. It is agreed that the business known as _____ is the individual and separate business of [*Name of Owner*], and is not to be deemed a jointly owned business of both parties.

X
Separate Accounts

In conformity with the intentions of the parties set forth herein, both parties agree to maintain separate bank accounts, insurance accounts (except "renter's" insurance to insure the contents of an apartment, house, etc., which the parties may jointly hold), tax returns, credit accounts, credit union accounts, medical accounts, automobile registration and ownership, and deeds to property, and to make all purchases of personal property, including furniture, appliances, records, books, works of art, stereo equipment, etc., separate, in order to avoid confusion as to the ownership of same, and also in order to avoid nullifying the general intent of this agreement.

—Continued

Cohabitation Agreement—*Continued*

XI
Duration of This Agreement

This agreement shall remain in effect from the date the parties start cohabiting until either party leaves or removes himself or herself from the common domicile with the intention not to return, or until they marry, or until they make a new written agreement that is contrary to the terms of this agreement.

XII
Attorney Fees and Costs

Each party agrees to act in good faith with the provisions of this agreement, and should one party breach the agreement or fail to act in good faith therewith, such party agrees to pay to the other such attorney fees and costs as may be reasonable in order to properly enforce the provisions herein.

XIII
No Common Law Marriage Intended

Even though the parties hereto are cohabiting under the same roof and may give the appearance of being married, or from time to time represent to the public that they are husband and wife, they do not intend by such acts to acquire the status of "common law" marriage, and expressly state herein that this is not an agreement to marry, that they are not now married, and that they understand they are not married to each other during the term of this agreement.

XIV
Waiver of Support

Both parties waive and relinquish any and all rights to "alimony," "spousal support," or other separate maintenance from the other in the event of a termination of their living together arrangement.

Dated: _____

_____

[*Name and Signature of Party*]

_____

[*Name and Signature of Party*]

Witnesses:

_____

_____

Notary Public:

_____   (SEAL)

My commission expires _____

■■■■ SUMMARY

The four main kinds of agreements parties enter before and after marriage are cohabitation agreement, antenuptial agreement, post-nuptial agreement, and separation agreement. An antenuptial agreement is a premarital contract that defines certain rights and obligations during marriage and upon the termination of marriage by death or divorce. To be enforceable, the agreement must meet the requirements for a valid contract, must be based on disclosure of assets, must not be unconscionable, and must not be against public policy.

A cohabitation agreement is a contract between two unmarried parties covering financial and related matters while they live together, upon separation, or upon death. Some states will enforce such agreements so long as they are not based solely on meretricious sexual services, or so long as the sexual aspect of their agreement is severable from the rest of the agreement. When one party sues the other for breaching the agreement, the media's misleading phrase for the litigation is palimony suit.

If the aggrieved party cannot establish the existence of an express or implied cohabitation contract, other theories might be used by the court to avoid the unfairness of one of the parties walking away from the relationship with nothing. These theories include quasi contract, trust, partnership, joint venture, and the putative-spouse doctrine.

■■■■ KEY CHAPTER TERMINOLOGY

Cohabitation Agreement	Fornication	Quasi Contract
Antenuptial Agreement	Adultery	Unjust Enrichment
Post-nuptial Agreement	Meretricious	Trust
Separation Agreement	Severable	Constructive Trust
Waiver	Cohabited	Partnership
Unconscionable	*Marvin v. Marvin*	Joint Venture
Public Policy	Palimony	Putative Spouse
Uniform Premarital Agreement Act	Implied Contract	

THE FORMATION OF CEREMONIAL MARRIAGES AND COMMON LAW MARRIAGES

8

Marriage is a coming together for better or for worse, hopefully enduring and intimate to the degree of being sacred. It is an association that promotes a way of life, not causes; a harmony in living, not political faiths; a bilateral loyalty, not commercial or social projects. Yet it is an association for as noble a purpose as any involved in our prior decisions. *Griswold v. Connecticut*, 381 U.S. 479, 486, 85 S. Ct. 1678, 1682, 14 L. Ed. 2d 510 (1965)—Justice Douglas.

■■■■ RAISING THE MARRIAGE ISSUE

A client is not likely to walk into a law office and ask, "am I married?" The existence of a marriage becomes an issue when the client is trying to obtain some other objective, such as seeking

- ☐ a divorce (you can't divorce someone to whom you are not married)
- ☐ pension benefits as the surviving spouse of a deceased employee
- ☐ social security survivor benefits through a deceased spouse
- ☐ worker's compensation death benefits as the surviving spouse of an employee fatally injured on the job
- ☐ assets as the spouse of a deceased person who died **intestate**
- ☐ assets under a clause in a will that gives property "to my wife" or "to my husband"
- ☐ a **forced share** of a deceased spouse's estate
- ☐ **dower** or **curtesy** rights
- ☐ entrance to the United States (or avoidance of deportation) as a result of being married to a U.S. citizen

Intestate Dying without leaving a valid will.

Forced Share A designated share of a deceased spouse's estate that goes to the surviving spouse despite what the will of the deceased spouse gave the surviving spouse.

Dower A widow's right to the lifetime use of one-third of the land her deceased husband owned during the marriage.

Curtesy A husband's right to the lifetime use of all the land his deceased wife owned during the marriage (if issue were born of the marriage).

Privilege for Marital Communication One spouse cannot disclose in court any confidential communications that occurred between the spouses during the marriage. (This privilege does not apply when the spouses are suing each other.)

Miscegenation Mixing the races. The marriage or cohabitation of persons of difference races.

□ The right to assert in a criminal case the **privilege for marital communications,** also called the husband-wife privilege.

■■■ REGULATING WHO CAN MARRY

Marital status may be achieved through one of two possible methods: ceremonial marriage or common law marriage. As we shall see in the next section, however, many states have abolished common law marriage.

The United States Supreme Court has held that marriage is a fundamental right. Consequently, a state is limited in its power to regulate one's right to marry. For example, a state cannot prohibit **miscegenation.** Nor can it withhold a marriage license pending proof that child-support payments (from an earlier marriage) are being met, and proof that any children due such payments are not likely to become public charges. Only "reasonable regulations that do not significantly interfere with decisions to enter into the marital relationship may legitimately be imposed" *Zablocki v. Redhail,* 434 U.S. 374, 386, 98 S. Ct. 673, 681, 54 L. Ed. 2d 618 (1978).

States have imposed two major kinds of requirements for entering marriage: (1) technical or formal requirements for ceremonial marriages, e.g., obtaining a license, and (2) more basic requirements relating to the intent and capacity to marry that apply to both ceremonial and common law marriages, e.g., being of minimum age to marry, and not being too closely related to the person you want to marry. The latter requirements will be discussed in chapter 9. Here our focus is primarily on the technical or formal requirements.

■ CEREMONIAL MARRIAGE

The requirements for a **ceremonial marriage,** found within the statutory code of your state, usually specify the following:

Ceremonial Marriage
A marriage that is entered in compliance with the statutory requirements, e.g., obtaining a marriage license, having the marriage performed (i.e., solemnized) by an authorized person.

☐ Marriage license (Exhibit 8.1)

☐ Ceremony performed by an authorized person (Exhibit 8.2)

☐ Witnesses to the ceremony (Exhibit 8.2)

☐ Waiting period

☐ Physical examination of the two parties

☐ Recording of the license in a designated public office following the ceremony

Not all states have the same requirements, and some may impose additional ones.

ASSIGNMENT 8.1

Go to your state statutory code and identify all of the technical requirements for entering a ceremonial marriage, e.g., obtaining a license, paying a fee. (See General Instructions for the State-Code Assignment in chapter 1.)

ASSIGNMENT 8.2

In Assignment 8.1, you identified all of the requirements for a ceremonial marriage in your state. In this assignment, you are to interview someone who was married in your state in order to determine whether all the requirements for a ceremonial marriage were met. You may interview your spouse or a married relative, friend, classmate, etc. Before you conduct the interview, draft a checklist of questions necessary to determine if the marriage is in compliance with state requirements. (These should be questions that could be part of a manual.) Make notes of the interviewee's answers. For all answers, ask the interviewee if any documents or other evidence exists to substantiate (or corroborate) information given. (See General Instructions for the Checklist-Formulation Assignment in chapter 1.) Hand in to your instructor a written account of the interview (including the questions you asked). Remember that one of the primary characteristics of such written work products should be specificity; the details of names, addresses, dates, who said what, etc., can be critical. (See General Instructions for the Interview Assignment in chapter 1.)

Suppose that the technical requirements for a ceremonial marriage have been violated. What consequences follow?

Assume, for example, that a statute requires a ten-day waiting period between the date of the issuing of the license and the date of the ceremony. Joe

Marriage License

NOT VALID After Sixty Days from Date

The State of Ohio, Adams County

To Any Person Legally Authorized to Solemnize Marriages in the State of Ohio:

I, the undersigned,

James W. Lang, Jr.

Judge of the Probate Court within and for the County and State aforesaid, have **Licensed**, and do hereby License and Authorize

Mr. Peter Steck   and

Miss Patricia Jane Farrell

to be joined in **Marriage**.

In Witness Whereof, I have hereunto subscribed my name and affixed the seal of said Court, at West Union, Ohio, this 18th day of June A.D. 19 68

JAMES W. LANG, JR.

Judge of the Probate Court

By A. C. Bailey

Deputy Clerk

The above marriage was solemnized by me this 22nd day of June 1968

(Rev.) John J. Marquardt

and Mary want to marry right away and find a minister who marries them on the same day they obtained the license. What result? Are they validly married? In most states, the marriage is valid even when there has been a failure to comply with one of the requirements discussed in this chapter for a ceremonial marriage. In such states, noncompliance with the requirements for a ceremonial marriage cannot later be used as a ground for annulment or divorce. Keep in mind, however, that we are *not* discussing age or relationship requirements that involve the *legal capacity* of parties to marry nor are we discussing requirements relating to *intent to marry*. Violations of such requirements can indeed be grounds for annulment or divorce, as we will see in the next chapter.

While noncompliance with technical requirements does not affect the validity of a marriage in most states, other consequences may result. The parties, for

Number _____ .

To _____ , authorized to celebrate (or witness) marriages in the state of _____ , greeting:

   You are hereby authorized to celebrate (or witness) the rites of marriage between _____ , of _____ , and _____ , of _____ , and having done so, you are commanded to make return of the same to the clerk's office of _____within ten days under a penalty of fifty dollars for default therein.

   Witness my hand and seal of said court this _____ day of _____ , anno Domini _____ .

_____ Clerk.

By _____ Assistant Clerk.

□ **EXHIBIT 8.2**
Authorization to Celebrate or Witness a Marriage

Number _____ .

   I, _____ , who have been duly authorized to celebrate (or witness) the rites of marriage in the state of _____ do hereby certify that, by authority of a license of corresponding number herewith, I solemnized (or witnessed) the marriage of _____ and _____ , named therein, on the _____ day of _____ , at _____ , in said state.

example, might be prosecuted for perjury if they falsified public documents in applying for the marriage. The person who performed the marriage ceremony without the authority to do so may be subjected to a fine. Other sanctions similar to these might also apply.

Over 2,000 followers of Rev. Sun Myung Moon go through a ceremonial marriage in Madison Square Garden, New York City.

a. In your state, is the validity of the marriage affected by a violation of any of the technical requirements for a ceremonial marriage that you identified in Assignment 8.1?

b. What penalties can be imposed for the violation of any of the technical requirements for a ceremonial marriage in your state?

To answer the above two questions, you may have to check both statutory law and case law. See General Instructions for the State-Code Assignment and for the Court-Opinion Assignment in chapter 1.

Suppose that a statute in a state provides as follows:

§ 10 No marriage shall be invalid on account of want of authority in any person solemnizing the same if consummated with the full belief on the part of the persons so married, or either of them, that they were lawfully joined in marriage.

George and Linda read a newspaper article stating that five of seven ministers connected with the Triple Faith Church in their state had been fined for illegally performing marriage ceremonies. A week later, they are married by Rev. Smith, who is in charge of Triple Faith Church but who has no authority to marry anyone. Can the validity of their marriage be called into question under § 10? (See General Instructions for the Legal-Analysis Assignment in chapter 1.)

☐ **Note on Proxy Marriage** Some states sanction a **proxy marriage** in which the ceremony takes place with one or both parties being absent (e.g., the groom is overseas). A third-party agent must be given the authority to act on behalf of the missing party or parties during the ceremony.

COMMON LAW MARRIAGE

Common Law Marriage
The marriage of two people who agree to be married, cohabit, and hold themselves out as husband and wife even though they do not go through a ceremonial marriage.

When parties enter a valid **common law marriage,** the marriage is as valid as a ceremonial marriage. Children born during a common law marriage, for example, are legitimate. To end such a marriage, one of the parties must die, or they both must go through a divorce proceeding in the same manner as any other married couple seeking to dissolve a marriage.

Most states have abolished common law marriages. Thirteen states and the District of Columbia still recognize them (see Exhibit 8.3). Even in states that have abolished common law marriages, however, it is important to know something about them for the following reasons:

1. Parties may enter a common law marriage in a state where such marriages are valid and then move to another state that has abolished such marriages. Under traditional **conflict of law** principles, as we shall see, the second state may have to recognize the marriage as valid. In our highly mobile society, parties who live together should be aware that if they travel through states that recognize common law marriages for vacations or for other temporary purposes, one of the parties might later try to claim that they entered a common law marriage in such a state.

Conflict of Law An inconsistency between the laws of different legal systems such as two states or two countries.

2. It may be that your state once recognized common law marriages as valid, but then, as of a certain date, abolished all such marriages for the future. A number of people may still live in your state who entered valid common law marriages before the law was changed, and hence, their marriages are still valid.

☐ **EXHIBIT 8.3   Common Law Marriage**

STATE	VALID IN STATE?	RECOGNIZED IF CURRENTLY VALID WHERE CONTRACTED?	STATE	VALID IN STATE?	RECOGNIZED IF CURRENTLY VALID WHERE CONTRACTED?
Alabama	Yes	Yes	Montana	Yes	Yes
Alaska	Not after 1/1/64	Yes	Nebraska	Not after 1923	Yes
Arizona	No	Yes	Nevada	Not after 3/29/43	Yes
Arkansas	No	Yes	New Hampshire	No	Yes
California	Not after 1895	Yes	New Jersey	Not after 1/12/39	Yes
Colorado	Yes	Yes	New Mexico	No	Yes
Connecticut	No	*	New York	Not after 4/29/33	Yes
Delaware	No	Yes	North Carolina	No	Yes
Dist. of Columbia	Yes	Yes	North Dakota	No	Yes
Florida	Not after 1/1/68	Yes	Ohio	Yes	Yes
Georgia	Yes	Yes	Oklahoma	Yes	Yes
Hawaii	No	Yes	Oregon	No	Yes
Idaho	Yes	Yes	Pennsylvania	Yes	Yes
Illinois	Not after 6/30/05	*	Rhode Island	Yes	*
Indiana	Not after 1/1/58	*	South Carolina	Yes	Yes
Iowa	Yes	Yes	South Dakota	Not after 7/1/59	*
Kansas	Yes	Yes	Tennessee	No	Yes
Kentucky	No	Yes	Texas	Yes	Yes
Louisiana	No	*	Utah	No	Yes
Maine	No	*	Vermont	No	*
Maryland	No	Yes	Virginia	No	Yes
Massachusetts	No	Yes	Washington	No	Yes
Michigan	Not after 1/1/57	Yes	West Virginia	No	Yes
Minnesota	Not after 4/26/41	*	Wisconsin	Not after 1913	*
Mississippi	Not after 4/5/56	*	Wyoming	No	Yes
Missouri	Not after 3/3/21	*			

*Legal status unclear.
SOURCE: U.S. Department of Labor, Women's Bureau.

Does your state have a statute abolishing common law marriages? If so, what is its effective date? If not, check court opinions to determine whether common law marriages are valid in your state. Give the full citation to the statute or case that you rely on. (See General Instructions for the State-Code Assignment and General Instructions for the Court-Opinion Assignment in chapter 1.)

ASSIGNMENT 8.5

What conditions must exist for a valid common law marriage in states that recognize such marriages? Not all states have the same requirements. Generally, however, the following conditions must be met.

Common Law Marriage

☐ The parties must have legal capacity to marry.

☐ There must be an intent to marry and a present agreement to enter a marital relationship—to become husband and wife to each other. (Some states require an express agreement; others allow the agreement to be inferred from the manner in which the man and woman relate to each other.)

☐ The parties must actually live together as husband and wife, i.e., there must be cohabitation.

☐ There must be an openness about the relationship; the parties must make representations to the world that they are husband and wife. (See interviewing questions in checklist below.)

A popular misconception about common law marriages is that the parties must live together for seven years before the marriage becomes legal. These is no such time requirement.

In some states, the courts are reluctant to find all these elements present in a particular case. Common law marriages may be disfavored by the court *even in a state where such marriages are legal.* It is too easy to fabricate a claim that the parties married, particularly after one of them has died.

■■■■ Interviewing and Investigation Checklist

Factors Relevant to the Formation of a Common Law Marriage between C (Client) and D (Defendant)

Legal Interviewing Questions

1. On what date did you first meet D?

2. When did the two of you first begin talking about living together? Describe the circumstances. Who said what, etc.?

3. Did you or D ever discuss with anyone else your plans to live together?

4. On what date did you actually move in together? How long have you been living together?

5. In whose name was the lease to the apartment or the deed to the house in which you lived?

6. Do you have separate or joint bank accounts? If joint, what names appear on the account?

7. Who pays the rent or the mortgage?

8. Who pays the utility bills?

9. Who pays the food bills?

10. Since you have been living together, have you filed separate or joint tax returns?

11. Have you ever made a written or oral agreement that you and D were going to be married?

12. Why didn't you and D have a marriage ceremony?

13. Did you ever introduce each other as "my husband" or "my wife"?

14. Name any relatives, neighbors, business associates, friends, etc., who think of you and D as husband and wife.

15. Did you and D ever discuss making individual or joint wills? Do you have them? Did you contact any attorneys about them? If so, what are their names and addresses?

16. Did you and D ever separate for any period of time? If so, describe the circumstances.

17. Did you and D ever have or adopt any children? If so, what last name did the children have?

18. On insurance policies, is either of you the beneficiary? How is the premium paid?

19. During your life with D, what other indications exist that the two of you treated each other as husband and wife?

20. In what other states did the two of you spend a significant amount of time? (Determine whether any of these states recognize common law marriages. See Exhibit 8.3.)

Possible Investigation Tasks

☐ Obtain a copy of the lease or deed.

☐ Obtain copies of bills, receipts, tax returns, etc., to determine how the names of C and D appear on them.

☐ Obtain copies of any agreements between C and D.

☐ Interview anyone C indicates would think of C and D as husband and wife.

☐ Obtain birth certificates of children, if any.

Two situations remain to be considered: *conflict of law* and *impediment removal.*

CONFLICT OF LAW

Bill and Pat live in State X, where common law marriages are legal. They enter such a marriage. Then they move to State Y, where common law marriages have been abolished. A child is born to them in State Y. Bill is injured on the job and dies. Pat claims worker's compensation benefits as the "wife" of Bill. Will State Y recognize Pat as married to Bill? Is their child legitimate?

The law of State X is inconsistent with the law of State Y on the validity of common law marriages. A conflict of law problem exists whenever a court must decide between inconsistent laws of different legal systems. There are conflict of law principles that guide a court in deciding which law to choose. In the case of marriages, the traditional "conflicts" principle is that the validity of a marriage is governed by the law of the place where the parties entered or contracted it.

Pat and Bill's marriage was contracted in State X, where it is valid. Since the marriage was valid where it was contracted, State Y will accept the marriage as valid (even though it would have been invalid had they tried to enter it in State Y). Pat is married to Bill and their child is legitimate. (In chapter 9, we will discuss the problem of parties moving to another state *solely* to take advantage of its more lenient marriage laws and returning to their original state after the marriage.)

IMPEDIMENT REMOVAL

In 1969 Ernestine enters a valid ceremonial marriage with John. They begin having marital troubles and separate. In 1975 Ernestine and Henry begin living together. Ernestine does not divorce John. She and Henry cohabitate and hold each other out as husband and wife in a state where common law marriages are valid. Except for the existence of the 1969 marriage to John, it is clear that Ernestine and Henry would have a valid common law marriage. In 1981 John obtains a divorce from Ernestine. Henry and Ernestine continue to live together in the same manner as they had since 1975. In 1989, Henry dies. Ernestine claims death benefits under the Worker's Compensation Act as his surviving "wife." Was she ever married to Henry?

Ernestine and Henry never entered a ceremonial marriage. Until 1981 a serious **impediment** existed to their being able to marry: Ernestine was already married to someone else. When the marriage was dissolved by the divorce in 1981, the impediment was removed. The issue is (1) whether Ernestine and Henry would be considered to have entered a valid common law marriage at the time the impediment was removed, or (2) whether at that time they would have had to enter a *new* common law marriage agreement, express or implied. In most states, a new agreement would not be necessary. An earlier agreement to marry (by common law) will carry forward to the time the impediment is removed so long as the parties have continued to live together openly as husband and wife. Accordingly, Ernestine automatically became the wife of Henry when the impediment of the prior marriage was removed, since she and Henry continued to live together openly as husband and wife after that time. As one court puts it:

> It is not to be expected that parties once having agreed to be married will deem it necessary to agree to do so again when an earlier marriage is ter-

Impediment A legal obstacle that prevents the formation of a valid marriage or other contract.

minated or some other bar to union is eliminated. *Matthews v. Britton,* 303 F.2d 408, 409 (D.C. Cir. 1962).

In the states that reach this conclusion, it makes no difference that either or both of the parties knew of the impediment at the time they initially agreed to live as husband and wife.

ASSIGNMENT 8.6

Examine the following sequence of events:

☐ Ann and Rich meet in State Y where they agree to live together as husband and wife forever. They do not want to go through a marriage ceremony, but they agree to be married and openly represent themselves as such. State Y does not recognize common law marriages.

☐ Rich accepts a job offer in State X, where common law marriages are legal, and they both move there.

☐ After three years in State X, Rich and Ann move back to State Y. One year later, Rich dies. In his will, he leaves all his property "to my wife." Ann is not mentioned by name in his will.

☐ From the time they met until the time of Rich's death, they lived together as husband and wife, and everyone who knew them thought of them as such.

a. Can Ann claim anything under the will? State Y provides tax benefits to "widows." Can Ann claim these benefits? (See the General Instructions for the Legal-Analysis Assignment in chapter 1.)

b. What further information would you like to have about this case? (See the General Instructions for the Investigation-Strategy Assignment in chapter 1.)

ASSIGNMENT 8.7

Vivian Hildenbrand and Tom Hildenbrand began living together in Oregon in 1975 and continuously did so until Tom's death in 1984. During this time, pursuant to mutual agreement, they cohabited and held themselves out as husband and wife, but never went through a marriage ceremony. They purchased real property in their joint names as husband and wife. On four different occasions, they went on vacation fishing trips to a resort in Idaho, where they registered as husband and wife, held themselves out as such, and lived together during their stay. Two trips in 1977 were of three days' duration each. Two trips were of seven day's duration each, one in 1978 and one in 1979. Oregon does not recognize common law marriages; Idaho does.

a. Were the parties married in 1984? (See General Instructions for the Legal-Analysis Assignment in chapter 1.)

b. Assume that Tom Hildenbrand died while he was working for the Oregon XYZ Chemical Company, due to an on-the-job accident. Vivian claims Oregon worker's compensation benefits. The state Worker's Compensation Board denies these benefits on the ground that she was not his wife. Draft a complaint for Vivian against the board. (See General Instructions for the Complaint-Drafting Assignment in chapter 1.)

☐ **Note on Putative Marriages** In chapter 7 we saw that some courts will treat unmarried parties as putative spouses for purposes of providing limited rights (page 135). Only a few states recognize putative marriages, however, and the requirements for establishing them are very strict:

A putative marriage is one which has been contracted in good faith and in ignorance of some existing impediment on the part of at least one of the contracting parties. Three circumstances must occur to constitute this species of marriage: (1) There must be bona fides. At least one of the parties must have been ignorant of the impediment, not only at the time of the marriage, but must also have continued ignorant of it during his or her life. (2) The marriage must be duly solemnized. (3) The marriage must have been considered lawful in the estimation of the parties or of that party who alleges the bona fides. *United States Fidelity & Guarantee Co. v. Henderson,* 53 S.W.2d 811, 816 (Tex. Civ. App. 1932).

An example might be a woman who goes through a marriage ceremony in good faith and does not find out until after her "husband" dies that he never even tried to obtain a divorce from his first wife who is still alive. In the few states that recognize putative marriages, such a woman would be given some protection, e.g., she would be awarded the reasonable value of the services she rendered or a share of the property the parties accumulated during the relationship.[1] Note, however, that only the innocent party can benefit from the putative marriage. If the woman had died first in our example, her bigamist "husband" could not claim benefits as her putative spouse.

■■■■■ HOMOSEXUAL "MARRIAGES"

Can a man marry a man? Can a woman marry a woman? Traditional marriage statutes neither specifically prohibit nor approve same-sex marriages. Such marriages, however, have been denied by the courts on the theory that marriage has always contemplated a man and a woman.

Denmark is one of the few countries of the world that has specifically authorized same-sex marriages. The parties, however, do not have all the rights of traditional marriages. For example, they cannot adopt minor children.

Proponents of same-sex marriages in America have attempted a number of strategies—all without success:

1. *Equal protection.* Since individuals of the opposite sex can marry, why treat gay individuals differently? Is this unequal treatment unconstitutional? Thus far the courts have said no. (See, however, the *Baehr* case below.)

2. *Fundamental right to marry.* The Supreme Court has said that there cannot be unreasonable restrictions on the right to marry since this is a fundamental right. (*Zablocki,* page 147) No court, however, has yet held that the prohibition against same-sex marriages is unreasonable.

3. *Common law marriage.* If gay people cannot enter ceremonial marriages, can they enter a common law marriage if all of the conditions for such a marriage are present, e.g., open cohabitation, intent to marry? No. Where this theory has been used, the courts have still insisted on a man-woman relationship.

4. *Putative spouse doctrine.* Here the parties acknowledge a legal impediment to the marriage but argue that they had a good-faith belief that they were legally married. Courts, however, have said that homosexuals could not possibly have such a good-faith belief.

---

1. Some states have enacted the Uniform Marriage and Divorce Act, which provides in section 209 that "Any person who has cohabited with another to whom he is not legally married in the good faith belief that he was married to that person is a putative spouse until knowledge of the fact that he is not legally married terminates his status and prevents acquisition of further rights. A putative spouse acquires the rights conferred upon a legal spouse, including the right to maintenance following termination of his status, whether or not the marriage is prohibited (Section 207) or declared invalid (Section 208). If there is a legal spouse or other putative spouses, rights acquired by a putative spouse do not supersede the rights of the legal spouse or those acquired by other putative spouses, but the court shall apportion property, maintenance, and support rights among the claimants as appropriate in the circumstances and in the interests of justice."

In many states, homosexual conduct among adults is a crime even if it is consensual. The United States Supreme Court has held that it is constitutional for states to impose criminal penalties for such conduct. *Bowers v. Hardwick*, 478 U.S. 186, 106 S. Ct. 2841, 92 L. Ed. 2d 140 (1986). Such states obviously have little sympathy for the argument that homosexuals should be allowed to marry.

Suppose that one of the parties is a transsexual (an individual, usually a man, who has had a sex-change operation). Can such an individual marry a man? Most courts would not permit the marriage, arguing that both parties to the marriage must have been *born* members of the opposite sex. A few courts, however, take the opposite position and allow such marriages.

A number of other special circumstances need to be considered in this area of the law:

□ Two homosexuals can enter a *Marvin*-type contract in which they agree to live together and share property acquired during the relationship. The major issue (as in a heterosexual relationship) is whether sexual services were an integral and inseparable part of the agreement. If so, as we saw in chapter 7, the contract will not be enforced.

□ In some states a gay adult can adopt another gay adult.

□ Assume that two lesbians live together. One is artificially inseminated and bears a child. In a few states, the other lesbian may be able to adopt the child, who then has two legal parents of the same sex.

□ In the above situation, if the other lesbian does not adopt the child and the adults separate, can the other lesbian be granted visitation rights? If the women entered a *co-parenting agreement* in which they agreed to raise and support the child together, would such an agreement be enforceable? In the absence of adoption, it is unlikely that a court would be sympathetic to the lesbian seeking visitation rights or asserting other parental rights under a co-parenting agreement.

□ Some universities have refused to allow gay student couples to live in *married* student housing, even if they can prove they are financially and domestically interdependent. The universities took the position that they had no authority to recognize unmarried couples.

□ Several large corporations (e.g., Levi Strauss & Co. and Lotus Development Corp.) have recently begun offering health coverage and other benefits to partners of their homosexual employees. The Levi plan applies to any worker who lives and shares finances with an unmarried lover.

□ Rent-control laws in New York City limit the right of a landlord to evict "the surviving spouse of the deceased tenant or some other member of the deceased tenant's family who has been living with the tenant." In a highly publicized case, the New York State Court of Appeals ruled that a man whose male lover died of AIDS was a "family" member of the deceased within the meaning of this law and therefore was entitled to remain in the apartment. *Braschi v. Stahl*, 74 N.Y.2d 201, 543 N.E.2d 49, 544 N.Y.S.2d 784 (1989).

□ A few cities allow same-sex couples to acquire some of the rights of married couples. To do so, they must register as **domestic partners.** This allows them health benefits, hospital visitation rights, bereavement leave from work, etc. In San Francisco, domestic partners are defined as two adults who have chosen "to share one another's lives in an intimate and committed

Domestic Partners
Two persons of the same sex who live together in an intimate relationship, who register with the government as domestic partners, and who thereby acquire limited rights enjoyed by a traditional married couple.

relationship of mutual caring, who live together, and who have agreed to be jointly responsible for basic living expenses incurred during the Domestic Partnership." They sign a Declaration of Domestic Partnership (see Exhibit 8.4). If they want to end this new legal relationship, they must file a Notice of Termination with the county clerk. New York City has a similar program (see Exhibit 8.5).

As indicated, however, no state has taken the drastic step of legalizing same-sex marriages. But in 1993, a thunderbolt came from Hawaii when the Hawaii Supreme Court wrote the controversial opinion of *Baehr v. Lewin*, which is excerpted below. While this opinion did not hold that same-sex couples have a fundamental right to marry, it did say that the denial of this right *might* constitute the denial of the equal protection of the law under the Hawaii Constitution. This case is still in litigation. It is not clear whether same-sex marriages will ultimately be legitimized. If it is, there is no reason to expect that the other forty-nine states will do likewise. These states fear, however, that they might be asked to recognize and enforce such marriages within their own boundaries.

Here is how this could happen. Assume that further litigation in *Baehr v. Lewin* ultimately leads to the right of same-sex couples to marry in Hawaii. Ted and Bob enter such a marriage. They then move to Ohio where they continue to live. Bob dies. Can Ted now go to an Ohio court and ask for a share of Bob's estate as his "spouse"? Or assume that they decide to separate. They go to an Ohio court to ask for a "divorce" and an order dividing their property. The traditional rule, as we have seen, is that the validity of a marriage is determined by the law of the state in which the marriage was entered or contracted. If this rule is applied, must Ohio recognize the validity of the Hawaii marriage even though it considers such marriages void and against its public policy? The problem is further compounded by the **Full Faith and Credit Clause** of the United States Constitution. Would this Clause *require* Ohio to give full recognition to the Hawaii marriage, especially if a Hawaii court renders a judgment that a particular marriage entered in Hawaii is valid? Such questions have no clear answers. The problem has not yet arisen because no state has sanctioned same-sex marriages. Will Hawaii be the first and thereby force other states to confront these questions? To get ready for this debate, the first step is to understand what started it all—the *Baehr v. Lewin* opinion.

Full Faith and Credit Clause Article IV of the *United States Constitution* provides that "Full Faith and Credit shall be given in each State to the public Acts, Records, and judicial Proceedings of every other State."

CASE

BAEHR V. LEWIN

74 Haw. 645, 852 P.2d 44 (1993)
Supreme Court of Hawaii.

Background: *Three couples were denied a marriage license by the Hawaii Department of Health (DOH). (They are referred to in the opinion as the "applicant couples.") Since they were same-sex couples, the DOH concluded that they could not meet the requirements for a valid marriage license specified in Hawaii Revised Statutes (HRS) § 572-1. The couples sued in circuit court, alleging a denial of their rights to privacy, due process of law, and equal protection of the law under sections 5 and 6 of the Hawaii Constitution. The circuit court dismissed the case, which is now on appeal before the Supreme Court of Hawaii.*

Decision on Appeal: *Reversed. It was an error to dismiss the complaint. There must be a new trial.*

In view of the complexity of the issues raised, read the following overview before examining the text of the opinion.

This is a constitutional law case. The two main constitutional arguments asserted in the case involve privacy and equal protection:

Privacy Argument. *There is a right to privacy in the Hawaii Constitution; this right is also implicit in the United States Constitution. Section 6 of the Hawaii Constitution explicitly says, "The right . . . to privacy is recognized." The Fourteenth Amendment of the United States Constitution guarantees "due process of law," which the courts have interpreted to include a* *right to privacy. The first question is whether the right to privacy in the state or federal constitution establishes a fundamental right of same-sex couples to marry. The court concludes that the United States Constitution does not. But a state constitution can give greater or broader rights to its citizens than does the federal constitution. The question then becomes whether the Hawaii Constitution allows same-sex couples to marry. The court concludes that it also does not.*

***Equal Protection Argument.** A state government can regulate marriage such as by writing statutes establishing who is eligible to marry and what rights married couples have in each other's property. But there are limits on the ability of a state to write such statutes. A state can't pass a statute that violates the constitution. Did Hawaii do that here? Section 5 of the Hawaii Constitution contains the state's equal protection clause. It says, "No person shall be . . . denied the equal protection of the laws, nor be denied the enjoyment of the person's civil rights or be discriminated against in the exercise thereof because of race, religion, sex, or ancestry." This section prohibits the state from passing statutes that discriminate against any person in the exercise of his or her civil rights on the basis of sex. Section 572–1 of the Hawaii Revised Statutes (HRS) discriminates on the basis of sex. It denies same-sex couples access to the marital status and its concomitant rights and benefits. The question then becomes whether § 572–1 violates the equal protection clause in § 5 of the Hawaii Constitution. Whenever a court is deciding whether discrimination in a statute is unconstitutional because of an alleged denial of equal protection, it applies a test or standard. There are two main tests: the rational basis test and the strict scrutiny test. The rational basis test says that the discrimination in the statute is constitutional if the statute rationally furthers a legitimate state interest. On the other hand, the more-difficult-to-meet strict scrutiny test presumes that the statute is unconstitutional unless the state shows compelling state interests that justify the discrimination, and also shows that the statute is narrowly drawn to avoid unnecessary abridgments of constitutional rights. The strict scrutiny test is often applied when the discrimination encroaches on a fundamental right or is against what is called a "suspect class" such as race. (The word "suspect" derives from the conclusion that certain kinds of discrimination create classifications that are inherently suspect or questionable.) The court had to decide which of these tests to apply in determining whether § 572–1 unconstitutionally denies same-sex couples the equal protection of the law. The court concluded that the strict scrutiny text should govern. Hence when this case is sent back to the circuit court for a new trial, the Department of Health must show that there are compelling state in-*

terests that justify the discrimination against same-sex couples in § 572–1 and that this statute is narrowly drawn to avoid unnecessary abridgments of constitutional rights.

The following excerpts from the opinion present the court's reasoning for these conclusions on the privacy and equal protection arguments.

Opinion of the Court:

Judge LEVINSON delivered the opinion of the court. . . .

[T]he United States Supreme Court has declared that "the right to marry is part of the fundamental 'right of privacy' implicit in the Fourteenth Amendment's Due Process Clause." *Zablocki v. Redhail,* 434 U.S. 374, 384 (1978). The issue in the present case is, therefore, whether the "right to marry" protected by . . . section 6 of the Hawaii Constitution extends to same-sex couples. . . .

The United States Supreme Court first characterized the right of marriage as fundamental [under the United States Constitution] in *Skinner v. Oklahoma ex rel. Williamson,* 316 U.S. 535 (1942). In *Skinner,* the right to marry was inextricably linked to the right of procreation. The dispute before the Court arose out of an Oklahoma statute that allowed the state to sterilize "habitual criminals" without their consent. In striking down the statute, the *Skinner* court indicated that it was "dealing . . . with legislation which involve[d] *one of the basic civil rights of man. Marriage and procreation are fundamental to the very existence and survival of the race."* Id. at 541 (emphasis added). [T]he Court . . . was obviously contemplating unions between men and women when it ruled that the right to marry was fundamental. This is hardly surprising inasmuch as none of the United States sanctioned any other marriage configuration at the time.

The United States Supreme Court has set forth its most detailed discussion of the fundamental right to marry in *Zablocki,* which involved a Wisconsin statute that prohibited any resident of the state with minor children "not in his custody and which he is under obligation to support" from obtaining a marriage license until the resident demonstrated to a court that he was in compliance with his child support obligations. 434 U.S. at 376. The *Zablocki* court held that the statute burdened the fundamental right to marry; . . . the Court invalidated it as violative of the fourteenth amendment to the United States Constitution. Id. at 390–91. . . .

[T]he precise question facing this court is whether we will extend the present boundaries of the fundamental right of marriage to include same-sex couples, or, put another way, whether we will hold that same-sex couples possess a fundamental right to marry. In effect, as the applicant couples frankly admit, we are being asked to recognize a new fundamental right. There is no doubt that . . . we are free to give broader privacy protection [under section 6 of the Hawaii Constitution] than that given by the federal constitution. . . .

In the case that first recognized a fundamental right to privacy, *Griswold v. Connecticut*, 381 U.S. 479 (1965), the Court declared that it was "deal[ing] with a right . . . older than the Bill of Rights[.]" Id. at 486. And in a concurring opinion, Justice Goldberg observed that judges "determining which rights are fundamental" must look not to "personal and private notions," but to the "traditions and [collective] conscience of our people" to determine whether a principle is "so rooted [there] . . . as to be ranked as fundamental." . . . The inquiry is whether a right involved "is of such a character that it cannot be denied without violating those 'fundamental principles of liberty and justice which lie at the base of all our civil and political institutions'. . . ." Id. at 493 (Goldberg, J., concurring).*

Applying the foregoing standards to the present case, we do not believe that a right to same-sex marriage is so rooted in the traditions and collective conscience of our people that failure to recognize it would violate the fundamental principles of liberty and justice that lie at the base of all our civil and political institutions. Neither do we believe that a right to same-sex marriage is implicit in the concept of ordered liberty, such that neither liberty nor justice would exist if it were sacrificed. Accordingly, we hold that the applicant couples do not have a fundamental constitutional right to same-sex marriage arising out of the right to privacy or otherwise.

Our holding, however, does not leave the applicant couples without a potential remedy in this case. . . . [T]he applicant couples are free to press their equal protection claim. If they are successful, the State of Hawaii will no longer be permitted to refuse marriage licenses to couples merely on the basis that they are of the same sex. . . . [T]he applicant couples contend that they have been denied the equal protection of the laws as guaranteed by . . . section 5 of the Hawaii Constitution. . . .

The power to regulate marriage is a sovereign function reserved exclusively to the respective states. *Salisbury v. List*, 501 F. Supp. 105, 107 (D. Nev. 1980). By its very nature, the power to regulate the marriage relation includes the power to determine the requisites of a valid marriage contract and to control the

qualifications of the contracting parties, the forms and procedures necessary to solemnize the marriage, the duties and obligations it creates, its effect upon property and other rights, and the grounds for marital dissolution.

In other words, marriage is a state-conferred legal status, the existence of which gives rise to rights and benefits reserved exclusively to that particular relationship. . . . So zealously has this court guarded the state's role as the exclusive progenitor of the marital partnership that it declared, over seventy years ago, that "common law" marriages—i.e., "marital" unions existing in the absence of a state-issued license and not performed by a person or society possessing governmental authority to solemnize marriages—would no longer be recognized in the Territory of Hawaii. *Parke v. Parke*, 25 Haw. 397, 404–05 (1920).

Indeed, the state's monopoly on the business of marriage creation has been codified by statute for more than a century. HRS (Hawaii Revised Statutes) § 572–1(7), descended from an 1872 statute of the Hawaiian Kingdom, conditions a valid marriage contract on "[t]he marriage ceremony be[ing] performed in the State by a person or society with a valid license to solemnize marriages[.]" HRS § 572–11 (1985) accords the DOH [Department of Health] sole authority to grant licenses to solemnize marriages, and HRS § 572-12 (1985) restricts the issuance of such licenses to clergy, representatives of religious societies (such as the Society of Friends) not having clergy but providing solemnization by custom, and judicial officers. Finally, HRS §§ 572–5 and 572–6 vest the DOH with exclusive authority to issue licenses to marriage applicants and to ensure that the general requisites and procedures prescribed by HRS chapter 572 are satisfied.

The applicant couples correctly contend that the DOH's refusal to allow them to marry on the basis that they are members of the same sex deprives them of access to a multiplicity of rights and benefits that are contingent upon that status. Although it is unnecessary in this opinion to engage in an encyclopedic recitation of all of them, a number of the most salient marital rights and benefits are worthy of note. They include: [state tax advantages for married couples, community property rights, spousal inheritance rights, the right to spousal support, etc.]. For present purposes, it is not disputed that the applicant couples would be entitled to all of these marital rights and benefits, but for the fact that they are denied access to the state-conferred legal status of marriage. . . .

Notwithstanding the state's acknowledged stewardship over the institution of marriage, the extent of permissible state regulation of the right of access to the marital relationship is subject to constitutional limitations or constraints. It has been held that a state

---

*In *State v. Mueller*, 66 Haw. 616, 671 P.2d 1351 (1983) . . . this court held that a prostitute did not have a fundamental right under article I, section 6 of the Hawaii Constitution to conduct business in her own home.

may deny the right to marry only for compelling reasons. *Salisbury*, 501 F. Supp. at 107.*

[S]ection 5 of the Hawaii Constitution provides in relevant part that "[n]o person shall ... be denied the *equal protection of the laws, nor be denied the enjoyment of the person's civil rights or be discriminated against in the exercise thereof because of* race, religion, *sex,* or ancestry." (Emphasis added.) Thus, by its plain language, the Hawaii Constitution prohibits state-sanctioned discrimination against any person in the exercise of his or her civil rights on the basis of sex.

"The freedom to marry has long been recognized as one of the vital personal rights essential to the orderly pursuit of happiness by free [people]." *Loving v. Virginia,* 388 U.S. 1, 12 (1967). So "fundamental" does the United States Supreme Court consider the institution of marriage that it has deemed marriage to be "one of the 'basic civil rights of [men and women.]'" Id. (quoting *Skinner,* 316 U.S. at 541). ...

HRS § 572–1 restricts the marital relation to a male and a female. ... Accordingly, ... HRS § 572–1 denies same-sex couples access to the marital status and its concomitant rights and benefits. It is the state's regulation of access to the status of married persons, on the basis of the applicants' sex, that gives rise to the question whether the applicant couples have been denied the equal protection of the laws in violation of ... section 5 of the Hawaii Constitution. ...

"Whenever a denial of equal protection of the laws is alleged, as a rule our initial inquiry has been whether the legislation in question should be subjected to 'strict scrutiny' or to a 'rational basis' test." *Nakano v. Matayoshi,* 68 Haw. 140, 151, 706 P.2d 814, 821 (1985) (citing *Nagle v. Board of Educ.,* 63 Haw. 389, 392, 629 P.2d 109, 111 (1981)). This court has applied "strict scrutiny" analysis to "'laws classifying on the basis of suspect categories or impinging upon fundamental rights expressly or impliedly granted by the [c]onstitution,'" in which case the laws are "'presumed to be unconstitutional unless the state shows compelling state interests which justify such classifications,'" *Holdman v. Olim,* 59 Haw. 346, 349, 581 P.2d 1164, 1167 (1978) (citing *Nelson v. Miwa,* 56 Haw. 601, 605 n. 4, 546 P.2d 1005, 1008 n. 4 (1976)), and that the laws are "narrowly drawn to avoid unnecessary abridgments of constitutional rights." *Nagle,* 63 Haw. at 392, 629 P.2d at 111.

By contrast, "[w]here 'suspect' classifications or fundamental rights are not at issue, this court has tradition-ally employed the rational basis test." Id. at 393, 629 P.2d at 112. "Under the rational basis test, we inquire as to whether a statute rationally furthers a legitimate state interest." *Estate of Coates v. Pacific Engineering,* 71 Haw. 358, 364, 791 P.2d 1257, 1260 (1990). "Our inquiry seeks only to determine whether any reasonable justification can be found for the legislative enactment." Id.

As we have indicated, HRS § 572–1 ... regulates access to the marital status and its concomitant rights and benefits on the basis of the applicants' sex. As such, HRS § 572–1 establishes a sex-based classification. ...

[W]e hold that sex is a "suspect category" for purposes of equal protection analysis under ... section 5 of the Hawaii Constitution and that HRS § 572–1 is subject to the "strict scrutiny" test.* It therefore follows, and we so hold, that (1) HRS § 572–1 is presumed to be unconstitutional (2) unless [the Department of Health] can show that (a) the statute's sex-based classification is justified by compelling state interests and (b) the statute is narrowly drawn to avoid unnecessary abridgements of the applicant couples' constitutional rights. ...

[W]hether the legislation under review is wise or unwise is a matter with which we have nothing to do. Whether it ... work[s] well or work[s] ill presents a question entirely irrelevant to the issue. The only legitimate inquiry we can make is whether it is constitutional. If it is not, its virtues, if it have any, cannot save it; if it is, its faults cannot be invoked to accomplish its destruction. If the provisions of the Constitution be not upheld when they pinch as well as when they comfort, they may as well be abandoned.

[W]e vacate the circuit court's order and judgment and remand this matter for further proceedings consistent with this opinion. On remand, in accordance with the "strict scrutiny" standard, the burden will rest on [the Department of Health] to overcome the presumption that HRS § 572–1 is unconstitutional by demonstrating that it furthers compelling state interests and is narrowly drawn to avoid unnecessary abridgements of constitutional rights. Vacated and remanded.

_____

*For example, states, including Hawaii, may and do prohibit marriage for such "compelling" reasons as consanguinity (to prevent incest), see, e.g., HRS § 572–1(1), immature age (to protect the welfare of children), see, e.g., HRS §§ 572–1(2) and 572–2 (1985), presence of venereal disease (to foster public health), see, e.g., HRS § 572–1(5), and to prevent bigamy, see, e.g., HRS § 572–1(3).

*[The United States Constitution also has an equal protection clause. When applying this clause to sex discrimination, *federal* courts might use a different standard. But a *state* has the right to adopt and apply the more stringent test of compelling state interest to sex-based classifications under the equal protection clause of the state's own constitution. We affirm "the longstanding principle that this court is free to accord greater protections to Hawaii's citizens under the state constitution than are recognized under the United States Constitution." 852 P.2d at 66. Ed.]

_____

See Assignment 8.8 on page 163 based on the Baehr *case.*

☐ **EXHIBIT 8.4   San Francisco Declaration of Domestic Partnership**

SAN FRANCISCO

DECLARATION OF

DOMESTIC PARTNERSHIP

We declare under penalty of perjury:

1. We have an intimate, committed relationship of mutual caring;

2. We live together (see definition on the other side of this page);

3. We agree to be responsible for each other's basic living expenses (see definition on the other side of this page) during our domestic partnership; we also agree that anyone who is owed these expenses can collect from either of us;

4. We are both 18 or older;

5. Neither of us is married;

6. Neither of us is related to the other as a parent, brother or sister, half brother or sister, niece, nephew, aunt, uncle, grandparent or grandchild;

7. Neither of us has a different domestic partner now;

8. Neither of us has had a different domestic partner in the last six months (this last condition does not apply if you had a partner who died; if you did, cross this out).

We declare under penalty of perjury under the laws of the State of California that the statements above are true and correct.

Signed on _____, 19____ in _____

Signature _____   Print Name _____

Signed on _____, 19____ in _____

Signature _____   Print Name _____

YOU MUST ALSO FILL OUT THE OTHER SIDE OF THIS FORM

DECLARATION OF DOMESTIC PARTNERSHIP

1. Definitions:

"**Live together**" means that the two of you share a place to live. You don't both have to be on the rental agreement or deed. It is okay if one or both of you has a separate place somewhere else. Even if one of you leaves the place you share, you still live together as long as the one who left intends to return.

"**Basic living expenses**" means the cost of basic food and shelter. It also includes any other expense which is paid by a benefit you or your partner gets because of the partnership. For example, if you get health insurance from your job, and the insurance covers your partner, you will be responsible for medical bills which the insurance does not pay. You don't have to split basic living expenses to be domestic partners. You just have to agree to provide these things for your partner if he or she can't provide for him or herself.

2. Address: Each of you should fill in your mailing address here:

Name _____

Address _____

City, State & Zip Code _____

Name _____

Address _____

City, State & Zip Code _____

3. The Last Step: To finish setting up a domestic partnership, you must EITHER:

(1) File this form with the San Francisco County Clerk; or
(2) Sign this form in front of a Notary Public and have the Notary fill in the notarization at the bottom of this page.

To be able to file this form with the County Clerk, one of you must work in San Francisco OR both of you live together in San Francisco (see explanation below).

[ ] Check here to state that one of you works in San Francisco.
[ ] Check here to state that you live together in San Francisco.

You don't have to check either space if you finish setting up your domestic partnership by getting this Declaration notarized.

4. Notarization: Use only if you do not file the Declaration with the county clerk

State of _____

County of _____ ss.

On this _____ day of _____ in the year 19 ___, before me _____ personally appeared _____, personally known to me (or proved to me on the basis of satisfactory evidence) to be the persons whose names are subscribed to this instrument, and acknowledged that they executed it.

_____
Notary Public

☐ **EXHIBIT 8.5 New York City's Executive Order Regarding Domestic Partnership**

Executive Order No. 123

August 7, 1989

BEREAVEMENT LEAVE FOR CITY EMPLOYEES

WHO ARE MEMBERS OF A DOMESTIC PARTNERSHIP

WHEREAS, there have been significant changes in our society resulting in diverse living arrangements among individuals and an expanded concept of what constitutes a family unit; and

WHEREAS, many of these living arrangements involve long-term committed relationships between unmarried persons; and

WHEREAS, the death of one individual in such a relationship, or the death of that individual's parent or child or other relative residing in the household, would have a profound personal impact upon the other individual in such a relationship;

NOW, THEREFORE, by the power vested in me as Mayor of the City of New York, it is hereby ordered:

Section 1. Bereavement Leave Established. Bereavement leave for all City employees is hereby established in the event of the death of a "domestic partner", as defined in Section 2, or the death of a parent or child of such domestic partner, or the death of a relative of such domestic partner residing in the household, and shall be afforded in accordance with existing rules and regulations and the terms of this Executive Order.

Section 2. Domestic Partnerships Defined. Domestic partners are two people, both of whom are 18 years of age or older and neither of whom is married, who have a close and committed personal relationship involving shared responsibilities, who have lived together for a period of one year or more on a continuous basis at the time of registration, and who have registered as domestic partners and have not terminated the registration in accordance with procedures to be established by the Department of Personnel of the City of New York.

Section 3. Registration. The Department of Personnel of the City of New York is directed to establish procedures and develop forms for the registration and termination of domestic partnerships. The Department of Personnel shall not register a domestic partnership if either member is currently a member of another domestic partnership or was previously a member of another domestic partnership and less than one year has expired since the termination of that domestic partnership.

Section 4. Effective Date. This Order shall take effect immediately.

Edward I. Koch

M A Y O R

---

a. Did the *Baehr* case hold that same-sex couples in Hawaii can be married?

b. Summarize the holding of the following opinions as they are presented in the *Baehr* case:

1. *Zablocki v. Redhail,* 434 U.S. 374, 384 (1978)

2. *Skinner v. Oklahoma ex rel. Williamson,* 316 U.S. 535 (1942)

c. What was the privacy argument the same-sex couples tried to assert in the *Baehr* case?

d. What is the difference between the rational basis test and the strict scrutiny test? Why did the *Baehr* court use the latter in this case?

e. The *Baehr* court did not adopt the rational basis test. If it had, can you think of a rational basis that might support the discrimination in § 572–1 against same-sex couples?

f. Shepardize the *Baehr* case. Has it been cited by courts of your state? If so, for what purposes? Do any state courts in your state agree or disagree with *Baehr?*

ASSIGNMENT 8.8

■ SUMMARY

Many material benefits derive from being married, particularly when a spouse dies, e.g., social security and pension benefits. To claim these benefits, one must establish the existence of a valid ceremonial marriage or, in states that allow them, a valid common law marriage.

States differ on the requirements that must be fulfilled to enter a ceremonial marriage. In many states, the requirements include obtaining a license, waiting a designated period of time, going through a physical examination, having the ceremony performed by an authorized person, having witnesses to the ceremony, and recording the license in the proper public office. Yet in most states, the failure to comply with such requirements is not a ground for an annulment.

In states where common law marriages are still possible, the requirements are a present agreement to enter a marital relationship, living together as husband and wife (cohabitation), and an openness about living together as husband and wife. As with ceremonial marriages, the parties must have the legal capacity to marry and must intend to marry. The latter conditions will be considered in chapter 9.

The validity of a marriage is governed by the state in which it was entered or contracted. Hence if a couple enters a common law marriage in a state where it is valid, but moves to a state where such marriages have been abolished, the latter state will recognize the marriage as valid.

Occasionally an impediment exists to an otherwise valid common law marriage, e.g., one of the parties is still married to someone else. If the impediment is removed while the parties are still openly living together, a valid common law marriage will be established as of the date of the removal.

Same-sex marriages are invalid in every American state. No legislature has passed a statute recognizing them, and all of the arguments made in court to force recognition have been unsuccessful. In some states, however, homosexuals have achieved limited rights in this area, e.g., to enter contracts governing nonsexual aspects of living together, to adopt a gay adult, and to register as "domestic partners" for purposes of being entitled to bereavement leave upon the death of one of the partners.

■ KEY CHAPTER TERMINOLOGY

Intestate
Forced Share
Dower
Curtesy
Privilege for Marital
  Communications

Miscegenation
Ceremonial Marriage
Proxy Marriage
Common Law Marriage
Conflict of Law

Impediment
Domestic Partners
Full Faith and Credit Clause

ANNULMENT

9

ANNULMENT, DIVORCE, AND LEGAL SEPARATION

When discussing an **annulment,** it is technically incorrect to refer to an "annulled marriage." The word "marriage" means the legal union of two people as husband and wife. If reasons (i.e., grounds) exist to substantiate the initial *illegality* of the union, then no marriage ever existed in spite of the license, the ceremony, consummation, and perhaps even children. While you will frequently see the phrase, "suit to annul a marriage," either "suit to annul an attempted marriage" or "suit to declare the validity or invalidity of a marriage" would be more technically accurate.

A **divorce,** on the other hand, is a dissolution of a marriage that once validly existed. In a divorce there is something to dissolve; in an annulment, there is simply a judicial statement or declaration that no marital relationship existed between the parties at the outset.

A **legal separation** (also called a judicial separation) gives the parties permission to end their "bed and board" relationship and live separately. They are still legally married. If they want to remarry, they must obtain a divorce.

Annulment A declaration by a court that a valid marriage never existed.

Divorce A declaration by a court that a marriage has been dissolved so that the parties are no longer married to each other.

Legal Separation A declaration by a court that parties can live separately and apart even though they are still married to each other.

THE VOID/VOIDABLE DISTINCTION

Certain grounds for annulment will render the marriage void, while other grounds will render it only voidable. *Void* means the marriage is invalid whether or not any court declares its invalidity. *Voidable* means the marriage is invalid only if a court declares that it is invalid. This distinction can be critical, as we will see in the *Miller* opinion later in the chapter.

Voidable Marriage A marriage that is invalid only if someone challenges it and a court declares it invalid.

Assume that two individuals have a **voidable marriage,** but that they die without anyone bringing an annulment action or challenging their marriage in any way. The practical effect of this inaction is that the entire world treats the marriage as if it were valid. In effect, there is no practical difference between a marriage that complies with all the legal requirements and a voidable marriage that no one ever challenges.

If, however, an annulment action *is* brought and a court declares a voidable marriage to be invalid, the invalidity generally "relates back" to the time when the parties tried to enter the marriage. The invalidity does not begin on the date the court declares the marriage invalid. A **void marriage** is considered **void ab initio.** Technically, if a marriage is void, there is no need to bring a court action to seek a declaration that it is invalid. Nevertheless, parties will usually want a court declaration in order to remove any doubt that the marriage is invalid.

Void Marriage A marriage that is invalid whether or not a court declares it so.

Void ab Initio Invalid from the very beginning.

States use different terminology to describe the proceeding:

- ☐ Action for annulment
- ☐ Suit to annul
- ☐ Libel for annulment
- ☐ Action for declaration of invalidity
- ☐ Action for a judgment of nullity
- ☐ Action for declaratory judgment (i.e., for a court pronouncement) that the marriage is invalid
- ☐ Action to affirm the validity of a marriage

■■■■ WHO CAN SUE?

Standing The right to bring a case and seek relief from a court.

Estopped Prevented from asserting a right or a defense because it would be unfair or inequitable to do so.

Dirty Hands Wrongdoing or other inappropriate behavior that would make it unfair or inequitable to allow a person to assert a right or a defense he or she would normally have.

Grounds Acceptable reasons for seeking a particular result.

As we study each of the grounds for annulment, one of the questions we must ask is, who can be the plaintiff to bring the annulment action? The wrongdoer (i.e., the party who knowingly did the act that constituted the ground for the annulment) is *not* always allowed to bring the action. This party may lack **standing** to bring the action. If the *innocent* party refuses to bring the action, it may be that the marriage can never be annulled. The wrongdoing party, in effect, is prevented (sometimes called **estopped**) from getting out of what might clearly be an invalid marriage. Such a marriage is sometimes referred to as a *marriage by estoppel.* The wrongdoing party has **dirty hands** and should not be allowed to "profit" from this wrongdoing through a court action seeking an annulment. Whether a wrongdoing party will be estopped from bringing the annulment action often depends on whether the marriage is void or voidable.

■■■■ OVERVIEW OF GROUNDS FOR ANNULMENT

There are essentially two kinds of **grounds** for annulment. First are those that relate to a party's *legal capacity* to marry:

- ☐ Preexisting marriage
- ☐ Improper relationship by blood or by marriage
- ☐ Nonage
- ☐ Physical disabilities

Second are those that focus on whether a party with legal capacity to marry formed the requisite *intent* to marry:

☐ Sham marriages
☐ Mental disabilities
☐ Duress
☐ Fraud

ASSIGNMENT 9.1

List the grounds for annulment in your state. (See General Instructions for the State-Code Assignment in chapter 1.)

■■■■ GROUNDS RELATING TO THE LEGAL CAPACITY TO MARRY

PRIOR EXISTING MARRIAGE (BIGAMY)

Here we will consider both the criminal and the civil consequences of **bigamy.**

CRIME Entering a second marriage or even attempting to enter such a marriage when the first marriage has not ended by death, annulment, or divorce is a felony in most states. **Polygamy**[1] or *bigamy* is a crime.

In some states, if a spouse has disappeared for a designated number of years, he or she will be presumed dead. This presumption is the foundation for what is called the **Enoch Arden defense,** which will defeat a bigamy prosecution following a second marriage. States may differ on the elements of the Enoch Arden defense, e.g., the length of the disappearance, the requirement of diligence in trying to locate the missing spouse before remarrying, etc.

ANNULMENT: THE CIVIL ACTION Our next concern is the existence of a prior undissolved marriage as a ground for an annulment of a second (attempted) marriage. In most states, a bigamous marriage is void; in only a few states is it voidable.

When a claim is made in an annulment proceeding that a second marriage is invalid because of a prior undissolved marriage, one of the common responses or defenses to this claim is that the *first* marriage was never valid or that this earlier marriage ended in a divorce or annulment. Yet marriage records, particularly old ones, are sometimes difficult to obtain, and for common law marriages, there simply are no records. Consequently, proving the status of a prior marriage can be a monumental task. Was it properly contracted? Was it dissolved? To assist parties in this difficult situation, the law has created a number of **rebuttable presumptions,** including:

☐ A marriage is presumed to be valid.
☐ When more than one marriage exists, the latest marriage is presumed to be valid.

Bigamy Entering or attempting to enter a second marriage when a prior marriage is still valid.

Polygamy Having more than one spouse at the same time, usually more than two.

Enoch Arden Defense The presumption that a spouse is dead after being missing for a designated number of years.

Rebuttable Presumption A presumption is an assumption of fact that can be drawn when another fact or set of facts is established. The presumption is rebuttable if a party can introduce evidence to try to show that the assumption is false.

---

1. Polygamy often means having more than one *wife* at the same time. Polyandry means having more than one *husband* at the same time.

The effect of the second presumption is that the court will treat the first marriage as having been dissolved by the death of the first spouse, by divorce, or by annulment. Note, however, that the presumption is *rebuttable*, which means that the party seeking to annul the second marriage can attempt to rebut (i.e., attack) the presumption by introducing evidence (1) that the first spouse is still alive, or (2) that the first marriage was *not* dissolved by divorce or annulment. The presumption favoring the validity of the latest marriage is so strong, however, that some states require considerable proof to overcome or rebut it.

Finally, we need to consider the impact of *Enoch Arden* in annulment cases. We have already looked at Enoch Arden as a defense to a criminal prosecution for bigamy. We now examine the consequences of Enoch Arden on the second marriage in a civil annulment proceeding. Paul marries Cynthia. Cynthia disappears. Paul has not heard from her for fifteen years in spite of all his efforts to locate her. Paul then marries Mary in the honest belief that his first wife is dead. Mary does not know anything about Cynthia. Suddenly Cynthia reappears, and Mary learns about the first marriage. Mary immediately brings an action against Paul to annul her marriage to him on the ground of a prior existing marriage (bigamy). The question is whether Paul can raise the defense of Enoch Arden. Can Paul contest the annulment action against him by arguing that he had a right to presume that his first wife was dead? States differ in their answer to this question. Here are some of the different approaches:

☐ Enoch Arden applies only to criminal prosecutions for bigamy; the presumption of death does not apply to annulment proceedings.

☐ Enoch Arden does apply to annulment proceedings; the missing spouse is presumed dead. The second marriage is valid and cannot be annulled even if the missing spouse later appears.

☐ Enoch Arden does apply to annulment proceedings; the missing spouse is presumed dead. If, however, the missing spouse later appears, the second marriage can be annulled. Hence, the Enoch Arden defense is effective only if the missing spouse stays missing.

▬▬ Summary of Ground for Annulment: Prior Existing Marriage

Definitions: The existence of a prior valid marriage that has not been dissolved by divorce, annulment, or the death of the first spouse.

Void or voidable: In most states, the establishment of this ground renders the second marriage void.

Who can sue: In most states, either party to the second marriage can bring the annulment action on this ground; both have standing.

Major defenses:

1. The first spouse is dead or presumed dead (Enoch Arden).

2. The first marriage was not validly entered.

3. The first marriage ended by divorce or annulment.

4. The plaintiff has "dirty hands" (available in a few states).

Is this annulment ground also a ground for divorce? Yes, in some states.

Consanguinity
Relationship by blood.

Affinity   Relationship by marriage.

CONSANGUINITY AND AFFINITY LIMITATIONS

There are two ways that you can be related to someone: by **consanguinity** and by **affinity.**

Examples of a marriage of individuals related by consanguinity would be:

☐ Father marries his daughter.

☐ Sister marries her brother.

Examples of a marriage of individuals related by affinity would be:

☐ Man marries his son's former wife.

☐ Woman marries her stepfather.

State statutes prohibit certain individuals related by consanguinity or related by affinity from marrying. Violating these prohibitions can be a ground for annulment of the marriage.

States generally agree that certain relationships involve **incest:** marriage of parent and child, brother and sister, grandparent and grandchild, etc. Some disagreement exists on whether this is also true of cousin-cousin marriages and affinity relationships.

The *crime* of incest is committed mainly by designated individuals related by consanguinity. Surprisingly, however, the crime can also be committed in some states by designated individuals related by affinity.

Incest Sexual intercourse between two people who are too closely related to each other as defined by statute.

In the following list, you will find pairs of individuals. For each pair, check your state code and answer three questions: Can the individuals marry? If the marriage is prohibited, is it void or voidable? What code section gives you the answer? (See General Instructions for the State-Code Assignment in chapter 1.

ASSIGNMENT 9.2

	Can They Marry?	Void or Voidable?	Code Section
a. Mother/son			
b. Father/daughter			
c. Brother/sister			
d. Grandparent/grandchild			
e. Uncle/niece or aunt/ nephew			
f. First cousin/first cousin			
g. Second cousin/second cousin			
h. Half brother/half sister			
i. Father-in-law/daughter-in- law or mother-in-law/son- in-law			
j. Brother-in-law/sister-in-law			
k. Stepparent/stepchild			
l. Adoptive parent/adoptive child			
m. Godparent/godchild			

(If your state code does not provide a direct answer to any of the above questions, you may have to check court opinions. See General Instructions for the Court-Opinion Assignment in chapter 1.)

ASSIGNMENT 9.3

Locate the sections in your state code that define criminal behavior. Determine how many, if any, of the marriages mentioned in Assignment 9.2 (a)–(m) would subject the parties to criminal prosecution. (See General Instructions for the State-Code Assignment in chapter 1.)

☐ **Notes on Consanguinity and Affinity**

1. Assume that a prohibition to a marriage exists because of an affinity relationship between the parties. What happens to the prohibition when the marriage ends by the death of the spouse who created the affinity relationship for the other spouse? Can the surviving spouse *then* marry his or her in-laws? (For example, John is the father-in-law of Mary, who is married to John's son Bill. After Bill dies, John marries Mary.) Some states allow such marriages, while others maintain the prohibition even after the death of the spouse who created the affinity relationship for the other spouse.

2. The Uniform Marriage and Divorce Act (§ 207) would prohibit all marriages between ancestors and descendants, brother-sister marriages, and adopted brother-sister marriages; it would permit first-cousin marriages and all affinity marriages.

3. States differ on whether two adopted children in the same family can marry.

4. As indicated above, the Supreme Court has held that marriage is a fundamental right and only "reasonable regulations" that interfere with the decision to enter a marriage can be imposed. (*Zablocki,* page 147). It is anticipated that some of the rules mentioned above regarding who can marry will be challenged as unreasonable regulations—particularly the rules prohibiting the marriage of individuals related by affinity.

▇▇ Summary of Ground for Annulment:
Prohibited Consanguinity or Affinity Relationship

Definition: State statutes provide that persons lack the legal capacity to marry if they are related by consanguinity (blood) or by affinity (marriage) in the manner specified in those statutes.

Void or voidable: In most states, the prohibited marriage is void.

Who can sue: Either party can be the plaintiff in the annulment action; both have standing.

Major defenses:

1. The parties are not prohibitively related by blood or marriage.

2. The spouse who created the affinity relationship for the other spouse has died (this defense is available only for affinity relationships and only in some states).

Is this annulment ground also a ground for divorce? Yes, in most states.

NONAGE

In order to marry, a party must be a certain minimum age. Marrying below that age constitutes the ground of **nonage**. The minimum age may differ, however, depending upon whether:

Nonage   Below the required minimum age to enter a designated relationship or to perform a particular task.

☐ Parental consent exists.

☐ The female is already pregnant.

☐ A child has already been born out of wedlock.

In some states, a court may have the power to authorize a marriage of parties under age even if a parent or guardian has refused to consent to the marriage.

In these states, the court will consider such factors as the maturity of the parties, their financial resources, whether children (to be born or already born) would be illegitimate if the marriage were not authorized, etc. Still another variation found in some states is that the courts have the authority to require that underage individuals go through premarital counseling as a condition of their being able to marry.

At one time, states imposed different age requirements for males and females. This has been changed either by statute or by a court ruling that this kind of sex discrimination is unconstitutional.

What age restrictions apply to marriages in your state? (See General Instructions for the State-Code Assignment in chapter 1.)

ASSIGNMENT 9.4

■ Summary of Ground for Annulment: Nonage

Definition: At the time of the marriage, one or both of the parties was under the minimum age to marry set by statute.

Void or voidable: In most states, the marriage is voidable.

Who can sue: Usually, only the underaged party is allowed to bring the annulment action. In some states, the parent or guardian of the underaged party also has standing.

Major defenses:

1. The parties were of the correct statutory age at the time of the marriage.

2. The underaged party affirmed or **ratified** the marriage by cohabitation after that party reached the statutory minimum age.

3. The wrong party is bringing the suit.

4. Even though the parties failed to obtain parental consent as specified in the statute, the absence of this consent is not a ground for annulment. (Note, however, that this is so only in some states.)

Is this annulment also a ground for divorce? Yes, in some states.

PHYSICAL DISABILITIES

The major physical incapacities or disabilities mentioned in marriage statutes are communicable venereal disease and incurable **impotence**. While several other physical problems are sometimes involved (e.g., epilepsy and pulmonary tuberculosis in advanced stages), most of the litigation centers on venereal disease and impotence.

As indicated in chapter 8, states often have a statutory requirement that parties contemplating marriage go through a medical examination as a condition of obtaining a marriage license. A major objective of this exam is to determine whether either or both of the parties have communicable venereal disease. Suppose that either or both of the parties do have such a disease at the time of their marriage. It may be that the medical exam failed to show this, or that they failed to take the exam (and entered a common law marriage in a state where such marriages are valid), or that they were able to falsify the results of the medical exam. States differ as to the consequences of marrying where one or both of the parties have the disease. While the marriage is valid in most states, in several states the marriage is not valid, and a ground for annulment can arise as a result. Furthermore, a state may make it a crime knowingly to marry or have sexual intercourse with someone who has an infectious venereal disease.

Ratified Approved retroactively by agreement, conduct, or inaction that should be interpreted as approval. The noun is *ratification.*

Impotence The inability to have sexual intercourse, often due to an inability to achieve or maintain an erection.

Copulate To engage in sexual intercourse.

Sterility Inability to have children; infertile.

Issues related to a discussion of impotence include:

□ Inability to **copulate**—incurable

□ Inability to copulate—curable

□ **Sterility**

□ Refusal to have sexual intercourse

In most states, only the first situation—an incurable inability to copulate—is a ground for annulment. The standard for incurability is not the impossibility of a cure; rather, it is the present unlikelihood of a cure. The standard for copulation is the ability to perform the physical sex act naturally, without pain or harm to the other spouse. The "mere" fact that a spouse does not derive pleasure from the act is not what is meant by an inability to copulate. The *refusal* to copulate is not an inability to copulate, although the refusal is sometimes used as an indication of (i.e., as evidence of) the inability to copulate. In most states, it makes no difference whether the inability is due to physical (organic) causes or to psychogenic causes, nor does it matter that the person is impotent only with his or her spouse. If normal coitus is not possible with one's spouse, whatever the cause, the ground exists.

It is a defense to an annulment action that the party seeking the annulment knew of the party's impotence at the time of the marriage and yet still went through with the marriage. Also, continued cohabitation (living as husband and wife) long after the party learned of the other partner's impotence may constitute the equitable defense of **laches** and thus bar the annulment action.

Laches Waiting an unreasonably long time to bring a suit or assert a right.

□ **Note on Testing for AIDS**

Some states require their officials to tell marriage applicants that the state will provide testing for human immunodeficiency virus (HIV). Rejecting the offer will not in itself lead to a denial of the license. At one time, however, Illinois mandated that the "medical examination shall include tests to determine whether either of the parties to the proposed marriage has been exposed to human immunodeficiency virus (HIV) or any other identified causative agent of acquired immunodeficiency syndrome (AIDS)" ILL. REV. STAT. ch. 40, § 204(b). The requirement was eventually repealed. Large numbers of people avoided the test by traveling to neighboring states to obtain a marriage license:

> During the first 6 months of legislatively mandated premarital testing for human immunodeficiency virus in Illinois, 8 of 70,846 applicants for marriage licenses were found to be seropositive, yielding a seroprevalance of 0.011%. The total cost of the testing program for 6 months is estimated at $2.5 million or $312,000 per seropositive individual identified. Half of the reported seropositive individuals reported a history of risk behavior. During the same period, the number of marriage licenses issued in Illinois decreased by 22.5%, while the number of licenses issued to Illinois residents in surrounding states increased significantly. We conclude that mandatory premarital testing is not a cost-effective method for the control of human immunodeficiency virus infection. Turnock and Kelly, *Mandatory Premarital Testing for Human Immunodeficiency Virus: The Illinois Experience,* 261 Journal of the American Medical Association 3415 (June 15, 1989).

▀▀▀ Summary of Ground for Annulment: Physical Disabilities (Impotence)

Definition: The incurable inability to copulate without pain or harm to the spouse.

Void or voidable: Voidable.

Who can sue: Either party; both have standing.

Major defenses:

1. The impotence is curable.

2. The nonimpotent party knew of the other's impotence at the time of the marriage.

3. Statute of limitations or laches (plaintiff waited too long to bring this annulment action).

Is this annulment ground also a ground for divorce? Yes, in some states.

Homosexual "Marriages"

Since people of the same sex cannot legally marry, annulment can never be an issue, since there is no accepted marital union to annul. See the earlier discussion of homosexual "marriages" in chapter 8.

▰▰▰ GROUNDS RELATING TO THE INTENT TO MARRY

SHAM MARRIAGES

An essential element of a marriage contract is the intent to enter a marriage. With this in mind, examine the following "marriages":

☐ Dennis and Janet enter a marriage solely to obtain permanent resident alien status for Dennis, who is not a U.S. citizen. Janet is a citizen. Dennis wants to use his marriage status to avoid deportation by immigration officials.

☐ Edna dares Stanley to marry her following a college party. After a great deal of laughing and boasting, they go through all the formalities (obtaining a license, having the blood test, etc.) and complete the marriage ceremony.

☐ Frank and Helen have an affair. Helen becomes pregnant. Neither wants the child to be born illegitimate. They decide to be married solely for the purpose of having the child born legitimate.

☐ Robin and Ken have been dating for a number of months. They decide to get married "just to try it out." They feel this is a modern and rational way of determining whether they will want to stay together, forever. Both fully understand that there will be "no hard feelings" if either of them wants to dissolve the marriage after six months.

All four of the above couples go through all the steps required to become married. To any reasonable outside observer of their outward actions, nothing unusual is happening. They all intended to go through a marriage ceremony; they all intended to go through the outward appearances of entering a marriage contract. Subjectively, however, they all had "hidden agendas."

According to traditional contract principles, if individuals give clear outward manifestations of mutual assent to enter a contract, the law will bind them to their contract even though their unspoken motive was *not* to enter a binding contract. Most courts, however, apply a different principle to marriage contracts than to other contracts. The first three couples above engaged in totally **sham** marriages. The parties never intended to live together as husband and wife; they had a limited purpose of avoiding deportation, displaying braggadocio, or "giving a name" to a child. Most courts would declare such marriages to be void and would grant an annulment to either party so long as the parties did not **consummate** their union or otherwise cohabit *after* the marriage. If, however, the couples in these three cases lived together as husband and wife even for a short period after the marriage, most courts would be reluctant to declare the marriage void. The subsequent **cohabitation** would be some evidence that at the time they entered the marriage they *did* intend to live as husband and wife. The central question is, what intention did the parties have at the time they entered the marriage? Did they intend to be married or not? It is, of course, very difficult to get into their heads to find out what they were thinking. Hence, the law must rely on objective conduct as evidence of intent. If parties cohabit

Sham Pretended, false, empty.

Consummate To engage in sexual intercourse for the first time as spouses.

Cohabitation Living together as husband and wife whether or not the parties are married.

after marriage, this is certainly some evidence that they intended to be married at the time they appeared to enter a marriage contract.

In the first three hypothetical cases, assume that the couples did not cohabit after they entered the marriage. Most courts would, therefore, find that at the time they entered the marriage contract, they did not have the intention to be married, i.e., to assume the duties of a marriage. It should be pointed out, however, that some courts apply a *different* rule and would hold that the marriage is valid whether or not cohabitation followed the marriage ceremony—so long as the parties went through all the proper procedures to be married.

What about the fourth hypothetical case, in which the parties entered a *trial marriage?* The fact that the parties cohabited is evidence that they did intend to be married at the time they entered the marriage contract. Most courts would find that this marriage is valid and deny an annulment to anyone who later claims that the parties never intended to assume the marital status. It cannot be said that they married in jest or that they married for a limited purpose. The fact that they did not promise to live together forever as husband and wife does not mean that they lacked the intent to be married at the time they entered the marriage.

▆▆▆ Summary of Ground for Annulment: Sham Marriage

Definition: The absence of an intention to marry in spite of the fact that the parties voluntarily went through all the formalities of a marriage.

Void or voidable: Void.

Who can sue: Either party; both have standing.

Major defense: The parties did have the intention to marry at the time they entered the marriage ceremony. A major item of evidence that this intention existed is that they cohabited after the ceremony. (NOTE: in some states, the annulment will be denied if the parties went through all the outward formalities of the marriage no matter what their unspoken objective was.)

Is this annulment ground also a ground for divorce? Usually not.

ASSIGNMENT 9.5

a. Elaine is twenty years old, and Philip, a bachelor, is seventy-five. Philip asks Elaine to marry him. Philip has terminal cancer and wants to die a married man. He and Elaine know that he probably has less than six months to live and that he will spend the rest of his life in a hospital bed. Under their arrangement, she does not have to continue as his wife after six months if he is still alive. They go through all the formal requirements to be married. On the day after the marriage ceremony, Elaine changes her mind and wants to end the marriage. Can she obtain an annulment? (See General Instructions for the Legal-Analysis Assignment in chapter 1.)

b. Interview Elaine. (See General Instructions for the Interview Assignment in chapter 1.)

c. Draft a complaint for Elaine for her annulment action. (See General Instructions for the Complaint-Drafting Assignment in chapter 1.)

d. Draft a set of interrogatories from Philip to Elaine. (See General Instructions for the Interrogatory Assignment in chapter 1.)

IN THE INTEREST
OF MELISSA MILLER

301 Pa. Super. 511, 448 A.2d 25 (1982)
Superior Court of Pennsylvania.

Background: *Edward Christoph is a thirty-six-year-old English teacher who began a romantic relationship with one of his eighth grade students, Melissa Miller (also called Missy). She was fourteen years old at the time. Her mother had been having difficulty with her at home. Melissa would sneak out of the house through her bedroom window in the early morning hours and stay away for three or four hours. Her mother found letters to Melissa from Christoph that said, "You gave yourself fully," and "I love you." When the police began investigating Christoph for sexual involvement with a minor, he consulted an attorney who advised him how to enter a common law marriage. He then entered a common law marriage with Melissa. (Common law marriages are allowed in Pennsylvania. Though you must be sixteen to enter a ceremonial marriage, the age of consent to enter a common law marriage is seven.) The mother asked the state to declare Melissa to be a dependent child because of her incorrigibility. The juvenile division of the lower court did so and ordered her placed in a foster home. Since Christoph's motive in marrying Melissa was to avoid criminal prosecution, the court also invalidated the common law marriage. Melissa, as appellant, is now appealing this decision in the Superior Court of Pennsylvania. She does not want the marriage invalidated.*

Decision on Appeal: *Reversed. The common law marriage was not invalid. Melissa should not have been declared a dependent child.*

Opinion of the Court:

Judge SPAETH delivered the opinion of the court.
. . .

Mr. Christoph testified that his motive [in entering the common law marriage] was that appellant should "be my wife" and that his understanding, when he told her this, was that no criminal charges were going to be brought against him:

Q. What did you say to Melissa . . . on that occasion? A. I said, "I marry you, Melissa."

Q. You say, I marry her? A. Yes.

Q. And what did you intend when you said you married her? A. I intended that she be my wife.

Q. And as your wife, what was your intention towards her? A. To take her home to live with me as my wife.

Q. Did you recognize any responsibility when you said those words? A. Yes.

Q. What were the responsibilities that you recognized? A. To take her, provide a home and all the necessities that you would normally provide for your wife.

Q. Mr. Christoph, at the time this alleged marriage is to have taken place between you and Missy, do you know—were you aware of the fact that the police were investigating you? A. I had talked to the police at the time, yes.

Q. Were you afraid that charges would be filed against you by the police as a result of your involvement with Missy. A. No.

Q. You were not afraid of that? A. No.

Q. The crime, corrupting the moral[s] of minors, have you ever heard of that at the time you got married to Missy? A. Yes, I did.

Q. Did you have any concerns at the time this alleged marriage is to have taken place with you being charged by the police. A. No.

Q. Why not? A. Because when I talked to Detective Slupski he said no charges would be brought.

Q. Isn't it a fact you got married to Missy to prevent her from testifying against you and as a result you wouldn't have to face criminal charges? A. No.

Q. Isn't that a fact? A. No, it is not. [The trial judge then questioned the witness.]

THE COURT: As far as the police investigation, you were aware of that because you talked to a police officer? THE WITNESS: Yes I did.

THE COURT: And you spoke to him about the charge of corrupting the morals of a minor? THE WITNESS: Yes, I did.

THE COURT: And how did that come about? THE WITNESS: I don't understand the question.

THE COURT: How did you speak to him? Did you go down to speak to him? THE WITNESS: He said he wanted to talk to me at a certain time.

THE COURT: What happened? THE WITNESS: We discussed the charges and he asked me questions about what had happened and at the end of the conversation he said he was going to recommend to the D.A. that no charges be brought.

THE COURT: When did this occur? THE WITNESS: I really don't know the day. It was a week maybe a week and a half before we got married.

It is true, as the lower court states in its opinion, that Mr. Christoph's sister, Virginia Byers, who was a witness to the marriage ceremony, testified that "one of Mr. Christoph's express motives in marrying Melissa Miller was to avoid criminal prosecution." Slip op. at 3–4. However, the sister also testified that another of Mr. Christoph's motives was that he loved appellant:

Q. [on cross-examination by counsel for appellant's mother]: Did that strike you as strange that he [Mr. Christoph] wanted to marry such a young girl that use[d] to be a student of his? A. A little bit, but he said he loved her, so—

Q. Was there any more of a discussion than that, other than the fact that he loved her and wanted to take her as his wife? A. What do you mean, sir?

Q. Was there any discussion as to any other reasons or any other motives as to why he wanted to marry her, other than love? A. Well, I think there were some legal problems.

Q. What legal problems? A. Her—Melissa's mother didn't approve of the situation.

Q. What other legal problems? A. I don't know. Possibly that—I guess, maybe, he would go to jail.

Q. Go to jail for what? A. Let me think of what the term is.

Q. Corrupting the morals of minors? A. Yeah, that's what I'm trying to think of—say.

Q. Is that what you are talking about? A. That crossed his mind. . . .

Q. Did he express that by marrying Missy, he would avoid criminal prosecution? A. Yes.

Q. When was this discussed with your brother? A. About the criminal charges? That would—

Q. Yes. A. —that would have been Saturday morning.

Q. That would have been two or three days prior to the marriage? A. That is correct.

Q. And in discussing these things with him, what was first mentioned as for his reasons for wanting to get married? A. His first reasons—uh—

Q. Did he give a priority? A. No, not really.

REDIRECT EXAMINATION BY MR. KOWNACKI:

Q. This was a general discussion with you? A. Right.

Q. Did he appear sincere in his stated reasons for love? A. Yeah. I was surprised, but yeah, he was serious.

Q. You have known your brother for how long? A. Twenty-five and a half years.

Q. You had a relation—good close relationship with him? A. Yes.

Q. You feel you know your brother well? A. Very well.

Q. Therefore, you know him when he is sincere and insincere? A. Yeah.

Q. He indicated he loved Melissa and wanted to marry her, you felt he was sincere? A. Yes, I did.

The lower court does not mention this portion of the sister's testimony. It seems to us that the fairest inference to be drawn from the evidence is that Mr. Christoph may have had at least two motives for marrying appellant—his love for her, and his desire to avoid criminal prosecution for his relationship with her. We find no support in the record for the lower court's assignment of priority to the second of these motives.

We may, however, put aside any difficulty with the inferences drawn by the lower court. Accepting the lower court's finding that Mr. Christoph married appellant to avoid criminal prosecution, still, we are unable to uphold its order. For contrary to the court's opinion, such a motive does not invalidate a common law marriage.

The controlling decision is *Estate of Gower*, 445 Pa. 554, 284 A.2d 742 (1971). In *Gower*, as here, the parties had by words in the present tense expressed their intent to marry one another. The lower court nevertheless held the marriage invalid because the appellant's motive in entering into the marriage was to avoid conscription for military service. Reversing, the Supreme Court held that "[t]he reason or motive underlying a decision to marry is not relevant to a finding of the *intention* to marry." Id. at 557, 284 A.2d at 744. (emphasis in original). Therefore, the appellant's motive to avoid conscription could not "render[ ] invalid his otherwise valid common law marriage." Id.

The record here establishes—and the lower court did not question—appellant's and Mr. Christoph's *intention* to marry. The fact—as the lower court found it to be—that Mr. Christoph's *motive* was to avoid prosecution could not render invalid their otherwise valid common law marriage. . . .

[T]here is a distinction, in both the common law* and the Pennsylvania Divorce Code, Act of April 2, 1980, P.L. 63, Act No. 26, 23 P.S. § 101 et seq., between a void marriage and a voidable marriage. The Code provides the following grounds for annulment or invalidity of void marriages, in Section 204:

(a) Where there has been no confirmation by cohabitation following the removal of an impediment, the supposed or alleged marriage of any person shall be deemed void in the following cases: . . . (3) Where either party to such marriage was incapable of consenting by reason of insanity or serious mental disorder, or otherwise lacked capacity to consent or did not intend to assent to such marriage. . . .

The Code provides the following grounds for annulment of voidable marriages, in Section 205: § 205.

---

*The distinction between a void marriage and a voidable marriage derives from the English ecclesiastical courts. A void marriage included unions so abhorrent as to be against public policy from their inception. Into this class belonged bigamous marriages and those in which one party was insane. Void marriages could be dissolved over the objection of the parties by interested persons. In contrast, voidable marriages contained some defect that could be removed by ratification, and were dissolvable only by the injured spouse. Perlberger, *Pennsylvania Divorce Code* § 3.2 (1980).

GROUNDS FOR ANNULMENT OF VOIDABLE MARRIAGES:

(a) The marriage of any person shall be deemed voidable and subject to annulment in the following cases: (1) Where either party to such marriage was under 16 years of age, unless such marriage was expressly authorized by a judge of the court. . . . (5) Where one party was induced to enter into such marriage due to the fraud, duress, coercion, or force attributable to the other party, and there has been no subsequent voluntary cohabitation after knowledge of such fraud or release from the effects of fraud, duress, coercion, or forces.

(b) In all such cases of marriages which are voidable, either party thereto may seek and obtain an annulment of such marriage, but unless and until such decree is obtained from a court of competent jurisdiction, such marriage shall be valid and subsisting. The validity of such a voidable marriage shall not be subject to attack or question by any person if it is subsequently confirmed by the parties thereto or if either party has died.

Section 203 of the Code authorizes a proceeding for the annulment of both void and voidable marriages: In all cases where a supposed or alleged marriage shall have been contracted which is void or voidable under this act or under applicable law, either party to such supposed or alleged marriage may bring an action in annulment to have it declared null and void in accordance with the procedures provided for under this act and the Rules of Civil Procedure. . . .

Section 204(a)(3) . . . makes a marriage void only where one of the parties "lacked capacity to consent or did not intend to assent" to the marriage. Since here neither party lacked capacity and both intended to assent, the section is inapplicable. The lower court's finding that "[Mr. Christoph's] sole purpose was to practice a fraud upon this Court and upon [appellant]" does not bring the marriage within Section 204(a)(3). For marriages induced by fraud are dealt with explicitly in Section 205(a)(5), which concerns voidable marriages.[†]

The distinction between a void marriage and a voidable marriage is not merely a matter of semantics. The Divorce Code, like the common law, provides that a voidable marriage may be annulled only by "either party thereto" and is "valid and subsisting" "unless and until" challenged by one of them. Section 205(b); Perlberger, *Pennsylvania Divorce Code* § 3.2.3 (1980) ("the legislature has expressly declared this crucial distinction between void and voidable marriages by enactment of section 205(b)"). If indeed appellant was induced to enter into marriage by Mr. Christoph's fraud, their marriage is not, as the lower court held, void, but voidable. In that event, appellant may seek to have it annulled. Not only, however, does she not make such a request; she has appealed to this court asking that her marriage be upheld.

We have not overlooked the arguments of counsel for appellant's mother, urging that we re-examine the doctrine of common law marriage, and either abolish it or align the age of consent to that required for statutory marriage. However, we have declined previous opportunities to abolish or modify the doctrine of common law marriage. . . . Past efforts in the Legislature to abolish common law marriage have failed. . . . The Marriage Law, Act of August 22, 1953, P.L. 1344, 48 P.S. § 1–23, explicitly preserves the right to contract a common law marriage, providing that "[n]othing herein shall be construed to change the existing law with regard to common law marriage." This remains the legislative intent. . . .

In conclusion, we wish to note that neither have we overlooked the anguish that this marriage has caused appellant's mother. We may hope that her fears are unfounded, as they may be, for the most devoted mother is sometimes mistaken about what is good for her child. But if we knew that the marriage would prove unhappy and short, that would not deflect us from our decision. Our responsibility is to interpret and apply the law. If a marriage is lawful, that is the end of our inquiry. For as judges, we are agents of the State, and whether a lawful marriage is happy or unhappy is none of the State's affair.

Reversed.

[†]We note that counsel for appellant's mother urges an entirely different reason for the application of section 204(a)(3), arguing that appellant lacked the capacity to consent to the marriage because she was under sixteen, as required by The Marriage Law, Act of Aug. 22,

1953, P.L. 1344, 48 P.S. § 1–1 et seq. However, the statutory age requirement is not applicable to common law marriages. *Buradus v. General Cement Products Co.*, 356 Pa. 349, 52 A.2d 205 (1949). Appellant did not lack capacity to consent to a common law marriage. . . .

---

a. After reading the *Miller* case, do you think common law marriage should be abolished? Why or why not?

b. Why couldn't this marriage be annulled?

c. What changes in the Pennsylvania law of annulment might have allowed the court to annul the marriage?

ASSIGNMENT 9.6

MENTAL DISABILITIES

Two related reasons have been attributed to the existence of *mental disability* as a ground for annulment. First, it is designed to prevent people from marrying who are incapable of understanding the nature of the marriage relationship. Second, it is designed to prevent or at least discourage such individuals from reproducing, since it is argued that many mentally ill parents are likely to be poor parents and their children are likely to become public charges.

Mental disability has been very difficult to define. The various state statutes use different terms to describe this condition: insane, idiot, weak-minded, feebleminded, unsound mind, lack of mental capacity, imbecile, lunatic, incapable of consenting to a marriage, mentally ill or retarded, legally incompetent, mental defective, etc. One court provided the following definition:

> While there has been a hesitancy on the part of the courts to judicially define the phrase "unsound mind," it is established that such term has reference to the mental capacity of the parties at the very moment of inception of the marriage contract. Ordinarily, lack of mental capacity, which renders a party incapable of entering into a valid marriage contract, must be such that it deprives him of the ability to understand the objects of marriage, its ensuing duties and undertakings, its responsibilities and relationship. There is a general agreement of the authorities that the terms "unsound mind" and "lack of mental capacity" carry greater import than eccentricity or mere weakness of mind or dullness of intellect. *Johnson v. Johnson,* 104 N.W.2d 8, 14 (N.D. 1960).

Not all states would agree with every aspect of this definition of mental disability, although in general it is consistent with the definitions used by most courts.

Suppose that a person is intoxicated or under the influence of drugs at the time the marriage contract is entered. In most states, this, too, would be a ground for annulment if the alcohol or drugs rendered the person incapable of understanding the marriage contract.

While the issue of mental health usually arises in annulment actions—when someone is trying to dissolve the marriage—it also becomes relevant in some states at the license stage. Before a state official can issue a license to marry, he or she may be required by statute to inquire into the prior mental difficulties, if any, of the applicants for the license, e.g., to ask whether either applicant has ever been in a mental institution. At one time, the license to marry in these states could be denied to any mentally disabled person unless that person was sterilized or the woman involved in the proposed marriage was over forty-five years old. (For more on sterilization, see page 417.) It is generally conceded, however, that these license restrictions have been ineffective in preventing the marriage of people with serious mental problems. They are also of questionable constitutionality in view of the *Zablocki* opinion (page 147).

Whenever the mental health question arises (at the license stage or as part of an annulment proceeding), it is often very difficult to prove that the "right" amount of mental illness is present. All individuals are presumed to be sane unless the contrary has been demonstrated. Suppose that someone was once committed to a mental institution and, upon release, seeks to be married. Surely, the fact of prior institutionalization does not conclusively prove that the person is *presently* incapable of understanding the marriage contract and the marriage relationship at the time he or she attempts to marry.

Assume that a person is mentally disabled but marries during a brief period of mental health before relapsing again to his or her prior state of mental disability. The marriage took place during what is called a **lucid interval,** and many states will validate such a marriage if there was cohabitation. Furthermore, some states will deny the annulment if the parties cohabited during a lucid interval at any time *after* the marriage was entered even if one or both parties was not "lucid" at the time of the marriage. The problems of trying to prove that any "interval" was "lucid" can be enormous, however.

Lucid Interval A period of time during which a person has the mental capacity to understand what he or she is doing.

□ Notes on Mental Illness

1. A state may have one standard of mental illness that will disable a person from being able to marry, another standard that will disable a person from being able to enter an ordinary business contract, and still another standard that will disable a person from being able to write a will.

2. Mental illness is, of course, also relevant in criminal proceedings where the defense of *insanity* is often raised in an attempt to relieve a defendant of criminal responsibility for what was done. Within criminal law, a great debate has always existed as to the definition of insanity. The M'Naghten "right-wrong" test is as follows: "at the time of the committing of the act, the party accused was laboring under such a defect of reason, from disease of the mind, as not to know the nature and quality of the act he was doing, or if he did know it that he did not know he was doing what was wrong." 10 Clark & F. 200, 8 Eng. Rep. 718 (1843). The Durham "diseased mind" test is as follows: "an accused is not criminally responsible if his unlawful act was the product of mental disease or mental defect." *Durham v. United States,* 214 F.2d 862, 874–75 (D.C. Cir. 1954). See also *United States v. Brawner,* 471 F.2d 969 (1972). The *Model Penal Code* test is as follows: "A person is not responsible for criminal conduct if at the time of such conduct as a result of mental disease or defect he lacks substantial capacity either to appreciate the criminality (wrongfulness) of his conduct or to conform his conduct to the requirements of the law." § 4.01.

▄▄▄▄ Summary of Ground for Annulment: Mental Disability

Definition: The inability to understand the marriage contract and the duties of marriage at the time the parties attempt to enter the marriage due to mental illness, the influence of alcohol, or the influence of drugs.

Void or voidable: Voidable in most states.

Who can sue: In some states, only the mentally ill person (or his or her parent or guardian) can sue for the annulment. In other states, only the mentally healthy person can sue. In many states, either can sue; both have standing.

Major defenses:

1. The person was never mentally disabled.

2. The marriage occurred during a lucid interval.

3. After the marriage began, there was a lucid interval during which the parties cohabited.

4. The plaintiff has no standing to bring this annulment action.

Is this annulment ground also a ground for divorce? Yes, in most states, if the mental disability arises after the marriage commences.

DURESS

If someone has been forced to consent to marry, it clearly cannot be said that that person had the requisite *intent* to be married. The major question of **duress** is what kind of force will be sufficient to constitute a ground for annulment. Applying physical force or threatening its use is clearly sufficient. If an individual is faced with a choice between a wedding and a funeral, and chooses the wedding, the resulting marriage will be annulled as one induced by duress.

Duress Coercion; acting under the pressure of an unlawful act or threat.

The same is true if the choice is between bodily harm and marriage. Suppose, however, that the choice does not involve violence or the threat of violence. The most common example is as follows:

> George is courting Linda. They have had sexual relations several times. Linda announces that she is pregnant. Linda's father is furious at George and threatens to "turn him in" to the county district attorney to prosecute him for the crimes of seduction and bastardy. (If Linda is underage, the charge of statutory rape may be involved as well.) Furthermore, Linda and her father will sue George in the county civil court for support of the child. On the other hand, no criminal prosecution will be brought and no civil action will be initiated if George agrees to marry Linda. George agrees, and the "shotgun wedding" promptly takes place. After the wedding, it becomes clear that Linda was not pregnant; everyone made an honest mistake. George then brings an action to annul the marriage on the ground of duress.

Here the threat is of criminal prosecution and of bringing a civil support action. If such threats are made *maliciously*, they will constitute duress and be a ground for annulment. The threat is malicious if it has no basis in fact. If the threats are not malicious, no annulment action can be based on them.

In most states, marriages induced by duress are voidable rather than void, but only the innocent party will have standing to bring the annulment action on that ground. If, however, this innocent party voluntarily cohabited with the "guilty" party (i.e., the one who did the coercing) after the effects of the duress have worn off, then the annulment action will be denied on the theory that the marriage has been ratified.

ASSIGNMENT 9.7

Do you think that any of the following marriages could be annulled on the ground of duress? (See General Instructions for the Legal-Analysis Assignment in chapter 1.)

a. Rita married Dan after Dan threatened to kill Rita's second cousin if she did not marry him. The only reason Rita married Dan was to save her cousin's life.

b. Tom married Edna after Tom's very domineering father ordered him to marry her. Tom had been in ill health lately. Tom married Edna solely because he has never been able to say no to his father.

c. Paula married Charles after Paula's mother threatened suicide if she would not marry him. Paula married Charles solely to prevent this suicide.

■■■ Summary of Ground for Annulment: Duress

Definition: The consent to marry was induced by (a) physical violence, or (b) threats of physical violence, or (c) malicious or groundless threats of criminal prosecution, or (d) malicious or groundless threats of civil litigation.

Void or voidable: Voidable in most states.

Who can sue? The party who was coerced.

Major defenses:

1. There was no physical violence or threat of it.

2. The plaintiff did not believe the threat of violence and hence was not coerced by it.

3. There was no threat of criminal prosecution or of civil litigation.

4. The threat of criminal prosecution or of civil litigation was not malicious; it was made in the good-faith belief that it could be won.

5. This is the wrong plaintiff (e.g., this plaintiff has "dirty hands" and lacks standing since this is the party who used duress).

6. The plaintiff freely cohabited with the defendant after the effect of the duress had gone (ratification).

Is this annulment ground also a ground for divorce? Yes, in some states.

FRAUD

The theory behind **fraud** as a ground for annulment is that if a party consents to a marriage where fraud is involved, the consent is not real. A party does not have an *intent to marry* if the marriage has a foundation in fraud. The party intends one thing and gets another! Generally, for this ground to succeed, the defendant must intentionally misrepresent or conceal an important fact and the person deceived must reasonably rely upon this fact in the decision to enter the marriage.

Not every fraudulent representation will be sufficient to grant an annulment. As one court put it:

> Surely every representation leading up to marriage cannot be material—the fact that a brunette turned to a blond overnight, or that the beautiful teeth were discovered to be false, or the ruddy pink complexion gave way suddenly to pallor, or that a woman misstated her age or was not in perfect health, would lead no court to annul the marriage for fraud. Ryan & Granfield, *Domestic Relations,* 136 (1963).

What kind of fraud *is* ground for an annulment? Most courts have used an **essentials test:** The fraud must involve the essentials of the marital relationship, usually defined as those aspects of the marriage that relate to sex and children. For example, a man misrepresents his intent to have children. This would clearly go to the essentials of the marriage.

A much broader definition of fraud (making annulment easier to obtain on this ground) is the **materiality test:** The fraud must be material, meaning "but for" the fraudulent representation (whether or not it relates to sex and children) the person deceived would not have entered the marriage. Fewer courts use the materiality test than those that continue to insist on the essentials test.

Although, in theory, the essentials test is usually deemed to be the stricter of the two tests, in reality, the two tests often overlap and are frequently applied inconsistently by the courts. If children have been born from the union, for example, courts often strain the application of the tests in order to deny the annulment since preserving the marriage may be the only way to legitimize the children in some states. Also, if the marriage has never been consummated, courts tend to be more liberal in finding fraud. Oddly, a few courts treat an unconsummated marriage as little more than an engagement to be married.

The state of mind of the deceiving party is critical. In most states there must be an *intentional misrepresentation* of fact or an *intentional concealment* of fact. Consider the following methods by which false facts are communicated:

Fraud Knowingly making a false statement of present fact with the intention that the plaintiff rely on the statement. The plaintiff's reasonable reliance on the statement harms him or her.

▇▇ **Forms of Communication**

1. Just before their marriage, Joe tells Mary that he is anxious to have children with her. In fact, he intends to remain celibate after their marriage.

1. Joe's statement about children is an *intentional misrepresentation* of fact.

2. Joe says nothing about his planned celibacy since he knows that if he tells Mary, she will not marry him. He says nothing about children or celibacy, and the subject never comes up prior to their marriage.

2. Joe's silence is an *intentional concealment* of fact.

3. Joe does not tell Mary that he intended to remain celibate because he incorrectly assumed that Mary already knew.

3. Joe's silence is an *innocent* (or *good-faith*) *nondisclosure* of fact.

4. Just before their marriage, Joe tells Mary that since he is physically unable to have sexual intercourse, he will

4. Joe's statement is an *innocent* (or *good-faith*) *misrepresentation* of fact.

—*Continued*

—Continued

have to stay celibate. To his surprise, Joe later finds out that he is not impotent.

5. One hour after Joe marries Mary, he gets on a bus and disappears forever. They never had sexual intercourse before or after marriage, and never discussed the subject.

5. From Joe's conduct we can draw an *inference* that at the time he married Mary, he probably never intended to consummate the marriage.

Generally, only the first, second, and fifth forms of communication mentioned in the above chart will support an annulment on the ground of fraud. *Innocent nondisclosure* or *innocent misrepresentation* will not be sufficient in most states. It should be pointed out, however, that in some states the innocence of the communication is not relevant so long as the other elements of fraud are present.

▬ Summary of Ground for Annulment: Fraud

Definition: The intentional misrepresentation or concealment of a fact that is essential or material to the marriage and that the person deceived reasonably relies on in the decision to enter the marriage.

Void or voidable: Voidable in most states.

Who can sue: The innocent party only.

Major defenses:

1. The fraud was not about an essential fact.

2. The fraud was not material: the plaintiff did not rely on the fraud in his or her initial decision to marry.

3. The fraud arose after the marriage was entered (again, no reliance).

4. The plaintiff may have relied on the fraud, but he or she was unreasonable in doing so.

5. After plaintiff discovered the fraud, he or she consummated the marriage or otherwise cohabited with the fraudulent party (ratification).

6. The misrepresentation or nondisclosure was innocent—made in good faith with no intention to deceive.

7. This plaintiff has no standing to bring the annulment action since the plaintiff was the deceiver.

8. This plaintiff has "dirty hands" (e.g., in a case involving fraud relating to pregnancy, the plaintiff had premarital sex with the defendant).

Is this annulment ground also a ground for divorce? Yes, in a few states.

□ **Note on Church Annulment**

The Roman Catholic Church has its own separate system of annulment. The Church does not recognize divorce. The only way to terminate a marriage (other than by death of one of the parties) is through a Church annulment. This will allow a Catholic to remarry in the church, to receive Communion, and to participate in all the other sacraments. Theoretically this participation is denied to a Catholic who remarries without obtaining a Church annulment—even if he or she obtains a civil annulment. Just as the Church does not recognize civil annulments, the state does not recognize Church annulments. The two proceedings are separate.

The Church defines an annulment as "a declaration by a competent tribunal of the Church that what had the appearance of marriage was in fact invalid according to canon law." The annulment, or *declaration of nullity,* is "granted as a result of some impediment or on various grounds related to defective consent or lack of form. The most frequent ground for marriage nullity is *defective consent,* especially lack of due discretion and lack of due competence." Huels, *The Pastoral Companion: A Canon Law Handbook for Catholic Ministry,* 259 (1986). [emphasis added] To determine whether grounds for annulment exist according to *canon law,* the following questions are critical:

First, when [the couple] said their vows, did both partners freely accept and clearly understand the lifelong commitment they were making? And secondly, at that time, did both partners have the personal capacity to carry out consent, to form a community of life with the chosen partner? *Catholic Update,* UPD 100 (St. Anthony Messenger Press, 1980).

The annulment procedure includes a formal hearing presided over by a tribunal judge. An advocate presents the case of the petitioner seeking the annulment. Also present is a "defender of the bond" who monitors the proceeding to ensure that rights are protected and Church law properly observed. The hierarchy in Rome has criticized American bishops for allowing too many church annulments. Over 50,000 annulments are granted each year in the 119 dioceses of the United States. This constitutes 80 percent of the annulments granted by the Church worldwide.

■■■■■ CONFLICT OF LAW

The conflict of law question requires us to compare the law of two states. The law that exists where the parties were married (the *state of celebration*) must be compared with the law that exists where the parties now live (the state of **domicile** or **domiciliary state**). The question arises as follows:

Jim and Jane marry in State X where their marriage is valid. They then move to State Y. If they had married in State Y, their marriage would not have been valid. Jim sues Jane in State Y for an annulment. What annulment law does the court in State Y apply—the law of State X or the law of State Y?

State "X" is the state of celebration or the state of contract, i.e., the state where the parties entered the marriage contract. State "Y" is the domiciliary state, i.e., the state where the parties are domiciled. State "Y" is also called the **forum** state. In this case the domiciliary state happens to be the same as the forum state.

To place this problem in a concrete perspective, assume that Jim dies **intestate.** Assume further that he has children from a prior marriage, but had no children with his second spouse. Under the intestacy laws of most states, his spouse and children receive designated portions of his estate. If there is no spouse, the children obviously have more of an estate to share. Hence, it is in the interest of the children to claim that Jane cannot be the surviving spouse of Jim because they were never validly married. The success of this claim may depend on which law applies—that of State X or State Y.

Before examining the question of what law applies, we need to keep in mind the public policy favoring marriages. Legislatures and courts tend to look for reasons to validate a marriage, rather than to create circumstances that make it easy to invalidate it. This is all the more so if the parties have lived together for a long time and if children are in the picture. We have already seen that the law has imposed a presumption that a marriage is valid. The public policy favoring marriage, however, is not absolute. Other public policies must also be taken into account. The conflict of law rules are a product of a clash of public policies.

General Conflict of Law Rule in Annulment Actions   If the marriage is valid in the state of celebration (even though it would have been invalid if it had been contracted in the domiciliary state), the marriage will be recognized as valid in the domiciliary state *unless* the recognition of the marriage would violate some strong public policy of the domiciliary state.

Domicile   The place where a person has been physically present with the intent to make that place a permanent home; the place to which one intends to return when away.

Domiciliary State   The state where a person is domiciled. (This person is referred to as the domiciliary.)

Forum   (1) The place where the parties are presently litigating their dispute. (2) A court or tribunal hearing a case.

Intestate   Die without leaving a valid will.

Thus, in the case of Jim and Jane above, the general rule would mean that State Y would apply the law of State X unless to do so would violate some strong public policy of State Y. Assuming that no such policy would be violated, the annulment would be denied, since the marriage was valid in the state of celebration, State X. Assuming, however, that a strong public policy is involved, State Y would apply its own law and grant the annulment.

What do we mean by a strong public policy, the violation of which would cause a domiciliary state to apply its own marriage law? Some states say that if the marriage would have been *void* (as opposed to merely voidable) had it been contracted in the domiciliary state, then the latter state will not recognize the marriage even though the state of celebration recognizes the marriage as valid. In other words, it is against the strong public policy of a domiciliary state to recognize what it considers a void marriage even though other states consider the marriage valid.

A marriage that the domiciliary state would consider bigamous or incestuous is usually not recognized. In such cases, the domiciliary state will apply its own marriage law and grant the annulment even though the marriage may have been valid in the state of celebration. When other grounds for annulment are involved, states differ as to whether they, as domiciliary states, will apply their own marriage law or that of the state of celebration.

MARRIAGE-EVASION STATUTES

Suppose that a man and woman live in a state where they cannot marry, e.g., they are underage. They move from their domiciliary state to another state *solely* for the purpose of entering or contracting a marriage since they can validly marry under the laws of the latter state, e.g., they are not underage in this state. They then move back to their domiciliary state. If an annulment action is brought in the domiciliary state, what law will be applied? The marriage law of the domiciliary state or that of the state of celebration? If the annulment action is brought in the state of celebration, what law will be applied? Again the conflict of law question becomes critical because the annulment will be granted or denied depending upon which state's marriage law governs. Note that the man and woman went to the state of celebration in order to *evade* the marriage laws of the domiciliary state. Several states have enacted *marriage-evasion* statutes to cover this situation. In such states, the choice of law depends upon the presence or absence of an intent to evade. The statute might provide that the domiciliary state will refuse to recognize the marriage if the parties went to the state of celebration for the purpose of evading the marriage laws of the domiciliary state to which they returned. It is sometimes very difficult to prove whether the parties went to the other state with the intent to evade the marriage laws of their domiciliary state. It may depend on circumstantial evidence such as how long they remained in the state of celebration, whether they returned to their initial domiciliary state or established a domicile in another state altogether. The interviewing and investigation checklist below is designed to assist you in collecting evidence on intent:

▮▮ Interviewing and Investigation Checklist

Factors Relevant to the Intent to Evade the Marriage Laws[2]

Legal Interviewing Questions

1. How long have the two of you lived in State Y?

2. Why didn't you marry in State Y?

3. When did you decide to go to State X?

4. Have you or D ever lived in State X?

5. Do you or D have any relatives in State X?

6. Were you or D born in State X?

7. On what date did you and D go to State X?

8. Did you sell your home or move out of your apartment in State Y?

9. When you left State Y, did you intend to come back?

10. After you arrived in State X, when did you apply for a marriage license?

11. On what date were you married?

12. While you were in State X, where did you stay? Did you have all your clothes and furniture with you?

13. Who attended the wedding ceremony in State X?

14. Did you and D have sexual relations in State X?

15. Did you or D work in State X?

16. How long did you and D stay in State X?

17. Did you and D vote or pay taxes in State X?

18. Did you and D open a checking account in any bank in State X?

19. Where did you and D go after you left State X?

Possible Investigation Tasks

☐ Obtain copies of all records that tend to establish the kind of contact the parties had with State X, e.g., motel receipts, bank statements, rent receipts, employment records.

☐ Interview friends, relatives, and associates of the parties to determine what light they can shed on the intent of the parties in going to State X.

_____

2. See also the interviewing and investigation checklist for establishing domicile, page 358.

Thus far our main focus has been on marriages that are valid in the state of celebration but invalid and annullable in the domiciliary state if they had been contracted in the latter state (see Exhibit 9.1). Suppose, however, that the marriage was invalid in the state of celebration. The parties then move to a new state where they establish a domicile. If they had been married in their new domicile state, their marriage would have been valid. An annulment action is brought in their new domicile state (Exhibit 9.2).

Our question now becomes, if a marriage is invalid where contracted, can it ever be considered valid in any other state? Will a present domiciliary state validate a marriage that is invalid according to the law of the state of celebration? Surprisingly, the answer is often yes. In some states, a domiciliary state will deny an annulment of a marriage that would have been valid if contracted in the domiciliary state but that is clearly invalid in the state where it was actually contracted. Such states take this position, in part, because of the public policy (and indeed the presumption) favoring the validity of marriages.

☐ **EXHIBIT 9.1**
Marriages Valid in State of Celebration

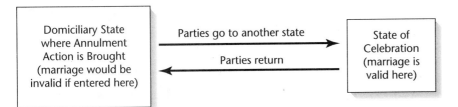

□ **EXHIBIT 9.2**
Marriages Invalid in
State of Celebration

| State of Celebration (marriage is invalid here) | Parties move to another state → | New Domiciliary State where Annulment Action is Brought (marriage would be valid if entered here) |

ASSIGNMENT 9.8

a. Is there a statute in your state that deals with marriages contracted out of state? If so, give its citation and state how it handles such marriages. (See General Instructions for the State-Code Assignment in chapter 1.)

b. Find a court opinion written by a state court in your state that involved an annulment action brought in your state concerning a marriage that was contracted in another state. (If no such action has ever been brought in your state, pick an opinion from any state.) Answer the following questions about the opinion you found:

1. In what state was the marriage contracted?

2. What was the alleged ground for the annulment?

3. What marriage law was applied in the opinion?

4. What reason did the court give for applying that law?

5. Was the annulment granted? Why or why not? (See the General Instructions for the Court-Opinion Assignment in chapter 1.)

■■■■ CONSEQUENCES OF AN ANNULMENT DECREE

In theory, an annulled marriage never existed. The major question that always arises as a result of this theory is: What effect does the annulment have on events occurring after the "marriage"?

The old rule was that once a marriage was declared invalid, the declaration "related back" to the time the parties attempted to enter the marriage. This relation-back doctrine meant that the annulment decree was retroactive. The doctrine, when strictly applied, resulted in some very harsh consequences. Children born to parents before their marriage was annulled were, in effect, born out of wedlock and were illegitimate. Suppose that a woman lives with a man for forty years before their marriage is annulled. She would not be entitled to any alimony or support payments since a man has no duty to support someone who was never his wife! Clearly, these were unfair consequences, and all states took steps to offset them. What follows is an overview of the present law in this area.

LEGITIMACY OF CHILDREN FROM AN ANNULLED MARRIAGE

Legitimize To formally declare that children born out of wedlock are legitimate.

With few exceptions, states have passed statutes that **legitimize** children from an annulled marriage. Some of the statutes, however, are not absolute, e.g., the statute might say that the children are legitimate only if one or both of the parents honestly believed that their marriage was valid when they entered it, or the statute might legitimize all the children born from an annulled marriage *except* when the annulment was granted on the ground of a prior existing marriage (bigamy).

ALIMONY AND DISPOSITION OF PROPERTY ACQUIRED BEFORE THE MARRIAGE WAS ANNULLED

In some states, alimony cannot be awarded in annulment proceedings. In other states, however, statutes have been passed that allow alimony in such actions. This includes temporary alimony pending the final outcome of the action and permanent alimony following the annulment decree. It may be, however, that alimony will be denied to the "guilty" party, e.g., the party who committed the fraud or who forced the other party to enter the marriage.

Another limitation on alimony in some states is that only defendants can receive it. By definition, the plaintiff seeking the annulment is saying that no marriage ever existed. A few courts say that it is inconsistent for the plaintiff to take this position and also to ask for alimony.

Where alimony is authorized, attorney fees might also be awarded. If so, the spouse able to pay, usually the husband, must pay the fees of the attorney for the other spouse in defending or initiating the annulment action.

Suppose it is clear in a particular state that alimony cannot be awarded in the annulment action. Courts have devised various theories to provide other kinds of relief such as allowing a party to bring a suit on a theory of *quasi contract* to prevent *unjust enrichment*. Under this theory, the party may be able to recover the reasonable value of the goods and services provided during the relationship. Other theories that might allow a division of property acquired during the relationship include *partnership, joint venture,* and *putative spouse.* For a discussion of these theories, see chapter 7 where we discussed similar theories to obtain relief for parties who cohabited but never married.

PROBLEMS OF REVIVAL

Bob is validly married to Elaine. They go through a valid divorce proceeding, which provides that Bob will pay Elaine alimony until she remarries. One year later, Elaine marries Bill; Bob stops his alimony payments. Two years later, Elaine's marriage to Bill is annulled.

In this case, what is Bob's obligation to pay alimony to Elaine? Several possibilities exist:

□ Bob does not have to resume paying alimony; his obligation ceased forever when Elaine married Bill; the fact that the second marriage was annulled is irrelevant.

□ Bob does not have to resume paying alimony; *Bill* must start paying alimony if the state authorizes alimony in annulment actions.

□ Bob must resume paying alimony from the date of the annulment decree; the annulment of the second marriage *revived* his earlier alimony obligation.

□ Bob must resume paying alimony for the future and for the time during which Elaine was married to Bill; the annulment *revived* the original alimony obligation.

The last option is the most logical. Since the technical effect of an annulment decree is to say that the marriage never existed, this decree should be retroactive to the date when the parties entered the marriage that was later annulled. While the last option is perhaps the most logical of the four presented, it is arguably as unfair to Bob as the first option is unfair to Elaine. States take different positions on this problem. Most states, however, adopt the second or third option mentioned above.

CUSTODY AND CHILD SUPPORT

When children are involved, whether considered legitimate or not, courts will make temporary and permanent custody decisions in the annulment proceeding. Furthermore, child-support orders are inevitable when the children are minors. Hence the fact that the marriage is terminated by annulment usually has little effect on the need of the court to make custody and child-support orders (see chapters 11 and 12).

INHERITANCE

Testate   Die leaving a valid will.

If a spouse dies **testate,** he or she can leave property to the surviving spouse. Suppose, however, that the marriage is annulled before the spouse died and that the will was never changed. In most states, an annulment (or a divorce) automatically revokes gifts to a surviving spouse unless the will specifically says otherwise.

Assume that one of the spouses of the annulled marriage dies *intestate.* In this event, the state's intestacy laws operate to determine who inherits the property of the deceased. The intestacy statute will usually provide that so much of the deceased's property will go to the surviving spouse, so much to the children, etc. If the marriage has already been annulled, there will be no surviving spouse to take a spouse's intestate share of the decedent's estate. An annulment (as well as a divorce) terminates mutual intestate rights between the former spouses.

SOCIAL SECURITY
AND WORKER'S COMPENSATION BENEFITS

Earlier we discussed the problem of revival in connection with alimony payments. The same problem exists with respect to certain statutory entitlement benefits. Suppose, for example, that Jane is entitled to social security or worker's compensation benefits following the death of her husband, Jim. Assume that these benefits will cease if and when she remarries. Jane then marries Tom, and the benefits stop. The marriage with Tom is subsequently annulled, however. Are the benefits now revived on the theory that Jane was never married to Tom? Case law is split on this question with some cases holding that the benefits do revive, and others concluding the opposite.

CRIMINAL LAW CONSEQUENCES

Ed marries Diane. He leaves her without obtaining a divorce. He now marries Claire. This marriage is then annulled. He is charged with the crime of bigamy. Can he use the defense that his marriage with Claire was annulled and therefore he was never married to Claire? Most of the cases that have answered this question have said that the subsequent annulment is *not* a defense to the bigamy charge.

INTERSPOUSAL IMMUNITY IN TORT ACTIONS

Interspousal Tort Immunity   One spouse cannot sue another for designated torts that grow out of the marriage relationship.

As we shall see in chapter 21, spouses may have the benefit of an **interspousal tort immunity** that prevents certain kinds of tort litigation between spouses. For example, assume George assaults his wife, Paulene, in a state where the immunity applies. She would not be able to sue him for the tort of assault. (She might be able to initiate a *criminal* action against him for the crime of assault and battery, but she could not bring a *civil* assault action against him.) An annulment of the marriage would not change this result. Even if George's marriage with Paulene was later annulled, she would still not be able to bring this tort action against him for conduct that occurred while they were together. The annulment does not wipe out the impact of the interspousal tort immunity.

PRIVILEGE FOR MARITAL COMMUNICATIONS

At common law, one spouse was not allowed to give testimony concerning *confidential communications* exchanged between the spouses during the marriage. The details of this prohibition will be explained in chapter 14. For now, our question is as follows:

> Sam is married to Helen. Their marriage is annulled. A year later Sam is sued by a neighbor who claims that Sam negligently damaged the neighbor's property. The alleged damage was inflicted while Sam was still married to Helen. At the trial, the neighbor calls Helen as a witness and asks her to testify about what Sam told her concerning the incident while they were still living together. According to the privilege for marital communications, Helen would be prohibited from testifying about what she and her husband told each other during the marriage. Their marriage, however, was annulled so that in the eyes of the law they were never married. Does this change the rule on the privilege? Can Helen give this testimony?

The answer is not clear; few cases have considered the issue. Of those that have, some have concluded that the annulment does not destroy the privilege, while others have reached the opposite conclusion.

TAX RETURN STATUS

A husband and wife can file a joint return so long as they were married during the taxable year. Suppose, however, that after ten years of marriage and ten years of filing joint returns, the marriage is annulled. Must the parties now file *amended* returns for each of those ten years? Should the returns now be filed as separate returns rather than joint ones, again on the theory that the annulment meant the parties were never validly married? According to the Internal Revenue Service, Publication 504, *Tax Information for Divorced or Separated Individuals,* p. 1 (1990 Edition):

> You are considered unmarried for the whole year [if you have] . . . obtained a decree of annulment which holds that no valid marriage ever existed. You also must file amended returns claiming an unmarried status for all tax years affected by the annulment not closed by the [three year] statute of limitations.

Answer the following questions by examining the statutory code of your state.

a. Is there a statute on whether children of annulled marriages are legitimate? If so, give the citation to the statute and explain how it resolves the question.

b. Is there a statute on whether temporary and permanent alimony can be granted in annulment proceedings? If so, give the citation to the statute and explain how it resolves the question.

(See General Instructions for the State-Code Assignment in chapter 1.)

ASSIGNMENT 9.10   How would the following two problems be resolved in your state? You may have to check both statutory law and case law. (See General Instructions for the State-Code Assignment and General Instructions for the Court-Opinion Assignment in chapter 1.)

a. Fred and Jill are married. Fred is killed in an automobile accident with the ABC Tire Company. Jill brings a wrongful death action against the ABC Tire Company. The attorney of ABC learns that Jill was married to someone else at the time she married Fred. The attorney claims that Jill cannot bring the wrongful death action since she was never validly married to Fred.

b. Bob and Mary are married. Bob dies intestate. Mary claims Bob's estate (i.e., his property) pursuant to the state's intestate law. Bob's only other living relative, Fred, claims that he is entitled to Bob's estate. Fred argues that Mary is not entitled to any of Bob's property because the marriage between Bob and Mary was invalid and should be annulled.

ASSIGNMENT 9.11   **a.** What is the name of the court in your state that can hear annulment actions?

b. How does this court acquire jurisdiction over the subject matter of annulment actions, e.g., residence or domicile requirements, place of celebration, etc.?

c. To what court(s) can a party appeal a trial court judgment on annulment?

(See General Instructions for the State-Code Assignment in chapter 1.)

ASSIGNMENT 9.12   Prepare a flowchart of annulment litigation in your state. (See General Instructions for the Flowchart Assignment in chapter 1.)

◼ SUMMARY

A divorce is a termination of a valid marriage. An annulment is an acknowledgment that the parties were never married, whether they lived together (and acted as if they were married) for thirty minutes or for thirty years after the "marriage" ceremony. To obtain an annulment, a party must establish grounds, and must have standing. Two categories of grounds exist: grounds relating to the legal capacity to marry, and grounds relating to the intent to marry. Some of these grounds will render the marriage void, while others will render it voidable.

There are four grounds relating to the legal capacity to marry:

1. *Prior existing marriage.* At the time of the marriage, a prior marriage had not been terminated.

2. *Consanguinity and affinity.* The parties married in violation of a prohibition against the marriage of certain individuals who are already related to each other.

3. *Nonage.* A party was underage at the time of the marriage.

4. *Physical disabilities.* A party had a specified disease or was impotent at the time of the marriage.

There are four grounds relating to the intent to marry:

1. *Sham marriage.* The parties never intended to live together as husband and wife.

2. *Mental disability.* At the time of the marriage, a party was incapable of understanding the nature of the marriage relationship.

3. *Duress.* A party was forced into the marriage.

4. *Fraud.* A party intentionally misrepresented or concealed certain facts from the other party that were either essential to the marriage or were material to the decision to enter the marriage.

Under conflict of law principles:

1. A marriage will be considered valid in a domiciliary state if (a) the marriage is valid according to the state where it was contracted, and (b) recognizing the validity of the marriage would not violate any strong public policy of the domiciliary state. If both conditions are met, the domiciliary state will deny the annulment even though the marriage could have been annulled if it had been contracted in the domiciliary state.

2. Generally, if a marriage would have been void had it been contracted in the domiciliary state, the latter state will not apply the law of the state of celebration where the marriage is valid.

3. Some states have statutes that invalidate marriages contracted in other states solely to evade the domiciliary state's marriage laws.

4. Some states have statutes that invalidate marriages contracted in their own state solely to evade the marriage laws of other states.

5. Some states will validate a marriage contracted in another state (even though the marriage is invalid in the state where it was contracted) so long as the marriage would have

been valid if it had been contracted in the state where the parties are now domiciled. In effect, this state will deny the annulment even though the state of celebration would have granted it.

In an annulment proceeding, the court must award custody of the children and provide for their support. Children born from an annulled marriage are usually considered legitimate. If the state does not allow alimony, the court may use a theory such as quasi contract to divide property acquired during the time the parties were together.

Suppose a divorced spouse remarries and thereby loses certain benefits granted by the divorce. But the second marriage is annulled. States do not always agree on whether the divorce benefits are revived. Revival issues might also arise in cases that involve inheritance, bigamy, tort liability, evidence, and income tax status.

■■■■■ KEY CHAPTER TERMINOLOGY

Annulment	Rebuttable Presumption	Lucid Interval
Divorce	Consanguinity	Duress
Legal Separation	Affinity	Fraud
Voidable Marriage	Incest	Essentials Test
Void Marriage	Nonage	Materiality Test
Void ab Initio	Ratified	Domicile
Standing	Impotence	Domiciliary State
Estopped	Copulate	Forum
Dirty Hands	Sterility	Intestate
Grounds	Laches	Legitimize
Bigamy	Sham	Testate
Polygamy	Consummate	Interspousal Tort Immunity
Enoch Arden Defense	Cohabitation	

SEPARATION AGREEMENTS: LEGAL ISSUES AND DRAFTING OPTIONS

Chapter 10 begins our comprehensive study of the separation agreement. Parts of chapter 11 (on child custody), chapter 12 (on child support), and chapter 15 (on taxation) also cover important dimensions of the separation agreement. Chapter 10, however, examines the document as a whole, setting the stage for the other chapters. Our focus throughout will be on the nature of the separation agreement, the drafting options available, and the response of a court *when the parties are not able to reach an agreement.*

Separation Agreement
A contract by two married individuals who have separated or are about to separate that covers support, custody, property division, and other terms of their separation.

▨ SEPARATION AGREEMENTS AND LITIGATION

The negotiation and drafting of the **separation agreement** are among the most important and difficult tasks of the family law practitioner. (For an overview of the kinds of agreements parties can enter before and during marriage, see Exhibit 7.1 in chapter 7.) Generally, a divorce is contemplated by both parties when they enter a separation agreement. This, however, is not always the case. Occasionally separation agreements are written by parties who never divorce and hence never remarry.

Separation agreements find their way into court in the following kinds of situations:

☐ One party sues the other for breach of contract, i.e., for violation of the separation agreement; the plaintiff in this suit wants the separation agreement enforced.

☐ The parties file for a divorce and ask the court either (1) to approve the terms of the separation agreement or (2) to approve the terms *and* to incorporate them into the divorce decree so that the decree and the agreement become merged.

☐ After the divorce, one of the parties brings a suit to set aside the separation agreement, e.g., because it was induced by fraud.

The law encourages parties to enter separation agreements. So long as certain basic public policies (to be discussed below) are not violated, the law gives a great deal of leeway to the parties to resolve their difficulties and, in effect, to decide what their relationship will be on such vital matters as alimony, property division, custody and visitation of the children, etc. The role of the lawyer and paralegal is to assist the client in this large endeavor.

A high priority of the family law practitioner must always be to avoid litigation, since it is often extremely time-consuming, expensive, and emotionally draining on everyone involved. The marital breakdown of the parties was probably a most painful experience for the entire family. Litigation tends to remind the parties of old sores and to keep the bitterness alive. While a separation agreement will not guarantee harmony between the spouses, it can help keep their disputes on a constructive level.

◼◼◼◼ NEGOTIATION FACTORS

An effective separation agreement is achieved through bargaining or negotiation by the parties on their own or, more commonly, through lawyers representing them. What is an effective, separation agreement? Obviously, this will vary according to individual circumstances. Nevertheless, some general observations can be made about the characteristics of an effective separation agreement:

◼◼◼ Characteristics of an Effective Separation Agreement

1. *Comprehensive.* It covers all major matters. Should a problem arise months or years later, the parties will not have to say, "We never thought of that when we drafted the agreement."

2. *Fair.* If the agreement is not fair to both sides, it may be unworkable, which will force the parties into expensive and potentially bitter litigation. Hence the worst kind of legal assistance a law office can provide is to "outsmart" the other side into "giving up" almost everything. Little is accomplished by winning the war, but losing the peace. "You gain no advantage in depriving your ex-spouse of what he/she is entitled to. Remember, your ex-spouse has the ability to make your life miser-

able." Mississippi State Bar, Family Law Section, *Consumers Guide to Divorce*, 4 (1990).

3. *Accurate.* The agreement should accurately reflect the intentions of the parties. What they orally agreed to do in formal or informal bargaining sessions should be stated in the written agreement.

4. *Legal.* Certain things can and cannot be done in a separation agreement; the agreement must not attempt to do anything that is illegal.

5. *Readable.* The agreement should be written in language that the parties can understand without having to hire or rehire a lawyer every time a question arises.

▇▇▇ CHECKLISTS FOR THE PREPARATION OF A SEPARATION AGREEMENT

Before an intelligent separation agreement can be drafted, a great deal of information is needed. First of all, a series of detailed lists should be compiled on the following items:

☐ All prior agreements between husband and wife, e.g., antenuptial agreement, loan agreement

☐ All property held by the husband in his separate name

☐ All property held by the wife in her separate name

☐ All property in one person's name that really "belongs" to the other

☐ All property held jointly—in both names

☐ All property acquired during the marriage

☐ All contracts during the marriage for the sale of real property

☐ All insurance policies currently in force

☐ All debts currently outstanding, with an indication of who incurred each one

☐ All income from any source earned by the husband

☐ All income from any source earned by the wife

☐ Projected future income of both parties, e.g., salary, dividends, interest, pension rights, royalties, loans that will be repaid, future trust income, expected inheritance

☐ All present and projected living expenses of the husband

☐ All present and projected living expenses of the wife

☐ All present and projected living expenses of the children

In addition to such lists, the following data should be collected:

☐ Names and addresses of both spouses and of the children

☐ Data on all prior litigation, if any, between the parties

☐ Name and address of present attorney of other spouse

☐ Names and addresses of prior attorneys, if any, retained by either party

☐ Copies of tax returns filed in prior five years

☐ Character references (if needed on questions of custody or credibility)

☐ Names and addresses of individuals who might serve as arbitrators or mediators

☐ Documentation of prior indebtedness

☐ Copy of will(s) currently in force, if any

The preliminary client interview in chapter 5 includes a great many categories of questions that should provide much of this background information within the knowledge of the client. The interrogatories in the next section focus on obtaining information from the *opposing* spouse and are also designed to identify critical information needed to negotiate and draft a separation agreement.

Here is a checklist covering individual clauses of a separation agreement. The checklist is an overview of topics that need to be considered by the parties and that we will consider in chapters 10, 11, 12, and 15. Some of the headings in the checklist are commonly used in the separation agreement itself.

1. *Alimony:*
   - ☐ Who pays
   - ☐ How much
   - ☐ Method of payment
   - ☐ Frequency of payment
   - ☐ Whether it terminates on the remarriage or the death of either spouse
   - ☐ Whether it fluctuates with income of payor
   - ☐ Whether it is modifiable
   - ☐ Security for payment
   - ☐ Method of enforcement
   - ☐ Tax consequences

2. *Child support:*
   - ☐ Who pays
   - ☐ How much (check the mandatory child support guidelines)
   - ☐ Whether amount of child support is modifiable
   - ☐ Method of payment
   - ☐ Security for payment
   - ☐ Frequency of payment
   - ☐ Whether it terminates when a child reaches a certain age
   - ☐ Whether it terminates if the child is otherwise emancipated
   - ☐ Day care expenses
   - ☐ Education expenses covering private schools, college, etc.
   - ☐ Tax consequences

3. *Custody:*
   - ☐ Which parent obtains custody and what kind, e.g., sole custody, joint custody, split custody
   - ☐ Visitation rights of noncustodial parent
   - ☐ Visitation rights of others, e.g., grandparent
   - ☐ Summer vacations and special holidays
   - ☐ Transportation expenses
   - ☐ Permissible removal of child from the state on a temporary or permanent basis
   - ☐ Changing the last name of the child
   - ☐ Consultation on all major educational and medical decisions
   - ☐ The child's participation in religious activity

4. *Health expenses (custodial parent and children):*
   - ☐ Medical
   - ☐ Dental
   - ☐ Drugs
   - ☐ Special needs
   - ☐ Expenses that are not covered by insurance

5. *Insurance:*
   - ☐ Life
   - ☐ Health
   - ☐ Automobile
   - ☐ Disability
   - ☐ Homeowner's

6. *Estate documents:*
   - ☐ Wills that are already in existence (individual or mutual)
   - ☐ Changes to be made in existing wills
   - ☐ Trust accounts for children

7. *Debts still to be paid:*
   - ☐ Incurred by whom
   - ☐ Who pays

8. *Personal property:*
   - ☐ Cash
   - ☐ Joint and separate bank accounts (savings, checking, certificates of deposit, etc.)
   - ☐ Stocks, bonds, and other kinds of securities
   - ☐ Motor vehicles
   - ☐ Art works
   - ☐ Household furniture
   - ☐ Jewelry

□ Rights to receive money in the future, e.g., retirement pay, stock options, royalties, rents, court judgment awards

9. *Real property:*

□ Residence

□ Vacation home

□ Business real estate

□ Tax shelters

□ Leases

10. *Income tax returns*

11. *Attorney fees and court costs*

12. *Incorporation of separation agreement into divorce decree (merger)*

13. *Arbitration*

14. *What happens to agreement if parties reconcile*

■■■■ UNCOVERING FINANCIAL ASSETS: INTERROGATORIES

Gaining access to all the personal and financial information needed to negotiate a separation agreement or to prepare for trial is not always easy. In fact, one of the major reasons separation agreements are later challenged is that one of the parties did not have or was not given a complete inventory of the other spouse's financial assets before signing. Later, in chapter 14, we will examine discovery devices that are designed to obtain this kind of information. One of the devices is **interrogatories,** which can be particularly effective when seeking financial assets.

The comprehensive set of interrogatories in Exhibit 10.1 are part of a law office's strategy to uncover facts. Reading them will give you a good idea of the kind of information that is the foundation of effective negotiation and drafting of a separation agreement. Without answers to these questions *prior* to negotiation, an attorney would, in most cases, not be able to negotiate and draft the agreement competently.

Interrogatories A written set of factual questions sent by one party to another before a trial begins.

■■■■ THE BEGINNING OF THE SEPARATION AGREEMENT

On the assumption that the law firm now has a comprehensive picture of the assets of the client (see chapter 5) and of the opposing spouse (see interrogatories in Exhibit 10.1), we turn to the separation agreement itself.

Exhibit 10.2 on page 209 presents some sample introductory clauses often found in separation agreements. It is good practice in the drafting of a separation agreement to number each paragraph separately (1, 2, 3, etc.) after the introductory clauses, and to use headings for each major topic, e.g., alimony, custody.

A number of issues relating to the introductory clauses in Exhibit 10.2 need to be discussed:

□ **Public policy and collusion**

□ **Capacity to contract**

□ **Duress and fraud**

□ **Consideration**

PUBLIC POLICY AND COLLUSION

The agreement in Exhibit 10.2 between Fred and Linda Jones is careful to point out that a separation has already occurred. When parties are still living

(text continues on p. 209)

☐ **EXHIBIT 10.1 Interrogatories**

The plaintiff, requests that the defendant answer under oath, in accordance with Section _____ , the following interrogatories:

NOTE: Questions concerning marriage and children pertain to the other party to this suit, unless otherwise indicated. Where a question or part of a question is inapplicable, indicate same.

1. State your full name, age, residence and post office address, home telephone number, social security number, business addresses and business phone numbers.

2. State:
   (a) The names, birth dates and present addresses of all children born or adopted during the marriage, indicating whether any children are emancipated, and who has legal custody of each unemancipated child.
   (b) Whether any dependent child is in need of unusual or extraordinary medical or mental care or has special financial needs, giving a detailed description of the condition which requires such care and the treatment required, to the best of your knowledge, including, but not limited to:
      (i)   Nature of treatment;
      (ii)   Name of treating doctors and/or other professionals;
      (iii) Cost of care; and
      (iv)   Estimated length of treatment.

3. As to yourself state:
   (a) Your present health;
   (b) Whether you have any need of unusual or extraordinary medical care or special financial needs;
   (c) Educational background, giving all schools attended and years of attendance, any degrees conferred, as well as any special training courses and employment skills;
   (d) If you were married at the time you attended school or any special training course, indicate whether your spouse contributed to the cost of your education and/or support and living expenses and the amount thereof, and, if your spouse did not contribute to these, who paid for your education and/or support and living expenses;
   (e) If you own or have been granted a license to practice any profession or other occupation in this or any other state, indicate the nature of such license(s) and the approximate monetary value of each license.

4. If you have any disability(ies) which at any time renders or rendered you unable to perform work or limits or limited your ability to perform work, either now, in the past, or in the future, state:
   (a) The nature of the disability(ies);
   (b) The name and address of each treating physician for the past ten years for said disability(ies);
   (c) The frequency of said treatment;
   (d) The cost of said treatment;
   (e) The nature of said treatment;
   (f) The method of payment for said treatment, including the name of the payor.
      *Attach any medical reports concerning the disability(ies).

PRIMARY AND MARITAL RESIDENCES

5. State your primary residence addresses for the past five (5) years, up to the present time, indicating periods of residence at each address.

6. If you are not currently residing with your spouse, state the names, ages and relationship to you of those persons with whom you reside at the above address, either on a permanent or periodic basis.

7. If your primary residence is rented or leased, state:
   (a) The monthly rental and term of the lease or agreement;
   (b) To whom the rental is paid, including name and address;
   (c) Whether any other persons are contributing to rental payments, the amount of the contribution, and the names of any such persons.
      *Attach copies of cancelled rent checks for the last twelve (12) months and a copy of your lease or rental agreement.

8. If your present primary residence is owned by you, state:
   (a) The date the residence was acquired;
   (b) From whom it was purchased;
   (c) The purchase price;
   (d) The amount of the downpayment;

Continued

☐ **EXHIBIT 10.1** Interrogatories—*Continued*

    (e) The source of the downpayment, showing contribution by both spouses, as well as any other persons;

    (f) The amount of the original mortgage(s);

    (g) The amount of the mortgage(s) as of the date of the separation of the parties;

    (h) The amount of the mortgage(s) at the present time if different from (f) or (g) above;

    (i) The name and address of the mortgagee(s) and the mortgage number(s), if any;

    (j) The market value of the property at the time of the separation of the parties;

    (k) The present market value of the property, if different from (j) above;

    (l) The tax basis of the property when acquired;

    (m) The adjusted tax basis of the property at the time of the separation of the parties;

    (n) The current adjusted tax basis, if different from your answer to (m) above;

    (o) The nature and dollar amount of any liens or other encumbrances on the property not indicated in previous answers;

    (p) The current assessed valuation assigned the property for real property taxation purposes.

       *Attach copies of closing statements, deeds, appraisals, as well as the most recent bill or bills for real estate taxes.

9. If the residence referred to in question 8 above is not the "marital residence," then supply the same information as requested in questions 8(a) through 8(p) above for the "marital residence."

      *Attach copies of closing statements, deeds, appraisals, as well as the most recent bill or bills for real estate taxes.

10. Who has been paying the mortgage and/or tax payments from the date of the separation of the parties?

OTHER REAL ESTATE

11. If you have an interest in any real property other than indicated in the previous section, for each such piece of real property, state:

    (a) Street address, county, and state where the property is located;

    (b) Type of property, deed references, and the nature of your interest in the property (full or partial; type of tenancy; restraints on alienation);

    (c) Zoning of the property;

    (d) Date property was acquired;

    (e) From whom it was purchased;

    (f) The amount of the downpayment;

    (g) The source of the downpayment, showing the contribution of both spouses and others;

    (h) The amount of the original mortgage(s);

    (i) The purchase price;

    (j) The amount of the mortgage(s) as of the date of the separation of the parties;

    (k) The amount of the present mortgage(s);

    (l) The name and address of the mortgagee(s) and the mortgage number(s), if any;

    (m) The present market value of the property;

    (n) The nature and dollar amount of any liens or other encumbrances on the property that are not listed in a previous answer;

    (o) The names and addresses of all co-owners and the nature of their interest in the property;

    (p) Itemize all operation expenses, including but not limited to taxes, mortgage payments, insurance, fuel oil, gas, electric, water and maintenance;

    (q) The present assessed valuation assigned the property for real property taxation purposes;

    (r) The exact nature and extent of your interest, if not listed in question 11(b);

    (s) The tax basis of the property when acquired;

    (t) The adjusted tax basis at the time of the separation of the parties;

    (u) The names and mailing addresses of all tenants and occupants and the annual and/or monthly rental paid by each, and their relationship to you (e.g., relative, friend) if any;

    (v) The source and amount of any income produced by the property, if not previously indicated.

      *Attach copies of the closing statements, deeds, and appraisals.

12. If you have sold or otherwise disposed of any real property in which you have had an interest within the last ten (10) years, state for each property, in detail, the same information as asked in interrogatory 11 above.

   *Attach copies of each closing statement and deed.

Continued

□ **EXHIBIT 10.1   Interrogatories—*Continued***

13. If you have executed any contracts to buy or sell real property within the last ten (10) years, indicate the location of the property, terms of the sale, and whether you were the purchaser or seller, and the name of the other party or parties.

    *Attach a copy of each such contract.

14. If you are the holder of an interest in any real property not disclosed in a previous interrogatory, state for each:
    (a) The type of such property (whether real or personal);
    (b) The location of such property;
    (c) The date acquired;
    (d) The net monthly rental to you from each piece of property;
    (e) The gross monthly rental to you from each piece of property;
    (f) The present value of such property.

INCOME AND EMPLOYMENT

15. State the names, addresses, and telephone numbers of all employers for the last ten (10) years and give the dates of such employment, position held, salary, other compensation, and reason for termination.

16. As to your present employment, state:
    (a) Name and address of your employer;
    (b) Type of work performed, position held, and nature of work or business in which your employer is engaged;
    (c) Amount of time you have been employed in your present job;
    (d) Hours of employment;
    (e) Rate of pay or earnings, gross and net average weekly salary, wages, commissions, overtime pay, bonuses, and gratuities.

       *Attach copies of all evidence of above payments, including pay stubs, W-2 forms, etc. for the past twelve months.

17. State what benefits your employer provides for you and/or your family inclusive but not limited to all of the following. Include a brief description of the benefit and whether your family is a beneficiary of the particular benefit:
    (a) Health insurance plan;
    (b) Life insurance;
    (c) Pension, profit sharing, or retirement income program;
    (d) Expense and/or drawing accounts;
    (e) Credit cards (include reimbursement for business expenses placed on your personal credit cards);
    (f) Disability insurance;
    (g) Stock purchase options;
    (h) Indicate whether you are required to pay for all or any part of the benefits listed in this interrogatory and the amount of those payments and/or contributions.

18. If you are furnished with a vehicle by any person, employer, or other entity, state:
    (a) The year, make, model, and license number;
    (b) The name and address of the legal owner;
    (c) The name and address of the registered owner;
    (d) The date you were furnished with such vehicle or replacement vehicle;
    (e) The amount paid for gas, repairs, maintenance, and insurance costs by you personally and by anyone other than yourself. Indicate whether you are reimbursed directly or indirectly for the expenses paid by you personally.

       *If this vehicle is leased, attach a copy of said lease.

19. Describe any other property or other benefit furnished to you as a result of your present employment.

20. State and itemize all deductions taken from your gross weekly earnings or other emoluments, including but not limited to taxes, insurance, savings, loans, pensions, profit sharing, dues, and stock options.

21. State if you have an employment contract with any company, corporation, partnership, and/or individual at the present time or at any time during the last three (3) years. If there is or was such a contract of employment, state the terms thereof, or if written, attach a copy hereto.

Continued

□ **EXHIBIT 10.1   Interrogatories—*Continued***

22. As a result of your employment at any time during the marriage, are you entitled to receive any monies from any deferred compensation agreement? If so, for each agreement state:
   (a) The date such agreement was made, or if in writing, executed. If written, attach a copy.
   (b) The parties making or executing such agreement.
   (c) The amount you are to receive under such deferred compensation agreement and when you are to receive same. Attach copies of evidence of such payment.

23. State whether you have filed federal, state, and/or local income tax returns during the last five (5) years. If so, indicate the years during which they were filed and whether federal, state, or local.
   *Attach copies of all returns filed during the past five (5) years.

24. State in which bank savings account or checking account your salary, bonus, or other compensation is deposited, giving the name of the bank, branch, and account number. If said salary, bonus, or other compensation checks are cashed or negotiated rather than deposited, indicate the name and branch of the bank(s) or other institutions where said checks are regularly cashed or negotiated.

25. State whether you have received or are receiving any form of compensation, monetary or otherwise, from any work and/or services performed for other individuals, companies, corporations, and/or partnerships outside the business in which you are regularly engaged. If so, state:
   (a) The name and address of the individual, company, corporation, and/or partnership from whom you are receiving or have received such compensation during the last five (5) years;
   (b) The amount of the compensation received;
   (c) The nature of the services rendered by you for said compensation.
       *Attach copies of all 1099 forms covering "miscellaneous income" received as a result of such work and/or services during the last five (5) years.

26. State whether your salary or other compensation will increase during the next year and/or contract period as a result of any union contract and/or employment contract, or as the result of any regular incremental increase, or as a result of a promotion you have received that is not yet effective.

27. Itemize all income benefits and other emoluments not already included in your answers to the preceding interrogatories, including but not limited to any other sources of income such as pensions, annuities, inheritances, retirement plans, social security benefits, military and/or veteran's benefits, lottery prizes, bank interest, dividends, showing the source, amount, and frequency of payment of each. Indicate whether each income benefit and/or other emolument is taxable or nontaxable.

SELF-EMPLOYMENT

28. If you are self-employed or conduct a business or profession as a sole proprietor, partner, or corporation, state the type of entity it is. (For purposes of this question, a corporation includes any corporation in which your interest exceeds twenty percent (20%) of the outstanding stock).

29. If a partnership, list the names and addresses of all partners, their relationship to you, and the extent of their interest and yours in the partnership.
   *Attach copies of any partnership agreements in effect at any time during the last five (5) years and all partnership tax returns filed during this period.

30. If a corporation, list the names and addresses of all directors, officers, and shareholders and the percentage of outstanding shares held by each. If any of the foregoing people are related to you, indicate the relationship.
   *Attach copies of all corporate tax returns filed by the corporation during the past five (5) years.

31. State whether you have had an ownership interest(s) in any other corporation, partnership, proprietorship, limited venture, or other business during the course of the marriage. If so, state:
   (a) The nature of such interest(s);
   (b) The market value of such interest(s);
   (c) The position held by you with respect to such interest(s) including whether you were an officer, director, partner, etc.;
   (d) The date of acquisition of your interest(s) and the market value of said interest(s) when acquired;
   (e) The value of said interest(s) on the date of your marriage if such interest(s) were acquired before your marriage;
   (f) The date of termination of your ownership interest, if terminated;

Continued

☐ **EXHIBIT 10.1 Interrogatories—*Continued***

(g) The total sale price of the business enterprise, if sold or transferred;

(h) The amount of the compensation received by you and the form of the compensation if other than cash or negotiable instrument as a result of the sale or transfer;

(i) The terms of each agreement of sale or transfer;

(j) The income received by you from the business during the last year prior to the sale or transfer.

32. State for each business, partnership, corporation, or other business entity in which you have an interest, the following:

(a) The amount of your contribution to the original capitalization;

(b) The amount of your contribution for any additional capitalization or loans to the business entity;

(c) The source from which monies were taken for capitalization and/or loans;

(d) The market value of the business entity at the time of the separation of the parties;

(e) The present market value of the business entity if different than (d) above;

(f) The market value of your share of the business entity at the time the separation of the parties if different than (d) above;

(g) The present market value of your share of the business entity if different than (f) above;

(h) The market value of your share of the total value of the business entity at the time of your marriage;

(i) Amount of loans and/or reimbursement of capitalization paid you by the business entity at any time during the past five (5) years; indicate the amount received, the date received, and the disposition of the proceeds;

(j) The present amount maintained in the capital account;

(k) The name and address of all banks or other institutions in which the business entity has or has had, during the past five (5) years, checking, savings, or other accounts, the account numbers of each account, the amount presently contained in each, the amount contained in each at the time of the separation of the parties, and the amount contained in each six (6) months prior to the separation of the parties. If an account was closed prior to the time periods mentioned in this question, that is, prior to six (6) months before the separation of the parties, indicate the amounts in each such account for a three (3) year period prior to the closing account. State the destination of the amount in the account when closed;

(l) The total value of your capital account;

(m) The total value of all accounts receivable;

(n) The dollar value of all work in progress;

(o) The appreciation in the true worth of all tangible personal assets over and above book value;

(p) The total dollar amount of accounts payable;

(q) A list of all liabilities.

33. State the name and address of the following:

(a) All personal and business accountants consulted during the last five (5) years;

(b) All personal, business, or corporate attorneys consulted during the past five (5) years;

(c) Your stockbroker(s);

(d) Your investment advisor(s).

PERSONAL ASSETS

34. Itemize all accounts in banks or other institutions, time deposits, certificates of deposit, savings clubs, Christmas clubs, and checking accounts in your name or in which you have an interest presently or have had an interest during the past five (5) years, stating for each:

(a) The name and address of each depository;

(b) The balance in those accounts as of the date of the separation of the parties;

(c) The present balance;

(d) The balance four (4) months prior to the separation of the parties;

(e) If there is any difference between your answers to (b), (c), and (d) above, specify when the withdrawals were made, who received the benefit of the withdrawals, who made the withdrawal, and where the proceeds of the withdrawals went;

(f) The name and address in which each account is registered, account numbers, and the present location and custodian of the deposit books, check registers, and certificates.

*Attach copies of the monthly statements of such accounts for the past five (5) years and copies of savings account books or savings books and check registers.

Continued

35. State whether you have a safe deposit box either in your name individually, or in the name of a partnership, corporation, or other business entity to which you have access, stating the following:
    (a) The location of the box and box number.
    (b) The name in which it is registered and who, in addition to yourself, has access to the box;
    (c) List the contents of said box in which you claim an interest.

36. If you have any cash in your possession or under your control in excess of one hundred dollars ($100), specify:
    (a) The amount of the cash;
    (b) Where it is located;
    (c) The source of said cash.

37. For each vehicle of any nature in which you have any interest, including, but not limited to, automobiles, trucks, campers, mobile homes, motorcycles, snowmobiles, boats, and airplanes, state:
    (a) The nature of each vehicle;
    (b) Your interest therein;
    (c) The name in which the vehicle is registered;
    (d) The make, model, and year of each;
    (e) The price paid, the date acquired, and the source of the funds used;
    (f) The principal operator of the vehicle since its purchase;
    (g) The present location of the vehicle;
    (h) The name and address of any co-owners;
    (i) The present value of the vehicle.

38. State whether you own any horses or other animals with a value in excess of two hundred fifty dollars ($250). If so, state:
    (a) The date of purchase, the purchase price, and the source of the funds used;
    (b) The type of animals;
    (c) The market value of the animals at the time of the separation of the parties;
    (d) Their present market value if different from (c);
    (e) The names and addresses of any co-owners and the percentage of their interest.

39. List all household goods, furniture, jewelry, and furs with a value in excess of two hundred fifty dollars ($250), in which you have an interest, stating for each:
    (a) The nature of each;
    (b) Your interest therein;
    (c) The price paid, the date acquired, and the source of the funds used;
    (d) The present value of the asset;
    (e) Whether the asset is "marital property," "separate property," or "community property." If you claim the asset is separate property, state your reasons therefor.

40. State whether you own or have an interest in any collections or hobbies, including but not limited to art, stamps, coins, precious metals, antiques, books, and collectibles with an aggregate value in excess of two hundred fifty dollars ($250). If so, state:
    (a) The nature of each;
    (b) Your interest therein and the interest of any co-owners. Also state the names and addresses of all co-owners and their relationship to you;
    (c) A complete itemization of each such collection, showing the price paid, the date acquired, and the source of the funds used;
    (d) The present value of each element of the asset (an "element" means a unit capable of being sold by itself);
    (e) If owned prior to the marriage, the value of each such element at the time of the marriage.

41. State whether you are receiving or are entitled to receive any royalty income. If so, state:
    (a) The basis for such income, including the nature of any composition, copyright, work, or patent from which such income arose;
    (b) The amount of such income during the past five (5) years;
    (c) The terms of any agreement in relation to such composition, copyright, work, or patent.
        *Attach copies of any royalty statement or other invoice verifying such income.

42. State whether you have any legal actions pending for money damages, or whether you are entitled to receive any legal settlements or insurance recoveries. If so, state:
    (a) The amount of money you are demanding in your pleadings, or to which you are entitled as an insurance recovery or legal settlement;

Continued

☐ **EXHIBIT 10.1   Interrogatories—*Continued***

    (b) The court in which the action is or was pending, the caption of the case, and the index or docket number;

    (c) Whether any other person has an interest in the insurance recovery, legal settlement, or pending action and, if so, state their name, address, and the nature of their interest;

    (d) The circumstances resulting in your becoming entitled to the insurance recovery or legal settlement, or the circumstances leading to the commencement of the legal action.

43. State whether you have any HR10 or IRA arrangements. If so, state:

    (a) The date of the creation of each such plan;

    (b) The amounts contributed by you or on your behalf to each such plan;

    (c) The current value of your account under each such plan.

44. State whether you are entitled to receive, or have received during the past five (5) years any gambling awards or prizes, indicating the nature thereof, the amount, when you are to receive the same, and the date you became entitled to the award or prize.

45. State the names and addresses of all persons who owe you money if not indicated in previous interrogatories. Also state as to each:

    (a) The amount thereof;

    (b) When said sum is due;

    (c) The nature of the transaction that entitled you to receive the money and when the transaction took place.

STOCK ASSETS

46. Itemize all shares of stock, securities, bonds, mortgages, and other investments, other than real estate revealed in previous interrogatories, stating for each:

    (a) Identity of each item indicating the type and amount of shares;

    (b) Whose name they are registered in, the names of any co-owners, their interest therein, and their relationship to you;

    (c) The source of the monies from which you purchased the item;

    (d) The original price of each item;

    (e) The market value at the time of the separation of the parties;

    (f) The present market value of each item if different from (e) above;

    (g) The amount of any dividends or other distribution received;

    (h) The present location and custodian of all certificates or evidences of such investments.

    *Attach hereto monthly statements of these securities for the past five (5) years.

47. State whether any of the shares of stock owned by you and listed in any of your previous answers to interrogatories is subject to any cross purchase or redemption agreement. If so, state:

    (a) The date of such agreements;

    (b) The parties to such agreements;

    (c) The event that will bring about the sale or transfer under the agreement;

    (d) The sale price under the agreement.

48. Itemize all shares of stock, securities, bonds, mortgages, and other investments, other than real estate and business entities previously listed in your name or in which you have an interest, which you have sold in the last five (5) years, stating for each:

    (a) The identity of each item indicating the type and amount of shares;

    (b) Whose name they were registered in, including the names of any co-owners, their interest therein, and their relationship to you;

    (c) The source of the monies from which you purchased each item;

    (d) The original price of each item and date of purchase;

    (e) The market value at the time of the separation of the parties;

    (f) The amount of dividends or other distribution received;

    (g) The date each was sold or transferred;

    (h) To whom each was sold or transferred;

    (i) The amount received for each such sale or transfer;

    (j) The disposition and destination of the proceeds of said sale;

    (k) If applicable, the value of each such item at the time of your marriage.

49. Itemize all shares of stock, securities, bonds, mortgages, and other investments purchased by you but held nominally by third persons, stating for each:

    (a) The manner in which the person is holding said investment;

Continued

☐ **EXHIBIT 10.1 Interrogatories—*Continued***

(b) The identity of each item as to type and amount of shares;

(c) Whose name they are registered in, including the names of any co-owners, their interest therein, and their relationship to you;

(d) The source of the monies from which you purchased each item;

(e) The original price of each item;

(f) The market value at the time of the separation of the parties;

(g) The present market value of each item;

(h) The value, if applicable, at the time of your marriage;

(i) The present location and custodian of all certificates or evidence of such investments;

(j) The amount of dividends or other distribution received.

*Attach hereto monthly statements of these securities for the past three (3) years.

50. Are you the holder of any mortgages, accounts receivable, notes, or other evidence of indebtedness not indicated in your answer to previous interrogatories? If so, for each such instrument, state:

(a) The type of instrument;

(b) The date of maturity of such instrument;

(c) The amount of interest payable to you under such instrument;

(d) The nature of the sale or transaction (including the type of merchandise sold) from which the said instrument arose;

(e) The date the instrument was acquired by you.

51. State whether you have any money invested in any business ventures not answered in previous interrogatories. For each such investment, state:

(a) The nature of such investment;

(b) Your share of the interest therein;

(c) The original cost of such investment and the source of monies used for said investment;

(d) The amount of income yielded from the said investment;

(e) The present value of said investment.

52. If, during the course of your marriage, you have received any inheritances, state:

(a) From whom you inherited;

(b) The nature and amount of the inheritance;

(c) The disposition of any of the assets of the inheritance, tracing them to the time of the separation of the parties;

(d) The value of the inheritance at the time of the separation of the parties;

(e) The present value of the inheritance.

53. State whether you expect to receive any future inheritances. If so, state:

(a) From whom you expect to inherit;

(b) The nature and amount of inheritance.

54. State whether you have, during the last five (5) years, sold or transferred any interest in personal property valued in excess of two hundred fifty dollars ($250), and for each such sale or transfer, state:

(a) The nature of the property;

(b) The date of the sale or transfer;

(c) The method of transfer;

(d) The name and address of each purchaser or person receiving title;

(e) The amount received for said transfer or sale;

(f) The disposition of the proceeds of said sale or transfer.

55. State whether you have made any gift of any money or other personal property to friends, relatives, or anyone else during the past five (5) years of a value in excess of two hundred fifty dollars ($250). If so, state:

(a) The name and address of said person and the relationship of that person to you;

(b) The nature and value of the gift or the amount of money given;

(c) The date each gift was given;

(d) The reason for such gift.

TRUSTS

56. State whether you are the grantor, beneficiary, or holder of a power of appointment for any trust created by you, the members of your family, or any other persons or corporations. If so, state:

Continued

☐ **EXHIBIT 10.1 Interrogatories—*Continued***

(a) The date of the trust instrument;

(b) The name of the settlor of each trust;

(c) The name of the beneficiary(ies) of each trust;

(d) The present amount of each trust corpus;

(e) The amount of the trust corpus at the time of the separation of the parties;

(f) The amount of the trust corpus at the time of your marriage, if applicable.

(g) Any restrictions on alienation to which such corpus is subject;

(h) The terms of each trust instrument;

(i) The income earned by the trust during the past five (5) years.

*If there is a trust instrument, attach a copy hereto. If the trustee has rendered an accounting during the past five (5) years attach a copy hereto.

57. List any and all property, assets, or other things of a value in excess of two hundred fifty dollars ($250) that you hold in trust for anyone, stating as to each:

(a) The description of the property, its location, the name and address of the person for whom you hold same, and his or her relationship to you;

(b) The conditions or terms of the trust, including the amounts you are paid as commissions or other compensation for holding such property;

(c) How such property was acquired by you and whether you paid any part of the consideration therefor.

58. List all property or other things of value of any nature or kind with a value in excess or two hundred fifty dollars ($250) that is held in trust for you or that is in the care or custody of another person, corporation, or entity for you, stating for each:

(a) The nature of the property or other thing of value, its location, and custodian;

(b) The name and address of the trustee, if different than above;

(c) The conditions or terms of the trust;

(d) How such property or other thing of value was acquired and who paid the consideration therefor;

(e) The original cost;

(f) The value at the time of the separation of the parties;

(g) The present value if different than (f) above.

*Attach copies of any trust instruments or writings evidencing the above.

INSURANCE

59. List each life insurance policy, annuity policy, disability policy, or other form of insurance not disclosed in a previous interrogatory, stating for each:

(a) The name and address of the insurance company;

(b) The policy number;

(c) The type of policy;

(d) The name and address of the owner of the policy;

(e) The name and address of the present beneficiary of the policy;

(f) If there has been a change of beneficiary in the last five (5) years, give the date of each change and the name and address of each former beneficiary;

(g) The date the policy was issued;

(h) The face amount of the policy;

(i) The annual premium and the name and address of the person paying the premium currently and for the past five (5) years;

(j) The cash surrender value of said policy;

(k) If any loans have been taken out against the policy, the date of each such loan, the person making such loan, the amount of the loan, and the purpose for which the proceeds were utilized;

(l) If said policy has been assigned, the date of the assignment, the name and address of each assignee;

(m) The present custodian of the policy;

(n) If any policy is supplied by an employer, whether it is a condition of employment and under what conditions it terminates.

60. State whether you have surrendered, transferred, or in any way terminated any form of insurance policy for the last five (5) years. If so, state:

(a) The name and address of the insurance company;

Continued

□ **EXHIBIT 10.1   Interrogatories—*Continued***

(b) The number of the policy;

(c) The type of policy;

(d) The name and address of the last or current owner of the policy;

(e) The name and address of the last or present beneficiary of the policy;

(f) The face amount of the policy;

(g) The cash surrender value of the policy at present or just prior to its being surrendered, transferred, or terminated;

(h) The person transferring, surrendering, or terminating said policy;

(i) If any cash was realized from the said transfer, termination, or surrender, the amount realized and for what purposes the proceeds were used.

PENSION AND DISABILITY

61. State whether you are entitled to any pension, profit sharing, or retirement plan. If so, state:

(a) The nature of the plan;

(b) The name and address of the entity or person providing the plan;

(c) Whether your interest in the plan is vested and, if not, the date and conditions under which the plan will vest;

(d) Whether the plan is contributory or noncontributory and, if contributory, the amount you contributed during the marriage;

(e) The amount you earned in the plan during the marriage;

(f) If you have the right to withdraw any monies from the plan, how much money you may withdraw and when;

(g) If you have withdrawn or borrowed any monies from the plan, indicate when and how much was borrowed and whether the money must be returned or repaid;

(h) If there are any survivor benefits, give a brief description thereof.

*Attach copies of all writings concerning the plan(s) in your possession or which are readily available from your employer or pension payor.

62. If you are entitled to any disability benefits, state:

(a) The nature of the disability;

(b) The dollar amount of the award;

(c) The date of payment of the award;

(d) Whether there are any survivor benefits, giving a brief description thereof;

(e) Whether any benefits or awards are presently being claimed by you, litigated, or are being reviewed, indicating the amount thereof if not included above.

EXPENSES

63. Itemize your average monthly expenses in detail [see chart below]. If any of the expenses include support of any other person outside your immediate family, set forth the name and address of such person, and the portion of each expense attributable to each such person supported. (NOTE: All weekly expenses must be multiplied by 4.333 to obtain the monthly expense.) If certain expenses are paid by your employer, spouse, or another party, so indicated by footnoting.

*   *   *   *   *

MONTHLY BUDGET EXPENSE FOR
interrogatory 63

Food _____	Dentists _____
Clothing _____	Orthodontists _____
Mortgage(s) _____	Psychiatrists _____
Property taxes _____	Attorney fees _____
Rent _____	Drugs _____
Utilities _____	Hair care _____
Fuel oil _____	Dry cleaners _____
Telephone _____	Laundry _____
Garbage Collection _____	Veterinarian _____
Water _____	Newspapers _____
Plumbing _____	Magazines _____
Electrician _____	Insurance _____
Doctors _____	Homeowner _____

Continued

☐ **EXHIBIT 10.1 Interrogatories—Continued**

Renter _____	Camp _____
Automobile _____	Household improvements _____
Life _____	Household repairs _____
Hospitalization _____	Apartment maintenance _____
Floater _____	Garden maintenance _____
Umbrella _____	Pool maintenance _____
Disability _____	Termite/pest service _____
Other _____	Tree service _____
Professional dues _____	Water softener _____
Club dues _____	Furniture & appliances _____
Babysitters _____	Furnishings _____
Domestics _____	Contributions _____
Burglar alarm service _____	Vacations _____
Voluntary support payments _____	Christmas presents _____
Court-ordered support payments _____	Chanukah presents _____
Past Due Installment Obligations	Other presents _____
Credit cards _____	Entertainment _____
Auto loans _____	Misc. spending money _____
Personal loans _____	Cable TV _____
Charge accounts _____	Emergencies _____
Credit card fees _____	
Education _____	DETAIL ALL OTHER EXPENSES
Allowances _____	BELOW:
Sports & hobbies _____	
Dancing lessons _____	_____
Music lessons _____	
Sport lessons _____	_____
Auto expenses _____	
Gas _____	_____
Maintenance _____	
Commuting _____	_____
Parking _____	
License & registration _____	_____
Transportation _____	

TOTAL MONTHLY EXPENSES _____

64. State whether anyone contributes to your support, income, or living expenses who has not been included in your answers to a previous interrogatory. If so, state:
    (a) Their names and address;
    (b) Their relationship to you;
    (c) The amount of support, income, or living expenses received by you during the last five (5) years and the frequency of said support, income, or living expenses;
    (d) The reason for said support;
    (e) The nature of said support.

LIABILITIES

65. Set forth a list of all credit card balances, stating:
    (a) The name of the obligor;
    (b) The total amount due at the present time and the amount due at the time of the separation of the parties;
    (c) The minimum monthly payment;
    (d) The name in which the card is listed and the names of all persons entitled to use the card;
    (e) The exact nature of the charges for which the money is owed;
    (f) Who incurred each obligation.
       *Attach copies of all credit card statements for the past twelve (12) months.
66. Set forth in detail any outstanding obligations, including mortgages, conditional sales contracts, contract obligations, promissory notes, or government agency loans not included in your answers to any previous interrogatories, stating for each:

Continued

☐ **EXHIBIT 10.1 Interrogatories—*Continued***

(a) Whether the obligation is individual, joint, or joint and several;
(b) The names and addresses of each creditor, and their relationship to you;
(c) The form of the obligation;
(d) The date the obligation was incurred;
(e) The consideration received for the obligation;
(f) A description of any security given for the obligation;
(g) The amount of the original obligation;
(h) The date of interest on the obligation;
(i) The present unpaid balance of the obligation;
(j) The date and the amount of each installment repayment due;
(k) An itemization of the disposition of the funds received for which the obligation was incurred.

67. List all judgments outstanding against you or your spouse not included in your answer to a previous interrogatory, and for each state:
(a) The names of the parties and their respective attorneys;
(b) The courts in which the judgments were entered and the index or docket number assigned to each case;
(c) The amount of each judgment.

68. If there is a wage execution, judgment, or order to pay out of income and earnings, state:
(a) How much is taken from your earnings each week;
(b) The name and address of obligors, and their relationship to you;
(c) The balance due.

69. State the nature of any lien or security interest not indicated in your answer to a previous interrogatory to which any of the assets listed by you in previous interrogatories are subject, indicating for each:
(a) The name and address of the holder thereof;
(b) The holder's relationship to you;
(c) The amount and frequency of the payments you make thereon;
(d) The balance due.

MISCELLANEOUS

70. If any money, property, and/or asset was acquired by you either before the marriage or after the separation of the parties, state for each with a value in excess of two hundred fifty dollars ($250) the following:
(a) The nature of the property;
(b) The date acquired;
(c) The source of the acquisition;
(d) Your interest therein;
(e) The present market value.

71. If any other money, property, or assets described in the above interrogatory was sold, transferred, or disposed of, state for each:
(a) The manner of the disposition;
(b) The date of the disposition;
(c) To whom sold, transferred, or disposed and their relationship to you;
(d) The amount received.

72. List all gifts received by you from your spouse with a value in excess of one hundred dollars ($100), giving for each:
(a) The date received;
(b) The nature of the gift;
(c) The market value of the gift when given, and currently.

73. List all gifts received by you from your family, your spouse's family, or any other party or entity, with a value in excess of one hundred dollars ($100), giving for each:
(a) The name of the donor and the relationship of the donor to you;
(b) The date received;
(c) The nature of the gift;
(d) The market value of the gift when given, and currently.

74. If you have prepared a financial statement of your assets and liabilities, either individually or for any business in which you have an interest within the past five (5) years, state:

Continued

☐ **EXHIBIT 10.1 Interrogatories—*Continued***

> (a) The dates of all such statements;
> (b) The name and address of the person, firm, company, partnership, corporation, or entity for whom they were prepared;
> (c) The name and address of all persons who worked on the preparation of such statements.
>
> *Attach copies of all such statements.
>
> 75. State what counsel fees you have paid or agreed to pay for services rendered in connection with the separation of the parties.
> 76. State whether you have made application for any loans with any lending institutions, individuals, companies, or corporations during the past five (5) years. If so state for each:
> (a) The name and address of the lending institution, individual, company, or corporation;
> (b) The date of the application;
> (c) The amount of the loan;
> (d) Whether your application was approved or denied.
>
> *Attach a copy of all such loan applications.
>
> 77. List any gift made by you in excess of two hundred fifty dollars ($250) within the past five (5) years. For each such gift, state:
> (a) The name of the donee;
> (b) The reason for the gift;
> (c) The amount of the gift.

(*text continued from p. 196*)

together despite their decision to separate, the law operates on the assumption that there is still hope. By definition, a separation agreement attempts to provide *benefits* to the parties in the form of money, freedom, etc. The very existence of such an agreement is viewed as an *inducement* to obtain a divorce unless the

☐ **EXHIBIT 10.2 Sample Introductory Clauses in a Separation Agreement**

Separation Agreement

THIS AGREEMENT is entered on this _____day of _____ , 19 ___ , by Fred Jones (referred to in this agreement as the Husband), residing at _____ , and by Linda Jones (referred to in this agreement as the Wife), residing at _____ .

Witnesseth:

WHEREAS, the parties were married on _____ , 19 ___ in the state of _____ _____ , city of _____ , and

WHEREAS, _____ children were born of this marriage: (here list each child with dates of birth)

WHEREAS, as a result of irreconcilable marital disputes, the parties have been voluntarily living apart since _____ , 19 ___ which both parties feel is in their own best interests and that of their children, and

WHEREAS, both parties wish to enter this agreement for the purpose of settling all custody, support, and property rights between them, and any other matter pertaining to their marriage relationship, and

WHEREAS, both parties acknowledge that they have had separate and independent legal advice from counsel of their own choosing on the advisability of entering this agreement, that they have not been coerced or pressured into entering the agreement, and that they voluntarily decide to enter it.

NOW THEREFORE, in consideration of the promises and the mutual commitments contained in this agreement, the parties agree as follows:

> [the full text of the agreement goes here in numbered paragraphs; sample clauses are found at the end of this chapter.]

Conducive to Divorce
Tending to encourage or contribute to divorce.

Public Policy The principles inherent in the customs, morals, and notions of justice that prevail in a state. The foundation of public laws. The principles that are naturally and inherently right and just.

parties have already separated or are about to do so shortly. A separation agreement between two parties who are still living together and who intend to remain together indefinitely might be declared unenforceable. It would be the equivalent of one spouse saying to another, "If you leave me now, I'll give you $25,000." The agreement is invalid because it is **conducive to divorce.** This is against **public policy.**

Another kind of illegal agreement is an attempted "private divorce." Suppose a husband and wife enter the following brief separation agreement:

> "We hereby declare that our marriage is over and that we will have nothing to do with each other henceforth. As we part, we ask nothing of each other."

Assume further that this agreement is not shown to anyone. To permit parties to make such a contract would be to enable them to divorce themselves without the involvement of a court. At the time the parties attempted to enter this contract, it may have seemed fair and sensible. Suppose, however, that months or years later, the wife finds herself destitute. If she sues her husband for support or alimony, he cannot defend the action by raising her contract commitment not to ask anything of him. If either of them later tries to marry someone else, he or she will have no defense against a charge of bigamy.

Collusion (1) An agreement to commit fraud. (2) An agreement between a husband and wife in a divorce proceeding that one or both will lie to the court to facilitate obtaining the divorce.

A more serious kind of illegal agreement between husband and wife involves **collusion.** An example would be a plaintiff in a divorce action who falsely asserts that the defendant deserted her on a certain date, and the defendant falsely admits to this or remains silent even though he knows that the assertion is false. Their *collusive* objective is usually to *facilitate* the granting of the divorce. Before no-fault divorce became part of our legal system (see chapter 13), this kind of falsehood was common. Another example is a clause in a separation agreement providing that if either party later seeks a divorce, the other party will not appear or will not raise any defenses to the divorce action even if the parties know that such defenses exist. Such an agreement would be invalid because it is collusive, improperly inducing divorce.

The rule that separation agreements are invalid if they are conducive to divorce has been criticized as unrealistic since it is difficult to imagine a mutually acceptable separation agreement involving future divorce that does *not* in some way facilitate or encourage the parties to go through with the divorce. Nevertheless, courts continue to watch for improper facilitation and collusion. The coming of no-fault divorce has lessened a court's inclination to invalidate a separation agreement for these reasons. Since divorce has been made much easier to obtain because of no-fault grounds, courts are more reluctant to try to save the marriage at all costs and more willing to let the separation agreement be the vehicle through which the parties confront the inevitable. This is not to say that courts will no longer be concerned with collusion and agreements that are conducive to divorce. These prohibitions are still on the books. The atmosphere, however, has changed with no-fault. Most of the court decisions on these prohibitions were decided before the arrival of no-fault. It is questionable how willing courts are to follow all of those decisions today.

Below are a series of clauses sometimes found in separation agreements with comments on how the courts have treated the issues of divorce facilitation and collusion raised by the clauses.

> "The wife agrees that she will file for a divorce against the husband within three months."
>
> "None of the terms of this separation agreement shall be effective unless and until either of the parties is granted a divorce."

The first clause is invalid; a party cannot promise to file for a divorce. The clause does not merely encourage divorce, it makes it almost inevitable. The second clause appears to be as bad as or worse than the first. Neither of the parties will obtain any of the benefits in the separation agreement unless one of them obtains a divorce. Arguably, this clause encourages one of the parties to file for divorce and the other party to refrain from contesting the divorce. Oddly, however, the courts have not interpreted the second clause in this way. It *is* legal to condition the entire separation agreement on the granting of a divorce. The logic of this result is not entirely clear, but the courts so hold.

> "The wife agrees that if the husband files for divorce, she will not raise any defenses to his action."
>
> "In the event that the wife travels to another state to file for divorce, the husband agrees to go to that state, appear in the action, and participate therein."

The first clause is collusive. If a party has a defense, it is improper to agree not to assert it. Even if you are not sure whether you have a defense, it is collusive to agree in advance to refrain from asserting whatever defense you *might* have. Courts consider this as improper as an agreement to destroy or to conceal important evidence.

The second clause is more troublesome. Here the parties are clearly contemplating an out-of-state divorce, perhaps because they both realize that they would have difficulty establishing the grounds for divorce in their own state. Such **migratory divorces** were once quite common. Is a clause conducive to divorce if it obligates the defendant to appear in the foreign divorce action? Some states think that it is and would invalidate the agreement. Other states, however, would uphold the agreement.

Migratory Divorce A divorce obtained in a state to which one or both parties traveled before returning to their original state.

ASSIGNMENT 10.1

Determine whether any of the following clauses improperly facilitate divorce or are collusive. (See General Instructions for the Legal-Analysis Assignment in chapter 1.)

a. "In the event that the wife files a divorce action, the husband agrees not to file any defenses to said action if and only if it is clear to both parties that the husband has no defense."

b. "In the event that the wife files a divorce action, the husband will pay in advance all expenses incurred by the wife in bringing said action."

c. "In the event that the wife files for a judicial separation, for separate maintenance, or for an annulment, the husband agrees to cooperate fully in the wife's action."

ASSIGNMENT 10.2

a. Locate a digest containing small paragraph summaries of court opinions from your state. (For the kinds of digests that exist, see chapter 2.) Find those parts of the digest that deal with separation agreements. List any ten key topics and numbers that cover any aspect of separation agreements.

b. Are there any statutes in your state code dealing with separation agreements? If so, briefly summarize any five. (See General Instructions for the State-Code Assignment in chapter 1.)

CAPACITY TO CONTRACT

There was a time in our history when the very thought of a wife entering a contract with her husband was anathema. A married woman lacked the *capacity to contract* with her husband. At common law, the husband and wife were one, and "the one" was the husband! You cannot make a contract with yourself. This rule, of course, has been changed. A wife can enter a contract with her husband (although the Internal Revenue Service and the husband's creditors are often suspicious of such contracts, especially when the result is to place property purchased by the husband in the name of the wife). Linda Jones is no longer denied the right to enter a separation agreement (a contract) with Fred Jones simply because she is his wife.

Today, the major question of capacity involves mental health. A separation agreement is invalid if either party lacked the capacity to understand the agreement and the consequences of signing it. The traditional test is as follows: The person must understand the nature and consequences of his or her act at the time of the transaction. This understanding may not exist due to insanity, mental retardation, senility, temporary delirium due to an accident, intoxication, drug addition, etc.

DURESS AND FRAUD

In the excerpt from the Jones separation agreement in Exhibit 10.2, you will note that several times at the beginning of the agreement the parties mention that they are entering it "voluntarily." According to traditional contract principles, if a party enters a contract because of **duress,** it will not be enforced. Suppose that a wife is physically threatened if she does not sign the separation agreement. Clearly the agreement would not be valid. The husband could not sue her for breaching it or attempt to enforce it in any other way.

Of course, simply because the separation agreement says that the parties enter it "voluntarily" does not necessarily mean that no duress existed. Either spouse could have been forced to say the agreement was signed "voluntarily." But to have the agreement say that it was "voluntarily" signed is at least *some* indication (however slight) that no duress existed, although an **aggrieved** party can introduce evidence to the contrary.

During discussions and negotiations, if a spouse lies about a major asset that he or she possesses, the separation agreement must be set aside for **fraud.** If the spouse fails to disclose or undervalues assets, many courts will again invalidate the agreement unless its terms are deemed to be fair to the other spouse.

Suppose that after signing the separation agreement, a party becomes destitute or near-destitute. Some courts will intervene and not allow him or her to suffer the consequences of a bad bargain in the separation agreement, even if there was no clear evidence of duress or fraud. At one time, many courts presumed that a husband took unfair advantage of his wife unless he demonstrated otherwise. These courts did not allow the husband to treat his wife **at arm's length** as he would a competitor in a commercial transaction. The women's movement has helped change this attitude. Courts no longer so blatantly protect women. Both sides will be forced to live with the agreement they signed, particularly if there was full disclosure of assets, no duress or fraud, both had the opportunity to seek independent advice before they signed, and neither is about to become a public charge.

The last WHEREAS clause in the beginning of the Jones separation agreement in Exhibit 10.2 states that both Fred and Linda had the benefit of separate legal advice on the advantages and disadvantages of signing the agreement. As indicated, this fact can be very significant in a court's deliberation on whether

Duress Coercion; acting under the pressure of an unlawful act or threat.

Aggrieved Injured or wronged; the person injured or wronged.

Fraud Knowingly making a false statement of present fact with the intention that the plaintiff rely on the statement. The plaintiff's reasonable reliance on the statement harms him or her.

At Arm's Length As between two strangers who are looking out for their own self-interests. At a distance; without trusting the other's fairness; free of personal bias or control.

to set the agreement aside on a ground such as duress. It is relatively difficult to challenge the validity of a separation agreement that was signed after both sides had the benefit of their own attorney—even though the spouse with most of the resources may have had to pay for both attorneys.

The following case of *Bell v. Bell* contains some of the factors that a court will consider when the validity of a separation agreement is called into question because of duress or other improper conduct:

CASE

BELL V. BELL

38 Md. App. 10, 379 A.2d 419 (1977)
Court of Special Appeals of Maryland

Background: *Diane and Stanley Bell entered a separation agreement and executed eleven deeds pursuant to the agreement. Diane asked the circuit court to cancel the agreement and the deeds on the ground that they were obtained by duress and undue influence. The chancellor in the circuit court denied this request. The case is now on appeal before the Court of Special Appeals of Maryland where Diane is the appellant and Stanley is the appellee.*

Decision on Appeal: *Decree of circuit court affirmed. The separation agreement and deeds should not be set aside.*

Opinion of the Court:

Justice THOMPSON delivered the opinion of the court. . . .

The facts that gave rise to this suit are as follows. Diane Bell consulted an attorney in July of 1975, concerning the preparation of a separation agreement. The agreement was prepared and Mrs. Bell presented it to Mr. Bell at home on the morning of August 27, 1975. After examining the agreement at his place of business Mr. Bell inserted several changes and gave it to his secretary for retyping. Two significant changes were made in the agreement. The original provided for child support in the amount of $700 per month. This figure in the amended agreement was reduced to $300. Mr. Bell's agreement also provided for the disposition of the eleven houses owned by the parties as tenants by the entireties. Under his agreement Mrs. Bell was to receive one of the houses while he retained the other ten. After his agreement was completed he telephoned the appellant and asked her to come to his office in Wheaton to sign the agreement. At that time no mention was made of the changes.

When Mrs. Bell arrived, Mr. Bell suggested that they go to the nearby offices of Ralph Duane Real Estate Co. so that they could discuss the agreement in private. Prior to Mrs. Bell's arrival Mr. Bell had prepared a series of sixteen 3 × 5 cards containing phrases such as "the man," "the kids," "his carrier," "your name," and "Ingrid (accessory)." During the course of the meeting he used these cards to inform the appellant of an investigation of her activities by private detectives and his knowledge of her adulterous affair with a police lieutenant. He also informed her that he knew that many of the contacts occurred at the apartment of her friend, Ingrid Gibson. He then presented his version of the separation agreement and made it clear that unless she signed it he would reveal her relationship to the Internal Affairs section of the police department and to the newspapers. Several times during the course of the conversation Mrs. Bell threatened to leave or requested an opportunity to consult with her attorney, but on each occasion, Mr. Bell threatened to "start the ball rolling" if such attempts were made before the agreement was signed. Mr. Bell placed a tape recorder in the office and recorded the entire conversation without the knowledge of Mrs. Bell. The tape was introduced into evidence.

After Mrs. Bell registered several protests, she read through the agreement and negotiated with Mr. Bell to make several changes. Among these changes was the receipt of a total of $15,000 in cash in addition to the one house. Under the agreement that was signed Mr. Bell received approximately $163,000 worth of property that was previously owned as tenants by the entireties while Mrs. Bell settled for approximately $45,000 in cash and property.*

The appellant argues that a confidential relationship existed between the parties and the burden was on the appellee to show the agreement was fair in all respects. In order to establish a confidential relationship one must show that by virtue of the relationship between them, he is justified in assuming the other party will not act in a manner inconsistent with his welfare. Unlike many jurisdictions, Maryland does not presume the existence of a confidential relationship in transactions between husband and wife. . . . In Maryland there has been a presumption that the husband is the dominant figure in the marriage. In *Manos v. Papachrist*, 199 Md. 257, 262, 86 A.2d 474, 476 (1951), the Court noted:

---

*The property Mr. Bell received had a gross value of $597,000 but was subject to mortgages totalling $434,339.

"Ordinarily the relationship of husband and wife is a confidential one. Of course, in any given case it is a question of fact whether the marital relationship is such as to give the husband dominance over his wife or to put him in a position where words of persuasion have undue weight. Generally, however, on account of the natural dominance of the husband over the wife, and the confidence and trust usually incident to their marriage, a court of equity will investigate a gift from a wife to her husband with utmost care, especially where it strips her of all her property; and the burden of proof is on the husband to show that there was no abuse of confidence, but that the gift was fair in all respects, was fully understood, and was not induced by fraud or undue influence."

We noted the questionable foundation upon which this presumption rests in light of Article 46 of the Maryland Declaration of Rights, better known as the Equal Rights Amendment, in *Trupp v. Wolff*, 24 Md. App. 588, n. 15, 335 A.2d 171 (1975). . . . Since that decision, the Court of Appeals has held that sex classifications are no longer permissible under the amendment. . . . Consequently, the presumption of dominance cannot stand.

When the presumption is disregarded the question of whether a confidential relationship exists between husband and wife becomes a question of fact. Among the various factors to be considered in determining whether a confidential relationship exists are the age, mental condition, education, business experience, state of health, and degree of dependence of the spouse in question. . . .

The testimony shows that Mrs. Bell was born in Europe, moved to this country when she was eleven years old, and left school at the age of fifteen. Although she is employed as a beautician, she has relatively little experience or expertise in business matters. On the other hand, Mr. Bell is an experienced businessman, possesses a real estate license, and has a college degree. The chancellor considered these facts, but found that no confidential relationship existed primarily because Mrs. Bell negotiated several changes in the agreement and questioned other provisions, as is clearly shown by the tape recording. He found there was a lack of trust and confidence in the other party necessary to the establishment of a confidential relationship. We are unable to say his decision on this issue was clearly erroneous. Md. Rule 1086.

Absent proof of a confidential relationship between the parties, separation agreements, not disclosing any injustice or inequity on their face, are presumptively valid and the burden is on the party challenging the agreement to show its execution resulted from coercion, fraud, or mistake. *Cronin v. Hebditch*, 195 Md. 607, 74 A.2d 50 (1950). . . .

The only inequity claimed by the appellant is that she relinquished her one half interest in approximately $210,000 worth of real estate for approximately $45,000 in property and cash. This disparity in consideration is not sufficient to show that the agreement was unjust or inequitable. The cases which have found agreements to be unjust or inequitable on their face involved agreements that were completely lacking in any reasonable consideration. *Cronin v. Hebditch*, supra; *Eaton v. Eaton*, 34 Md. App. 157, 366 A.2d 121 (1976). In *Cronin* the wife signed an agreement releasing all her rights in property totalling more than $700,000 for a mere $10,000 and the Court of Appeals voided the agreement. More recently, in *Eaton* we struck down an agreement in which rights in $200,000 to $250,000 worth of property were released for $4,300. There we said:

" '[The] defendant in this case has ostensibly purchased far more cheaply than a Court of Equity can condone all of the plaintiff's rights "of whatsoever kind or nature originating in and growing out of the marriage status." ' " 34 Md. App. at 162, 366 A.2d at 124.

As we are unable to say the agreement in question was lacking in any reasonable consideration, *Cronin* and *Eaton* cannot be used to relieve the appellant from proving the agreement was the product of duress or undue influence.*

The appellant's claim of duress or undue influence rests on the threats of Stanley Bell to notify the Internal Affairs section of the Police Department and the newspapers of her adulterous relationship unless the agreement was signed. Mr. Bell also stated that such disclosures would ruin the career of her lover and Ingrid Gibson, as well as her reputation in the community. The chancellor construed these statements as being no more than a threat to institute a divorce action on the grounds of adultery.

In order to establish duress there must be a wrongful act which deprives a person of the exercise of his

---

*We are aware that some cases in other jurisdictions have created a presumption of invalidity where the consideration given is grossly disproportionate to the consideration received or is otherwise unfair. See *Le Bert-Francis v. Le Bert-Francis*, 194 A.2d 662 (D.C. 1963) (where separation agreement is unfair it is presumed to be invalid and the burden is on the party seeking to enforce it to prove otherwise); *Demaggio v. Demaggio*, 317 So. 2d 848 (Fla. App. 1975) (presumption of fraud created where agreement was grossly disproportionate, husband concealed assets, and wife was unrepresented by counsel); *Davis v. Davis*, 24 Ohio Misc. 17, 258 N.E.2d 277 (1970) (where provisions are disproportionate burden is on party seeking to uphold agreement to show there was full disclosure and the agreement was signed voluntarily).

In the absence of a confidential relationship, we see no reason to shift the burden of proof because the parties were husband and wife and one of them made a bargain which now seems unfair, but is not grossly unfair.

free will. . . . Although we have found no Maryland case discussing the issue whether a threat to institute a civil suit can furnish a legally sufficient basis for duress, the question has been considered by a number of courts in other jurisdictions. Under these cases such suits do not form a legally sufficient basis for duress where the threat to institute the suit is made in good faith. . . . The courts have stated the assertion of a claim with the knowledge there is no reasonable belief of success or that it is false, amounts to bad faith and is a sufficient basis for a claim of duress. . . . Even though a particular act is legal, if it is wrongful in the moral sense a number of authorities have held that it can be used to establish a claim of duress. . . . *Link v. Link,* 278 N.C. 181, 179 S.E.2d 697 (1971).

The appellant argues that a threatened civil suit can be wrongful in a moral sense where it is used to coerce a settlement in a transaction unrelated to the subject matter of the suit. In support of this argument she relies on *Link v. Link,* supra. In *Link* the husband threatened to institute divorce proceedings against the wife and seek custody of their children unless the wife signed an agreement transferring her individual property to the husband. In deciding the case the Court noted the general rule that threats to institute civil proceedings are not wrongful but went on to state:

"The law with reference to duress has, however, undergone an evolution favorable to the victim of oppressive action or threats. The weight of modern authority supports the rule, which we here adopt, that the act done or threatened may be wrongful even though not unlawful, per se; and that the threat to institute legal proceedings, criminal or civil, which might be justifiable, per se, becomes wrongful, within the meaning of this rule, if made with the corrupt intent to coerce a transaction grossly unfair to the victim and not related to the subject of such proceedings." 179 S.E.2d at 705. . . .

We find the reasoning of *Link* to be persuasive. Applying this approach to the case before us we think there was a legally sufficient basis for a finding of duress.

Mr. Bell threatened an action for divorce on the grounds of adultery to force a property settlement be-tween the parties. Although the threatened action and the separation agreement both relate to the marital status of the parties, their substance is significantly different. . . . Mr. Bell's threats of a civil suit for divorce were unrelated to the dispute over the property and were made to obtain Mrs. Bell's signature on an agreement.

Even though the chancellor concluded that there was no wrongful conduct he went on to note in his opinion that even if the actions were considered wrongful, they did not deprive Mrs. Bell of her free will. . . . In support of this finding he noted that Mrs. Bell actively negotiated with Mr. Bell concerning various provisions in the agreement. At one point in the conversation she stated: "Umm, I'm just trying to get you know as much as I can which is, you have to admit, you'd do the same thing." Although there was testimony that Mrs. Bell was extremely upset after the agreement was signed, there was other testimony to the contrary. The chancellor considered this evidence and concluded:

"[T]he negotiations and the tenor of the parties' meeting indicate quite clearly that the Plaintiff, in order to avoid an embarrassing incident involving her and close friends, freely and voluntarily negotiated with her husband."

The question of whether Mrs. Bell was deprived of her free will was one of fact and as there is ample evidence to support this finding, we are unable to say it was clearly erroneous. . . . In other words, there is no rule of law that precludes a woman from giving away a substantial portion of her property to save her reputation, if it is her voluntary act. Although on the evidence we may have found the act involuntary, we must accept the chancellor's findings because of his superior position to make this subtle distinction. . . .

[T]he chancellor found on the merits that the appellant did not act under duress or undue influence. We have accepted his finding because there was evidence to support it. . . .

DECREE AFFIRMED.

APPELLANT TO PAY THE COSTS.

---

a. Was Diane Bell coerced into signing the separation agreement? Was there coercion?

b. Conduct a debate in class on whether the separation agreement should have been enforced. Assume that there is a higher court in Maryland and that Diane appeals to this higher court. Make arguments to this court on behalf of Diane and on behalf of Stanley.

c. Assume that the facts of *Bell v. Bell* arose in your state. How would the case be decided? (If your state is Maryland, answer this question based on the law of any other state. See General Instructions for the Court-Opinion Assignment in chapter 1.)

ASSIGNMENT 10.3

d. Does a separation agreement have to be fair to both parties to be enforceable in your state? Check the statutes and the court opinions of your state. (See General Instructions for the State-Code Assignment and General Instructions for the Court-Opinion Assignment in chapter 1.)

CONSIDERATION

Consideration
Something of value that is exchanged between the parties, e.g., an exchange of promises to do something or to refrain from doing something.

Contracts must be supported by **consideration** to be valid. The separation agreement is a set of promises by the parties of what they will do. The exchange of these promises (some of which may have already been performed, at least in part, at the time the agreement is signed) is the consideration for the separation agreement. A wife's promise to relinquish all claims she may have against her husband's estate when he dies is an example of her consideration to him. A husband's promise to transfer to his wife full title to land he solely owns is an example of his consideration to her.

We have already seen, however, that certain kinds of consideration are improper. A couple, for example, cannot exchange promises that one party will file for divorce and the other party will refrain from asserting any defenses he or she might have. Such consideration is illegal because it is conducive to divorce, and may be collusive.

Perhaps the main consideration in the separation agreement involves the separation itself. A husband and wife have the right to live with each other as husband and wife, i.e., the right of cohabitation. By reason of the separation agreement, the parties promise each other that they will never again claim this cohabitation right.

■■■■ ALIMONY PAYMENTS AND PROPERTY DIVISION: INTRODUCTION

Alimony The amount of money or other property paid in fulfillment of a duty to support one's spouse after a separation or divorce.

Property Division The distribution of property accumulated by spouses as a result of their joint efforts during the marriage. (Sometimes referred to as a **property settlement**.)

Arrears Payments that are due but have not been made. (Also called **arrearages**.)

Outstanding Unpaid.

Discharged Released; forgiven so that the debt is no longer owed.

We now begin our coverage of **alimony** and **property division.** These two concepts are sometimes confused. A separation agreement (or a court opinion) may refer to a property division but mean *both* support and property division. In part, the confusion may be due to the fact that in the minds of the husband and wife, there is not always a clear distinction between these two concepts.

Exhibit 10.3 presents some major consequences of the distinction between alimony and property division. These consequences must be understood before examining the options available to the parties in drafting those clauses of the separation agreement that cover alimony and property division.

EFFECT OF BANKRUPTCY

Under most forms of bankruptcy, citizens can eliminate all or most of their debts in order to make a fresh start. If a husband has fallen behind on his obligation under a separation agreement or a divorce decree, all **arrears** constitute a debt to his wife. Each time an alimony payment becomes due, a new debt is created. All **outstanding** obligations under a property division agreement are also debts. When a debtor goes into bankruptcy, some of his or her debts are **discharged.** Which ones? The Bankruptcy Act of Congress provides as follows:

A discharge . . . does not discharge an individual debtor from any debt . . . to a spouse, former spouse, or child of the debtor, for alimony to, maintenance for, or support of

☐ **EXHIBIT 10.3 Alimony and Property Division Terms of a Separation Agreement**

EFFECT OF BANKRUPTCY	
Alimony	*Property Division*
If the spouse with the obligation to pay alimony goes into bankruptcy, his or her obligation to pay alimony is *not* discharged. All unpaid or delinquent alimony debts are still owed.	Under certain circumstances, a spouse may be able to discharge his or her property division debt through bankruptcy.

EFFECT OF REMARRIAGE AND DEATH	
Alimony	*Property Division*
If the person receiving alimony obtains a divorce and remarries, the alimony payments stop unless the separation agreement specifically provides otherwise. If the person paying alimony remarries, the alimony payments to the first spouse must continue unless a court provides otherwise. If the husband or wife dies, alimony payments cease unless the separation agreement specifically provides otherwise.	Remarriage or death of either party does not affect the terms of the property division. All remaining obligations under the property division must be fulfilled regardless of remarriage or death.

AVAILABILITY OF CONTEMPT	
Alimony	*Property Division*
If a party fails to fulfill an alimony obligation and falls into arrears, the power of the court to punish for contempt can be used as an enforcement device if the separation agreement has been incorporated and merged into a later divorce decree.	If either party fails to fulfill the obligations under the property division, states differ on whether the contempt power of the court can be used as an enforcement device. Many states say that it cannot.

THE COURT'S POWER TO MODIFY TERMS	
Alimony	*Property Division*
If the alimony terms of the separation agreement later prove to be seriously inadequate, the court sometimes has the power to modify those terms in order to require more alimony to be paid.	If either party later becomes dissatisfied with the terms of an otherwise valid property division, the court will rarely, if ever, modify those terms.

FEDERAL INCOME TAX TREATMENT	
Alimony	*Property Division*
Alimony payments are includible in the gross income of the payee and are deductible for the payor.	Transfers of property incident to a divorce are not reportable as income by the transferee nor deductible by the transferor. The basis of the property in the hands of the transferee is the same as the transferor's basis.

such spouse or child, in connection with a separation agreement, divorce decree or other order of a court of record. . . . 11 U.S.C.A. § 523(a)(5).

Hence, debts in the nature of spousal or child support survive bankruptcy; they are not discharged. Property division debts, however, are treated differently. In general, they also are not dischargeable. But under two special circumstances, they *are* dischargeable: first, the spouse who owes the obligation (the debtor) proves that he or she does not have enough assets to pay the property division debt plus all his or her other legitimate debts, *or* second, the debtor proves that the benefit of discharging the property division debt outweighs the harm or detriment to the other spouse.[1]

This has a number of practical consequences. Assume that the husband is in serious financial difficulties and that bankruptcy is a possibility (a fact that must be carefully investigated by the lawyer and paralegal representing the wife). The wife may be advised in the negotiation stage of the separation agreement to accept a small property division in exchange for a high amount of alimony. In the event that a bankruptcy does occur, she does not want to take the risk that he will be able to prove to the Bankruptcy Court that he fits within one of the two special circumstances that allow a discharge of property division debts. If he can, she loses everything still owed under the property division, whereas the alimony debt always survives the bankruptcy.

EFFECT OF REMARRIAGE AND DEATH

Normally a spouse will want to stop paying alimony in the event that the receiving spouse remarries. But alimony that ends upon the receiving spouse's remarriage can be an incentive *not* to remarry. To offset this, at least to some extent, the separation agreement might provide that alimony payments will continue after the remarriage of the receiving spouse, but at a lower amount.

If the paying spouse remarries, his or her alimony obligation continues unless modified by a court.

If either party dies, alimony payments cease, unless the separation agreement specifically provides otherwise. The separation agreement, for example, could provide that the alimony payments will continue after the death of the husband at which time the wife would collect the alimony from his **estate** or from a trust fund set up by him. Furthermore, the husband might take out a life insurance policy payable on his death to his wife. This, in effect, continues some measure of support for the wife after he dies. Absent such provisions, the death of the paying spouse terminates the alimony obligation in most states.

Estate All the property left by the deceased. After being used to pay debts, this property is distributed to those entitled under the will or the intestacy laws.

The situation is entirely different with respect to property division commitments; they continue no matter who dies or remarries. For example, as part of a property division (having nothing to do with support), John agrees to pay Mary $25,000. After John has paid Mary $1,000 of this amount, he dies. Mary can make a claim against John's estate for $24,000. If Mary died after John paid the $1,000, her estate could require John to pay the remaining $24,000 to it (i.e., to Mary's estate) for distribution according to Mary's will or according to the laws of intestacy. The same is true if either party remarries. The funds or other property owed under the property division clauses of the separation agreement remain due and owing no matter who remarries.

AVAILABILITY OF CONTEMPT

When one of the parties breaches a term of the separation agreement, ensuing legal action may depend upon whether the agreement is incorporated

---

1. 11 U.S.C.A. § 523 (a)(15): An individual debtor will not be discharged from any non-support debt incurred by the debtor in the course of a divorce or separation or in connection with a separation agreement unless:

    (A) the debtor does not have the ability to pay such debt from income or property of the debtor not reasonably necessary to be expended for the maintenance or support of the debtor or a dependent of the debtor and, if the debtor is engaged in a business, for the payment of expenditures necessary for the continuation, preservation, and operation of such business; or

    (B) discharging such debt would result in a benefit to the debtor that outweighs the detrimental consequences to a spouse, former spouse, or child of the debtor. . . .

and merged into a subsequent divorce decree. If it is not, the regular breach-of-contract remedies are available, e.g., suit for damages, suit to rescind the contract. The sanctions for **contempt** (e.g., fine, prison) are *not* available. To some extent, the picture changes if the divorce decree incorporates and merges with the separation agreement. Alimony provisions *can* be enforced by the contempt powers of the court when there is incorporation and merger. States differ on whether the property division terms of a separation agreement can also be enforced by contempt. Many states say that it cannot. The sanction of contempt, however, is usually available when a party has violated a specific court order to transfer property.

Contempt Obstructing or assailing the authority or dignity of the court such as by intentionally violating a court order.

COURT'S POWER TO MODIFY TERMS

Courts will not modify an alimony term unless the ex-spouse is about to become a public charge or is facing serious financial difficulties due to a change of circumstances since the time he or she signed the separation agreement containing the original alimony term. A property division term, on the other hand, is rarely, if ever, modifiable by a court.

FEDERAL INCOME TAX TREATMENT

The federal tax implications of alimony and property division in a separation agreement will be treated in detail in chapter 15.

DISTINGUISHING BETWEEN ALIMONY AND PROPERTY DIVISION

As you can see, it can make a great deal of difference whether a term of a separation agreement is classified as alimony or as property division. The classification hinges on the intent of the parties at the time they entered the separation agreement. For example, did the parties intend a five-year annual payment of $50,000 to be alimony or property division? Unfortunately, it is often difficult to answer this question. As indicated earlier, the parties may either be confused about the distinction or pay no attention to it. At a later date, however, when the parties realize the importance of the distinction (e.g., at tax time or when bankruptcy occurs), they will probably make conflicting claims about what their intentions were. It is the court's job to turn the clock back to when they were negotiating the separation agreement and determine what their intent was at that time. In making this determination, the court will consider a number of factors:

☐ Labels used in the agreement

☐ Contingencies

☐ Method of payment

☐ The nature of what is transferred

Usually none of these factors is conclusive by itself. All of them must be considered. One of the factors may clearly indicate an intent that a term is alimony. If, however, the other factors clearly suggest that the term is part of the property division, the court may conclude that it is the latter. Unhappily, the factors often point in opposite directions.

LABELS USED IN THE AGREEMENT   Sometimes the separation agreement will explicitly label a provision as "alimony" or as a "property settlement" or "property division." These labels, however, do not always control. For example, suppose that an annual payment of $10,000 given to the wife is labeled "Property Division." If it is otherwise clear to the court that this money was in the nature of support, the court will classify it as alimony in spite of the label.

Contingent
Conditional; dependent on something that may not happen.

CONTINGENCIES   Terms that are **contingent** on the occurrences of certain events are often interpreted as alimony rather than as a property division, e.g., $10,000 a year to the wife until she remarries or dies. The presence of such contingencies suggests an intent to provide support while needed rather than an intent to divide property.

METHOD OF PAYMENT   A term may provide a single *lump-sum payment* (e.g., $10,000), *periodic payment* (e.g., $10,000 a year), or a *fluctuating payment* (e.g., $10,000 a year to be increased or decreased depending upon earnings in a particular year). Single lump-sum payments often suggest a property division. Periodic and fluctuating payments often suggest alimony.

THE NATURE OF WHAT IS TRANSFERRED   A conveyance of property other than cash (e.g., a house, a one-half interest in a business) often suggests a property division. Cash alone, however, usually suggests alimony.

Again, these are only guides. All of the circumstances must be examined in order to determine the intent of the parties. It may be that a court will conclude that a transfer of a house was intended as alimony or support. The court might also conclude that a single lump-sum payment was intended as alimony. While a court will be inclined to rule otherwise in these examples, specific proof of intent will control.

■■■■ ALIMONY

We will now examine individual clauses in the separation agreement, starting with alimony. Keep in mind, however, that no individual clause of a separation agreement can be fully understood in isolation. The negotiation process involves a large variety of factors. A party may agree to a term in the agreement not so much because that term in and of itself gives the party what he or she wants, but rather because the party decided to concede that term in order to gain another term, e.g., a wife may accept a lower alimony provision in exchange for the husband's agreement to the term giving her sole custody of their child. This is the nature of the bargaining process.

Alimony, as we have seen, is the amount of money or other property paid in fulfillment of a duty to support one's spouse after a separation or divorce. (Later, in chapter 15 on taxation, we will see that the Internal Revenue Service uses a broader definition of alimony to determine when it is deductible.) While the parties are still married, the payments are sometimes referred to as *spousal support* or as *separate maintenance*. The word *alimony* is more commonly used when the divorce has occurred or is imminent.

Traditionally, it was the husband's duty to support the wife. Today, however, the duty is mutual in the sense that it will be imposed on the party who has the resources for the benefit of the party in need. To impose the duty only on a man would amount to unconstitutional sex discrimination in violation of the Equal Protection Clause of the U.S. Constitution and in violation of many state constitutions. In the vast majority of situations, however, it is the woman who is the recipient of support through a separation agreement and/or through a court order.

First, we will examine some of the major negotiating options that must be considered in drafting the support provisions of the separation agreement. Then we turn to how a court will handle spousal support if the parties have not been able to negotiate an agreement.

SUPPORT PROVISIONS IN A SEPARATION AGREEMENT

PERIODIC PAYMENTS OR LUMP SUM? In a few states, it is illegal for a husband and wife to agree on a lump-sum payment in satisfaction of the support duty. In most states, however, it is permissible. From the perspective of the recipient, collectibility is an important factor in deciding whether to seek a single lump-sum alimony payment. The wife may find it safer to take the lump-sum payment now rather than hassle with installment or periodic payments if there is any likelihood that the husband will fall behind in his payments. It can be expensive and psychologically draining to have to go after a delinquent husband.

FIXED OR FLUCTUATING PERIODIC PAYMENTS? If periodic payments are agreed to, a number of questions need to be considered and resolved. Should the payments have a fixed dollar amount, e.g., $300 per month or per week? On what day of the month or week is each payment due? Another major option is the flexible periodic payment. The amount of the payment may fluctuate up or down depending upon the income of the husband, of the wife, or of both. An alimony payment of 25 percent of the husband's earnings, for example, provides an automatic fluctuating standard.

MEDICAL AND DENTAL EXPENSES Does the alimony payment cover medical, dental, or mental health expenses (e.g., psychiatrist)? If not, do the parties want to include a term in the separation agreement on how these expenses are to be covered? They must also consider the tax consequences of paying these expenses.

LIFE INSURANCE Even though the duty of support usually ends at the death of the **payor** or of the **payee,** the parties might agree that the support payments will continue after the payor dies. If so, one way to do this is through a life insurance policy on the life of the party with the support duty. The beneficiary would be the other spouse and/or the children. If a life insurance policy already exists, the parties may decide to include a term in the separation agreement that requires a spouse to continue paying the premiums, to increase the amount of the policy, to name the other spouse as the irrevocable beneficiary, etc. The agreement should also specify whether an existing policy remains in force if either side remarries. If no life insurance policy exists, the parties need to decide whether to take one out.

Payor One who makes a payment of money or is obligated to do so.

Payee One to whom money is paid or is to be paid.

MODIFICATION The separation agreement may contain a clause that the terms of the agreement shall not be modified unless both parties agree in writing to do so. Will a court honor such a clause? The answer is no where children are involved. As we shall see later, judges will change custody and child support clauses when they feel the best interest of the children warrants it. This is so whether or not the separation agreement is later incorporated and merged into the divorce decree.

What about the *alimony* term of the separation agreement? Will a court modify this term if the separation agreement has been incorporated and merged into the divorce decree even though the agreement has a no-modification clause? States differ on their answer to this question. Some state courts *will* modify the alimony term if a change of circumstances since the divorce decree justifies it, e.g., the payee is about to become destitute. We will return to the subject of modification later in this chapter.

TERMINATION OF SUPPORT PAYMENTS   The circumstances that will terminate the support obligation should be explicitly spelled out in the separation agreement. For example, it might say that payments end when:

☐ The payee dies.

☐ The payor dies.

☐ The payee remarries. (If the second marriage is later annulled, states differ on whether the original support obligations of the first husband revive. See chapter 9.)

☐ The payee commits adultery or fornication.

☐ The payee fails to abide by the custody terms of the separation agreement.

☐ The payee competes with the payor in business. (In most states, however, such a term will *not* be enforced since a payee's support payments cannot be conditioned on something that is not reasonably related to the marriage relationship.)

Of course, the separation agreement can provide the opposite. It may state, for example, that the support payments will *continue* when:

☐ The payor dies. (The payor's estate would then have the obligation to continue the support payments. Life insurance is often used as a method of continuing support payments after the payor's death.)

☐ The payee remarries. (Rather than continue the support payments in full after the payee remarries, the separation agreement usually provides for a reduced support payment. Some payors fear that if the total support payment ends upon remarriage, the payee will have little incentive to remarry. It should be pointed out, however, that a few states forbid support payments to continue after the payee remarries.)

The termination of alimony payments does not affect arrears, i.e., unpaid back payments. All delinquent payments that accrued before the support obligation terminated must be paid. If they terminated upon the death of the husband, for example, all payments he failed to make before he died can be enforced against his estate.

Escrow   Property is delivered by one person to another who will hold it until a designated condition or contingency occurs; then the property is delivered to the person for whose benefit the escrow was established.

SECURITY   When a payor fails to make a support payment, the payee can sue, but this is hardly an adequate remedy. Litigation can be expensive, lengthy, and emotionally draining. Preferable would be a term in the separation agreement that provides *security* to the payee for the performance of the support obligation. This security can be provided in a number of forms:

1. Escrow. The payor deposits a sum of money with an escrow agent, e.g., a bank, with instructions to pay the payee a designated amount of money in the event that the payor falls behind in a payment.

2. Surety bond. The payor gives the payee a surety bond. The payor pays premiums to the surety company. The surety company guarantees that if the payor fails to fulfill the support obligation, the company will fulfill it up to the amount of the bond.

3. Annuity. The payor purchases an annuity contract that provides a fixed income to the payee (annuitant) in the amount of the support obligation.

4. Trust. The payor transfers property (e.g., cash) to a trustee (e.g., a bank) with instructions to pay a fixed income to the payee (the beneficiary) in the amount of the support obligation.

The last two forms of security do not depend upon a breach by the payor of the support obligation clause of a separation agreement in order to come into effect.

Surety Bond An obligation by a guarantor to pay a second party if a third party defaults in its obligation to the second party.

Annuity A fixed sum payable to an individual at specified intervals for a limited period of time or for life.

Trust A method of holding property by which legal title is given to one party (the trustee) for the benefit of another (the beneficiary).

COURT-ORDERED ALIMONY
IN THE ABSENCE OF A SEPARATION AGREEMENT

How will a court decide the question of support if the parties have not been able to reach agreement on the matter? The major factors considered by the court are outlined in Exhibit 10.4. In some states, these factors are spelled out in the statutory code. Once a court decides to grant alimony, it will consider many of the same options discussed above, e.g., whether the amount should fluctuate, whether security should be provided.

ASSIGNMENT 10.4

Answer the following questions after examining your state code. (See General Instructions for the State-Code Assignment in chapter 1.)

a. What standards will a court use in awarding alimony, e.g., is marital fault relevant?

b. When can alimony be awarded to a man?

c. Are there any limitations on the form that alimony can take, e.g., periodic payments, lump sum, etc.?

d. When alimony is awarded, is it always for an indefinite period?

e. If the court denies the divorce to both parties, can alimony still be awarded?

ASSIGNMENT 10.5

Find an opinion decided within the last ten years by a court in your state that awarded alimony. List all the considerations that the court used in making its alimony decision. Try to find an opinion in which the court mentioned a specific dollar amount as alimony. If you cannot find such an opinion written by a court sitting in your state, select a neighboring state. (See General Instructions for the Court-Opinion Assignment in chapter 1.)

▆▆▆▆ PROPERTY DIVISION: GENERAL PRINCIPLES

CATEGORIZING PROPERTY

A property division should be based on a fair allocation of the property accumulated by the spouses during the marriage due to their joint efforts. Whether the property division is agreed to by the parties or imposed by a court

☐ **EXHIBIT 10.4   Factors a Court Will Consider in the Alimony Decision**

1. **The Needs of the Payee**
   ☐ The traditional general guideline is that alimony should enable the payee to maintain substantially the same standard of living enjoyed during the marriage.
   ☐ The payee's needs may vary according to his or her age and health.
   ☐ Most courts will provide a lower alimony award, or none at all, if the person requesting alimony has independent income and property. They will consider all resources of the payee, e.g., the expectation of inheritances.
   ☐ Most courts consider the payee's current employability. The presence of young children, of course, substantially limits the employment prospects of parents with custody.
   ☐ Many states authorize a court to grant **rehabilitative alimony.** In other states, however, the alimony award is granted for an indefinite period until modified by court order.
2. **The Length of the Marriage**
   ☐ Courts are very reluctant to grant significant alimony for a marriage of a short duration, e.g., under two years.
3. **The Ability of the Payor to Pay**
   ☐ The age and health of the payor.
   ☐ The payor's standard of living during and after the marriage.
   ☐ The payor's present and anticipated debts and other financial obligations.
   ☐ The voluntariness of the payor's financial condition. A husband, for example, cannot voluntarily enter a state of poverty by quitting a high-paying job solely to avoid alimony. The focus is not simply on the payor's present resources. The test is the payor's "earning capacity." (A similar issue arises when the parties confront the property division. One spouse cannot destroy or *dissipate* the property accumulated during the marriage and thereby prevent the other spouse from obtaining his or her share. We will examine this in the football case *(Gastineau)* later in the chapter.)
4. **Marital Fault**
   ☐ In most states, marital fault of the payee will *not* disqualify him or her from receiving alimony, although it can sometimes be taken into consideration in determining the amount of the alimony award.
   ☐ In some states, however, only if the payee was granted the divorce based on the payor's fault will the payee be entitled to alimony.
   ☐ In a few states, if the payor is found at fault, his or her alimony obligation may be increased.
5. **Other Factors**
   ☐ Some courts say that a factor in the award of alimony is the contribution (financial or otherwise) of the payee in helping the payor generate assets during the marriage. This factor, however, is more relevant to property division. Yet, as indicated, there are courts that tend to blur the distinction between alimony and property division.
   ☐ The court's decision on property division is sometimes a factor in awarding alimony. A court may be inclined to give a lower alimony award if it feels that the payee has been given "a good deal" in the property division. Some courts take the position that the adequacy of a support award can be determined only after the marital assets have been divided—again supporting the view that no single item in a separation agreement or court decree should be examined in isolation.

Rehabilitative Alimony
Alimony for a limited time until the payee can go to school or pursue employment on the way to becoming financially self-sufficient. (Also known as *durational maintenance.*) Designed to combat the notion that alimony is a permanent pension.

Real Property Land and anything permanently attached to the land.

Personal Property
Movable property; any property other than real property.

in the absence of agreement, the following preliminary questions must be examined:

1. What kind of property do the parties have?
2. How was the property acquired?
3. How is the property held? Who has title?

WHAT KIND OF PROPERTY DO THE PARTIES HAVE?   Real property can include a main home, a vacation home, land and building used in a business, condominium, etc. **Personal property** consists of cars, boats, cash, stocks, bonds, royalties, furniture, jewelry, art objects, books, records, clothes, photographic equipment, sports equipment, pets, business supplies (inventory), credits, accounts receivable, exclusive options to buy, insurance policies, etc.

Later we will examine three categories of assets that have generated considerable controversy in recent years: future pensions, professional degrees, and the goodwill of a business or profession.

☐ **Note on Embryos as "Property"** Assume that a woman is unable to conceive because damaged tubes prevent her eggs from reaching the womb. The eggs can be removed surgically, fertilized with her husband's sperm in the laboratory **(in vitro fertilization),** and reimplanted in the uterus at a later time during a normal ovulation cycle, hopefully to mature to a healthy fetus. Billig, *High Tech Earth Mothering,* 9 DIS-TRICT LAWYER 57 (July/August 1985). The procedure is known as an embryo transplant. In chapter 20 we will examine the question of what happens when the implantation is made in a "rented womb" of a surrogate mother. Here our concern is the "property" status of the embryos themselves.

What happens if the woman and her husband separate and file for divorce *before* the embryo is reimplanted in her? An embryo can be frozen between fertilization and implantation. What is the status of the *frozen embryo?* Who "owns" it? Is the embryo "property" to be divided upon divorce? Does the court have to decide its "custody"? Should the embryo be treated as potential life? When does life begin? Is the embryo a potential child?

The problem arises when the parties disagree about what should be done with the embryo. Suppose the husband wants it destroyed because he does not want to become the father of a child with his soon-to-be-ex-wife, but she wants the embryo kept alive so that a reimplantation can be attempted in her at a later time. Can he be forced to be a father against his will? Is this question any different from whether a man can force the woman he impregnates to have an abortion because he does not want to become a father? The courts have held that a man cannot force a woman to have an abortion. Is this any different from whether he can force a doctor to destroy a frozen embryo?

Definitive answers to such questions do not exist. Medical technology is moving much faster than the development of law and ethics in our society. The experts are at loggerheads:

> "We're talking about four-celled embryos—they haven't developed into organs or anything. They are too rudimentary; . . . therefore, they can't really be harmed, and there should be no requirement that unwanted embryos be saved."

> "Obviously, embryos are not property. These entities should not be defined as being property in terms of being able to be bought and sold. They are potential beings and declaring the embryos as property comes up to the threshold of crossing the barrier of assaulting the value of a potential person."

Curriden, *Frozen Embryos,* American Bar Association Journal 69–70 (August 1980).

More than 5,000 in vitro fertilization babies have been born in this country, and more than 20,000 "frozen embryos" remain in storage in laboratories across the United States. Clearly, there is a need for legislatures and courts to provide guidance on their status.

A major breakthrough came in 1992 with the Tennessee case of *Davis v. Davis,* 842 S.W.2d 588 (Tenn. 1992). Junior Lewis Davis sought a divorce from his wife, Mary Sue Davis. The parties were able to agree on all terms of dissolution, except one: who was to have "custody" of the seven "frozen embryos" (also referred to as preembryos) stored in a Knoxville fertility clinic that had attempted to assist the Davises in achieving a much-wanted pregnancy during a happier period in their relationship. Mary did not want to use the "frozen embryos" herself, but wanted authority to donate them to a childless couple. Junior was adamantly opposed to such donation and wanted the "frozen embryos" discarded. When the Davises signed up for the IVF program at the Knoxville clinic, they did not execute a written agreement specifying what disposition should be made of any unused embryos that might result from the cryopreservation

In Vitro Fertilization
The surgical removal of a woman's eggs and their fertilization with a man's sperm in the laboratory.

process. Nor were there any Tennessee statutes to guide the court on what to do in this situation.[2]

The Tennessee Supreme Court established its own guidelines on what to do when the parties cannot agree. The party wishing to avoid procreation should ordinarily prevail, assuming the other party has a reasonable possibility of achieving parenthood by means other than use of the preembryos in question. If no other reasonable alternatives exist, then the argument in favor of using the preembryos to achieve pregnancy should be considered. However, if the party seeking control of the preembryos intends merely to donate them to another couple, the objecting party has the greater interest and should prevail.

Junior Lewis Davis was "ecstatic" over this ruling. "I think this is a great step for men regarding our biological rights," he said.[3]

ASSIGNMENT 10.6

What is the status of a frozen embryo in your state? Is it divisible property? (See General Instructions for the State-Code Assignment and for the Court-Opinion Assignment in chapter 1.)

HOW WAS THE PROPERTY ACQUIRED?   Real and personal property can be acquired in a variety of ways:

- ☐ As a gift to one of the spouses
- ☐ As a gift to both of the spouses
- ☐ As a **bequest** to one or both spouses
- ☐ As a **devise** to one or both spouses
- ☐ Through **intestate succession**
- ☐ Through funds from the salary of one of the spouses
- ☐ Through funds from the salaries of both of the spouses

Bequest A gift of personal property in a will.

Devise A gift of real property in a will.

Intestate Succession Obtaining the property from a deceased who died without leaving a valid will. The persons entitled to this property are identified in the statute on intestate distribution.

Timing is important. When did the party or parties receive the property? Was it brought into the marriage or was it acquired during the marriage? If the property was separately owned before the marriage, was its value increased due to mutual efforts during the marriage?

HOW IS THE PROPERTY HELD? WHO HAS TITLE?   Property can be held in a number of ways:

1. *Legal title in name of one spouse only.* The title to the property is in the name of only one of the parties. This could be because the property was purchased with the funds of that one spouse. Or, it may be that the property was purchased with the funds of one spouse but placed in the name of the other spouse (perhaps in the hope of insulating the property from the claims of the creditors of the spouse who purchased the property). Finally, title may be in the name of one spouse even though both contributed funds for its purchase.

---

2. Louisiana has a statute entitled "Human Embryos." It forbids the intentional destruction of a cryopreserved IVF embryo and declares that disputes between parties should be resolved in the "best interest" of the embryo. 1986 La. Acts R.S. 9:121 et seq. Under the Louisiana statute, unwanted embryos must be made available for "adoptive implantation."

3. Mark Curriden, *No Forced Fatherhood,* 78 American Bar Association Journal 35 (September 1992).

2. *Joint tenancy.* In a **joint tenancy,** each joint tenant has an equal right to possess the entire property. They do not each own a piece of the property; each joint tenant owns it all. When one joint tenant dies, his or her interest passes to the surviving joint tenants by the **right of survivorship.**

3. *Tenancy by the entirety.* Under a **tenancy by the entirety,** each spouse has a right of survivorship, as with any joint tenancy.

4. *Tenancy in common.* In a **tenancy in common,** all parties have a right to possession of the property, but their share in the property may not be equal. There is no right of survivorship. When one tenant dies, the property goes to whomever the deceased designated by will, or to the heirs of the deceased by intestate succession if the deceased died without leaving a valid will. Hence, a major distinction between (1) a joint tenancy and a tenancy by the entirety and (2) a tenancy in common is that the property of a deceased tenant passes through the estate of that tenant only in the case of a tenancy in common. In the other tenancies, the property passes immediately to the surviving tenant(s) by **operation of law.**

5. *Community property.* The following information is taken from Clark, *The Law of Domestic Relations in the United States*, 512–515 (2d ed., Practitioner's Edition 1987):

> [Nine] states have adopted **community property** as a means of providing equitably for the property interests of married persons.* [Most of the other states in the country are generally classified as *common law property* states.] The principle underlying community property is that the efforts of both spouses are instrumental in contributing to the welfare of the family, and that therefore property acquired by either spouse during the marriage, with certain exceptions, should belong to both spouses. Community property was originally a Spanish institution and was enacted first in those states whose law was influenced by Spanish law, spreading later to other states. . . .
>
> [C]ommunity property . . . arises when the spouses are married and includes property acquired by either spouse during the marriage, except property acquired by gift, devise or inheritance.† Property which does not fall within the definition of community property is characterized as **separate property** of the spouse who has acquired it. The difficulty of applying this ostensibly simple definition to the many forms in which property is acquired has led to the development of a rebuttable presumption that property acquired by either spouse during the marriage, whether title is taken in the name of either spouse or of both, is community property.‡ The presumption may be rebutted if it can be proved that the funds with which the property was acquired were the separate funds of one of the spouses.
>
> In most community property states the parties may by agreement vary the usual rules. They may agree that all property acquired by either of them is separate property, or that it is all community property, or they may agree on the characterization of particular items of property.
>
> Some examples indicate the difficulties of determining whether particular property is community or separate property. Thus veterans' education benefits have been held

---

*These are Arizona, California, Idaho, Louisiana, Nevada, New Mexico, Texas, Washington, and Wisconsin. 4A R. Powell, Real Property § 625[2] (Rev.ed.1982).

†Id. at § 625.2[1]. The Uniform Marital Property Act § 4, 9A Unif.L.Ann. 29 (Supp.1985) defines marital property in substantially the same way. Under that Act the parties may by agreement vary the manner in which property is held. Uniform Marital Property Act § 3, 9A Unif.L.Ann. 28 (Supp. 1985) Community property states permit this also.

‡There may be other presumptions, such as the statutory presumption in California that where a single family residence is acquired by husband and wife as joint tenants it is community property.

Joint Tenancy Property that is owned equally by two or more persons with the *right of survivorship.*

Right of Survivorship When one owner dies, his or her share goes to the other owners; it does not go through the estate of the deceased owner.

Tenancy by the Entirety A joint tenancy held by a husband and wife.

Tenancy in Common Property owned by two or more persons in shares that may or may not be equal, with no right of survivorship.

Operation of Law Automatically because of the law. (A result occurs by operation of law when it happens because the law mandates the result, not because a party agrees to produce the result.)

Community Property Property in which each spouse has a one-half interest because it was acquired during the marriage, regardless of who earned it or who has title to it. **Common law property** is property owned by the spouse who earned it.

Separate Property Property totally owned by one spouse; noncommunity property.

to be separate property when they were earned before marriage, but paid after marriage, even though the statute provided for increased benefits for dependents, including spouses. There is a conflict in the decisions concerning damages for personal injury. The Texas authorities classify such damages as separate property, but they hold that the medical expenses and loss of earnings recovered in such a suit are community property. Other courts hold that the entire recovery is community property. Where property is purchased before marriage but paid for in part after marriage out of community funds, its classification as community or separate varies among the community property states. Some would characterize it as separate property, some as separate or community depending upon when title vested, and some would apply complex calculations to establish the proportion of separate to community funds going into the purchase.

The diversity in characterization of property as community or separate, and the differences between the community property states and the common law states, have created difficult questions of the conflict of laws. An early case, *Saul v. His Creditors,**
established the rule that when the marriage occurred in a common law state, where the parties were then domiciled, but they later became domiciled in the community property state, property acquired after the change in domicile had the status of community property. California has carried this a step further by enacting a statute creating the institution of **quasi-community property**. . . . Quasi-community property is divisible on divorce in the same fashion as community property.

The right to manage and control community property is a subject for differing statutory provisions among the various community property states. Traditionally the husband alone had this power. The United States Supreme Court, in *Kirchberg v. Feenstra,*[†] was presented with an Equal Protection Clause challenge to the former Louisiana statute which made the husband the "head and master" of the community and gave him the power to convey community property without the wife's consent. The Court held that such gender-based classifications cannot stand in the absence of proof that they further some important governmental interest. Finding no such interest in this case, the Court held that the statute violated the [Equal Protection Clause of the] Fourteenth Amendment. Within the constitutional limit so laid down, the states have provided for management and control by each spouse, have required the consent of both spouses for certain transfers of community property, and have authorized joint management of at least some forms of community property. The obvious analogy here is to the law of partnership, since the spouses owe each other **fiduciary** duties of good faith and fair treatment in dealing with community property, as do partners with respect to partnership property.

Quasi-Community Property Property acquired by the spouses when they lived in a non-community property state before moving to a community property state. If they had acquired it in a community property state, it would have been community property.

Fiduciary Pertaining to good faith, loyalty, trust, and candor; pertaining to the obligation to protect another's interest and to provide fair treatment.

WHAT PROPERTY IS DIVIDED AND WHO GETS WHAT?

The general rule in community property states and in common law property states is that property acquired by a party *before the marriage* is deemed to be the separate property of that party and therefore not divisible upon divorce unless both parties agree to divide it. The same is usually true of property obtained solely by one spouse through gift or inheritance during the marriage, e.g., from a relative of that spouse. During the marriage, however, such property will undoubtedly increase in value. This **appreciation** may be deemed to be divisible property regardless of the manner in which the property was acquired or when it was acquired.

All other property obtained during the marriage is potentially divisible upon divorce, depending upon the special laws of individual states.

After identifying which property is divisible, the next question is how the division is made. In community property states like California, the division is

Appreciation An increase in the value of property.

---

*Mart. (N.S.) 569, 16 Am.Dec. 212 (La.1827).
†450 U.S. 455, 101 S. Ct. 1195, 67 L. Ed. 2d 428 (1981).

usually 50/50 unless the parties agree otherwise in a separation agreement. In common law property states, courts have considerably more discretion. If the parties cannot agree on how to divide marital assets, the goal of the court in a common law property state is to achieve an **equitable distribution** (see Exhibit 10.5). The court will weigh a number of factors such as

☐ who earned the asset;

☐ what the other spouse did to contribute to the household while the asset was being earned;

☐ any interruption of personal career or educational opportunities of either spouse (especially the one who stayed at home with the kids);

☐ the length of the marriage;

☐ the desirability of keeping the marital home for use as a residence for any dependent;

☐ any intentional dissipation of marital assets;

☐ any other factor necessary to do equity and justice to the parties.

In a common law property state that applies the principle of equitable distribution, most courts will seek a property division that reflects the proportionate contribution made by each spouse. Often a court will presume that the division should be equal unless the factors listed above would suggest a different allocation. A major theme in this area of family law is the recognition of the contribution made by the stay-at-home spouse to the acquisition and growth (i.e., appreciation) of marital assets. It is clear, for example, that a husband would not be able to earn $150,000 a year, study the stock market, and buy two homes out of his salary if he also had to stay home to care for the three kids and worry about the washing machine that is not working! Since permanent alimony is becoming less common, courts use property division as the primary vehicle of achieving "equity and justice."

Once the decision is made on how to divide the property in a community property state or in a common law property state, the next concern is to identify

Equitable Distribution
The fair, but not necessarily equal, division between former spouses of property acquired during the marriage.

☐ **EXHIBIT 10.5 Property Division upon Divorce**

KIND OF PROPERTY	COMMON LAW PROPERTY STATES	COMMUNITY PROPERTY STATES
Property acquired before marriage	This is separate property. All of it goes to the spouse who acquired it unless he or she agrees otherwise.	This is separate property. All of it goes to the spouse who acquired it unless he or she agrees otherwise.
Property acquired by one spouse during marriage by gift or inheritance	This is separate property. All of it goes to the spouse who acquired it unless he or she agrees otherwise.	This is separate property. All of it goes to the spouse who acquired it unless he or she agrees otherwise.
Property acquired during marriage other than by gift or inheritance	If the spouses cannot agree, each gets a fair (equitable) share, which may or may not be equal.	50/50 split between the spouses unless they agree otherwise.
Increased value (appreciation) of separate or community property that occurs during marriage	If the spouses cannot agree, each gets a fair (equitable) share of the amount of the appreciation, which may or may not be equal.	50/50 split of the amount of the appreciation between the spouses unless they agree otherwise.

the most *practical* way to accomplish the division. A 50/50 split or a 60/40 split of cash is easy. Not so for the division of homes, vehicles, and businesses. They can't be conveniently chopped up. Sometimes it is practical to sell an asset and divide the proceeds according to the allocation that applies. When this is not practical, other options are negotiated and/or ordered by the court:

☐ The wife will keep the house, and the husband will keep the car and his business.

☐ The wife will live in the house, but the husband will retain a designated amount of the equity in the house, which must be paid to him if the house is sold.

☐ The wife receives $25,000 as a lump-sum payment, and the husband receives everything else.

Many factors can play a role in the negotiations. For example, the wife may agree to a lower property division in exchange for the husband's agreement to let her have custody of the children. She may agree to a higher alimony award in exchange for a relatively lower property division out of fear that he is on the brink of bankruptcy (in which the property division debts, but not the alimony debts, might be discharged). He may be able to convince her to take more alimony and less property so that he can take advantage of the alimony tax deduction. She may agree even though she must pay taxes on the alimony received. They both know that his higher income would cause the same money to be taxed at a higher rate. He may find ways to compensate her for this in other terms of the separation agreement.

| **ASSIGNMENT 10.7** | When parties are not able to agree on a property division, what standards will a court in your state use to do it for them? (See General Instructions for the State-Code Assignment in chapter 1.) |

UNLAWFUL DISSIPATION

Dissipate Waste, destroy, or squander.

As we saw when discussing alimony, a spouse cannot avoid a support obligation by voluntarily becoming poor. The amount of the obligation will be based on earning capacity, not necessarily actual earnings. A similar principle is at work in the property division. One spouse cannot squander—**dissipate**—marital property so that there is nothing left to divide in the separation agreement. These concerns are at the heart of the *Gastineau* decision, to which we now turn.

CASE

GASTINEAU V. GASTINEAU
151 Misc. 2d 813, 573 N.Y.S.2d 819 (1991)
New York Supreme Court, Suffolk County

Background: *Marcus Gastineau was a professional football player for the New York Jets. His wife, Lisa, sued him for divorce and charged that he dissipated some of the*

marital assets. While the trial was in progress (i.e., pendente lite), the court ordered Marcus to make payments to Lisa to cover expenses. He fell $71,707 behind in these payments. The court then ordered the sequestration of his net severance pay of $83,000. This removed it from his possession and control until the court rendered its decision.

Decision: *Marcus dissipated marital assets. In the equitable distribution of the marital assets, a court can treat dissipated assets as if they still exist.*

Opinion of the Court:

Justice LEIS delivered the opinion of the court.

This action for divorce, equitable distribution and other ancillary relief was tried on February 25, 28, March 5, and 6, 1991. The Plaintiff, Lisa Gastineau, is represented by counsel. The Defendant, Marcus Gastineau appeared pro se. . . .

The parties were married in December of 1979. This action was commenced in September 1986. Consequently, this is a marriage of short duration. The Plaintiff is thirty-one years old and the Defendant is thirty-four. The parties have one child, Brittany, born on 11/6/82.

At the beginning of the trial the Plaintiff testified as to specific allegations of cruel and inhuman treatment allegedly committed by the Defendant. The Defendant remained mute, neither admitting nor denying these allegations. The Court thereupon granted the Plaintiff a divorce based on cruel and inhuman treatment [Domestic Relations Law (DRL) § 170(1)].

The parties married just after Marc Gastineau had been drafted by the New York Jets to play professional football. The Plaintiff, at that time, was a sophomore at the University of Alabama. The Plaintiff never completed her college education, nor did she work during the course of the marriage.

In 1982, when Brittany was born, the parties purchased a house in Huntington, New York for $99,000.00. In addition to the purchase price, the Plaintiff and Defendant spent another $250,000.00 for landscaping and other renovations. This money came from the Defendant's earnings as a professional football player.

According to the uncontroverted testimony of the Plaintiff, in 1979 (the Defendant's first year in professional football) the Defendant earned a salary of $55,000.00. In his second year, 1980, the Defendant's salary was approximately $75,000.00. In 1981 it was approximately $95,000.00 and in 1982 he earned approximately $250,000.00. The Defendant's tax returns (which were not available for the years 1979 through 1982) indicate that the Defendant earned $423,291.00 in 1983, $488,994.00 in 1984, $858,035.00 in 1985, $595,127.00 in 1986, $953,531.00 in 1987 and in 1988, his last year with the New York Jets, his contract salary was $775,000.00 plus $50,000.00 in bonuses. It must be noted that in most years the Defendant earned monies in excess of his contract salary as a result of promotions, advertisements and bonuses.

In 1985 the parties purchased a home in Scottsdale, Arizona for $550,000.00. During the course of the parties' marriage Plaintiff and Defendant acquired many luxury items including a power boat, a BMW, a Corvette, a Rolls Royce, a Porche, a Mercedes and two motorcycles. They continually had a housekeeper who not only cleaned the house but prepared the parties' meals. In addition, the parties frequently dined out at expensive restaurants. The Plaintiff testified that as a result of this life style she has become accustomed to buying only the most expensive clothes and going to the best of restaurants.

In 1988 the Defendant began an illicit relationship with Brigitte Nielsen. When Ms. Nielsen was diagnosed as having cancer the Defendant testified that he could no longer concentrate on playing football. At that time the Defendant was under contract with the New York Jets at a salary of $775,000.00. He left professional football in October 1988 (breaking his contract) after the sixth game of the 1988 season. The Defendant went to Arizona and remained with Ms. Nielsen while she underwent treatment for cancer.

Regardless of whether the Defendant wanted to be with his girl friend while she underwent treatment for cancer, he had a responsibility to support his wife and child. The Court cannot condone Mr. Gastineau's walking away from a lucrative football contract when the result is that his wife and child are deprived of adequate support.

According to the testimony adduced at trial, there are sixteen games per season in the NFL. Players are paid one-sixteenth of their contract salary at the end of each game. Based on the Defendant's salary for 1988 ($775,000.00), he received $48,437.00 per game. The Defendant played six games in the 1988 season and received approximately $290,622.00 plus $50,000.00 in bonuses. He was entitled to an additional $484,437.00 for the ten games remaining in the season. This Court finds that by walking away from his 1988–89 contract with the NFL the Defendant dissipated a marital asset in the amount of $484,437.00 (DRL § 236(B)(5)(d)(11)).*

Whether or not the Defendant would have been offered a contract by the New York Jets for the 1989/90 football season if he had not broken his 1988/89 contract is pure speculation. In professional football there are no guarantees. Variables such as age, how an athlete plays, the ability of other players seeking to fill his position, as well as possible injuries sustained during the season, make it impossible to determine with certainty whether or not the Defendant would have been re-signed by the New York Jets had he finished the 1988/89 season. It must also be noted that there has been no testimony offered by the Plaintiff to establish that the Defendant would have been re-signed by the New York Jets for the 1989/90 season had he not broken his contract.

---

*["5. a. Except where the parties have provided in an agreement for the disposition of their property . . . the court . . . shall determine the respective rights of the parties in their separate or marital property, and shall provide for the disposition thereof in the final judgment. . . . d. In determining an equitable disposition of property. . . , the court shall consider: . . . (11) the wasteful dissipation of assets by either spouse. . . ."]

The speculative nature of the Defendant's future in professional football is highlighted by the fact that in 1989 he tried out for the San Diego Chargers, the LA Raiders and the Minnesota Vikings, without success. The New York Jets also refused to offer him a contract. In 1990 the Defendant did acquire a position with the British Colombia Lions in the Canadian Football League at a salary of $75,000.00. He was cut, however, less than half way through the season. The Defendant played five of the 18 scheduled games and was paid approximately $20,000.00. The Defendant's performance in the Canadian Football League lends credence to his claim that he no longer has the capacity to earn the monies that he once made as a professional football player. Under these circumstances the court is limited to considering the dissipation of a marital asset valued at $484,437.00, to wit: the remaining amount of money that the Defendant was eligible to collect pursuant to his 1988/89 contract.

While Defendant admits that he has name recognition, he claims that his name has a negative rather than a positive connotation. The Defendant testified that because of his antics on the field (such as his victory dance after sacking a quarterback), the fact that he crossed picket lines during the NFL player's strike and because he walked away from his professional football career, his name has no value for promotions or endorsements. There has been no evidence presented to the contrary by the Plaintiff.

The Defendant testified that his chances of obtaining employment with a professional football team are almost nil. Although he is presently attempting to obtain a position at a Jack LaLanne Health Spa he could not provide details as to the potential salary. The Defendant has also attempted to enter professional boxing. No testimony has been elicited by the Plaintiff, however, as to the Defendant's financial potential as a professional boxer. Since the Defendant left professional football he has not worked or earned any money (except for the $20,000.00 that he earned when he played football in Canada). According to the Defendant, Ms. Nielsen paid for all of the Defendant's expenses during the period of time that they lived together.

After the Defendant failed to appear for a number of court dates and also failed to comply with this Court's pendente lite order, the Court directed that the Defendant's NFL severance pay be sequestered pursuant to DRL § 243 and the Plaintiff be appointed receiver and sequestrator of said funds (which amounted to approximately $83,000.00 after deducting taxes).

According to Plaintiff the entire $83,000.00 (reflecting the Defendant's total net severance pay from the NFL) was spent by her as follows: Thirty-two thou-sand dollars ($32,000.00) was used to pay mortgage arrears on the Huntington house (which still has approximately $15,000.00 outstanding in arrears), $22,000.00 went to the Plaintiff's attorneys, $15,000.00 went to repay loans taken out by the Plaintiff to pay necessary expenses and the rest, approximately $14,000.00, went for landscaping, medical insurance, electricity, fuel oil, telephone bills, dental and doctor bills.

PRIMARY MARITAL ASSETS

With all of the money that the Defendant earned throughout the course of his professional football career he has retained only three significant marital assets. (1) The Huntington house, which has been valued at approximately $429,000.00 and has an outstanding mortgage of $150,000.00. (2) A house located in the state of Arizona which was purchased for approximately $550,000.00 and has a $420,000.00 mortgage (which in all probability will be sold at foreclosure); (3) The Defendant's severance pay from the NFL of approximately $83,000.00.

It is clear that the Defendant has also dissipated a marital asset worth approximately $324,573.00 (to wit: $484,437.00 the Defendant was entitled to receive pursuant to his 1988/89 contract tax effected by 33%, reflecting approximate federal and state income tax). Although neither the Plaintiff nor the Defendant attempted to tax effect this dissipated marital asset, it is clear that the Defendant would not have actually received $484,437.00 had he finished the 1988/89 season. The Court therefore, on its own, has tax effected this amount by 33%, approximately what the defendant would have paid in federal and state taxes had he actually received the $484,437.00. In this regard the Court has considered the tax returns of the parties (which are in evidence) with reference to their tax consequences and takes judicial notice of the fact that compensation for service constitutes income (IRC [26 USC] § 61(a)(1)) which is taxable (IRC [26 USC] §§ 1 and 63); New York Tax Law § 620 et seq., *Richardson on Evidence* §§ 17 and 18 [10th Ed.].

EQUITABLE DISTRIBUTION

It is a guiding principle of equitable distribution that parties are entitled to receive equitable awards which are proportionate to their contributions, whether direct or indirect, to the marriage, *Ullah v. Ullah*, 555 N.Y.S.2d 834 (2nd Dep't 1990).

In this case, the Plaintiff testified that during the course of the marriage she supervised the renovations made on the Huntington house, traveled with the Defendant wherever he trained and, with the assistance of a full-time nanny, raised and cared for their child.

This is not a long term marriage, and there has been minimal testimony elicited concerning the Plaintiff's direct or indirect contributions to the Defendant's acquisition of marital assets. Although it was the defendant's own athletic abilities and disciplined training which made it possible for him to obtain and retain his position as a professional football player, equity dictates, under the facts of this case, that the Plaintiff receive one-third of the marital assets. The Defendant's decision to voluntarily terminate his contract with the New York Jets, depriving Plaintiff and the parties' child of the standard of living to which they had become accustomed, his failure to obtain meaningful employment thereafter and the indirect contributions made by the Plaintiff during the course of the marriage warrant an award to the Plaintiff of one third of the parties' marital assets. The Court is also mindful of the fact that during the years of the Defendant's greatest productivity, the Plaintiff enjoyed the fruits of Defendant's labors to the fullest (*Parlow v. Parlow*, 548 N.Y.S.2d 373 (Sup. Ct. Westchester Co. 1989)), unlike the landmark *O'Brien* case (*O'Brien v. O'Brien*, 66 N.Y.2d 576, 498 N.Y.S.2d 743, 489 N.E.2d 712 (1985)), where a newly licensed professional discarded his wife after she provided years of contributions to the attainment of his medical license.

There are only two marital assets to be considered in granting Plaintiff her one-third distributive award, (1) the Huntington house, and (2) the $324,573.00 dissipated marital asset. The Arizona house has no equity.

The Huntington house is valued at $429,000.00. It has a $150,000.00 mortgage with $15,000.00 owed in back mortgage payments. It thus has an equity of $264,000.00. One third of the equity would entitle the Plaintiff to $87,120.00. When one adds $107,109.00 (1/3 of the $324,573.00 tax effected marital asset which was dissipated), the Plaintiff would be entitled to $194,229.00. This would encompass Plaintiff's 1/3 distributive award of the parties' sole remaining marital asset (the Huntington house) and her 1/3 share of the marital asset dissipated by the Defendant. If one adds this $194,229.00 to the arrears owed by the Defendant on the pendente lite order ($71,707.00) Plaintiff could be awarded the total equity ($264,000.00) in the Huntington house in full satisfaction of her one-third distributive award of the parties' marital assets and still have approximately $1,936.00 remaining as a credit. The Court awards Plaintiff the Huntington house and grants her a Judgment for $1,936.00 for the remaining arrears owed to her.

Neither side has offered proof as to the present value of the Arizona house or the extent of arrears on mortgage payments (*Gluck v. Gluck*, 520 N.Y.S.2d 581 (2nd Dep't 1987)). It would appear however, that there is no equity remaining in the Arizona house. The Court awards the Arizona house to the Defendant. The Court directs that each party take whatever steps are required to effect the transfer of the deed to the real property awarded to the other party so as to convey title to said property in said other's name alone.

---

a. Who was treated unfairly by the *Gastineau* case: Marcus? Lisa? Neither? Was her one-third share too high, too low, or just right? Have a debate in class on this question. (Note that this case did not cover child support. The court must make a separate decision on who pays child support and how much.)

b. How much would Lisa have gotten if New York were a community property state?

PENSIONS, DEGREES, AND GOODWILL

Three recent areas of contention involving property division are pensions, professional degrees (or occupational licenses), and the goodwill of a business. Until fairly recently, parties negotiating a separation agreement did *not* include these items in their bargaining. They were either considered too intangible or were simply assumed to belong to one of the parties separately, usually the husband. Litigation and legislation, however, have forced drastic changes in these views. As a result, the negotiations for a separation agreement now regularly take account of these items in one way or another.

DIVIDING A PENSION   Many workers are covered by **pension** plans at work. Employer-sponsored plans may be financed entirely by the employer or by the employer with employee contributions. There are two main kinds of pension plans, the **defined-benefit plan** and the **defined-contribution plan.**

☐ **Defined-Benefit Plan** The amount of the benefit is fixed, but not the amount of contribution. The formula for such plans usually gears the benefits to years of service and earnings (e.g., a benefit of $10 a month for each year of employment) or a stated dollar amount.

☐ **Defined-Contribution Plan** Each employee has his or her own individual account. The amount of contribution is generally fixed, but the amount of the benefit is not. Such plans usually involve profit-sharing, stock-bonus, or money-purchase arrangements where the employer's contribution (usually a percentage of profits) is divided among the participants based on the individual's wages and/or years of service and accumulations in the individual's pension account. The eventual benefit is determined by the amount of total contributions and investment earnings in the years during which the employee is covered.

Vested Fixed so that it cannot be taken away by future events or conditions; accrued so that you now have a right to present or future possession or enjoyment.

Accumulated benefits in these plans are not **vested** until the employee has a nonforfeitable right to receive the benefits, whether or not the employee leaves the job before retirement.

Can pension benefits be divided upon divorce? Assume that a wife stayed home to care for the children while her husband worked. Is she entitled to any of his pension benefits? The question is important because retirement benefits may be the largest portion of the marital estate in many marriages.

Yes, it is possible for a spouse, an ex-spouse, or a child to receive some or all of these pension benefits if the court so directs in a special order called a **Qualified Domestic Relations Order (QDRO).** Any one of these individuals can become an **alternate payee** under the plan. If the parties cannot agree in their separation agreement on how to divide pension benefits, a judge can issue a QDRO to enforce an obligation of child support (see chapter 12), alimony, or other marital property right of the alternate payee. Before this dramatic change in the law became effective in 1984, individuals other than the employee could not demand that pension benefits be paid directly to them. QDROs have now made this practice commonplace. Exhibit 10.6 provides an example of a typical QDRO provided by an employer as guidance to its employees in drafting proposed QDROs to be signed by a judge. The example assumes that the alternate payee will receive one-half of the employee's pension benefits. It is certainly possible for a different allocation to be ordered, however.

Qualified Domestic Relations Order A court order that allows a nonemployee to reach pension benefits of an employee or former employee to satisfy a support or other marital obligation to the nonemployee.

Alternate Payee A nonemployee entitled to receive pension benefits of an employee or former employee pursuant to a Qualified Domestic Relations Order.

How much does the nonemployee receive from the employee's pension fund? What amount or percentage will be ordered in the QDRO? The parties can negotiate this in their separation agreement. If they cannot reach an agreement, the court will decide. It is possible for an alternate payee to receive up to 100 percent of the employee's pension benefits.

Employees and employers do not like QDROs—the former because they had thought their pension could never be touched by anyone, and the latter because of the extra administrative burden imposed. During negotiations, the employee will usually try to get the other side to accept some other benefit in lieu of asking the court for a QDRO. If, however, nothing else of comparable value is available, dividing pension benefits through a QDRO is unavoidable. (In chapter 12, we will consider a similar device called a Qualified Medical Child Support Order—QMCSO—that covers health insurance for children.)

A great deal depends on the *value* of the employee's pension plan. Without knowing this value, the negotiations are meaningless. Yet determining value

☐ **EXHIBIT 10.6   Qualified Domestic Relations Order (QDRO)**

This sample QDRO is provided by Apex Company, Inc., to its employees as an example of an order the company will treat as a QDRO. You may include the language in a separate order or as part of the divorce decree itself. The company does not give individual tax advice or advice about the marital property rights of either party.

1. Pursuant to Section 414(p) of the Internal Revenue Code, this qualified domestic relations order ("Order") assigns a portion of the benefits payable in the Apex Company, Inc. Annuity Plan ("the Plan") from _____ [Member's Name] _____ (Member No. _____) to _____ [Spouse's Name] in recognition of the existence of his/her marital rights in _____ [Member's Name] _____ retirement benefits.

2. The Member in the Plan is _____ [Member's Name] _____ , whose last known mailing address is _____ , Social Security No. _____ .

3. The Alternate Payee is _____ [Spouse's Name] _____ , whose last known mailing address is _____ , Social Security No. _____ .

[Use the following paragraph if the Member is <u>not</u> already receiving retirement benefits:]

4. Apex Company, Inc. is hereby ORDERED to assign a portion of the accumulations so that each party as of the date of the assignment has a retirement account of approximately the same value. The date of assignment is _____ .

[Use the following paragraph if the Member <u>is</u> already receiving retirement benefits:]

4. Apex Company Inc. is hereby ORDERED to make monthly payments equal to one-half of the amount payable to _____ [Member's Name] _____ directly to _____ [Spouse's Name _____ . These direct payments to _____ [Spouse's Name] _____ shall be made beginning after the date of this order and ending at _____ [Member's Name] _____ 's death.

5. This qualified domestic relations order is not intended to require the Plan to provide any type or form of benefits or any option not otherwise provided by the Plan, nor shall this Order require the Plan to provide for increased benefits not required by the Plan. This Order does not require the Plan to provide benefits to the Alternate Payee that are required to be paid to another Alternate Payee under another order previously determined to be a qualified domestic relations order.

6. All benefits payable under the Apex Company, Inc. Annuity Plan other than those payable to _____ [Spouse's Name] _____ shall be payable to _____ [Member's Name] _____ in such manner and form as he/she may elect in his/her sole and undivided discretion, subject only to plan requirements.

7. _____ [Spouse's Name] _____ is ORDERED AND DECREED to report any retirement payments received on any applicable income tax return. The Plan Administrator of Apex Company, Inc. is authorized to issue the appropriate Internal Revenue Form for any direct payment made to _____ [Spouse's Name] _____ .

8. While it is anticipated that the Plan Administrator will pay directly to _____ [Spouse's Name] _____ the benefit awarded to her, _____ [Member's Name] _____ is designated a constructive trustee to the extent he receives any retirement benefits under the Plan that are due to _____ [Spouse's Name] _____ but paid to _____ [Member's Name] _____ . _____ [Member's Name] _____ is ORDERED AND DECREED to pay the benefit defined above directly to _____ [Spouse's Name] _____ within three days after receipt by him.

_____   _____
[NAME OF COURT]   [NAME OF JUDGE]

---

can be a complex undertaking, often requiring the services of actuarial and accounting specialists. Value will depend on factors such as:

☐ Type of pension plan

☐ Amount contributed to the plan by the employee and by the employer

☐ How benefits are determined, e.g., when they accrue or are vested

☐ Age of employee

☐ Employee's earliest retirement date

☐ Employee's life expectancy

Often the parties must calculate the **present value** of a benefit. Assume that at the beginning of the year you become entitled to $1,000 by the end of the year. On January 1, you are *not* given $1,000; you are given the present value

Present Value The amount of money an individual would have to be given now to produce or generate a certain amount of money in a designated period of time.

of $1,000. The present value of $1,000 is $909.09 if we assume that you could invest $909.09 in a local bank (or in some other investment entity) at 10 percent interest. When a benefit is distributed, what is actually received may be the present value of the benefit, calculated in this way. If a 10 percent rate of interest is too high in today's market, the parties will have to assume a lower interest percentage and a higher present value. At 5 percent interest, for example, the present value of $1,000 is $952.38 (If you brought $952.38 to a bank offering 5 percent interest, at the end of the year you would have $1,000 in your account.)

A number of companies have been formed that help parties value pensions. One such company is Legal Economic Evaluations, Inc., whose application is presented in Exhibit 10.7.

□ **EXHIBIT 10.7   Pension Valuation Form**

**LEGAL
ECONOMIC
EVALUATIONS, INC.**
1000 Elwell Court, #203
Palo Alto, CA 94303
(415)969-7682

PENSION VALUATION

ATTORNEY INFORMATION

Name _____   Today's Date ___ / ___ / ___

Name of Firm _____   Representing: □ Petitioner's Spouse

Street _____   □ Pensioner

City, State & Zip Code _____   □ Both

Telephone Number (   ) _____ How Did you Hear of Us? _____

CASE INFORMATION

(For Faster Service, please collect the information below and call one of our Economists at (800)221-6826 or (800)648-9900 inside California.)

Pensioner Name _____ Gender   M   F   Birthdate ___ / ___ / ___

Employer _____ Occupation _____

Date of Employment ___ / ___ / ___   Date Entered Plan ___ / ___ / ___   Termination Date ___ / ___ / ___

Spouse Name _____   Birthdate ___ / ___ / ___

Date of Marriage ___ / ___ / ___

If the pensioner is already receiving benefits, how much are they ($ ___) and when did they begin (___ / ___ / ___)?

Have you enclosed a copy of the pension plan booklet?   □ Yes

Have you enclosed the pensioner's most recent benefits statement?   □ Yes

Is there any other recent correspondence regarding pension benefits?   □ Yes   □ No   If so, please enclose a copy.

If no information regarding benefit amounts is available, please list the pensioner's salary for the last five years below: (Also state any other relevant information below.)

_____

_____

_____

_____

In addition to the present value of the pension, do you wish us to show the spouse's net interest based on the ratio of service during marriage to total plan service (also known as the "Time Rule" or "Coverture Percentage")?

□ Yes   □ No

BILLING

□ Enclosed is a check for $100 payable to Legal Economic Evaluations, Inc.
    Please mail remittance and this completed form to the above address.

M3

Find a friend or relative who works at a place where he or she is covered by a pension. Assume that you work at an office where your friend or relative is a client who is seeking a divorce in which one of the issues is the division of pension benefits. (If you are covered by an employee pension plan, use yourself as the client in this assignment.)

Your supervisor asks you to do two things. First, obtain as much information as you can about the client's pension, e.g., the kind of plan it is, when benefits become available. Second, obtain an employer-approved copy of a sample QDRO. Ask the client to call the personnel office at work in order to speak to the "plan administrator" (the person in charge of administering the pension plan) and request the information and the sample.

Prepare a report that summarizes the plan's features, pointing out whatever you think will be relevant to later negotiations on dividing the pension benefits. (You can change the name of your friend or relative.) Attach the copy of the sample QDRO to your report.

DIVIDING A DEGREE

Bill and Pat are married in 1973. While Bill goes through college, medical school, and internship to become a doctor, Pat works full-time to support the two of them. On the day he obtains his license to practice medicine, they decide to divorce. During the long years of Bill's education, they have accumulated almost no property. Pat earns $25,000 a year at her job. Since she is fully capable of supporting herself, the court decides that she should receive no alimony. They have no children.

Many would consider it an outrage that Pat walks away from the marriage with nothing. She is not eligible for alimony, and there is no tangible property to divide. He walks away with a professional degree and a doctor's license ready to embark on a lucrative career. Courts are slowly coming to the realization that the supporting spouse should be given a remedy in such a situation.

In our example, what financial factors are involved?

1. The amount Pat and/or her family contributed to Bill's support while he was in school

2. The amount Pat and/or her family contributed to the payment of Bill's education expenses

3. The amount Bill would have contributed to the marriage if he had worked during these years rather than gone to school

4. Any increased earnings Pat would have had if she had taken a different job, e.g., by moving to a different location

5. Any increased earnings Pat would have had if she had continued her education rather than working to support Bill through his education

6. The increased standard of living Pat would have enjoyed due to Bill's expected high earnings if they had stayed married

7. The share of his increased earnings to which Pat would have been entitled if they had stayed married

Some courts will consider only items (1) and (2) in providing Pat with a remedy. As a matter of equity, she is entitled only to **restitution**—a return of what she and/or her family contributed while Bill was acquiring his degree and license. A degree and license are not considered divisible property by such courts. They are personal to the holder. Under this view, it logically follows that she is not entitled to a share of his increased earnings as a result of the degree and license. All of the above items (1–7) are taken into consideration in deciding the question of *spousal support*. Increased earnings as a result of the degree and license are taken into consideration because one of the factors in an

Restitution An equitable remedy in which a person is restored to his or her original position prior to the loss or injury. Restoring to the plaintiff the value of what he or she parted with.

alimony or maintenance decree is the spouse's ability to pay. The problem, however, is that the wife may not be eligible for alimony because of her own employability. Nor can equity be done by giving the wife a generous share of tangible property since no such property may have been accumulated due to the fact that the husband had high educational expenses and little or no income of his own. In such situations, one minimal remedy is a direct award for items (1) and (2) above, which again amounts to little more than restitution. A few courts, however, will deny even this remedy, taking the position that the wife, in effect, was making a gift of her money and other resources to the husband during his education.

A growing number of cases, however, have ruled that the degree and license *do* constitute divisible marital property and that more than restitution is called for. The *Woodworth* case is one example:

CASE

WOODWORTH V. WOODWORTH

126 Mich. App. 258, 337 N.W.2d 332 (1983)
Court of Appeals of Michigan

Background: *While Michael Woodworth went through law school, his wife Ann was a nursery school teacher. In their divorce action, she claimed that his law degree was a marital asset that should be divided. The trial court agreed. It valued the degree at $20,000 and ruled that he must pay her $2,000 per year for ten years. The case is now on appeal before the Court of Appeals of Michigan. On appeal, Michael is the plaintiff and Ann is the defendant.*

Decision on Appeal: *A former husband's law degree, which was the end product of a concerted family effort, was marital property subject to distribution upon divorce. The case is remanded to the trial court to recalculate the value of the degree.*

Opinion of the Court:

Judge BURNS delivered the opinion of the court.

On January 6, 1982, the parties' divorce was finalized. Both parties appeal as of right.

The parties were married on June 27, 1970, after plaintiff had graduated from Central Michigan University with a bachelor's degree in secondary education and defendant had graduated from Lansing Community College with an associates degree. They then moved to Jonesville, where plaintiff worked as a teacher and coach for the high school and defendant worked as a nursery school teacher in Hillsdale. In the Fall of 1973, they sold their house, quit their jobs,* and moved to Detroit, where plaintiff attended Wayne State Law School. Three years later, they

moved to Lansing where plaintiff took and passed the bar exam and accepted a job as a research attorney with the Court of Appeals. Plaintiff is now a partner in a Lansing law firm.

For all intents and purposes, the marriage ended on August 25, 1980, when the parties separated. The [chart at the top of the next page] summarizes each party's earnings during the marriage.

The basic issue in this case is whether or not plaintiff's law degree is marital property subject to distribution. The trial court held that it was, valued it at $20,000, and awarded this amount to defendant in payments of $2,000 over ten years. Plaintiff contends that his law degree is not such a marital asset. We disagree.

The facts reveal that plaintiff's law degree was the end product of a concerted family effort. Both parties planned their family life around the effort to attain plaintiff's degree. Toward this end, the family divided the daily tasks encountered in living. While the law degree did not preempt all other facets of their lives, it did become the main focus and goal of their activities. Plaintiff left his job at Jonesville and the family relocated to Detroit so that plaintiff could attend law school. In Detroit, defendant sought and obtained full time employment to support the family.

We conclude, therefore, that plaintiff's law degree was the result of mutual sacrifice and effort by both plaintiff and defendant. While plaintiff studied and attended classes, defendant carried her share of the burden as well as sharing vicariously in the stress of the [law school] experience known as the "paper chase."

We believe that fairness dictates that the spouse who did not earn an advanced degree be compensated whenever the advanced degree is the product of such concerted family investment. The degree

---

*Defendant had already quit her job the year before after the parties' first child was born.

SUMMARY OF EARNINGS DURING THE MARRIAGE

YEAR	PLAINTIFF		DEFENDANT	
1970	$ 2,591	Jonesville HS teacher/coach	$ 1,422	Nursery School Teacher
			$ 2,549	Grant Company (clerk)
1971	$ 7,989	Teacher	$ 4,236	Teacher
	$ 410	St. Anthony Ch. (instructor)	$ 280	St. Anthony Ch. (instructor)
1972	$ 9,691	Teacher	$ 2,525	Teacher
1973	$ 6,557	Teacher	$ 986	Bank Teller
1974	$ 2,483	Legal Aid (student lawyer)	$ 6,572	Bank Teller
1975	$ 2,588	Legal Aid (student lawyer)	$ 1,050	Bank Teller
			$ 8,191	Dept/Social Services (case worker)
1976	$ 6,342	Court of Appeals (attorney)	$10,276	Dept/Social Services (case worker)
1977	$12,493	Court of Appeals (attorney)	$ 1,586	Dept/Social Services (case worker)[†]
	$ 5,595	Assistant Prosecuting Attorney		
1978	$21,085	Assistant Prosecuting Attorney	$—0—	
1979	$27,247	Assistant Prosecuting Attorney	$—0—	
1980	$ 2,057	Assistant Prosecuting Attorney	$—0—	
	$30,000	Private Practice		

[†]Defendant quit this job in January after the parties' third child was born.

---

holder has expended great effort to obtain the degree not only for him or herself, but also to benefit the family as a whole. The other spouse has shared in this effort and contributed in other ways as well, not merely as a gift to the student spouse nor merely to share individually in the benefits but to help the marital unit as a whole. . . .

We are aware that numerous other cases have held that an advanced degree is not a marital asset and may be considered only (if at all) in determining alimony.

However, we reject the reasons given in these cases to support their conclusions. The cases first contend that an advanced degree is simply not "property":

"An educational degree, such as an M.B.A., is simply not encompassed by the broad views of the concept of 'property'. It does not have an exchange value or any objective transferable value on an open market. It is personal to the holder. It terminates on death of the holder and is not inheritable. It cannot be assigned, sold, transferred, conveyed, or pledged. An advanced degree is a cumulative product of many years of previous education, combined with diligence and hard work. It may not be acquired by the mere expenditure of money. It is simply an intellectual achievement that may potentially assist in the future acquisition of property. In our view, it has none of the attributes of property in the usual sense of that term." *Graham v. Graham,* 194 Colo. 432, 374 P.2d 75 (1978).

Yet whether or not an advanced degree can physically or metaphysically be defined as "property" is beside the point. Courts must instead focus on the most equitable solution to dissolving the marriage and dividing among the respective parties what they have.

"[T]he student spouse will walk away with a degree and the supporting spouse will depart with little more than the knowledge that he or she has substantially contributed toward the attainment of that degree." Comment, *The Interest of the Community in a Professional Education,* 10 Cal. West. L. Rev. 590 (1974).

In *DeLa Rosa v. DeLa Rosa,* 309 N.W.2d 758, (1981), the Minnesota Supreme Court added:

"[O]ne spouse has forgone the immediate enjoyment of earned income to enable the other to pursue an advanced education on a full time basis. Typically, this sacrifice is made with the expectation that the parties will enjoy a higher standard of living in the future."

Where, as in this case, the family goal of obtaining the law degree was the purpose of the substantial contribution and sacrifice, both the degree holder and his or her spouse are entitled to share in the fruits of the degree. The trial judge recognized as much:

"Here the plaintiff quit his job and entered law school. The defendant secured employment so plaintiff could become a professional with far greater earning capacity than he had, which would benefit him and their children. To permit this, upon divorce, to benefit only the party who secured the professional degree is unconscionable."

The next argument is that a marriage is not a commercial enterprise and that neither spouse's expectations are necessarily going to be met after the divorce:

"I do not believe that a spouse who works and contributes to the education of the other spouse during marriage normally does so in the expectation of compensation." *Sullivan v. Sullivan,* 184 Cal. Rptr. 801 (1982) (Kaufman, P. J., concurring).

Furthermore:

"They do not nor do they expect to pay each other for their respective contributions in any commercial sense. Rather, they work together, in both income and nonincome producing ways, in their joint, mutual and individual interests.

"The termination of the marriage represents, if nothing else, the disappointment of expectations, financial and nonfinancial, which were hoped to be achieved by and during the continuation of the relationship. It does not, however, in our view, represent a commercial investment loss. Recompense for the disappointed expectations resulting from the failure of the marital entity to survive cannot, therefore, be made to the spouses on a strictly commercial basis which, after the fact seeks to assign monetary values to the contributions consensually made by each of the spouses during the marriage. . . .

"If the plan fails by reason of the termination of the marriage, we do not regard the supporting spouse's consequent loss of expectation by itself as any more compensable or demanding of solicitude than the loss of expectations of any other spouse who, in the hope and anticipation of the endurance of the relationship in its commitments, has invested a portion of his or her life, youth, energy and labor in a failed marriage." *Mahoney v. Mahoney,* 182 N.J. Super. 612–614, 442 A.2d 1062 (1982).

We agree that a marriage is not intrinsically a commercial enterprise. Instead, it is a relationship sanctioned by law governed as its essence by fidelity and troth. Neither partner usually expects to be compensated for his or her efforts. But that consideration does not end the discussion. We are not presently concerned with how best to characterize a marriage while it endures. Instead, we are concerned with how best to distribute between the parties what they have once the marriage has for all intents and purposes dissolved. In other words:

"To allow a student spouse . . . to leave a marriage with all the benefits of additional education and a professional license without compensation to the spouse who bore much of the burdens incident to procuring these would be unfair. . . ." *O'Brien v. O'Brien,* 452 N.Y.S.2d 801, 805 (1982).

Furthermore, we also agree that divorce courts cannot recompense expectations. However, we are not talking about an expectation here. Defendant is not asking us to compensate for a failed expectation that her husband would become a wealthy lawyer and subsequently support her for the rest of her life. Instead, she is merely seeking her share of the fruits of a degree which she helped him earn. We fail to see the difference between compensating her for a degree which she helped him earn and compensating her for a house in his name which her earnings helped him buy.

The third argument against including an advanced degree as marital property is that its valuation is too speculative. In *Lesman v. Lesman,* 452 N.Y.S.2d 938-939 (1982), the Court stated:

"Gross inequities may result from predicating distribution awards upon the speculative expectations of enhanced future earnings, since distributive awards, unlike maintenance, once fixed may not be modified to meet future realities. It is almost impossible to predict what amount of enhanced earnings, if any, will result from a professional education. The degree of financial success attained by those holding a professional degree varies greatly. Some, even, may earn less from their professional practices than they could have earned from non-professional work. Moreover, others, due to choice or factors beyond their control, may never practice their professions."

Michigan has already recognized that:

"Interests which are contingent upon the happening of an event which may or may not occur are not distributable. The party seeking to include the interest in the marital estate bears the burdens of proving a reasonably ascertainable value; if the burden is not met, the interest should not be considered an asset subject to distribution." *Miller v. Miller,* 83 Mich. App. 672, 677, 269 N.W.2d 264 (1978).

However, future earnings due to an advanced degree are not "too speculative." While a degree holder spouse might change professions, earn less than projected at trial, or even die, courts have proved adept at measuring future earnings in such contexts as personal injury, wrongful death, and workers' compensation actions. In fact, pain and suffering, professional goodwill and mental distress, within these general legal issues, have similar valuation "problems". . . . We, therefore, do not believe that the *Miller* contingency caveat applies to future earnings.

The last argument is that these matters are best considered when awarding alimony rather than when distributing the property. . . . A trial judge is given wide discretion in awarding alimony.... However, alimony is basically for the other spouse's support. The considerations for whether or not a spouse is entitled to support are different than for dividing the marital property. *McLain v. McLain,* 108 Mich. App. 166, 310 N.W.2d 316 (1981), listed eleven factors that the trial judge is to consider in determining whether or not to award alimony. Some of these deal with the parties' financial condition and their ability to support themselves. If the spouse has already supported the other spouse through graduate school, he or she is quite possibly already presently capable of supporting him or herself. Furthermore, M.C.L.A. § 552.13; M.S.A. § 25.93 gave the trial court discretion to end alimony if the spouse receiving it remarries. We do not believe that the trial judge should be allowed to deprive the spouse who does not have an advanced degree of the fruits of the marriage and award it all to the other spouse merely because he or she has remarried. Such a situation would necessarily cause that spouse to think twice about remarrying.

Having determined that the defendant is entitled to compensation in this case, we must next determine how she is to be compensated. Two basic methods have been proposed—a percentage share of the present value of the future earnings attributable to the degree or restitution.

[Some courts limit] the recovery to restitution for any money given to the student spouse to earn the degree. While this solution may be equitable in some circumstances, we do not believe that restitution is an adequate remedy in this case. Limiting the recovery to restitution "would provide [the supporting spouse] no realization of [his or] her expectation of economic benefit from the career for which the education laid the foundation." Pinnel, *Divorce After Professional School: Education and Future Earning Capacity May Be Marital Property,* 44 Mo.L.Rev. 329, 335 (1979). Clearly, in this case, the degree was a family investment, rather than a gift or a benefit to the degree holder alone. Treating the degree as such a gift would unjustly enrich the degree holder to the extent that the degree's value exceeds its cost. ... We note that this case does not involve the situation where both parties simultaneously earned substantially similar advanced

degrees during the marriage. In such a situation, equity suggests that the parties have already amply compensated each other.

The trial court in this case valued plaintiff's law degree at $20,000 and ruled that plaintiff must pay defendant $2,000 per year for ten years. We are unable to determine how this value was reached and therefore, remand to the trial court to permit that court to revalue the degree in light of the following factors: the length of the marriage after the degree was obtained, the sources and extent of financial support given plaintiff during his years in law school, and the overall division of the parties' marital property. In determining the degree's present value, the trial court should estimate what the person holding the degree is likely to make in that particular job market and subtract from that what he or she would probably have earned without the degree. ... The ultimate objective in a property distribution is to be fair. ... Both parties may present new evidence on these matters and the degree's valuation.

One of the tragedies of this divorce, as in so many others, is that what used to be financially adequate is no longer enough. As the trial court aptly stated: "The tablecloths ... will not cover both tables." We, therefore, note that the trial court has discretion to order that the payments be made on an installment basis. ... If the trial court should order such a payment schedule, the trial court should also consider the possibility of insuring these payments by a life insurance policy on plaintiff's life benefitting defendant.

Plaintiff has also appealed the overall property division while defendant has cross-appealed from the alimony determination. If the trial court alters the value placed on plaintiff's law degree, the property division and alimony award must also be reassessed. We, therefore, refrain from addressing these issues at this time.

Pursuant to GCR 1963, 726.1, we order plaintiff to pay defendant reasonable attorney fees for this appeal. Costs to defendant.

Remanded with instructions to proceed in a manner consistent with this opinion. We do not retain jurisdiction.

---

a. Was *Woodworth v. Woodworth* correctly decided? Why or why not?

b. Frank and Elaine are married in your state. Both work at low-paying jobs at a fast-food restaurant. Elaine wishes to become a paralegal, and Frank would like to become an electrician. A local institute has a one-year paralegal training program, and a nine-month electrician training program. Frank and Elaine decide that only one of them can go to school at a time. Frank volunteers to let Elaine go first, keeping his job at the restaurant to support them both while she is at the institute. A month before Elaine is scheduled to

ASSIGNMENT 10.10

graduate, Frank has a serious accident at the restaurant. He will not recover fully from his injury or be able to go to school for at least five years. When Elaine is graduated, she obtains a good job as a paralegal. The parties seek a divorce a month after graduation. There are no children from the marriage, and no tangible property to divide. In the divorce proceeding, Frank tells the court that the only asset that can be divided is Elaine's paralegal certificate. He asks the court to award him a percentage of the earnings that Elaine will have during the next five years as a paralegal.

i. How would *Woodworth v. Woodworth* apply to this case? (See General Instructions for the Legal-Analysis Assignment in chapter 1.)

ii. How would your state resolve the case of Elaine and Frank? (See General Instructions for the Court-Opinion Assignment in chapter 1.)

DIVIDING A BUSINESS   When a divorce occurs, one of the assets to be divided may be a business acquired during the marriage or at least developed during this time even if one of the parties had the business before the marriage. The business could be a large corporation, a small sole proprietorship, a partnership, a law practice, a medical practice, etc. Business appraisers are often hired to place a value on the business. In addition to plant and equipment, a number of intangible items must be valued, e.g., patents, trademarks, employment agreements, copyrights, securities, and goodwill.

Many standard business documents[4] must be collected when valuating a business. For example:

- ☐ Federal, state, and local income tax returns for the last five years
- ☐ Annual and interim financial statements
- ☐ Bank statements
- ☐ Depreciation schedules
- ☐ Articles of incorporation and bylaws or partnership agreements, including amendments
- ☐ Minutes of meetings of shareholders and directors
- ☐ Buy/sell agreements of shareholders or partners, including amendments
- ☐ Loan applications
- ☐ W-2 statements (or the equivalent) for the highest paid employees
- ☐ Leases
- ☐ Production schedules
- ☐ Inventory reports
- ☐ Management reports
- ☐ Billing records

Goodwill The favorable reputation of a business that causes it to generate additional business.

One aspect of a business that is sometimes particularly difficult to evaluate is its **goodwill.** Because of goodwill, the company is expected to have earnings beyond what is considered normal for the type of business involved. Individuals providing services, such as accountants and lawyers, may also have goodwill:

> If you are a lawyer facing divorce, it is open season on your practice. . . . Like it or not, law practices and lawyer's goodwill are assets. That you can't sell your practice doesn't mean it has no value. And there are almost no legal limits on the methods an appraiser

4. Part of the following list comes from Business Valuation Research, Inc., of Seattle, Washington.

may use in assigning a value to a law practice. . . . One approach is called the excess earnings method. An appraiser looks at published surveys to find the average income for a lawyer of your experience and type of practice, then compares your earnings with the average. If your earnings are higher than the average, the increment is said to be attributable to goodwill. If your ability to attract clients and collect substantial fees from them brings you more income than you would earn working for an average salary, you have built real goodwill. Gabrielson & Walker, *Surviving Your Own Divorce,* 76, 77 CALIF. LAWYER (June 1987).

If goodwill was developed during the marriage, the spouse who stayed at home may be deemed to have contributed to it (as well as to the rest of the business). In community property states, spouses have a 50/50 interest in the portion of the business (including goodwill) that materialized during the marriage. In other states, the court might reach a different equitable allocation.

The fact that a business (with or without goodwill) is a divisible part of the marital estate does not necessarily mean that upon divorce the business must be sold so that the proceeds can be physically divided. The separation agreement may provide, for example, that the husband gives the wife $150,000 in exchange for the release of any interest that the wife may have in his business. Or vice versa, if she is the one primarily responsible for the business. Similarly, a court may order such an exchange if the parties are not able to agree on dividing the business in their separation agreement.

Does your state have any statutes on the division of a business or profession following a divorce? If so, briefly summarize their terms. (See General Instructions for the State-Code Assignment in chapter 1.)

ASSIGNMENT 10.11

▇▇▇ INSURANCE

A number of questions must be considered by the parties:

☐ What kinds of insurance do the parties now have?

☐ How have the insurance premiums been paid?

☐ Following the separation, what will happen to the policies?

☐ Is there a need for additional insurance?

Several different kinds of insurance policies could be in effect at the time the parties draft the separation agreement:

☐ Life insurance

☐ Homeowners' insurance

☐ Hospitalization or other medical insurance

☐ Liability insurance (for business)

☐ Car insurance

☐ Umbrella insurance

Each kind of policy should be carefully identified with notations as to how much the premiums are, who has paid them, who the beneficiaries are, whether the beneficiaries can be changed and, if so, by whom, etc. Unfortunately, parties often neglect such important details. Insurance policies can be as crucial as other "property" items that must be divided or otherwise negotiated as part of the separation agreement. The parties may opt to leave the policies as they are with no changes. This is fine if it is a conscious decision of *both* parties after *all* the facts are known about each policy, the tax consequences are explained, and the economic advantages and disadvantages of the various ways of handling each policy are discussed.

As we have seen, one spouse usually has no obligation to support the other spouse or the children after the payor spouse dies. The latter, however, may want to assume this obligation voluntarily. Life insurance on the payor's life, with the beneficiaries being the other spouse and/or the children, is a common way of doing this. If such a life insurance policy already exists, then the payor may agree to keep it effective (e.g., pay the premiums) after the separation. The payee and children, however, may not gain much protection from such an agreement if the payor can change the beneficiaries. Hence, as part of the bargaining process, the payee may ask that the designation of the beneficiaries be made irrevocable.

■■■■■ DEBTS

The parties must discuss how to handle:

☐ Debts outstanding (i.e., unpaid) at the time the separation agreement is signed

☐ Debts incurred after the separation agreement is signed

A great variety of debts may be outstanding:

☐ Debts between the spouses (e.g., a loan made by one spouse to the other during the marriage)

☐ Business debts incurred by the husband

☐ Family debts incurred by the husband

☐ Business debts incurred by the wife

☐ Family debts incurred by the wife

Joint and Several Liability More than one person is legally responsible. They are responsible together and individually for the entire amount.

☐ Business or family debts incurred by both the husband and wife (i.e., the debts are in both names so that there is **joint and several liability** on the debts, meaning that a creditor could sue the husband and wife *together* on the debt, or could sue *either* the husband or the wife for payment of the whole debt).

The parties must decide who is going to pay what debts, and the separation agreement should specifically reflect what they have decided.

The extent to which the parties are in debt is relevant to (1) the necessity of using present cash and other resources to pay these debts, (2) the availability of resources to support spouse and children, and (3) the possibility of bankruptcy now or in the immediate future. As for the husband's personal or business debts, for example, the wife should not take the attitude that such debts are "his problem." His bankruptcy might cause her to lose whatever he still owes her under the property division agreement. (As we have seen, however, a bankruptcy would not discharge alimony and child support obligations. See Exhibit 10.3.)

As to future debts (i.e., those incurred after the separation agreement is signed), the normal expectation of the parties is that they will pay their own debts. A cautious spouse will often cancel all joint credit cards. Except for the obligations that arise out of the separation agreement itself, the parties are on their own. A clause should be inserted in the agreement providing that each party promises not to attempt to use the credit of the other.

TAXES

In chapter 15 we will discuss the tax consequences of separation agreements. Our focus here is on the question of who pays the taxes and who will be able to take advantage of certain tax benefits. The following are the kinds of situations the parties need to anticipate:

☐ If the Internal Revenue Service (IRS) assesses a tax deficiency and penalty for a prior year during which the parties filed a joint return, who pays the deficiency and penalty?

☐ If the parties file their last joint return in the current tax year, and then, many months later, the IRS assesses a tax deficiency and penalty on that last tax return, who pays this deficiency and penalty?

☐ In the year in which the separation agreement is signed, if the parties file separate returns, with whose resources are each person's taxes paid?

☐ In the current and in future years, who takes the tax deduction for the payment of interest on the mortgage and for the payment of property taxes?

☐ In the current and in future years, who takes the tax exemption for each of the dependent children?

☐ What happens to any tax refunds for the current tax year and for any prior year?

Often, the husband will agree to a clause in the separation agreement that he will **indemnify** the wife against any tax deficiencies and penalties that may arise out of the joint returns filed in any year during their marriage. Under such a clause, he will have to pay the entire deficiency and penalty for which they both may be jointly and severally liable. Similarly, the parties must also agree on how tax refunds, if any, are to be divided. Such refunds are usually payable by government check to both of the parties. Two signatures are required to sign such checks. Years after a particular return is filed, the IRS might institute an audit. It is a good idea to insert a clause in the separation agreement that both parties agree to cooperate with each other in responding to the issues raised during any possible audits in the future.

Indemnify To compensate another for any loss or expense incurred.

There are laws on who can receive the tax benefits of exemptions and deductions from alimony, interest payments, and property-tax payments. The parties do not have total freedom in deciding who can use these tax benefits. The point, however, is that one of the parties will be entitled to the benefits. This is an economic advantage that should be taken into consideration in the overall evaluation of who is getting what from the separation agreement. The parties make a big mistake when they fail to take account of such matters. The separation agreement may specify a dollar amount to be transferred pursuant to a support clause or a property division clause. If, however, all the tax factors have not been considered, the parties may later be surprised by the discrepancy between such stated dollar figures and the *real* amounts that they receive and pay out.

WILLS

The parties must consider a number of questions involving wills and estates:

☐ Do the spouses already have wills naming each other as beneficiaries? If so, are these wills to be changed? In most states, a divorce automatically revokes gifts to a surviving spouse unless the will specifically says otherwise.

Nevertheless, the parties may want to make this explicit in their separation agreement and also cover the period between separation and the issuance of the final divorce decree.

☐ Have they named each other as **executor** of their estates? If so, is this to be changed?

☐ Is the husband going to agree to leave his wife and/or children something in his will? If so, and this requires a change in his will, when is this change to be made?

☐ Is either spouse mentioned as a beneficiary in the will of a relative of the other spouse? If so, is this likely to be changed?

When a spouse dies, the surviving spouse has important rights in the property of the deceased spouse, sometimes in spite of what the latter intended or provided for in a will. Assume that a spouse dies **testate** leaving nothing to the surviving spouse. In most states, a surviving spouse who is dissatisfied with a will can **elect against the will** and receive a **forced share** of the deceased's property. This share is often the same share that the surviving spouse would have received if the deceased had died **intestate.**

The separation agreement should specify what happens to the right to elect against a will and similar rights such as **dower** and **curtesy.** The normal provision is that each side *releases* all such rights in the other's property.

◼ MISCELLANEOUS PROVISIONS

A number of other items need to be considered:

LEGAL EXPENSES

One spouse is often ordered by the court to pay the attorney fees of the other in a divorce action. The parties may want to specify this in the separation agreement itself. They should consider not only the legal costs (counsel fees, filing fees, etc.) of a potential divorce, but also the legal costs incurred in connection with the preparation of the separation agreement itself. Of course, if both have adequate resources of their own, the parties may agree that they will pay their own legal bills.

NONMOLESTATION CLAUSE

Most separation agreements contain a **nonmolestation clause,** in which both parties agree, in effect, to leave each other alone. Specifically, they will not try to live with the other person, interfere with each other's lifestyle, or bother each other in any way.

◼ MODIFICATION OF THE SEPARATION AGREEMENT

Generally, a court has no power to alter the terms of a valid contract. A separation agreement is a contract. Can its terms be modified? Clearly, the parties to any contract can mutually agree to modify its terms. But can the court *force* a modification on the parties when only one party wants it?

The answer may depend on which terms of the separation agreement are in question. *Property division* terms, as indicated earlier, are rarely modifiable (see

---

Executor The person designated in a will to carry out the terms of the will and handle related matters.

Testate Die leaving a valid will.

Elect against the Will To obtain a designated share of a deceased spouse's estate in spite of what the latter provided or failed to provide for the surviving spouse in a will.

Forced Share The share of a deceased spouse's estate the surviving spouse receives in spite of what the deceased provided or failed to provide for the surviving spouse in a will.

Intestate Die without leaving a valid will.

Dower The right of a widow to the lifetime use of one-third of the land her deceased husband owned during the marriage.

Curtesy The right of a husband to the lifetime use of all the land his deceased wife owned during the marriage (if issue were born of the marriage).

Nonmolestation Clause A clause in an agreement that the parties will not bother each other.

Exhibit 10.3). *Child custody* and *child support* terms, however, are almost always modifiable according to the court's perception of the best interest of the child (see chapters 11 and 12). The area of greatest controversy concerns *alimony* or *spousal-support* terms.

First, consider two extreme and relatively rare circumstances where the court can modify spousal-support terms:

□ The separation agreement itself includes a provision allowing a court to modify its terms.

□ The needy spouse has become so destitute that he or she will become a public charge unless a modification is ordered.

If neither of these situations exists, can the court order a modification of the spousal-support terms of the separation agreement? This involves two separate questions. Does the court have the power to modify, and if so, when will it exercise this power?

THE POWER TO MODIFY

In a few states a court has no power to modify a spousal-support term unless the parties have agreed in the separation agreement to allow the court to do so. Most states, however, will allow their courts to modify a separation agreement even if it expressly says that modification is not allowed. A number of theories have been advanced to support this view. Some states hold that the separation agreement is merely advisory to the court and that as a matter of public policy, the court cannot allow the question of support to be determined solely by the parties. The state as a whole has an interest in seeing to it that this sensitive question is properly resolved. What the parties have agreed upon will be a factor in the court's determination, but it will not be the controlling factor. Other states advance the theory of merger. When a court accepts the terms of a separation agreement, it can *incorporate* and *merge* them into the divorce decree. The agreement loses its separate identity. The question is not whether the separation agreement can be modified, but whether the decree can be modified. Courts are much less reluctant to modify their own decrees than they are to modify the private contracts of parties. Under the merger doctrine, the contract no longer exists. Suppose, however, that a court incorporates but does *not* merge the separation agreement into the decree. Here the court simply refers to the separation agreement in its decree and usually approves the spousal-support terms the parties agreed to. Since there is no merger, the separation agreement remains as an independent—and nonmodifiable—contract.

THE EXERCISE OF THE POWER TO MODIFY

Assuming the court has the power to modify spousal-support orders, when will the court use it? The general rule is that a modification will be ordered only when there has been a substantial change of circumstances of a continuing nature that is not due to voluntary action or inaction of the parties. Furthermore, some courts limit the exercise of their modification power to periodic or ongoing alimony payments; they will not modify a *lump-sum* support award.

Tom and Mary enter a separation agreement that is approved, incorporated, and merged by the court in its divorce decree. Tom is required to pay Mary $750 a month alimony. Assume that Tom comes to the court a year later seeking a decrease, and/or Mary comes seeking an increase.

Unfortunately, courts are not always consistent as to when they will allow a modification in such a case. Consider the following circumstances:

1. *The ex-husband becomes sick and earns substantially less.* Most courts would modify the decree to lessen the amount he must pay—at least during the period when his earning capacity is affected by the illness.

2. *The ex-husband suddenly starts earning a great deal more.* The ex-wife will usually not be able to increase her alimony award simply because her ex-husband becomes more wealthy than he was at the time of the divorce decree. The result might be different if she can show that the *original* alimony award was inadequate due to his weaker earning capacity at that time.

3. *The ex-wife violates the terms of the separation agreement relating to the visitation rights of the ex-husband/father.* Some courts feel that alimony payments and visitation rights are interdependent. If the ex-wife interferes with the father's visitation rights with the children, these courts will reduce or terminate her alimony. For such a result, however, the interference must be substantial.

4. *The ex-wife engages in "immoral" conduct, e.g., has a live-in lover.* When the ex-husband finds out about the lover, his concern is that his alimony payments are being used to support his ex-wife's lover. Most states will not reduce the alimony payments for this reason. In the states that will, the ex-wife's affair usually must be flagrant and ongoing.

5. *The ex-husband wants to retire, change jobs, or go back to school.* When his income is reduced in this way, the courts will consider a downward modification of the alimony obligation only if the proposed change in lifestyle is made in good faith and not simply as a way to avoid paying the original amount of alimony. A rich executive, for example, cannot "drop out" and become a poor farmer. Such an executive, however, may be able to take a lower paying job if this is required for his health.

6. *The ex-husband remarries.* In most states, his alimony obligation to his first wife is not affected by his remarriage. A few states, however, will consider a reduction if it is clear that he cannot meet the burden of supporting two families, particularly when there are children from the second marriage.

7. *The ex-wife remarries.* If the ex-wife remarries, most courts will terminate his alimony obligation unless the parties agreed in the separation agreement that alimony would continue in some form after she remarried.

8. *The ex-husband dies.* Alimony ends on the death of the ex-husband unless the separation agreement provides for its continuance and/or the divorce decree imposes his obligation on the ex-husband's estate.

ASSIGNMENT 10.12

Find authority (e.g., a statute or a court opinion) in your state for the court's power to modify an alimony award. When will such a modification be made? (See also General Instructions for the State Code Assignment and the Court-Opinion Assignment in chapter 1.)

ASSIGNMENT 10.13

Karen and Jim obtain a divorce decree that awards Karen $500 a month in alimony "until she dies or remarries." A year after the divorce decree becomes final, Karen marries Paul. Jim stops the alimony payments. A year later, this marriage to Paul is annulled. Karen now wants Jim to resume paying her $500 a month alimony and to pay her $6,000 to cover the period when she was "married" to Paul ($500 × 12). What result? (See General Instructions for the Legal-Analysis Assignment in chapter 1.)

ARBITRATION AND MEDIATION

Many separation agreements contain a clause providing that disputes arising in the future about the agreement shall be subject to **arbitration.** Normally, a professional arbitration organization, such as the American Arbitration Association, is specified as the arbitrator who will resolve the dispute. A professional group, however, is not necessary. The parties may select a mutually trusted friend or associate as the arbitrator. The agreement should specify who the arbitrator will be and who will pay the arbitration expenses.

An alternative to arbitration is **mediation.** In arbitration, the parties agree in advance to abide by the decision rendered by the arbitrator. A mediator, however, does not make a decision. He or she tries to guide the parties to reach a decision *on their own* in much the same manner as a labor mediator tries to assist union and management to reach a settlement. If mediation does not work, the parties either agree to submit the dispute to an arbitrator or are forced to litigate it in court.

Arbitration The process of submitting a dispute to a third party outside the judicial system who will render a decision that resolves the dispute.

Mediation The process of submitting a dispute to a third party outside the judicial system who will help the parties reach their own resolution of the dispute. The mediator will not render a decision that resolves the dispute.

RECONCILIATION

What happens if the parties become reconciled to each other after they execute the separation agreement but before they divorce? They certainly have the power to cancel or rescind their contract so long as both do so voluntarily. If it is clear that they want to cancel, no problem exists. Legally, the separation agreement goes out of existence. The problem arises when the parties say nothing about the separation agreement after they reconcile and resume cohabitation. Sometime thereafter the parties separate again, and one of them tries to enforce the separation agreement while the other argues that it no longer exists. Courts handle the problem in different ways:

☐ The reconciliation will cancel the alimony or spousal-support terms of the separation agreement, but will not cancel the property division terms.

☐ The reconciliation will cancel the **executory** terms of the separation agreement, but will not cancel the executed (already performed) terms.

Executory Unperformed as yet.

Reconciliation usually means the full and unconditional resumption of the marital relationship; occasional or casual contact will not suffice. The intent must be to abandon the separation agreement and to resume the marital relationship permanently.

Interviewing and Investigation Checklist

Have the Parties Reconciled?

Legal Interviewing Questions

1. On what date did you both sign the separation agreement?

2. When did you stop living together?

3. Where did you both live when you were separated?

4. Was the separation bitter? Describe the circumstances of the separation.

5. After you signed the separation agreement, when did the two of you have your first contact? Describe the circumstances.

6. Have the two of you had sexual intercourse with each other since the separation agreement was signed? How often?

7. Did you ever discuss getting back together again? If so, describe the circumstances, e.g., who initiated the discussion, was there any reluctance?

8. During this period, did the two of you abide by the terms of the separation agreement? Explain.

9. Did you move in together? If so, where did you both stay? Did one of you give up a house or apartment in order to live together?

—Continued

—*Continued*

10. Did you discuss what to do with the separation agreement?

11. Did the two of you assume that it was no longer effective?

12. After you came together again, did either of you continue abiding by any of the terms of the separation agreement?

13. Did either of you give back whatever he or she received under the terms of the separation agreement?

14. When you resumed the relationship, did you feel that the reunion was going to be permanent? What do you think your spouse felt about it?

15. Did either of you attach any conditions to resuming the relationship again?

16. What have the two of you done since you came together again to indicate that you both considered

each other to be husband and wife, e.g., both sign joint tax returns, make joint purchases, spend a lot of time together in public, etc.?

17. Have you separated again? If so, describe the circumstances of the most recent separation.

Possible Investigation Tasks

☐ Interview people who know the plaintiff (P) and defendant (D) well to find out what they know about the alleged reconciliation.

☐ Obtain any documents executed after the separation agreement was signed that may indicate the extent to which P and D did things together during this time, e.g., rent receipts with both of their names on them, opening or continuing joint checking or savings accounts.

ASSIGNMENT 10.14

Tom and Mary execute a separate agreement on February 17, 1978, in which they mutually release all rights (dower, curtesy, right of election, etc.) in each other's estate. They ceased living together on February 2, 1978. On March 13, 1978, Tom moves out of the city. On the next day, he makes a long distance call to Mary in which he says, "This is ridiculous. Why don't you come live with me? You know I still love you." Mary answers, "I guess you're right, but if we are going to live together again, I want you to come back here." Tom then says, "I'm sure we can work that out." They agree to meet next week to discuss it further. Before they meet, Tom dies. Tom's will makes no provision for Mary. Mary now seeks a forced share of his estate, electing against his will. What result? At the time of Tom's death, he was still married to Mary. (See General Instructions for the Legal-Analysis Assignment in chapter 1.)

■■■■■ COMPUTER HELP

Computer companies have designed software to assist the law office in managing the large volume of data involved in the negotiation of a separation agreement. Let's look at one software package that has features common to many. California Family Law Report (CFLR) describes its software, called PRO-Pertizer™, as follows:

PRO*ertizer*™ is a software program designed to help the family law professional divide the client's marital assets.

You can enter a list of up to 500 marital assets for possible division during the dissolution of a marriage, along with the present fair market value and any encumbrances [See Exhibit 10.8]. The program automatically calculates each item's equity (fair market value [FMV] less debt). With a keystroke, you can see the result of assigning an item's full value to either party, or of assigning the item to each in equal or unequal parts. The constant, instantaneous recalculations keep totals accurate and save hours of running and rerunning calculator tapes when formulating and considering negotiation proposals made by both sides.

TUTORIAL	CFLR PROPERTIZER(tm) V.1.0 (c)1987 CFLR Cmb Brkt H: 34.7 W: 39.2							
16		JOINT			BEFORE TAX		TAX	AFTER TAX	
Items	FMV	Debt	Equity	To H	To W	Basis	H Net	W Net
1 Real Estate	200000	50000	150000	75000	75000	25000	44641	40673
2 Furniture	20000	0	20000	0	20000	40000	0	20000
3 Jewelry/Art	15000	0	15000	0	15000	30000	0	15000
4 Vehicles	45000	22000	23000	0	23000	60000	0	23000
5 Cash	100000	0	100000	100000	0	FMV	100000	0
6 Life Ins	1000	0	1000	0	1000	FMV	0	1000
7 Inventory	15000	5000	10000	10000	0	3000	5836	0
8 Securities	27000	0	27000	27000	0	10000	21182	0
9 Retirement	100000	0	100000	20000	80000	FMV	20000	80000
10 Receivables	15000	0	15000	15000	0	0	9796	0
11 Business	200000	75000	125000	125000	0	5000	57343	0
12 MasterCard	0	3500	-3500	-3500	0	FMV	-3500	0
13 Visa	0	4000	-4000	-4000	0	FMV	-4000	0
14 Sears	0	500	-500	-500	0	FMV	-500	0
15 H Credit	2500	0	2500	2500	0	FMV	2500	0
16 W Credit	2500	0	2500	0	2500	FMV	0	2500
17								
18								
Press (F1) for help								
TOTALS:	743000	160000	583000	366500	216500	379000	253218	182173
Equalizing payment due to spouse:				H->W	75000		H->W	35522

When each party's combined marginal bracket (CMB) is entered, each item's tax basis may be entered to view the after-tax effect for both parties as a result of the way in which assets are negotiated.

□ **EXHIBIT 10.8 Propertizer™ Data Entry Screen**

Items can be temporarily blanked out to remove them from consideration and to see how they affect a possible settlement. Rows can be inserted or deleted anywhere, and at any time, within the list of items. To arrive at an equalizing payment of $0, or as close to $0 as possible, any item can be considered separately in order to redistribute equity. You can quickly redistribute an asset to minimize or zero out the before-tax equalizing payment. A *Moore/Marsden* calculation for separating joint and separate interests in real property can be performed for any or all items.

For more information on computer software used in the calculations of child-support payments, see chapter 12. Many software programs have the ability to turn financial data into interesting and effective graphics presentations. For example, the first charts in Exhibit 10.9 compare the income of a husband and wife over a seven-year period. Other charts in Exhibit 10.9 depict bank deposits and withdrawals over a twelve-month period. A dry listing of numbers can come alive when used in conjunction with such charts.

Contact a lawyer or paralegal who works in a law office that practices family law in whole or part, and find out what computer software programs they use on family law cases other than basic word-processing programs used in any kind of case. Write a report about one such program, including its name, functions, cost, level of difficulty, and strengths and weaknesses. Try to obtain the address and phone number of the company that wrote the program. (Perhaps you can write the company and ask for promotional literature on the product. Use its 800 number, if available.)

ASSIGNMENT 10.15

☐ **EXHIBIT 10.9   Graphics Presentations: Seven-Year Comparative Income; 1994 Deposits and Withdrawals (Husband vs. Wife)**

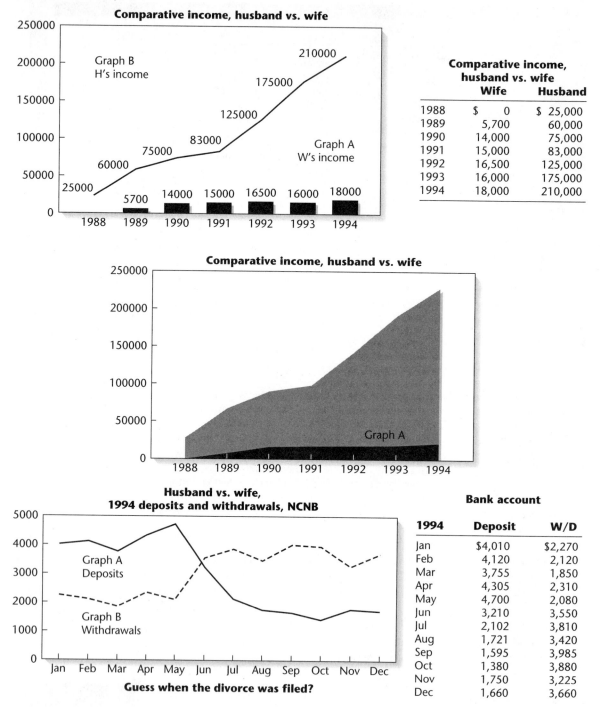

Comparative income, husband vs. wife		
	Wife	**Husband**
1988	$ 0	$ 25,000
1989	5,700	60,000
1990	14,000	75,000
1991	15,000	83,000
1992	16,500	125,000
1993	16,000	175,000
1994	18,000	210,000

Bank account		
1994	**Deposit**	**W/D**
Jan	$4,010	$2,270
Feb	4,120	2,120
Mar	3,755	1,850
Apr	4,305	2,310
May	4,700	2,080
Jun	3,210	3,550
Jul	2,102	3,810
Aug	1,721	3,420
Sep	1,595	3,985
Oct	1,380	3,880
Nov	1,750	3,225
Dec	1,660	3,660

SOURCE: Raggio, "Lawyer-Proof Presentation Graphics," 12 *Family Advocate* 41 (Summer, 1989).

■■■■ SAMPLE SEPARATION-AGREEMENT CLAUSES

Stone B., Modern Legal Forms
§ 4515ff., p. 274ff. West Publishing Co. (1977)

I

Separation Agreement—Significant Clauses*

Agreement made this 19th day of November, 19___ , between John Jones, presently residing at 10 South Street, _____ , hereinafter sometimes referred to as "the Husband," and Mary Jones, presently residing at 25 North Street, _____ , hereinafter sometimes referred to as "the Wife."

Witnesseth:

Whereas, the parties are husband and wife and were married in _____ , on June 15, 19 ___ , and

Whereas, there are two children of the marriage, namely a daughter, Elizabeth Ann Jones, hereinafter referred to as "Elizabeth," born on April 1, 19 ___ , and a son, William Roe Jones, hereinafter referred to as "William," born on August 15, 19 ___ and

Whereas, in consequence of disputes and irreconcilable differences, the parties have separated, and are now living separate and apart, and intend to continue to live separate and apart for the rest of their natural lives; and

Whereas the parties desire to confirm their separation and make arrangements in connection therewith, including the settlement of all questions relating to their property rights, the custody of their children (which the parties recognize as paramount), and other rights and obligations growing out of the marriage relation;

Now, Therefore, in consideration of the premises and of the mutual covenants and undertakings herein set forth, the parties covenant and agree as follows:

Separation

1. The parties may and shall at all times hereafter live and continue to live separate and apart for the rest of their natural lives. Each shall be free from interference, authority and control, direct or indirect, by the other as fully as if he or she were single and unmarried. Subject to the provisions of this agreement, each may reside at such place or places as he or she may select. The parties shall not molest each other or compel or endeavor to compel the other to cohabit or dwell with him or her, by any legal or other proceedings for the restoration of conjugal rights or otherwise.

Wife's Debts

2. The Wife covenants and represents that she has not heretofore incurred or contracted, nor will she at any time in the future incur or contract, any debt, charge or liability whatsoever for which the Husband, his legal representatives, or his property or estate is now or may become liable, and the Wife further covenants at all times to keep the Husband free, harmless and indemnified of and from any and all debts, charges and liabilities heretofore and hereafter contracted by her.

Mutual Release

3. Subject to the provisions of this agreement, each party has remised, released and forever discharged and by these presents does for himself or herself, and his or her heirs, legal representatives, executors, administrators and assigns, remise, release and forever discharge the other of and from all cause or causes of action, claims, rights or demands whatsoever, in law or in equity, which either of the parties hereto ever had or now has against the other, except any or all cause or causes of action for divorce.

Waivers of Claims against Estate

4. Subject to the provisions of this agreement, each of the parties may in any way dispose of his or her property of whatsoever nature, real or personal, and each of the parties hereto, for himself or herself, and for his or her heirs, legal representatives, executors, administrators and assigns, hereby waive any right of election which he or she may have or hereafter acquire

*From a lecture by John Scully, Jr., on *Significant Clauses in a Separation Agreement,* published in 7 Record of the Bar Association of the City of New York 236–250.

regarding the estate of the other, or to take against any last will and testament of the other, whether heretofore or hereafter executed, and renounces and releases all interest, right or claim of right to dower, or otherwise, that he or she now has or might otherwise have against the other, on the property of whatsoever nature, real or personal, of the other, under or by virtue of the laws of any State or country, and each will at the request of the other, or his or her legal representatives, executors, administrators and assigns, execute, acknowledge and deliver any and all deeds, releases, or any other instruments necessary to bar, release or extinguish such interests, rights and claims, or which may be helpful for the proper carrying into effect of any of the provisions of this agreement. Each of the parties renounces and relinquishes any and all claims and rights that he or she may have or may hereafter acquire to act as executor or administrator of the other party's estate.

Division of Personal Property

5. The parties have heretofore divided their personal property to their mutual satisfaction. Henceforth, each of the parties shall own, have and enjoy, independently of any claim or right of the other party, all items of personal property of every kind, nature and description and wheresoever situate, which are now owned or held by or which may hereafter belong or come to the Husband or the Wife, with the full power to the Husband or the Wife to dispose of same as fully and effectually, in all respects and for all purposes, as if he or she were unmarried.

Custody of Children

6. (a) The Wife shall have sole custody of Elizabeth and shall have sole custody of William, except that the Husband may at his option have the custody of either child or both, concurrently or at different or overlapping periods, as follows:

(1) between the 1st day of June and the 30th day of September in each year for a continuous period not to exceed three months; and
(2) during the Christmas holidays each year, for a period of not more than 5 days; and
(3) during the Easter school vacations, for a period of not more than 5 days; and
(4) for one weekend, consisting of Saturday and Sunday, in each calendar month.

(b) The Husband shall exercise his option by notifying the Wife in writing of his intention so to do at least 30 days before the beginning of any such period referred to in subparagraph (1) of paragraph 6(a) and at least 10 days before the beginning of any such period referred to in subparagraphs (2), (3) or (4) of paragraph 6(a).

(c) It is the Husband's intent to exercise the right of custody each year and from time to time, but the Husband's custody as provided in subparagraph 6(a) shall be entirely optional with him and his waiver thereof on any occasion, and for any reason, shall not constitute a waiver of his right to insist thereafter upon compliance with the provision thereof.

(d) The Husband shall have the right to meet with the children at any time on reasonable notice, and the Wife shall afford the Husband the opportunity to do so.

(e) Neither the Husband nor the Wife shall have the right to take or send the children or either of them outside of the continental territorial limits of the United States of America without obtaining the prior written consent of the other.

(f) Each of the parties agrees to keep the other informed at all times of the whereabouts of the children while the children or either of them are with the Husband or Wife respectively, and they mutually agree that if either of them has knowledge of any illness or accident or other circumstances seriously affecting the health or welfare of either of the children, the Husband or the Wife, as the case may be, will promptly notify the other of such circumstances.

(g) The parties shall consult with each other with respect to the education and religious training of the children, their illnesses and operations (except in emergencies), their welfare and other matters of similar importance affecting the children, whose well-being, education and development shall at all times be the paramount consideration of the Husband and the Wife.

(h) The parties shall exert every reasonable effort to maintain free access and unhampered contact between the children and each of the parties, and to foster a feeling of affection between the children and the other party. Neither party shall do anything which may estrange either child from the other party, or injure the opinion of the children as to their mother or father, or which may hamper the free and natural development of either child's love and respect for the other party.

Support of Wife and Children

7. If the Wife has not remarried (should the parties be divorced), the Husband shall make the following payments to the Wife for her life and for the support and maintenance of the Wife and for the support, maintenance and education of the children:
(a) Wife _____ (b) Children _____ .

Wife's Counsel Fees

8. The Husband will pay the reasonable counsel fees and legal expenses of the Wife in connection with negotiation and preparation of this agreement.

Acceptance and Release by Wife

9. The Wife recognizes and acknowledges that the foregoing provisions for her benefit are satisfactory and that they are reasonable and adequate for her support and maintenance, past, present and future, and in keeping with her accustomed mode of living, reasonable requirements and station in life. The Wife accordingly releases and discharges the Husband, absolutely and forever, for the rest of her life from any and all claims and demands, past, present and future for alimony or for any provision for maintenance and support except as contained in this agreement.

Subsequent Divorce

10. In the event that an action for divorce is instituted at any time hereafter by either party against the other in this or any other state or country, the parties hereto agree that they shall be bound by all the terms of this agreement and this agreement shall *not* be merged in any decree or judgment that may be granted in such action but shall survive the same and shall be forever binding and conclusive on the parties and nothing herein contained shall be construed to prevent the decree of judgment in any such action from incorporating in full or in substance the terms of this agreement.

Entire Agreement

11. Both the legal and practical effect of this agreement in each and every respect and the financial status of the parties has been fully explained to both parties by their respective counsel and they both acknowledge that it is a fair agreement and is not the result of any fraud, duress, or undue influence exercised by either party upon the other or by any other person or persons upon either, and they further agree that this agreement contains the entire understanding of the parties. There are no representations, promises, warranties, convenants, or undertakings other than those expressly set forth herein.

Additional Instruments

12. Each of the parties agrees further at any time and from time to time to make, execute, and deliver all instruments necessary to effectuate the provisions of this agreement.

Notices

13. For the purpose of this agreement, all notices or other communications given or made hereunder shall, until written notice to the contrary, be given or mailed to the Wife at 25 North Street, _____ , and to the Husband at 10 South Street, _____ .

Each party shall at all times keep the other party informed of his or her place of residence and business and shall promptly notify the other party of any change, giving the address of any new place of residence or business.

Situs

14. All matters affecting the interpretation of this agreement and the rights of the parties hereto shall be governed by the laws of the State of _____ .

Binding Effect

15. All the provisions of this agreement shall be binding upon the respective heirs, next of kin, executors, administrators, and assigns of the parties hereto.

Counterparts

16. This agreement shall be executed in triplicate, each of which so executed shall be deemed an original and shall constitute one and the same agreement.

In Witness Whereof, the parties hereto have hereunto set their respective hands and seals and initialed each page of this agreement the day and year first above written.

Witnesses:

———————————————— .   ———————————————— . [L.S.]

———————————————— .   ———————————————— . [L.S.]

[Add acknowledgments]

II
Separation Agreement—Fixed Monthly
Payments—Custody and Support of Children

This Agreement is made the _____ day of _____ , 19 ___ , between _____ , herein called the Husband, and _____ , his wife, herein called the Wife.

Whereas the Husband and Wife were married on the _____ day of _____ , 19___ , and have two children, _____ and _____ ;

Whereas differences have arisen between the Husband and Wife as the result of which they are now living separate and apart;

Whereas the Husband and Wife have entered into this Agreement freely, with the advice of counsel, and acknowledge that its provisions are fair.

The parties agree as follows:

Separation

1. The Husband and Wife may live apart from each other as if they were unmarried. Each shall be free from the control of the other and may reside at such place as he or she shall think fit.

No Interference

2. The Husband and Wife will not in any manner annoy, molest, or disturb the other, or compel or endeavor to compel the other to cohabit or dwell with him or her.

Wife's Debts

3. The Wife will at all times keep the Husband indemnified against all debts and liabilities she may hereafter contract and from all actions, claims, demands, costs, damages, and expenses on account thereof. In case the Husband shall at any time be called on to and shall pay any debt or debts she may hereafter contract, then it shall be lawful for the Husband to retain out of the next amount payable to the Wife hereunder the amount of such debt or debts with all costs and expenses he may incur on account thereof.

Division of Household Goods

4. The Husband and Wife have divided between them to their mutual satisfaction the personal effects, household furniture and furnishings, and all other articles of personal property used by them in common, in accordance with the Schedule attached hereto.

Transfer of Home

5. The Husband has conveyed to the Wife by deed, executed, acknowledged, and delivered simultaneously with the execution of this Agreement, the property which was the former home of the parties and in which the Wife now resides.

Support of Wife

6. The Husband shall during the life of the Wife and until she remarries pay to the Wife, or to such person as she shall from time to time appoint in writing, the yearly sum of _____ dollars by equal monthly payments beginning on the _____ day of _____ , 19 ___ , for the support and maintenance of herself.

Custody of the Children in Wife

7. The Wife shall have the sole custody and control of the children, _____ and _____ , without any interference on the part of the Husband except as herein provided.

Right of Husband to Visit Children

8. The Husband shall have the right to visit the children or either of them one day every two weeks if he so desires at reasonable times and places. Further, the Husband shall at his

option have the custody of the children or either of them during the summer school holidays for a continuous period of one month.

Duty to the Wife to Care for Children

9. The Wife shall properly care for, educate, and maintain the children until they respectively reach the age of 18 years.

Support of Children

10. The Husband shall pay to the Wife as long as she shall have custody of the children or either of them the sum of _____ dollars each month beginning on the _____ day of _____ , 19 ___ , for the support and education of each child so in the custody of the Wife until such child reaches the age of 18 years.

Mutual Release

11. Except as herein otherwise provided, the Husband and Wife release and forever discharge the other of and from all causes of action, claims, rights, or demands whatsoever in law or in equity which either of the parties hereto ever had or now has against the other except all causes of action for divorce.

Subsequent Divorce

12. If the Husband and Wife shall hereafter apply for a divorce and the court shall grant the same, this Agreement shall be submitted to the court for approval. If it is approved by the court, the terms thereof shall be carried into the decree of divorce and operate as a final determination of the property rights of the parties.

Wife's Attorney's Fees

13. The Husband shall pay to _____ the sum of _____ dollars for his services as attorney to the Wife in connection with the negotiation and preparation of this Agreement.

Additional Instruments

14. The Husband and Wife shall at the request of the other execute, acknowledge, and deliver to the other party any and all further instruments that may be reasonably required to give full force and effect to the provisions of this Agreement.

Binding Effect

15. This Agreement shall be binding on the heirs, executors, administrators, and assigns of the parties hereto.

In witness whereof the parties have signed and sealed this Agreement.

_____ [*Seal*]
_____ [*Seal*]

[*Add acknowledgments*]

III
Separation Agreement—Dismissal of
Pending Action for Separation—Lump
Sum Cash and Property Settlement—No Children

This agreement, made this _____ day of _____ , 19 ___ , between _____ , the Husband and _____ , the Wife.

Whereas, the parties were married on _____ day of _____ , 19 ___ , and thereafter, on or about the _____ day of _____ , 19 ___ , separated and have since lived apart;

Whereas, an action was instituted by the Wife against the Husband in the _____ Court of _____ , for a separation and provision for the maintenance of the Wife;

Whereas, the parties have agreed upon what is a reasonable provision for the support and maintenance of the Wife, past, present, and for the remainder of her natural life; and

Whereas, the parties have agreed on a reasonable and just disposal of all of the property of the Husband, free and discharged of any and all past, present, and future claims, demands, charges, dower estate rights, interests, liens, or other property rights of any kind whatsoever of the Wife.

Now, therefore, the parties agree as follows:

Separation

1. The parties agree to continue to live separate and apart from each other the same as if unmarried. Each may reside from time to time at such place or places, and, conduct, carry on and engage in any employment, business, or trade he or she shall deem fit, free from any control, restraint, or interference direct or indirect by the other.

Dismissal of Action

2. The parties agree that the said action for separation and maintenance now pending in the _____ Court shall be immediately dismissed without costs to either party.

Wife's Support

3. Simultaneously with the signing of this agreement the Husband agrees to pay to the Wife the sum of _____ dollars, and to pay her attorney's bills and court disbursements in said action, amounting to _____ dollars, and further to convey to her by warranty deed the following described property: [*Description*]. It is understood that said money and property is given to the Wife for her support and maintenance. The Wife agrees that such provision is ample and will in fact provide her with a support and maintenance befitting her station in life, and she accepts said money and property in full satisfaction and in lieu of support and maintenance by the Husband during her life.

No Future Liability

4. Neither party shall contract any debts in the name of the other, or in any way attempt to charge the other with liability therefor, nor will either party claim or demand maintenance or support from the other.

Each Spouse Releases Right in Property of Deceased Spouse

5. The Wife agrees that the estate of the Husband, after the payment of the consideration herein mentioned to the Wife, shall belong to the person or persons who would have become entitled thereto if the Wife had died during the lifetime of the Husband; and the Wife further agrees that she will permit any will of the Husband to be probated, and allow administration upon his personal estate to be taken out by the person or persons who would have been entitled so to do, had the Wife died during the lifetime of the Husband. The Husband agrees that the estate of the Wife, including the consideration herein mentioned, shall belong to the person or persons who would have become entitled thereto if the Husband had died during the lifetime of the Wife; and the Husband further agrees that he will permit any will of the Wife to be probated, and allow administration upon her personal estate to be taken out by the person or persons who would have been entitled so to do, had the Husband died during the lifetime of the Wife.

Further Assurance

6. The parties shall make, execute, and deliver any and all such further assurances as the other of the parties shall reasonably require, for the purpose of giving full effect to the provisions of this agreement.

Effect of Divorce

7. The Wife agrees that in case the marriage between the parties should be dissolved by order of a court, then the consideration passing to the Wife under this agreement shall stand as full satisfaction and discharge of alimony, counsel fees, and other claims and demands that might be made by the Wife against the Husband for any cause whatever.

In Witness Whereof, *etc.*

[*Signatures*]

IV
Separation Agreement Incident
to Divorce Action—Lump Sum Cash Settlement—No Children

This agreement made _____ , 19 ___ , between _____ , the Husband, and _____ , the Wife.

Whereas on _____ , 19 ___ , the parties were married in _____ County, _____ , and lived together as husband and wife until _____ , 19 ___ , and have reached the conclusion that it will be impossible for them to continue to live together;

Whereas a bill for divorce has been prepared and the parties are desirous of settling any and all claims for alimony that the Wife might have against the Husband; and

Whereas each party acknowledges that this agreement has been entered into freely with full knowledge of the facts, and each party believes that under the circumstances the sum of $ _____ is a fair and adequate settlement of all alimony;

Now, therefore, in consideration of the payment to the Wife of the sum of $ _____ , the receipt of which is hereby acknowledged, the Wife does hereby release the Husband from any and all claims, now and hereafter, that might arise by way of alimony. The said settlement of alimony is hereby accepted as a full release of any and all liability, present and future, in so far as any alimony or property adjustment between the Husband and the Wife is concerned.

The foregoing settlement is approved by the undersigned _____ as attorney for the Wife. In Witness Whereof, *etc.*

[*Signatures*]

V

Separation Agreement—Divorce Action Pending—Fixed Monthly Payments—Deposit of Property to Secure Such Payments— Release of Wife's Interest in Community Property—No Children*

This agreement made this _____ day of _____ , 19 ___ , between _____ , herein called the Husband, and _____ , herein called the Wife.

Whereas, the parties were united in marriage at _____ , on the _____ day of _____ , 19 ___ , and lived together as husband and wife until the _____ day of _____ , 19 ___ ; and

Whereas, during the time the parties lived together as husband and wife they acquired certain real and personal property which comprises their community estate and which is not susceptible of partition; and

Whereas, on the _____ day of _____ , 19 ___ , the Wife filed her petition in the ___ Court of _____ County, _____ , praying that the marriage relation between herself and the Husband be dissolved, and the parties have agreed that in the event said marriage relation is dissolved by judgment of said Court as prayed for in said petition, in lieu of a partition of said community estate the Husband shall pay to the Wife the sum of _____ dollars per month so long as she shall live, and the Wife shall transfer, assign, and convey to the Husband all her right, title, and interest in and to said community estate;

Now, therefore, it is agreed as follows:

1. The Husband agrees to pay to the Wife the sum of _____ dollars on the first day of _____ , 19 ___ , and the sum of _____ dollars on the first day of each and every month thereafter so long as she shall live, said payments to be made by the Husband to the _____ National Bank of _____ , with instructions to said bank to promptly pay the same to the Wife. For the purpose of guaranteeing such payments the Husband shall deposit with said bank the sum of _____ dollars in cash and _____ shares of the capital stock of _____ Corporation, of the approximate present value of _____ dollars; provided that the Husband

---

*Adapted from the record in *Farrell v. Commissioner of Internal Revenue*, 134 F.2d 193 (C.C.A. Tex. 1943) certiorari denied 64 S. Ct. 47, 320 U.S. 745, 88 L. Ed 442, a proceeding to collect a deficiency in income taxes from one of the parties to this agreement.

The community property released in this contract consisted in part of oil leases that subsequently turned out to be very valuable. Shortly after this agreement was executed, Mrs. Farrell secured a divorce from her husband and the decree embodied the terms of the contract with respect to the monthly payments and the transfer of the community interest to the husband. Four days later she married again.

About two years later she brought suit in the Texas courts to have the property provisions of the divorce decree set aside on the ground that she was induced to enter into this agreement by fraud. The Court of Civil Appeals in *Burguieres v. Farrell*, 85 S.W.2d 952 (Tex. Civ. App. 1935) upheld the agreement, holding that the entire transaction was fair, that the wife was fully informed and there was no fraud.

shall have the right at any time to withdraw such shares of stock upon depositing with said bank the further sum of _____ dollars in cash in lieu thereof; and provided further that in the event the Husband shall fail to make any of the payments herein provided for, said _____ bank shall have the right to sell said shares of stock for cash and make such payments to the Wife out of such fund, and in such event the Wife shall have the right to require the Husband to deposit the amount of such payment or payments with said bank in order that such fund shall at all times be maintained at the sum of _____ dollars or at the sum of _____ dollars and said _____ shares of the capital stock of _____ Corporation.

2. The Wife agrees that all property, belonging to the community estate of the parties, shall be and become the separate property of the Husband, and any and all rights, title, and interest in and to said property now belonging to the Wife, or which might be claimed by her, shall be, and the same hereby is, transferred, assigned, and conveyed to the Husband, free from any and all liens or claims on the part of the Wife, and the Wife further agrees that she will, upon demand, execute and deliver to the Husband proper deeds, assignments, or conveyances for any and all of such property conveying the title therein to the Husband.

In Witness Whereof, *etc.*

VI
Separation Agreement—Divorce Action Pending—Lump Sum and Fixed Monthly Payments to Wife—Transfer of Community Property to Husband—Custody and Support of Children

This agreement made the _____ day of _____ , 19 ___ , between _____ , herein called the Husband, and _____ , herein called the Wife.

Whereas, disputes have arisen between the parties, and by reason thereof they have agreed to live separate and apart from each other during their natural lives; and

Whereas, the Husband as plaintiff filed a suit for divorce in the _____ Court of _____ County, _____ , numbered _____ on the docket of said Court, which suit is now pending, and the Wife has filed her cross-action for divorce in said suit, and regardless of the outcome of the trial thereof, the parties recognize that their differences are so great that a reconciliation is impossible; and

Whereas, the Husband has furnished to the Wife a list of all principal assets and liabilities as of _____ , 19 ___ , and has also furnished additional information as to change of assets and liabilities as of this date, and the Wife has investigated and appraised these assets and liabilities with the aid of her legal counsel and is thoroughly conversant with all facts; and

Whereas, the parties desire to completely and forever settle their property rights in and to their community property, which is all of the property that either of them possesses.

The parties agree as follows:

Separation

1. They shall live separate and apart from each other the remainder of their natural lives, and neither shall have any right in any way to control the personal actions or conduct of the other, or to complain about such actions or conduct except in so far as the same may affect the right of custody of their children, and neither shall in any way molest, disturb, or trouble the other.

Alimony to Wife

2. In full, final, and complete settlement of all the rights of the Wife in and to the community property of the parties, as well as any and all other claims which she may now or hereafter have against the Husband arising out of the marriage relationship, the Husband has paid and promises to pay to the Wife the following amounts:

(a) *Lump Sum Payment.* The Husband has this day paid to the Wife the sum of $ _____ , receipt of which is hereby acknowledged.

(b) *Fixed Monthly Payments.* The Husband promises to pay to the Wife at _____ , the sum of $ _____ per month for _____ years, the first payment being due _____ and one payment being due on the _____ day of each month thereafter for _____ full years. Such payments may be made by check mailed to the Wife on or before the due dates, addressed to the last address that the Wife may have given in writing to the Husband.

(c) *Insurance Policies to Secure Monthly Payments.* The Husband shall at all times carry life insurance in solvent companies, payable to the Wife as beneficiary, for the amount of the then unpaid installments hereinabove provided, discounted at _____ per cent per year compounded for the period of prepayment; and upon the Husband's death, the Wife shall accept payment of said insurance money in full payment and satisfaction of all of the then unpaid monthly payments provided for in paragraph (b) hereof. The husband shall have the right to discharge his obligations under said paragraph (b) at any time after the expiration of _____ years from this date by paying the value of unmatured installments discounted at _____ per cent per year compounded for the period of prepayment.

(d) *Upon Death of Wife, Wife's Monthly Payments to Be Made to Children.* Should the Wife die before the monthly installments are all paid, the then remaining installments shall be paid as they mature to the _____ children of the parties in equal parts, or to their guardian if they are then minors.

(e) *Transfer to Wife of Personal Belongings.* The Wife shall have as her property all of the silverware, dishes, glassware, linens, rugs, drapes, furniture, pictures, and furnishings now in the home at _____, except [*description*], which excepted articles shall belong to the Husband. The Wife shall vacate the home on or before _____, 19 ___, but agrees that the Husband may keep all of her said personal property in the home until _____, 19 ___, at which time she shall remove the same, provided however that if the home is sold at an earlier date she shall upon demand remove her personal property.

Transfer of Community Property to Husband

3. All other property, rights, claims, and choses in action belonging to the Husband or to their community estate, whether or not herein specifically mentioned, shall belong absolutely to the Husband, as his separate property, and the Wife agrees to execute to the Husband upon demand general warranty deeds covering her interest in all real property owned by them and bills of sale or other conveyances of title to such personal property. The principal items of property to be conveyed are as follows: [*description*].

Wife's Debts

4. The Wife agrees to pay promptly all bills incurred by her since _____, 19 ___. Should the Wife fail to pay any of such bills, and demand for payment is made on the Husband, he may pay same and deduct the amount so paid from the monthly payments owing by him to the Wife.

Community Debts

5. The Husband agrees to pay all of the community indebtedness of the parties not herein assumed by the Wife.

Custody of Children

6. The two children, _____ and _____, shall remain with the Wife, subject to the orders of the Court as is provided by law in such cases. The Husband shall have the right to visit his children and to have their company and companionship at reasonable times to be arranged.

Support of Children

7. The Husband shall pay to the Wife the sum of $ _____ per month for each child on the first day of each month for the support and maintenance of the two children, which payments shall continue until the Husband's legal obligation to support them ends, or until changed as to amount by agreement of the parties or by order of the Court. Such payments shall cover all living expenses of the children that could be chargeable to the Husband, except tuition to schools to be selected by agreement of the parties which the Husband shall also pay, and such medical expenses as the Husband may first approve in writing. If one or both of the children shall at any time, by agreement of the parties, be sent to boarding schools or to summer camps, the Husband shall pay their reasonable expenses while there, but during such times he shall not be required to make the monthly payments otherwise required to be made to the Wife for their support and maintenance.

Mutual Release

8. In consideration of the payments now made and agreed to be hereafter made, the parties do each declare this to be a full, final, and complete settlement of all of their property rights, and each party does hereby release and relinquish to the other all of his or her rights, title,

claim, interest, and demand, accrued or accruing in and to the property of the other whether now in being or hereafter acquired; and this shall be a full and complete settlement of the controversy over the property rights of the parties, involved in cause No. _____ in the _____ Court of _____ County, and, except for the right of either party to prosecute his or her suit for complete divorce, this settlement shall be a bar to any suit at law or otherwise for anything growing out of the marriage relation of the parties as well as the property rights of the one against the other.

Witness our hands, in triplicate, at _____ , this _____ day of _____ , 19 ___ .

_____

_____

Witnesses:

_____

_____

[*Add Acknowledgments*]

VII
Separation Agreement—Divorce
Action Pending—Alimony Based on
Oil Royalties—Custody and Support of Child

This agreement, made this _____ day of _____ , 19 ___ , between _____ , of _____ , herein called the Husband, and _____ , of _____ , herein called the Wife, witnesseth:

Whereas, the parties are husband and wife, but are now living separate and apart from each other, and it is their intention to continue to live separate and apart; and,

Whereas, the Wife has this day instituted suit for divorce against the Husband in the _____ Court of _____ County, _____ , under cause numbered _____ in said Court, and has asked that she be awarded the custody, care, control, and education of _____ , minor child of the parties and for the ratification and approval of this property settlement and agreement concerning the support and maintenance of said child; and,

Whereas, the parties have this day reached a satisfactory agreement between themselves out of Court concerning the custody, support, and maintenance of said child, and the support, maintenance, and alimony of the Wife, as well as for a division of and settlement of property rights, claims, or demands of any nature, either past, present, or future, as hereinafter set out.

Now, therefore, the parties agree as follows:

Custody of Child

1. The Wife is to have the care, custody, and control of _____ , minor child of the parties, subject to the approval of the _____ Court of _____ County, _____ , subject to any future orders of said Court concerning the custody of said child and subject to the right of the Husband to visit said child at any and all reasonable times and occasions; and the Wife, subject to the conditions hereinafter stated, accepts the custody of said child and agrees to properly care for, support, rear, train, and educate said child to the best of her ability, it being understood that the Wife shall have the right to select the residence for said child at whatsoever place within the State of _____ she may desire, but that she will inform the Husband of any change in said place of residence.

Support of Wife and Child

2. The Husband shall turn over to the Wife for the support of and maintenance of herself and _____ , minor child of the parties, until such time as the Wife may remarry, all of the proceeds arising from his interest in oil and gas royalties from wells now producing, and one half of all of the proceeds arising from his interest in oil and gas royalties from any wells which may be hereafter drilled upon any and all land now owned by the Husband, or in which he may own any interest, either legal or equitable, said land being particularly described as follows: [*Here describe*].

Remarriage or Death of Wife

3. It is further agreed that in the event of the remarriage of the Wife to any person other than the Husband during the lifetime of _____ , minor child of the parties, then all of said

oil and gas royalties, oil and gas runs, or proceeds from same arising from said lands shall be paid to said child, or to her duly appointed guardian. In the event the Husband and the Wife remarry each other, or in the event the Wife marries someone other than the Husband during the lifetime of said child, and said child thereafter dies, or in the event of the remarriage of the Wife after the death of said child, or in the event of the death of the Wife at any time, then immediately upon the happening thereof, the Husband shall be entitled to, and shall have and receive all such oil and gas royalties, oil and gas runs, or other proceeds arising from the same not already paid over to the Wife or to said child under this agreement; and the Wife agrees that in the event of any such remarriage she will promptly make, execute, and deliver any necessary and proper transfer orders, division orders, or other instruments necessary to enable such person as is entitled thereto under this agreement to collect and receive same, and that in the event she should refuse or neglect to do so, then this instrument shall be treated and construed as a compliance and assignment of said interests, runs, and royalties.

Sale of Royalty Interest

4. It is further agreed that the Husband shall have the full and unrestricted use of all of the lands in any manner acquired by him and the rents and profits thereof, except the royalties and oil and gas runs above mentioned, but that in the event of the sale by the Husband of any of said real estate herein described during the lifetime of _____ , minor child of the parties, the Husband shall pay over to said child, or to her duly appointed guardian, for her use, support, maintenance and education, one third of any and all sums realized from the sale of any or all of said property and that the Wife will, upon request, join with the Husband, or will execute, acknowledge, and deliver any and all necessary and proper instruments in writing to effectuate the sale and conveyance of any such property; it being understood, however, that nothing in this paragraph shall be construed as conferring the right upon the Husband to make any sale or conveyance of any oil or gas royalty in, to, or under any of the land above described, but that said oil and gas royalty interests in said land shall be held for the use, support, and maintenance of the Wife and said child, as herein provided.

Release by Wife

5. The Wife agrees that she will not at any time undertake to hold the Husband liable for, or undertake to collect from him any sums for alimony, court costs, attorneys' fees, support, and maintenance for herself or said child, and that this agreement may be pleaded in any suit as a defense to any action for alimony, court costs, attorneys' fees, support, and maintenance.

Witness our signatures in duplicate the day and year above written.

_____

_____

[Add acknowledgments]

_____

Sample Property Agreement

California Judicial Council Form Manual
3-99 to 3-82 (Jan. 1988)

I. We are Waldo P. Smedlap, hereafter called Husband, and Lydia T. Smedlap, hereafter called Wife.[1] We were married on October 7, 1978 and separated on December 5, 1979. Because irreconcilable differences have caused the permanent breakdown of our marriage,[2] we have made this agreement together to settle once and for all what we owe to each other and what we can expect from each other. Each of us states here that nothing has been held back, that we have honestly included everything we could think of in listing the money and goods that we own; and each of us states here that we believe the other one has been open and honest in writing this agreement. And each of us agrees to sign and exchange any papers that might be needed to complete this agreement.

Each of us also understands that even after a Joint Petition for Summary Dissolution is filed, this entire agreement will be cancelled if either of us revokes the Dissolution Proceeding.[3]

[1] *Wherever the word Husband appears anywhere in this agreement, it will stand for Waldo P. Smedlap; wherever the word Wife appears, it will stand for Lydia T. Smedlap.*

[2] *This means that there are problems in your marriage which you think can never be solved.* **Irreconcilable differences** *are the only legal grounds for getting a* **Summary Dissolution.**

[3] *This means that the property agreement is a part of*

the divorce proceedings. If either of you decides to stop the Dissolution proceedings by turning in a **Notice of Revocation of Summary Dissolution,** this entire agreement will be cancelled.

[4]Community property is property which you own as a couple. If you have no community property, replace part II with the simple statement, **"We have no community property."**

[5]If furniture and household goods in one apartment are to be divided, then they may have to be listed item by item.

[6]If you have no unpaid debts, replace part III with the simple statement, **"We have no unpaid community obligations."**

[7]A general rule for dividing debts is to give the debt over to the person who benefited most from the item. In the sample agreement, since the Husband received the education, you could agree that he should pay off the loan.

[8]In this clause you are giving up the right to have your spouse support you.

II. Division of Community Property[4]
We divided our community property as follows:

1. Husband transfers to Wife as her sole and separate property:
   A. All household furniture and furnishings located at her apartment at 180 Needlepoint Way, San Francisco.[5]
   B. All rights to cash in savings account #08-73412-085 at Home Savings.
   C. All cash value in life insurance policy #798567 Sun Valley Life Insurance, insuring life of Wife.
   D. All retirement and pension plan benefits earned by Wife during marriage.
   E. 2 U.S. Savings Bond Series E.
   F. Wife's jewelry.
   G. 1972 Chevrolet 4-door sedan, License No. EXL 129.

2. Wife transfers to Husband as his sole and separate property:
   A. All household furniture and furnishings located at his apartment on 222 Bond Street, San Francisco.
   B. All retirement and pension plan benefits earned by Husband during the marriage.
   C. Season tickets to Golden State Terriers Basketball games.
   D. 1 stereo set.
   E. 1 set of Jack Nicklaus golf clubs.
   F. 1 RAC color television.
   G. 1973 Ford station wagon License No. EPX 758.
   H. 1 pet parrot named Arthur, plus cage and parrot food.
   I. All rights to cash in Checking Account #1721-319748-07, Bank of America.

III. Division of Community Property (Debts)[6]

1. Husband shall pay the following debts and will not at any time hold Wife responsible for them:
   A. Mister Charge account #417-38159 208-094.
   B. Debt to Dr. R. C. Himple.
   C. Debt to Sam's Drugs.
   D. Debt to U.C. Berkeley for college education loan to Husband.[7]

2. Wife shall pay the following debts and will not at any time hold Husband responsible for them:
   A. Cogwell's charge account #808921.
   B. Debt to Wife's parents, Mr. and Mrs. Joseph Smith.
   C. Debt to Green's Furniture.
   D. Debt to Dr. Irving Roberts.

IV. Waiver of Spousal Support[8]
Each of us waives any claim for spousal support now and for all time.

V. Dated: _____ Dated: _____

_____   _____
Waldo P. Smedlap   Lydia T. Smedlap

ASSIGNMENT 10.16

Two members of the class will role-play in front of the rest of the class a negotiation session involving a husband and wife who want to enter a separation agreement. The spouses are representing themselves. They have two children, ages two and three. Each member of the class (including the two role-players) will draft a separation agreement based upon the understandings reached at the negotiation session. The role-players can make up the facts as they go along, e.g., names of the parties, addresses, kinds of assets involved. Use the checklist on pages 195–196 as an overview of the topics to be negotiated. In the negotiation session, the role-players should not act hostile toward each other. They should be courteous but anxious to protect their own rights. Finally, they should not leave any matters hanging—everything discussed should result in some form of agreement through the process of bargaining and compromise. (See General Instructions for the Agreement-Drafting Assignment in chapter 1.)

SUMMARY

A major goal of the law office is to prepare an effective separation agreement that will avoid litigation. The first step is the collection of extensive information, particularly financial information pertaining to everyone involved. Elaborate checklists can be helpful in this effort, as well as detailed interrogatories sent to the other spouse.

For a separation agreement to be valid, the parties must have the capacity to contract. The agreement must not violate public policy by inducing the parties to divorce, and it must not be the product of collusion, duress, or fraud. Finally, the consideration for the agreement must be proper.

The separation agreement should clearly distinguish alimony from property division. The distinction can be relevant in a number of areas, e.g., the effect of bankruptcy, the effect of remarriage and death, the availability of enforcement by contempt, the power of the court to modify terms, and federal tax treatment. The distinction is not simply a matter of labels. The question is, what did the parties intend?

In negotiating alimony, the parties should consider a number of factors, e.g., method of payment, coverage, relationship to child support, modification, termination, and security. The principal focus of the court will be the needs of the recipient, the length of the marriage, and the ability of the payor to pay. In most states marital fault is not relevant.

In negotiating property division, the first step is to categorize all the property to be divided as personal or real. What resources were used to acquire it? How is title held? The division that is made depends on the bargaining process and on whether the parties live in a community property state or in a common law property state. Pension assets can be divided, particularly through a Qualified Domestic Relations Order (QDRO). Businesses are also divisible, including their goodwill. Not all states agree, however, as to whether a license or degree can be divided.

The parties need to consider the continuation of insurance policies, debts incurred before and after the separation agreement is signed, the payment of taxes, whether wills need to be changed, the payment of counsel fees, and the need for a nonmolestation clause.

Child custody and child support terms of a separation agreement are modifiable by a court, unlike property division terms. Spousal support terms are often modifiable, particularly if the separation agreement has been incorporated and merged into the divorce decree

When problems arise that involve an interpretation of the separation agreement, the parties may decide to submit the controversy to arbitration or mediation in lieu of litigation. If the parties reconcile and resume cohabitation after they sign the separation agreement, the spousal support terms (but not the property division terms) are automatically canceled in some states. In others, both support and property division terms are canceled if they are executory.

KEY CHAPTER TERMINOLOGY

Separation Agreement	Arrearages	In Vitro Fertilization
Interrogatories	Outstanding	Bequest
Conducive to Divorce	Discharged	Devise
Public Policy	Estate	Intestate Succession
Collusion	Contempt	Joint Tenancy
Migratory Divorce	Contingent	Right of Survivorship
Duress	Payor	Tenancy by the Entirety
Aggrieved	Payee	Tenancy in Common
Fraud	Escrow	Operation of Law
At Arm's Length	Surety Bond	Community Property
Consideration	Annuity	Common Law Property
Alimony	Trust	Separate Property
Property Division	Rehabilitative Alimony	Quasi-Community Property
Property Settlement	Real Property	Fiduciary
Arrears	Personal Property	Appreciation

Equitable Distribution
Dissipate
Pension
Defined-Benefit Plan
Defined-Contribution Plan
Vested
Qualified Domestic Relations
  Order (QDRO)
Alternate Payee

Present Value
Restitution
Goodwill
Joint and Several Liability
Indemnify
Executor
Testate
Elect against the Will
Forced Share

Intestate
Dower
Curtesy
Nonmolestation Clause
Arbitration
Mediation
Executory

CHILD CUSTODY

KINDS OF CUSTODY

Few issues in family law are as emotionally draining as child custody. In divorce cases, judges sometimes tell the parties, "I can dissolve the marriage, but I cannot dissolve the family." A party can be an ex-spouse, but cannot be an ex-parent.[1] A major premise of the law of child custody is that it is important to try to preserve as much of the parental-child relationship as possible after the original family unit has disintegrated due to divorce. Before examining how this is done, we need to understand some basic custody terminology.

☐ **Legal Custody** Legal custody is the right and the duty to make the decisions about raising a child, e.g., decisions on the child's health, education, religion, and discipline. While married and living together, both parents have legal custody of their children. Upon divorce or separation, if both parents continue to make the major decisions together about the health, education, religion, and discipline of the child, they are sharing legal custody, a situation known as joint custody, or joint legal custody.

☐ **Physical Custody** Physical custody simply refers to the parent with whom the child lives. If a court awards custody to one parent only, that parent is called the **custodial parent.** The other is the **noncustodial parent,** who usually has visitation rights.

☐ **Sole Custody** Sole custody exists when one parent has both legal custody and physical custody. The other parent has visitation rights. About 70 percent of all custody decisions today are sole-custody arrangements.[2]

---

1. Unless, of course, there has been a termination of parental rights because of severe parental unfitness or a consent to adoption. See chapter 19.
2. Some states distinguish between *sole physical custody* (child resides full-time with one parent) and *sole legal custody* (one parent makes all the decisions on health, education, and welfare). In Texas, the person with primary responsibility for decisions on the child's upbringing is called the *managing conservator*. A child can have joint managing conservators.

☐ **Joint Custody**   Joint custody means that each parent shares legal custody (joint legal custody) and/or shares physical custody (joint physical custody) over alternating but not necessarily equal, periods of time. These arrangements are sometimes referred to as shared custody, shared parental responsibility, shared parenting, or co-parenting. Bird's-nest custody is joint custody where the child remains in a single home and each parent moves in and out during alternate periods of time.

☐ **Split Custody**   Split custody has two meanings. First, it refers to an arrangement in which one parent has legal custody, with physical custody going to each parent in alternating periods when the child lives with him or her. Second, it refers to a situation involving more than one child. Each parent receives sole custody of at least one child with visitation rights to the other children. This second definition is also referred to as *divided custody*.

None of these categories is static. One kind of custody arrangement may eventually evolve into another kind, either by formal agreement or by informal mutual understanding. For example, one side may have sole custody, but because of circumstances (e.g., illness or job change), visitation becomes so extensive that the parents end up with the equivalent of a joint-custody arrangement.

▰▰▰ SEPARATION AGREEMENT

CUSTODY

In negotiating the custody term of a separation agreement, the parties must consider many circumstances:

☐ The kind of custody they want.

☐ The age and health of the child.

☐ The age and health of the parents. Which parent is physically and mentally more able to care for the child on a day-to-day basis?

☐ The parent with whom the child has spent the most time up to now. With whom are the emotional attachments the strongest?

☐ Which parent must work full-time?

☐ The availability of backup assistance, e.g., from the grandparents or close friends who can help in emergencies.

☐ The availability of day-care facilities.

☐ How will the major decisions on the child's welfare be made, e.g., whether to transfer schools, whether to have an operation? Must one parent consult the other on such matters? Is joint consent ever needed?

☐ The religious upbringing of the child.

☐ The child's surname. Can the name be changed if the mother remarries?

☐ Can the child be moved from the area?

☐ Who would receive custody if both parents died?

☐ If disputes arise between the parents concerning custody, how are they to be resolved? Arbitration? Mediation?

☐ What happens if one parent violates the agreement on custody? For example, the custodial parent interferes with the visitation rights of the noncustodial parent. Can the latter stop paying alimony?

☐ Mutual respect. Do the parties specifically agree to encourage the child to love both parents?

In recent years, *joint custody* has received a good deal of attention. Advocates of this option claim that it is psychologically the most healthy alternative for the child. It arguably produces less hostility between parents, less hostility between child and individual parent, less confusion in values for the child, less sexual stereotyping of parental roles (one parent "works," the other cares for the children), less manipulation of the child by one or both parents, less manipulation of one or both parents by the child, etc. Others, however, argue that the decision on joint custody should be approached with great caution since it will work only in exceptional circumstances. The parents have just separated. By definition, therefore, they are not able to cooperate in the manner called for by a joint-custody arrangement. A recent study of 700 divorce cases in Massachusetts concluded that couples with joint legal custody are more than twice as likely to reopen lawsuits over child-care arrangements than couples where only one parent had custody.[3]

The following factors are relevant to a decision on whether joint custody will work. Any one of these factors might tip the scale *against* its feasibility.

1. Is each parent fit and suitable as a custodial parent?

2. Do both parents agree to joint custody, or is one or both opposed?

3. Have the parents demonstrated that they are able to communicate at least to the extent necessary to reach shared decisions in the child's best interest?

4. Is there geographical proximity so that there will be no substantial disruption of the child's schooling, association with friends, religious training, etc.?

5. Do the parents' homes present similar environments, or will the child be confronted with vastly different or potentially disruptive environmental changes when moving between the two homes of his or her parents?

6. Is there any indication that the psychological and emotional needs and development of the child will suffer due to the joint custodial arrangement?

7. Does each parent have a work schedule and home routine that is compatible with the child's needs so that either can assume full parental duties when with the child?

8. Is joint custody in accord with the child's wishes or does the child have strong opposition to such an arrangement?

VISITATION

In negotiating visitation rights in a separation agreement, a number of details must be worked out:

☐ When can the noncustodial parent have the child visit? Alternating weekends? School vacations? Holidays? Which ones? How much advance notice is needed if additional time is desired?

☐ At what time is the child to be picked up and returned?

☐ Can the noncustodial parent take the child on long trips? Is the consent of the custodial parent needed?

☐ Can the custodial parent move out of the area even though this makes visitation more burdensome and costly?

---

3. The Wall Street Journal, July 15, 1991 at p. B1; The Compleat Lawyer, 13 (Fall 1991).

☐ Who pays the transportation costs, if any, when the child visits the non-custodial parent?

☐ Is the noncustodial parent required to be available for visits? Will it be a violation of the separation agreement if he or she does *not* visit? Or, is visitation at the sole discretion of the noncustodial parent?

☐ When the noncustodial parent decides not to visit at a given time, must he or she notify the custodial parent in advance, or attempt to?

☐ Do any third parties have visitation rights, e.g., grandparents?

☐ If disputes arise between parents on visitation, how are they resolved? Arbitration? Mediation?

☐ What happens if one of the parties violates the agreement on visitation?

☐ Does this breach justify nonperformance by the other party of another term of the separation agreement, e.g., alimony payments?

There are two major choices in selecting visitation times. The parties can simply state in their separation agreement that visitation will be at "reasonable" times to be mutually agreed upon by the parties in the future, with adequate advance notice to be given by the noncustodial parent when he or she wants visitation. Alternatively, the agreement can spell out precise times for visitation. The following article advocates the latter position in cases where both parents have relatively stable work schedules.

"Fixing Definite Schedules"
By Fain
The Matrimonial Strategist 2 *(May 1983).*

The traumatic and emotional issues that often dominate determination of custody and visitation ... rights of parents of minor children continue to provoke much litigation. This has perhaps been measurably improved by constructive mediation efforts that have now been initiated by many courts of this country.

As much as it would be preferable to maintain a degree of flexibility in allowing parents to agree on reasonable visitation rights, it is the opinion of most family-law practitioners that it is more important to fix visitation or shared physical custody rights as specifically as possible. ... This will minimize friction and ensuing disputes between parents who are frequently in a hostile posture to begin with. When visitation rights are set down with particularity, it is more likely that arguments will be discouraged, and less likely that the custodial parent will attempt to limit or defeat the noncustodial parent's visitation rights.

Problems Can Arise
In certain situations, though, specifying visitation rights ... can lead to problems for parents and child. For example, if a non-custodial parent has an occupation or job with defined hours during the week and regular vacations every year, specificity is fine. But, if the non-custodial parent has an occupation or profession which frequently requires travel, or in which the work requirements do not permit vacations to be planned in advance, specifying rigid visitation rights can often lead to conflict. Such situations should be resolved by tailor-made provisions in the separation agreement.

It is clear that regularity and consistency of visits ... is better for children because it promotes stability and security of the children's lives, as well as for the parents. However, as with all theories of custody and visitation, even these theories are now being challenged, as exemplified by the continued stress on joint legal and physical custody arrangements. ...

In a typically traditional visitation arrangement the following schedule has been found reasonably effective in agreements. As with all example clauses, it should be varied or modified by the attorneys and parties to comport with the facts and circumstances of a given case.

SAMPLE VISITATION SCHEDULE: CUSTODY AND VISITATION RIGHTS

Custody of the minor children, Jane X and Joe X, is awarded *Wife.*

I. **Husband** shall have the children with him at the following times:

  A. Regular Visitation:

    1. On alternate weekends from seven (7:00)

p.m. Friday to seven (7:00) p.m. Sunday, commencing Friday, _____ , 19XX.

2. The entire month of **July,** 19XX, the entire month of **August,** the following year, and alternating July and August in subsequent years.

B. Holidays and Special Days:

1. Lincoln's Birthday, 19XX, from seven (7:00) p.m. the day before said holiday to seven (7:00) p.m. the day of said holiday, and thereafter on alternate years.

2. Washington's Birthday, 19XX, from seven (7:00) p.m. the day before said holiday to seven (7:00) p.m. the day of said holiday, and thereafter on alternate years.

3. Memorial Day, 19XX, from seven (7:00) p.m. the day before said holiday to seven (7:00) p.m. the day of said holiday, and thereafter on alternate years.

4. Independence Day, 19XX, from seven (7:00) p.m. the day before said holiday to seven (7:00) p.m. the day of said holiday, and thereafter on alternate years.

5. Labor Day, 19XX, from seven (7:00) p.m. the day before said holiday to seven (7:00) p.m. the day of said holiday, and thereafter on alternate years.

6. Columbus Day, 19XX, from seven (7:00) p.m. the day before said holiday to seven (7:00) p.m. the day of said holiday, and thereafter on alternate years.

7. Veterans Day, 19XX, from seven (7:00) p.m. the day before said holiday to seven (7:00) p.m. the day of said holiday, and thereafter on alternate years.

8. Thanksgiving Day, 19XX, from seven (7:00) p.m. the day before said holiday to seven (7:00) p.m. the day of said holiday, and thereafter on alternate years.

9. Christmas 19XX, the first week of the Christmas school vacation, commencing seven (7:00) p.m. the last day of school before the vacation and ending at eleven (11:00) a.m. Christmas Day to five (5:00) p.m. New Year's Day, and thereafter on alternate years.

10. Christmas Day, 19XX, the second week of Christmas school vacation, commencing eleven (11:00) a.m. Christmas Day to five (5:00) p.m. New Year's Day, and thereafter on alternate years.

11. The entire Easter school vacation in the year 19XX, including Easter Sunday, commencing seven (7:00) p.m. the last day of school before the vacation and ending at

seven (7:00) p.m. the day before school resumes, and thereafter during the Easter vacation on alternate years.

12. On the children's birthdays in the year 19XX, and thereafter on alternate years.

13. Every Father's Day.

14. On Husband's birthday

15. Religious Holidays (where applicable):

   a. Good Friday of 19XX, from noon (12:00) p.m. to six (6:00) p.m. of said day, and thereafter on alternate years, or

   b. The first day of the Jewish Holidays of Yom Kippur, Rosh Hashannah and Passover during 19XX, commencing at five (5:00) p.m. on the eve of each such day and terminating at seven (7:00) p.m. on such day, and thereafter on alternate years.

II. **Wife** shall have the children with her on the holiday and special days listed in Clause I-B in the years alternate to the years in which Husband has the children with him pursuant to Clause I-B; Wife shall also have the children on every Mother's Day and on Wife's birthday.

[*Editor's Note: A common variation would be to split the holidays between Husband and Wife and have them switch halves in alternate years. Another suggested addition if the children are young is Halloween in alternating years.*]

III. **Priorities:**

The rights of Wife under Clause II shall override the regular visitation rights of Husband set forth in Clause I-A, in the event of conflict between Clause I-A and Clause II, except that Husband shall not be limited in his right to take the children out of the Home-City area during the period set forth in Clause I-A2 above, even though Wife shall thereby be deprived of the right she would otherwise have under Clause II to have the children with her during said period. In the event of conflict between Clause I-B and Clause II, the rights of Husband under Clause I-B shall override the rights of Wife under Clause II.

[*Editor's Note: The significance of Clause III cannot be overrated. A key function of any drafter is to avoid argument over meaning and intention. A provision establishing a hierarchy of clauses will help avoid problems.*]

ASSIGNMENT 11.1

Richard and Helen Dowd have been married for six years. They are both computer consultants who work out of their home. They have one child, Kevin, aged four. Recently, they decided to separate. Draft a joint-custody agreement for them. Assume that both want to be active in raising Kevin. (See General Instructions for the Agreement-Drafting Assignment in chapter 1.)

■■■■■ COURT-ORDERED CUSTODY: THE CHILD'S PERSPECTIVE

When they brought the sword before him, he said, "Cut the living child in two, and give half to one woman and half to the other." 1 Kings 3:24–25 (NAB)

When parents cannot agree on custody, the courts must resolve the matter. Judges, forced into the role of King Solomon, say that child custody is one of the most painful issues they face. In a custody battle, it is often difficult for a court to force parents to focus on the best interest of the child rather than on their own hostility toward each other.

In a few states, parties are *required* to go through a parenting class for divorcing parents. For example, Tarant County, Texas, has a four-hour seminar on how parents can help their children cope with separation and visitation. Using video and role-playing, the seminar emphasizes the emotional harm that fighting parents can continue to inflict on their children.

Most courts have guidelines they distribute to the parties on the effect of divorce on children. Sometimes these guidelines are made part of the court's custody decree. Before examining how courts make the custody decision, we should examine some of these guidelines. The following (written on the assumption that the mother is awarded custody) are used in Wisconsin:

GUIDELINES
Dade County Family Court Counseling Service Staff, Madison, Wisconsin.

Relation toward Children
Although the court does have the power to dissolve the bonds of matrimony, the court does not have the power to dissolve the bonds that exist between you as parents and your children. Both of you, therefore, are to continue your responsibility to emotionally support your children. You are to cooperate in the duty and right of each other to love those children. By love, the court means the training, the education, the disciplining and motivation of those children. Cooperation means to present the other party to the children with an attitude of respect either for the mother or for the father. Neither of you should in any way downplay, belittle or criticize the other in the presence of those children because you may emotionally damage your children and/or you may develop a disappointment or hatred in the minds of those children for the party that attempts to belittle or demean the other in the presence of those children. It is of utmost importance you both recognize your children's right to love both parents without fear of being disloyal to either one of you.

In support of this admonition, the courts have drafted written guidelines on your future conduct relating to the best interest of your children. I sincerely urge that you preserve them, periodically read them and always be guided by them.

Guidelines for Separated Parents
As you know, your children are usually the losers when their parents separate. They are deprived of full-time, proper guidance that two parents can give—guidance and direction essential to their moral and spiritual growth.

It is highly desirable that you abstain from making unkind remarks about each other. Recognize that such remarks are not about a former spouse but are about a parent of your children. Such comments reflect adversely upon the children.

It is urged that both parties cooperate to the end that mutual decisions concerning the interest of the children can be made objectively. Parents should remember that the mother who has custody should urge the children to find time to be with the father and encourage them to realize that their father has affection for them and contributes to their support. The father should recognize that his plans for visitation must be adjusted from time to time in order to accommodate the planned activities of the child. Visitation should be a pleasant experience rather than a duty. Cooperation in giving notice and promptness in maintaining hours of visitation are important to avoid ruffled feelings.

Although there is probably some bitterness between you, it should not be inflicted upon your children. In every child's mind there must and should be an image of two good parents. Your future conduct with your children will be helpful to them if you will follow these suggestions.

i. *Do Not's*

a. Do not poison your child's mind against either the mother or father by discussing their shortcomings.

b. Do not use your visitation as an excuse to continue the arguments with your spouse.

c. Do not visit your children if you have been drinking.

ii. *Do's*

a. Be discreet when you expose your children to [anyone] with whom you may be emotionally involved.

b. Visit your children only at reasonable hours.

c. Notify your spouse as soon as possible if you are unable to keep your visitation. It's unfair to keep your children waiting—and worse to disappoint them by not coming at all.

d. Make your visitation as pleasant as possible for your children by not questioning them regarding the activities of your spouse and by not making extravagant promises which you know you cannot or will not keep.

e. Minimize the amount of time the children are in the care of strangers and relatives.

f. Always work for the spiritual well-being, health, happiness and safety of your children.

iii. *General*

a. The parent with whom the children live must prepare them both physically and mentally for the visitation. The children should be available at the time mutually agreed upon.

b. If one parent has plans for the children that conflict with the visitation and these plans are in the best interests of the children, be adults and work out the problem together.

c. Arrangements should be made through visitation to provide the mother with some time "away" from the family. She needs the time for relaxation and recreation. Upon her return, she will be refreshed and better prepared to resume her role as mother and head of the household. Therefore, provide for extended periods of visitation such as weekends and vacations.

Bill of Rights for Children in Divorce Action

1. The right to be treated as important human beings, with unique feelings, ideas and desires and not as a source of argument between parents.

2. The right to a continuing relationship with both parents and the freedom to receive love from and express love for both.

3. The right to express love and affection for each parent without having to stifle that love because of fear of disapproval by the other parent.

4. The right to know that their parent's decision to divorce is not their responsibility and that they will live with one parent and will visit the other parent.

5. The right to continuing care and guidance from both parents.

6. The right to honest answers to questions about the changing family relationships.

7. The right to know and appreciate what is good in each parent without one parent degrading the other.

8. The right to have a relaxed, secure relationship with both parents without being placed in a position to manipulate one parent against the other.

9. The right to have the custodial parent not undermine visitation by suggesting tempting alternatives or by threatening to withhold visitation as a punishment for the children's wrongdoing.

10. The right to be able to experience regular and consistent visitation and the right to know the reason for a cancelled visit.

Many courts force parents into **mediation** to try to construct a workable custody plan they both can support. The mediator is a private counselor or a trained government employee who meets with the parents to try to help them reach agreement. The mediator does not force a decision on them. While he or she may ultimately recommend a custody/visitation arrangement to the court, the primary objective of mediation is to pressure the parents to reach their own agreement, which they can take before the judge for approval.

Mediation The process of submitting a dispute to a third party (other than a judge) who will help the parties reach their own resolution of the dispute.

▨ PARENT VS. PARENT:
CONSIDERATIONS IN THE CUSTODY DECISION

First, we consider the custody decision when the dispute is between the two *biological parents* who cannot agree on custody. The standard used by the court is the **best interest of the child.** In the vast majority of cases, the court will award sole custody to *one* of the parents and give visitation rights to the other. Earlier, we examined other kinds of custody such as joint custody. As indicated, there is considerable debate on the feasibility of a joint-custody decree. Unless the parties mutually agree to try joint custody, it is unlikely that a court will order it. The primary focus of the following discussion, therefore, will be on the kind of custody that is most commonly awarded: sole custody.

Contested Disputed; challenged. If the parties agree, the matter is *uncontested.*

Guardian Ad Litem A special guardian appointed by the court to represent the interests of another.

In a **contested** custody case of this kind, the main participants are the mother and her lawyer against the father and his lawyer. (The parent with all or most of the financial resources will often be ordered to pay the reasonable attorney fees of the other parent.) In most states, the court has the power to appoint *separate* counsel for the child. A **guardian ad litem** is an individual (often a lawyer) who is appointed to represent the interests of a third party— here, the child. This lawyer is to act independently of the other lawyers in the case.

How does the court decide who receives custody? What factors go into the decision? Earlier in this chapter you found a list of factors that parties negotiating a separation agreement must consider in arriving at a mutually acceptable custody arrangement. A court will usually consider these same factors in rendering a custody decision when the parties have not been able to reach agreement, or in deciding whether to approve a custody arrangement that they have agreed upon.

- ☐ **Court discretion**
- ☐ **Stability**
- ☐ **Availability**
- ☐ **Emotional ties**
- ☐ **Legal preferences**
- ☐ **Morality and lifestyle**
- ☐ **Religion**
- ☐ **Cultural continuity**
- ☐ **Wishes of the child**
- ☐ **Expert witnesses**

THE COURT'S DISCRETION

Of necessity, trial judges are given great discretion in making the custody decision. There are no rigid formulas that can be followed. The standard is very broad: the best interest of the child. Inevitably, the judge's personal views and philosophy of life help shape his or her concept of what is in the best interest of a child, e.g., views on the traditional family, alternate lifestyles, working women, child discipline. Of course, a judge would never admit that he or she is following his or her own personal views and philosophy; judges are supposed to be guided by "the law" and not by their individual biases. In reality, however, they are guided by both.

STABILITY

By far the most important consideration is stability. There is almost a presumption that it is in the best interest of the child to award custody to the parent who will cause the least amount of disruption to the disintegrating life of the child. The loss of a household with two functioning parents is a shattering experience for most children. They will need as much stability as possible in their living arrangement, schooling, religious practice, access to relatives and friends, etc. While their lives will never be the same again, a court will want to know how each parent proposes to maintain maximum stability and continuity in these areas.

AVAILABILITY

Which parent will be available to spend the time required to respond to the day-to-day needs of the child? There is a danger that the child will feel abandoned and responsible for the divorce. To offset this danger, it is important that at least one of the parents be available to the child to provide reassurance and comfort. The court will want to know which parent in the past:

- ☐ Took the child to doctor's appointments
- ☐ Met with teachers
- ☐ Took the child to church
- ☐ Helped with homework
- ☐ Attended school plays with the child
- ☐ Involved the child in athletic activities
- ☐ Arranged and attended birthday parties
- ☐ Changed diapers
- ☐ Stayed up with the sick child during the night

Then the court will want to know what *plan* each parent has for the future as to these needs. The health, age, and employment responsibilities of each parent are obviously relevant to this plan.

Immediately after the separation, it is common for one of the parents to have temporary custody. Upon filing for divorce, the court may formally order a temporary-custody arrangement (with visitation rights) pending the final court proceeding, which may take place months later. During this interval, the court will inquire into the amount and kind of contact each parent had with the child. Again, the above list of questions becomes important, particularly with respect to the parent who moved out. How much time has this parent spent with the child? Have letters and gifts been sent? What about visits and telephone calls? To what extent has this parent gone out of his or her way to be with the child?

EMOTIONAL TIES

Closely related to time availability is the emotional relationship that has developed in the past between a parent and child and the future prospects for this development. Which parent has been sensitive or insensitive to the psychological crisis that the child has experienced and will probably continue to experience because of the divorce? Of particular importance is the extent to which one parent has tried and succeeded in fostering the child's love for the *other* parent. A qualification to become a custodial parent is the ability and inclination to cooperate in arranging visitations by the other parent. Hence, a major issue will be which parent can separate his or her own needs and lingering bitterness from the need of the child to maintain emotional ties with both parents. (Children who have been pressured by one parent to be hostile toward the other might suffer from what is called the **parental alienation syndrome**.)

A number of other factors are relevant to the emotional needs of the child:

☐ The level of education of the parent

☐ The psychological health of the parent: Has the parent been in therapy for any reason? Has it been helpful? What is the parent's attitude about seeking such help? Positive? Realistic? Does the parent think that the *other* parent is the only one who needs help?

☐ The stability of the parent's prior work history

☐ Views on discipline, TV watching, studying, religious activities, cleaning the child's room, etc.

☐ How siblings get along in the home

☐ General home and neighborhood environment: Cramped apartment conditions? Residential area? Easy accessibility to school, friends, and recreational facilities?

Also, does the parent seeking sole custody plan to move from the area? If so, into what kind of environment? How will the proposed move affect the other parent's ability to visit the child? Depending upon the circumstances of the case, a court might award custody to a parent on condition that he or she *not* move out of a designated area without the consent of the other parent.

LEGAL PREFERENCES

Until the 1850s, fathers had a near-absolute right to the custody of their children. Following this period, most states adopted the **tender years presumption.** The court presumed that a young child's best interest was to be with its mother. This presumption was justified on the basis of biological dependence, socialization patterns, and tradition. "There is but a twilight zone between a mother's love and the atmosphere of heaven, and all things being equal, no child should be deprived of that maternal influence." *Tuter v. Tuter,* 120 S.W.2d 203, 205 (Mo. App. 1938). A very strong case had to be made against the mother to overcome the presumption, e.g., proof that the mother was unfit.

Within the last twenty years, more and more fathers have been seeking sole custody. They have argued that it is unconstitutional for a court to give preference to one parent over the other solely on the basis of sex. Recent courts have tended to agree and have been granting custody to fathers in increasing numbers. Some states have passed statutes that specifically outlaw the use of sex-based presumptions in custody cases. Yet courts continue to grant custody to mothers in the overwhelming number of cases. A 1990 study of divorce in nineteen states conducted by the National Center for Health Statistics found that:

☐ Mothers were awarded sole custody in 71 percent of the cases.

☐ Fathers were awarded sole custody in 8.5 percent of the cases.

☐ Custody was shared in 15.5 percent of the cases.

Parental Alienation Syndrome A disorder suffered by some children at the center of a custody dispute. They idealize one parent while expressing hatred for the other, even though the relationship with both parents was relatively positive before the dispute.

Tender Years Presumption Young children are better off living with their mother than with their father.

☐ Custody was awarded to other relatives or friends in 5 percent of the cases.

Most of the judges now sitting on the bench grew up with full-time moms at home. Some experts feel it is difficult for these judges to accept the notion of giving sole custody to working fathers. But new judges are on the way. It "will take a generation of judges who are brought up by, or married to career women" before there is more sympathy for granting custody to working parents—particularly fathers.[4]

In place of the tender years presumption, many courts have substituted a **primary caregiver presumption** by which the court presumes that custody should go to the parent who has been the primary person taking care of the child over the years. This, of course, usually means that the mother continues to receive sole custody in most cases since she is usually the one who stays home to care for the child. Even when both the mother and father work outside the home, the mother is more likely to be awarded custody as the primary caregiver or caretaker. Some, therefore, have argued that this presumption is simply the tender years presumption in disguise.

One preference favored the father: it was presumed to be in the best interest of older boys to be placed with their fathers. Today, very few courts even mention this presumption. Although it has not been as controversial as the tender years presumption, it is subject to the same criticisms.

A less controversial presumption is that brothers and sisters are best kept together with the same parent whenever possible. Finally, courts widely accept the idea that the preference of older, more mature children as to their own custody should be given great, though not necessarily controlling, weight.

Primary Caregiver Presumption The primary person who has taken care of the child should have custody.

MORALITY AND LIFESTYLE

"A judge should not base his decision upon [a] disapproval of the morals or other personal characteristics of a parent that do not harm the child. . . . We do not mean to suggest that a person's associational or even sexual conduct may not be relevant in deciding a custody dispute where there is compelling evidence that such conduct has a significant bearing upon the welfare of the children." *Wellman v. Wellman,* 104 Cal. App. 3d 992, 998, 164 Cal. Rptr. 148, 151–52 (1980).

Is it possible to separate the private morality (particularly sexual morality) of parents from the welfare of their children? If a parent engages in what the community considers immoral conduct, can we presume (conclusively presume?) that this parent is unfit and that it is in the best interest of the child to be placed with the other parent? In *Stanley v. Illinois,* 405 U.S. 645, 92 S. Ct. 1208, 31 L. Ed. 2d 551 (1972), the United States Supreme Court held that a state cannot presume that a father is unfit simply because he never married the mother of his illegitimate child. Such a father must be given a hearing to determine his *actual* fitness or unfitness. Examine the following highly publicized opinion of *Jarrett v. Jarrett.* Do you think that the majority opinion violates *Stanley?*

---

4. Jan Hoffman, *Divorced Fathers Make Gains in Battles to Increase Rights,* New York Times, April 26, 1995, at p. A11.

CASE

JARRETT V. JARRETT

78 Ill. 2d 337, 36 Ill. Dec. 1, 400 N.E.2d 421 (1979)
Supreme Court of Illinois

Background: *In 1976 the circuit court of Cook County (an Illinois trial court) granted Jacqueline Jarrett a divorce from Walter Jarrett on grounds of extreme and repeated cruelty. It also awarded her custody of the three Jarrett children. When her boyfriend, Wayne Hammon, moved in, Walter went back to the circuit court to ask that it modify its order by giving him custody. The court granted this request, but the change was reversed by the appellate court. Walter then appealed. The case is now before the Supreme Court of Illinois.*

Decision on Appeal: *Reversed. The trial court properly transferred custody to the father because of the mother's open and continuous cohabitation with her boyfriend.*

Opinion of the Court:

Justice UNDERWOOD delivered the opinion of the court. . . .

During their marriage, Walter and Jacqueline had three daughters, who, at the time of the divorce, were 12, 10 and 7 years old. In addition to custody of the children, the divorce decree also awarded Jacqueline the use of the family home, and child support; Walter received visitation rights at all reasonable times and usually had the children from Saturday evening to Sunday evening. In April 1977, five months after the divorce, Jacqueline informed Walter that she planned to have her boyfriend, Wayne Hammon, move into the family home with her. Walter protested, but Hammon moved in on May 1, 1977. Jacqueline and Hammon thereafter cohabited in the Jarrett home but did not marry.

The children, who were not "overly enthused" when they first learned that Hammon would move into the family home with them, asked Jacqueline if she intended to marry Hammon, but Jacqueline responded that she did not know. At the modification hearing Jacqueline testified that she did not want to remarry because it was too soon after her divorce; because she did not believe that a marriage license makes a relationship; and because the divorce decree required her to sell the family home within six months after remarriage. She did not want to sell the house because the children did not want to move and she could not afford to do so. Jacqueline explained to the children that some people thought it was wrong for an unmarried man and woman to live together but she thought that what mattered was that they loved each other. Jacqueline testified that she told some neighbors that Hammon would move in with her but that she had not received any adverse comments. Jacqueline further testified that the children seemed to develop an affectionate relationship with Hammon, who played with them, helped them with their homework, and verbally disciplined them. Both Jacqueline and Hammon testified at the hearing that they did not at that time have any plans to marry. In oral argument before this court Jacqueline's counsel conceded that she and Hammon were still living together unmarried.

Walter Jarrett testified that he thought Jacqueline's living arrangements created a moral environment which was not a proper one in which to raise three young girls. He also testified that the children were always clean, healthy, well dressed and well nourished when he picked them up, and that when he talked with his oldest daughter, Kathleen, she did not object to Jacqueline's living arrangement.

The circuit court found that it was "necessary for the moral and spiritual well-being and development" of the children that Walter receive custody. In reversing, the appellate court reasoned that the record did not reveal any negative effects on the children caused by Jacqueline's cohabitation with Hammon, and that the circuit court had not found Jacqueline unfit. It declined to consider potential future harmful effects of the cohabitation on the children. . . .

Both parties to this litigation have relied on sections 602 and 610 of the new Illinois Marriage and Dissolution of Marriage Act (Ill.Rev.Stat.1977, ch. 40, pars. 602, 610), which provide:

"Sec. 602. Best interest of child.

(a) The court shall determine custody in accordance with the best interest of the child. The court shall consider all relevant factors including:

   (1) the wishes of the child's parent or parents as to his custody;

   (2) the wishes of the child as to his custodian;

   (3) the interaction and interrelationship of the child with his parent or parents, his siblings and any other person who may significantly affect the child's best interest;

   (4) the child's adjustment to his home, school and community; and

   (5) the mental and physical health of all individuals involved.

(b) The court shall not consider conduct of a present or proposed custodian that does not affect his relationship to the child."

"Sec. 610. Modification.

(a) No motion to modify a custody judgment may be made earlier than 2 years after its date, unless the court permits it to be made on the basis of affidavits that there is reason to believe the child's present environment may endanger seriously his physical, mental, moral or emotional health.

(b) The court shall not modify a prior custody judgment unless it finds, upon the basis of facts that have arisen since the prior judgment or that were unknown to the court at the time of entry of the prior judgment, that a change has occurred in the circumstances of the child or his custodian and that the modification is necessary to serve the best interest of the child. In applying these standards the court shall retain the custodian appointed pursuant to the prior judgment unless: . . .

> (3) the child's present environment endangers seriously his physical, mental, moral or emotional health and the harm likely to be caused by a change of environment is outweighed by its advantages to him. . . .

The chief issue in this case is whether a change of custody predicated upon the open and continuing cohabitation of the custodial parent with a member of the opposite sex is contrary to the manifest weight of the evidence in the absence of any tangible evidence of contemporaneous adverse effect upon the minor children. . . . [W]e conclude that under the facts in this case the trial court properly transferred custody of the Jarrett children from Jacqueline to Walter Jarrett.

The relevant standards of conduct are expressed in the statutes of this State: Section 11–8 of the Criminal Code of 1961 (Ill.Rev.Stat.1977, ch. 38, par. 11–8) provides that "[a]ny person who cohabits or has sexual intercourse with another not his spouse commits fornication if the behavior is open and notorious." In *Hewitt v. Hewitt*, 77 Ill. 2d 49, 394 N.E.2d 1204 (1979), we emphasized the refusal of the General Assembly in enacting the new Illinois Marriage and Dissolution of Marriage Act . . . to sanction any nonmarital relationships and its declaration of the purpose to "strengthen and preserve the integrity of marriage and safeguard family relationships". . . .

Jacqueline argues, however, that her conduct does not affront public morality because such conduct is now widely accepted, and cites 1978 Census Bureau statistics that show 1.1 million households composed of an unmarried man and woman, close to a quarter of which also include at least one child. This is essentially the same argument we rejected last term in *Hewitt v. Hewitt*, and it is equally unpersuasive here. The number of people living in such households forms only a small percentage of the adult population, but more to the point, the statutory interpretation urged upon us by Jacqueline simply nullifies the fornication statute. The logical conclusion of her argument is that the statutory prohibitions are void as to those who believe the proscribed acts are not immoral, or, for

one reason or another, need not be heeded. So stated, of course, the argument defeats itself. The rules which our society enacts for the governance of its members are not limited to those who agree with those rules—they are equally binding on the dissenters. The fornication statute and the Illinois Marriage and Dissolution of Marriage Act evidence the relevant moral standards of this State, as declared by our legislature. The open and notorious limitation on the former's prohibitions reflects both a disinclination to criminalize purely private relationships and a recognition that open fornication represents a graver threat to public morality than private violations. Conduct of that nature, when it is open, not only violates the statutorily expressed moral standards of the State, but also encourages others to violate those standards, and debases public morality. While we agree that the statute does not penalize conduct which is essentially private and discreet, . . . Jacqueline's conduct has been neither, for she has discussed this relationship and her rationalization of it with at least her children, her former husband and her neighbors. It is, in our judgment, clear that her conduct offends prevailing public policy. . . .

Jacqueline's disregard for existing standards of conduct instructs her children, by example, that they, too, may ignore them, . . . and could well encourage the children to engage in similar activity in the future. That factor, of course, supports the trial court's conclusion that their daily presence in that environment was injurious to the moral well-being and development of the children.

It is true that, as Jacqueline argues, the courts have not denied custody to every parent who has violated the community's moral standards, nor do we now intimate a different rule. Rather than mechanically denying custody in every such instance, the courts of this State appraise the moral example currently provided and the example which may be expected by the parent in the future. We held in *Nye v. Nye*, 411 Ill. 408, 105 N.E.2d 300 (1952) that past moral indiscretions of a parent are not sufficient grounds for denying custody if the parent's present conduct establishes the improbability of such lapses in the future. This rule focuses the trial court's attention on the moral values which the parent is actually demonstrating to the children.

Since the decision in *Nye*, the appellate courts of this State have repeatedly emphasized this principle, particularly when the children were unaware of their parent's moral indiscretion. . . . At the time of this hearing, however, and even when this case was argued orally to this court, Jacqueline continued to cohabit with Wayne Hammon and had done nothing to indicate that this relationship would not continue in the future. Thus the moral values which Jacqueline currently represents to her children, and those which she may be expected to portray to them in the future, contravene statutorily declared standards of conduct and endanger the children's moral development.

Jacqueline argues, however, that *Rippon v. Rippon*, 64 Ill. App. 3d 465, 381 N.E.2d 70 (1978) indicate[s] that the moral indiscretion of a parent is not sufficient ground for denial of custody. In *Rippon* the mother who had committed the indiscretion planned to marry her paramour and there was no indication of future misconduct. *Rippon* therefore falls within the rule set out in *Nye*. . . .

Jacqueline also argues, and the appellate court agreed . . . that the trial court's decision to grant custody of the children to Walter Jarrett was an improper assertion by the trial judge of his own personal moral beliefs. She further argues that the assertion of moral values in this case, as in *Hewitt v. Hewitt*, is a task more appropriately carried out by the legislature. As pointed out earlier, however, it is the legislature which has established the standards she has chosen to ignore, and the action of the trial court merely implemented principles which have long been followed in this State.

The mother argues, too, that . . . the Illinois Marriage and Dissolution of Marriage Act requires the trial court to refrain from modifying a prior custody decree unless it finds that the children have suffered actual tangible harm. The statute, however, directs the trial court to determine whether "the child's present environment *endangers* seriously his physical, mental, moral or emotional health." [Emphasis added.] In some cases, particularly those involving physical harm, it may be appropriate for the trial court to determine whether the child is endangered by considering evidence of actual harm. In cases such as this one, however, such a narrow interpretation of the statute would defeat its purpose. At the time of the hearing the three Jarrett children, who were then 12, 10 and 7 years old, were obviously incapable of emulating their mother's moral indiscretions. To wait until later years to determine whether Jacqueline had inculcated her moral values in the children would be to await a demonstration that the very harm which the statute seeks to avoid had occurred. Measures to safeguard the moral well-being of children, whose lives have already been disrupted by the divorce of their parents, cannot have been intended to be delayed until there are tangible manifestations of damage to their character.

While our comments have focused upon the moral hazards, we are not convinced that open cohabitation does not also affect the mental and emotional health of the children. Jacqueline's testimony at the hearing indicated that when her children originally learned that Wayne Hammon would move in with them, they

initially expected that she would marry him. It is difficult to predict what psychological effects or problems may later develop from their efforts to overcome the disparity between their concepts of propriety and their mother's conduct. Nor will their attempts to adjust to this new environment occur in a vacuum. Jacqueline's domestic arrangements are known to her neighbors and their children; testimony at the hearing indicated that Wayne Hammon played with the Jarrett children and their friends at the Jarrett home and also engaged in other activities with them. If the Jarrett children remained in that situation, they might well be compelled to try to explain Hammon's presence to their friends and, perhaps, to endure their taunts and jibes. In a case such as this the trial judge must also weigh these imponderables, and he is not limited to examining the children for current physical manifestations of emotional or mental difficulties.

Finally, we do not believe that the United States Supreme Court's opinion in *Stanley v. Illinois* (1972), 405 U.S. 645, 92 S. Ct. 1208, 31 L. Ed. 2d 551, requires a different result. In *Stanley* the Supreme Court found that Illinois statutes created a presumption that an unwed father is unfit to exercise custody over his children. The court held that depriving an unwed father of his illegitimate children without a prior hearing to determine his actual rather than presumptive unfitness, when the State accords that protection to other parents, deprives him of equal protection of the law.

The case before us is fundamentally different. The trial court did not presume that Jacqueline was not an adequate parent, as the juvenile court in effect did in *Stanley*. Rather the trial court recognized that the affection and care of a parent do not alone assure the welfare of the child if other conduct of the parent threatens the child's moral development. Since the evidence indicated that Jacqueline had not terminated the troublesome relationship and would probably continue it in the future, the trial court transferred custody to Walter Jarrett, an equally caring and affectionate parent whose conduct did not contravene the standards established by the General Assembly and earlier judicial decisions. Its action in doing so was not contrary to the manifest weight of the evidence.

Accordingly, we reverse the judgment of the appellate court and affirm the judgment of the circuit court of Cook County.

Appellate court reversed; circuit court affirmed.

GOLDENHERSCH, Chief Justice, with whom THOMAS J. MORAN, Justice, joins, dissenting:

The majority states, "The chief issue in this case is whether a change of custody predicated upon the open and continuing cohabitation of the custodial parent with a member of the opposite sex is contrary to the manifest weight of the evidence in the absence of any tangible evidence of contemporaneous adverse effect upon the minor children." An examination of the opinion fails to reveal any other issue, and the effect of the decision is that the plaintiff's cohabitation with Hammon *per se* was sufficient grounds for changing the custody order previously entered. This record shows clearly that the children were healthy, well adjusted, and well cared for, and it should be noted that both the circuit and appellate courts made no finding that plaintiff was an unfit mother. The majority, too, makes no such finding and based its decision on a nebulous concept of injury to the children's "moral well-being and development." I question that any competent sociologist would attribute the increase of "live in" unmarried couples to parental example. . . .

[C]ourts should not impose the personal preferences and standards of the judiciary in the decision of this case. Courts are uniquely equipped to decide legal issues and are well advised to leave to the theologians the question of the morality of the living arrangement into which the plaintiff had entered.

As a legal matter, simply stated, the majority has held that on the basis of her presumptive guilt of fornication, a Class B misdemeanor, plaintiff, although not declared to be an unfit mother, has forfeited the right to have the custody of her children. This finding flies in the face of the established rule that, in order to modify or amend an award of custody, the evidence must show that the parent to whom custody of the children was originally awarded is unfit to retain custody, or that a change of conditions makes a change of custody in their best interests. This record fails to show either. Mr. Justice Moran and I dissent and would affirm the decision of the appellate court.

MORAN, Justice, with whom GOLDENHERSCH, Chief Justice, joins, dissenting:

I join in the dissent of the chief justice, but also dissent separately. My primary disagreement with the majority lies with its countenancing a change of custody based solely on a *conclusive presumption* that

harm to the Jarrett children stemmed from Jacqueline's living arrangements. The majority purports to follow the Illinois Marriage and Dissolution of Marriage Act. Yet, under that act, only on the basis of fact can there be a finding that a change in circumstances has occurred and that modification of the prior custody judgment is necessary to serve the best interest of the children. The court is not to consider conduct of a custodian if that conduct does not affect his relationship to the child. In this case, not one scintilla of actual or statistical evidence of harm or danger to the children has been presented. To the contrary, all of the evidence of record, as related by the majority, indicates that under Jacqueline's custodianship the children's welfare and needs were met. Also, the trial court expressly declined to find Jacqueline unfit. Nevertheless, the majority's finding of a violation of the seldom-enforced fornication statute effectively foreclosed any further consideration of the custody issue. Instead of focusing solely on the best interest of the children—the "guiding star"—the majority has utilized child custody as a vehicle to punish Jacqueline for her "misconduct." Such selective enforcement of a statute is inappropriate and, especially in the child-custody context, unfortunate.

The majority decision also is at odds with the principle of *Stanley v. Illinois* (1972), 405 U.S. 645, 92 S. Ct. 1208, 31 L. Ed. 2d 551. The constitutional infirmity of the statutory presumption in *Stanley* casts doubt on the validity of the judicially created conclusive presumption in this case. After *Stanley*, an unwed father may not be deprived of his illegitimate children without a prior hearing to determine his actual fitness. Similarly, Jacqueline should not be deprived of the children in the absence of evidence that a change is necessary to serve the best interest of the children. A hearing at which custody is determined on the basis of the conclusive presumption sanctioned by the majority amounts to no hearing at all.

ASSIGNMENT 11.2

a. What did the dissenting opinion of Chief Justice Goldenhersch mean when he charged that the majority opinion of Justice Underwood was applying theology rather than law? Do you agree with the Chief Justice? Explain.

b. Is the majority opinion inconsistent with *Stanley v. Illinois?* Explain.

c. In chapter 7 on cohabitation contracts, we studied *Hewitt v. Hewitt.* The court in *Jarrett* said that its opinion is consistent with *Hewitt.* Is it? Explain.

What happens if one of the parents seeking custody is homosexual? There are some courts that would never grant custody to a gay parent, especially if the other parent follows a more traditional lifestyle. Other courts, however, take a different view. They will want to know whether:

☐ The gay parent has a live-in lover.

☐ The parent's sexual activities are open and obvious to the child.

☐ The child is psychologically able to handle the parent's homosexuality.

☐ The child's social life will be adversely affected. (For example, will the child be teased by classmates?)

These courts will award custody of the child to a gay parent if all of the factors point to a healthy home environment for the child and there is no evidence that the homosexuality will have an adverse impact on the child. At one time, there was fear that a parent's homosexuality would cause the child to be homosexual. Many studies have rejected this conclusion, particularly since a child's sexual preferences are developed during its infancy and very early years. This is usually well before the homosexual parent seeks custody. It must be acknowledged, however, that a gay parent has a substantial uphill battle in gaining custody (or in keeping custody if the homosexuality is revealed only after the parent has been awarded custody). Gay parents have been most successful in winning custody when the heterosexual parent is either no longer available or is demonstrably unfit. In such cases, the homosexual parent wins by default unless his or her conduct is so offensive that the court will grant custody to neither biological parent.

RELIGION

Under our Constitution, a court cannot favor one religion over another or prefer organized religion over less orthodox forms of religious beliefs. To do so could amount to an unconstitutional "establishment" of religion. The state must remain neutral. In the law of custody, the question is what effect the practice of religion is likely to have on the child, not which religion is preferable or correct according to the judge's personal standards, or according to the standards of the majority in the community, or according to "respectable" minorities in the community. The court will want to know what religion, if any, the child has practiced to date. Continuity is highly desirable. Also, will the practice of a particular religion tend to take the child away from other activities? For example, will the child be asked to spend long hours in door-to-door selling of religious literature and hence be unable to attend regular school? If so, the court will be reluctant to award custody to the parent who would require this of the child.

ASSIGNMENT 11.3

When Helen married John, she converted from Catholicism to his religion, Judaism. Neither Helen nor John was a very religious person, however. To a moderate extent, their two children were raised in the Jewish faith. The couple divorced when the children were ages four and five. Because of John's job, he could not be the sole custodian of the children. Hence he agreed that Helen receive sole custody. But he asked the court to order Helen to continue raising the children in the Jewish faith.

a. Under what circumstances do you think a court can grant this request so that, in effect, John will be granted *spiritual custody* of the children even though physical custody and legal custody (in all matters except religion) will be granted to Helen? (See General instructions for the Legal-Analysis Assignment in chapter 1.)

b. Suppose that Helen returns to her original religion and starts taking the children to Catholic Mass. What options does John have in your state? (See General Instructions for the State-Code Assignment in chapter 1.)

CULTURAL CONTINUITY

The following assignment and the case of *Carle v. Carle* address the role of cultural continuity in the custody decision.

ASSIGNMENT 11.4

Richard and Lisa have been married three years. Richard is black; Lisa is white. They have one child, Donald, who is twenty months old. In a divorce proceeding, both parents are seeking custody of David.

a. What facts do you think are needed to represent Richard or Lisa? (See General Instructions for the Investigation-Strategy Assignment in chapter 1.)

b. Assume that Richard and Lisa are equally competent and able to care for Donald. When the divorce is final, Richard plans to marry Mary (who is also black), and Lisa plans to marry Ted (who is also white). How should the custody decision be made?

c. If all the parties lived in Alaska, how do you think the court would apply *Carle v. Carle* that follows?

CASE

CARLE V. CARLE

503 P.2d 1050 (1972)
Supreme Court of Alaska

Background: In a divorce proceeding between George and Charlotte Carle, the trial court awarded custody of their seven-year-old son, George Carle, Jr., to the mother. The father appealed. The case is now on appeal before the Supreme Court of Alaska where the father is the appellant and the mother is the appellee.

Decision on Appeal: Reversed. In the custody award, the trial judge may have used inappropriate cultural criteria. The case is remanded for a redetermination of custody. A guardian ad litem should be appointed to represent the child.

Opinion of the Court:

Chief Justice RABINOWITZ delivered the opinion of the court. . . .

George Carle and Charlotte Carle were married in 1963, when George was 21 and Charlotte 16. George is a Haida Indian whose family is from Hydaburg. Charlotte is a Tlinget Indian with family ties at Klawock.* George's primary source of income is employment on commercial fishing boats, although he has worked at other jobs. During the fishing off-season, he leads the traditional subsistence existence of village Alaska, hunting, trapping, fishing, and picking berries. Since the marriage of the parties, Charlotte has held many different jobs and has also attended school. At the time the custody hearing was held in this case, she had been employed in Juneau for some 6 months.

When the matter was before the trial court, Charlotte was living in Juneau with Tom Hughes, a non-native, with whom she had been living since shortly after she separated from George in 1965. Charlotte and Hughes expressed their intent to marry after her divorce. They also indicated that they hoped to be able to bring Hughes' three children from an earlier marriage into their home in addition to George Jr. and two children of their own union. Hughes and Charlotte work alternate shifts at their respective employments and have outside help for the brief period when their shifts overlap and neither can be home.

George Jr. was born at Mt. Edgecumbe, Alaska, December 20, 1964. He first lived with Charlotte's grandmother in Klawock when Charlotte was working in a cannery for a short time in the summer of 1965. He returned to this home when his father brought him back from San Diego where Charlotte had taken him in 1965, and remained there until 1968. In October, 1968, Charlotte's grandmother became ill, so one of her daughters took the boy to Charlotte in Juneau. He stayed with Charlotte about 9 months until her financial situation became so bad that she could not adequately care for her two children.† To see that they were properly cared for, she sent them to her grandmother who was at home again in Klawock.** George Jr. remained in Klawock until after the 1970 fishing season. His father then came to get him because the grandmother was too old and sick to be able to care for the child any longer. After visiting various relatives, George Sr. took his son to Hydaburg to live with one of the boy's paternal aunts briefly during the fishing season. At the end of the season, George Sr. made

---

*From the time of their marriage in 1963 through the summer of 1965, George and Charlotte lived in Klawock off and on with Charlotte's grandmother. From 1966 to 1968, when the grandmother was taking care of his son, George spent the off-seasons in her home also. In September 1970, George took his son with him to Hydaburg where the boy lived with two of George's sisters—with one during the fall fishing season and with the other from the end of the season through the time of the custody hearing. The custody decree left the child with the latter married sister temporarily so that the boy could finish the year in the Headstart program he had been attending.

---

†By that time she and Hughes had had one baby. Hughes had gone to Hawaii to work in the summer of 1969, but did not stay much more than a month because of Charlotte's financial status.

**When Charlotte sought the return of the two children two weeks later, her grandmother would only send back the baby. The grandmother refused to give up George Jr. to Charlotte once before in 1967. Recognizing her grandmother's great attachment to the boy, Charlotte did not insist on recovering custody either time.

more permanent living arrangements for the boy; placing him with another aunt and her family where he could live next door and participate in the boy's upbringing. Had custody been awarded to the father, the boy would have continued to live with this married aunt indefinitely.

In our jurisdiction it is well established that the trial court is possessed of broad discretion to determine where custody should be placed. We will disturb the trial court's resolution of custody issues only if convinced that the record shows an abuse of discretion, or if controlling findings of fact are clearly erroneous. In the case at bar, the trial court recognized that the paramount consideration in any custody determination is what appears to be for the best interests of the child.[††]

The facts have been set forth in some detail because of appellant George Carle's contentions that the trial court erred in its evaluation of the relevant facts for the purpose of deciding what custody disposition would be in the best interests of the minor child, George Jr. George Carle's argument before this court is two-pronged: first, the trial court failed to give adequate consideration to the "actual interests" of the child, defined essentially as his psychological well-being; and second, that the trial judge's custody decision was the result of his cultural bias against the Native village way of life. In regard to this latter argument, appellant contends that the trial judge erroneously employed a presumption that the Native village culture is "inevitably succumbing" to the caucasian, urban culture.

We turn first to the asserted failure of the trial court to consider the actual interest or psychological well-being of the child. George Carle contends that the interests of the child in a custody dispute merit constitutional protection and that due process requires courts to "determine custody according to criteria which assure full and meaningful consideration of the child's actual interest."[***] According to the father, this would mean focusing primarily on "the actual psychological interests of the child," and more particularly, on "the existence and quality of . . . emotional relationships between the child and his possible custodian." We agree that the nature of the child's existing relationships should be a significant factor in choosing his custodian. Nevertheless, we believe that the "best interests" criterion adequately encompasses this factor.

Even were we to adopt the father's position and focus primarily on the actual psychological interests of the child the evidence does not clearly require a different result as to the choice of custody. The child's most stable, continuous, and long-lasting relationship was with his great-grandmother who can no longer care for him. He has spent relatively little time in 7 years with his mother, but his contacts with his father have been transitory also.[†††] The child has related well to both parents and to the respective living situations they offered him. Moreover, the trial court's decision frequently touched on elements of the child's relationship with others—with his aunt and her family, with Hughes, with his school in Hydaburg. In fact, it was precisely his concern for the child's psychological development that led the judge to place him and his mother in Juneau. In his decision the trial judge found that the child's mother had obtained stable employment and possessed the means of providing good care for the child; that the mother and Hughes provided a sense of family and home for the child, "a settled place of security and safety"; that the paternal aunt could not fulfill the necessary filial relationship; that placing the child in the mother's custody provided greater assurance of a settled, stable, family environment for the child; and that the mother was in a position to materially aid the child's development of a sense of identity, worth, and self confidence. The trial court was also of the view that the transition from the village to urban way of life could be more easily accomplished while the child was still young than if delayed until his character and personality were more rigidly formed.[*] In short the trial court concluded that

---

[††]AS 09.55.205 provides that in deciding custody, the trial courts should be guided by the following considerations:

"(1) by what appears to be for the best interests of the child and if the child is of a sufficient age and intelligence to form a preference, the court may consider that preference in determining the question;

(2) as between parents adversely claiming the custody neither parent is entitled to it as of right."

[***]Whether or not a constitutional right of the child is involved, parents have standing to challenge on appeal a determination of what is in the best interests of the child. . . . We deem this an appropriate occasion to reiterate the point we made in *Sheridan v. Sheridan*, 436 P.2d 821, 825 n. 16 (Alaska 1970) to the effect that in contested custody cases the trial court, in its discretion, is empowered to appoint a guardian ad litem to represent the interests of the minor child. . . .

[†††]While there might be some preference for leaving the child in the custody of the person with whom he has most recently and continuously resided, we decline to establish such a presumption lest it lead to pre-hearing maneuvering for possession of the child. In any event such a rule would have been no help in the instant case where neither party actually has lived with George Jr. for long or continuous periods.

[*]As to the quality of emotional relationships between the child and his possible custodian, in his decision the trial judge alluded to the fact that the father's hearing loss and speech difficulties hampered his ability to readily communicate; that the father's occupation as a commercial fisherman requires that he be absent for several months during fishing season; that the father did not have a home of his own in which to care for the child; that the father's capacity to provide the necessities of life for himself and his son was limited; and that the father's married sister cared for and loved the child and that it was not an unusual facet of Native village culture to provide care and a home when the child's natural parents are unable to do so.

the child would be emotionally and economically more secure in an urban setting.

The father asserts that the trial court failed "to give sufficient recognition to the traditional manner of care and upbringing of Native children" in weighing the custody alternatives available to the minor child of the parties. This assertion is not borne out by the record. Throughout the custody hearing the trial judge allowed evidence bearing on the nature and quality of village life. Before hearing final argument, the trial judge indicated what he thought was the most important question for counsel to discuss. In doing so, he said that the custody alternatives offered were perhaps somewhat unique, and that

> "I'm most fundamentally faced with a decision whether this child is to be reared in a Native culture in a village or in the Anglo-Saxon culture in a developed community. And I'm concerned about the basic differences between the environmental circumstances of the village life on the one hand, where his family associations are offered, apart from the specific capabilities of the [father], and on the other hand, the advantages and disadvantages of a different way of life."

Finally, in his oral decision the trial judge explicitly recognized that it is common in villages for members of the extended family to assist the natural parents of a child in his rearing, and that the village offered certain advantages to children raised there.† More particularly, the trial court recognized that George Jr. was then being well and lovingly cared for in his aunt's home.

From an overall appraisal of the record, it appears that the trial court's decision to award custody to the mother was influenced by the view that there existed a great probability of a more stable home, emotionally and economically, if the mother was awarded custody.

This brings us to appellant's second argument to the effect that the trial court's custody decision was dictated by the court's cultural bias against the Native village way of life and denied the child the "right of cultural survival." This contention arises out of the

trial judge's statement made in the course of his decision that

> "Inevitably, the village way of life is succumbing to the predominate [sic] caucasian, urban society of the land, and of necessity the youth of the villages must confront and adjust to this new lifestyle. That transition can more easily be accomplished in the case of this child at his young age than if delayed until his character and personality are more rigidly formed."

In light of these comments, the closeness of the custody questions and the fact that the child's best interests were not independently protected by the appointment of a guardian ad litem,** we have concluded that the case should be remanded for further proceedings. We are reluctant to finalize the decree in this case, given the possibility that an improper criterion was employed by the court in its resolution of the custody issue. Admittedly, the precise meaning of the trial judge's assertion that "the village way of life is succumbing to the predominate [sic] caucasian, urban society" is not free of ambiguity. Similarly, it is not clear whether the trial judge was suggesting that the Native youth must necessarily adopt urban lifestyles. Yet, on the basis of the trial judge's questioned remarks, we think a cogent argument can be advanced that the custody issue here was decided in part through the utilization of an impermissible criteria.

Both judicial decision and statutory provision mandate that the paramount consideration in any custody determination is "what appears to be for the best interests of the child." We think it is not permissible, in a bicultural context, to decide a child's custody on the hypothesis that it is necessary to facilitate the child's adjustment to what is believed to be the dominant culture. Such judgments are, in our view, not relevant to the determination of custody issues. Rather, the focus should be on the fitness of the parent and the parent's ability to accord the child the most meaningful parent-child relationship. It is not the function of our courts to homogenize Alaskan society. Recently we had occasion to observe that, "The United States of America, and Alaska in particular, reflect a pluralistic society, grounded upon such basic values as the preservation of maximum individual choice, protection of minority sentiments, and appreciation for divergent lifestyles." *Breese v. Smith*, 501 P.2d 159, 169 (Alaska 1972). Since we are unable to conclude with any degree of certainty that custody was decided

---

†The trial court's findings of fact, where pertinent, read as follows: "The evidence indicated that it is not unusual in the village culture for the relatives of a child, such as the paternal aunt here, to provide a home and care for a child where for some reason the natural parents are not suitably situated to do so. In this case, the boy does appear to be loved and accepted in his aunt's home and family in Hydaburg. The evidence also indicated that he is currently doing well in a so-called 'Headstart' program in the village school. . . .

From the evidence it may be said there are indeed, some significant and praiseworthy values in the Native village cultural environment in which the boy would be reared under defendant's custody. These include a rapport with nature and with a community of people which is perhaps less characteristic of urban life. The village environment may well nurture a sense of pride and self-worth in this Native child which a community such as Juneau could tend to suppress in his status as a member of a minority race."

**During the course of the trial the trial judge remarked that the issue before him "really concerns a party who is in a sense not represented in this suit." Although counsel was not appointed to represent the child, the trial judge alluded to the fact that in the past he contemplated such appointments.

without taking into consideration impermissible factors, we hold that the case must be remanded for further proceedings.

We think it necessary to comment on one other facet of the proceedings below. Here the differing lifestyles flowing from the two cultures have significance in determining which parent could provide the best possible parent-child relationship. In such circumstances, we deem it inappropriate to decide the custody issue on the basis of cultural assumptions which are not borne out by the record. Rational decision-making requires, as a necessary prerequisite, a solid evidentiary base upon which evaluation can be made of these factors as they relate to the primary question of what custody disposition is in the best interests of the child.

We therefore reverse and remand to the superior court for further proceedings not inconsistent with the foregoing. Upon remand, the superior court is empowered to appoint a guardian ad litem for the child, and to take such other steps as are deemed appropriate, including the taking of additional evidence in the event any party raises issues as to changed circumstances arising since trial that bear on the custody issue.

WISHES OF THE CHILD

Older children are almost always asked where they would want to live. Courts are understandably reluctant, however, to ask young children to take sides in custody disputes. If this becomes common practice, there would be an incentive for both parents to pressure the child to express preferences. If, however, the court is convinced that the child is mature enough to state a rational preference and that doing so would not harm the child, evidence of such a preference will be admissible. Great caution must be used in questioning the child. The judge may decide to speak to the child outside the formal courtroom (with the lawyers but not the parents present), or the judge may allow a professional (e.g., child psychologist, social worker) to interview the child at home.

EXPERT WITNESSES

Psychologists, psychiatrists, social workers, and other experts can be called as expert witnesses by either parent to testify on the child's home environment and emotional development, the mental stability of the parents, the suitability of various custody plans, etc. Either parent, or the guardian at litem for the child, can make a motion that the court order a custody evaluation by an expert. An example of a custody-evaluation report by such an expert is provided in Exhibit 11.1.

ASSIGNMENT 11.5

a. What standards exist in your state code to guide the judge on the decision to grant custody when the dispute is between the two biological parents? (See General Instructions for the State-Code Assignment in chapter 1.)

b. Find an opinion written by a court in your state in which the court granted custody to one of the parents following a divorce or legal separation. Pick an opinion in which both parents sought sole custody. State the factors that the court used in making this decision. Why did the judge decide not to give custody to the other parent? Do you agree with the judge's decision on the custody issue? Are there other facts about the case that you would like to know, but were not provided in the opinion? Do you think the investigators for each side did a good job of gathering all the facts? (See General Instructions for the Court-Opinion Assignment in chapter 1.)

□ **Note on Frozen Embryos** A husband and wife participate in *in vitro fertilization* resulting in an embryo that is frozen for later implantation. Before this can occur, the parties file for divorce. What is the status of the frozen embryo? Is it "property" to be divided between the parties? Does the court have to make a "custody" decision? See the discussion on page 225.

□ **EXHIBIT 11.1 Sample Custody Evaluation by an Expert**

Psychiatric Custody Evaluation

August 25, 1981

Honorable James K. O'Brien
Supreme Court of New York
New York County
60 Centre Street
New York, New York 10007

Re: Johnson v. Johnson
Docket No. M-3784-81

Dear Judge O'Brien:

This report is submitted in compliance with your court order dated June 9, 1981, requesting that I conduct an evaluation of the Johnson family in order to provide the court with information that would be useful to it in deciding which of the Johnson parents should have custody of their children Tara, Elaine, and Charles.

My findings and recommendations are based on interviews conducted as itemized below:

July 6, 1981—Mrs. Carol Johnson and Mr. Frank Johnson, seen jointly	2 hours
July 7, 1981—Mr. Frank Johnson	1 hour
July 11, 1981—Mrs. Carol Johnson	1 hour
July 13, 1981—Tara Johnson	1 1/2 hours
July 14, 1981—Mr. Frank Johnson	1 hour
July 20, 1981—Mrs. Carol Johnson	1 hour
July 21, 1981—Charles Johnson	3/4 hour
Elaine Johnson	3/4 hour
July 22, 1981—Tara Johnson	1/2 hour
Mrs. Carol Johnson and Tara Johnson, seen jointly	1/2 hour
July 24, 1981—Mrs. Carol Johnson	1 hour
July 27, 1971—Mrs. Carol Johnson and Mr. Frank Johnson, seen jointly	1 hour
Aug. 3, 1981—Elaine Johnson	3/4 hour
Aug. 4, 1981—Tara Johnson	1/4 hour
Mr. Frank Johnson and Tara Johnson, seen jointly	1/2 hour
Aug. 10, 1981—Tara Johnson Mr. Frank Johnson and Mrs. Carol Johnson, seen jointly	3/4 hour
Aug. 11, 1981—Tara Johnson Elaine Johnson Charles Johnson Mrs. Carol Johnson and Mr. Frank Johnson, seen jointly	3/4 hour
Aug. 14, 1981—Tara Johnson Elaine Johnson Charles Johnson Mrs. Carol Johnson and Mr. Frank Johnson, seen jointly	1 hour
	16 hours

In addition, on Aug. 16, 1981, Mr. and Mrs. Johnson were seen together for the purpose of my presenting these findings and recommendations to them. This interview lasted two hours, bringing to 18 the total number of hours spent with the Johnson family in association with this evaluation.

Continued

☐ **EXHIBIT 11.1   Sample Custody Evaluation by an Expert—*Continued***

Mr. Frank Johnson, an airline pilot, is 43 years old. His first wife died soon after the delivery of Tara, who is now 16 years of age. He married Mrs. Carol Johnson when Tara was 2 years old. Mrs. Johnson, a housewife, who was formerly an elementary school teacher, is now 40. Her first marriage ended in divorce. A child of this relationship died soon after birth. There are two children of the Johnson marriage: Elaine, 11 and Charles, 7. Mrs. Johnson adopted her stepdaughter Tara in July 1980. In October 1980, Mr. Johnson initiated divorce proceedings because he felt that his wife no longer respected him and that she was a poor mother for the children, especially his daughter Tara. However, Mr. and Mrs. Johnson are still occupying the same domicile.

Both parents are requesting custody of all three children. It is this examiner's recommendation that Mr. Frank Johnson be granted custody of Tara and that Mrs. Carol Johnson be granted custody of Elaine and Charles. The observations that have led me to these conclusions will be divided into four categories: 1) Mr. Frank Johnson's assets as a parent, 2) Mr. Frank Johnson's liabilities as a parent, 3) Mrs. Carol Johnson's assets as a parent, and 4) Mrs. Carol Johnson's liabilities as a parent. Following these four presentations I will comment further on the way in which my observations brought about the aforementioned recommendations. Although much information was obtained in the course of the evaluation, only those items specifically pertinent to the custody consideration will be included in this report.

Mr. Frank Johnson's Assets as a Parent

Mr. Frank Johnson is Tara's biological father. The special psychological tie that this engenders is not enjoyed by Mrs. Carol Johnson and Tara. It is not the genetic bond per se that is crucial here; rather, it is the psychological attachment that such a bond elicits. Mr. Johnson had already started to develop a psychological tie with Tara while his first wife was pregnant with her. He was actually present at her birth and assumed an active role in her rearing—almost from birth because of the illness and early death of his first wife. This situation prevailed until the time of his marriage to Mrs. Johnson when Tara was 2 years of age. Although Mrs. Johnson has been Tara's primary caretaker since then, Mr. Johnson's early involvement with Tara during these crucial years of her development contributes to a very strong psychological tie between them that has continued up to the present time.

My observations have convinced me, and both parents agree, that at this time, Tara has a closer relationship with her father than her mother. Her relationship with Mrs. Johnson at this time is characteristically a difficult one in that there are frequent battles and power struggles. Although Tara is not completely free of such involvement with her father, such hostile interaction is far less common. In my interviews with Mr. Johnson and Tara, I found her to be far more friendly with him than I observed her to be with Mrs. Johnson in my joint interviews with them.

In every interview, both alone and in joint sessions with various members of the family, Tara openly and unswervingly stated that she wished to live with her father: "I want to live with my father. I am closer to him." "When I was younger, my mother did more things; but since I'm older, my father does more things." "My father listens to what I say; my mother doesn't."

Mr. Johnson and Tara both utilize a similar method of communication. Neither feels a strong need to give confirmation of examples to general statements that they make, and they are therefore comfortable with one another. Mrs. Johnson, on the other hand, is much more specific in her communications and this is a source of difficulty, not only in her relationship with Tara, but in her relationship with her husband as well.

All five family members agree that Mr. Johnson spends significant time with Charles, involved in typical father-son activities, sports, games, etc. It is also apparent that Charles has a strong masculine identification and this arose, in part, from his modeling himself after his father.

Mr. Frank Johnson's Liabilities as a Parent

Mr. Johnson states that he would not have involved himself in the custody evaluation conducted by this examiner if he had to contribute to its financing. Accordingly, Mrs. Johnson assumed the total financial obligation for this evaluation. I conclude from this that with regard to this particular criterion for comparing the parents, Mr. Johnson's position is less strong than Mrs. Johnson's.

On many occasions Mr. Johnson made general comments about his superiority over his wife with regard to parental capacity. For example, "She's a very poor mother," "She neglects the children," and "If you had all the information you would see that I'm a better parent." However, it was extremely

Continued

☐ **EXHIBIT 11.1 Sample Custody Evaluation by an Expert—*Continued***

difficult to elicit from Mr. Johnson specific examples of incidents that would substantiate these statements. I not only considered this to be a manifestation of Mr. Johnson's problem in accurately communicating, but also considered it to be a deficiency in his position. One cannot be convinced of the strength of such statements if no examples can be provided to substantiate them.

In the hope that I might get more specific information from Mr. Johnson I asked him, on at least three occasions, to write a list of specifics that might help corroborate some of his allegations. He came to three subsequent interviews without having written anything in response to my invitation. I consider such failure to reflect a compromise in his motivation for gaining custody of the three children. When he did finally submit such a list it was far less comprehensive than that which was submitted by Mrs. Johnson and in addition, the issues raised had far less significance, e.g., "She's late once in a while," "She's sometimes forgetful," and "She doesn't like playing baseball with Charles."

Although I described Mr. Johnson's communication problem as a factor supporting his gaining custody of Tara, I would consider it a liability with regard to his gaining custody of Elaine and Charles. Tara (possibly on a genetic basis) communicates in a similar way and so, as mentioned, is comfortable with her father when they communicate. Elaine and Charles, however, appear to be identifying with their mother with regard to communication accuracy. Accordingly, intensive exposure to Mr. Johnson might compromise what I consider a healthier communicative pattern.

Mr. Johnson's profession as an airline pilot has not enabled him to have predictable hours. Not only is his schedule variable, but there are times when he is required to work on an emergency basis. All three children agree that Mrs. Johnson is more predictably present. Mr. Johnson's irregular schedule is not a significant problem for Tara who, at 16, is fairly independent and would not suffer significantly from her father's schedule. The younger children, however, are still in need of predictability of parental presence and Mr. Johnson has not demonstrated his capacity to provide such predictability. In my final interview with Mr. Johnson he stated that he would change his work pattern to be available to his children during non-school hours. Mrs. Johnson was very dubious that this could be arranged because his job does not allow such flexibility. Both parents agreed, however, that it had not occurred in the past and that such predictability was not taking place at the time of this evaluation.

Both Charles and Elaine stated that they wanted to live with their mother and not live with their father. Charles stated, "I want to be with my mother. I'd be alone when my father goes to work." Elaine stated, "I want to live with my mother. I'm closer to my mother. I'm not as close to my father."

In a session in which I was discussing his future plans with Mr. Johnson, he stated that he was considering moving to California because he could earn more money there by supplementing his income with certain business ventures that he had been invited to participate in. He stated also that he would still move even if he were only to be granted custody of Tara. Although I appreciate that a higher income could provide Mr. Johnson's children with greater financial flexibility, I believe that the disadvantages of such a move would far outweigh its advantages from their point of view. Specifically, the extra advantages they might enjoy from such a move would be more than offset by the even greater absence of their father who, his liabilities notwithstanding, is still an important figure for them.

In an interview in which I discussed with Mr. Johnson how he would react to the various custodial decisions, he was far more upset about the prospect of losing Tara than he was about the possibility of losing Charles and Elaine. In fact, he appeared to be accepting of the fact that Elaine would go to her mother. Although somewhat distressed about the possibility of Charles' living with his mother, he did not show the same degree of distress as his wife over the prospect of losing the younger two children.

Mrs. Carol Johnson's Assets as a Parent

Mrs. Carol Johnson was far more committed to the custody evaluation than her husband. As mentioned, she was willing to make the financial sacrifices involved in the evaluation. I consider this to be a factor reflecting greater motivation than her husband for gaining custody of the children. Mrs. Johnson is more available to the children during non-school hours than her husband and this is one element in her favor regarding gaining custody, especially of the younger children. Mrs. Johnson is a more accurate and clearer communicator than her husband and this is an asset. As mentioned, the younger children do not seem to have been affected by their father's communication difficulty. Having them live with him might result in their acquiring this maladaptive trait.

During her pregnancy with Elaine, Mrs. Johnson suffered with toxemia and associated high blood pressure and convulsions. Most physicians generally discourage women with this disorder from becoming pregnant again because it is genuinely life endangering. However, Mrs. Johnson did wish to have a third child, primarily because her husband, she states, was so desirous of having a son. Her pregnancy

Continued

☐ **EXHIBIT 11.1 Sample Custody Evaluation by an Expert—Continued**

with Charles was complicated by the exacerbation of a preexisting asthmatic condition from which she states that she almost died. A less maternal woman would not have become pregnant again.

Elaine stated on many occasions, and in every interview, both alone and with other family members, that she wished to live with her mother: "I'm closer to my mother," "She's home more than my father," "They call my father to do things at work all the time," and "My mother has more feelings for me than my father."

Charles also, both in individual session and in joint interviews, emphatically stated that he wished to live with his mother: "I want to stay with my mother because she doesn't work as much as my father." "If you get sick the father might not know what to do, but the mother does." "My mother knows how to take care of me." "She doesn't work that much." "She reads me books more than my father."

On one occasion Mr. Johnson stated: "Carol is closer to Elaine than I am. They are similar. They're both sore losers. Both get emotional if they don't have their way." Mrs. Carol Johnson agrees that she and her daughter Elaine have these traits, but not to the degree described by her husband. Although there are certainly negative elements regarding the reasons why Mr. Johnson sees Elaine to be closer to his wife, this statement is an admission of his recognition of this preference of Elaine for her mother. The situation is analogous to Mr. Johnson's involvement with Tara. They are closer to one another, yet maladaptive and undesirable factors are contributing to the closeness.

Mrs. Carol Johnson's Liabilities as a Parent

Tara is not Mrs. Johnson's biological daughter. Although she has raised Tara from her infancy, as if she were her own biological child, and although she has adopted her, Mrs. Johnson is at a certain disadvantage regarding the development of a strong psychological parent-child tie. As mentioned, I believe that a biological relationship increases the strength of the psychological bond. Accordingly, Mrs. Johnson is at a disadvantage when compared to Mr. Johnson regarding this aspect of the custody consideration.

Mrs. Johnson and Tara have a poor relationship at this point. In my interviews with Mrs. Johnson and Tara I found the latter to view her mother scornfully and to be openly resentful of her authority. On one occasion Tara said: "She has a lot of nerve telling me what to do." Were this an isolated statement, it would probably not have much significance. However, all agreed that it epitomized her general attitude toward her mother. Although some of the scornful attitude Tara exhibits toward her mother can be viewed as age-appropriate, I believe the extent goes beyond what is to be expected for teen-agers.

Mrs. Johnson cannot provide Charles with the same kind of father model and father-type involvement that her husband can. Although she claims an interest in sports and a greater degree of facility than the average woman, it is still clear that her husband has been far more involved in this type of activity with his son than has Mrs. Johnson.

Mr. Johnson accuses Mrs. Johnson of being excessively punitive and too strong a disciplinarian. Mrs. Johnson claims that her husband is too lax with the children and does not implement proper disciplinary measures. I believe that it is most likely that Mrs. Johnson is a little too punitive and that Mr. Johnson is a little too lenient. However, neither parent exhibits these difficulties to a degree that would be significantly injurious to the children, nor would I consider this to be a factor compromising either of their capacities as parents. It is probable, however, that these differences are playing a role in Tara's antagonism to her mother and her gravitating toward her father.

In every interview, both individual and joint, Tara openly stated that she wished to live with her father. "I would be very unhappy if the judge made me go with my mother." "He can't make me live with my mother. I'd run away to my father if he did."

Conclusions and Recommendations

Weighing the above factors as best I can, I believe that the evidence is strongly in favor of Mr. Johnson being given custody of Tara. I believe, also, that the above evidence strongly supports the conclusion that Elaine should be given to Mrs. Johnson. Although there are certain arguments supporting Mr. Johnson's gaining custody of Charles, I believe that these are greatly outweighed by arguments in favor of Mrs. Johnson's gaining custody. Were the court to conclude that Tara would be better off living with Mrs. Johnson, I believe that there would be a continuation of the present hostilities, and this could be disruptive to the healthy psychological development of the younger children—if they were exposed to such hostile interactions over a long period. I believe that if Mr. Johnson were to be granted custody of Elaine and Charles it is most likely that they would suffer psychological damage. All things considered, I believe he is the less preferable parent for the young children and, if they had to live with him, they would suffer emotional deprivations that could contribute to the development of psychiatric disorders.

Richard A. Gardner, M.D.

SOURCE: R. Gardner, M.D., *Family Evaluation in Child Custody Litigation,* 318–25 (1982).

COURT DECISION ON VISITATION

Courts want to preserve as much of the child's relationship with both parents as possible. Hence, visitation rights are almost always granted to the noncustodial parent even if they must be exercised in the presence of third parties (*supervised visitation*). Failing to grant such rights would be a step in the direction of terminating the parental rights of that parent (see Chapter 19). Moreover, as indicated earlier, one of the criteria that a court will use in awarding sole custody to a parent is whether the latter will cooperate in the exercise of visitation rights by the other parent. Custodial parents who fail to provide such cooperation are sometimes dealt with harshly by the court, e.g., terminating spousal support, transferring custody to the other parent, contempt orders. It is never permissible, however, for the noncustodial parent to terminate child-support payments in retaliation for the custodial parent's violation of visitation rights.

Whenever possible, the court will favor frequent and regular visitation by the noncustodial parent, e.g., every other weekend, alternating holidays, substantial summer vacation time. When the custody battle is between two relatively fit parents, the court is even more inclined to grant greater visitation rights to the loser so long as the court is convinced that the losing parent had the proper motivation in seeking custody.

An essential component of successful visitation in most cases is physical proximity between the child and the noncustodial parent. A great deal of litigation has centered on the right of the custodial parent to move the child substantial distances away. Some courts flatly forbid such moving. A few states have statutes that cover this problem. For example:

Minn.Stat.Ann. § 518.175(3) (1969) The custodial parent shall not move the residence of the child to another state except upon the order of the Court or with the consent of the non-custodial parent, when the non-custodial parent has been given visitation rights by the decree.

In extreme cases, the court might order the custodial parent to post a bond to secure compliance with the visitation rights of the noncustodial parent.

Another issue that is occasionally litigated is whether *third parties* can be given rights of visitation, e.g., grandparents, stepparents. Factors considered by the court in deciding this question include:

☐ The language of the statute in the state that governs who can visit. A court will want to know if it has statutory power to grant visitation rights to third parties.

☐ Whether the custodial parent objects to granting the visitation rights. And if so, why.

☐ Whether the child has lived with the third party for a substantial period of time in the past or has otherwise formed close emotional ties with the third party.

The best interest of the child is again the standard the court will use if it has the power to grant visitation rights to anyone other than biological parents. Even when the power exists, however, it is rarely used except in situations such as the following:

The father dies soon after the divorce in which the mother was given sole custody of the child. The paternal grandparents are granted visitation rights. The child had a warm relationship with these grandparents in the past. If visitation is not allowed, the child may lose all contact with the father's side of the family.

A stepparent has been supporting his wife's child by a prior marriage. When the stepparent and mother divorce, he seeks visitation rights, even though he never adopted the child. Visitation rights are granted if the stepparent had a close relationship with the child while together, and it would be very disruptive to end the relationship abruptly.

■■■■■ THE NEW "TERROR WEAPON"

"I had to face the fact that for one year [during the exercise of unsupervised visitation rights by the father], I sent my child off to her rapist."[5]

"For many parents engaged in seriously contested child custody disputes, false allegations of child abuse have become an effective weapon for achieving an advantage in court."[6]

In alarming numbers, parents are being accused of sexually abusing their children, usually during visitation. The issue can also arise during an initial custody proceeding where one parent claims that the other committed sex abuse during the marriage, and hence should not be granted custody, or should not be granted visitation rights in unsupervised settings.

The level of bitterness generated by this accusation is incredibly high. It is the equivalent of a declaration of total war between the parties. The chances of reaching a settlement or of mediating the custody dispute—or anything else that is contested—often vanishes the moment the accusation is made. Protracted and costly litigation is all but inevitable.

Nor does litigation always resolve the matter. Assume that a mother with sole custody is turned down when she asks a court to terminate the father's right to visit the child because of an allegation of child abuse. The court finds the evidence of abuse to be insufficient and orders a continuation of visitation. Unable to accept this result, the mother goes underground out of desperation and a total loss of faith in the legal system. She either flees with the child, or she turns the child over to sympathetic third parties who agree to keep the child hidden from the authorities. The child might be moved from one "safe house" to another to avoid detection. This underground network consists of a core of dedicated women who at one time were in a similar predicament or who are former child-abuse victims themselves.

If the mother remains behind, she is hauled back into court. If she refuses to obey an order to produce the child, she faces an array of possible sanctions, including imprisonment for civil contempt or even prosecution for criminal kidnaping. Unfortunately, the media have an excessive interest in cases of this kind. Once reporters and cameras become involved, a circus atmosphere tends to develop.

Attorneys can find themselves in delicate situations. The first question they face is whether to take the case. When an alleged child abuser—usually the father—seeks representation, the attorney understands the father's need for a

---

5. Szegedy-Maszak, *Who's to Judge*, New York Times Magazine, 28 (May 21, 1989).
6. Gordon, *False Allegations of Abuse in Child Custody Disputes*, 2 Minnesota Family Law Journal 225 (1985).

vigorous defense. What if he didn't do it? Yet attorneys tend to place cases of this kind in a different category. Many need to believe in his innocence before they will take the case. According to a prominent matrimonial attorney, "I have a higher duty to make sure some wacko doesn't get custody of his child." Before proceeding, therefore, the attorney might ask him to:

☐ Take a lie detector test

☐ Take the *Minnesota Multiphasic Personality Index test* **(MMPI),** which may be able to reveal whether someone has a propensity to lie and is the kind of person who statistically is likely to be a child abuser

☐ Be evaluated by a knowledgeable psychologist or psychiatrist.

Some attorneys have even insisted that the father undergo hypnosis as a further aid in trying to assess the truth of the allegation.

Attorneys representing the mother face similar concerns. Is she telling the truth? Is she exaggerating, knowingly or otherwise? Is she trying to seek some other strategic advantage from the father, e.g., more financial support? (Custody blackmail?) What advice should the attorney give her when she first reveals the charge of sexual abuse, particularly when the evidence of abuse is not overwhelming? Should she be advised to go public with the charge? As indicated, the consequences of doing so—and of not doing so—can be enormous. Bitter litigation is almost assured. What if the attorney talks her out of going public with the charge in order to settle the case through negotiation, "and a month or two later something terrible happens?" Faced, therefore, with a need to know if the accusation is true, the attorney may ask *her* to go take a polygraph test or an MMPI test, or to undergo an independent evaluation by a psychologist or psychiatrist.

Other attorneys disagree with this approach. They do not think that clients should be subject to such mistrust by their own attorney. And they fail to see much value in some of the devices used to assess the truth. Some typical comments from such attorneys are that professionals "trained in sexual abuse are wrong very often"; "Frankly I trust my horse sense more than I trust psychiatrists"; and "There is no research that says the polygraph or MMPI is of any use." [7]

Of course, attorneys for both sides will have to interview the child. This can be a very delicate task. There is a danger of emotional damage every time the child is forced to focus on the events in question. Even though children are generally truthful, many are susceptible to suggestion and manipulation. Very often, the charge is made that the child has been "brainwashed" into believing that abuse did or did not occur. Clearly, the child needs protection. A separate attorney (guardian at litem) is usually appointed by the court to represent the child in the litigation. Guidelines may exist in the state on who can interview the child and in what setting. Trained child counselors are commonly used. Using special, anatomically correct dolls, the counselor will ask the child to describe what happened. These interviews are usually videotaped. When the time comes for a court hearing, the judge will often interview the child outside the courtroom, e.g., in the judge's chambers without either parent present.

---

7. Fisk, *Abuse: The New Weapon,* The National Law Journal, 20 (July 17, 1989).

ASSIGNMENT 11.6

Diane and George are the parents of Mary. When the child is two years old, the parents divorce. The decree awards Diane sole custody with visitation rights to George (on alternating weekends). Diane soon suspects that George is sexually abusing Mary during the visits. Answer the following questions for your state. (See General Instructions for the State-Code Assignment and General Instructions for the Court-Opinion Assignment in chapter 1.)

a. What options does Diane have?

b. Under what circumstances can the child be interviewed about the alleged molestation? Are there any restrictions on such interviews?

c. Can Diane be jailed for contempt of court if she refuses to obey an order to disclose Mary's location following a court decision that there was no sexual abuse by George? If so, for how long? Indefinitely?

■■■■ BIOLOGICAL PARENT VS. PSYCHOLOGICAL PARENT

Thus far our main focus has been the custody dispute where the main combatants are the two biological parents. Suppose, however, that the dispute is between one biological parent and a third party such as a/an:

☐ Grandparent

☐ Other relative

☐ Stepparent (who never adopted the child)

☐ Foster parent (who is temporarily caring for the child at the request of the state)

☐ Neighbor

☐ Friend

Assume that the other biological parent is out of the picture because he or she has died, has disappeared, or does not care. The third party is usually someone with whom the child has established close emotional ties. Frequently, the child has lived with the third party for a substantial period of time. This may have occurred for a number of reasons:

☐ The biological parent was ill, out of the state, out of work, etc.

☐ The biological parent was in prison.

☐ The state asked the third party to care for the child temporarily.

☐ The child could not stay at home because of marital difficulties between the biological parents.

☐ The biological parent was in school for substantial periods of time.

☐ The biological parent once considered giving the child up for adoption.

Psychological Parent
An adult who is not legally responsible for the care of a child, but who has formed a substantial emotional bond with the child.

Third parties who have formed such emotional ties with a child are referred to as **psychological parents.** See Goldstein, Freud, and Solnit, *Beyond the Best Interests of the Child* (1979).

There are two main schools of thought among courts when the custody dispute is between a biological parent and a psychological parent:

1. It is in the best interest of the child to be placed with its biological parent (this is a strong presumption).

2. It is in the best interest of the child to be placed with the adult who will provide the most wholesome, stable environment.

The emphasis of the first approach is on parental rights: unless you can show that the biological parent is *unfit*, he or she has the right to custody. The emphasis of the second approach is on the child's needs. Most states follow the first approach. In these states, the question is not whether the biological parent or the psychological parent can provide the best home for the child. The question is whether it is clear that placement with the biological parent would be harmful to the child. While the child may suffer some damage if his or her relationship with the psychological parent is severed, this does not necessarily overcome the biological parent's overriding right to have the child. The law is very reluctant to take children away from their natural parents because of a determination that someone else could do a better job raising them.

In practice, courts sometimes tend to blur the two approaches listed above. While maintaining allegiance to the doctrine of parental rights, the court might still undertake a comparison between the benefits to the child of living with the biological parent, as opposed to the benefits of living with the psychological parent. When the benefits to be derived from the latter are overwhelming, the court might be more inclined to find unfitness in the biological parent or to conclude that giving custody to the biological parent would be detrimental to the child. The interpretation of the evidence can be very subjective. There is often enough data to support any conclusion the court wants to reach. A person's mistakes in raising children can be viewed either as an inability to be a competent parent or as an inevitable component of the nearly impossible job of parenting in today's society.

ASSIGNMENT 11.7

a. Are there any statutes in your state on how the court is to resolve a custody dispute between a biological parent and a psychological parent? If so, what do they say? (See General Instructions for the State-Code Assignment in chapter 1.)

b. Find an opinion written by a court in your state in which the dispute was between a biological parent and a psychological parent. Who won? Why? What standards did the judge apply? Were there other facts about the case that you wish the court had provided? If so, what facts and why would you want them? (See General Instructions for the Court-Opinion Assignment in chapter 1.)

c. Make up a fact situation involving a custody dispute between a biological parent and a psychological parent. Make it a close case. Include facts that would strongly favor each side. Now write a memorandum in which you discuss the law that would apply in your state to your case. Assume that you are working for the office that represents the psychological parent. (See General Instructions for the Legal-Analysis Assignment in chapter 1.)

▰▰▰ MODIFICATION OF THE CUSTODY ORDER BY THE STATE THAT ISSUED THE ORDER

In this section we consider the modification of a custody order by the *same* state that issued the order. Later we will examine the special jurisdiction problems that arise when a party with a custody order from one state tries to have it modified in another state. While our discussion will focus on the two biological parents, the same principles apply no matter who is given custody by the original order.

Two reasons justify a court in modifying its own custody order:

☐ There has been a significant change in circumstances since the original order, or

□ Relevant facts were not made available to the court at the time of its original order.

In either situation, new facts are now before the court. The question becomes whether it is in the best interest of the child for the court to change its mind and award custody to the other parent. Given the disruption of such a change, the answer is no, unless the new facts *substantially* alter the court's perception of the child's welfare. For example:

□ The custodial parent has been neglecting or abusing the child.

□ The custodial parent has moved from the area, contrary to the court's order, thus making visitation extremely difficult or impossible.

□ The custodial parent has adopted an unorthodox lifestyle that has negatively affected the child's physical or moral development (or there is a danger that this lifestyle will have this effect). See, for example, the *Jarrett* case presented earlier in which the mother began an open relationship with a live-in lover.

It is not enough that the custodial parent has experienced hard times such as sickness or loss of a part-time job since the original order. Nor is it enough to show that mistakes have been made in raising the children. To justify a modification, the adverse circumstances or mistakes must be (1) ongoing, (2) relatively permanent, (3) serious, and (4) detrimental to the children.

ASSIGNMENT 11.8

a. Are there any statutes in your state specifying the conditions for modifying a custody order that was issued within your state? If so, what are they? (See General Instructions for the State-Code Assignment in chapter 1.)

b. Find an opinion in which a custody order issued in your state was modified by a court in your state. What was the modification? Why was it ordered? What standards did the court use? Were there other facts about the case that you would have liked to have had? If so, what facts and why would you want to know about them? (see General Instructions for the Court-Opinion Assignment in chapter 1.)

c. Make up a fact situation involving a case in which sole custody was granted to one parent, but the other parent is now seeking a modification. Make it a close case. Include facts that support a modification and facts that support a continuation of the status quo. Now write a memorandum in which you discuss the law that would apply in your state to your case. Assume that you are working for the office that represents the party who wants to prevent the other side from modifying the order. (See General Instructions for the Legal-Analysis Assignment in chapter 1.)

d. Read Exhibit 11.2 containing an affidavit in support of a motion to modify a custody decree. Do you think the court should reconsider the custody order as requested? What further facts, if any, would you like to have? (See General Instructions for the Investigation-Strategy Assignment in chapter 1.)

▄▄▄ JURISDICTIONAL PROBLEMS AND CHILD SNATCHING

Earlier we discussed the modification of a child-custody order by the state that issued the order. Suppose, however, that a party tries to have the order modified by *another* state. Consider the following sequence:

Dan and Ellen are divorced in New York where they live. Ellen receives custody of their child. Dan moves to Delaware. During a visit of the child in Delaware, Dan petitions

☐ **EXHIBIT 11.2 Affidavit in Support of a Motion to Modify the Custody Decree**

AFFIDAVIT IN SUPPORT
Index No. 3

STATE OF NEW YORK
COUNTY OF _____ } ss.

_____ , being duly sworn, deposes and says:

1. I am the defendant herein. This affidavit is submitted in support of an application for reconsideration of the decision of the court made in this action on _____ , 19 ___ , insofar as custody of my children is concerned.

2. Custody of the children has been awarded to my ex-wife, plaintiff. I did not contest her claim in the divorce. When I reported this to the children, they became extremely upset. My son told me that he did not want to live with his mother and that he felt it was unfair for a boy of his age to be forced to live with a parent contrary to his desires. My daughter had a similar reaction.

3. I tried to convey the situation to the Court by an informal application of reconsideration, on the strength of simple notes written to the Court by my children. My attorney advised me that the Court would not alter its determination.

4. I love my children very much. A history of prior proceedings between my wife and myself indicates that she had been awarded custody of the children under a Family Court order several years ago. At that time, she lived with the children in our house in Peekskill. I paid support, as directed for the children and my wife, and for the upkeep of the house. About two years ago my wife ousted my son from the house and sent him to live with me. At that time, I occupied a small apartment in Peekskill so that I could be near the children. I would see them quite often and would take them to school on many mornings. When my son came to me, I made room for him and we lived together until my daughter came to live with us about a year ago. We made room for her. My wife made no objections to the children living with me and made no attempts to get them to come back to her. While we all lived in my small apartment, my wife continued to live in the Peekskill house all by herself. I continued paying the upkeep on the house, although my wife permitted it to fall into a state of deteriorating disrepair. I contributed to her support.

5. I took care of my children as best I could. They were grown and attended school most of the day. In the evening we enjoyed a family life. We were together on the week-ends. There were many week-ends when their mother would not attempt to spend any time with them. My son stayed away from the Peekskill house. My daughter visited there with her mother on occasion. I know that on many occasions my wife stayed away from the Peekskill house for days at a time.

6. I have devoted my non-working hours to my children. I altered my schedule so that I would see them off to school each morning when I was not away from the City. If I was to be away, I would arrange adult supervision. I worked with my children on their homework and on anything else where they sought my participation. We shopped together and played together. My children were encouraged to maintain their friendships and to bring their friends to our home. Because of cramped quarters, my children would often visit with their friends and I encouraged them to maintain relationships with companions of their respective ages. I shared their problems and their joys. I tried to set responsible examples for them. My son had demonstrated to me that he is growing into a responsible young man who aspires to attend Massachusetts Institute of Technology. I am proud of his seriousness and of his healthy outlook in times like this. I have tried to maintain a closely knit family between my children and myself so that they should know the advantages of love, companionship, and security. I know that they did not find any such relationship at their mother's bosom.

7. My children have revealed to me that they were wrong in not having made a definite choice during this interview with the court on the matter of their preference of a home. I understand that they will still love their mother and I have not attempted to sway them from that plateau. They told me that they wanted the court to decide the problem for them and that they had hoped that they could be the force which could solve the rift between plaintiff and myself. They were unaware that at the time of the interview, my wife's prayer for divorce had already been granted. My son told me that he indicated to the court that he preferred to live with me although he did not state, unequivocally, that he did not desire to live with his mother.

8. I gather from my children's reaction and from what they have told me that they misunderstood what was required of them during their interview with the court. I submit that another interview should be granted if the court feels that my children's affidavits are insufficient to establish their desires. Had I not seen the effect of the custody decision on my children and had they not indicated their grief over it, I would sit back and abide by the will of the court.

9. I seriously question my wife's fitness as our children's custodian. She voluntarily relinquished their custody, as aforesaid. Under adverse living conditions (cramped quarters), my children have thrived and demonstrated a progression toward adulthood. I believe that my wife's having been competitive instead of being cooperative with the children operated to compromise their welfare. I believe that using the children as a pawn has lost our children's respect. I feel that my pleasures must be subservient to the welfare of my children. They deserve as real a home as can be possible under the circumstances. They are entitled to eat a meal in peace and one which shows concern in its preparation. I believe that the children deserve some security in the knowledge that they have the genuine care and love of a parent. I believe that they cannot get this from their mother.

10. WHEREFORE, I respectfully pray that this application be granted and that upon reconsideration I be awarded custody of my children.

[Signature]

SOURCE: Marino, J., McKinney's Forms, Form 14:24B and Form 14:33A West Publishing Co. (1976).

a Delaware court for a modification of the New York custody order. Ellen does not appear in the Delaware proceeding. Dan tells the Delaware court a horror story about the child's life with Ellen in New York. The Delaware court modifies the New York order on the basis of changed circumstances, awarding custody to Dan.

Or worse:

While their child is in a New York school yard, Dan takes the child out of the state without telling Ellen. Dan petitions a Delaware court for a modification of the custody order. If he loses, he tries again in Florida. If he loses, he tries again in another state until he finds a court that will grant him custody.

Forum Shopping
Seeking a court that will be favorable to you. Traveling from court to court until you find one that will provide a favorable ruling.

The latter situation involves what has been commonly called *child snatching.* The parent "grabs" the child and then "shops" for a favorable forum **(forum shopping).** For years the problem reached epidemic proportions.

Courts are caught in a dilemma. When a custody order is made, it is not a final determination by the court. Custody orders are always modifiable on the basis of changed circumstances that affect the welfare of the child. This rule is designed to help the child by making the court always available to protect the child. But if an order is not final, it is not entitled to *full faith and credit* by another state, i.e., another state is not required to abide by it. Hence, other states are free to reexamine the case to determine whether new circumstances warrant a modification. To maintain flexibility, states require very little to trigger its jurisdiction to hear a custody case, e.g., the domicile or mere presence of the child in the state along with one of the parents. The result is chaos: scandalous child snatching and unseemly forum shopping.

The question, therefore, is how to cut down or eliminate child snatching and forum shopping without taking away the flexibility that courts need to act in the best interest of the child. Two major statutes need to be discussed:

☐ The *Uniform Child Custody Jurisdiction Act* (see Appendix B)
☐ The *Parental Kidnaping Prevention Act* (see Appendix C)

UNIFORM CHILD CUSTODY JURISDICTION ACT (UCCJA)

In 1968 the **Uniform Child Custody Jurisdiction Act (UCCJA)** was issued by the National Conference of Commissioners on Uniform Laws. This conference proposes laws for adoption by the various state legislatures. When first proposed, only a small number of states adopted the UCCJA. But after a top-rated television program (*60 Minutes*) gave national exposure to the problem, many of the states fell in line.

Two important questions are covered in the UCCJA:

☑ When does a court in the state have the power or jurisdiction to make the *initial* decision on child custody?

☐ When will a court modify a custody order of another state?

A goal of the UCCJA is to "avoid jurisdictional competition and conflict with courts of other states in matters of child custody which have in the past resulted in the shifting of children from state to state with harmful effects on their well-being" (§ 1).

JURISDICTION TO MAKE THE INITIAL CHILD-CUSTODY DECISION

The foundation of the UCCJA is § 3, which specifies the conditions that must exist for a court to hear a child-custody case. Without one of these conditions being present, the court will have no jurisdiction to decide the case. Any *one* of the following four conditions will be sufficient to confer such jurisdiction:

1. *Home state.*
   - This is the **home state** of the child at the time the case is brought. A home state is where the child has lived for at least six consecutive months (or since birth if the child is less than six months old). These time periods can include temporary absence from the state. *Or*
   - This state was the home state of the child (as defined above) within six months of the commencement of the custody suit, but the child is now being kept out of state and at least one parent or person claiming the right to custody still lives in this state.

2. *Significant connection/substantial evidence.* Even though this is not the home state of the child, it is in the best interest of the child for this state to take jurisdiction because:
   - The child and parents, or the child and at least one person claiming custody, have a significant connection with this state, *and*
   - There is substantial evidence in this state concerning the child's present or future care, protection, training, and personal relationships.

3. *Physical presence/abandonment/emergency.* Even though this is not the home state of the child and even though there is not significant connection with or substantial evidence in this state, the state can still take jurisdiction if:
   - The child is physically present in the state and has been abandoned, *or*
   - The child is physically present in the state and an emergency exists because the child has been subjected to or threatened with mistreatment, abuse, neglect, etc.

4. *No other state has jurisdiction.* Even though this is not the home state of the child, even though there is no significant connection with or substantial evidence in this state, and even though there is no abandonment or emergency, this state can still take jurisdiction if:
   - It is in the best interest of the child for this state to take jurisdiction, and no other state would have jurisdiction under any of the conditions substantially similar to those listed above: (1) No other state is the home state. (2) There is no significant connection with or substantial evidence in another state. (3) The child is not physically present in another state faced with abandonment or an emergency. *Or*
   - It is in the best interest of the child for this state to take jurisdiction, and another state has declined to accept jurisdiction because this state is the more appropriate forum to determine custody.

Section 8(a) of the UCCJA also has a *"clean hands"* provision. A court can decline to exercise jurisdiction if the petitioner for custody has "wrongfully taken the child from another state or has engaged in similar reprehensible conduct" and it is "just and proper" for the court to decline jurisdiction under the circumstances.

Thus, simply because a court has jurisdiction to take a custody case, it will not necessarily use that jurisdiction. In addition to refusing jurisdiction in a case where the petitioner has **dirty hands,** a court can also decline to use its jurisdiction if it is clear under the circumstances that another state would be a more convenient forum to resolve the custody dispute (§ 7). For example, it may be

Home State The state where a child has lived for at least six consecutive months, or since birth if the child is less than six months old.

Dirty Hands Wrongdoing or other inappropriate behavior that would make it unfair or inequitable to allow a person to assert a right or a defense he or she would normally have.

possible for *two* states to have a significant connection with the parties. Substantial evidence on the child's welfare may exist in *both* states. One of these states, however, could decline to exercise its jurisdiction because the other state has a *more* significant connection and *more* substantial evidence. The UCCJA, therefore, encourages states to defer to the most convenient and appropriate state available.

ASSIGNMENT 11.9

a. Fred and Jane were married in Ohio on January 1, 1980. On March 13, 1980, they had a child, Bob. From the first day of their marriage, however, they began having marital difficulties. On July 4, 1980, Fred moved to Kentucky. Bob continued to live with his mother in Ohio. By mutual agreement, Fred can occasionally take the child to Kentucky for visits. After a scheduled one-day visit on November 5, 1980, Fred decides not to return the child. He keeps Bob until November 1, 1981, when he returns him to Jane. Fred then joins the Army. When he returns on October 6, 1985, he discovers that Jane has been beating Bob.

Assume that both Ohio and Kentucky have adopted the UCCJA. Under § 3 and § 8(a) of the UCCJA, which state would have jurisdiction to determine the custody of Bob on the following dates:

April 4, 1980
November 6, 1980
January 1, 1981
September 1, 1981
October 6, 1985

See General Instructions for the Legal-Analysis Assignment in chapter 1.

b. Interview Fred. See General Instructions for the Interviewing Assignment in chapter 1.

JURISDICTION TO MODIFY A CUSTODY ORDER OF ANOTHER STATE

Thus far we have examined the jurisdiction of a state to make an *initial* custody order. We have addressed the questions of when does a court have jurisdiction to decide the custody question for the first time, and if more than one state has jurisdiction, which is the most convenient forum? We now turn to the question of *modification:* when does one state have jurisdiction to modify a custody order of another state? Section 14 of the UCCJA governs:

> A court in this state (where a modification is being sought) can modify the custody order of another state only if:
>
> (i) The state that issued the custody order no longer appears to have jurisdiction under conditions substantially similar to § 3 (i.e., it is no longer the home state, or it no longer has significant connection/substantial evidence, or the child is not physically present in the state faced with abandonment or an emergency), *or*, the state has declined to assume jurisdiction to modify its own custody order. And,
>
> (ii) This state (where a modification is being sought) has jurisdiction under § 3 (i.e., it is the home state, or it has significant connection/substantial evidence, or the child is physically present in the state faced with abandonment or an emergency).

For example, before a California court can modify a New York custody order, the California court must first determine whether New York would now have jurisdiction under § 3 (or under provisions substantially similar thereto), *and* whether California now has jurisdiction under § 3.

Again, however, even though a state has jurisdiction to modify the order of another state, the state may decline to exercise this jurisdiction. Section 8(b) is the dirty hands provision for modification cases:

> Unless required in the interest of the child, the court shall not exercise its jurisdiction to modify a custody decree of another state if the petitioner, without consent of the

person entitled to custody, has improperly removed the child from the physical custody of the person entitled to custody or has improperly retained the child after a visit or other temporary relinquishment of physical custody. If the petitioner has violated any other provision of a custody decree of another state the court may decline to exercise its jurisdiction if this is just and proper under the circumstances.

Reread the facts in Assignment 11.9(a). Assume that in 1981, an Ohio court awarded custody of Bob to Jane. On October 10, 1985, Fred asks a Kentucky court to grant him custody. Assume further that both Ohio and Kentucky have adopted the UCCJA. Can Kentucky modify? (See General Instructions for Legal-Analysis Assignment in chapter 1.)

ASSIGNMENT 11.10

---

a. Find a court opinion in your state in which your state refused to modify the custody order of another state. Why did it refuse?

b. Find a court opinion of your state in which your state modified the custody order of another state. Why did it do so? (See General Instructions for the Court-Opinion Assignment in chapter 1.)

c. Is the opinion you discussed in part (a) consistent with the opinion you discussed in part (b)?

ASSIGNMENT 11.11

Exhibit 11.3 shows the form used to file a declaration under the UCCJA.

PARENTAL KIDNAPING PREVENTION ACT (PKPA)

Not all states had adopted the UCCJA by 1980, and some states that did adopt it changed several of its key provisions. This meant that there were still opportunities for forum shopping. To combat this, Congress passed the **Parental Kidnaping Prevention Act (PKPA)** to give added clout to the anti-child snatching movement. Congress was concerned that the lack of nationwide consistency in state custody laws contributed to a tendency of parties "to frequently resort to the seizure, restraint, concealment, and interstate transportation of children, the disregard of court orders, excessive relitigation of cases, obtaining of conflicting orders by the courts, . . . and interstate travel and communication that is so expensive and time consuming." To remedy this problem, Congress enacted the PKPA, the essential terms of which are reprinted in Appendix C.

The PKPA addresses the question of when one state *must* enforce (without modification) the custody decree (or visitation order) of another state. Phrased another way, when must one state give *full faith and credit* to the custody decree of another state? In answering this question, the PKPA adopts many of the principles of the UCCJA. The essential question is whether the state that rendered the custody decree had jurisdiction to do so based on provisions very similar to § 3 of the UCCJA, discussed earlier. First, this state must have had jurisdiction according to its own laws. Additionally, one of the following conditions must be met as of the time the state rendered its custody decree:

"(A) such state (i) is the home State of the child on the date of the commencement of the proceeding, or (ii) had been the child's home State within six months before the date of the commencement of the proceeding and the child is absent from such State because of his removal or retention by a contestant or for other reasons, and a contestant continues to live in such State;

"(B)(i) it appears that no other State would have jurisdiction under subparagraph (A), and (ii) it is in the best interest of the child that a court of such State assume jurisdiction because (I) the child and his parents, or the child and at least one contes-

☐ **EXHIBIT 11.3**   **Declaration under Uniform Child Custody Jurisdiction Act (UCCJA)**

ATTORNEY OR PARTY WITHOUT ATTORNEY *(Name and Address)*:	TELEPHONE NO.:	FOR COURT USE ONLY

ATTORNEY FOR *(Name)*:

SUPERIOR COURT OF CALIFORNIA, COUNTY OF
STREET ADDRESS:
MAILING ADDRESS:
CITY AND ZIP CODE:
BRANCH NAME:

CASE NAME:

DECLARATION UNDER UNIFORM CHILD CUSTODY JURISDICTION ACT (UCCJA)	CASE NUMBER:

1. **I am a party** to this proceeding to determine custody of a child.
2. *(Number)*:   minor children are subject to this proceeding as follows:
   (Insert the information requested below. The residence information must be given for the last FIVE years.)

a. Child's name		Place of birth		Date of birth		Sex
Period of residence	Address		Person child lived with *(name and present adress)*		Relationship	
to present						
to						
to						
to						
to						

b. Child's name		Place of birth		Date of birth		Sex
☐ Residence information is the same as given above for child a. *(If NOT the same, provide the information below.)*						
Period of residence	Address		Person child lived with *(name and present address)*		Relationship	
to present						
to						
to						
to						

c. ☐   Additional children are listed on Attachment 2c. *(Provide requested information for additional children on an attachment.)*

(Continued on reverse)

☐ **EXHIBIT 11.3 Declaration under Uniform Child Custody Jurisdiction Act (UCCJA)—*Continued***

SHORT TITLE:	CASE NUMBER:

3. Have you participated as a party or a witness or in some other capacity in another litigation or custody proceeding, in California or elsewhere, concerning custody of a child subject to this proceeding?

  ☐ No ☐ Yes *(If yes, provide the following information:)*

  a. Name of each child:

  b. Capacity of declarant: ☐ party ☐ witness ☐ other *(specify)*:

  c. Court *(specify name, state, location)*:

  d. Court order or judgment *(date)*:

4. Do you have information about a custody proceeding pending in a California court or any other court concerning a child subject to this proceeding, other than that stated in item 3?

  ☐ No ☐ Yes *(If yes, provide the following information:)*

  a. Name of each child:

  b. Nature of proceeding: ☐ dissolution or divorce ☐ guardianship ☐ adoption ☐ other *(specify)*:

  c. Court *(specify name, state, location)*:

  d. Status of proceeding:

5. Do you know of any person who is not a party to this proceeding who has physical custody or claims to have custody of or visitation rights with any child subject to this proceeding?

  ☐ No ☐ Yes *(If yes, provide the following information:)*

a. Name and address of person	b. Name and address of person	c. Name and address of person
☐ Has physical custody ☐ Claims custody rights ☐ Claims visitation rights	☐ Has physical custody ☐ Claims custody rights ☐ Claims visitation rights	☐ Has physical custody ☐ Claims custody rights ☐ Claims visitation rights
Name of each child	Name of each child	Name of each child

I declare under penalty of perjury under the laws of the State of California that the foregoing is true and correct.

Date:

▶

. . . .
(TYPE OR PRINT NAME)   (SIGNATURE OF DECLARANT)

6. ☐ Number of pages attached after this page:

NOTICE TO DECLARANT: You have a continuing duty to inform this court if you obtain any information about a custody proceeding in a California court or any other court concerning a child subject to this proceeding.

MC-150 [Rev. January 1, 1987]
  [Cor. 1/2/87]

DECLARATION UNDER
UNIFORM CHILD CUSTODY JURISDICTION ACT (UCCJA)

Page two

tant, have a significant connection with such State other than mere physical presence in such State, and (II) there is available in such State substantial evidence concerning the child's present or future care, protection, training, and personal relationships;

"(C) the child is physically present in such State and (i) the child has been abandoned, or (ii) it is necessary in an emergency to protect the child because he has been subjected to or threatened with mistreatment or abuse;

"(D)(i) it appears that no other State would have jurisdiction under subparagraph (A), (B), (C), or (E), or another State has declined to exercise jurisdiction on the ground that the State whose jurisdiction is in issue is the more appropriate forum to determine the custody of the child, and (ii) it is in the best interest of the child that such court assume jurisdiction; or

"(E) the court has continuing jurisdiction. . . ."

In these circumstances, the custody order shall be given full faith and credit by another state. Another state "shall not modify" it. Once a court has proper jurisdiction to render a custody decree, this jurisdiction continues so long as this state remains the residence of the child *or* of any party claiming a right to custody.

Congress also made available to the states the *Federal Parent Locator Service,* which will help to locate an absent parent or child for the purpose of enforcing laws on the unlawful taking or restraint of a child or for the purpose of making or enforcing a child-custody determination. Previously, this service has been used mainly in child-support cases (see chapter 12).

ASSIGNMENT 11.12   Is it a crime for a parent in your state to take his or her child from the other parent without the consent of the latter? Check the statutes and cases of your state. (See General Instructions for the State-Code Assignment and General Instructions for the Court-Opinion Assignment in chapter 1.)

■■■■ CHILDREN ABROAD: SPECIAL PROBLEMS

The following material deals with child abduction over international borders. As we have seen, parental kidnaping within the United States can lead to complex jurisdictional problems. These problems multiply when the child is taken out of the country.

LOCATING A MISSING CHILD ABROAD
United States Department of State,
Office of Citizens Consular Services, Washington, D.C.

The resolution of child custody disputes is a private legal matter in which the Department of State may not properly intervene. Our role is limited to questions concerning the welfare and whereabouts of the American citizen children abducted by one parent and transported to a foreign jurisdiction and the issuance of passports to children who are the subject of custody disputes.

Consular Welfare/Whereabouts Search
When a child has been abducted by a parent, the American embassy or consulate can conduct a welfare/whereabouts check for the child. Under this procedure, the consular officer attempts to locate the child and ascertain the child's state of health. The consular officer will endeavor to either personally interview the child or enlist the services of local authorities to determine the child's health and welfare. The consular officer may begin by contacting local authorities to verify the child's entry and/or residence in the country. When the child is located, the consular officer may telephone the parent/guardian abroad or speak directly to the child. A personal visit to the child by the consular officer may be requested by the parent in the United States. If difficulty ensues when the parent/guardian refuses the consular officer access to the child, local officials, family services agencies or police authorities may be requested to determine the child's

well-being. A report of the child's condition is then relayed to the requesting parent. If the welfare/whereabouts check convinces the consular officer that the child may have been abused or if evidence provided by the parent in the U.S. such as police reports, medical records or school records supports allegations of child abuse, the consular officer will make strong representations to the local authorities for a thorough investigation and, if necessary, request the removal of the child into the protective custody of the local courts or child welfare service. Consular officers cannot, however, take custody or force the return of the child to the deprived parent in the United States.

AFTER AN ABDUCTION— A CHECKLIST FOR PARENTS

International Parental Child Abduction, 3d ed., United States Department of State, Bureau of Consular Affairs (1989).

This list assumes that you know, or strongly suspect, that your child has been abducted abroad.

1. Emergency Action—What to Do Right Away

□ If you do not know where your child is, have you filed a *missing person report* with your local police department?

□ Have you reported the abduction to the National Center for Missing and Exploited Children?

□ Have you obtained a decree of sole custody or one that prohibits your child from traveling without your permission? In most states you can obtain such a decree even after a child is abducted. A custody decree in your favor is necessary for any legal action.

□ Has your child's name been entered in the U.S. passport name-check system?

□ If your child is a dual national, have the embassy and consulates of the foreign country been informed of your custody decree and asked not to issue a foreign passport to your child?

□ If your child is a U.S. citizen only but the other parent has close ties to a particular country, have the embassy and consulates of that country been informed of your custody decree and asked not to issue a visa to your child?

□ Have you asked the Department of State's Office of Citizens Consular Services (CCS) to initiate a welfare/whereabouts search for your child overseas?

2. The Search

□ Have you obtained certified copies of your custody decree from the court that issued it? You may need to furnish proof of your custody rights at various stages in your search and recovery effort.

□ Have you obtained a copy of the National Center for Missing and Exploited Children's publication, *Parental Kidnapping: How to Prevent an Abduction and What to Do if Your Child Is Abducted?*

□ Have you tried to establish contact with relatives or friends of the abducting parent?

□ Has the Federal Parent Locator Service been contacted?

□ Have you contacted the principal of your child's school and asked to be informed of requests for transfer of your child's school records?

□ Have you prepared a poster of your child?

□ Have you asked local law enforcement authorities to ask the U.S. Postal Inspection service to put a "mail cover" on addresses in the U.S. to which the abductor might write?

□ Have you asked local law enforcement authorities to help you obtain information from telephone and credit card companies on the whereabouts of the abductor?

3. After Your Child Has Been Located Abroad

□ Have you retained the services of a foreign attorney?

□ Have you sent certified copies of the custody decree, court orders, state and Federal warrants, copies of state custody and parental child abduction laws, and the Federal Parental Kidnaping Prevention Act to the foreign attorney?

4. Legal Proceedings: Possible Criminal Remedies

□ Is parental child abduction a crime in the state where your child resides or was abducted?

□ Has a state warrant been issued for the arrest of the abductor?

□ Has a Federal Unlawful Flight to Avoid Prosecution (UFAP) warrant been issued for the arrest of the abductor?

□ If a warrant has been issued, has the abductor's name been entered in the *wanted persons* section of the National Crime Information Center (NCIC) computer?

□ Is it possible or useful to take legal action against agents or accomplices to the abduction?

☐ If the abductor is a U.S. citizen, have you considered seeking to have his or her passport revoked?

☐ Would extradition of the abductor, if possible, be effective in your case?

ONE POSSIBLE SOLUTION: THE HAGUE CONVENTION

International Parental Child Abduction, 3d ed., United States Department of State, Bureau of Consular Affairs (1989).

The most difficult and frustrating element for most parents whose child has been abducted abroad is that U.S. laws and court orders are not directly enforceable abroad. Each sovereign country has jurisdiction within its own territory and over persons present within its border, and no country can force another to decide cases or enforce laws within its confines in a particular way. Issues that have to be resolved between sovereign nations can only be handled by persuasion, or by international agreement.

The increase in international marriages since World War II increased international child custody cases to the point where 23 nations, meeting at the Hague Conference on Private International Law in 1976, agreed to seek a treaty to deter international child abduction. Between 1976 and 1980, the United States was a major force in preparing and negotiating the Hague Convention on the Civil Aspects of International Child Abduction. The Convention came into force for the United States on July 1, 1988, and applies to abductions or wrongful retentions that occurred on or after that date.

Thirty-seven countries have now ratified the Hague Convention, and other countries are working toward ratification. Call or write Citizens Consular Service to learn which countries have joined.

What Is Covered by the Convention

The countries that are parties to the Convention have agreed with each other that, subject to certain limited exceptions, a child wrongfully removed or retained in one of these countries shall promptly be returned to the other member country where the child habitually resided before the abduction or wrongful retention. The Convention also provides a means for helping parents to exercise visitation rights abroad.

There is a treaty obligation to return an abducted child below the age of 16 if application is made less than one year from the date of wrongful removal or retention. After one year, the court is still obligated to order the child returned unless the person resisting return demonstrates that the child is settled in the new environment. A court may refuse to order a child returned if there is a grave risk that the child would be exposed to physical or psychological harm or oth-erwise placed in an intolerable situation. A court may also decline to return the child if the child objects to being returned and has reached an age and degree of maturity at which the court can take account of the child's views. Finally, the return of the child may be refused if the return would violate the fundamental principles of human rights and freedoms of the country where the child is being held.

How to Invoke the Hague Convention

You do not need to have a custody decree to invoke the Convention. However, to apply for the return of your child, you must have been actually exercising custody at the time of the abduction and you must not have consented to the removal or retention of the child. You may apply for the return of your child or the ability to exercise your visitation rights. You can also ask for assistance in locating your child and for information on your child's welfare. See Exhibit 11.4.

Each country that is a party to the Convention has designated a Central Authority to carry out specialized duties under the Convention. You may submit an application either to the U.S. Central Authority or directly to the Central Authority of the country where the child is believed to be held. The Central Authority for the United States is the Department of State's Office of Children's Issues, which is part of the Department's Overseas Citizens Services and Bureau of Consular Affairs.

Since the late 1970's, the Bureau of Consular Affairs has taken action in over 8,000 cases of international parental child abduction. It also provided information in response to thousands of additional inquiries pertaining to international child abduction, enforcement of visitation rights and abduction prevention techniques. The Office of Children's Issues works closely with parents, attorneys, other government agencies, and private organizations in the United States to prevent international abductions. In 1994, the Office of Children's Issues received over 800 applications under the Hague Convention. About half involved children abducted from the United States to other countries. Most of the cases involved Canada, Mexico, Germany and the United Kingdom.

There are still many countries, however, where the Hague Convention has not been accepted. In 1994, the office handled the cases of more than 250 children abducted to non-Hague countries. In the event of an abduction to a non-Hague country one option for a

☐ **EXHIBIT 11.4   Hague Convention Application**

UNITED STATES DEPARTMENT OF STATE

**APPLICATION FOR ASSISTANCE UNDER THE
HAGUE CONVENTION ON CHILD ABDUCTION**

SEE PRIVACY STATEMENT ON REVERSE

OMB NO. 1405–0076
EXPIRES: 6–91
Estimated Burden – 1 Hour

I. IDENTITY OF CHILD AND PARENTS

CHILD'S NAME *(LAST, FIRST, MIDDLE)*	DATE OF BIRTH	PLACE OF BIRTH	
ADDRESS *(Before removal)*	U.S. SOCIAL SECURITY NO.	PASSPORT/IDENTITY CARD COUNTRY: NO. :	NATIONALITY
HEIGHT WEIGHT	COLOR OF HAIR		COLOR OF EYES

FATHER	MOTHER
NAME *(Last, First, Middle)*	NAME *(Last, First, Middle)*
DATE OF BIRTH PLACE OF BIRTH	DATE OF BIRTH PLACE OF BIRTH
NATIONALITY OCCUPATION PASSPORT/IDENTITY CARD COUNTRY: NO. :	NATIONALITY OCCUPATION PASSPORT/IDENTITY CARD COUNTRY: NO. :
CURRENT ADDRESS AND TELEPHONE NUMBER	CURRENT ADDRESS AND TELEPHONE NUMBER
U.S.SOCIAL SECURITY NO.	U.S.SOCIAL SECURITY NO.
COUNTRY OF HABITUAL RESIDENCE	COUNTRY OF HABITUAL RESIDENCE

DATE AND PLACE OF MARRIAGE AND DIVORCE, IF APPLICABLE

II. REQUESTING INDIVIDUAL OR INSTITUTION

NAME *(Last, First, Middle)*	NATIONALITY	OCCUPATION
CURRENT ADDRESS AND TELEPHONE NUMBER		PASSPORT/IDENTITY CARD COUNTRY: NO. :

COUNTRY OF HABITUAL RESIDENCE

RELATIONSHIP TO CHILD	NAME, ADDRESS, AND TELEPHONE NO. OF LEGAL ADVISER, IF ANY

III. INFORMATION CONCERNING THE PERSON ALLEGED TO HAVE WRONGFULLY REMOVED OR RETAINED CHILD

NAME *(Last, First, Middle)*	KNOWN ALIASES	
DATE OF BIRTH PLACE OF BIRTH	NATIONALITY	
OCCUPATION, NAME AND ADDRESS OF EMPLOYER	PASSPORT/IDENTITY CARD COUNTRY: NO. :	U.S. SOCIAL SECURITY NO.

CURRENT LOCATION OR LAST KNOWN ADDRESS IN THE U.S.

HEIGHT WEIGHT	COLOR OF HAIR	COLOR OF EYES

FORM
6–88   **DSP–105**

☐ **EXHIBIT 11.4   Hague Convention Application—*Continued***

OTHER PERSONS WITH POSSIBLE ADDITIONAL INFORMATION RELATING TO THE WHEREABOUTS OF CHILD
(Name, address, telephone number)

IV.   TIME, PLACE, DATE, AND CIRCUMSTANCES OF THE WRONGFUL REMOVAL OR RETENTION

V.   FACTUAL OR LEGAL GROUNDS JUSTIFYING THE REQUEST

VI.   CIVIL PROCEEDINGS IN PROGRESS, IF ANY

VII.   CHILD IS TO BE RETURNED TO:

NAME *(Last, First, Middle)* | DATE OF BIRTH | PLACE OF BIRTH

ADDRESS | TELEPHONE NUMBER

PROPOSED ARRANGEMENTS FOR RETURN TRAVEL OF CHILD

VIII.   OTHER REMARKS

IX.   DOCUMENTS ATTACHED (PREFERABLY CERTIFIED)

☐ DIVORCE DECREE   ☐ PHOTOGRAPH OF CHILD   ☐ OTHER
☐ CUSTODY DECREE   ☐ OTHER AGREEMENT CONCERNING CUSTODY

SIGNATURE OF APPLICANT AND/OR STAMP OF CENTRAL AUTHORITY | DATE | PLACE

PRIVACY ACT STATEMENT

THIS INFORMATION IS REQUESTED UNDER THE AUTHORITY OF THE INTERNATIONAL CHILD ABDUCTION REMEDIES ACT, PUBLIC LAW 100–300. THE INFORM-
ATION WILL BE USED FOR THE PURPOSE OF EVALUATING APPLICANTS' CLAIMS UNDER THE HAGUE CONVENTION ON THE CIVIL ASPECTS OF INTER-
NATIONAL CHILD ABDUCTION, LOCATING ABDUCTED CHILDREN, AND ADVISING APPLICANTS ABOUT AVAILABLE LEGAL REMEDIES. WITHOUT THE
REQUESTED INFORMATION, U.S. AUTHORITIES MAY BE UNABLE EFFECTIVELY TO ASSIST IN LOCATING ABDUCTED CHILDREN.

Comments concerning the accuracy of the burden hour estimate on page 1 may be directed to OMB, OIRA, State Department Desk Officer, Wash., D.C. 20503 left-behind parent is to obtain legal assistance in the country of the abduction and follow through a court action. Of non-Hague countries, the largest number of cases involved children who were abducted to Egypt, Japan, Jordan, the Philippines, and Saudi Arabia.

WHAT THE STATE DEPARTMENT
Can Do:
□ In cases where the Hague Convention on the Civil Aspects of International Child Abduction applies, assist parents in filing an application with foreign authorities for return of the child

□ In other cases, through our Embassies and Consulates abroad, attempt to locate, visit and report on the child's general welfare

□ Provide the left-behind parent with information on the country to which the child was abducted, including its legal system, family laws, and a list of attorneys there willing to accept American clients

□ Provide a point of contact for the left-behind parent at a difficult time

□ Monitor judicial or administrative proceedings overseas

□ Assist parents in contacting local officials in foreign countries or contact them on the parent's behalf

□ Provide information on domestic remedies, such as warrants, extradition and passport revocation

□ Alert foreign authorities to any evidence of child abuse or neglect

Cannot Do:
□ Reabduct the child

□ Help a parent to violate host country laws

□ Pay legal expenses or court fees

□ Act as a lawyer or represent parents in court

□ Give refuge to a parent involved in a reabduction

▆▆▆ SUMMARY

Legal custody and physical custody can be given to one parent (sole custody) or to both parents (joint custody). In negotiating custody and visitation terms of a separation agreement, many factors need to be considered, such as the age and health of the parents and child, the emotional attachments of the child, the work schedules of the parents, etc. If negotiations fail and the parties cannot agree, litigation is necessary. This can be a stressful experience, not only for the parents, but also for the person caught in the middle—the child.

The court has considerable discretion in resolving a custody battle between two biological parents according to the standard of the best interest of the child. It will consider a number of relevant factors such as stability in the child's life, availability to respond to the child's day-to-day needs, emotional ties that have already developed, etc. At one time, courts applied evidentiary guidelines such as the presumption that a child of tender years is better off with his or her mother. Today, many courts reject such presumptions, although fathers continue to complain that the mother is still given an undue preference.

The moral values and lifestyles of the parent seeking custody are generally not considered by the court unless they affect the welfare of the child. If the parents practice different religions, the court cannot prefer one religion over another, but can consider what effect the practice of a particular religion will have on the child. To the extent possible, the court will try to maintain continuity in the child's cultural development. If the child is old enough to express a preference, it will be considered. Often the court will also consider the testimony of expert witnesses.

The court will generally favor liberal visitation rights for the noncustodial parent. Occasionally, such rights will be granted to individuals other than biological parents, e.g., grandparents. One of the most distressing issues in this area is the charge by the custodial parent that the child has been sexually molested during visitation. This may lead to a denial of visitation or to visitation only when supervised by another adult, usually a professional.

When the custody battle is between a biological parent and a nonparent (often called a psychological parent), the biological parent usually wins unless he or she can be shown to be unfit.

Occasionally, it is in the best interest of the child for a court to modify an earlier custody decision because of changed circumstances. Frantic parents will sometimes engage in forum shopping and child snatching in order to find a court that will make a modification order. To cut down on this practice, two important laws have been enacted:

the state Uniform Child Custody Jurisdiction Act, and the federal Parental Kidnaping Prevention Act. When the child has been taken to a foreign country, the aid of the Hague Convention on Child Abduction might be enlisted.

■■■■■ KEY CHAPTER TERMINOLOGY

Legal Custody
Physical Custody
Custodial Parent
Noncustodial Parent
Sole Custody
Joint Custody
Split Custody
Mediation

Best Interest of the Child
Contested
Guardian ad Litem
Parental Alienation Syndrome
Tender Years Presumption
Primary Caregiver Presumption
MMPI
Psychological Parents

Forum Shopping
Uniform Child Custody Jurisdiction Act (UCCJA)
Home State
Dirty hands
Parental Kidnaping Prevention Act (PKPA)

CHILD SUPPORT

SEPARATION AGREEMENT

When the parties are negotiating the child support terms of a separation agreement, they need to consider a wide range of factors:

☐ According to state guidelines, what is the minimum amount of child support that must be paid to the custodial parent? Do the parties want to exceed the minimum?

☐ What standard of living was the child accustomed to during the marriage?

☐ Do the providers of support have the financial resources to maintain this standard of living?

☐ What are the tax considerations? Unlike alimony, child support payments are not deductible by the provider (see chapter 15). Consequently, the provider or payor may try to convince the other parent to agree to a lower child support payment in exchange for a higher alimony payment in order to take advantage of the deduction. Alimony payments, unlike child support payments, are taxable to the recipient. Hence, the alimony recipient (payee) will usually want some other benefit to compensate for the increased taxes that will result from agreeing to the higher alimony and lower child support payments, e.g., some extra benefit in the property division terms of the separation agreement.

☐ On what day is each payment to be made?

☐ How many payments are to be made? One covering everyday expenses and a separate one covering large, emergency expenses, e.g., hospitalization?

☐ Will there be security for the payments, e.g., a trust account, an escrow account that can be used in the event of nonpayment?

☐ Is the child to be covered by medical insurance? If so, who pays the premiums?

☐ When the provider dies, is his or her estate obligated to continue payments? If so, must the provider's will so state?

☐ Is the child to be the beneficiary of a life insurance policy on the life of the provider? If so, how much, who pays the premiums, and can the beneficiaries be changed by the provider? Does the payment of premiums (and hence the insurance coverage) end when the child reaches the age of majority?

☐ Is there an escalation clause? Do the support payments fluctuate with the income of either of the parents?

☐ Do the support payments fluctuate with the income of the child, e.g., summer jobs, inheritance?

☐ Do they fluctuate in relationship to the Consumer Price Index?

☐ Do the payments end or change when the child reaches a certain age, marries, moves out of the house, or becomes disabled?

☐ What educational expenses will be covered by the provider? Tutors, preparatory school, college, graduate/professional school, room, board, books, transportation, entertainment expenses while at school, etc.?

☐ When the child is away at school, does the provider have to continue sending child support payments to the custodial parent?

☐ Do school payments go to the custodial parent or directly to a child away at school?

☐ If disputes arise between the parents concerning child support payments, what happens? Arbitration? Mediation?

There are limits, however, on what the parties can agree to in their separation agreement, as the *Straub* case demonstrates.

CASE

STRAUB V. B.M.T.

626 N.E.2d 848 (1993)
Court of Appeals of Indiana

Background: *Edward Straub and Francine Todd are having an affair. Straub impregnates her after she agreed not to hold him responsible for children born from the union. But three years after the birth of a child to them (referred to as B.M.T. by the court), Todd sued Straub for child support. The trial court ordered him to pay $130 per week. Straub appealed. The case is now on appeal before the Court of Appeals of Indiana.*

Decision on Appeal: *Affirmed. The agreement to relieve a father of financial responsibility was void as a matter of public policy.*

Opinion of the Court:

Judge MILLER delivered the opinion of the court.
. . .

Straub and Todd began dating in 1985 when both were teachers at the same elementary school. In late 1986, Todd [aged 33] discussed her desire to have a child with Straub after her doctor informed her that artificial insemination would not work. Straub told

Todd that he did not want the responsibility of another family due to his age [58] and the fact that he already had children from a previous marriage. However, when Todd threatened to end their relationship, he agreed to try to impregnate her providing she would sign a "hold harmless" agreement. On December 15, 1986, Straub presented Todd with a holographic agreement purporting to hold Straub harmless from financial and emotional support of a child which might result from the couple's sexual relations. . . . That document, Petitioner's Exhibit #8, reads in its entirety as follows:

"To Whom it may concern. I Francine Todd in sound mind & fore thought have decided not to marry, but would like to have a baby of my own. . . . I have approached several men who will not be held responsible financially or emotionally who's [sic] names will be kept secret for life. Signed *Francine Todd*. . . .

Edward continued to have sexual relations with Francine after the child's birth but did not establish a relationship with the child. He stopped seeing Francine after she filed this action. . . .

I. IS THE AGREEMENT AGAINST INDIANA'S PUBLIC POLICY?

Indiana has long recognized the obligation of both parents to support their children. In *Matter of M.D.H.* (1982), Ind. App., 437 N.E.2d 119, 126, the court noted that current statutory provisions relating to support orders for legitimate and illegitimate children are virtually identical. The court stated, "[A] parent's obligation to support his minor child, legitimate or illegitimate, is *a basic tenet recognized in this state by statutes* that provide civil and criminal sanctions against parents who neglect such duty. . . ." Id. at 127 (emphasis added).* . . .

Straub first claims that "fundamental contract principles" allow him to contract around his statutory and common-law duty to provide support to his daughter. . . . It is well settled that a parent cannot, by his own contract, relieve himself of the legal obligation to support his minor children. In *Ort v. Schage* (1991), Ind. App., 580 N.E.2d 335, we held that an agreement to forego court ordered child support even in exchange for a benefit (social security payments) to the child is unenforceable because a parent has no right to contract away a child's support benefits. *Pickett v. Pickett* (1984), Ind. App., 470 N.E.2d 751. . . .

Public policy considerations mandate that the state take an active interest in providing for the welfare of illegitimate children in order to avoid placing an undue financial burden on its taxpayers. "The duty of parents to provide necessary support, care, and maintenance for their children, although arising out of the fact of their relationship, may be rested upon the interest of the state as *parens patriae* of children and of the community at large in preventing them from becoming a public burden, and is, therefore, a duty not only to themselves, but to the public as well. This duty is at the same time a legal and natural obligation, *the consistent enforcement of which is equally essential to the well-being of the state, the morals of the community, and the development of the individual.*" 59 Am. Jur. 2d Parent and Child § 51 (emphasis added). . . .

Finally, Straub argues that the agreement signed by Todd should be enforced because he was acting merely as a "sperm donor." He argues that we should follow cases from other jurisdictions which look to the pre-conception intent of the parties involved in deciding whether to enforce their agreement. Straub's Brief at 25–27 citing *Davis v. Davis* (1993), Tenn., 842 S.W.2d 588.† We are not persuaded.

We first note, of course, arguing that Straub's and Todd's relationship was that of a sperm donor and donee ignores the facts. It is undisputed that Straub and Todd had an ongoing affair, one which began before Todd decided to become pregnant and only ended three years after B.M.T.'s birth when she decided to have a second child by Straub—after Straub had married someone else. Secondly, both parties testified, and the trial court found, that Straub and Todd continued to have intercourse after Todd became pregnant with B.M.T. and their relationship continued for a number of years after B.M.T.'s birth. We know of no medical requirements—or of any sperm donor program—that continues to give insemination injections after the donee becomes pregnant. . . . The trial court did not err in finding Straub's and Todd's agreement was void because it is against Indiana's public policy.

II. INDEMNIFICATION

Straub argues that he should be indemnified against any support claims because: 1) Todd is capable of supporting the child on her own; and 2) the "economic injury" to Straub due to her "breach of contract" would exceed $100,000.00. Because this argument merely seeks to circumvent public policy, it too must fail. First, because the agreement between the parties is void, there is no enforceable contract to breach. Second, Todd's present ability to care for the child on her own and the cost of the support to Straub do not change the law—Straub must provide his share of his daughter's support as determined by the trial court under the Guidelines, which take into account both parent's incomes.** . . .

The judgment of the trial court is affirmed.

Judge CONOVER, dissenting. . . .

Todd, an unmarried adult female teacher, wanted to have a child but did not want to remarry to accom-

---

*Ind. Code 35-46-1-5(a) provides: A person who knowingly or intentionally fails to provide support to his dependent child commits nonsupport of a child, a Class D felony.

†If we were to accept Straub's argument, this type of contract would arguably be binding in a variety of situations. For example, a couple desirous of having a child, but for some reason—religious or other-

wise—feels the child should be born in wedlock, could enter into a valid and binding antenuptial agreement absolving one of the parents from the duty to support the child after divorce. Similarly, an agreement made after marriage (and in contemplation of divorce) would also be binding.

**We must be ever mindful of the best interests of this child. Thus, B.M.T. has a right to more than the basic necessities of life. Specifically, she has a right to the lifestyle that her parent's combined income will furnish. This right may not be contracted away by her parents, and to do so is a violation of public policy. However, while we are not able to address every factual possibility, we recognize an exception may lie where the custodial parent is so affluent as to render the contribution of the non-custodial parent's income irrelevant to the child's lifestyle. In that case, the child's lifestyle may not be an issue, and it might be argued that the parents would not be contracting away the best interests of the child. Here, however, because Todd's only apparent income is her salary for teaching school, this appears to be a typical case wherein the child is entitled to the lifestyle that the combination of her parent's incomes will afford.

plish that end. When she was medically advised artificial insemination would not work in her case, she asked her current lover Straub, a 56 year old adult male teacher, to cease using condoms during intercourse and impregnate her. Straub already had raised 5 children of his own. While willing to help, Straub neither wanted to raise another child nor assume the financial obligations concomitant with child rearing. Straub told Todd he would accommodate her if he could be free of the obligation to support the child-to-be and his name as inseminator would remain a secret. Agreeing, Todd, an employed teacher fully capable of supporting the child, signed a written agreement to that effect that Straub had prepared. In the normal course of things thereafter, Todd became pregnant. Three years after the child was born, Todd changed her mind. . . .

Today, the general public almost universally looks with understanding and approval upon a single woman's desire to bear and nurture a child without male interference. A financially responsible modern woman, at her option, has an unqualified right to do so, it perceives. In other words, our declarations on this subject are currently incorrect. They reflect policy which has been dead since the 1960's. Accordingly, they must be changed, in my view, because we are subject to the public's will in such matters.

I find no better statement of the vagaries of public policy than this: Public policy has been described as a will-o'-the-wisp of the law which varies and changes with the interests, habits, needs, sentiments, and fashions of the day; the public policy of one generation may not, under changed conditions, be the public policy of another. Thus, the very reverse of that which is public policy at one time may become public policy at another time. Hence, no fixed rules can be given by which to determine what is public policy for all time. When an alteration of public policy on any given point of general interest has actually taken place, and such alteration is indicated by long-continued change of conduct on the part of the people affected and has become practically universal, the court may recognize the fact and declare the public policy accordingly. . . .

I believe this change in public policy is readily discernible. . . . [A]n Indiana woman in this modern age has had an inalienable right to contract in any manner she chooses in the pursuit of her happiness. . . . Since the last obstructions to contractual equality due to womanhood have been removed, women are now irrevocably bound to perform the obligations they incur when contracting just as men are. Courts have neither the right nor the power in the name of public policy to intervene simply because the contracting woman with the benefit of hindsight determines she has made a bad bargain by entering into a contract of this kind. The courts now must leave the parties where they find them in such cases.

Thus, in my opinion, the contract in question is valid and enforceable because it is conversant with current public policy. Todd had an absolute right to contract with Straub as she did, and is absolutely bound by the obligations she incurred under that contract. . . . Todd is gainfully employed and fully capable of providing for all the needs of the child she so desperately wanted. Under current public policy, the contract she signed here is valid and enforceable. Neither the legislature nor the judiciary can act to impair the obligations she incurred thereunder because the record demonstrates the child will never become a ward of the state.

I would reverse.

ASSIGNMENT 12.1

a. Did this court hold that it would have reached a different result if Todd had been rich?

b. Who is correct? Judge Miller or Judge Conover? Is the majority opinion anti-woman?

c. George and Helen are not married but are living together. George impregnates Helen. He asks her to have an abortion. She refuses. When the child is born, can she force George to support it? Would it make any difference if Helen became pregnant after lying to George about using contraceptives? (See General Instructions for the Legal-Analysis Agreement in chapter 1.)

INITIAL DECISION BY A COURT

Pendente Lite While the litigation is going on.

Often the first request of the custodial parent is to ask the court to issue a temporary order for child support while the divorce litigation is pending **(pendente lite)**. Later, a permanent support order will be part of the final divorce decree. We turn now to an examination of how the court makes these preliminary and permanent child support decisions.

JURISDICTION TO ORDER CHILD SUPPORT

A court must have **personal jurisdiction** (sometimes called *in personam jurisdiction*) over the noncustodial parent from whom child support is being sought. This usually means that this parent must be served with process (service of process) while physically in the state. When child support is sought in a divorce proceeding, service of process occurs when the following documents are delivered to the defendant: a copy of the divorce complaint or petition and a summons to appear in court at a designated time to answer the complaint. In the vast majority of cases, the defendant is a resident of the state, so it is relatively easy to obtain personal jurisdiction over him or her. If such a defendant is difficult to find within the state, alternative methods of service are usually available, e.g., publishing a notice of the litigation in a newspaper.

Problems arise, however, if the defendant is a nonresident of the state. If personal jurisdiction is not obtained over such a defendant, then a child support order rendered by the state is invalid and cannot be enforced. A different result is reached if the issue before the court is whether the parties can be divorced. Personal jurisdiction over a nonresident is *not* necessary for the court to grant a divorce so long as one of the spouses is domiciled in the state. Later, we will consider the enforceability of a decree that divorces the parties (see chapter 14). Here our focus is the enforceability of a child support decree.

> Ted and Wilma are married in New York. They have one child. Wilma takes the child and moves to California where she establishes a **domicile.** Wilma files for divorce in California. Ted remains in New York. He has never been in California and therefore is not served in California. The California court grants the divorce and orders Ted to pay child support.

The support order in the California court is invalid since California never had personal jurisdiction over Ted. The divorce itself, however, is valid since Wilma was domiciled in California. Personal jurisdiction over the defendant is not necessary for a court to have the power to terminate a marriage. Domicile of one of the spouses is sufficient. The parties have a **divisible divorce.** The part of the divorce that dissolved the marriage is enforceable (because of the presence of the plaintiff's domicile in California). The part of the divorce that ordered child support is not enforceable (because of the absence of personal jurisdiction over the defendant in California).[1]

How, then, does a court acquire personal jurisdiction over a nonresident defendant? The defendant, of course, can always consent to a court's assertion of personal jurisdiction by agreeing to appear in the court and fully litigate all the issues in the case. Can personal jurisdiction be obtained in the absence of such consent?

Most states have what is called a **long arm statute** that enables a state to acquire jurisdiction over nonresident defendants who have sufficient purposeful contact with the state so that it is fair and reasonable for the state to resolve (i.e., adjudicate) the disputes involved. Not all contacts will be sufficient to confer personal jurisdiction through the long arm statute, however. In the situation above involving Ted and Wilma, for example, the fact that Ted may

Personal Jurisdiction The power of a court to render a decision that binds an individual defendant.

Domicile The place where a person has been physically present with the intent to make that place a permanent home.

Divisible Divorce A divorce decree that is enforceable in another state only in part.

Long Arm Statute A law that gives a state court personal jurisdiction over a nonresident based on his or her purposeful contact with the state.

---

1. As we will see in chapter 14, a *spousal*-support order and a property division order also require personal jurisdiction over any defendant against whom such orders are sought to be enforced. The only order that does not require personal jurisdiction of the defendant is the dissolution order itself, which simply requires the domicile of the plaintiff.

often call or write his child in California is not sufficient to confer personal jurisdiction on a New York state resident. Nor would it be sufficient if Ted originally had custody of the child and agreed to send the child to California to live with its mother. Suppose, however, that Ted often visited the child in California, arranged for the child to attend a certain school in California, and opened a bank account for the child in California. Of course, if Ted is personally served with process while physically in California, the latter state would acquire personal jurisdiction over him for purposes of rendering a child support order. The question is whether personal jurisdiction can be acquired in the absence of such service. Did he have enough contact with California to make it fair and reasonable for him to be forced to defend a child support action in California? The answer is *probably yes*. The courts are still developing standards for determining when a nonresident defendant has sufficiently minimal contacts with a state for the purpose of acquiring personal jurisdiction through a long arm statute. Each case must be decided on its own facts. When Ted visited the child in California and arranged for a school and a bank account there, he in effect took advantage of the services of the state of California. He arguably became purposefully involved with the state. It therefore seems fair and reasonable to expect him to come to California and litigate the child support issue.

It again must be emphasized, however, that the law does not inevitably point to this result. The United States Supreme Court has not yet given us clear guidelines on when a long arm statute can validly confer personal jurisdiction over a nonresident in a family law case of this kind. See *Kulko v. Superior Court,* 436 U.S. 84, 98 S. Ct. 1690, 56 L. Ed. 2d 132 (1978).

WHO PAYS CHILD SUPPORT?

The traditional rule was that only the father had the legal duty to support his children. Today, each parent has an equal duty of support regardless of who has custody and day-to-day control of the children. The essential question is, who has the ability to pay? The mother, the father, or both? In practice, it is usually the father who is ordered to pay. He is the one who often controls most of the financial resources. Furthermore, the prejudice of the traditional rule still lingers in the minds of many judges.

What about a stepparent (someone who has married one of the natural parents)? If the stepparent has adopted the child formally or equitably (see chapter 19), there is a duty to support the child even after the marriage ends in divorce. Without adoption, however, most states say that the stepparent has no duty of support unless he or she has agreed otherwise.

STANDARDS TO DETERMINE AMOUNT OF SUPPORT

A child has many needs that must be paid for: shelter, food, clothing, education, medical care, transportation, recreation, etc. A court will consider a number of factors in determining the amount of child support. These factors are quite similar to what the parties must assess on this issue in their separation agreement:

☐ State guidelines—the most important (see discussion below).

☐ Standard of living enjoyed by child before the separation or divorce.

☐ Child's age.

☐ Child's own financial resources, e.g., from a trust fund set up by a relative, from part-time employment.

☐ Financial resources of custodial parent.

☐ Financial resources of noncustodial parent.

☐ Earning potential of both parents.

☐ Child's need and capacity for education, including higher education.

☐ Financial needs of noncustodial parent.

☐ Responsibility of noncustodial parent to support others, e.g., a second family from a second marriage.

Note that marital fault is not on the list. Which parent was at fault in "causing" the divorce is not relevant and should not be considered in assessing the need for child support.

Since 1987 every state has been under a federal mandate to adopt **child support guidelines** for the determination of child support by its courts.[2] The guidelines establish a rebuttable presumption on the amount of child support that should be awarded. A judge is required to use this amount unless to do so would be inequitable to the parties or the child.

Child Support Guidelines A required method of determining the amount of child support that must be paid.

While the guidelines are not the same in every state, many states have based their guidelines on the *Income Shares Model,* which operates on the principle that the children should receive the same proportion of parental income that they would have received had the parents lived together. Studies have shown that individuals tend to spend money on their children in proportion to their income, and not solely on need. Child support is calculated as a *share* of each parent's income that would have been spent on the children if the parents and children were living in the same household. The calculation of these shares is based on the best available economic data on the amount of money ordinarily spent on children by their families in the United States. This amount is then adjusted to the cost of living for a particular state.

Exhibits 12.1 and 12.2 provide further information on how this amount is calculated in one particular state, South Carolina.

COMPUTATION OF CHILD SUPPORT [see Exhibit 12.2] A South Carolina court can determine a total child support obligation in line 7 of Worksheet A by adding the basic child support obligation (line 5), health insurance (line 6a), and work-related child care costs (line 6b).

The total child support obligation is divided between the parents in proportion to their income. Line 8 calculates each parent's proportional share of combined monthly adjusted gross income. After the adjustments of line 10, line 11 computes the net child support to be paid to the custodial parent.

A monetary obligation is computed for each parent. The guidelines presume that the custodial parent will spend that parent's share directly on the child in that parent's custody. In cases of joint custody or split custody where both parents have responsibility of the child for a substantial portion of the time, there are provisions for adjustments. Line 11 reflects that portion of the calculated total child support obligation to be paid by the parents.

---

2. 42 U.S.C.A. 667; 45 C.F.R. 302.52, 302.56.

☐ **EXHIBIT 12.1   South Carolina Schedule of Basic Child Support Obligations**

Important: These figures are *not* child support payments to be made by either parent. They are the amounts of child support to be contributed by *both* parents. An individual parent's share of this amount must be computed by use of the formula found on the Child Support Obligation Worksheet [Exhibit 12.2].

MONTHLY COMBINED GROSS INCOME	ONE CHILD	TWO CHILDREN	THREE CHILDREN	FOUR CHILDREN	FIVE CHILDREN	SIX CHILDREN
500.00	50	50	50	50	50	50
550.00	57	58	58	59	60	60
600.00	94	95	96	97	98	99
650.00	123	124	126	127	128	130
700.00	151	154	155	157	159	160
750.00	159	183	185	187	189	191
800.00	168	216	218	221	223	225
850.00	176	248	251	254	257	259
900.00	185	270	284	287	290	293
950.00	194	282	317	320	324	327
1000.00	202	295	349	353	357	360
1050.00	211	307	364	385	390	394
1100.00	219	320	378	418	423	427
1150.00	228	332	393	434	456	461
1200.00	236	344	408	450	488	494
1250.00	245	357	422	466	506	527
1300.00	253	369	437	483	523	560
1350.00	261	381	450	498	539	577
3250.00	518	751	886	979	1061	1135
3300.00	522	756	891	985	1067	1142
3350.00	525	761	897	991	1074	1149
5250.00	665	959	1125	1243	1347	1442
5300.00	670	966	1133	1252	1357	1452
5350.00	675	973	1141	1261	1367	1463
7250.00	843	1213	1420	1569	1701	1820
7300.00	847	1219	1427	1577	1710	1829
7350.00	852	1225	1435	1585	1718	1839
9250.00	999	1441	1693	1871	2028	2170
9300.00	1002	1446	1699	1877	2035	2177
9350.00	1006	1451	1705	1884	2042	2185
11250.00	1127	1629	1916	2117	2295	2456
11300.00	1130	1633	1921	2123	2302	2463
11350.00	1133	1637	1927	2129	2308	2469

If the obligor's income and corresponding number of children fall into a shaded area, compute the support obligation using obligor's income only.

A number of computer companies have devised software for lawyers who need to calculate child support under state guidelines (see Exhibit 12.3).

COST OF COLLEGE   A good deal of litigation has centered on the issue of educational expenses, particularly higher education. Does a divorced parent have a duty to send his or her child to college? Arguments *against* imposing this duty are as follows:

☐ A parent's support duty is limited to providing the necessities to the child, e.g., food, shelter, clothing. College is not a necessity; it is a luxury.

☐ A parent's support duty terminates when the child reaches the age of majority in the state, e.g., eighteen. A child in college will be over the age of majority during some or most of the college years.

_____)
Name of Plaintiff   )
                    vs.   )
_____)
Name of Defendant   )

_____
File Number
Child Support Obligation

Worksheet A

	Father	Mother
1. **Monthly Gross Income**	_____	_____

2. Monthly Alimony (this action)
   a. To be received .... + _____   + _____
   b. To be paid .... − _____   − _____

3. Other monthly alimony or child
   support paid (if having priority over
   this action .... − _____   − _____

Combined Monthly Adjusted Gross Income

= | 4(C) |

4. **Adjusted Monthly Gross Income** ...$\underline{4(F)}$ _____ + $\underline{4(M)}$ _____

$4(F) + 4(M) = 4(C)$

Number of Children to be supported by Order in this Action: [____]

5. Basic Combined Child Support Obligation (Gross)
   (from Schedule, using Combined Monthly Adjusted Gross Income (Line (4C)) .... $\underline{5(C)}$ _____

	Father	Mother

6. Adjustments to Basic Child Support
   Obligation
   a. Health insurance premium (portion
      covering children only) .... + _____   + _____
   b. Work-related child care costs
      (net of tax credit) .... + _____   + _____

   Total adjustments to Basic Combined
   Child Support Obligation .... $\underline{6(F)}$ _____ + $\underline{6(M)}$ _____ = $6(C)$ + _____

7. **Total Combined Monthly Child Support Obligation (Net)** .... | 7(C) |

$5(C) + 6(C) = 7(C)$

	Father	Mother

8. Proportional share of combined monthly
   adjusted gross income .... $\underline{8(F)}$ _____ % $\underline{8(M)}$ _____ %

   $4(F)/4(C) = 8(F)$ $4(M)/4(C) = 8(M)$

9. Gross child support obligation of
   individual parent (monthly) .... | 9(F) | | 9(M) |

   $7(C) \times 8(F) = 9(F)$ $7(C) \times 8(M) = 9(M)$

Complete Items 10–11 _for Non-Custodial Parent Only_

Non-Custodial Parent is (check one):   Father ☐   Mother ☐

10. Credit for adjustments to basic
    combined child support obligation $\underline{10(F)}$ _____ $\underline{10(M)}$ _____
    (from item 6(F) or item 6(M)) ....   (same as item 6(F))   (same as item 6(M))

11. **_Net Child Support to be paid_**
    to custodial parent .... | 11(F) | | 11(M) |

    $9(F) − 10(F) = 11(F)$ $9(M) − 10(M) = 11(M)$

Worksheet Prepared by:

Date: _____   _____

For: Father ☐   Mother ☐

☐ **EXHIBIT 12.3   Advertisement for Software That Calculates Child Support Payments**

☐ Children of parents who are still married have no right to force their parents to send them to college. Why should children of divorced parents have the right to be sent to college?

Some states, however, have rejected these arguments and have required the divorced parent to pay for a college education as part of the child support payments if the parent has the ability to pay and the child has the capacity to go to college. Arguments supporting this position:

☐ In today's society, college is not a luxury. A college degree, at least the first one, is a necessity.

☐ A parent's duty to provide child support does not terminate in all cases when the child reaches majority. For example, a physically or mentally handicapped child may have to be supported indefinitely. Some courts take the position that the support duty continues so long as the child's need for support continues, i.e., so long as the child remains dependent. This certainly includes the period when the child is in college.

☐ It is true that married parents have no obligation to send their children to college. But there is a strong likelihood they will do so if they have the means and their children have the ability. When the court requires a divorced parent to send his or her children to college, the same tests are applied: ability to pay and capacity to learn. Thus, the court, in effect, is simply trying to equalize the position of children of divorced parents with those of married parents.

THE SECOND FAMILY   Another area of controversy concerns the noncustodial parent's responsibility of supporting others. Should the amount of child support be less because this parent has since taken on the responsibility of supporting a second family? Suppose there is a remarriage with someone who already has children and/or they have additional children of their own. The old view was that the parent's primary responsibility was to the first family. No adjustment would be made because the parent has voluntarily taken on additional support obligations. Many courts, however, no longer take this hard line.

While they will not permit the parent to leave the first family destitute, they will take into consideration the fact that a second family has substantially affected the parent's ability to support the first. Given this reality, an appropriate adjustment will be made. It must be emphasized, however, that not all courts are this understanding. Some continue to adhere to the old view.

ASSIGNMENT 12.2

a. How does a court determine the amount of child support in your state? Describe the main features of whatever guidelines exist and explain how they are used.

b. Under what circumstances, if any, does a noncustodial parent have an obligation to pay for his or her child's college education in your state?

To answer these questions, check, your state code and opinions of courts in your state. (See General Instructions for the State-Code Assignment and General Instructions for the Court-Opinion Assignment in chapter 1.)

ASSIGNMENT 12.3

Jim and Carla have one child, George, who is two years old at the time they seek a divorce. By mutual agreement, Carla will have custody of George. When the issue of child support arises in the divorce proceeding, Carla asks the court to take into consideration the fact that Jim has already announced his engagement to a rich widow. Carla feels that this should prompt the court to require Jim to make higher child support payments. Should it? Would it make any difference if Carla were the one about to marry a wealthy new spouse? Would this affect the amount of child support that Jim should pay? (See General Instructions for the Legal-Analysis Assignment in chapter 1.)

■■■ MODIFICATION OF CHILD SUPPORT ORDERS

The standard rule is that a child support order can be modified on the basis of a substantial change of circumstances that has arisen since the court granted the order, assuming, of course, that the court has personal jurisdiction over the parent from whom a modification is sought. The changed circumstances must be serious enough to warrant the conclusion that the original award has become inequitable, e.g., the child's welfare will be jeopardized if the child support award is not increased due to an unexpected illness of the child, requiring costly medical care. Alternatively, the child support award can be decreased if it is clear that the need no longer exists at all or to the same degree—e.g., if the child has died, acquired independent resources, moved out on his or her own. A recent federal law allows the parties to request a review of a child support order every three years to make sure that it complies with the guidelines.

Frequently, the custodial parent claims that child support should be increased because the noncustodial parent's ability to pay has increased since the time of the original order, e.g., by obtaining a much better paying job. This is a ground to increase child support only when it is clear that the original decree was inadequate to meet the needs of the child. At the time of the original decree, a lesser amount may have been awarded because of an inability to pay more *at that time.* Hence, a later modification upward is simply a way for the court to correct an initially inadequate award. Since many initial awards *are* inadequate, courts are inclined to grant the modification.

Note that we have been discussing the modification of *future* child support payments. What about **arrearages?** Can a court modify a delinquent obligation? There was a time when courts were sympathetic to requests by delinquent ob-

Arrearage Payments that are due but have not been made (also called **arrears**).

ligors to forgive past due debts, particularly when the court was convinced that future obligations would be met. Congress changed this in 1986 when the Bradley Amendment banned retroactive modification of child support arrearages.[3]

What happens when the noncustodial parent seeks a modification downward because he or she can no longer afford the amount originally awarded? If the circumstances that caused this change are beyond the control of the parent, e.g., a long illness, the courts will be sympathetic. Suppose, however, that the change is voluntary. For example:

> At the time of a 1990 child support order, Dan was a fifty-year-old sales manager earning $120,000 a year. The order required him to pay his ex-wife $3,000 a month in child support. In 1991, Dan decides to go to evening law school. He quits his job as a sales manager and takes a part-time job as an investigator earning $10,000 a year. He then petitions the court to modify his child support payments to $250 a month.

In many courts, Dan's petition would be denied because he has not lost the *capacity* to earn a high salary. Self-imposed poverty is not a ground to reduce child support in such courts. Other courts are not this dogmatic. They will grant the modification petition, if:

☐ The child will not be left in a destitute condition, and,

☐ The petitioner is acting in good faith.

The court will want to know whether a legitimate change-of-career or change-of-lifestyle is involved. Is it the kind of change that the party would probably have made if the marriage had not ended? If so, the court will be inclined to grant a modification downward, so long as the child is not seriously harmed thereby. On the other hand, is the parent acting out of *bad faith* or malice, e.g., to make life more miserable for the custodial parent? If so, the modification request will be denied.

CASE

GOLDBERGER V. GOLDBERGER

96 Md. App. 313, 624 A.2d 1328 (1993)
Court of Special Appeals of Maryland

Background: *The Circuit Court awarded Esther Goldberger a divorce from Aron Goldberger and custody of their six children: Chana Frumit, Mamele, Meir, Chaim Tzvi, Eliezer, and Yaacov. The court also ordered Aron to pay $4,066 per month in child support for the six children. It found that he had impoverished himself voluntarily and that his potential income was $60,000 per year. The court based this figure on the amount of money others had contributed to his litigation expenses. The case is now on appeal before the Court of Special Appeals of Maryland. Aron is the appellant and Esther is the appellee.*

Decision on Appeal: Affirmed in part; reversed in part. The trial court correctly concluded that Aron voluntarily impoverished himself but failed to properly calculate the amount he should pay for child support.

Opinion of the Court:

Judge LEVITZ delivered the opinion of the court.
The odyssey of the young children of Aron and Esther Goldberger has led them from Lakewood, New Jersey, to Israel, to Belgium and England, and finally to Baltimore, Maryland. These children have been the subject of the attention of various courts including: The High Court of Justice, Family Division, London, England; the Ecclesiastical Court of the Chief Rabbi of London (Beth Din); and, finally, the Circuit Court for Baltimore City. [Eight judges of the Circuit Court

---

3. This prohibition does not apply for any period during which there was a pending petition to modify child support, but only from the date that notice of the petition was given to the other party. 42 U.S.C.A. § 666(a)(9).

(nearly 30% of the Bench) have been involved in the case to date.]

Prior to the trial of this matter before the Circuit Court, the parties and their children had been examined and evaluated by ten physicians or psychologists. When the trial began, Esther and Aron Goldberger were fighting only about the custody of their children and related matters of support and visitation. Allegations of sexual child abuse, kidnapping, insanity and unfitness were made by one or the other of the parents. Other extended family members were brought into the conflict and took an active part in it. Since both parties are devout Orthodox Jews, noted Rabbis in this country and in Europe and Israel were consulted by the parties for advice, guidance and support. . . .

[T]he evidence revealed that appellant was 32 years old and healthy, with many years of higher education. It was undisputed that appellant had earned no actual income, as he had never worked at any income-producing vocation. Appellant planned his life to be a permanent Torah/Talmudic student.* He was a student before he was married and before any of his children were born. Appellant testified that he studies "for the sake of studying, which is a positive commandment to study the Torah for the sake of studying it." Further, appellant testified that it was his intention to continue his life of study forever: ". . . I should continue to study the rest of my life, to always be in studying. . . ." Throughout his life appellant has been supported by others, first, his parents, thereafter, his father-in-law, and most recently, friends in the Orthodox community. Nevertheless, appellant fathered six children whom he has refused to support, arguing that he has no means to support and never will have the means to provide support.†

A life devoted to study is viewed by many in the Orthodox community as a true luxury that very few can enjoy.** Unfortunately for the appellant's children, permanent Torah/Talmudic students must depend on the charity of others to provide the necessities of life. Those who support a Torah student have no legal obligation to continue such support in either duration or amount.

Nevertheless, through a network of family and Orthodox communities in Europe and the United States, approximately $180,000 had been contributed to appellant over a three year period to enable him to pursue his custody claim. Approximately $3,000 of that sum was once used to purge appellant of contempt for failing to pay child support.

Based on these facts, the court determined (1) that appellant had voluntarily impoverished himself, and (2) that his potential income was equivalent to the money that had been contributed by others to his cause. It therefore regarded his income, for purposes of paying child support as $60,000 per year and ordered that he pay $4,066 per month for the support of his six children. Appellant challenges both the finding of voluntary impoverishment and the calculation of potential income.

The obligation of parents to support their minor children has been consistently upheld by the Court of Appeals of Maryland. In *Carroll County v. Edelman*, 320 Md. 150, 577 A.2d 14, 23 (1990), the Court stated,

> Parenthood is both a biological and a legal status. By nature and by law, it confers rights and imposes duties. One of the most basic of these is the obligation of the parent to support the child until the law determines that he is able to care for himself. . . .

The legislature of Maryland has made it a crime for parents to fail to support their minor children. Md. Code Ann., Fam. Law § 10–203 (1991). . . .

In view of the above authorities, there can be no question that appellant has a legal obligation to financially support his children until they reach the age of legal majority. The more difficult question is how to calculate the proper amount of that support. Fortunately, that question has been answered by the Legislature of Maryland. Md. Code Ann., Fam. Law § 12–202(a)(1) (1991) states, "[I]n any proceeding to establish or modify child support, whether pendente lite or permanent, the court shall use the child support guidelines set forth in this subtitle." In order to use the guidelines as required by § 12–202(a)(1), it is necessary to calculate the income of the parents. "Income" is defined in § 12–201(b) of the Family Law Article as: (1) actual income of a parent, if the parent is employed to full capacity; or (2) potential income of a parent, if the parent is voluntarily impoverished.

The legislature's purpose in including potential income was to implement state and federal policy of requiring adequate support by precluding parents from avoiding their obligation by deliberately not earning what they could earn.

---

*The Torah is the "fundamental" law of the Jewish people. It consists of the five books of Moses (the Pentateuch): Genesis, Exodus, Leviticus, Numbers and Deuteronomy. It is considered to be of divine origin. The Talmud is an exposition of the fundamental oral and written law. It contains the rabbinic interpretation of the "fundamental" and "common" law.

†Rabbi Jacob ben Asher (1270–1340), known as the "Ba'al Ha Turim" and considered one of the great authorities on Jewish Law, stated in his authoritative digest, "A man can be forced to work in order to maintain his wife and infant children." Tur, Even Ha'ezec 70. Horwitz, *Spirit of Jewish Law*. Central Book Co. 1973.

**Even Teveya, the fictional lead character of *Fiddler on the Roof*, recognizes that a life of study is a luxury when he sings, "*If I were a rich man.* . . . Wouldn't have to work hard. . . . I'd discuss the Holy books with the learned men seven hours every day; that would be the sweetest thing of all." (Emphasis added).

While the Code does not define the term "voluntarily impoverished," in *John O. v. Jane O.,* 90 Md. App. 406, 601 A.2d 149 (1992), we had occasion to address the meaning of that term. We noted that neither the Legislature nor the Courts in existing case law had defined what "voluntarily impoverished" meant. We noted that no clear definition was found in any Maryland resource materials. Accordingly, we looked to the dictionary definitions of the words "voluntarily" and "impoverished." We noted that "voluntarily" means "done by design or intention; proceeding from the free and unrestrained will of the person; produced in or by act of choice. . . ." "Impoverished" means "to make poor, reduce to poverty or to deprive . . . of resources, etc." . . .

The issue of voluntary impoverishment most often arises in the context of a parent who reduces his or her level of income to avoid paying support by quitting, retiring or changing jobs. The intent of the parent in those cases is often important in determining whether there has been voluntary impoverishment. Was the job changed for the purpose of avoiding the support obligation and, therefore, voluntary, or was it for reasons beyond the control of the parent, and thus involuntary? . . . A parent who chooses a life of poverty before having children and makes a deliberate choice not to alter that status after having children is . . . "voluntarily impoverished." Whether the voluntary impoverishment is for the purpose of avoiding child support or because the parent simply has chosen a frugal lifestyle for another reason, doesn't affect that parent's obligation to the child. Although the parent can choose to live in poverty, that parent cannot obligate the child to go without the necessities of life. A parent who brings a child into this world must support that child, if he has or reasonably could obtain, the means to do so. The law requires that parent to alter his or her previously chosen lifestyle if necessary to enable the parent to meet his or her support obligation.

Accordingly, we now hold that, for purposes of the child support guidelines, a parent shall be considered "voluntarily impoverished" whenever the parent has made the free and conscious choice, not compelled by factors beyond his or her control, to render himself or herself without adequate resources. To determine whether a parent has freely been made poor or deprived of resources the trial court should look to the factors enunciated in *John O. v. Jane O.,* 90 Md. App. 406, at 422:

1. his or her current physical condition;

2. his or her respective level of education;

3. the timing of any change in employment or financial circumstances relative to the divorce proceedings;

4. the relationship of the parties prior to the divorce proceedings;

5. his or her efforts to find and retain employment;

6. his or her efforts to secure retraining if that is needed;

7. whether he or she has ever withheld support;

8. his or her past work history;

9. the area in which the parties live and the status of the job market there; and

10. any other considerations presented by either party.

Based on a review of the evidence before the circuit court, there was no error in finding that appellant was "voluntarily impoverished."

Once a court determines that a parent is voluntarily impoverished, the court must then determine the amount of potential income to attribute to that parent in order to calculate the support dictated by the guidelines. Some of the factors the court should consider in determining the amount of potential income include:

1. age;

2. mental and physical condition;

3. assets;

4. educational background, special training or skills;

5. prior earnings;

6. efforts to find and retain employment;

7. the status of the job market in the area where the parent lives;

8. actual income from any source;

9. any other factor bearing on the parent's ability to obtain funds for child support.

After the court determines the amount of potential income to attribute to the parent, the court should calculate the amount of support by using the standardized worksheet authorized in Family Law § 12–203(a) and the schedule listed in Family Law § 12–204(e). Once the guideline support figure is determined, the court must then determine whether the presumptive correctness of the guideline support figure has been overcome by evidence that application of the guidelines would be unjust or inappropriate. Md. Code Ann., Fam. Law § 12–202(a)(2) (1991).

Unfortunately, the court below erred in determining that appellant's potential income was $60,000 per year, based solely on his ability to raise funds to support and carry on this litigation. Although the court may consider the ability of appellant to persuade others to provide him with funds to pay child support in the future, the court cannot assume this will occur merely because appellant has been able to convince others to support this litigation up until now. The court needs to hear testimony and make findings regarding the factors relating to potential income previously enunciated. No such findings were made in this case. After calculating the guidelines using appellant's realistic potential income, the court must decide whether the presumptive correctness of the guidelines has been overcome. Accordingly, this matter must be remanded to the trial court for such determinations. . . .

We vacate the court's child support order and remand the matter to the trial court to recalculate the appellant's child support obligation in light of this opinion. Judgment affirmed in part and vacated in part. Appellant to pay the costs.

ASSIGNMENT 12.4

a. Did the court violate Aron Goldberger's First Amendment right to freedom of religion by forcing him to pay child support?

b. Assume you work for the law firm that represents Esther Goldberger. To determine how much child support Aron should pay, what facts would you investigate as a result of the *Goldberger* opinion? (See General Instructions for the Investigation-Strategy Assignment in chapter 1.)

We saw in chapter 10 that separation agreements are often sloppily written in that they fail to distinguish between property division terms (which are not modifiable by a court) and support terms (which are). For example, suppose that the parties agree to give the "wife the exclusive use of the marital home until the youngest child reaches the age of twenty-one." Is this a division of property or a child support term? If it is the former, then the husband cannot modify it on the basis of changed circumstances (e.g., her remarriage). If it is a child support term, then a modification is possible. Most courts would interpret the above clause as a child support term since it is tied to a period of time when the child would most likely need support. Yet a court *could* rule the other way. Needless litigation often results from poor drafting.

ASSIGNMENT 12.5

a. What standards apply to a request to modify child support payments in your state? (See General Instructions for the State-Code Assignment in chapter 1.)

b. Sara pays her ex-husband, Harry, $800 a month in child support under a 1995 court order that granted custody to Harry but gave liberal visitation rights to Sara. Due to continuing bitterness, Harry refuses to allow Sara to see their child. Sara then petitions the court to reduce her child support payments. How would her request for a modification be handled in your state? (See General Instructions for the Court-Opinion Assignment in chapter 1.)

c. Reread the facts involving Dan, the former sales manager who wants to go to law school, page 322. How would this request for a modification be handled in your state? (See General Instructions for the Court-Opinion Assignment in chapter 1.)

ASSIGNMENT 12.6

Assume the same facts as Assignment 12.3 except that Jim does not announce his marriage to the rich widow until after the initial child support order is made in the divorce proceeding. Once the marriage occurs, Carla asks the court to modify the order by increasing the amount paid for child support. What result? Would it make any difference if Carla were the one to marry a wealthy new spouse? Can Jim ask the court to modify his child support payments downward? (See General Instructions for the Legal-Analysis Assignment in chapter 1.)

ASSIGNMENT 12.7

In a 1989 divorce decree, Frank was ordered to pay $1,000 a month in child support to his former wife, Irene, who was granted custody of their child. He makes all of his payments in 1989. When he loses his job on January 1, 1990, however, he can afford only $500 a month, which he now pays every month. In June of 1990, he asks a court to modify the child support order to $500 a month. Assume that the court agrees that he can pay only $500 a month and modifies the order to this effect on July 1, 1990. By the end of 1990, what is the total amount of child support payments that he would be legally obligated to make in 1990? (See General Instructions for the Legal-Analysis Assignment in chapter 1.)

■ ENFORCEMENT OF CHILD SUPPORT ORDERS

Nonpayment of child support has reached epidemic proportions. Every year billions of dollars go uncollected. The Census Bureau found that in 1991:

□ 11.5 million families with children had a parent living outside the home (this represents almost one-third of all families with children);

□ 9.9 million families (out of the 11.5 million total) consist of women with custody, and 1.6 million consist of men with custody;[4]

□ 6.2 million custodial parents had child support court awards or child support agreements with the noncustodial parent; 5.3 million custodial parents had neither;

□ $17.7 billion in child support was ordered, but only $11.9 billion was paid;

□ 50 percent of the 6.2 million parents with child support awards or agreements received the full payment, 25 percent received partial payment, and 25 percent received nothing.

Predictably, there has been a dramatic increase in the number of families enrolled in the main public assistance program for families: Aid to Families with Dependent Children (AFDC). Many families are on AFDC because of parents who fail to pay child support. In response to the crisis, Congress added Title IV-D to the Social Security Act[5] to encourage the creation of enforcement agencies, remedies, and procedures throughout the country. In each state, an agency now exists whose function is to carry out the mandate of Title IV-D by providing new enforcement tools that can be used along with the more traditional ones. The agencies have different names, e.g., Child Support Enforcement Branch or Division, Office of Recovery Services, Child Support and Paternity Unit. Collectively, they are all known as **IV-D agencies** (see Appendix F). They assist AFDC recipients, as well as non-AFDC recipients, although the latter may be charged a nominal fee for the services provided. Exhibit 12.4 shows one state's application for child support enforcement services.

IV-D Agency A state agency that attempts to enforce child support obligations.

ASSIGNMENT 12.8

What is the name of the IV-D agency in your state? Contact the closest branch. Ask for a copy of a brochure describing its services.

---

4. Since more than 85 percent of custodial parents are mothers, in our discussion we will often refer to the delinquent parent/obligor as the father, although there is still a significant number of cases in which the delinquent parent is the mother.
5. 42 U.S.C.A. §§ 651–665.

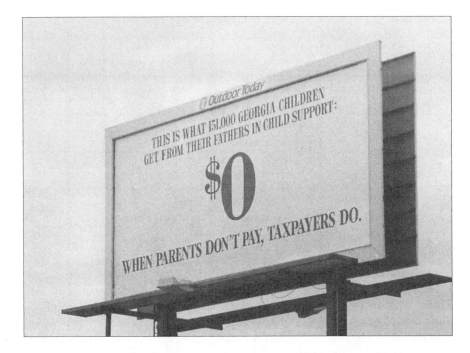

If a woman receives AFDC, she must **assign** or transfer her support rights   **Assign** To transfer rights
to the state IV-D agency or other county welfare agency that attempts to collect   or property.
support from the father. This simply means that she gives the agency the right
to keep any support money that it collects on her behalf. This money is then
used to offset the AFDC money she receives on an ongoing basis for herself
and her children. If she fails to cooperate in assigning these rights, her share
of the AFDC benefits can be terminated, and the AFDC benefits of her children
can be sent to some other responsible adult who will agree to make them available for the children.

One of the valuable services provided by the state IV-D agency is its attempt
to keep careful records on when the noncustodial parent pays and fails to pay
child support. The availability of this data helps to keep the pressure on. Furthermore, many IV-D agencies can be quite persistent in going after the noncustodial parent through automatic billing, telephone reminders, delinquency
notices, etc. Other enforcement tools are also available through the IV-D agency
as outlined below.

A new *federal* agency was created to coordinate, evaluate, and assist state
IV-D agencies—the Office of Child Support Enforcement within the U.S. Department of Health and Human Services.

But, first things first. A very large number of noncustodial parents simply
disappear. Problem number one is to *find* the noncustodial parent in order to
obtain a child support order, and/or in order to enforce it. Another service
provided by the IV-D agency is its **State Parent Locator Service** (SPLS). At the
national level, there is a comparable **Federal Parent Locator Service** (FPLS) that
operates through the Office of Child Support Enforcement. The FPLS can be
very helpful if the search for the parent involves more than one state.

The starting point in the search is the custodial parent who is asked to provide the following leads to the state IV-D agency on the whereabouts of the noncustodial parent:

☐ Social security number (check old state and federal tax returns, hospital records, police records, bank accounts, insurance policies, credit cards, loan applications, pay slips, union records, etc.)

☐ Last known residential address

☐ Current or recent employer's name and address

☐ Prior employers' names and addresses

☐ Place of birth

☐ Names and addresses of relatives and friends

☐ Local clubs and organizations to which he once belonged

☐ Local banks, public utilities, and other creditors he may have had or now has

The State Parent Locator Service of the IV-D agency will use the leads provided by the custodial parent to try to locate the noncustodial parent. (See Exhibit 12.4) It will check the records of other state agencies for a current address, e.g., Department of Motor Vehicle Registration, Unemployment Compensation Commission, Tax Department, and prisons. If the noncustodial parent has moved to another state, the IV-D agency in that state can be asked to provide comparable search services, or the Federal Parent Locator Service can be asked to help. The latter can also search the records of federal agencies for leads, e.g., Internal Revenue Service, Department of Defense, Selective Service Commission, National Personnel Records Center, Veterans Administration, and Social Security Administration.

ASSIGNMENT 12.9   How does the State Parent Locator Service of the IV-D agency in your state operate? Describe how the service functions. (See General Instructions for the State-Code Assignment in chapter 1.)

Once the noncustodial parent is located, the next step is to secure a child support order against him. A paternity proceeding may be needed to establish the obligation of support. (Paternity is discussed in chapter 17.) If the parent has moved to another state, URESA (the Uniform Reciprocal Enforcement of Support Act) and UIFSA (the more recent Uniform Interstate Family Support Act) can be used by a custodial parent in one state to obtain and enforce a child support (or alimony) order in another state without ever having to travel to the latter state. URESA and UIFSA are discussed in chapter 14.

The court has the following enforcement options available to it:[6]

☐ **Civil contempt proceeding**

☐ **Execution**

☐ **Prosecution for criminal nonsupport**

☐ **Income withholding**

(*text continued at bottom of p. 331*)

---

6. Some of these options also apply to the enforcement of alimony obligations. See chapter 14.

☐ **EXHIBIT 12.4 Massachusetts Application for Child Support Enforcement Services**

**Massachusetts Department of Revenue
Child Support Enforcement Division**

**Application for
Child Support Enforcement Services**

• • • •
Absent Parent Background and Financial Information:

a. Is the absent parent currently married? Yes ☐ No ☐ Don't Know ☐
(If no or don't know, skip to question #b.)
What is his or her spouse's name? _____
Does his or her spouse work? Yes ☐ No ☐ Don't Know ☐
  If yes, where does she or he work, if you know? _____
  What is her or his income $ _____ per _____ Don't Know ☐
                          (Week, Month or Year)

b. If not married, does the absent parent share his or her household with another adult?
Yes ☐ No ☐ Don't Know ☐

c. Does the absent parent have any children who are not also your children?
Yes ☐ No ☐ Don't Know ☐

If yes, please list their names and ages here, along with the name of the adult with whom they live.

Name	Age	Living With:
_____	_____	_____
_____	_____	_____

d. Is the absent parent providing support for children who are not also your children?
Yes ☐ No ☐ Don't Know ☐
If yes, how much is he/she paying? $ _____ per _____ Don't Know ☐
                                 (Week, Month or Year)

e. To your knowledge, does the absent parent have any of the following sources of income?

Type of Income	Amount (if known)	Week/Month/Year
Worker's compensation	$ _____ per	_____
Unemployment compensation	_____	_____
Social Security retirement (over 62, green check)	_____	_____
Other pension	_____	_____
Social Security disability (green check)	_____	_____
Supplemental Security Income (SSI) (gold check)	_____	_____
Other disability	_____	_____
Welfare	_____	_____
Veteran's benefits	_____	_____
Commissions	_____	_____
Trust income	_____	_____
Rental income (from houses/apartments he or she owns)	_____	_____
Annuities	_____	_____
Interest income	_____	_____
Dividend income	_____	_____

f. To your knowledge, does he or she have—or has he or she ever had in the last three years:

	Yes	No	When	Amount
Royalties	☐	☐	19___	$ _____
Severance pay	☐	☐	19___	_____
Capital gains	☐	☐	19___	_____
Prizes and awards	☐	☐	19___	_____
Lottery winnings	☐	☐	19___	_____
Gambling winnings	☐	☐	19___	_____
Bonuses	☐	☐	19___	_____

Continued

☐ **EXHIBIT 12.4   Massachusetts Application for Child Support Enforcement Services—*Continued***

g. Does the absent parent:

Own any houses or other real estate? Yes ☐ No ☐ Don't Know ☐

If yes, please describe and indicate location if you can. _____
_____

Own any motor vehicle? Yes ☐ No ☐ Don't Know ☐

If yes, for each vehicle, please identify the model, color, state where it is registered, and license plate number, if you can.
_____
_____

Own a boat? Yes ☐ No ☐ Don't Know ☐

If yes, please indicate the registration number, if you can. _____

Where is it moored? _____
                              City or Town   State

Own any stocks or bonds? Yes ☐ No ☐ Don't Know ☐

If yes, please use a separate sheet of paper to identify the name and address of the absent parent's stock broker and list any stocks and/or bonds owned by the absent parent if that information is available to you. Indicate the name of the company, the number of shares, and the date the stock was purchased, if possible.

Have any bank accounts? Yes ☐ No ☐ Don't Know ☐

List the name(s) of the bank(s), location(s), and type(s) of account(s) if that information is available to you.

Bank Name	Location	Type of Account

If you need additional space, please continue on a separate piece of paper.

Have any credit cards? Yes ☐ No ☐ Don't Know ☐

If yes, please list the names of the companies and account numbers if that information is available to you.

Credit Company	Account Number

Have any outstanding loans? Yes ☐ No ☐ Don't Know ☐

If yes, please identify the name of the bank(s) or financial institution(s), location(s) and account number(s).

Lending Institution	Location	Account Number
	City/Town State	
	City/Town State	

h. Have you ever filed a joint income tax return with the absent parent? Yes ☐ No ☐

If yes, for which state(s) and for what year(s)?

    State   Tax Years

_____ 19 ___ to 19 ___ If you filed a joint *federal* return, for what years? 19 ___ to 19 ___

i Does the absent parent have any disabilities or handicaps? Yes ☐ No ☐ Don't Know ☐

j. Does the absent parent have a driver's license? Yes ☐ No ☐ Don't Know ☐

If yes, from what state? _____ What is the license number? _____ Don't Know ☐

k. Does the absent parent have any trade or commercial licenses? Yes ☐ No ☐ Don't Know ☐

If yes, what sort of license is it? _____

From what state was it issued? _____

l. Has the absent parent ever belonged to any labor unions? Yes ☐ No ☐ Don't Know ☐

If yes, enter the name of the union, local number, city and state.
_____

Continued

☐ **EXHIBIT 12.4 Massachusetts Application for Child Support Enforcement Services—*Continued***

m. Does the absent parent go by any other names or aliases? Yes ☐ No ☐ Don't Know ☐

If yes, please identify. _____

n. Has the absent parent ever been a member of the armed forces? Yes ☐ No ☐ Don't Know ☐

If yes, what branch of service? _____

_____/_____/_____   _____/_____/_____   _____   _____
    Date Entered   Date Discharged   Service Number   Last Duty Station

o. What high school, trade school and/or college did the absent parent attend? Please indicate the name and address of each school, the dates attended and the degree earned.

Name	Address	Dates of Attendance	Degree
_____	_____	_____	_____
_____	_____	_____	_____

Please attach an additional piece of paper if you need more space.

p. Does the absent parent have a criminal record?

Yes ☐ No ☐ Don't Know ☐ If yes, in which state? _____

q. Please identify the names and addresses of as many of the absent parent's past employers as you can. (Do not include the most recent employer which you have already identified earlier.)

Name	Address
_____	_____
_____	_____

Please attach an additional piece of paper if you need more space.

r. What are the names of the absent parent's parents? (Please indicate their names even if they are deceased.)

Father's Name	Mother's Maiden Name
Street or P.O. Box	Street or P.O. Box
City State Zip	City State Zip
( )	( )
Telephone	Telephone

s. Please provide the names and addresses of others who might know the whereabouts of the absent parent.

Name	Relationship	Phone
Street or P.O. Box	City State	Zip
Name	Relationship	Phone
Street or P.O. Box	City State	Zip

SOURCE: Massachusetts Department of Revenue Child Support Enforcement Division.

☐ **License denial or revocation**

☐ **Tax Refund Intercept Program (TRIP)**

☐ **Unemployment compensation intercept**

☐ **Qualified Domestic Relations Order (QDRO)**

☐ **Qualified Medical Child Support Order (QMSCO)**

☐ **Credit bureau referral ("credit clouding")**

☐ **Posting security**

☐ **Protective order**

Obligor   Someone who is legally obligated to another. The latter is the *obligee.*

Contempt   Obstructing or assailing the authority or dignity of the court.

In our discussion of these options the person obligated to make child support payments will be referred to as the **obligor.**

CIVIL CONTEMPT PROCEEDING

Contempt of court exists when the authority or dignity of the court is obstructed or assailed. The most glaring example is an intentional violation of a court order. There are two kinds of contempt proceedings, civil and criminal, both of which can lead to the jailing of the offender. The purpose of a *civil contempt* proceeding is to compel future compliance with the court order, whereas the purpose of a *criminal contempt* proceeding is to punish the offender.[7] Criminal contempt in child support cases is rare because of the cumbersome nature of any criminal proceeding.

When civil contempt occurs in child support cases, the offender is jailed until he agrees to comply with the court order. Suppose, however, that the offender has no resources and thus cannot comply. In effect, such a person would be imprisoned because of his poverty. This is illegal. Imprisonment for debt is unconstitutional because it amounts to a sentence for an indefinite period beyond the control of the offender. To bypass this constitutional prohibition, a court must determine that the offender has the *present ability* to pay the child support debt but simply refuses to do so. Such an individual is in control of how long the sentence will be. In effect, the keys to jail are in his own pocket. Release occurs when he pays the child support debt.

In addition to jailing the obligor, most courts have the power to order the less drastic sanction of imposing a fine when the obligor is found to be in civil contempt.

ASSIGNMENT 12.10

What steps must be taken in your state to use a civil contempt proceeding to enforce a child support order? (See General Instruction for the Flowchart Assignment in chapter 1.)

Writ of Execution   A document directing a court officer to seize the property of someone who lost a judgment, sell it, and pay the winner of the judgment.

Lien   An encumbrance or claim on property imposed for the payment of a debt.

EXECUTION

Once an obligor fails to pay a judgment ordering child support, the sheriff can be ordered to seize the personal or real property of the obligor in the state. All of this occurs through a **writ of execution.** Its initial effect is to create a **lien** on the property that prevents the obligor from disposing of it. The property seized can then be sold by the sheriff. The proceeds from this *forced sale* are used to pay the judgment and the expenses of the execution. Not all property of the obligor, however, is subject to execution in every state. Certain property, e.g., clothes and cars, may be exempt from execution.

ASSIGNMENT 12.11

Describe the steps that are taken in your state when a plaintiff seeks execution of a judgment ordering child support payments that are not paid. Also state what property of the obligor, if any, is exempt from execution. (See General Instructions for the State-Code Assignment in chapter 1.)

Suppose that the obligor moves to another state after failing to pay a child support order. To answer the question of whether the mother can go to the

---

7. Homer Clark, *The Law of Domestic Relations in the United States,* § 18.3, p. 390 (Practitioner's Ed. 2d 1987).

obligor's new state and seek execution or other enforcement remedies against him there, see page 386, where there is a discussion of when one state must give full faith and credit (i.e., enforce) to the court order of another state.

PROSECUTION FOR CRIMINAL NONSUPPORT

In most states, the willful failure to support a child is a *state* crime for which the obligor can be prosecuted. (In 1992, willful nonpayment of support for a child residing in another state became a *federal* crime.) There must be an ability to provide support before the obligor can be tried and convicted of *criminal nonsupport* or desertion. The range of punishment includes probation, fine, and imprisonment. Except for relatively wealthy offenders, imprisonment is seldom an effective method of enforcing child support. Most obligors are wage earners, and once they are jailed, their primary source of income obviously dries up. One way out of this dilemma is for the judge to agree to suspend the imposition of the jail sentence on condition that the obligor fulfill the support obligation, including the payment of arrearages. The obligor would be placed on *probation* under this condition.

The threat of prosecution has encouraged some delinquent obligors to come forward. Several states have launched highly publicized amnesty programs (see Exhibit 12.5).

---

a. Is it a crime in your state to fail to pay child support? If so, quote the essential elements of the crime. (See General Instructions for the State-Code Assignment in chapter 1.)

b. Prepare a checklist of questions you would ask in order to help determine whether this crime was committed. (See General Instructions for the Investigation-Strategy Assignment in chapter 1.)

c. What steps must be taken in your state to prosecute someone for violating this crime? (See General Instructions for the Flowchart Assignment in chapter 1.)

ASSIGNMENT 12.12

INCOME WITHHOLDING

Income withholding is a mandatory, automatic deduction from the obligor's income when he falls behind in child support payments. Wages of an employee are the most common example of income that is subject to withholding, although other kinds may qualify as well, e.g., commissions, retirement pay-

---

DO YOU OWE CHILD SUPPORT?
—Has your luck run out?—

Beginning Monday morning, December 6, a substantial number of Kansas City area parents who have failed to make their court-ordered child support payments will be arrested, jailed, and prosecuted. Could you be one of those parents?

Rather than gamble, you can receive amnesty from criminal prosecution by coming in person to the child support enforcement office at 1805 Grand Avenue in Kansas City and making immediate payment arrangements. You only have until this Friday at 5 p.m. Next Monday, you may be in jail, and then it will be too late.

Come in—let's talk.
Missouri Division of Child Support Enforcement
1805 Grand Ave., Suite 300
Kansas City, MO

☐ **EXHIBIT 12.5**
Ad Placed in Sports Section of Local Paper

ments. In most cases, a child support order from the court will mandate immediate wage withholding for all current support obligations and for all arrearages unless a better form of payment is agreed to by the parties and approved by the court. Wage withholding is the most effective method of collection available. The amount collected in this way increased from $26 million in 1985 to almost $4 billion in 1992 (see Exhibit 12.6).

Some employers are irritated by the record keeping involved in income withholding even though they are usually entitled to a small fee for this service. But employers do not have a choice on whether to participate. Furthermore, they can be fined or otherwise sanctioned by the state for subjecting an obligor-employee to any discipline because of income withholding. Exhibit 12.7 outlines government guidelines to employers regarding this matter.

Garnishment A process whereby a debtor's property under the control of another is given to a third person to whom the debtor owes a debt.

Income withholding is similar to the more traditional **garnishment** process under which a third party, e.g., a bank or employer, who owes the obligor money or other property is ordered by a court to turn it over to a debtor of the obligor, such as the custodial parent. Garnishment, however, is usually less effective than income withholding because of the more cumbersome procedures for instituting garnishment and the restrictions that may exist on how long it can be in effect.

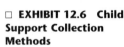

ASSIGNMENT 12.13

a. Who can use income withholding in your state through the state IV-D agency? How does this enforcement mechanism operate?

b. Compare income withholding to the garnishment process in your state. How do they differ?

c. Jim is subject to a child support order in your state to pay his ex-wife, Wanda, $900 a month for their fifteen-year-old daughter, Paula. Jim fails to make payments for three months. Wanda then goes to the state IV-D agency to seek help. Income withholding is commenced through Jim's employer, the ABC Truck Company. Six months later, Paula gets married. Jim goes to his supervisor and asks that income withholding terminate because he no longer has a duty to support his daughter. Assume he is correct that a parent does not have to support a child who has been emancipated through marriage. Can the company stop the withholding?

(See General Instructions for the State-Code Assignment in chapter 1.)

☐ **EXHIBIT 12.6 Child Support Collection Methods**

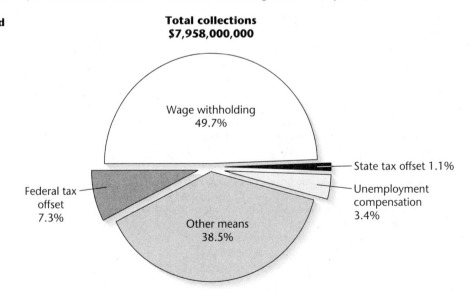

Total collections $7,958,000,000

Wage withholding 49.7%

State tax offset 1.1%

Unemployment compensation 3.4%

Federal tax offset 7.3%

Other means 38.5%

SOURCE: Eleanor Landstreet, *Enforcing Child Support Against the Self-Employed and Nonwage Earners* (Office of Child Support Administration, 1994).

☐ **EXHIBIT 12.7   Wage Withholding for Child Support: An Employer's Guide**

Employer's Guide for Universal Wage Withholding
The following is a brief summary of your legal responsibilties as an employer:

You may already be familiar with wage withholding for child support orders administered by the Child Support Enforcement agency in your State. Now you could be receiving wage withholding orders for almost *every* employee who has a child support order issued against him or her—regardless of whether the case is administered by the State Child Support Enforcement agency or is privately handled through an attorney, a court, or another office; regardless of whether payments are in arrears; and regardless of whether the parent has been regularly paying his or her child support obligation.

In addition to ensuring that child support is received on time, wage withholding has advantages for the employee ordered to pay child support. It offers a clear record that child support payments have been made in full, on time, and as ordered. It is a convenient way for a parent to fulfill a legal responsibility: a parent paying by wage withholding does not have to write checks or take payments to the former spouse, child support office, or court every week or month. Wage withholding avoids missed payments. Employers, such as yourself, also benefit when employees are under less stress and don't have to take time off to resolve child support issues. You will be able to use electronic funds transfer/electronic data interchange technology to transmit wage withholdings, if you choose.

This Guide presents answers to questions that you may have about your responsibilities under Federal wage withholding laws.

How will I know if I have to start withholding child support from an employee's wages?
You will receive a notice that tells you when to begin, how much to deduct, and where to send the money.

How long after I receive the notice do I begin the withholding?
Withholding is to begin no later than the first pay period that occurs 14 days after the mailing date of the order.

The withholding may add administrative fees to my business. May I charge a fee for this service?
If your State law allows, you may collect a fee to help offset your costs. The fee can be deducted each time a payment is withheld. The fee is an additional amount to be deducted from the employee's wages and is not to be deducted from the support payment.

If I don't want to get involved in collecting child support, can I dismiss someone who has a withholding order against his wages?
No. If you refuse to hire, or if you discipline or discharge an employee because of wage withholding for child support, you will be subject to a fine under your State's law.

And if I don't carry out the withholding?
If you fail to withhold child support as specified in the notice, you will be liable for the full amount you should have withheld from the employee's wages.

If the employee tells me the amount to be deducted is wrong, what should I do?
Continue to withhold wages according to the notice. The employee must contest the facts with the withholding agency, not the employer. Until you are notified otherwise by the withholding agency, you should proceed with the withholding as ordered.

Is there a limit to the amount that can be withheld?
The total amount that can be withheld from any employee's paycheck is limited by the Consumer Credit Protection Act unless further limited by State law. The limits provided in the Consumer Credit Protection Act are 50 percent of disposable earnings if an obligated parent has a second family and 60 percent if there is no second family. These limits are each increased by five percentage points (to 55 and 65) if payments are in arrears for a period equal to 12 weeks or more.

Will I be responsible for determining how to apply the Consumer Credit Protection Act limits?
Yes. However, your State Child Support Enforcement agency will help you if you need assistance.

Several of my employees already have garnishments against their paychecks and, if I deduct for child support, the total deducted will be more than allowed under law. How do I handle this?
Withholding for child support takes priority over other legal processes carried out under State law against the same wages. In fact, the only withholding that takes precedence is a prior Federal tax levy. This means that child support must be withheld first, then deductions for other garnishments or attachment orders can be made. If you have any questions, contact your State Child Support Enforcement agency.

How do I know when to stop the withholding?
The withholding remains in effect until you are notified by the withholding agency of *any* changes to the order.

What do I do if the employee quits the job?
You must notify the Child Support Enforcement agency *promptly* when the employee leaves and give the employee's last known home address and the new employer's name and address, if known.

SOURCE: U.S. Department of Health and Human Services, Office of Child Support Administration (June 1994).

LICENSE DENIAL OR REVOCATION

To engage in certain occupations, a person must obtain a license from the state. Examples include plumber, hairdresser, real estate broker, accountant, electrician, teacher, doctor, and lawyer. Many states will deny an initial application for a license, deny an application for a renewal of a license, or revoke the license of a parent who is delinquent in making child support payments. In Maine, for example, revocation notices are sent to parents who are at least ninety days behind. A few states include the revocation of the *driver's* license of a delinquent obligor.

ASSIGNMENT 12.14   Under the state code of your state, can licenses be revoked for the failure to pay child support? If so, what licenses? What are the conditions that will trigger a revocation? (See General Instructions for the State-Code Assignment in chapter 1.)

TAX REFUND INTERCEPT PROGRAM (TRIP)

Income tax refunds owed by state and federal tax authorities to obligors can be intercepted and used to fulfill past-due child support obligations. During the first four years of the **Tax Refund Intercept Program** (TRIP), 1.5 million such tax refunds were intercepted for this purpose.

The collection occurs through the state IV-D agency. It is not possible for a woman with four hungry children to call the Internal Revenue Service and ask that it send her the father's refund check. She must first apply to the IV-D agency in the state. A notice (Exhibit 12.8) is then sent to the taxpayer that his tax refund is about to be intercepted to meet the child support debt. If the taxpayer contests the interception, a hearing is held.

ASSIGNMENT 12.15   How are *state* income tax refunds intercepted to meet child support needs in your state? Describe the steps involved. (See General Instructions for the State-Code Assignment in chapter 1.)

UNEMPLOYMENT COMPENSATION INTERCEPT

The unemployment compensation benefits of the obligor can also be intercepted to meet ongoing (not just past-due) child support payments. This method of withholding enables the state IV-D agency to collect at least some support from an unemployed obligor. Nothing is left to chance. Computers at the unemployment compensation agency and at the state IV-D agency communicate with each other to identify delinquent parents who have applied for or who are eligible for unemployment compensation. An investigator from the IV-D agency will then contact the surprised obligor. It may even be possible to intercept benefits across state lines pursuant to reciprocal agreements among cooperating states. (In most states a similar intercept program can reach an obligor's worker's compensation benefits.)

ASSIGNMENT 12.16   Can unemployment compensation benefits be intercepted to meet child support needs in your state? If so, describe the steps involved. (See General Instructions for the State-Code Assignment in chapter 1.)

□ **EXHIBIT 12.8 Notice of Collection of Income Tax Refund**

Department of the Treasury
Internal Revenue Service

If you have any questions, refer to this information:

Date of This Notice: January 4, 1994
Social Security Number: 215-32-2726
Document Locator Number:
Form   Tax Year Ended: 1992

Call:

Sam Jones
999 Peachtree Street   or
Doraville, CO 99999

Write: Chief, Taxpayer Assistance Section
Internal Revenue Service Center

If you write, be sure to attach this notice.

THIS IS TO INFORM YOU THAT THE AGENCY NAMED BELOW HAS CONTACTED US REGARDING AN OUTSTAND-ING DEBT YOU HAVE WITH THEM.

UNDER AUTHORITY OF SECTION 6402(c) OF THE INTERNAL REVENUE CODE, ANY OVERPAYMENT OF YOUR FED-ERAL INCOME TAX WILL BE APPLIED TO THAT OBLIGATION BEFORE ANY AMOUNT CAN BE REFUNDED OR APPLIED TO ESTIMATED TAX. IF YOU HAVE ANY QUESTIONS ABOUT THE OBLIGATION OR BELIEVE IT IS IN ERROR, YOU SHOULD CONTACT THAT AGENCY IMMEDIATELY.

NAME OF AGENCY

DEPT. OF SOCIAL SERVICES
DIV. OF INCOME AND SUPPORT
CHILD SUPPORT ENFORCEMENT
1575 OBLIGATION STREET
TIMBUKTU, CO 92037

CONTACT: CHILD SUPPORT
PHONE: 619-456-9103

QUALIFIED DOMESTIC RELATIONS ORDER (QDRO)

Very often an obligor will have pension and other retirement benefit plans through his employer. A special court order, called a **Qualified Domestic Relations Order (QDRO),** allows someone other than the obligor to reach some or all of these benefits in order to meet a support obligation of the obligor, such as child support. The child becomes an *alternate payee* under these plans.[8] This person cannot receive benefits under the plan that the obligor himself would not have been able to receive. For example, if the obligor is not entitled to a lump-sum payment, the child as alternate payee is also subject to this limitation.

Qualified Domestic Relations Order A court order that allows a nonemployee to reach pension benefits of an employee or former employee in order to satisfy a marital obligation to the nonemployee.

QUALIFIED MEDICAL CHILD SUPPORT ORDER (QMCSO)

Many children of a noncustodial parent have no health insurance. Assume that this parent is working for a company that has a group health plan. But the parent either refuses to add the child to the plan, or the insurance company tells the parent that the child is ineligible because he or she does not live with the parent, does not live in the insurer's service area, is not claimed as a dependent on the parent's tax return, or was born to unmarried parents. In 1993 Congress passed a law that made it illegal for insurance companies to use such reasons to

---

8. For an example of a Qualified Domestic Relations Order in which the ex-spouse is the alternate payee seeking support through alimony, see Exhibit 10.6 in chapter 10.

Qualified Medical Child Support Order A court order requiring that a group health plan provide benefits for the child of a parent covered under the plan.

deny coverage to children. A court order can now be obtained to require coverage. It is called the **Qualified Medical Child Support Order (QMCSO)**. The child becomes an *alternate recipient* under the health plan. The employer can deduct the cost of adding the child to the plan from the parent's pay.

CREDIT BUREAU REFERRAL ("CREDIT CLOUDING")

An obligor may be warned that a credit bureau (e.g., TRW, Trans Union, CBI-Equifax) will be notified of a delinquency in making child support payments unless the delinquency is eliminated by payment or unless satisfactory arrangements are made to pay the debt. Once the computers of a credit bureau have information on such payment problems, a "cloud" on the obligor's credit rating is created *(credit clouding)*, which notifies potential creditors that the obligor may be a bad credit risk. This method of pressuring compliance with child support obligations is particularly effective with self-employed obligors who often don't have regular wages that can be subjected to income withholding or garnishment. Many states now routinely report child support debts to credit bureaus. (See Exhibit 12.9.)

POSTING SECURITY

In some cases, a noncustodial parent may be asked to post security in the form of a bond or other guarantee that will cover future support obligations.

☐ **EXHIBIT 12.9   States Routinely Reporting Child Support Debts to Credit Bureaus as of December 31, 1993**

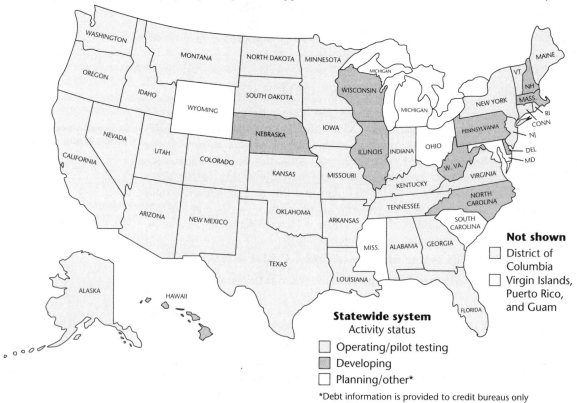

Not shown
☐ District of Columbia
☐ Virgin Islands, Puerto Rico, and Guam

Statewide system
Activity status
☐ Operating/pilot testing
▨ Developing
☐ Planning/other*

*Debt information is provided to credit bureaus only upon their request

SOURCE: 16 *Child Support Report* 3 (Office of Child Support Enforcement, 1994).

PROTECTIVE ORDER

Some men do not react kindly to requests from the mothers of their children that they meet their child support obligations. Occasionally, they may even physically assault the mother or threaten to do so. The police may be called in, although some have complained that the police do not take so-called domestic disputes seriously. Usually, the woman can obtain through the local prosecutor or district attorney a **protective order,** which threatens the man with arrest and jail unless he stays away from the children and their mother.

Protective Order A court order designed to protect a person from harm or harassment.

Under what circumstances can a woman obtain a protective order against her husband in your state? Describe the steps involved. (See General Instructions for the State-Code Assignment in chapter 1.)

ASSIGNMENT 12.17

An unmarried couple lives together. The woman promises the man that she will use birth control, but has no intention of keeping this promise. When a child is born, can the father refuse to support it because of the mother's "fraud"?

ASSIGNMENT 12.18

■■■■■ NECESSARIES

A seldom used but still available method for a spouse and child to obtain support is to go to merchants, make purchases of **necessaries,** and charge them to the credit of the nonsupporting husband/father. The latter must pay the bills, whether or not he knows about them or authorizes them so long as:

Necessaries The basic items needed by family members to maintain a standard of living.

☐ They are in fact for necessaries, and,

☐ The husband/father has not already provided them for the family

Since the definition of necessaries is not precise, and since a merchant has difficulty knowing whether a husband/father has already made provision for the necessaries of his family, few merchants are willing to extend credit in these circumstances without express authorization from the husband/father. Some states, however, have eliminated the requirement that there be evidence of a failure of the husband/father to provide necessaries before his credit can be charged.

What are necessaries? Generally, they encompass what is needed and appropriate to maintain the family at the standard of living to which it has been accustomed, e.g., home, food, clothing, furniture, medical care. The educational expenses of minor children are necessaries. A college education, on the other hand, is not in many states.

a. Find two opinions written by courts in your state that address the doctrine of necessaries. Try to find one opinion that reached the conclusion that the spouse or father was liable, and one that reached the opposite conclusion. (If you cannot find such opinions written by courts in your state, try neighboring states.)

b. Would a college education be considered one of the necessaries in your state so that a parent would be required to pay the expenses of the education?

c. Suppose that a wife wishes to complete her undergraduate degree. Would a husband in your state have to pay for it?

(See General Instructions for the Court-Opinion Assignment in chapter 1.)

ASSIGNMENT 12.19

□ **Note** Some states have tried to enforce the support obligation through their marriage-formulation statutes. The statute may provide, for example, that no individual will be allowed to enter a marriage if that person has failed to support his or her child in the custody of someone else. The United States Supreme Court has held, however, that such statutes are an unconstitutional interference with the fundamental right to marry. *Zablocki v. Redhail,* 434 U.S. 374, 98 S. Ct. 673, 54 L. Ed. 2d 618 (1978). (See chapter 8.)

■ SUMMARY

In negotiating the child support terms of a separation agreement, the parties must consider a number of factors, the most important of which are the state guidelines on child support, the standard of living to which the child was accustomed during the marriage, and the financial resources available for support. A court will consider the same factors in deciding whether to approve what the parties have negotiated.

Before the court can make a child support order, it must have personal jurisdiction over the defendant. This is acquired through in-person service of process or through the long arm statute. The defendant can be the father, the mother, or anyone who has formally adopted the child. Child support orders for future payments can be later modified if changed circumstances are serious enough to warrant it.

The major problem in this area is enforcement: a very large number of noncustodial parents are not making their child support payments. Title IV-D agencies have been established to combat this problem by locating delinquent parents (obligors) and by using new enforcement tools to make them pay what they owe.

In a civil contempt proceeding, an obligor with the present ability to pay can be jailed for nonpayment. A writ of execution can be levied against his property. Other options include criminal prosecution, income withholding, wage garnishment, license revocation, tax-refund intercept, unemployment-compensation intercept, Qualified Domestic Relations Orders, Qualified Medical Child Support Orders, credit clouding, and posting security. If the obligor physically threatens the custodial parent, a protective order can be sought.

In some states, the custodial parent or child can make purchases of necessaries and charge them to the credit of the obligor.

■ KEY CHAPTER TERMINOLOGY

Pendente Lite
Personal Jurisdiction
Domicile
Divisible Divorce
Long Arm Statute
Child Support Guidelines
Arrearages
IV-D Agencies

Assign
State Parent Locator Service
Federal Parent Locator Service
Obligor
Contempt
Writ of Execution
Lien
Garnishment

Tax Refund Intercept Program
Qualified Domestic Relations
  Order (QDRO)
Qualified Medical Child Support
  Order (QMCSO)
Protective Order
Necessaries

DIVORCE, JUDICIAL SEPARATION, AND SEPARATE MAINTENANCE

▆▆▆▆ DIVORCE: HISTORICAL BACKGROUND

In order to obtain a divorce that dissolves the marital relationship, specified reasons must exit. These reasons, called **grounds,** are spelled out in statutes. The two categories of grounds are no-fault and fault. The major **no-fault grounds** are as follows:

☐ Living apart
☐ Incompatibility
☐ Irreconcilable differences, irretrievable breakdown

The major fault grounds are as follows:

☐ Adultery
☐ Cruelty
☐ Desertion

Although these are the main three, a number of other fault grounds also exist in most states.

For many years, fault grounds were the only grounds for divorce, the premise being that a marriage should not be terminated unless there was evidence of serious wrongdoing by one of the spouses—blame had to be established. Many believed that such stringent divorce laws would help prevent the failure of marriages. In colonial America, it was common to deny the guilty spouse the right of remarriage if a divorce was granted. The payment of alimony was sometimes used to punish the guilty spouse rather than as a way to help the other become reestablished. In short, guilt, wrongdoing, and punishment were predominant themes of our divorce laws. (Exhibit 13.1 shows how the divorce rate has changed since 1941.)

Grounds Acceptable reasons for seeking a particular result.

No-Fault Grounds Reasons for granting a divorce that do not require proof that either spouse committed marital wrongs.

□ **EXHIBIT 13.1**
Number of Divorces
and Divorce Rates

YEAR	NUMBER OF DIVORCES	PERCENTAGE CHANGE FROM PREVIOUS YEAR	RATE PER 1,000 TOTAL POPULATION
1992	1,210,000	+ .01	4.7
1991	1,187,000	+ .01	4.7
1990	1,175,000	− .01	4.7
1989	1,186,000	.00	4.8
1988	1,183,000	+ .02	4.8
1987	1,157,000	− .03	4.8
1986	1,192,000	+ .01	5.0
1985	1,172,000	+ .01	4.9
1984	1,156,000	− .005	4.9
1983	1,158,000	− .01	4.9
1982	1,170,000	− .03	5.0
1981	1,213,000	+ .03	5.3
1980	1,182,000	.00	5.2
1979	1,181,000	+ .04	5.3
1978	1,130,000	+ .03	5.1
1977	1,090,000	+ .006	5.0
1976	1,083,000	+ 4.5	5.0
1975	1,036,000	+ 6.0	4.9
1974	977,000	+ 6.8	4.6
1973	915,000	+ 8.3	4.4
1972	845,000	+ 9.3	4.1
1971	773,000	+ 9.2	3.7
1965	479,000	+ 6.4	2.5
1960	393,000	− .5	2.2
1955	377,000	− .5	2.3
1950	385,000	− 3.0	2.6
1946	610,000	+25.8	4.3
1941	293,000	+11.0	2.2

SOURCE: B. Wilson, National Center for Health Statistics. December 17, 1992. See also F. Cox, *Human Intimacy,* 596 (6th ed. 1993)

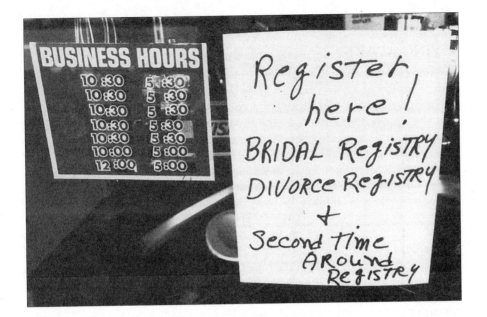

During this period of fault-based divorce, the system was frequently criticized as irrelevant and encouraging fraud. Over 90 percent of the divorces were **uncontested,** meaning that there was no dispute between the parties. Since both spouses wanted the divorce, they rarely spent much time fighting each other about whether adultery, cruelty, or other fault grounds existed. In fact, parties often flagrantly lied to the courts about the facts of their case in order to quickly establish that fault did exist. While such **collusion** was obviously illegal, the parties were seldom caught. Since both sides wanted the divorce, there was little incentive to reveal the truth. The system also encouraged **migratory divorces,** where one of the parties would "migrate," or travel, to another state solely to take advantage of its more lenient divorce laws. Some of these states gained the reputation of being divorce mills.

Reform was obviously needed. In 1969 California enacted the first no-fault divorce law in the country. Soon other states followed. Today, no-fault grounds (or their equivalent) exist in every state. Some states have eliminated the word "divorce" and replaced it with the word **dissolution** as a symbolic gesture that a new day has arrived. This does not mean, however, that fault grounds have been abolished. Most states have retained them, and oddly enough, at times fault becomes relevant to a court's discussion of a no-fault ground, as we will see in a moment. Yet in the main, fault is largely ignored in current practice, except when child custody and parental fitness are in issue.

Uncontested Not disputed; not challenged.

Collusion An agreement between spouses in a divorce proceeding that one or both will lie to the court to facilitate the obtaining of the divorce.

Migratory Divorce A divorce obtained in a state to which one or both spouses traveled before returning to their original state.

ASSIGNMENT 13.1

a. In your state code, find the statute that lists the grounds for divorce. Give the citation to this statute and list all the grounds for divorce provided therein. See also Assignment 1.3(d) in chapter 1. (See General Instructions for the State-Code Assignment in chapter 1).

b. For each ground of divorce identified in part (a), draft a checklist of questions to help determine whether those grounds exist. (See General Instructions for the Checklist-Formulation Assignment in chapter 1.)

■■■■ NO-FAULT GROUNDS FOR DIVORCE

LIVING APART

Living Apart A no-fault ground of divorce that exists when the spouses live separately for a designated period of consecutive time.

Living "separate and apart" is a ground for divorce in many states. The statutes authorizing this ground of **living apart** must be carefully read since slight differences in wording may account for major differences in meaning. The simplest statute authorizes the divorce if the parties have lived separate and apart for a designated period of consecutive time, as outlined below. While this requirement exists in all the statutes, some states impose additional and more restrictive requirements. For example, living separate and apart may have to be pursuant to a court order or a separation agreement, or it may have to be consensual or "voluntary."

TIME   In all states where living apart is a ground, the statute requires that the parties live apart for a designated period of time, ranging from six months to three years. The purpose of the time limitation is, in effect, to force the parties to think seriously about whether a reconciliation is possible.

CONSECUTIVENESS   If the parties have separated off and on over a period of time, the living-apart ground is not established, even if the sum total of time the parties were actually separated exceeds the designated time required for separation under the statute. The separated time must be consecutive, and it must continue right up to the time one of the spouses brings the divorce action on the ground of living apart. Hence, if the parties reconcile and resume cohabitation, even if only temporarily, the period of separation will not be considered consecutive. If, following cohabitation, the parties separate again, the requisite consecutiveness of the period of living apart will be calculated as of the time when the most recent cohabitation ended.

CONSENT   Several states require that the period of separation be consensual or voluntary on the part of *both* spouses. Thus, if one spouse is drafted into the service or is hospitalized for an extended period of time, the separation is surely not by consent.

Sometimes the *cause* of the separation may be relevant to its voluntariness. Suppose, for example, that Bob deserts his wife Linda and they live apart for a period in excess of that required by the statute. Arguably, the parties did not separate voluntarily; they separated as a result of the *fault* of Bob. Some states will deny the divorce on the ground of living apart because the separation was not voluntary. Others will deny the divorce on this ground only when the plaintiff seeking the divorce is the "guilty" party. Most states, however, will grant the divorce to either party on the basis that voluntariness and marital fault are irrelevant so long as there was a living apart for the requisite period of time.

■■■■ Interviewing and Investigation Checklist

Divorce on the Ground of Living Apart

Legal Interviewing Questions

1. How long have you lived apart?

2. On what date did you separate?   —*Continued*

—*Continued*

3. Since that date, what contact have you had with D (defendant)?

4. Have you ever asked D to live with you again? Has D ever asked you?

5. Have you had sexual intercourse with D since you separated?

6. Describe the circumstances of your separation with D.

7. When you separated, did you intend a permanent separation? If so, what indications of this did you give?

8. Did D intend a permanent separation? If so, what indications did D give?

9. What was the condition of your marriage at the time of separation?

10. Did you leave D? Did D leave you? Did you both leave at the same time by mutual agreement?

11. When the separation occurred, did either of you protest? Were you or D dissatisfied with the separation?

12. Since you separated, have either of you asked or suggested that the two of you get back together again? If so, what was the response of the other?

13. Have either of you obtained a judicial separation or a decree of separate maintenance? If so, when? Have you been living separate since that time? Have both of you abided by the terms of the judicial separation or of the maintenance decree?

14. Are you now living separate from D?

15. Since you separated, at what address have you lived? (Same question about D.)

16. Do you and D have a separation agreement?

Possible Investigation Tasks

☐ Collect evidence that the parties have lived separate and apart, e.g., rent receipts from the apartments of the client and of D, copies of separate utility bills.

☐ Obtain witness statements from people aware of the separation.

ASSIGNMENT 13.2

Assume that a statute provides that one of the grounds for divorce is voluntary separation for a period of two consecutive years. This living-apart ground is the only one authorized in the state. Could a divorce be granted on the ground of living apart in the following three situations? (See General Instructions for the Legal-Analysis Assignment in chapter 1.)

a. Fred and Gail are married. On June 10, 1985, they agree to separate. Fred moves out. On May 15, 1987, when he learns that she is thinking about filing for divorce, he calls Gail and pleads with her to let him come back. She refuses. On July 25, 1987, she files for divorce on the ground of living apart.

b. Tom and Diane are married. On November 1, 1985, Diane deserts Tom. Tom did not want her to go. On March 13, 1986, Tom meets Karen. They begin seeing each other regularly. On June 14, 1986, Tom tells Karen that he hopes he never sees Diane again. On December 28, 1987, Tom files for divorce on the ground of living apart.

c. Bill and Susan are married. For over three years they have been living separate lives due to marital difficulties, although they have continued to live in the same house. They have separate bedrooms and rarely have anything to do with each other. One of them files an action for divorce on the ground of living apart.

ASSIGNMENT 13.3

a. In your answer to Assignment 13.1, you made a list of the grounds for divorce in your state. If one of the grounds for divorce in your state is living apart, determine whether the divorce actions sought above in Assignment 13.2(a), (b), and (c) would be granted in your state. (See the General Instructions for the Legal-Analysis Assignment in chapter 1.) Try to find opinions written by courts in your state that have interpreted the law governing the same facts, or facts similar to those involving Fred and Gail, Tom and Diane, Bill and Susan. (See General Instructions for the State Code Assignment and the General Instructions for the Court-Opinion Assignment in chapter 1.)

b. Pick one of the three fact situations involved in Assignment 13.2(a), (b), or (c). Draft a complaint for the party seeking the divorce. (See General Instructions for the Complaint-Drafting Assignment in chapter 1.)

As we shall see, many states allow parties to seek a *judicial separation*, which is a court authorization that the parties can live separate lives under specified terms, e.g., alimony, custody order. In some states, this judicial separation can be *converted* into a divorce after a designated period of time. Similarly, a decree of *separate maintenance* can often be converted into a divorce after this period of time.

☐ Note on Enoch Arden

Enoch Arden Defense
The presumption that a spouse is dead after being missing for a designated number of years.

When a spouse has disappeared for a certain period of time, the **Enoch Arden defense** presumes that the missing spouse is dead, and in some states, this enables the spouse left behind to remarry without being charged with bigamy or having the second marriage annulled if the missing spouse returns after the statutory period (see chapter 9).

■■■ Summary of Ground for Divorce: Living Apart

Definition: Living separate and apart for a designated, consecutive period of time. (In some states, the separation must be mutual and voluntary.)

Who can sue: In most states, either party. In a few states, the party at fault cannot bring the divorce action, i.e., the party who wrongfully caused the separation.

Major defenses:

1. The parties have never separated.

2. The parties have not been separated for the period designated in the statute.

3. The parties reconciled and cohabitated before the statutory period was over, i.e., the separation was not consecutive.

4. The separation was not voluntary (this defense is available in only a few states).

5. The agreement to separate was obtained by fraud or duress.

6. The court lacks jurisdiction (see chapter 14).

7. Res judicata (see chapter 14).

8. Statute of limitations or laches.

Is this also a ground for annulment? No.

Is this also a ground for judicial separation? Yes, in many states.

Is this also a ground for separate maintenance? Yes, in many states.

INCOMPATIBILITY

Incompatibility Such discord exists between the spouses that it is impossible for them to live together in a normal marital relationship.

Some states list **incompatibility** as a ground for divorce. Courts often say that "petty quarrels" and "minor bickerings" are not enough to grant the divorce on this ground. There must be such rift or discord that it is impossible to live together in a normal marital relationship. For most of the states that have this ground, fault is not an issue; the plaintiff does not have to show that the defendant was at fault in causing the incompatibility, and the defendant cannot defend the action by introducing evidence that the plaintiff committed marital wrongs. In a few states, however, the courts *are* concerned about the fault of the defendant and the plaintiff.

Suppose that the plaintiff alleges that the parties are incompatible. Can the defendant defend by disagreeing? Do *both* husband and wife have to feel that it is impossible to live together? Assuming that the plaintiff is able to establish that more than "petty quarrels" are involved, most courts will grant the divorce to the plaintiff even though the defendant insists that they can still work it out. Each state's statute, however, must be carefully examined to determine whether this is a proper interpretation.

The ground of incompatibility and the ground of cruelty appear to be rather similar. Even though cruelty is a fault ground while incompatibility is not, the same or similar kind of evidence is used to establish both grounds. The major difference in most states is that for cruelty, unlike incompatibility, the plaintiff must show that the acts of the defendant endangered the plaintiff's physical health.

■■■■ Interviewing and Investigation Checklist

Divorce on the Ground of Incompatibility

(This checklist is also relevant to the breakdown ground, discussed next.)

Legal Interviewing Questions

1. Are you and D (defendant) now living together? If not, how long have you been separated?

2. Have you ever sued D or been sued by D for separate maintenance or for a judicial separation? If so, what was the result?

3. Describe your relationship with D at its worst.

4. How often did you argue? Were the arguments intense or bitter? Explain.

5. Did you or D ever call the police?

6. Did you or D receive medical attention as a result of your arguments or fights?

7. Did you or D have a drinking or drug problem?

8. How did D act toward the children? What is your relationship with them?

9. Have you and D had any sexual problems?

10. Do you feel that there is any possibility that you and D could reconcile your differences?

11. Do you think D feels that the two of you can solve your problems?

12. Have you or D ever sought counseling or therapy of any kind?

13. Are you now interested in any such help in order to try to save the marriage? Do you feel it would work? How do you think D feels about this?

Possible Investigation Tasks

☐ Obtain copy of judicial separation judgment, separate maintenance decree, police reports, hospital records, if any.

---

a. Is incompatibility a ground for divorce in your state? If so, what is the exact language of this ground in the statute? (See General Instructions for the State-Code Assignment in chapter 1.)

b. One married partner says to the other, "I no longer love you." By definition, are they incompatible for purposes of this ground for divorce? (See General Instructions for the Legal-Analysis Assignment in chapter 1.)

ASSIGNMENT 13.4

■■■■ Summary of Ground for Divorce: Incompatibility

Definition: The impossibility of two parties being able to continue to live together in a normal marital relationship because of severe conflicts or personality differences.

Who can sue: Either party in most states.

Major defenses:

1. The differences between the parties are only minor.

2. The defendant was not at fault in causing the incompatibility (this defense is *not* available in most states).

3. The court lacks jurisdiction.

4. Res judicata.

5. Statute of limitations or laches.

Is this also a ground for annulment? No.

Is this also a ground for judicial separation? Yes, in many states.

Is this also a ground for separate maintenance? Yes, in many states.

IRRECONCILABLE DIFFERENCES, IRREMEDIABLE BREAKDOWN

Irreconcilable Differences Such discord exists between the spouses that the marriage has undergone an irremediable breakdown.

The newest and most popular version of the no-fault ground for divorce adopted in many states provides that the marriage can be dissolved for **irreconcilable differences** that have caused the *irremediable breakdown* of the marriage. The goal of the legislatures that have enacted this ground has been to focus on the central question of whether it makes any sense to continue the marriage.[1] The statutes often have similar language and content. For example:

☐ Discord or conflict of personalities that destroys the legitimate ends of marriage and prevents any reasonable expectation of reconciliation

☐ Irretrievable breakdown of the marriage

☐ Breakdown of marriage to such an extent that the legitimate objects of marriage have been destroyed and there remains no reasonable likelihood that the marriage can be preserved

☐ Substantial reasons for not continuing the marriage

This ground for divorce is obviously quite similar to the incompatibility ground just considered.

What happens if the defendant denies that the breakdown of the marriage is irremediable and feels that marriage counseling would help? In most states, this is simply one item of evidence that the court must consider in deciding whether remediation is possible. It is likely, however, that if one party absolutely refuses to participate in any reconciliation efforts, the court will conclude that the breakdown of the marriage is total even if the other party expresses a conciliatory attitude. Again, the language of individual statutes would have to be examined on this issue.

■■■ Interviewing and Investigation Checklist

Divorce on the Ground of Irremediable Breakdown

Legal Interviewing Questions

1. How long have you been married to D (defendant)? How many children do you have?

2. How does D get along with the children?

3. How often do you and D communicate meaningfully?

4. Does D insult you, ridicule your religion, your political views, your family?

5. Does D do this in front of anyone? Who else knows that D does this? How do they know?

6. Has D ever ridiculed or criticized you to your friends, relatives, or other associates?

7. Do you think that D has ever tried to turn the children against you? If so, how do you know? What specifically have the children or others said or done to make you think so?

8. Does D drink or use drugs? If so, how much, how often, and how has it affected your marriage?

—Continued

---

1. One court phrased the test as follows: "The new statutory test for determining if a marriage is irretrievably broken is simply whether for whatever reason or cause (no matter whose 'fault') the marriage relationship is for all intents and purposes ended, no longer viable, a hollow sham beyond hope of reconciliation or repair." *Ryan v. Ryan,* 277 So. 2d 266, 271 (Fla. 1977).

—*Continued*

9. Has D ever hit you? If so, describe the circumstances. How often has D done this? Did the children see it? Has anyone else ever seen it?

10. Were there any other major events or scenes that were unpleasant for you? If so, describe them.

11. How would you describe your sexual relationship with D? Has D ever refused your request for sex? Has D ever made any unreasonable sexual demands on you?

12. Has D ever accused you of infidelity?

13. Does D stay away from home often? Does D ever not come home at night?

14. Have you ever had to call the police because of what D did?

15. Has D ever sued you, or have you ever sued D?

16. How often do you fight or argue with D?

17. Is D now living with you? If not, explain the circumstances of the separation.

18. Has D's behavior affected your health in any way? Have you had to see a doctor?

19. Have you seen or have you considered seeing a psychiatrist or some other person in the field of mental health?

20. Have you ever experienced any behavior like this before?

21. How was your health before D started behaving this way?

22. Do you have any difficulty sleeping?

23. Do you have any difficulty doing your regular work because of D?

24. What is D's opinion of you as a spouse?

25. Do you think that you will ever be able to live in harmony with D? Explain why or why not.

26. Does D think the two of you will ever be able to get back together again? Explain why or why not.

Possible Investigation Tasks

☐ Obtain all of C's (client's) medical records, if any, from doctors, hospitals, etc., that have treated her as a result of what D has done.

☐ If the children are old and mature enough, interview them to see how they viewed D's relationship with C and, specifically, how D treated them.

☐ Obtain police records, if any, resulting from any fights or disturbances.

---

a. Is irreconcilable differences or irremediable breakdown a ground for divorce in your state? If so, what is the exact language of this ground in the statute? (See General Instructions for the State-Code Assignment in chapter 1.)

b. Dan and Helen were married in your state. Helen does not want to be married anymore. She loves Dan and enjoys being his wife, but simply wants to live alone indefinitely. Dan does not want a divorce. Can she obtain a divorce in your state? (See General Instructions for the State-Code Assignment and the Court-Opinion Assignment in chapter 1.)

ASSIGNMENT 13.5

■■■ Summary of Ground for Divorce: Irreconcilable Differences, Irremediable Breakdown

Definition: The breakdown of the marriage to the point where the conflicts between the spouses are beyond any reasonable hope of reconciliation.

Who can sue: Either party.

Major defenses:

1. The breakdown is remediable.

2. The court lacks jurisdiction.

3. Res judicata.

4. Statute of limitations or laches.

Is this also a ground for annulment? No.

Is this also a ground for judicial separation? Yes, in many states.

Is this also a ground for separate maintenance? Yes, in many states.

Adultery Voluntary sexual intercourse between a married person and someone to whom he or she is not married.

Co-respondent The person who allegedly had voluntary sexual intercourse with a spouse charged with adultery.

Corroboration Additional evidence of a point beyond that offered by the person asserting the point.

Fornication Sexual intercourse between unmarried persons.

Illicit Cohabitation Fornication between two persons who live together.

Criminal Conversation A tort committed by a person who has sexual relations with the plaintiff's spouse.

▆▆▆ FAULT GROUNDS FOR DIVORCE

Although fault grounds are less often considered in today's courts, they remain in force. They include:

☐ Adultery   ☐ Desertion
☐ Cruelty   ☐ Others

ADULTERY

Adultery is voluntary sexual intercourse between a married person and someone to whom he or she is not married. This person is called the **co-respondent.** The intercourse is not voluntary, of course, if the defendant is raped or if the defendant is insane at the time. Since direct evidence of adultery is seldom available, circumstantial evidence must be relied upon. Specifically, the plaintiff must prove that the defendant had the *opportunity* and the *inclination* to commit adultery. **Corroboration** is often required to support the plaintiff's testimony.

☐ Notes on Sexual Relations as a Crime and as a Tort

1. In most states adultery (as defined above), fornication, and illicit cohabitation are crimes. **Fornication** is sexual intercourse between unmarried persons. **Illicit cohabitation** is fornication between two individuals who live together. It is rare, however, for the state to prosecute anyone for these crimes.

2. Criminal conversation is a tort brought against a third party who has had sexual intercourse (adultery) with the plaintiff's spouse (see chapter 21).

ASSIGNMENT 13.6

Is adultery, fornication, or illicit cohabitation a crime in your state? If so, what are their elements? (See General Instructions for the State-Code Assignment in chapter 1.)

Cruelty The infliction of serious physical or mental suffering on another.

CRUELTY

In most marriage ceremonies, the parties take each other "for better or worse." This concept was viewed quite literally early in our history, particularly when the woman was the one claiming to have received too much of the "worse." It was expected that a good deal of fighting, nagging, and mutual abuse would occur within the institution of marriage. The concept of permitting the marriage to be dissolved because of "mere" cruelty or indignities was alien to our legal system for a long time. The change in the law came slowly. When **cruelty** was allowed as a ground for divorce, the statute would often require that it be "extreme" or "inhuman" before the divorce could be granted. Furthermore, some states limited the ground to actual or threatened *physical* violence. Later, *mental anguish* came to be recognized as a form of cruelty and indignity, but there was often a requirement that the psychological cruelty must result in some impairment of the plaintiff's health. Some courts will accept a minimal health impairment, e.g., a loss of sleep. Other courts require more serious impairment. Whether a court will accept a minimum impairment or will require something close to hospitalization, most courts have insisted on at least some physical effect from the cruelty. Only a few states will authorize a divorce on the ground of cruelty or indignity where the mental suffering does not produce physical symptoms.

DESERTION

Desertion (also called *abandonment*) occurs when (1) one spouse voluntarily leaves another, (2) for an uninterrupted statutory period of time, e.g., two years, (3) with the intent not to return to resume cohabitation, and when (4) the separation occurred without the consent of the other spouse and (5) there was no justification or reasonable cause for the separation. **Constructive desertion** exists when the conduct of the spouse who stayed home justified the other spouse's departure, or when the spouse who stayed home refuses a sincere offer of reconciliation (within the statutory period) from the other spouse who initially left without justification. In effect, the spouse who stayed home becomes the deserter! The spouse who left would be allowed to sue the other spouse for divorce on the ground of desertion.

OTHERS

A number of closely related and sometimes overlapping grounds exist in some states. Here is a partial list (some of which are also grounds for annulment):

- Bigamy
- Impotence
- Nonage
- Fraud
- Duress
- Incest
- Imprisonment for three consecutive years
- Conviction of a serious crime
- Insanity; mental incapacity for three years
- Habitual drunkenness
- Drug addiction
- Nonsupport
- Unexplained absence
- Neglect of duty
- Obtaining an out-of-state divorce that is invalid
- Venereal disease or AIDS
- Unchastity
- Pregnancy by someone else at the time of the marriage
- Treatment injurious to health
- Deviate sexual conduct
- Any other cause deemed by the court sufficient, if satisfied that the parties can no longer live together

■■■ DEFENSES TO THE FAULT GROUNDS FOR DIVORCE

The basic defenses to the fault grounds for divorce may be defined as follows:

- **Collusion**
Parties to a divorce committed fraud on the court by agreeing on a story to be told to the court by one or both parties even though both know the story is untrue.

- **Connivance**
There was a willingness or a consent by one spouse that the marital wrong be done by the other spouse.

- **Condonation**
There was an express or implied forgiveness by the innocent spouse of the marital fault committed by the other spouse.

□ **Recrimination**

The party seeking the divorce (the plaintiff) has also committed a serious marital wrong.

□ **Provocation**

The plaintiff incited the acts constituting the marital wrong by the other spouse.

These defenses are rarely used today, however, since the fault grounds are themselves seldom used.

□ **Note on Religious Divorces**

> When a man hath taken a wife, and married her, and it come to pass that she find no favor in his eyes, because he hath found some uncleanliness in her: then let him write her a bill of divorcement, and give it in her hand, and send her out of his house. Deuteronomy 24:1, (KJV)

A Jewish couple that wants a religious divorce can go to a special court called a *Beth Din* presided over by a rabbi who is aided by scribes and authorized witnesses. There the husband delivers a **get,** or bill of divorcement, to his wife. Fault does not have to be shown. Both the husband and wife must consent to the divorce, but it is the husband who gives the get, and the wife who receives it. In New York, a religious divorce is allowed only if a secular (i.e., civil) divorce or annulment is underway or has already been granted. If a Jewish man has a civil divorce but not a religious divorce, he can still be remarried by a rabbi. But a Jewish woman without a get—even if divorced in a civil court—is called an *agunah,* or abandoned wife, and cannot be remarried by a rabbi. Markoff, *How Couples "Get" a Religious Divorce,* 8 National Law J. (August 15, 1988).

A Moslem divorce is traditionally performed by a husband pronouncing the word **Talak** (I divorce you) three times. The wife need not be present. In some countries, however, the process is more public. In Pakistan, for example, the husband must notify the chairman of an arbitration council that he has pronounced the *Talak.* The council will then attempt to reconcile the parties. If this fails, the divorce becomes absolute 90 days after the husband pronounced the *Talak.* In Egypt, the husband must pronounce the *Talak* in the presence of two witnesses who are usually officers of a special court. *The Religious Effect of Religious Divorces,* 37 Modern Law Review, 611–613 (1974).

■■■■ JUDICIAL SEPARATION

Judicial Separation A declaration by a court that parties can live separate and apart even though they are still married to each other.

A **judicial separation** is a decree by a court that two people can live separately—from bed and board—while still remaining husband and wife. The decree also establishes the rights and obligations of the parties while they are separated. A judicial separation is also known as a:

□ Legal separation   □ Separation from bed and board

□ Limited divorce   □ Divorce from bed and board

□ Divorce a mensa et thoro

Parties subject to a judicial separation are not free to remarry. The marriage relationship remains until it is dissolved by the death of one of the parties, by annulment, or by an absolute divorce, or a *divorce a vinculo matrimonii,* as the "full" divorce is called.[2]

Perhaps the main function of a judicial separation is to secure support from the other spouse. In this sense, an action for judicial separation is very similar

---

2. In some community property states (see page 227), the "community estate" is dissolved by a separation from bed and board. See Internal Revenue Service, *Community Property and the Federal Income Tax,* p. 2 (1988 Edition).

to an action for separate maintenance, to be discussed in the next section. For religious or family reasons, the parties may not wish to end the marriage by obtaining a divorce. If support is needed, a judicial separation is an alternative in many states.

We should distinguish a judicial separation from a *separation agreement.* The latter is a private contract between a husband and wife. The agreement may or may not become part of (i.e., be incorporated and merged in) the judicial separation decree or the absolute divorce decree if one is later sought. Also, it is important that the word "separated" or "separation" be used carefully. Alone, these words mean simply a *physical* separation between the husband and wife. If, however, a court-sanctioned or court-ordered separation is involved, then the reference should be to a *legal* or *judicial* separation.

To obtain a judicial separation, *grounds* must be established in the same manner as grounds must be established to obtain an absolute divorce. In fact, the grounds for judicial separation are often very similar if not identical to the grounds for an absolute divorce, e.g., no-fault grounds such as incompatibility or irretrievable breakdown, and fault grounds such as adultery or cruelty.

ASSIGNMENT 13.7

a. Does your state have an action for a judicial separation?

b. If so, what is the action called?

c. What is the citation of the statute authorizing this action?

d. What are the grounds in your state for a judicial separation?

e. Are there any grounds for judicial separation that are *not* grounds for divorce?

f. What defenses exist for an action for judicial separation?

(See General Instructions for the State-Code Assignment and General Instructions for the Court-Opinion Assignment in chapter 1.)

In a judicial separation decree, the court can award alimony and can issue custody and child support orders, all of which are enforceable through traditional execution and contempt remedies. If the parties have drafted a separation agreement, the court will consider incorporating and merging the terms of this agreement into the judicial separation decree. The separation agreement, of course, will reflect the wishes of the parties on the critical issues of alimony, property division, child custody, and child support.

After a judicial separation decree has been rendered, the fact that the parties reconcile and resume cohabitation does not mean that the decree becomes inoperative. It remains effective until a court declares otherwise. Hence, a husband who is under an order to pay alimony to his wife pursuant to a judicial separation decree must continue to pay alimony even though the parties have subsequently reconciled and are living together again. To be relieved of this obligation, a petition must be made to the court to change the decree.

The major consequence of a judicial separation decree in many states is its *conversion* feature. The decree can be converted into a divorce—an absolute divorce. In effect, the existence of the judicial separation decree for a designated period of time can become a ground for a divorce.

Prepare a flowchart of the procedural steps that are necessary for a judicial separation in your state. (See General Instructions for the Flowchart Assignment in chapter 1.)

ASSIGNMENT 13.8

■■■■ SEPARATE MAINTENANCE

Separate Maintenance
Court-ordered spousal support while the spouses are separated.

An action for **separate maintenance** (sometimes called an action for *support*) is a proceeding brought by a spouse to secure support. The action is usually filed by wives, but an increasing number of husbands are seeking spousal support by this route. Like the judicial separation decree, a separate maintenance decree does not alter the marital status of the parties; they remain married to each other while living separately. To the extent that both decrees resolve the problem of support, there is very little practical difference between them.

Since the main objective of the separate maintenance action is to reach the property (e.g., cash, land) of the defendant for purposes of support, the court must have personal jurisdiction over the defendant (see chapter 12).

The major ground for a separate maintenance decree is the refusal of one spouse to support the other without just cause. In addition, most states provide that all of the grounds for divorce will also be grounds for a separate maintenance award. Furthermore, in a divorce action, if the court refuses to grant either party a divorce, it usually can still enter an order for separate maintenance.

If the plaintiff refuses a good faith offer by the defendant to reconcile, the plaintiff becomes a wrongdoer, which may justify the defendant in refusing to provide support. If the separate maintenance action is still pending, the plaintiff will lose it. If a separate maintenance decree has already been awarded, the defendant may be able to discontinue making payments under it.

The court determines the amount and form of a separate maintenance award in the same way that it makes the alimony determination in a divorce (see chapter 10). If needed, the court can also make child support and child custody decisions in the separate maintenance action.

Separate maintenance decrees can be enforced in the same manner as alimony awards in divorce decrees, e.g., contempt, execution (see chapters 10, 12, 14).

ASSIGNMENT 13.9

a. Does your state have an action for separate maintenance or its equivalent? If so, on what grounds will the action be granted?

b. Prepare a flowchart of all the procedural steps required in a proceeding for separate maintenance or its equivalent.

(See General Instructions for the State-Code Assignment, for the Court-Opinion Assignment, and for the Flowchart Assignment in chapter 1).

■■■■ SUMMARY

The three major court proceedings that can be used when a marriage is in deep trouble are divorce, judicial separation, and separate maintenance. Grounds must exist before parties can use any of these three actions.

There are three major no-fault grounds for divorce: living apart, incompatibility, and irreconcilable differences that cause the irremediable breakdown of the marriage. The major fault grounds for divorce are adultery, cruelty, and desertion. Fault grounds, and the defenses to them, are less commonly used today.

Actions for judicial separation and separate maintenance are primarily designed to secure spousal support in a marriage that will continue to exist, at least for the time being.

■■■■ KEY CHAPTER TERMINOLOGY

Grounds	Uncontested	Migratory Divorce
No-Fault Grounds	Collusion	Dissolution

Living Apart
Enoch Arden Defense
Incompatibility
Irreconcilable Differences
Adultery
Co-respondent
Corroboration

Fornication
Illicit Cohabitation
Criminal Conversation
Cruelty
Desertion
Constructive Desertion
Connivance

Condonation
Recrimination
Provocation
Get
Talak
Judicial Separation
Separate Maintenance

14 DIVORCE PROCEDURE

KINDS OF DIVORCE

Uncontested Not disputed; not challenged.

Over 90 percent of divorce cases are **uncontested** since the parties are in agreement on the termination of the marital relationship, alimony, property division, child custody, and child support. In such cases, divorce procedure is often relatively simple. If, however, the bitterness of the past has not subsided and agreements have not been reached, the technicalities of procedure can occupy center stage in costly and complicated proceedings.

The following terms are often used in connection with divorce procedure:

☐ **Migratory Divorce** A divorce obtained in a state to which one or both spouses traveled before returning to their original state. The husband and/or wife travels (migrates) to another state in order to obtain a divorce—usually because it is procedurally easier to divorce there. He or she establishes domicile in the state, obtains the divorce, and then returns to the "home" state, where at some point there will be an attempt to enforce the "foreign" divorce judgment. If the domicile was valid, this divorce is entitled to full faith and credit (i.e., it must be enforced) by the home state or any other state.

☐ **Foreign Divorce** A divorce decree obtained in a state other than the state where an attempt is made to enforce that decree. For example, a divorce decree that is granted in Iowa or in France would be a foreign divorce when an attempt is made to enforce it in New York.

☐ **"Quickie" Divorce** A migratory divorce obtained in what is often called a *divorce mill* state, i.e., a state where the procedural requirements for divorce are very slight in order to encourage out-of-state citizens to come in for a divorce and, while there, to spend some tourist dollars.

☐ **Collusive Divorce** A divorce that results from an agreement or "conspiracy" between a husband and wife to commit fraud on the court by falsely letting it appear that they qualify procedurally or substantively for a divorce.

☐ **Default Divorce** A divorce granted to the plaintiff because the defendant failed to appear to answer the complaint of the plaintiff. (In most states, the divorce is not granted automatically; the plaintiff must still establish grounds for the divorce.)

☐ **Divisible Divorce** A divorce decree does two things: (1) dissolves the marital relationship, and (2) resolves the questions of alimony, property division, child custody, and child support. The divorce decree is thus *divisible*, or "dividable" into these two objectives. A *divisible divorce* is a divorce decree granted in one state but enforceable in another state only as to the dissolution of the marriage, not as to support, property division, etc. The other state does not have to give full faith and credit to other parts of the divorce decree. The divorce is divisible because only part of it must be recognized in another state.

☐ **Bilateral Divorce** A divorce granted by a court when both parties were present before the court.

☐ **Ex Parte Divorce** A divorce granted by a court when only one party (the plaintiff) was present before the court. The court did not have personal jurisdiction over the defendant.

☐ **Dual Divorce** A divorce granted to both husband and wife. A court might award the divorce decree to one party only—to the plaintiff or to the defendant, if the latter has filed a counterclaim for divorce against the plaintiff. A dual divorce, however, is granted to *both* parties.

☐ **Uncontested Divorce** A divorce granted to parties who had no disagreements. The defendant does not appear at the divorce proceeding (see *default divorce* above) or appears without disputing any of the plaintiff's claims.

☐ **Contested Divorce** A divorce granted after the defendant appeared and disputed some or all of the claims made by the plaintiff at the divorce proceeding.

☐ **Divorce a Mensa et Thoro** A *judicial separation* (see chapter 13); a *limited divorce*. The parties are not free to remarry since they are still married after receiving this kind of "divorce."

☐ **Limited Divorce** A *judicial separation;* a *divorce a mensa et thoro.*

☐ **Divorce a Vinculo Matrimonii** An *absolute divorce.* The parties are no longer married. They are free to remarry.

One of our objectives in this chapter is to have you prepare a flowchart of divorce procedure for your state. There will be a number of individual assignments to be answered mainly by reference to the state code and court rules of your state and, to a lesser degree, by reference to court opinions of your state. The answers to these assignments on pieces of the procedural picture will also be used to complete divorce flowchart Assignment 14.22 at the end of this chapter.

▰▰▰▰ DOMICILE

The word *domicile* is often confused with the word *residence*. Many divorce statutes use the word *residence* even though the meaning intended is *domicile*. Except for such oddities, there are distinct differences between the two words:

☐ **Residence** The place where someone is living at a particular time. A person can have many residences, e.g., a home in the city, plus a beach house, plus an apartment in another state or country.

□ **Domicile**   The place (1) where someone has physically been (2) with the intention to make that place his or her permanent home, or with no intention to make any other place a permanent home. It is the place to which one would intend to return when away. With rare exceptions, a person can have only one domicile.

It is important to be able to determine where one's domicile is, particularly in our mobile society. Here are two specific reasons why:

□ In most states, a court does not have divorce jurisdiction to dissolve a marriage unless one or both spouses are domiciled in the state where that court sits.

□ Liability for inheritance taxes may depend upon the domicile of the decedent at the time of death.

Emancipated   Legally independent of one's parent or legal guardian.

Operation of Law   A result occurs by operation of law when it happens because the law mandates the result, not because a party agrees to produce the result.

Domicile by Choice   A domicile chosen by a person with the capacity to choose.

Generally, children cannot acquire a domicile of their own until they reach majority (e.g., eighteen years of age) or become otherwise **emancipated.** In effect, a child acquires a domicile by **operation of law** rather than by choice. The law operates to impose a domicile on the child regardless of what the child may want (if the child is old enough to form any opinion at all). The domicile of a child is the domicile of its parents. If they are separated, the child's domicile is that of the parent who has legal custody.

An emancipated child and an adult can pick any domicile they want **(domicile by choice)** so long as they are physically present in a place (even if only momentarily) and have the intention to make it their permanent home at the time of their presence there. This intention can sometimes be very difficult to prove. Intention is a state of mind, and the only way to determine a state of mind is by interpreting external acts.

A person's verbal statements are not necessarily conclusive evidence of his or her state of mind of the person making those statements. Suppose, for example, that Bill is domiciled in Ohio and, while visiting California, becomes violently ill. He knows that if he dies domiciled in California, his beneficiaries will pay a lower inheritance tax than if he had died domiciled in Ohio. While lying in a California sick bed just before he dies, Bill openly says, "I hereby declare that I intend California to be my permanent home." This statement in itself fails to prove that Bill was domiciled in California at the time of his death. Other evidence may show that he made the statement simply to give the appearance of changing his domicile and that, if he had regained his health, he would have returned to Ohio. If this is so, then his domicile at death is Ohio in spite of his declaration, since he never actually intended to make California his permanent home.

The following chart seeks to identify some of the factors courts will consider in determining whether the requisite state of mind on intention existed.

■■■ Interviewing and Investigation Checklist

How to Determine When a Person Has Established a Domicile

Legal Interviewing Questions

1. When did you come to the state?
2. How often have you been in the state in the past? (Describe the details of your contacts with the state.)

3. Why did you come to the state?
4. Was your intention to stay there for a short period of time? A long period of time? Indefinitely? Forever?
5. While you were in the state, did you also have homes elsewhere in the state, and/or in another state,

—Continued

—*Continued*

and/or in another country? If so, give details, e.g., addresses, how long you spent at each home, etc.

6. Where do you consider your permanent home to be?

7. Have you ever changed your permanent home in the past? (If so, give details.)

8. Do you own a home in the state? Do you rent a home or apartment? How long have you had the home or apartment? Do you own any other land?

9. Where are you registered to vote?

10. Did you inform the board of elections in your old state that you moved?

11. Where is your job or business?

12. In what state is your car registered?

13. What state issued your driver's license?

14. In what states do you have bank accounts?

15. In what states do you have club memberships?

16. In what state do you attend church or synogogue?

17. Did you change your will to mention your new state?

18. When you register at hotels, what address do you give?

19. What is your address according to the credit card companies you use?

20. Where do your relatives live?

Possible Investigation Tasks

☐ Interview persons with whom the client may have discussed the move to the state, e.g., relatives, neighbors, business associates.

☐ Obtain copies of records that would indicate the extent of contact with the state, e.g., state tax returns, bank statements, land ownership papers, leases, hotel receipts, voting records, library cards.

In some states—Florida, for example—it is possible to make a formal declaration, or affidavit, of domicile that is filed with an official government body (Exhibit 14.1).

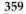

ASSIGNMENT 14.1

a. For purposes of obtaining a divorce, how is domicile determined in your state? (See General Instructions for the State-Code Assignment and General Instructions for the Court-Opinion Assignment in chapter 1.)

b. Using the index volume(s) of your state code, find as many references as you can to *domicile* (up to a maximum of ten). Briefly state the context in which the word is used in each of the statutes to which you were referred by the index.

ASSIGNMENT 14.2

Try to find an individual (e.g., relative, friend, classmate) who now lives, or who in the past lived, in more than one state at the same time, e.g., for business purposes, for school purposes, for vacation purposes, etc. Interview this individual with the objective of determining where his or her domicile is (or was). List all the facts that would tend to show that the person's domicile was in one state, and then list all the facts that would tend to show that his or her domicile was in another state.

ASSIGNMENT 14.3

In each of the following situations, determine in what state the person was domiciled at the time of death. (See General Instructions for the Legal-Analysis Assignment in chapter 1.)

a. While living in Illinois, Fred hears about a high-paying job in Alaska. He decides to move to Alaska, since he is tired of Illinois. He sells everything he owns in Illinois and rents an apartment in Alaska. There he discovers jobs are not easy to find. He decides to leave if he cannot find a job in three months. If this happens, he arranges to move in with his sister in New Mexico. Before the three months are over, Fred dies jobless in Alaska.

b. Gloria lives in New York because she attends New York University. Her husband lives in Montana. Gloria plans to rejoin her husband in Montana when she finishes school in six months. Two months before graduation, her husband decides to move to Oregon. Gloria is opposed to the move and tells him that she will not rejoin him if he does not return to Montana. Her husband refuses to move back to Montana. One month before graduation, Gloria dies in New York.

▮▮▮▮ JURISDICTION

Before discussing the nature of jurisdiction, some definitions that apply to this area of the law must be examined:

☐ **Adversarial Hearing** Both the plaintiff and the defendant appear at the hearing or other court proceeding to contest all the issues.

☐ **Ex Parte Hearing** Only one party appears at the hearing or other court proceeding; the defendant is not present.

☐ **Direct Attack vs. Collateral Attack** Two kinds of challenges or attacks can be made on a judgment: direct and collateral. The difference depends on when the attack is made and on what kind of court proceeding the challenge is raised in. Assume, for example, that Mary goes to a state trial court to sue Ed for child support. He does not

☐ **EXHIBIT 14.1** **Florida Declaration of Domicile**

DECLARATION OF DOMICILE

TO THE STATE OF FLORIDA AND COUNTY OF _____ :

This is my Declaration of Domicile in the State of Florida that I am filing this day in accordance, and in conformity with Section 222.17, Florida Statutes.

I, _____ , was formerly a legal resident of

_____ , and I resided at _____
　　　　　City　　　　　　　　　　State　　　　　　　　　　　　　　　　　Street and Number

_____ ,

however, I have changed my domicile to and am and have been a bona fide resident of the State of Florida since the _____ day of _____ , 19 _____ . I now reside at
_____ _____ , _____ County, Florida, and this statement is to be taken as my declaration of actual legal residence and permanent domicile in this State and County to the exclusion of all others, and I will comply with all requirements of legal residents of Florida.

I understand that as a legal resident of Florida: I am subject to intangible taxes; I must purchase Florida license plates for motor vehicles, if any, owned by me and/or my spouse; I must vote in the precinct of my legal domicile (if I vote), and that my estate will be probated in the Florida Courts.

I was born in the U.S.A.: Yes _____ No _____ Place of Birth: _____

Naturalized citizen—Where: _____ Date _____ No. _____

Permanent Visa: Yes _____ No _____ Date _____ No. _____

Sworn and subscribed before me this _____ day of _____ , A.D. 19 ___ . PAUL F. HARTSFIELD, Clerk of Circuit Court By _____ 　　　　　Deputy Clerk	_____ 　　　　　　Signature _____ 　　　　(Mailing Address) (To be executed and filed with Clerk of Circuit Court)

Penalty for perjury—up to 20 years in state prison—(Section 837.01, Florida Statutes) appear in the action. Mary wins a judgment. But Ed refuses to pay any child support under the judgment. He believes the trial court lacked personal jurisdiction to render its child support judgment against him. If he raises this challenge to the judgment in a normal appeal immediately after the trial court rendered its judgment, he would be bringing a *direct attack* against the judgment. Suppose, however, that the time for bringing a normal appeal has passed. In the same state or in a different state, Mary brings a separate suit against Ed to enforce the child support judgment. In this new suit, Ed says the child support judgment is invalid because the court that rendered it lacked personal jurisdiction over him. This is a *collateral attack* against the judgment. In general, an attack against a judgment is collateral when it is brought in a court proceeding that is outside the normal appeal process.

☐ **Res Judicata** When a judgment on its merits has been rendered, the parties cannot relitigate the same dispute (i.e., the same cause of action); the parties have already had their day in court.

☐ **Estop or Estoppel** Stop or prevent.

☐ **Equitable Estoppel** Equitable estoppel means that a party will be prevented from doing something because it would be unfair to allow him or her to do it. A party will be *equitably estopped* from attacking the validity of a judgment—even a clearly invalid judgment—when:

■ The party obtained the judgment or participated in obtaining it, *or*

■ The party relied on the judgment by accepting benefits based on it, *or*

■ The party caused another person to rely on the judgment to the detriment of the other person.

☐ **Foreign** Another state or country. A foreign divorce decree, for example, is one rendered by a state other than the state where one of the parties is now seeking to enforce the decree.

☐ **Forum State** The state in which the parties are now litigating a case.

☐ **Full Faith and Credit** Under Article IV of the U.S. Constitution, a valid public act of one state must be recognized and enforced by other states. Hence a divorce granted by a state with proper jurisdiction must be recognized by every other state, i.e., it must be given full faith and credit by other states.

☐ **Service of Process** Providing a formal notice to a defendant that orders him or her to appear in court to answer allegations in claims made by a plaintiff. The notice must be delivered in a manner prescribed by law.

☐ **Substituted Service** Service of process other than by handing the process documents to the defendant in person, e.g., service by mail, service by publication in a local newspaper.

The word **jurisdiction** has two main meanings: a *geographic* meaning and a *power* meaning. A specific geographic area of the country is referred to as the jurisdiction. A Nevada state court, for example, will often refer to its entire state as "this jurisdiction." The more significant definition of the word, which we will examine below, relates to power—the power of a court to resolve a particular controversy. If a citizen of Maine wrote to a California court and asked for a divorce through the mail, the California court would be without jurisdiction (without power) to enter a divorce decree if the husband and wife never had any contact with that state. The issue of how a court acquires the power—the jurisdiction—to hear a divorce case can sometimes be a complicated one, as we will see.

Jurisdiction (1) The geographic area over which a particular court has authority. (2) The power of a court to act.

Our study of jursidiction will focus on the different attacks or challenges a party will often try to assert against the jurisdiction of a divorce court. In particular, we will examine the following themes:

☐ Kinds of jurisdiction

☐ What part of the divorce decree is being attacked

☐ Who is attacking the divorce decree

☐ In what court the divorce decree is being attacked

☐ How jurisdiction is acquired

To a very large extent, the success of a jurisdictional attack on a divorce decree depends on the kind of jurisdiction involved, the part of the divorce decree being attacked, the identity of the person bringing the attack, etc. We now turn to a discussion of these critical factors.

KINDS OF JURISDICTION

1. Subject-matter jurisdiction. The power of the court to hear cases of this kind. A criminal law court would not have subject-matter jurisdiction to hear a divorce case. So too, a divorce decree rendered by a court without subject-matter jurisdiction over divorces is void.

Res A thing, object, or status.

2. In rem jurisdiction. The power of the court to make a decision affecting the **res,** which is a thing, object, or status. In divorce actions, the *res* is the marriage status, which is "located" in any state where one or both of the spouses are domiciled. A state with in rem jurisdiction because of this domicile has the power to terminate the marriage. (Another kind of jurisdiction is *personal* jurisdiction over the defendant. If a court does not have personal jurisdiction, it will not have the power to grant alimony, child support, or a property division; it can only dissolve the marriage.) A court lacks in rem jurisdiction if it renders a divorce judgment when neither party was domiciled in that state. Such a judgment is not entitled to full faith and credit (see discussion below); therefore, another state is not required to enforce the divorce.

3. Personal jurisdiction (also called *in personam jurisdiction*). The power of the court over the person of the defendant. If a court has personal jurisdiction over a defendant, it can order him or her to pay alimony and child support and can divide the marital property. If a court makes such an order without personal jurisdiction, the order can be attacked on jurisdictional grounds; it is not entitled to full faith and credit.

Exhibit 14.2 summarizes the kinds of divorce jurisdiction.

PART OF DIVORCE DECREE BEING ATTACKED

A divorce decree usually accomplishes three objectives:

1. *Dissolves the marriage.* For a court to have jurisdiction to dissolve a marriage, one or both of the spouses must be domiciled in the state. When this is so, the court has in rem jurisdiction, which is all that is needed to dissolve the marriage. Personal jurisdiction of both parties is not needed.

2. *Alimony, child support, and property division.* Alimony, child support, and property division cannot be ordered by the court unless it has personal jurisdiction over the defendant. Hence, it is possible for the court to have

☐ **EXHIBIT 14.2   Kinds of Divorce Jurisdiction**

KIND OF JURISDICTION THE COURT CAN ACHIEVE	HOW THIS KIND OF JURISDICTION IS ACQUIRED	POWER THIS KIND OF JURISDICTION GIVES THE COURT
Subject-matter jurisdiction	A state statute or constitutional provision gives the court the power to hear cases involving the subject matter of divorce.	The court can hear divorce cases.
In rem jurisdiction	One or both of the spouses are domiciled in the state.	The court can dissolve the marriage.
Personal jurisdiction	Process is personally delivered to the defendant—service of process. (Alternatives may include substituted service, the long arm statute, etc.)	The court can order the defendant to comply with alimony, child support, or property division obligations.

(The special problems involved in acquiring jurisdiction to render child custody decisions are discussed in chapter 11.)

jurisdiction to dissolve the marriage (because of domicile) but not have jurisdiction to make alimony, child support, and property division awards (because the plaintiff was not able to take the necessary steps, such as service of process, to give the court personal jurisdiction over the defendant). This is the concept of the *divisible divorce*—a divorce that is effective for some purposes but not for others.

3. *Child custody.* On the jurisdictional requirements to make a child custody award, see chapter 11.

PERSON ATTACKING DIVORCE DECREE

1. *The person who obtained the divorce.* A person should not be allowed to attack a divorce decree on jurisdictional grounds if that person was the plaintiff in the action that resulted in the divorce. This person will be estopped in any action to deny the validity of a divorce. The same result will occur if this person helped his or her spouse obtain the divorce or received benefits because of the divorce. (The effect of this rule, sometimes known as *equitable estoppel,* is to prevent a person from attacking a divorce decree that is clearly invalid. Note, however, that a few courts do not follow this rule and *will* allow a person to attack a divorce he or she participated in obtaining earlier.)

2. *The person against whom the divorce was obtained.* If the person now attacking the divorce on jurisdictional grounds was the defendant in the action that led to the divorce and made a personal appearance in that divorce action, he or she will not be allowed to attack the divorce. He or she should have raised the jurisdictional attack in the original divorce action.

If the original divorce was obtained *ex parte* (i.e., no appearance by the defendant), the defendant *will* be able to attack the divorce on jurisdictional grounds, such as the fact that the plaintiff was not domiciled in the state that granted the divorce, or the court that granted the divorce had no subject-matter jurisdiction.

If the person against whom the divorce was obtained has accepted the benefits of the divorce (e.g., alimony payments), many courts will estop that person from now attacking the divorce on jurisdictional grounds.

If the person against whom the divorce was obtained has remarried, he or she will be estopped from claiming that the second marriage is invalid because of jurisdictional defects in the divorce decree on the first marriage. Some states, however, will allow the jurisdictional attack on the divorce if the person making the attack did not know about the jurisdictional defect (e.g., no domicile), at the time.

3. *A person who was not a party to the divorce action.* A second spouse who was not a party to the prior divorce action cannot challenge the validity of that divorce on jurisdictional grounds. This second spouse relied on the validity of that divorce when he or she entered the marriage and should not now be allowed to upset the validity of that marriage by challenging the validity of the divorce.

A child of the parties of the prior divorce action cannot challenge the validity of the divorce on jurisdictional grounds if that child's parent would have been estopped from bringing the challenge.

COURT IN WHICH DIVORCE DECREE IS BEING ATTACKED

Many of the disputes in this area arise when a divorce decree is obtained in one state and brought to another state for enforcement. Is the *forum state* (where enforcement of the divorce decree is being sought) required to give *full faith and credit* to the foreign divorce? The answer may depend on which of the three aspects of the divorce decree a party is attempting to enforce:

1. *The dissolution of the marriage.* If either the plaintiff or the defendant was domiciled in the state where the divorce was granted, every other state must give full faith and credit to the part of the divorce decree that dissolved the marriage. The forum state must decide for itself whether there was a valid domicile in the foreign state. The person attacking the foreign divorce decree has the burden of proving the jurisdictional defect, i.e., the absence of domicile in the foreign state.

2. *Alimony, child support, and property division awards.* If the state where the divorce was obtained did not have personal jurisdiction over the defendant, then that state's award of alimony, child support, and property division is *not* entitled to full faith and credit in another state. Again we see the divisible-divorce concept: only part of the divorce decree is recognized in another state if the court had jurisdiction to dissolve the marriage because of domicile but had no jurisdiction to grant alimony, child support, and a property division due to the absence of personal jurisdiction over the defendant.

3. *Custody award.* See chapter 11.

HOW JURISDICTION IS ACQUIRED

1. *Subject-matter jurisdiction.* The only way a court can acquire subject-matter jurisdiction over a divorce is by a special statute or constitutional provision giving the court the power to hear this kind of case. A divorce decree rendered by a court without subject-matter jurisdiction over divorces is void.

2. *In rem jurisdiction.* All that is needed for a court to acquire in rem jurisdiction is the domicile of at least one of the spouses in the state. The case can proceed so long as reasonable notice of the action is given to the defendant. If the defendant is not domiciled in the state, notice can be by substituted service, e.g., mail, publication of notice in a newspaper.

3. *Personal jurisdiction.* A court can acquire personal jurisdiction over the defendant in several ways:

a. Personal service of process on the defendant in the state. This is effective whether or not the defendant is domiciled in the state.[1]

b. Consent. The defendant can always consent to personal jurisdiction simply by appearing in the action and defending the entire case. But if the defendant is a nondomiciliary, he or she can appear solely to contest the jurisdictional issue without being subjected to full personal jurisdiction. *Any* appearance by a *domiciliary*, however, will confer full personal jurisdiction on the court.

c. Substituted service, e.g., mail, publication in a newspaper. Substituted service of process will confer personal jurisdiction if the defendant is domiciled in the state. For nondomiciliaries, see the following discussion on the long arm statute.

d. Long arm statute. This is used to acquire personal jurisdiction over a defendant who is not domiciled in the state. This defendant must have sufficient minimum contacts with the state so that it is reasonable and fair to require the defendant to appear and be subjected to full personal jurisdiction in the state. What constitutes sufficient minimum contacts to meet this standard has not been answered clearly by the courts. Here are some of the factors that a court will consider, no one of which is necessarily conclusive: the defendant was domiciled in the state at one time before he or she left, the defendant cohabitated with his or her spouse in the state before the defendant left the state, the defendant visits the state, the defendant arranges for schooling for his or her children in the state, etc. In addition to these minimum contacts, the defendant must be given reasonable notice of the action.

e. URESA (Uniform Reciprocal Enforcement of Support Act) and UIFSA (Uniform Interstate Family Support Act) can be used to acquire personal jurisdiction over a defendant. These statutes are discussed later in the chapter.

JURISDICTIONAL ANALYSIS: EXAMPLES

Here are some examples of how divorce jurisdiction is determined:

1. Tom and Mary are married. Both are domiciled in Massachusetts. Mary moves to Ohio, which is now her state of domicile. She obtains a divorce decree from an Ohio state court. The decree awards Mary $500 a month alimony. Tom was notified of the action by mail but did not appear. He has had no contacts with Ohio. Mary travels to Massachusetts and brings an action against Tom to enforce the alimony award of the Ohio court.

☐ **Jurisdictional Analysis**

▪ The Ohio court had jurisdiction to dissolve the marriage because of Mary's domicile in Ohio. This part of the divorce decree is entitled to full faith and credit in

---

1. The United States Supreme Court has said: "Among the most firmly established principles of personal jurisdiction in American tradition is that the courts of a State have jurisdiction over nonresidents who are physically present in the State. The view developed early that each State had the power to hale before its courts any individual who could be found within its borders, and that once having acquired jurisdiction over such a person by properly serving him with process, the State could retain jurisdiction to enter judgment against him, no matter how fleeting his visit." *Burnham v. Superior Court of California,* 495 U.S. 604, 610, 110 S. Ct. 2105, 2110 (1990).

Massachusetts, i.e., Massachusetts *must* recognize this aspect of the Ohio divorce decree if Massachusetts determines that Mary was in fact domiciled in Ohio at the time of the divorce decree.

▪ The Ohio court did not have jurisdiction to render an alimony award since it did not have personal jurisdiction over Tom. This part of the divorce decree is not entitled to full faith and credit in Massachusetts, i.e., the Massachusetts court does not have to enforce the Ohio alimony award.

▪ Suppose that Tom had an out-of-state divorce in a state where he alone was domiciled. Suppose further that the divorce decree provided that Mary was *not* entitled to alimony. If this court did not have personal jurisdiction over Mary, she would not be bound by the no-alimony decision even though she would be bound by the decision dissolving the marriage.

2. Bill and Pat are married in New Jersey. Bill brings a successful divorce action against Pat in a New Jersey state court. Bill is awarded the divorce. Pat was not served with process or notified in any way of this divorce action. Bill then marries Linda. Linda and Bill begin having marital difficulties. They separate. Linda brings a support action (separate-maintenance action) against Bill. Bill's defense is that he is not married to Linda because his divorce with Pat was invalid due to the fact that Pat had no notice of the divorce.

☐ **Jurisdictional Analysis**

▪ Bill is raising a collateral attack against the divorce decree. He is attacking the jurisdiction of the court to award the divorce because Pat had no notice of the divorce action.

▪ Bill is the person who obtained the divorce decree. In most states, he will be estopped from attacking the decree on jurisdictional grounds. Whether or not the court in fact had jurisdiction to render the divorce decree, Bill will not be allowed to challenge it. He relied on the divorce and took the benefits of the divorce when he married Linda. He should not be allowed to attack the very thing he helped accomplish.

3. Joe and Helen are married in Texas. Helen goes to New Mexico and obtains a divorce decree against Joe. Joe knows about the action but does not appear. Helen has never been domiciled in New Mexico. Joe marries Paulene. When Helen dies, Joe claims part of her estate. His position is that he is her surviving husband because the New Mexico court had no jurisdiction to divorce them since neither was ever domiciled there.

☐ **Jurisdictional Analysis**

▪ Joe was not the party who sought the New Mexico divorce. The divorce proceeding was ex parte. Normally, he would be allowed to attack the divorce decree on the ground that no one was domiciled in New Mexico at the time of the divorce.

▪ But Joe relied upon the divorce and accepted its benefits by marrying Paulene. It would be inconsistent to allow him to change his mind now, and it could be unfair to Paulene. Hence, Joe will be estopped from attacking the divorce on jurisdictional grounds.

ASSIGNMENT 14.4

John and Sandra were married in Florida but live in Georgia. Sandra returns to Florida with their two children. John never goes back to Florida. He often calls his children on the phone, and they come to visit him pursuant to arrangements he makes with Sandra. Once he asked his mother to go to Florida to look after the children while Sandra was sick. Sandra files for a divorce in Florida. John does not appear, although he is given notice of the action. (Florida has a long arm statute.) Sandra is granted the divorce and $840 a month in child support. No alimony is awarded. She later travels to Georgia and asks a

Georgia court to enforce the child support order, which John has been ignoring. What result? (See General Instructions for the Legal Analysis Assignment in chapter 1.) What would the result be in your state? Check your state code and court opinions. (See General Instructions for the State-Code Assignment and General Instructions for the Court-Opinion Assignment in chapter 1.)

The remaining assignments in this section focus on the mechanics of jurisdiction—specifically, what courts have subject-matter jurisdiction over divorce, and what the residency requirements and service of process rules are for your state.

You cannot go into a United States District Court or any federal court to obtain a divorce. Federal courts do not have subject-matter jurisdiction over divorces. Parties who want to dissolve their marriage must use their local state courts.

Identify each court in your state with subject-matter jurisdiction over divorces. See Assignment 2.2 at the end of chapter 2. Write your answer in step 1 of the Divorce Litigation Flowchart in Assignment 14.22 at the end of the chapter. (See General Instructions for the State-Code Assignment in chapter 1.)

ASSIGNMENT 14.5

Most states require that the plaintiff be a resident of the forum state for a designated period of time before a divorce can be granted, e.g., six weeks, a year. In a few states, it is sufficient that the defendant is a resident even if the plaintiff is not. While the word "residence" is frequently used in the state statutes, the meaning intended by most of the statutes is domicile: one's permanent home where one intends to stay indefinitely. As we saw in the preceding pages, for a court to have jurisdiction to divorce a couple, domicile must exist. The statutes on residency (domicile) state the length of time during which there must be residence (domicile) in the state.

---

a. What is the residency requirement for a divorce action in your state? Write your answer in step 2 at the end of the chapter. (See General Instructions for the State-Code Assignment in chapter 1.)

b. If your state code uses the word *residence* in its divorce statute without defining it, find a court opinion in your state that does define it. (See General Instructions for the Court-Opinion Assignment in chapter 1.)

ASSIGNMENT 14.6

Tara, a member of the armed services is temporarily stationed in your state. She and her husband George are domiciled in another state. Under what circumstances, if any, can Tara obtain a divorce in your state? Assume that George has never been in your state. (See General Instructions for the State-Code Assignment in chapter 1.)

ASSIGNMENT 14.7

Complaint A pretrial document filed by one party against another that states a grievance, called a cause of action.

■■■■ MISCELLANEOUS PRETRIAL MATTERS

COMPLAINT

The divorce action begins when the plaintiff completes service of process on the defendant by giving him or her the **complaint** (the pleading that states the cause of action for divorce—see Exhibit 1.3 in chapter 1) and the **summons** (a

Summons A formal notice from the court ordering the defendant to appear and answer the allegations of the plaintiff.

☐ **EXHIBIT 14.3 Divorce Summons**

STATE OF MAINE   SUPERIOR COURT
CUMBERLAND COUNTY   Civil Action, Docket Number _____

A.B., Plaintiff
   of Bath,
   Sagadahoc County,
        v.
C.D., Defendant
   of Portland,
   Cumberland County,

     To the Defendant _____ :
     The Plaintiff _____ has begun a divorce action against you in this Court. If you wish to oppose the divorce, you or your attorney must prepare and file a written Answer to the attached Complaint within 20 days from the day this summons was served upon you. You or your attorney must file your Answer by delivering it in person or by mail to the office of the Clerk of the Superior Court, Cumberland County Courthouse, 142 Federal Street, Portland, Maine. On or before the day you file your Answer, you or your attorney must mail a copy of your Answer to the Plaintiff's attorney, whose name and address appear below.
     IMPORTANT WARNING: IF YOU FAIL TO FILE AN ANSWER WITHIN THE TIME STATED ABOVE, OR IF, AFTER YOU FILE YOUR ANSWER, YOU FAIL TO APPEAR AT ANY TIME THE COURT NOTIFIES YOU TO DO SO, A JUDGMENT MAY IN YOUR ABSENCE BE ENTERED AGAINST YOU FOR THE DIVORCE. IF AN ORDER FOR PAYMENT OF MONEY IS ENTERED AGAINST YOU, YOUR EMPLOYER MAY BE ORDERED TO PAY PART OF YOUR WAGES TO THE PLAINTIFF OR YOUR PERSONAL PROPERTY, INCLUDING BANK ACCOUNTS, AND YOUR REAL ESTATE MAY BE TAKEN TO SATISFY THE JUDGMENT. IF YOU INTEND TO OPPOSE THE DIVORCE, DO NOT FAIL TO ANSWER WITHIN THE REQUIRED TIME.
     If you believe you have a defense to the Plaintiff's Complaint or if you believe you have a claim of your own against the Plaintiff, you should talk to a lawyer.

[Seal of the Court]

Dated _____   _____
                                                                          Clerk of Said Superior Court
_____   Served on _____
Name of Plaintiff's Attorney   Date

_____   _____
Address   Deputy Sheriff

_____
Telephone

Petition Another name for complaint in some states.

In Forma Pauperis As a poor person.

document that orders the defendant to appear and answer the complaint—see Exhibit 14.3). The complaint is sometimes called the **petition.** The plaintiff also files the complaint or petition with the court along with the appropriate filing fees. If the plaintiff is poor, he or she can ask the court to waive the fees and proceed **in forma pauperis.**

ASSIGNMENT 14.8

Answer the following questions by examining your statutory code. Your answers will also become part of the Divorce Litigation Flowchart at the end of this chapter. (See General Instructions for the State-Code Assignment in chapter 1.)

a. What is the fee for filing a divorce complaint in your state? Write your answer in step 3 at the end of the chapter.

b. What happens if a party seeking a divorce cannot afford the filing fee or any court costs? Can he or she proceed as a poor person and thereby have these fees and costs waived?

c. Who may serve process in your state? Write your answer in step 4 at the end of the chapter.

d. How is personal service made on an individual? Write your answer in step 5 at the end of the chapter.

e. In a divorce action, when can substituted service be used?

f. How is substituted service made? By publication of a notice? By posting a notice? Other methods? Summarize your answer in step 6 at the end of the chapter.

g. How is proof of service made? Write your answer in step 7 at the end of the chapter.

h. Does your state have a long arm statute for divorce actions? If so, when can it be used?

In some states it is possible to obtain a divorce primarily through the mail without going through elaborate court procedures. Such a divorce is often referred to as a *summary dissolution* (see Exhibit 14.4) or a *simplified dissolution*. The requirements for taking advantage of this option are quite strict. In California, for example, the couple must be childless, married for five years or less, have no interest in real property (other than a lease on a residence), waive any rights to spousal support, etc. Cal. Civil Code § 4550 (1983). In short, there must be very little need for courts, lawyers, and the protection of the legal system. The less conflict between parties over children, property, and support, the easier it is to obtain a divorce.

A party who represents him or herself in a divorce action (summary or traditional) is proceeding **pro se.**

Pro Se On one's own behalf. Representing oneself.

GUARDIAN AD LITEM

If the husband or wife is a minor or if the defendant is insane at the time of the divorce action, the court may require that the individual be represented by a **guardian ad litem** or *conservator* to ensure that the interests of the individual are protected during the proceeding. In a disputed child-custody case, the state might appoint a guardian ad litem to represent the child.

Guardian ad Litem A special guardian appointed by the court to represent the interests of another.

Under what circumstances can a guardian ad litem be appointed in a divorce action in your state? Write your answer in step 8 at the end of the chapter. (See General Instructions for the State-Code Assignment in chapter 1.)

ASSIGNMENT 14.9

VENUE

Venue refers to the place of the trial. Within a state, it may be that the divorce action could be brought in a number of different counties or districts because each one of them has or could acquire the necessary jurisdiction. The *choice of venue* is the choice of one county or district among several where the trial could be held. The state's statutory code will often specify the requirements for the selection of venue. The requirements often relate to the residence (usually meaning domicile) of the plaintiff or defendant. For example, the statute might specify that a divorce action should be filed in the county in which the plaintiff has been a resident (meaning domiciliary) for three months preceding the commencement of the action.

Venue The place of the trial. The county, district, or state where the trial is held.

☐ **EXHIBIT 14.4 Joint Petition for Summary Dissolution of Marriage**

3-57

ATTORNEY OR PARTY WITHOUT ATTORNEY *(Name and Address):* TELEPHONE NO.	*FOR COURT USE ONLY*
ATTORNEY FOR *(Name):*	

SUPERIOR COURT OF CALIFORNIA, COUNTY OF

STREET ADDRESS:

MAILING ADDRESS:

CITY AND ZIP CODE:

BRANCH NAME:

MARRIAGE OF

HUSBAND:

WIFE:

JOINT PETITION FOR SUMMARY DISSOLUTION OF MARRIAGE	CASE NUMBER:

We petition for a summary dissolution of marriage and declare that all the following conditions exist on the date this petition is filed with the court:

1. We have read and understand the Summary Dissolution Information booklet.

2. We were married on *(date):*
   [A SUMMARY DISSOLUTION OF YOUR MARRIAGE WILL NOT BE GRANTED IF YOU FILE THIS PETITION MORE THAN FIVE YEARS AFTER THE DATE OF YOUR MARRIAGE.]

3. One of us has lived in California for at least six months and in the county of filing for at least three months preceding the date of filing.

4. There are no minor children born of our relationship before or during our marriage or adopted by us during our marriage and the wife, to her knowledge, is not pregnant.

5. Neither of us has an interest in any real property anywhere. *(You may have a lease for a residence in which one of you lives. It must terminate within a year from the date of filing this petition. The lease must not include an option to purchase.)*

6. Except for obligations with respect to automobiles, on obligations either or both of us incurred during our marriage, we owe no more than $4,000.

7. The total fair market value of community property assets, excluding all encumbrances and automobiles, is less than $14,000.

8. Neither of us has separate property assets, excluding all encumbrances and automobiles, in excess of $14,000.

9. *(Check whichever statement is true)*
   a. ☐ We have no community assets or liabilities.

   b. ☐ We have signed an agreement listing and dividing all our community assets and liabilities and have signed all papers necessary to carry out our agreement. A copy of our agreement is attached to this petition.

10. Irreconcilable differences have caused the irremediable breakdown of our marriage and each of us wishes to have the court dissolve our marriage without our appearance before a judge.

11. ☐ Wife desires to have her former name restored. Her former name is *(specify name):*

12. Upon entry of final judgment of summary dissolution of marriage, we each give up our rights as follows:
    a. to appeal, and
    b. to move for a new trial.

(Continued on reverse)

Form Adopted by Rule 1295.10
Judicial Council of California
1295.10 (Rev. January 1, 1987)

**JOINT PETITION FOR SUMMARY
DISSOLUTION OF MARRIAGE
(Family Law - Summary Dissolution)**

Civil Code, §§ 4550-4556

Continued

☐ **EXHIBIT 14.4—Continued**

HUSBAND:	CASE NUMBER:
WIFE:	

JOINT PETITION FOR SUMMARY DISSOLUTION OF MARRIAGE

13. EACH OF US FOREVER GIVES UP ANY RIGHT TO SPOUSAL SUPPORT FROM THE OTHER.

14. We stipulate that this matter may be determined by a commissioner sitting as a temporary judge.

15. **Mailing Address of Husband**
Name:
Address:

City:
State:
Zip Code:

   I declare under penalty of perjury under the laws of the State of California that the foregoing is true and correct.

16. **Mailing Address of Wife**
Name:
Address:

City:
State:
Zip Code:

   I declare under penalty of perjury under the laws of the State of California that the foregoing is true and correct.

Date:

► _____
(SIGNATURE—HUSBAND)

Date:

► _____
(SIGNATURE—WIFE)

> YOU HAVE A RIGHT TO REVOKE THIS PETITION ANY TIME BEFORE A REQUEST FOR FINAL JUDGMENT IS FILED. YOU WILL REMAIN MARRIED UNTIL ONE OF YOU FILES FOR AND OBTAINS A FINAL JUDGMENT OF DISSOLUTION. YOU MAY NOT REQUEST A FINAL JUDGMENT OF DISSOLUTION SOONER THAN SIX MONTHS FROM THE DATE THIS PETITION IS FILED.

ASSIGNMENT 14.10

In a divorce action in your state, how is venue determined? Write your answer in step 9 at the end of the chapter. (See General Instructions for the State-Code Assignment in chapter 1.)

PLEADING

As we have seen, the complaint (or petition) is the **pleading** that states the nature of the action, the fact that the parties are married, the basis of the court's jurisdiction, the grounds for the divorce, the relief sought, etc. (See the sample divorce complaint in Exhibit 1.3 in chapter 1 and Exhibit 14.4 in this chapter.) The response of the defendant is stated in the pleading called the **answer** (often referred to as the *response*). In most states, the defendant can **counterclaim** for divorce in his or her answer.

Pleading A formal document that contains allegations and responses of the parties in litigation.

Answer The pleading filed by the defendant that responds to the complaint of the plaintiff.

Counterclaim A claim made by the defendant against the plaintiff.

ASSIGNMENT 14.11

Answer the following questions on pleading after examining your state code and your court rules. (See General Instructions for the State-Code Assignment in chapter 1.)

a. What must a complaint for divorce contain? Write your response in step 10 at the end of the chapter.

b. Must the complaint be subscribed and/or verified? If so, by whom? Write your response in step 11 at the end of the chapter.

c. Where is the complaint filed and served? Write your response in step 12 at the end of the chapter.

d. How many days does the defendant have to answer the complaint? Write your response in step 13 at the end of the chapter.

e. Where and how is the answer filed and served? Write your response in step 14 at the end of the chapter.

f. Must the defendant specifically plead all available affirmative defenses (i.e., a defense that raises facts not stated in the complaint) in the answer? Write your response in step 15 at the end of the chapter.

g. Must the defendant's answer be subscribed and/or verified? If so, by whom? Write your response in step 16 at the end of the chapter.

h. How many days does the plaintiff have to reply to the defendant's counterclaim? Write your response in step 17 at the end of the chapter.

i. Where and how is the reply of the plaintiff to be filed and served? Write your response in step 18 at the end of the chapter.

WAITING PERIOD

Some states have a compulsory *waiting period* or "cooling-off" period (e.g., sixty days) that usually begins to run from the time the divorce complaint is filed. During this period of time, no further proceedings are held in the hope that tempers might calm down, producing an atmosphere of reconciliation.

ASSIGNMENT 14.12

Is there a waiting period in your state? If so, how long is it and when does it begin to run? Write your answer in step 19 at the end of the chapter. (See General Instructions for the State-Code Assignment in chapter 1.)

▬▬▬ DISCOVERY

Discovery Steps that a party can take before trial to obtain information from the other side in order to prepare for trial.

Discovery refers to a series of devices designated to assist the parties prepare for trial, particularly in reference to the financial status of the parties. For example, when the plaintiff is the wife who needs alimony, she might use some of the discovery devises to identify her defendant-husband's assets. The standard devices are as follows:

☐ **Interrogatories**   A written set of factual questions sent by one party to another before a trial begins (see page 197).

☐ **Deposition**   A deposition is an in-person, question-and-answer session conducted outside the courtroom, e.g., in one of the attorney's offices. The person questioned is said to be *deposed.*

☐ **Request for Admissions**   If a party believes that there will be no dispute over a certain fact at trial, it can request that the other party admit (i.e., stipulate) the fact. This will avoid the expense and delay of proving the fact at trial. The party can also be asked to admit that a specific document is genuine. The other party, of course, need not make the admission if it feels that there is some dispute over the fact.

☐ **Mental or Physical Examination**   If the mental or physical condition of a party is relevant to the litigation, many courts can order him or her to undergo an examination. If paternity is at issue, for example, the court might order the husband to undergo a blood-grouping test.

☐ **Request for Production**   One party can ask another to allow the inspection, testing, or copying of documents or other tangible things relevant to the case, e.g., tax returns, credit card receipts, diaries, business records.

Answer the following questions for a divorce action after examining your statutory code and your court rules. (See General Instructions for the State-Code Assignment in chapter 1.)

a. Who can be deposed? When must a deposition be requested? How must the request be made? Write your response in step 20 at the end of the chapter.

b. Are there any restrictions on the use of depositions in divorce actions? Write your response in step 21 at the end of the chapter.

c. When and on whom can interrogatories be filed? Write your response in step 22 at the end of the chapter.

d. When must interrogatories be answered? Write your response in step 23 at the end of the chapter.

e. When can a request for admission be made? Write your response in step 24 at the end of the chapter.

f. When will a court order a physical or mental examination? Write your response in step 25 at the end of the chapter.

g. What sanctions can be imposed if a party improperly refuses to comply with valid discovery requests? Summarize your response in step 26 at the end of the chapter.

ASSIGNMENT 14.13

Pick any well-known married couple in the media. Assume that they are getting a divorce and that you work for the law firm that is representing the wife. You are asked to draft a set of interrogatories meant to elicit as much relevant information as possible about the husband's personal and business finances. The information will be used in the firm's representation of the wife on alimony and property division issues. Draft the interrogatories. (See General Instructions for the Interrogatories Assignment in chapter 1.)

ASSIGNMENT 14.14

■ PRELIMINARY ORDERS

Obtaining a divorce can be time-consuming even when the matter is uncontested. The court's calendar may be so crowded that it may take months to have the case heard. If the case is contested and some bitterness exists between the parties, the litigation can seemingly be endless. While the litigation is going on (or to use the Latin phrase, **pendente lite**), the court may be asked to make a number of *preliminary* orders (sometimes called temporary orders) that remain in effect only until final determinations are made later:

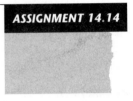

Pendente Lite While the litigation is going on.

- ☐ Granting physical and legal custody of the children
- ☐ Granting exclusive occupancy of the marital home to the custodial parent
- ☐ Granting a child support order
- ☐ Granting alimony
- ☐ Granting attorney's fees and related court costs in the divorce action
- ☐ Enjoining (preventing) one spouse from bothering or molesting the other spouse and children
- ☐ Enjoining a spouse from transferring any property, which might make it unavailable for the support of the other spouse and children
- ☐ Appointing a receiver over a spouse's property until the court decides what his or her obligations are to the other spouse and children
- ☐ Enjoining the parties from changing any insurance policies
- ☐ Ordering an inventory and appraisal of all family assets and debts
- ☐ Granting control of any business operated by the spouses

☐ Enjoining the defendant from leaving the state or the country

☐ Enjoining either spouse from taking the children out of the state

☐ Enjoining the defendant from obtaining a foreign divorce

ASSIGNMENT 14.15

In a divorce action in your state, what preliminary orders can be granted by the court pendente lite? Summarize your response in step 27 at the end of the chapter. (See General Instructions for the State-Code Assignment in chapter 1.)

For an example of a request for preliminary or temporary orders, see Exhibit 14.5.

▰▰▰ TRIAL

Voir Dire Jury selection.

Some states do not permit jury trials in divorce cases. If there is no jury, the judge decides the questions of fact as well as the questions of law. If a jury trial is allowed, the jurors are selected through a procedure known as **voir dire.** During this procedure, the lawyers and/or judge ask questions of prospective jurors to assess their eligibility to sit on the jury.

The lawyers begin the trial by making opening statements outlining the evidence they intend to try to prove during the trial. The plaintiff's side will usually present its case first. The lawyer will call the plaintiff's witnesses and directly examine them. The other side can cross-examine these witnesses. Physical evidence such as documents are introduced as exhibits. Some evidence may have to be **corroborated,** meaning that additional evidence must be introduced to support the position taken by the party. The plaintiff's side will "rest" its case after presenting all of its witnesses and evidence. The defendant's lawyer then begins his or her case through direct examination of witnesses, introduction of exhibits, etc.

Corroborated
Providing additional evidence of a point beyond that offered by the person asserting the point.

Preponderance of Evidence A standard of proof that is met if the evidence shows it is more likely than not that an alleged fact is true or false as alleged.

When a party has the burden of proving a fact, the standard of proof is usually a **preponderance of evidence:** the fact finder must be able to say from the evidence introduced and found admissible that it is *more likely than not* that the fact has been established as claimed. Occasionally, however, the law requires a fact to meet a higher standard of proof, e.g., clear and convincing evidence. Who has the burden of proof? In general, the party asserting a fact has the burden of proof on that fact. For example, a spouse who claims that the other spouse has a hidden bank account and physically assaulted the children has the burden of proof on these facts.

Privilege for Marital Communications One spouse cannot disclose in court any confidential communications that occurred between the spouses during the marriage.

Within the marriage, there is a **privilege for marital communications,** which prevents one spouse from testifying about confidential communications between the spouses during the marriage. This privilege, however, does not apply to:

☐ Criminal proceedings in which one spouse is alleged to have committed a crime against the other or against the children

☐ Civil cases between the spouses such as a divorce action

The privilege is limited to cases in which a third party is suing one or both of the spouses and attempts to introduce into evidence what one spouse may have said to another. Such evidence is inadmissible.

Default Judgment A judgment rendered when the other side failed to appear.

A **default judgment** can be entered against a defendant who fails to appear. The plaintiff, however, is still required to introduce evidence to establish his or her case. Unlike other civil proceedings, the default judgment is not automatic.

☐ **EXHIBIT 14.5 Motion and Affidavit for Temporary Alimony, Maintenance of Support, or Custody of Minor Children**

SUPERIOR COURT OF THE DISTRICT OF COLUMBIA
FAMILY DIVISION
DOMESTIC RELATIONS BRANCH

- *Plaintiff*

                                    v.   Jacket No. -

- *Defendant*

MOTION AND AFFIDAVIT

| Note:
| **FINANCIAL STATEMENT REQUIRED**
| **FILL OUT AND ATTACH HERETO.**

For ☐ TEMPORARY ALIMONY, MAINTENANCE OR SUPPORT
☐ TEMPORARY CUSTODY OF MINOR CHILDREN

Now comes ☐ Plaintiff   and moves the Court that -
☐ Defendant   (name)

be required to pay such amount as seems just and reasonable for the support and maintenance of

the ☐ Plaintiff (and - minor children) pending the final disposition of this cause (and
☐ Defendant

to award ☐ her the temporary custody of said minor children). Note: *Strike out portions of the preceding that do not apply.*
☐ him

The following facts are submitted in support of the above motion:

1. Marriage:	Date:	Place:	2. Are you agreeable to a reconciliation: ☐ Yes ☐ No

3. Children by this marriage:			Living with			Amounts Contributed to family
Name	Age	Name	Address	Relation		

4. WIFE			5. HUSBAND		
Age:	Married before: ☐ Yes—How terminated? ☐ No		Age:	Married before: ☐ Yes—How terminated? ☐ No	
Occupation:	Employer:		Occupation:	Employer:	
Living with	Name:	Relation:	Living with	Name:	Relation:
	Address:			Address:	

6. Wife asks for support of self (and - - - - minor children):	Amount: $	7. Husband willing to contribute as such support:	Amount: $
	Per: ☐ Week ☐ Month		Per: ☐ Week ☐ Month

8. Husband's support to family:	Before Separation: $	9. Previous divorce proceedings between parties. ☐ Yes ☐ No Alimony awarded: ☐ Yes ☐ No
	After Separation: $	

10. Juvenile Court proceedings: ☐ Yes ☐ No Explain:	11. Remarks

ASSIGNMENT 14.16

Answer the following questions after examining your state code and court rules. (See General Instructions for the State Code Assignment in chapter 1.)

a. In a divorce action, what evidence, if any, must be corroborated? Write your response in step 28 at the end of the chapter.

b. In a divorce action, are there any limitations on testimony that one spouse can give against the other? Write your answer in step 29 at the end of the chapter.

c. Can there be a jury trial in a divorce case? If so, when must the request for one be made? Write your response in step 30 at the end of the chapter.

d. What happens if the defendant fails to appear? Can there be a default judgment? Write your response in step 31 at the end of the chapter.

ASSIGNMENT 14.17

In your state, can one spouse use wiretap evidence against the other spouse at the divorce hearing, e.g., the wife taps her husband's phone and wants to introduce into evidence the conversation he had with his business partner about large assets that he has previously denied he owned. Check the code of your state as well as the federal code: the *United States Code* or the *United States Code Annotated* or the *United States Code Service.* (See General Instructions for the State-Code Assignment in chapter 1.)

ASSIGNMENT 14.18

Go to a court hearing in your state on divorce. In Assignment 14.5, you identified what court(s) in your state have the power to grant divorce. Attend a divorce hearing in one of these courts and answer the following questions concerning what you observe:

a. What court heard the case?

b. What was the name of the case?

c. Were both sides represented by counsel?

d. Were both parties present?

e. What kind of evidence, if any, was introduced?

☐ **Note on Alternative Dispute Resolution (ADR)** The following are alternatives to traditional litigation of a family law dispute in court, or at least alternatives that can be attempted before resorting to traditional litigation.

Arbitration

Both sides agree to submit their dispute to a neutral third person who will listen to the evidence and make a decision. This individual is usually a professional arbitrator hired through an organization such as the American Arbitration Association. An arbitration proceeding is not as formal as a court trial. Generally, the decision of an arbitrator is not appealable to a court. If a party is dissatisfied, he or she must go to court and start all over again.

Rent-a-Judge

This is actually another form of arbitration. A retired judge is hired by both sides to listen to the evidence and to make a decision that has no more or less validity than any other arbitrator's decision.

Mediation

Both sides agree to submit their dispute to a neutral third person who will try to help the disputants reach a resolution on their own. In some states, mediation is mandatory; the parties are required to try to work out their differences before final action by the court. The mediator does not render a decision, although occasionally he or she may make suggestions or recommendations to the parties and ultimately to the court. The most common issues that are handled in mediation are custody and visitation arrangements.

Med-Arb

First mediation is tried. Those issues that could not be mediated are then resolved through arbitration. Often, the same person serves as mediator and arbitrator in a Med-Arb proceeding.

REVELATIONS OF A FAMILY LAW MEDIATOR: WHAT GOES ON BEHIND CLOSED DOORS TO HELP DIVORCING COUPLES REACH AGREEMENT?

by Joshua Kadish
Oregon State Bar Bulletin 27 (February/March 1992).

Over the past seven or eight years, I have mediated a substantial number of family law cases. My office mates often inquire, "Just what happens behind those closed doors, anyway?" "What was the loud screaming about, followed by hysterical laughter and silence?" "How do you get these embattled couples to agree on anything if they hate each other so much?" I usually parry these questions with a crafty smile and a muttered, "I have my ways . . ." as I scuttle down the hallway.

Bowing to pressure from various fronts, I have decided that the time has come to tell all. What follows is fiction, which I hope reveals the truth.

Fred and Wilma were a young couple in the process of divorcing. They had significant disagreement about custody of their two children, ages 1½ and 6. Both had consulted with attorneys and, after receiving estimates of the cost of a custody battle, had followed their attorneys' recommendation to at least try mediation. Wilma had called me to set up an appointment, and at the appointed hour I ushered them into my office.

My office is somewhat different from many lawyers' offices. I do have a desk in one corner. Most of the office is given over to a sitting area consisting of a large, comfortable couch and two chairs grouped around a coffee table. I always let the couple enter my office first and seat themselves as they wish. Depending upon how they arrange themselves, I can get a preliminary idea of how hotly the battle is raging. Some couples will sit together on the couch. Most position themselves as far away from each other as possible. Fred and Wilma put a good deal of distance between themselves.

After we were settled, I spent a few minutes describing mediation to them. First, my job was to remain neutral and to help them reach agreements for themselves. My job was not to reach decisions for them. Second, what transpired in the mediation sessions was confidential and would not later be disclosed in a courtroom. Third, the process was voluntary and anyone was free to terminate the mediation at any time. Fourth, we would consider the interests of their children to be of paramount importance.

Without looking at either one of them, I then asked them to tell me about their current situation while I studiously looked down at my legal pad. I like to see who will start talking first. This gives me a clue about where the balance of power may lie in the relationship. I am always concerned about one party overpowering the other in mediation.

Fred started talking. Speaking angrily, he told me about their 10-year marriage, the two children and Wilma's affair and withdrawal from the marriage. He stated that although he worked hard, he spent more than an average amount of time caring for the children. He felt that in having an affair, Wilma had proved herself to be an unstable person and that he would be a preferable custodial parent. He pointed out that Wilma had worked during the course of the marriage and that parenting duties had been shared between them more or less equally.

During the course of his statement, Wilma had interrupted Fred to point out that although she had had an affair, it occurred after they had separated and that Fred had been emotionally distant and withdrawn from the marriage for a number of years. Her statement ignited a loud argument between them. I let them argue for a minute or two to get a sense of their style of arguing. This argument was a well-rehearsed one which they must have been through a hundred times. As each one spoke, I could see that neither party was listening but was marshaling arguments with which to respond, making sure that his or her position was well defended.

I interrupted the argument by stating that I suspected they had had this argument before. This brought a slightly sheepish smile to both faces. Humor is often useful in easing tension and getting people on another track. I then borrowed an idea from an excellent mediator, John Haynes, and asked each of them to take a few minutes to think about what was the absolute worst outcome they could imagine in mediation. By asking this question, I wanted to get them further off the track they had been racing down and to give them a few minutes to calm down. After a few minutes, I asked each to answer. Fred said he was afraid of losing everything, including his children. Wilma stated that she was afraid of the same thing.

I remarked that it was interesting that they were both afraid of exactly the same thing, specifically a loss of their children to the other party. I then asked whether it would be possible for them to agree that whatever the outcome of mediation was, it would not result in a complete loss of the children to the other person. They both indicated that they would agree to this.

From that point, the atmosphere eased considerably. Both Fred and Wilma had dramatically realized that each was concerned about exactly the same thing. When people realize that they have the same concerns, it makes them feel closer or at least less adversarial. Moreover, they had been able to reach their first agreement. They realized they had a common interest in not becoming estranged from their children and that they could agree this would not be a result of the mediation.

I then asked what the current situation was regarding the children. Fred stated that he had moved out and was living in a small apartment. He was seeing the children every other weekend. However, he emphasized that he was a very involved father and he wanted the children to spend at least half of their time with him on an alternating weekly basis. Wilma thought this would be bad for the children. She wanted them to be at home with her and see Fred every other weekend. She clearly wished to be the primary parent and felt that the children needed a mother's love. She was quite concerned about the children being in Fred's care for more than one overnight at a time. Fred interrupted her to state that he felt he was just as good a parent as she was. Wilma responded by telling an anecdote about Fred forgetting to feed the children lunch about three weeks ago.

Again, I interrupted. Taking a bit of a risk, I asked whether each parent thought the children loved and needed the other parent. Again, each parent responded affirmatively. My asking this question had the effect of derailing the disagreement and again bringing Fred and Wilma back to some common ground of understanding. Most parents will at least admit the children love and need the other parent.

The next task was to help Fred and Wilma learn to listen to each other and to start separating their positions from their interests. I asked them each if they thought they could state what the other person's position was regarding custody and visitation and the reasons for it. Fred thought he could, but when he tried, Wilma felt he was inaccurate. I then asked Wilma to tell him again what she was concerned about, which she did. Fred was then able to repeat Wilma's position back to her. We then reversed the

process, and after a couple of tries, Wilma was able to state Fred's concerns back to him.

This is a simple technique known as "active listening" which I borrowed from the field of psychology. It is not too difficult to learn the rudiments, particularly when you are married to a clinical psychologist, as I am. The goal in active listening is to make each person feel understood. There is great power in helping each party feel his or her position is genuinely understood by the other person. In most marital disputes, as one party talks, the other party is not listening, but is preparing arguments to respond to the other. This results in long, well worked out and pointless disputes. Active listening slows the pace down and helps couples improve their communication; if you are assured that you will be listened to, you will be much more likely to be able to listen to another.

At this point Fred and Wilma understood not only each other's positions, but the interests and reasons behind the positions. Wilma was concerned about being separated from the children for too many overnight periods in a row. Fred was concerned about long periods of time going by without seeing the children. I pointed out that although their positions (alternating weekly versus every other weekend visitation) conflicted, their interests did not necessarily conflict. Perhaps it would be possible to work out a schedule where Fred saw the children frequently, but not for a long string of overnights. Perhaps every other weekend visitation with some shorter but frequent mid-week visitations, plus frequent telephone contact would be acceptable.

I then hauled out a blank calendar. Using the calendar as the focus of discussion, we worked out a visitation schedule that seemed acceptable to both of them. During this discussion, I emphasized to them that they were fortunate to have the opportunity to experiment with different patterns of visitation because it is very difficult to sit in a room and decide what will and will not work in the long run. I suggested that they should commit to trying a certain pattern of visitation for perhaps two months and also commit to reviewing it and altering it as indicated by their needs and the children's.

By finally working out a schedule, I was trying to do several things. First, I was trying to show them that in some ways their interests could be meshed. Second, big problems can be broken down into small, manageable pieces. Rather than creating a visitation schedule which was engraved in stone and would last for the next 20 years, they could try something for two months. Finally, I had introduced the idea of experimentation and flexibility. They could adjust the situation based upon how they and the children actually reacted to the plan.

I ended the session by telling them I would write their agreement in memo form, which they could review with their attorneys. I then asked each of them to comment on the process of the session. Did either of them have any concerns about what had happened? What did they like about the session? What could we do differently next time when we moved to a discussion of financial issues? I try to make people feel that they are in control of the process. Fred and Wilma both stated that they were pleased with the session and surprised that they had been able to reach agreement. Fred asked how I had done it. "I have my ways . . ." I muttered as I ushered them to the door.

▬▬ DIVORCE JUDGMENT

An **interlocutory** decree (or a *decree nisi*) is one that will not become final until the passage of a specified period of time. In some states, after the court has reached its decision to grant a divorce, an interlocutory decree of divorce will be issued. During the period that this decree is in force, the parties are still married. The divorce decree could be set aside if the parties reconcile.

Interlocutory Not final; interim.

In many states, the parties may not remarry while the trial court's divorce judgment is being appealed. Finally, in a few states, even a final divorce judgment will not automatically enable a party to remarry. The court may have the power to prohibit one or both of the parties from remarrying for a period of time.

An absolute, or final, judgment (as opposed to an interlocutory judgment) will determine whether the marriage is dissolved. If it is, the divorce may be granted to the plaintiff, or to both parties (dual divorce) if both initially filed for the divorce. The judgment will also resolve the questions of alimony, child custody, child support, and property division. (All of this, of course, assumes that the court had proper jurisdiction to make these determinations as outlined earlier in this chapter.) In addition, the judgment will often restore the woman's maiden name, if that is her wish, and determine what the surname of the children will be as part of the custody decision.

Exhibit 14.6 shows a notice of entry of judgment, and Exhibit 14.7 shows a record of dissolution of marriage.

Answer the following questions after examining your state code. (See General Instructions for the State-Code Assignment in chapter 1.)

ASSIGNMENT 14.19

a. Is there an interlocutory decree or a decree nisi in your state? If so, how long is it effective and how does the divorce become final? Write your answer in step 32 at the end of the chapter.

b. After the divorce becomes final, can the court forbid either party to remarry?

c. While the divorce decree is being appealed, can the parties remarry?

d. To what court can the divorce decree be appealed? Write your answer in step 33 at the end of the chapter.

e. How many days does a party have to appeal? Write your answer in step 34 at the end of the chapter.

f. Where and how is the notice of appeal filed and served? Write your answer in step 35 at the end of the chapter.

▬▬ ENFORCEMENT OF DIVORCE JUDGMENT

In chapter 12, we covered the enforcement of child support. Here, our main focus is the enforcement of the alimony portion of a divorce judgment and, to

☐ **EXHIBIT 14.6   Notice of Entry of Judgment**

3-41

ATTORNEY OR PARTY WITHOUT ATTORNEY *(Name and Address):*	TELEPHONE NO.	**FOR COURT USE ONLY**

ATTORNEY FOR *(Name):*

SUPERIOR COURT OF CALIFORNIA, COUNTY OF

STREET ADDRESS:

MAILING ADDRESS:

CITY AND ZIP CODE:

BRANCH NAME:

MARRIAGE OF

PETITIONER:

RESPONDENT:

NOTICE OF ENTRY OF JUDGMENT	CASE NUMBER:

You are notified that the following judgment was entered on *(date):*

1. ☐ Dissolution of Marriage

2. ☐ Dissolution of Marriage — Status Only

3. ☐ Dissolution of Marriage — Reserving Jurisdiction over Termination of Marital Status

4. ☐ Legal Separation

5. ☐ Nullity

6. ☐ Other *(specify):*

Date: Clerk, by _____ , Deputy

— NOTICE TO ATTORNEY OF RECORD OR PARTY WITHOUT ATTORNEY —
Pursuant to the provisions of Code of Civil Procedure section 1952, if no appeal is filed the court may order the exhibits destroyed or otherwise disposed of after 60 days from the expiration of the appeal time.

Effective date of termination of marital status *(specify):*
WARNING: NEITHER PARTY MAY REMARRY UNTIL THE EFFECTIVE DATE OF THE TERMINATION OF MARITAL STATUS AS SHOWN IN THIS BOX.

CLERK'S CERTIFICATE OF MAILING
I certify that I am not a party to this cause and that a true copy of the Notice of Entry of Judgment was mailed first class, postage fully prepaid, in a sealed envelope addressed as shown below, and that the notice was mailed

at *(place):*   California,

on *(date):*

Date: Clerk, by_____ , Deputy

some extent, the property division portion as well.[2] A good deal of this section, however, will also be relevant to child support enforcement.

_____

2. While either party can be challenged for failure to abide by alimony and property division orders, it is usually the ex-husband who is in this position. The examples used herein reflect this.

☐ **EXHIBIT 14.7   Record of Dissolution of Marriage**

OREGON DEPARTMENT OF HUMAN RESOURCES
HEALTH DIVISION
Vital Records Unit
RECORD OF DISSOLUTION
OF MARRIAGE, OR ANNULMENT

SAMPLE

CO. FILE NO. _____

136- _____ State File Number

TYPE OR PRINT PLAINLY IN BLACK INK

HUSBAND

1. HUSBAND'S NAME (First, Middle, Last)

2. RESIDENCE OR LEGAL ADDRESS | STREET AND NUMBER | CITY OR TOWN | COUNTY | STATE

3. SOCIAL SECURITY NUMBER (Optional) | 4. BIRTHPLACE (State or Foreign Country) | 5. DATE OF BIRTH (Month, Day, Year)

6a. WIFE'S NAME (First, Middle, Last) | 6b. MAIDEN SURNAME

7. FORMER LEGAL NAMES (IF ANY) | (1) | (2) | (3)

WIFE

8. RESIDENCE OR LEGAL ADDRESS | STREET AND NUMBER | CITY OR TOWN | COUNTY | STATE

9. SOCIAL SECURITY NUMBER (Optional) | 10. BIRTHPLACE (State or Foreign Country) | 13. DATE OF BIRTH (Month, Day, Year)

12a. PLACE OF THIS MARRIAGE - CITY, TOWN OR LOCATION | 12b. COUNTY | 12c. STATE OR FOREIGN COUNTRY | 13. DATE OF THIS MARRIAGE (Month, Day, Year)

MARRIAGE

14. DATE COUPLE LAST RESIDED IN SAME HOUSEHOLD (Month, Day, Year) | 15. NUMBER OF CHILDREN UNDER 18 IN THIS HOUSEHOLD AS OF THE DATE IN ITEM 14   Number _____ ☐ None | 16. PETITIONER   ☐ Husband ☐ Wife ☐ Both

17a. NAME OF PETITIONER'S ATTORNEY (Type/Print) | 17b. ADDRESS (Street and Number or Rural Route Number, City or Town, State, Zip Code)

ATTORNEY

18a. NAME OF RESPONDENT'S ATTORNEY (Type/Print) | 18b. ADDRESS (Street and Number or Rural Route Number, City or Town, State, Zip Code)

19. MARRIAGE OF THE ABOVE NAMED PERSONS WAS DISSOLVED ON: (Month, Day, Year) | 20. TYPE OF DECREE   DISSOLUTION OF MARRIAGE ☐   ANNULMENT ☐ | 21. DATE DECREE BECOMES EFFECTIVE (Month, Day, Year)

22. NUMBER OF CHILDREN UNDER 18 WHOSE PHYSICAL CUSTODY WAS AWARDED TO   Husband _____ Wife _____   Joint (Husband/Wife) _____ Wife _____   ☐ No children | 23. COUNTY OF DECREE | 24. TITLE OF COURT

DECREE

25. SIGNATURE OF COURT OFFICIAL | 26. TITLE OF COURT OFFICIAL | 27. DATE SIGNED (Month, Day, Year)

ORS 432.010 REQUIRED STATISTICAL INFORMATION. THE INFORMATION BELOW WILL NOT APPEAR ON CERTIFIED COPIES OF THE RECORD.

28. NUMBER OF THIS MARRIAGE—First, Second, etc. (Specify below)	29. IF PREVIOUSLY MARRIED, LAST MARRIAGE ENDED		30. RACE - American, Indian, Black, White, etc. (specify below)	31. EDUCATION (Specify only highest grade completed)	
	By Death, Divorce, Dissolution, or Annulment (Specify below)	Date (Month, Day, Year)		Elementary/Secondary (0–12)	College (1–4 or 5+)
HUSBAND 28a.	29a.	29b.	30a.	31a.	
WIFE 28b.	29c.	29d.	30b.	31b.	

THE PETITIONER OR LEGAL REPRESENTATIVE OF THE PETITIONER IS RESPONSIBLE FOR COMPLETING THE PERSONAL INFORMATION ON THIS FORM AND SHALL PRESENT THIS FORM TO THE CLERK OF THE COURT WITH THE PETITION.
IN ALL CASES THE COMPLETED RECORD SHALL BE A PREREQUISITE TO THE GRANTING OF THE FINAL DECREE   45-5 (2-89)

A number of enforcement options can be used against a delinquent party:

- □ Civil contempt
- □ Execution
- □ Garnishment
- □ Attachment
- □ Posting security
- □ Receivership
- □ Constructive trust

- □ Criminal nonsupport
- □ Qualified Domestic Relations Order (QDRO)
- □ Qualified Medical Child Support Order (QMCSO)
- □ Uniform Reciprocal Enforcement of Support Act (URESA)

CIVIL CONTEMPT

A delinquent party who must pay a money judgment, e.g., an alimony order, is called the *judgment debtor*. The person in whose favor the judgment is rendered is the *judgment creditor*. For disobeying the order, the judgment debtor can be held in civil contempt, for which he will be jailed until he complies with the order. This remedy, however, is not used if the judgment debtor does not have the present financial ability to pay the alimony obligation. Inability to pay does not mean burdensome or inconvenient to pay. Using all resources currently available or those that could become available with reasonable effort, he must be able to comply with the alimony order. (Exhibit 14.8 shows an affidavit in support of a motion to punish for contempt.)

Contempt is generally not available to enforce property division orders. The latter are more often enforced by execution, attachment, posting security, receivership, and constructive trust, which are discussed below.

EXECUTION

Writ of Execution A document directing a court officer to seize the property of someone who lost a judgment, sell it, and pay the winner of the judgment.

A judgment is *executed* when the court orders the sheriff to carry it out by seizing the property of the judgment debtor, selling it, and turning the proceeds over to the judgment creditor. This is done pursuant to a **writ of execution.**

Execution is usually possible only with respect to support orders that are *final* and *nonmodifiable.* Such orders can become final and nonmodifiable in two ways:

- □ In some states, each unpaid installment automatically becomes a final and nonmodifiable judgment of nonpayment to which execution will be available.
- □ In other states, each unpaid installment does not become a final and nonmodifiable judgment of nonsupport until the wife makes a specific application for such a judgment and one is entered. Execution is available only after the judgment is so entered or docketed.

As we saw in chapter 12, federal law places severe restrictions on the ability of a court to modify child support arrearages retroactively.

GARNISHMENT

Garnishment A process whereby a debtor's property under the control of another is given to a third person to whom the debtor owes a debt.

When **garnishment** is used, the court authorizes the judgment creditor to reach money or other property of the judgment debtor that is in the hands of the third party, e.g., the employer or bank of the judgment debtor.

ATTACHMENT

Property of the judgment debtor is *attached* when the court authorizes its seizure to bring it under the control of the court so that it can be used to satisfy a judgment.

POSTING SECURITY

The court may require the judgment debtor to post a bond, i.e., *post security,* which will be forfeited if he fails to obey the judgment.

RECEIVERSHIP

The court can appoint a *receiver* over some or all the judgment debtor's property to prevent him from squandering it or otherwise making it unavailable to satisfy the judgment.

CONSTRUCTIVE TRUST

The court could impose a trust on property that the judgment debtor conveys to a "friendly" third party (e.g., the judgment debtor's mother) in an effort to make it appear that he no longer owns the property. A **constructive trust** is a trust created by the law, rather than by the parties, in order to prevent a serious inequity or injustice.

Constructive Trust A trust created by operation of law against one who has obtained legal possession of property (or legal rights to property) through fraud, duress, abuse of confidence, or other unconscionable conduct.

☐ **EXHIBIT 14.8 Affidavit in Contempt Proceeding**

SUPREME COURT OF THE STATE OF NEW YORK
COUNTY OF _____

_____ ,
                   Plaintiff,
    -against-
_____ ,
                   Defendant,

AFFIDAVIT IN SUPPORT OF MOTION
TO PUNISH FOR CONTEMPT

Index No. _____

STATE OF NEW YORK ⎱ ss.:
COUNTY OF _____ ⎰

_____ , being duly sworn, deposes and says:

That I am the plaintiff in the above entitled action and make this application to punish the defendant for contempt of Court for willfully neglecting and refusing to comply with the Judgment of this Court dated _____ , 19 ____ , directing the defendant, among other things, to pay to the plaintiff the sum of _____ ($ _____) Dollars per week as alimony, plus the sum of _____ ($ _____) Dollars per week per child for the maintenance and support of the infant children _____ , _____ , and _____ , for a total sum of _____ ($ _____) Dollars per week by check or money order at the residence of the plaintiff.

That hereto annexed is a copy of the Judgment of Divorce herein. That the defendant was duly personally served with a copy of said Judgment on the _____ day of _____ , 19 ____ .

That defendant has failed, neglected, and refused to pay me the amounts of money set forth in said Judgment of Divorce during the period commencing _____ , 19 ____ to date.

That the above named defendant has willfully neglected and failed to comply with said Judgment of this Court and he is now in arrears in the sum of _____ ($ _____) Dollars, and no part of which has been paid although duly demanded. That the neglect and refusal of the above named defendant to comply with said Judgment of the Court was calculated to and did defeat, impair, impede, and prejudice the rights and remedies of the above named plaintiff.

That the arrears are computed as follows:

Continued

☐ **EXHIBIT 14.8   Affidavit in Contempt Proceeding—*Continued***

DATE	AMOUNT DUE	AMOUNT PAID	ARREARS
_____	$ _____	$ _____	$ _____
_____	$ _____	none	$ _____
_____	$ _____	$ _____	$ _____
_____	$ _____	none	$ _____
_____	$ _____	none	$ _____
_____	$ _____	$ _____	$ _____
_____	$ _____	none	$ _____
_____	$ _____	$ _____	$ _____
_____	$ _____	none	$ _____
_____	$ _____	$ _____	$ _____
_____	$ _____	none	$ _____
		TOTAL ARREARS	$ _____

That total arrears are therefore due me in the sum of _____ ($ _____) Dollars.

That it is respectfully submitted that the defendant deliberately does this to defeat and prejudice the rights and remedies of myself and my infant children.

That defendant is employed as a school teacher with the same position that he held at the time of the trial on _____ , 19 ____ , which was only _____ months ago. His income is at least as much as he was earning then, if not more. The defendant is also engaged in private tutoring.

That no order of sequestration has been made herein for the reason that there is no property to sequestrate.

That no bond or security has been given for the payment of said alimony.

That your deponent has been unable to obtain steady employment and is in dire financial straits by reason of the defendant's willful refusal to comply with said Judgment of Divorce.

That no previous application for the relief herein prayed for has been made.

That the reason that an order to show cause herein is requested is that the same is required on an application of this matter by virtue of section 245 of the Domestic Relations Law.

WHEREFORE, an order to show cause is respectfully prayed requiring the defendant to show cause why he should not be punished for contempt for willfully disobeying the Judgment of this Court.

[Signature] _____

[Type Name of Deponent]

SOURCE: J. Marvins, *McKinney's forms*, 13:131A (1976).

CRIMINAL NONSUPPORT

The state can criminally prosecute the judgment debtor for the willful failure to meet his support obligation—*criminal nonsupport.*

QUALIFIED DOMESTIC RELATIONS ORDER (QDRO)

Under a **QDRO,** the court authorizes the judgment creditor to receive all or a portion of the pension or other retirement benefits that the judgment debtor has available through his employer. The ex-spouse, as judgment creditor, becomes an *alternate payee* under these plans. She cannot, however, receive benefits under the plan that the obligor himself would not have been able to receive. For example, if the obligor is not entitled to a lump-sum payment, the ex-spouse as alternate payee is also subject to this limitation. A child in need of support can also be an alternate payee through a QDRO. For an example of a QDRO, see Exhibit 10.6 in chapter 10.

QUALIFIED MEDICAL CHILD SUPPORT ORDER (QMCSO)

Under a **QMCSO,** a court can require parents to include their children on available group health plans where they work. Insurance companies cannot deny coverage because the child does not live with the parent, does not live in the insurer's service area, is not claimed as a dependent on the parent's tax return, or was born to unmarried parents. The child becomes an *alternate recipient* under the health plan.

UNIFORM RECIPROCAL ENFORCEMENT OF SUPPORT ACT (URESA)

What happens when the defendant leaves the state? As we have seen, a court must have personal jurisdiction over a defendant in order to obtain and enforce an alimony or child support order against him. When the parties no longer live in the same state, the state of the wife or ex-wife may not be able to obtain personal jurisdiction over the husband/father if the latter is not domiciled in the state, or is not physically present in the state (and hence cannot be served with process in the state), or does not have sufficient minimal contacts with the state for the long arm statute to apply. Furthermore, it may be quite impractical for her to travel to the new state of the husband/father to try to find him and obtain a support order against him there.

One remedy in that situation is the *Uniform Reciprocal Enforcement of Support Act* **(URESA).** (See Appendix E). It authorizes a two-state lawsuit without requiring the aggrieved party to leave her own state. The two states involved are the initiating state and the responding state. The *initiating state* is the state of the *obligee,* the party claiming child support and/or spousal support. The obligee can also be a government agency that wants to be reimbursed for the public assistance it has already paid the obligee(s). The *responding state* is the state of the obligor, the party allegedly owing support.

The obligee starts the process by filing a petition or complaint in a court in the initiating state. The petition identifies the obligor, provides facts that will help locate the obligor, and alleges a support obligation that is currently owed to the obligee.

If the court in the intitiating state determines that further proceedings are warranted, it will send the petition to a court in the responding state. Up to this point, the obligor is not involved. No notice has been sent to the obligor, and there has been no hearing at which the obligor has denied or admitted the support duty.

The responding state now acts to acquire personal jurisdiction over the obligor, e.g., by the service of process on the obligor within the state. The obligee does *not* have to travel to the responding state. The beauty of URESA is that a state official acts on the obligee's behalf in the responding state.

The case against the obligor now proceeds in the court of the responding state. The obligor raises any defenses he may have to the claim that he owes a duty of support to the obligee. Under URESA, the responding state can litigate the question of paternity if it is an issue. Once the court concludes that the duty does exist, it enters a support order against the obligor. The traditional enforcement mechanisms discussed earlier are used where appropriate, e.g., civil contempt, execution, garnishment.

Support payments made by the obligor are sent to the court that issued the order in the responding state. The latter then forwards them to the court in the initiating state, which in turn gives them to the obligee(s).

URESA has been very successful. After some relatively minor revisions, it became known as RURESA: the Revised Uniform Reciprocal Enforcement of Support Act. In 1994 every state had the opportunity to replace RURESA with the Uniform Interstate Family Support Act (**UIFSA**). Though this revision was more substantial, the main features of the interstate collection process remained the same.

ASSIGNMENT 14.20

Answer the following questions after examining your state code. (See General Instructions for the State-Code Assignment in chapter 1.)

a. What remedies (enforcement devices) exist to collect unpaid alimony payments?

b. What procedures must be followed to seek enforcement of an alimony order by contempt? Write your answer in step 36 at the end of the chapter.

c. Has your state enacted URESA, RURESA, or UIFSA? If so, give the citation of the act and briefly describe how it works.

d. What is the statute of limitations for bringing an action to enforce an alimony award? Write your answer in step 37 at the end of the chapter.

e. What procedures must be followed to set aside a divorce judgment on the ground that it was obtained by fraud? Write your answer in step 38 at the end of the chapter.

� ▬ FULL FAITH AND CREDIT

Assume that an obligee obtains a support judgment in one state and then travels to another state where the obligor now lives (rather than use URESA) to try to enforce the judgment. Can the obligor relitigate the support issue in his state, or is his state required to enforce the earlier judgment against him?

Full Faith and Credit Clause "Full Faith and Credit shall be given in each State to the public Acts, Records, and judicial Proceedings of every other State." Art. IV.

Under the **Full Faith and Credit Clause** of the United States Constitution, one state must give effect to the public acts, e.g., the court judgments, of another state. For example:

> Phyllis obtains a divorce from Bob in Ohio. Bob falls behind in the alimony and child support payments he is obligated to make under the terms of the Ohio divorce judgment. Bob then moves to Kentucky. Phyllis goes to Kentucky to bring a suit against Bob to collect all unpaid installments.

The question is whether Kentucky can relitigate the alimony and child support issues, or whether it must give *full faith and credit* to the Ohio judgment by allowing Phyllis to sue on the Ohio judgment. The answer depends upon the status of the Ohio divorce judgment:

☐ Did the Ohio court have subject-matter jurisdiction over divorce actions?

☐ Did the Ohio court have personal jurisdiction over Bob?

☐ In Ohio, would each unpaid installment (of alimony and child support) be automatically considered a final and nonmodifiable judgment?

If the answer to each of these questions is yes, then the Kentucky court *must* give full faith and credit to the Ohio judgment and permit Phyllis to enforce it against Bob without allowing him to relitigate the alimony and child support obligation. Suppose, however, that no Ohio final judgment exists on unpaid installments until Phyllis makes specific application to an Ohio court for such a judgment and that at the time she brought her Kentucky action, she had not obtained such a judgment. Under these circumstances, a Kentucky court would not be *obliged,* under the Full Faith and Credit Clause, to force Bob to pay all unpaid installments.

Under the doctrine of **comity,** however, a state can decide to give full faith and credit to a foreign judgment even though it is not obliged to do so. It may decide to do so to reduce the burden on an ex-wife seeking back alimony and child support payments. Another example of the application of the comity doctrine involves foreign land decrees. Suppose that as part of the Ohio divorce decree, the Ohio court ordered Bob to transfer title to land he owned in Kentucky to Phyllis. Phyllis then brings an action in Kentucky to force Bob to convey his Kentucky land to her. Generally, a forum state (here, Kentucky) does not have to give full faith and credit to the judgment of a foreign state (Ohio) that affects the title to land in the forum state. The latter state, however, may nevertheless decide to enforce that foreign judgment affecting its land as a matter of comity.

Comity Following the law of another state out of mutual respect, rather than obligation.

ASSIGNMENT 14.21

Interview a paralegal, a lawyer, or legal secretary who has been involved in divorce actions in your state. (See General Instructions for the Systems Assignment in chapter 1.) Obtain answers to the following questions:

a. Approximately how many divorce cases have you worked on?

b. How many of them have been uncontested?

c. Approximately how long does it take to process an uncomplicated, uncontested divorce?

d. Is there a difference between working on a divorce case and working on another kind of case in the law office? If so, what is the difference?

e. What are the major steps for processing a divorce action in this state? What documents have to be filed? What court appearances must be made? Etc.

f. What formbook, manual, or other legal treatise do you use, if any, that is helpful? Who is the publisher?

g. Does your office have its own internal manual that covers any aspect of divorce practice?

h. In a divorce action, what is the division of labor among the attorney, the paralegal, and the legal secretary?

i. What computer software, if any, is used? What is its function and how useful is it? What would the office have to do if such software did not exist?

ASSIGNMENT 14.22

Divorce Litigation Flowchart for Your State

(Fill in each step after checking the law of your state, particularly your state statutory code. You may also need to refer to court rules and judicial opinions. See General Instructions for the Flowchart Assignment in chapter 1. For each step, cite the statute, court rule, or other law that you are relying upon as authority for your answer.)

☐ **Step 1**
Name the court or courts that have subject-matter jurisdiction over divorces.

Citation:

☐ **Step 2**
What is the residency requirement for a divorce action?

Citation:

☐ **Step 3**
What is the filing fee for a divorce?

Citation:

☐ **Step 4**
Who may serve process?

Citation:

☐ **Step 5**
How is personal service made on an individual?

Citation:

☐ **Step 6**
In divorce actions, how is substituted service made?

Citation:

☐ **Step 7**
How is proof of service made?

Citation:

☐ **Step 8**
When can a guardian ad litem be appointed in a divorce action?

Citation:

☐ **Step 9**
In a divorce action, how is venue determined?

Citation:

☐ **Step 10**
What must a complaint for divorce contain?

Citation:

☐ **Step 11**
Must the complaint be subscribed and/or verified? If so, by whom?

Citation:

☐ **Step 12**
Where is the complaint filed and served?

Citation:

☐ **Step 13**
How many days does the defendant have to answer the complaint?

Citation:

☐ **Step 14**
Where and how is the answer filed and served?

Citation:

☐ **Step 15**
Must the defendant specifically plead all available affirmative defenses in the answer?

Citation:

☐ **Step 16**
Must the defendant's answer be subscribed and/or verified? If so, by whom?

Citation:

☐ **Step 17**
How many days does the plaintiff have to reply to the counterclaim of the defendant?

Citation:

☐ **Step 18**
Where and how is the reply to the plaintiff filed and served?

Citation:

☐ **Step 19**
Is there a waiting period? If so, how long is it and when does it begin to run?

Citation:

☐ **Step 20**
Who can be deposed? When must a deposition be requested? How is the request made?

Citation:

☐ **Step 21**

Are there any restrictions on the use of depositions in divorce actions?

Citation:

☐ **Step 22**

When and on whom can interrogatories be filed?

Citation:

☐ **Step 23**

When must interrogatories be answered?

Citation:

☐ **Step 24**

When can a request for admissions be made?

Citation:

☐ **Step 25**

When will a court order a physical or mental examination?

Citation:

☐ **Step 26**

Summarize the sanctions that can be imposed if a party improperly refuses to comply with valid discovery requests:

Citation:

☐ **Step 27**

In a divorce action, summarize the preliminary orders that can be granted by the court pendente lite.

Citation:

☐ **Step 28**

In a divorce action, what evidence, if any, must be corroborated?

Citation:

☐ **Step 29**

Are there any limitations on testimony that one spouse can give against the other?

Citation:

☐ **Step 30**

Can there be a jury trial in a divorce case? If so, when must the request for one be made?

Citation:

☐ **Step 31**

What happens if the defendant fails to appear? Can there be a default judgment?

Citation:

☐ **Step 32**

Is there an interlocutory decree or decree nisi? If so, how long is it effective, and how does the divorce become final?

Citation:

☐ **Step 33**

To what court can the divorce decree be appealed?

Citation:

☐ **Step 34**

How many days does a party have to appeal?

Citation:

☐ **Step 35**

Where and how is the notice of appeal filed and served?

Citation:

□ **Step 36**

Summarize the procedures that must be followed to seek enforcement of an alimony or child support order by contempt.

Citation:

□ **Step 37**

What is the statute of limitations for bringing an action to enforce an alimony award?

Citation:

□ **Step 38**

Summarize the procedures that must be followed to set aside a divorce judgment on the ground of fraud.

Citation:

SUMMARY

A person's residence is the place where he or she is living at a particular time. Domicile is the place where a person has been physically present with the intent to make that place a permanent home; it is the place to which one intends to return when away. In divorce laws, however, the word residence often has the meaning of domicile.

A divorce decree is divisible when only part of it is enforceable. The decree will dissolve the marriage. This part of the decree is enforceable if the court had in rem jurisdiction. If the court also orders alimony, child support, or property division without having personal jurisdiction over the defendant, this part of the decree is not enforceable. There are times, however, when a party with a valid jurisdictional challenge to a divorce decree will be estopped from bringing the challenge.

Once a court grants a divorce, one of the major concerns of the judgment debtor is how to enforce it. The remedies that are often available include civil contempt, execution, garnishment, attachment, posting security, receivership, constructive trust, prosecution for criminal nonsupport, QDRO, QMCSO, URESA, and UIFSA.

KEY CHAPTER TERMINOLOGY

Uncontested
Migratory Divorce
Foreign Divorce
"Quickie" Divorce
Collusive Divorce
Default Divorce
Divisible Divorce
Bilateral Divorce
Ex Parte Divorce
Dual Divorce
Uncontested Divorce
Contested Divorce
Divorce a Mensa et Thoro
Limited Divorce
Divorce a Vinculo Matrimonii
Residence
Domicile
Emancipated
Operation of Law
Domicile by Choice

Adversarial Hearing
Ex Parte Hearing
Direct Attack
Collateral Attack
Res Judicata
Estoppel
Equitable Estoppel
Foreign
Forum State
Full Faith and Credit
Service of Process
Substituted Service
Jurisdiction
Subject-Matter Jurisdiction
In Rem Jurisdiction
Res
Personal Jurisdiction
Long Arm Statute
Complaint
Summons

Petition
In Forma Pauperis
Pro Se
Guardian ad Litem
Venue
Pleading
Answer
Counterclaim
Discovery
Interrogatories
Deposition
Request for Admissions
Mental or Physical
  Examination
Request for Production
Pendente Lite
Voir Dire
Corroborated
Preponderance of Evidence
Privilege for Marital

Communications
Default Judgment
Alternative Dispute Resolution
  (ADR)
Interlocutory

Writ of Execution
Garnishment
Constructive Trust
QDRO
QMCSO

URESA
UIFSA
Full Faith and Credit Clause
Comity

15 TAX CONSEQUENCES OF SEPARATION AND DIVORCE

▰▰▰ THE ROLE OF TAX LAW IN THE BARGAINING PROCESS

Tax law should play a major role in the representation of divorce clients. Clauses in a separation agreement, for example, may have little relationship to the real world of dollars and cents if their tax consequences are not assessed (and to the extent possible, *bargained for*) before the agreement is signed. Income that once supported one household must now support two (or more) households. Careful tax planning can be of some help in accomplishing this objective.

We need to examine the three major financial components of a separation and divorce: alimony, child support, and property division. In general, the tax law governing these categories is as follows:

☐ The person who pays alimony (the payor) can deduct it.

☐ The person who receives alimony (the recipient or payee) must report it as income.

☐ Child support payments are not deductible to the payor nor reportable as income by the recipient.

☐ Payments pursuant to a property division are not deductible to the payor nor reportable as income by the recipient.

Since alimony is deductible, but child support and property division payments are not, attempts are often made to disguise child support or property division payments as alimony. A major theme of this chapter is to determine when such attempts are legal and when they will be challenged by the Internal Revenue Service (IRS).

Under our *progressive tax system*, every taxpayer does not pay the same tax *rate*. A high-income taxpayer will pay a higher percentage of income as tax than a low-income taxpayer. We refer to these individuals as being in different *tax brackets*. Generally, a deduction is worth more to someone in a high-income bracket than to someone in a lower bracket. The question at the bargaining table is whether the latter will cooperate in allowing the former to take such a deduction. Since a tax advantage to one side may be a distinct tax *disadvantage* to the other side, cooperation will probably be withheld unless something else is offered to offset the disadvantage. To understand the scope of what is negotiable between the parties, we need to understand the fundamentals of tax law and practice in this area.

■ ALIMONY

When certain conditions or tests are met, alimony (or separate-maintenance) payments are deductible to the payor and taxable to the recipient. The payments are:

□ Reported as taxable income on line 11 of the recipient's 1040 return (see Exhibit 15.1), and

□ Deducted from gross income on line 29 of the payor's 1040 return to obtain the latter's **adjusted gross income (AGI)** (refer again to Exhibit 15.1)

Adjusted Gross Income (AGI) The total amount of income received by a taxpayer less allowed deductions.

Since the deduction comes through the determination of adjusted gross income, there is no need to itemize deductions in order to take advantage of it.

Note that line 29 requires the payor to give the name and social security number of the recipient. Failure to do so can result in a $50 penalty fine and a disallowance of the deduction. Providing this information will make it easier for the IRS to check its own records to make sure that the recipient is reporting as income what the payor is deducting as alimony.

Unfortunately, defining alimony can be a complex undertaking. The IRS has its definition *for tax purposes,* and as we shall see, this definition is broader than the traditional notion of alimony as spousal support.

DEDUCTIBLE ALIMONY: THE SEVEN TESTS

When does a payment qualify as alimony for tax purposes?[1] When it meets the seven requirements for alimony listed in Exhibit 15.2. A more thorough discussion of each requirement follows:

□ **Divorce or Separation Agreement**
□ **No Joint Return**
□ **Parties Are Not Members of the Same Household**
□ **Payment in Cash**
□ **No Payment after Death of Recipient**
□ **Payment Is Not Treated as Child Support**
□ **Parties Have Not Exercised Nonalimony Option**

DIVORCE OR SEPARATION AGREEMENT The payment must be to a spouse or former spouse pursuant to and required by a divorce decree or a separation agreement. The decree does not have to be final. A payment ordered

---

1. The rules discussed here on the tax treatment of alimony payments pursuant to a decree of divorce also apply to payments pursuant to a decree of separate maintenance and a decree of annulment. The rules are also limited to payments made after 1984. Different rules apply to payments made before 1985.

□ **EXHIBIT 15.1   1040 Income Tax Form**

Form **1040**
Department of the Treasury–Internal Revenue Service
U.S. Individual Income Tax Return (T) **1994**

IRS Use Only–Do not write or staple in this space.

For the year Jan. 1–Dec. 31, 1994, or other tax year beginning _____ , 1994, ending _____ , 19 ___   OMB No. 1545-0074

Label
(See instructions on page 12.)
Use the IRS label. Otherwise, please print or type.

L A B E L   H E R E

Your first name and initial	Last name	Your social security number
If a joint return, spouse's first name and initial	Last name	Spouse's social security number
Home address (number and street). If you have a P.O. box, see page 12.	Apt. no.	For Privacy Act and Paperwork Reduction Act Notice, see page 4.
City, town or post office, state, and ZIP code. If you have a foreign address, see page 12.		

Presidential Election Campaign ►
(See page 12.)

Yes   No   Note: Checking "Yes" will not change your tax or reduce your refund.

Do you want $3 to go to this fund?
If a joint return, does your spouse want $3 to go to this fund?

Filing Status
(See page 12.)

Check only one box.

1   Single
2   Married filing joint return (even if only one had income)
3   Married filing separate return. Enter spouse's social security no. above and full name here. ►
4   Head of household (with qualifying person). (See page 13.) If the qualifying person is a child but not your dependent, enter this child's name here. ►
5   Qualifying widow(er) with dependent child (year spouse died ► 19___). (See page 13.)

Exemptions
(See page 13.)

6a ☐ Yourself. If your parent (or someone else) can claim you as a dependent on his or her tax return, *do not* check box 6a. But be sure to check the box on line 33b on page 2
  b ☐ Spouse

No. of boxes checked on 6a and 6b

  c Dependents:

(1) Name (first, initial, and last name)	(2) Check if under age 1	(3) If age 1 or older, dependent's social security number	(4) Dependent's relationship to you	(5) No. of months lived in your home in 1994

No. of your children on 6c who:
● lived with you
● didn't live with you due to divorce or separation (see page 14)

If more than six dependents, see page 14.

Dependents on 6c not entered above

  d If your child didn't live with you but is claimed as your dependent under a pre-1985 agreement, check here ► ☐
  e Total number of exemptions claimed

Add numbers entered on lines above ►

Income

Attach Copy B of your Forms W-2, W-2G, 1099-R here.

If you did not get a W-2, see page 15.

Enclose, but do not attach, any payment with your return.

7   Wages, salaries, tips, etc. Attach Form(s) W-2 7
8a **Taxable** interest income (see page 15). Attach Schedule B if over $400 .... 8a
  b **Tax-exempt** interest (see page 16). DON'T include on line 8a   8b
9   Dividend income. Attach Schedule B if over $400 9
10 Taxable refunds, credits, or offsets of state and local income taxes (see page 16) 10
11 Alimony received ◄ 11
12 Business income or (loss). Attach Schedule C or C-EZ 12
13 Capital gain or (loss). If required, attach Schedule D (see page 16) 13
14 Other gains or (losses). Attach Form 4797 14
15a Total IRA distributions .   15a _____   b Taxable amount (see page 17)   15b
16a Total pensions and annuities   16a _____   b Taxable amount (see page 17)   16b
17 Rental real estate, royalties, partnerships, S corporations, trusts, etc. Attach Schedule E   17
18 Farm income or (loss). Attach Schedule F 18
19 Unemployment compensation (see page 18) 19
20a Social security benefits   20a _____   b Taxable amount (see page 18)   20b
21 Other income. List type and amount–see page 18 _____ 21
22 Add the amounts in the far right column for lines 7 through 21. This is your total income ► 22

> Recipient reports alimony as income.

Adjustments to Income

Caution: See instructions . . ►

23a Your IRA deduction (see page 19) 23a
  b Spouse's IRA deduction (see page 19) .   23b
24 Moving expenses. Attach Form 3903 or 3903-F .   24
25 One-half of self-employment tax   25
26 Self-employed health insurance deduction (see page 21)   26
27 Keogh retirement plan and self-employed SEP deduction   27
28 Penalty on early withdrawal of savings   28
29 Alimony paid. Recipient's SSN ► _____   29
30 Add lines 23a through 29. These are your **total adjustments** .... ► 30

> Payor of alimony reports payments as adjustment to income. You deduct alimony from gross income to obtain your adjusted gross income.

Adjusted Gross Income

31 Subtract line 30 from line 22. This is your **adjusted gross income**. If less than $25,296 and a child lived with you (less than $9,000 if a child didn't live with you), see "Earned Income Credit" on page 27 ► 31

Cat. No. 11320B

Form **1040** (1994)

A payment qualifies as alimony when:

1. The payment is to a spouse or former spouse under a divorce decree or separation agreement.
2. The parties do not file a joint return with each other.
3. The parties are not members of the same household when the payment is made. (This third requirement applies only if the parties are separated under a decree of divorce or separate maintenance.)
4. The payment is in cash.
5. There is no obligation to make any payment (in cash or other property) after the death of the recipient.
6. The payment is not treated as child support.
7. The parties have not exercised the option of treating qualifying alimony payments as nonalimony.

by an *interlocutory* (interim or nonfinal) decree or a decree *pendente lite* (while awaiting the court's final decree) can also qualify.

Note that there is no specific requirement that the payment of alimony be for the *support* of the recipient, although we normally think of this as the purpose of alimony. *To qualify as alimony, a payment does not have to discharge an obligation of support.* The great attraction of alimony to the payor is its deductibility. The fact that alimony, for tax purposes, is not limited to spousal support is an open invitation to payors to try to fit different kinds of payments under the rubric of alimony to take advantage of this deductibility feature. Later we will examine the extent to which such efforts can succeed.

Finally, if a spouse makes an *additional* payment beyond what is required by the divorce or separation agreement, the additional payment is not alimony for tax purposes.

EXAMPLE 1 A 1994 separation agreement requires Linda to pay her ex-husband, Fred, a total of $1,000 per month in alimony. Assume that this amount fulfills all the requirements of deductible alimony. Hence, Linda can deduct each $1,000 payment and Fred must report it as income. During the last seven months of the year, Linda decides to increase her alimony payments to $3,000 each month in order to cover some extra expenses Fred is incurring.

Linda may *not* deduct the extra $14,000 ($2,000 × 7 months) she voluntarily added, and Fred does not have to report this $14,000 as income on his return. This is so even if state law considers the entire $3,000 payment each month to be alimony. Under *federal tax* law, voluntary alimony payments are not deductible.

NO JOINT RETURN   The parties must not file a joint return with each other at the time the attempt is made to deduct the alimony.

PARTIES ARE NOT MEMBERS OF THE SAME HOUSEHOLD   The *same-household* requirement applies when the parties have been separated under a decree of divorce.[2] (Note that two people living in physically separate rooms

---

2. As indicated earlier, references to a divorce decree include decrees of separate maintenance. See footnote 1.

are still considered part of the same household.) If there is no divorce decree, alimony payments can be deductible even if the parties are still living in the same household, so long as the other requirements for *deductible alimony* are met.

There is a one-month grace period for those separated by divorce. A payment made while the parties are together in the same household can be deductible if one party is preparing to move and does, in fact, move within one month after the payment.

EXAMPLE 2 Jack and Tara live at 100 Elm Street. They are divorced on January 1, 1995. Jack is obligated to pay Tara $500 a month in alimony on the first of each month. He makes his first payment January 1, 1995. He moves out of the Elm Street house on February 15, 1995.

The January 1, 1995, payment is *not* deductible. Since the parties have a divorce decree, they must not be living in the same household at the time of the alimony payment. Jack and Tara were both living at 100 Elm Street—the same household—at the time of that payment. The one-month grace period does not apply since Jack did not move out within a month of this payment. If he had left earlier (e.g., January 29, 1995), the payment *would* have been deductible. Of course, all payments after February 15, 1995 (when they opened separate households) are deductible, if the other requirements for deductible alimony are met.

PAYMENT IN CASH   Only *cash* payments, including checks and money orders, qualify.

EXAMPLE 3 Under the terms of a separation agreement and divorce decree, Bob:
- ☐ Gives Mary, his ex-wife, a car
- ☐ Paints her house
- ☐ Lets her use his mother's house
- ☐ Gives her stocks, bonds, or an annuity contract

The value of these items cannot be deducted as alimony since they are not in cash.

Can cash payments made by the payor to a third party be deducted as alimony?

EXAMPLE 4 Bob sends $1,000 to Mary's landlord to pay her rent. He also sends $800 to Mary's college to cover part of her tuition costs and $750 to Mary's bank to pay the mortgage on the house she owns.

Can Bob deduct any of these payments as alimony, and does Mary have to report them as income? The answer is yes, if the cash payment to the third party is required by the divorce decree or by the separation agreement, or, when not so required, if Mary sends Bob a written request to make the cash payment to the third party. The written request must state that Bob and Mary both intend the payments to the third party to be treated as alimony. If all the other tests for alimony are met, the payment to the third party is deductible by the payor and includible in the income of the recipient on whose behalf the payment is made.

Suppose that the third party is an insurance company.

EXAMPLE 5 Bob pays an annual premium of $1,700 on a life insurance policy on his life with Mary as the beneficiary.

Can he deduct these premiums as alimony? The answer is yes, but only if two conditions are met:

☐ The payor (Bob) is obligated to make these premium payments by the divorce decree or separation agreement.

☐ The beneficiary (Mary) *owns* the policy so that the payor cannot change the beneficiary.

No Payment after Death of Recipient

If the payor is obligated (under the divorce decree or separation agreement) to make payments after the death of the recipient, none of the payments made after *or before* the death of the recipient qualify as alimony. Here the IRS is trying to catch a blatant and improper attempt to disguise property division as alimony in order to take advantage of a deduction.

EXAMPLE 6 Under the terms of a separation agreement, Bob agrees to pay Mary $20,000 a year "in alimony" for ten years. If Mary dies within the ten years, Bob will make the remaining annual payments to Mary's estate. In the sixth year of the agreement, after Bob has paid Mary $120,000 (6 years × $20,000), Mary dies. For the next four years, Bob makes the remaining annual payments totaling $80,000 (4 years × $20,000) to Mary's estate.

All of the payments made by Bob will be disallowed as alimony—the entire $200,000 covering the periods before and after Mary's death. It makes no difference that the separation agreement called the payments "alimony." To qualify as deductible alimony, one of the tests is that the payor must have no liability for payments after the death of the recipient.

Whenever the payor must make payments beyond the death of the recipient, there is a strong suspicion that the payments are really part of a property division arrangement. Most normal debts continue in effect after the death of either party. If, for example, I pay you $3,500 to buy your car, and you die before delivering the car to me, it is clear that your obligation to give me the car survives your death. Your estate would have to give me the car. The same is true of a property division debt. Assume that Bob is obligated under a property division agreement to transfer a house to Mary, his ex-wife. If Bob dies before making this transfer, his estate can be forced to complete the transfer to Mary. Property division debts survive the death of either party. On the other hand, it is very rare for a "real" alimony debt to continue after the death of the recipient. After the recipient dies, he or she does not need alimony!

EXAMPLE 7 At the time of their separation, Mary had a separate career in which she earned a high salary. Bob owned a going business valued at $400,000, which he started when he married Mary. Bob and Mary agreed that she should have a substantial share of this business as part of the property division between them. But Bob does not want to sell the business in order to give Mary her share. In the negotiations, Mary asks for $150,000, payable immediately. Bob agrees that $150,000 is a fair amount, but he doesn't have it. Hence, he counters by offering her $200,000 payable over ten years in $20,000 annual payments to be labeled as "alimony" in their separation agreement. If Mary dies within the ten years, Bob will make the annual payments to Mary's estate. The extra $50,000 is added to offset the fact that Mary will have to wait in order to receive all her money and will have to pay income tax on whatever Bob declares as deductible alimony.

Again, this arrangement will not work. There are ways to disguise property division as alimony, but this is not one of them. The $200,000 can never be deductible alimony since the parties planned to continue the payments after the death of the recipient.

The IRS will reach the same conclusion if the payor agrees to make a substitute payment to a third party on the death of the recipient or a lump-sum payment to the estate of the recipient after his or her death.

PAYMENT IS NOT TREATED AS CHILD SUPPORT Child support is neither deductible by the payor nor includible in the income of the recipient. But what is child support? This question is easy to answer if the divorce decree or separation agreement specifically designates or fixes a payment (or part of a payment) as child support.

EXAMPLE 8 Under the terms of a divorce decree, Jane must pay Harry $2,000 a month, of which $1,600 is designated for the support of their child in the custody of Harry.

The $1,600 has been fixed as child support. Hence, it is not deductible by Jane nor includible in the income of Harry. This remains true even if the amount so designated varies from time to time.

Suppose, however, payments are made to the parent with custody of the children, but the parties say nothing about child support in their separation agreement, and the divorce decree is equally silent. The payments may even be labeled "alimony." In such a case, the IRS will suspect that the parties are trying to disguise child support payments as alimony in order to trigger a deduction for the payor. The suspicion will be even stronger if the separation agreement or divorce decree states that the payments are to be *reduced* upon the happening of certain events or contingencies that relate to the child's need for support.

EXAMPLE 9 Under the terms of a separation agreement, Bill will pay Grace $2,000 a month, "in alimony," which will be reduced to $800 a month when their child leaves the household and gets a job.

The parties are trying to disguise $1,200 a month as alimony, although it is fairly obvious that this amount is child support. Otherwise, why would the parties reduce the payment at a time when the child would no longer need support? What other reason would the parties have to add such a **contingency?** The device will not work.

Contingency An event that may or may not occur.

□ **Child Support Improperly Disguised as Alimony** The IRS will conclude that a payment is child support rather than alimony when the amount of the payment is to be reduced:

1. On the happening of a contingency relating to the child, or

2. At a time that can be clearly associated with a contingency relating to the child.

A contingency relates to a child when the contingency depends on an event that relates to that child.

EXAMPLE 10 The separation agreement of Bill and Mary Smith says that an "alimony" payment from Bill to Mary will be reduced by a designated amount when their son, Bob does any of the following:

☐ Reaches a specified age (see discussion below on when the reduction is to occur at the age of majority)

☐ Attains a specified income level

☐ Dies

☐ Marries

☐ Leaves school

☐ Leaves home (temporarily or permanently)

☐ Gains employment

Since each of these contingencies depends on an event that obviously relates to the child, no alimony deduction is allowed.

A payor will often want to reduce a payment when the child reaches the age of majority, which is usually 18 under state law. Will the IRS treat this reduction as an indication that alimony is being improperly disguised as child support? From what we have said thus far, one would expect the answer to be an unqualified "yes." But this is not necessarily so. The rule is as follows:

☐ **Reduction upon Age of Majority: Presumption of Child Support** The IRS will *presume* that a payment is child support if the reduction is to occur not more than six months before or after the child reaches the age of majority in the state.

Thus, if the reduction is to occur *more* than six months before or after the child reaches the age of majority, it will be treated as an alimony reduction.

EXAMPLE 11 Leo, Elaine, and their son Fred live in a state where the age of majority is 18. Fred was born on March 13, 1972. Leo and Elaine are divorced on January 12, 1980. Under the terms of the divorce decree, Elaine gets custody of Fred, and Leo must pay Elaine $2,000 a month in "alimony" until July 1, 1990, when the monthly payments are reduced to $1,200.

On these facts, the IRS will presume that the amount of the reduction is child support. Fred reaches the age of majority on March 13, 1990, when he turns 18. The reduction occurs on July 1, 1990, four months afterward. Since this reduction occurs "not more than six months . . . after the child reaches the age of majority," the presumption of child support applies.[3] The IRS will presume that the amount of the reduction ($800) is child support.

EXAMPLE 12 Same facts as in Example 11 except that the reduction is to occur on March 13, 1991.

On these facts, the presumption of child support does not apply. The reduction occurs one year after Fred reaches the age of majority, which of course is more than six months. The entire $2,000 can be deductible alimony.

---

3. This presumption can be rebutted by showing that the time at which the payments are to be reduced was determined independently of any contingencies relating to the children. For example, the payment period might be one customarily provided in the state, such as a period equal to one-half the duration of the marriage.

PARTIES HAVE NOT EXERCISED NONALIMONY OPTION Assume that all of the first six tests for determining alimony (see Exhibit 15.2) are met by the parties. As a result, the payor can deduct the payments and the recipient must include them in income. But suppose the parties do *not* want the payments to be deductible/includible. It may be, for example, that both parties are in the same tax bracket and hence neither would benefit significantly more than the other by having the tax alimony rules apply. They can decide to treat otherwise qualifying alimony payments as *nonalimony*. This is done by including a provision in the separation agreement or by asking the court to include a provision in the divorce decree that the payments will *not* be deductible to the payor and will be excludible from the income of the recipient.

The designation of nondeductibility/nonincludibility must be attached to the recipient's tax return for every year in which it is effective.

THE RECAPTURE RULE: FRONT LOADING OF PAYMENTS

A common tactic of a party who wants to try to disguise property division payments as alimony is to make substantial payments shortly after the divorce or separation, i.e., to **front load** the payments.

Front Load To try to disguise alimony as property division by making substantial "alimony" payments shortly after the separation or divorce.

EXAMPLE 13 Jim runs a cleaning business, which he developed during his marriage to Pat. The value of the business is $180,000 on the date of their divorce. During their negotiations for the separation agreement, they both agree that each should receive an equal share of the business, which Jim wants to continue to run after the divorce. They are clearly thinking about a property division. Of course, any payments pursuant to a property division are not deductible. Jim suggests a different route: he will pay Pat $30,000 a year in "alimony" for the first three years after their separation in return for a release of all her interest in the business. To secure this arrangement, Jim gives Pat a lien on the business until he pays the $90,000. For each of the three years, the payor (Jim) takes a $30,000 deduction, and the recipient (Pat) includes $30,000 in her income.

We said earlier there is no requirement that alimony be for the support of the recipient. Accordingly, in theory it is not improper to try to disguise property division payments as deductible alimony. But the parties must not go too far. The **recapture rule** is designed to catch parties who have gone too far through excessive front loading. To this end, the rule limits the extent to which large payments made over a relatively short period can qualify as deductible alimony. When the rule applies, its effect is to change the tax treatment of past payments by:

Recapture Rule Tax liability will be recalculated when the parties improperly attempt to disguise property division as alimony by front loading.

□ Requiring the payor to remove the deduction previously taken for payments, and hence to include such payments in the calculation of the payor's income, and

□ Allowing the recipient who previously included the alimony in income (and paid taxes on it) to deduct it from income so that taxes do not have to be paid on it

To apply the rule, let us look at a three-year period, beginning with the first calendar year that a payment qualifies as alimony. (This first year is sometimes referred to as the first *post-separation year*, which is not necessarily the year the parties separated.) The second and third years are the next two calendar years whether or not payments are made during these years.

EXAMPLE 14 Al and Jane were divorced on February 3, 1992. Under the terms of the divorce decree, Jane pays Al the following amounts of "alimony:"

Year	Amount
1992	$60,000
1993	40,000
1994	20,000

To figure the amounts that must be recaptured, if any, use the worksheet in Exhibit 15.3. In our example, $22,500 must be recaptured by Jane, the payor. She must show this amount as income on line 11 of her 1994 return. (Line 11 now says "Alimony received." She must cross out the word "received" and write in the word "recapture," so that 11 will read "Alimony recapture.") Al, the payee, can deduct $22,500 on line 29 of his 1994 return. (Line 29 now says "Alimony paid." He must cross out the word "paid" and write in the word "recapture" so that line 29 will read "Alimony recapture.")[4]

▬ PROPERTY DIVISION

In this section our focus will be the division of property between spouses that fairly accounts for their mutual efforts in obtaining and/or improving the property during the marriage. Before discussing the tax consequences of such a property division, we need to review some basic terminology. The following example at the top of page 402 will be used to help explain this terminology.

□ **EXHIBIT 15.3 Recapture Worksheet**

WORKSHEET FOR RECAPTURE OF ALIMONY		
Note: Do not enter less than zero on any line.		
1. Alimony paid in **2nd year**		$40,000
2. Alimony paid in **3rd year**	$20,000	
3. Floor	$15,000	
4. Add lines 2 and 3		35,000
5. Subtract line 4 from line 1		$ 5,000
6. Alimony paid in **1st year**		60,000
7. Adjusted alimony paid in **2nd year** (line 1 less line 5)	35,000	
8. Alimony paid in **3rd year**	20,000	
9. Add lines 7 and 8	55,000	
10. Divide line 9 by 2	27,500	
11. Floor	$15,000	
12. Add lines 10 and 11		42,500
13. Subtract line 12 from line 6		*17,500
14. **Recapture alimony.** Add lines 5 and 13		$22,500
*If you deducted alimony paid, report this amount as income on line 11, Form 1040.		
If you reported alimony received, deduct this amount on line 29, Form 1040.		

---

4. There are a number of important exceptions to the recapture rule. Regardless of the amount of the payment, the recapture rule does not apply (a) to payments under a temporary support order before the divorce or separation, (b) to payments required over a period of at least three calendar years of a fixed part of the payor's income from a business or property, or from compensation for employment or self-employment, or (c) to payments that end because the payor or recipient dies or the recipient remarries.

EXAMPLE 15 Tom buys a house in 1970 for $60,000. He spends $10,000 to add a new room. In 1981, he sells the house to a stranger for $100,000.

☐ **Transferor** The person who transfers property. Tom is the transferor.

☐ **Transferee** The person to whom property is transferred. The stranger is the transferee.

☐ **Appreciation** An increase in value. Tom's house appreciated by $40,000 (from $60,000 to $100,000). He has made a profit, called a *gain.* The gain, however, is *not* $40,000. See the definition for *adjusted basis* below.

☐ **Depreciation** A decrease in value. If the highest price Tom could have obtained for his house had been $55,000, the house would have depreciated by $5,000.

☐ **Realize** To benefit from or receive. Normally, *income, gain,* or *loss* are realized when they are received. If Tom could sell his house for $100,000, but he decides not to do so, he has not realized any income. He has a "paper" gain only. He does not have to pay taxes on a gain until he has realized a gain, e.g., by actually selling the house.

☐ **Fair Market Value** The price that could be obtained in an open market between a willing buyer and a willing seller dealing *at arm's length.* A sale between a parent and a child will usually not be at fair market value since the fact that they are related will probably affect the price paid. It is possible for a happily married husband and wife to sell something to each other at fair market value, but the likelihood is that they will not. In our example, Tom sold his house for $100,000 to a stranger. There is no indication that the buyer or seller was pressured into the transaction or that either had any special relationship with each other that might have affected the price or the terms of the deal. The price paid, therefore, was the fair market value.

☐ **Basis** The initial capital investment, usually the cost of the property. Tom's basis in his house is $60,000.

☐ **Adjusted Basis** The basis of the property after adjustments are made. The basis is either adjusted upward (increased) by the amount of *capital improvements* (i.e., structural improvements on the property) or adjusted downward. Tom added a room to his house—a structural improvement. His basis ($60,000) is increased by the amount of the capital expenditure ($10,000), giving him an adjusted basis of $70,000.

When Tom sold his house for $100,000, he *realized* income. To determine whether he realized a gain or profit, we need to compare this figure with his adjusted basis. The amount of gain for tax purposes is determined as follows:

SALE PRICE − ADJUSTED BASIS = TAXABLE GAIN
($100,000)   ($70,000)   ($30,000)

Tom must declare this gain of $30,000 on his tax return. Of course, if the sale price had been *less* than the adjusted basis, he would have realized a loss. If, for example, he had sold the house for $65,000, his loss would have been $5,000 ($70,000 − $65,000).

TAX CONSEQUENCES OF A PROPERTY DIVISION

A property division can be in cash or in other property. To illustrate:

CASH: Ex-wife receives a lump sum of $50,000 (or five yearly payments of $10,000) in exchange for the release of any rights she may have in property acquired during the marriage.

OTHER PROPERTY: Ex-wife receives the marital home, and the ex-husband receives stocks and the family business. They both release any rights they may have in property acquired during the marriage.

Cash property divisions rarely pose difficulties unless the parties are trying to disguise property division as alimony in order to take advantage of the deductibility of alimony. We already discussed when such attempts will be unsuccessful. A true property division in cash is a nontaxable event; nothing is deducted and nothing is included in the income of either party. The IRS will assume that what was exchanged was of equal value.

Suppose, however, that property other than cash is transferred in a property division and that the property so transferred had *appreciated* in value since the time it had been acquired by the transferor. Our problem is twofold:

☐ When *appreciated* property is transferred as part of a property division, is any gain or loss realized?

☐ What is the basis of such property in the hands of the transferee?

To examine these questions in concrete terms, let us return to Tom and his house in Example 15. Suppose that instead of selling the house to a stranger, he transfers it to his wife.

EXAMPLE 16 Tom buys a house in 1970 for $60,000. He spends $10,000 to add a new room. In 1981, on the date of his divorce, he transfers the house to his wife, Tara, as part of a property division that they negotiated. Tara releases any rights, e.g., dower, that she may have in his property. On the date of the transfer, the fair market value of the house is $100,000.

Note that all of this occurred before 1984. The law changed in 1984, but in order to understand the change, we need to understand the old law. The first question in Example 16 is whether Tom realized a gain of $30,000 at the time of the transfer to his ex-wife. Prior to 1984, the answer was yes. The United States Supreme Court so held in *United States v. Davis*, 370 U.S. 65, 82 S. Ct. 1190, 8 L. Ed. 2d 335 (1962). Hence, when Tom transferred a $100,000 home to his ex-wife as part of a property division, he received no deduction, since the transfer did not qualify as alimony, and he had to pay tax on his realized gain of $30,000. In answer to the second question, the basis of the property in the hands of Tara, the transferee, was the fair market value of the property at the time of the transfer, here $100,000. What Tara gave Tom (i.e., a release of her rights in his property) was assumed to be equal in value to what she received.

EXAMPLE 17 Same facts as in Example 16. In 1983 Tara sells the home to a stranger for $105,000. Assume that she made no capital improvements in the property since she acquired it from her ex-husband, Tom, in 1981.

Tara has realized a gain of $5,000. When she received the property, her basis was its fair market value, $100,000. Since she did not improve the property, this was her adjusted basis when she sold it in 1983:

SALE PRICE − ADJUSTED BASIS = TAXABLE GAIN
($105,000)   ($100,000)   ($5,000)

Everybody was unhappy about these tax rules—except the transferee, who was delighted to have fair market value as the basis. Transferors complained about being hit twice. "It's bad enough having to turn over property to my ex-wife that I can't deduct. On top of it all, I owe tax to the IRS on the appreciation." The IRS was also unhappy, because many transferors were neglecting to report the gain that resulted from the appreciation. Furthermore, the high basis of the property in the hands of the transferee (i.e., fair market value) meant that the IRS often collected very little tax when the transferee sold the property to someone else. See Example 17.

In 1984 Congress made a radical change in the law, which had the effect of overruling *United States v. Davis*. Under the new law, no gain or loss is recognized upon the transfer of appreciated property, and the adjusted basis in the property of the transferor is carried over to become the transferee's basis.

EXAMPLE 18 Use the same facts as in Examples 16 and 17 except that the date of the divorce, when Tom transferred the house to Tara, is 1985 (rather than 1981), and the date Tara sold the house to a stranger is 1986 (rather than 1983).

The new rules apply. Tom does *not* pay a tax on the appreciation at the time of the transfer to Tara. And the tax picture at the time Tara sells the property is substantially different:

SALE PRICE − ADJUSTED BASIS = TAXABLE GAIN
($105,000)   ($70,000)   ($35,000)

Tara takes over Tom's adjusted basis at the time she receives the property from him—$70,000. This becomes her basis when she sells it to someone else.

Needless to say, it is essential that a spouse know the adjusted basis of the property in the hands of the other spouse before accepting that property as part of a property division. It is meaningless, for example, to be told that property is "worth $150,000" on the market unless you are also told what the adjusted basis of that property is.

These new rules do not apply to every transfer of property between spouses or ex-spouses. We turn now to those that are covered.

PROPERTY TRANSFERS COVERED

In general, the new tax rules governing a property division apply to property transfers that are *incident to a divorce*. A property transfer is incident to a divorce when the transfer:

☐ Occurs within one year after the date on which the marriage ends, *or*
☐ Is related to the ending of the marriage

A property transfer is related to the ending of the marriage *if* it occurs within six years after the date on which the marriage ends *and* is made under a divorce or separation instrument.

A property transfer that is not made under a divorce or separation instrument, or that does not occur within six years after the end of the marriage is *presumed* to be unrelated to the ending of the marriage, unless the parties can show that some business or legal factors prevented an earlier transfer of the property.

EXAMPLE 19 Gabe solely owns a garage and a residence. He and his wife, Janet, are divorced on January 10, 1985. Pursuant to a property division that is spelled out in their separation agreement, Gabe will keep the residence but will transfer the garage to Janet on March 13, 1992.

Was the transfer of the garage incident to a divorce? It did not occur within a year of the ending of the marriage. But was it related to the ending of the marriage? It did not occur within six years of the ending of the marriage. The transfer was made just over seven years after the divorce. We are not told why the parties waited this long after the divorce, but there is no evidence of business or legal factors that prevented an earlier transfer. Hence the IRS will *presume* that the transfer was not related to the ending of the marriage, and the new tax rules discussed above will *not* apply to the transfer.

☐ **Tax Treatment of Payments and Transfers Pursuant to Post-1984 Divorce Agreements and Decrees**

	Payor	**Recipient**
Alimony	Deduction from gross income.	Included in gross income.
Alimony recapture	Included in gross income of the third year.	Deducted from gross income of the third year.
Child support	Not deductible.	Not includible in income.
Property settlement	Not included in gross income. Not deductible.	Not included in gross income. Not deductible; basis for the property is the same as the transferor's basis if the transfer is incident to a divorce.

SOURCE: West's Federal Taxation: Individual Income Taxes, 4–22 (1994).

■■■■■ LEGAL AND RELATED FEES IN OBTAINING A DIVORCE

Obtaining a divorce can be expensive. In addition to attorney fees, one or both parties may have to hire an accountant, actuary, and appraiser. Only two types of such fees are deductible:

☐ Fees paid for *tax* advice in connection with a divorce

☐ Fees paid to obtain *alimony* included in gross income

Other fees are not deductible. For example, you cannot deduct legal fees paid to negotiate the most advantageous or financially beneficial property division.

Bills from professionals received by a taxpayer should include a breakdown showing the amount charged for each service performed.

EXAMPLE 20

For representation in divorce case $9,000
For tax advice in connection with the divorce 800
Total bill..$9,800
Only $800 is deductible.

EXAMPLE 21

For representation in divorce case $6,500
For services in obtaining alimony 1,200
Total bill $7,700
Only $1,200 is deductible.

ASSIGNMENT 15.1

John and Carol are divorced on September 1, 1991. Their separation agreement requires John to pay Carol $500 a week for her support until she dies. Use the guidelines of this chapter to answer the following questions that present a number of variations in the case of John and Carol. (See General Instructions for the Legal-Analysis Assignment in chapter 1.)

a. Carol has an automobile accident. To help her with medical bills, John sends her a check for $900 with the following note: "Here's my monthly $500 payment plus an extra $400 alimony to help you with your medical bills." Can John deduct the entire $900 as alimony?

b. A year after the divorce, Carol has trouble paying her state income tax bill of $1,200. John wants to give her a gift of $1,200 in addition to his regular $500 monthly alimony. He sends $1,200 to the state tax department on her behalf. Can John deduct the $1,200 as alimony?

c. Assume that in the September 1, 1991 divorce, Carol is awarded $1,500 a month in alimony, effective immediately and payable on the first of each month. John makes a payment on September 1, 1991. (He also paid her $1,000 for her support on August 1, 1991, before they went to court.) During all this time, John lived in the basement of their home, which has a separate entrance. He moves into his own apartment in another town on October 25, 1991. Which of the following 1991 payments, if any, are deductible: $1,000 (on August 1), $1,500 (on September 1), and $1,500 (on October 1)?

d. Assume that under the divorce decree, John must make annual alimony payments to Carol of $30,000, ending on the earlier of the expiration of fifteen years or the death of Carol. If Carol dies before the expiration of the fifteen-year period, John must pay Carol's estate the difference between the total amount he would have paid her if she survived, minus the amount actually paid. Carol dies after the tenth year in which payments are made. John now pays her estate $150,000 ($450,000 − $300,000). How much of the $300,000 paid before her death is deductible alimony? How much of the $150,000 lump sum is deductible alimony?

e. Assume that under the terms of the separation agreement, John will pay Carol $200 a month in child support for their only child, Nancy, and $900 a month as alimony. If Nancy marries, however, the $900 payment will be reduced to $400 a month. What is deductible?

f. Assume that under the terms of the separation agreement, John will pay Carol $200 a month as child support for their only child, Nancy, and $900 a month as alimony. While Nancy is away at boarding school, however, the $900 payment will be reduced to $400 a month. What is deductible?

ASSIGNMENT 15.2

a. Greg was born on July 31, 1980. He is the only child of Bill and Karen. Under the terms of their separation agreement, which becomes effective on December 5, 1995, Bill is to have custody of Greg, and Karen is to pay him $4,000 a month in alimony. The agreement specifies that "none of the alimony is to be used for child support." On April 15, 1998, the alimony payment is to be reduced to $2,200 a month. What will be deductible?

b. Millie pays Paul the following amounts of alimony under the terms of her 1987 divorce decree:

Year	Amount
1987	$25,000
1988	4,000
1989	4,000

What amounts, if any, must be recaptured?

c. Under a 1989 separation agreement and divorce decree, Helen transfers a building she solely owns to her ex-husband, Ken, in exchange for his release of any rights he has in other property that Helen acquired during the marriage. The transfer is made on the day of the divorce. Helen had bought the building in 1986 for $1,000,000. In 1987 she made $200,000 worth of capital improvements in the building. Its fair market value on the date she transfers it to Ken is $1,500,000. A week later, however, the market crashes and Ken is forced to sell the building for $800,000. What are the tax consequences of these transactions?

d. Same facts as (c) except assume that all of these transactions occurred before 1984. What are the tax consequences of the transactions?

e. Dan and Karen are negotiating a separation agreement in contemplation of a divorce that they expect to occur within six months of today's date. Karen wants $1,000 a month in alimony, and she wants Dan to pay all of her legal fees. Dan agrees to do so. Assume that there will be no difficulty deducting the $1,000 a month under the alimony rules. Dan would also like to deduct what he pays for her legal fees, which are anticipated to be $12,000, of which $3,000 will be for obtaining alimony from Dan. What options exist for Dan?

▉▉▉▉ SUMMARY

Since a husband and wife are often in different tax brackets, the issue of who receives a tax deduction for a certain payment can be extremely important. Tax consequences, therefore, should be a part of the negotiation process in a separation and divorce.

If seven tests are met, alimony can be deducted by the payor but then must be declared as income by the recipient:

1. The payment must be to a spouse or former spouse and must be required by a divorce decree or separation agreement.

2. The parties must not file a joint return with each other.

3. The parties must not be members of the same household if they are separated under a decree of divorce.

4. The payment must be in cash.

5. The payor must be under no obligation to make payments after the death of the recipient.

6. The payment must not be improperly disguised as child support.

7. The parties must not elect to treat qualifying alimony payments as nonalimony.

If substantial payments are made shortly after a divorce or separation, the IRS will suspect that the parties are trying to disguise nondeductible, property division payments as deductible alimony payments. Such excessive front loading may result in a recalculation of taxes paid in prior years in order to recapture improper deductions for alimony.

In a property division incident to a divorce, property is transferred from one ex-spouse to the other. The property can be cash (e.g., $50,000) or noncash (e.g., a house). When there is a transfer of cash, none of it is deducted by the transferor, and none of it is included in the income of the transferee. When there is a transfer of noncash property that has appreciated in value, the following rules apply:

1. The transferor does not deduct anything.

2. The transferee does not include anything in income.

3. The transferor does not have to pay taxes on the amount of the appreciation.

4. The basis of the property in the hands of the transferee is the same basis that the property had in the hands of the transferor.

A fee paid to your own attorney, accountant, or other professional is deductible if for tax advice in connection with a divorce, or if paid to help you obtain alimony that is included in gross income.

▮▮▮ KEY CHAPTER TERMINOLOGY

Adjusted Gross Income (AGI)
Contingency
Front Load
Recapture Rule

Transferor
Transferee
Appreciation
Depreciation

Realize
Fair Market Value
Basis
Adjusted Basis

THE LEGAL RIGHTS OF WOMEN

16

Man is, or should be, woman's protector and defender. The natural and proper timidity and delicacy which belongs to the female sex evidently unfits it for many of the occupations of civil life. The constitution of the family organization, which is founded in the divine ordinance, as well as in the nature of things, indicates the domestic sphere as that which properly belongs to the domain and function of womanhood . . . The paramount destiny and mission of woman are to fulfill the noble and benign offices of wife and mother. This is the law of the Creator. *Bradwell v. Illinois,* 83 U.S. (16 Wall.) 130, 140–41, 21 L. Ed. 442 (1872)

No longer is the female destined solely for the home and the rearing of the family, and only the male for the marketplace, and the world of ideas. *Stanton v. Stanton,* 412 U.S. 7, 15, 95 S. Ct. 1373, 1378, 43 L. Ed. 2d 688 (1975).

THE STATUS OF WOMEN AT COMMON LAW

Today, a married woman would consider it condescending to be told that she has the right to:

☐ Make her own will
☐ Own her own property
☐ Make a contract in her own name
☐ Be a juror
☐ Vote
☐ Bring a suit and be sued
☐ Execute a deed

There was a time in our history, however, when a married woman could engage in none of these activities, at least not without the consent of her husband. For example, she could not bring a suit against a third party unless her husband agreed to join in it. Upon marriage, any personal property that she owned automatically became her husband's. If she committed a crime in the presence of her husband, the law assumed that he forced her to commit it. If she worked outside the home, her husband was entitled to her earnings. In short, at common law, the husband and wife were considered one person, and the one person was the husband![1]

While a great deal has happened to change the status of married women, not all sex discrimination has been eliminated.

Married Women's Property Acts Statutes removing all or most of the legal disabilities imposed on women as to the disposition of their property.

■■■■ OWNING AND DISPOSING OF PROPERTY

Most states have enacted **Married Women's Property Acts** that remove the disabilities married women suffered at common law. Under the terms of most of these statutes, women are given the right to own and dispose of property in the same manner as men.

ASSIGNMENT 16.1

Mary and Thad are married. Mary is a doctor and Thad is an architect. Before the marriage, Thad incurred a $35,000 debt at a local bank for his own education expenses. He is now in default on the loan. To collect this debt in your state, can the bank reach a vacation home that is solely owned by Mary? (See General Instructions for the State-Code Assignment and for the Court-Opinion Assignment in chapter 1.) Answer this question based on the following assumptions:

a. Mary acquired title to the vacation home as an inheritance from her uncle before she married Thad.

b. Mary acquired title to the vacation home as an inheritance from her uncle during her marriage to Thad.

c. Mary acquired title to the vacation home by buying it from a stranger solely from her own earnings as a doctor during her marriage to Thad.

d. Mary acquired title to the vacation home by buying it from Thad for $1 during the marriage. Thad inherited it from his mother before he married Mary. The sale to Mary was made just before Thad discovered that he was going to default on the bank loan. (See the next section on "Contracts and Conveyances.")

Conveyance The transfer of an interest in land.

■■■■ CONTRACTS AND CONVEYANCES

Today women have the power to enter into all forms of contracts and **conveyances** in their own names, independent of their husbands. If, however, both spouses own property together, the wife normally must have the consent of her husband—and vice versa—to convey the property to someone else.

What about contracts and conveyances between the spouses? Are there any restrictions on the ability of one spouse to enter into agreements with the other? If they are still living together, they cannot enter a contract concerning one spouse's duty to support the other (although such a contract will be valid after the parties have separated, see chapter 10).

Courts tend to be very suspicious of conveyances of property between husband and wife. Suppose, for example, that a husband transfers all his property

---

1. An unmarried woman at common law was not as handicapped, since she could own property and enter into contracts in her own name. But she could not vote or serve on juries, and her inheritance rights were limited. H. Clark, *The Law of Domestic Relations in the United States,* § 8.1, p. 498 (Practitioner's Ed. 2d ed. 1987).

into his wife's name, for which she pays nothing, so that when he is sued by his creditors, he technically does not own any assets from which they can satisfy their claims. The transfers would be considered fraudulent and would be invalidated by a court.

Two other situations can cause difficulty:

☐ The husband buys property with his separate funds but places the title in his wife's name. (Assume this is not a fraudulent transfer—he is not trying to defraud his creditors.)

☐ The wife buys property with her separate funds but places the title in her husband's name. (Again, assume no intent to defraud her creditors.)

Some courts treat the above two situations differently. In the first, most courts presume that the husband intended to make a gift of the property to his wife. In the second circumstance, however, a few courts do *not* presume a gift of the wife to her husband. Rather, the presumption is that the husband is holding the property in trust for his wife. Arguably, however, this is an unconstitutional discrimination based on sex, and some courts have so held. In these courts, whatever either spouse contributes to the purchase price is considered a gift to the other spouse unless it is clear that they had a different intention.

ASSIGNMENT 16.2

For the following questions, you will need to consult the statutory code of your state and/or the opinions of the courts sitting in your state. (See General Instructions for the State-Code Assignment and for the Court-Opinion Assignment in chapter 1.)

a. In your state, is there a Married Women's Property Act or an equivalent statute? If so, what is the citation?

b. Is the consent of the husband required when his wife wishes to convey her separately owned property to a third person?

c. What restrictions, if any, exist in your state on the capacity of one spouse to enter into a contract with the other?

d. Suppose that a wife worked for her husband in the latter's business in your state. Does the husband have to pay her or would such work be considered part of the "services" that she owes him?

■■■■ DEATH OF THE HUSBAND

DOWER

At common law, when a husband died, the surviving wife was given the protection of **dower,** although not all states defined dower in the same way. In many states, it was the right of a surviving wife to use one-third of all the real estate her deceased husband owned during the marriage.[2] The practical impact of this law was that the husband could not sell or give his property to others without accounting for her dower right. Very often she was paid to "waive her dower rights" so that others could obtain clear title to this property.

Dower The right of a widow to the lifetime use of one-third of the land her deceased husband owned during the marriage.

---

2. Some states imposed the requirement that she die leaving issue capable of inheriting the estate. If the wife died, the surviving husband was protected by **curtesy,** which was the right of a husband to the lifetime use of all the land his deceased wife owned during the marriage (if issue were born of the marriage).

RIGHT OF ELECTION

Forced Share The share of a deceased spouse's estate that a surviving spouse elects in lieu of provisions for the latter in the deceased's spouse's will.

Dower has been abolished in most states. In its place, the wife is given a share of her deceased husband's estate, often called a **forced share** because she can elect to take it in place of, and in spite of, what he gives her in his will. In exercising this **right of election,** she usually receives whatever the state would have provided for her if her husband had died **intestate.**

ASSIGNMENT 16.3

For the following questions, examine the statutory code of your state. (See General Instructions for the State-Code Assignment in chapter 1.)

a. Has dower been abolished in your state? If so, give the citation to the statute that abolished it.

b. If a widow is not satisfied with the property left her in the will of her deceased husband, what can she do in your state? Can she elect against the will?

c. If her husband dies intestate, what proportion of his estate will his widow receive in your state?

d. Does curtesy still exist in your state? If so, what is it? If not, what has replaced it, if anything?

Right of Election The right to take a designated share of a deceased spouse's estate in spite of what the latter provided or failed to provide for the surviving spouse in a will.

Intestate Dying without leaving a valid will.

▰▰▰ NAME

Many women change their surname to that of their husband at the time of marriage. This is done for one of two reasons:

☐ The law of the state gives her a choice on keeping her maiden name or taking her husband's name, and she chooses the latter.

☐ The law of the state gives her a choice that she does not know about; she uses her husband's name simply because that is the custom.

At one time, the law of some states *required* her to use her husband's name. Such laws have either been repealed or are clearly subject to constitutional attack since husbands are not required to take the name of their wife and no rational reason exists for the distinction. If she decides not to use her husband's name, she does not have to go through any special steps to exercise this choice. Once she is married, she simply continues using her maiden name, or she starts using a totally new name (other than her husband's). In such states, her legal name is whatever name she uses after her marriage so long as she is not trying to defraud anyone (e.g., to make it difficult for her creditors to locate her), and so long as her use of the name is exclusive and consistent.

Once there has been a divorce, most states permit the woman to request that the court allow her to resume using her maiden name or another name. Some states, however, place restrictions on resuming a maiden name or selecting a new name if there are children of the marriage. Suppose that she makes the request that her child's name be changed to her maiden name or to the name of her new husband. Many courts are reluctant to authorize this change unless it can be shown to be in the best interest of the child.

Independent of marriage or divorce, every state has a statutory procedure that must be used when citizens (male or female) wish to change their name. This *change-of-name* procedure involves several steps, e.g., filing a petition to change one's name in the appropriate state court, stating the reasons for the change, paying a fee to the court, publishing a notice of the court proceeding in a local newspaper. The process is usually not complicated so long as the court is convinced that the name change will not mislead anyone who may need to contact the individual, e.g., police officials, a former spouse, creditors.

ASSIGNMENT 16.4

For most of the following assignments, you will need to examine your state statutory code. You may also need to check opinions written by your state courts. (See General Instructions for the State-Code Assignment and for the Court-Opinion Assignment in chapter 1.)

a. When a woman marries in your state, does she have to take her husband's name?

b. After a divorce, how can a woman change her name to her maiden name?

c. Make a list of three different administrative agencies situated in your state that require some kind of application to be filled out, e.g., for a driver's license, for state employment, for food stamps, for worker's compensation. Assume that a recently married woman is filling out all three applications, and she wants to use her maiden name, not her husband's name, on the application. She has not been through a change-of-name statutory procedure. Contact each agency and ask if a woman can use her maiden name on the application.

d. Prepare a flowchart of all the steps that an individual must go through to change his or her name in your state through the appropriate statutory procedure. (See General Instructions for the Flowchart Assignment in chapter 1.)

e. Assume that you want to change your name. Pick a new name. Draft all the necessary court papers to acquire your new name via the statutory procedure outlined in the flowchart prepared in part (d).

f. Mary Jones married Tom Smith in your state. Her name then became Mary Smith. They had one child, Paul Smith. Tom abandons Mary. Can Mary have Paul's name changed to Paul Jones in your state? Assume that Paul is five years old and that Mary does not want to bring a divorce proceeding against Tom.

▬▬▬ CREDIT

Federal law prohibits discrimination on the basis of sex or marital status in a credit application.[3] Creditors such as banks or department stores that violate this prohibition can be sued and subject to punitive damages. In addition, a successful plaintiff can force the defendant to pay her court costs and reasonable attorney's fees in bringing the suit. Some of the specific prohibitions are as follows:

☐ A creditor cannot refuse to grant a woman an individual account because of her sex or marital status. For example, a woman cannot be required to open a joint account with her husband if she wants her own account and otherwise qualifies for one.

☐ A creditor cannot refuse a woman's request to open an account in her maiden name or in her hyphenated surname with her husband.

☐ A creditor cannot ask a woman for information about her husband or ex-husband unless she is relying on his income in seeking credit.

☐ A creditor cannot ask about a woman's plans to have children. In order to estimate her expenses, however, the creditor may ask how many children she has, their ages, and the cost of caring for them.

☐ A creditor cannot require that a woman disclose income from alimony, child support, or separate maintenance in her application for credit. If, how-

---

3. Or on the basis of race, color, religion, national origin, or age. 15 U.S.C.A. § 1691.

ever, she decides to disclose such items, the creditor cannot refuse to consider them. Furthermore, she can be asked how regularly she receives them in order to determine whether they are dependable sources of income.

☐ A creditor cannot require that a woman use a courtesy title (Miss, Ms., or Mrs.) on the application form.

☐ A creditor cannot request a woman's marital status in an application for an individual, unsecured account (such as a bank credit card or an overdraft checking account) where no community property is involved. A creditor cannot discriminate against a woman because of her marital status, but may consider her marital status in deciding whether to extend credit to her if she lives in a state where differences in her marital status may affect the creditor's ability to collect if she defaults, e.g., in a community property state.

☐ A creditor cannot consider a woman's sex as a factor in deciding whether she is a good risk.

▰▰▰ EMPLOYMENT

JOB DISCRIMINATION

There are a good many laws that in theory have eliminated job discrimination against women. The Equal Protection Clause of the United States Constitution provides that:

> No State shall . . . deny to any person within its jurisdiction the equal protection of the laws.

If a state passes a law that treats women differently from men, it will be invalidated unless there is a reasonable purpose for the differentiation. Only *unreasonable* discrimination violates the Constitution. Title VII of the 1964 Civil Rights Act provides that:

> It shall be an unlawful employment practice for an employer . . . to fail or refuse to hire or to discharge any individual, or otherwise to discriminate against any individual with respect to his compensation, terms, conditions, or privileges of employment, because of such individual's . . . sex; . . . 42 U.S.C.A. § 2000e–2(a)(1)(1974).

Again, this does not mean that all sex discrimination in employment is illegal. If men and women are doing the same job in a company but are being paid differently, the practice would be invalid, since they are both performing the same job. Job-related sex discrimination is permitted, however, if sex is a **Bona Fide Occupational Qualification (BFOQ),** meaning that sex discrimination is reasonably necessary to the operation of a particular business or enterprise. For example, it would be proper for a state prison to exclude women from being guards in all-male prisons where a significant number of the inmates are convicted sex offenders. It is reasonable to anticipate that some of the inmates would attack the female guards, creating a security problem. In this instance, the discrimination based on sex (i.e., being a male) in an all-male prison would be a BFOQ. An even clearer example of a BFOQ would be an acting job that required someone to play a mother. On the other hand, a BFOQ does *not* exist simply because customers or co-workers prefer a person of a particular sex to fill a position.

An employer cannot refuse to hire a woman because of her pregnancy-related condition so long as she is able to perform the major functions necessary to the job. Also, an employer may not terminate workers because of pregnancy, force them to go on leave at an arbitrary point during pregnancy if they are

Bona Fide Occupational Qualification Sex discrimination that is reasonably necessary for the operation of a particular business or enterprise.

still able to work, or penalize them in reinstatement rights, including credit for previous service, accrued retirement benefits, and accumulated seniority.

Finally, men and women who perform substantially equal work in the same establishment are covered by the Equal Pay Act. This law prohibits employers from discriminating in pay because of sex if the job performed by men and women requires equal skill, effort, and responsibility under similar working conditions. There can, however, be pay differences based on seniority or merit. It is illegal for an employer to retaliate against an employee who files a charge of equal pay discrimination.

SEXUAL HARASSMENT

Sexual harassment is also an unlawful employment practice under Title VII of the Civil Rights Act. Unwelcome sexual advances, requests for sexual favors, and other verbal or physical conduct of a sexual nature constitute sexual harassment when:

☐ Submission to such conduct is either explicitly or implicitly made a term or condition of an individual's employment; or

☐ Submission to or rejection of such conduct by an individual is used as the basis for employment decisions affecting that person; or

☐ Such conduct has the purpose or effect of unreasonably interfering with an individual's work performance or creating an intimidating, hostile, or offensive working environment.

It is not a defense for an employer to say that it did not know that one of its employees engaged in sexual harassment of another employee, or that the harassment took place in spite of an explicit company policy forbidding it. If it *should have known of the harassing conduct*, the employer must take immediate and appropriate corrective action, which usually entails more than merely telling all employees not to engage in sexual harassment.

ENFORCEMENT

The Equal Employment Opportunity Commission (EEOC) is a federal agency with the primary responsibility of enforcing Title VII of the Civil Rights Act. A charge of employment discrimination (see Exhibit 16.1) can be made to the EEOC in its offices throughout the country.

Most states have a *fair employment practices* (FEP) law that also provides protection against sex discrimination in employment. A complaint can be initiated at an EEOC office or at the state or city agency that administers the local FEP law.

The major complaint leveled against the laws outlawing sex discrimination in employment is that they have been very inadequately enforced. The law of discrimination can be complex and confusing. Bringing a discrimination case is usually time-consuming and expensive. Many feel we have a long way to go before the problem is solved.

▆▆▆▆ SEXUALITY AND REPRODUCTIVE RIGHTS

Topics relevant to a discussion of sexuality and reproductive rights include:

☐ Contraception

☐ Sterilization

☐ Abortion

☐ **EXHIBIT 16.1 Charge of Discrimination**

CHARGE OF DISCRIMINATION	ENTER CHARGE NUMBER
This form is affected by the Privacy Act of 1974; see Privacy Act Statement on reverse before completing this form.	☐ FEPA ☐ EEOC

_____ and EEOC
(State or local Agency, if any)

NAME (*Indicate Mr., Ms., or Mrs.*)	HOME TELEPHONE NO. (*Include Area Code*)
STREET ADDRESS CITY, STATE AND ZIP CODE	COUNTY

NAMED IS THE EMPLOYER, LABOR ORGANIZATION, EMPLOYMENT AGENCY, APPRENTICESHIP COMMITTEE, STATE OR LOCAL GOVERNMENT AGENCY WHO DISCRIMINATED AGAINST ME (*If more than one list below.*)

NAME	NO. OF EMPLOYEES/MEMBERS	TELEPHONE NUMBER (*Include Area Code*)
STREET ADDRESS		CITY, STATE AND ZIP CODE

NAME	TELEPHONE NUMBER (*Include Area Code*)
STREET ADDRESS	CITY, STATE AND ZIP CODE

CAUSE OF DISCRIMINATION BASED ON (*Check appropriate box(es)*) ☐ RACE ☐ COLOR ☐ SEX ☐ RELIGION ☐ NATIONAL ORIGIN ☐ AGE ☐ RETALIATION ☐ OTHER (*Specify*)	DATE MOST RECENT OR CONTINUING DISCRIMINATION TOOK PLACE (*Month, day, year*)

THE PARTICULARS ARE (*If additional space is needed, attached extra sheet(s)*):

■ I also want this charge filed with the EEOC. I will advise the agencies if I change my address or telephone number and I will cooperate fully with them in the processing of my charge in accordance with their procedures.	NOTARY—(When necessary to meet State and Local Requirements)
	I swear or affirm that I have read the above charge and that it is true to the best of my knowledge, information and belief.
I declare under penalty of perjury that the foregoing is true and correct.	SIGNATURE OF COMPLAINANT SUBSCRIBED AND SWORN TO BEFORE ME THIS DATE (Day, month, and year)
Date Charging Party (*Signature*)	

EEOC FORM 5. PREVIOUS EDITIONS OF THIS FORM ARE OBSOLETE AND MUST NOT BE USED. MAR 84

FILE COPY

□ New routes to motherhood

□ Lesbianism

The first three topics are discussed below. New routes to motherhood, such as surrogate motherhood, in vitro fertilization, and similar themes, are examined in chapter 20. Legal problems involving homosexuality and lesbianism are covered in chapter 8 on marriage and chapter 19 on adoption.

CONTRACEPTION

Married and unmarried individuals cannot be denied access to contraceptives. "If the right of privacy means anything, it is the right of the *individual*, married or single, to be free from unwarranted governmental intrusion into matters so fundamentally affecting a person as the decision whether to bear or beget a child." *Eisenstadt v. Baird*, 405 U.S. 438, 453, 92 S. Ct. 1029, 1038, 31 L. Ed. 2d 349 (1972).

STERILIZATION

Some states have laws that authorize the forced sterilization of persons legally considered mentally retarded or insane to prevent them from reproducing. Over sixty years ago, the United States Supreme Court decided that a state could legally sterilize a person it termed "feeble-minded." The woman in question was an institutionalized eighteen-year-old who was the daughter of a feeble-minded woman in the same institution; the eighteen-year-old had already had a baby that was feeble-minded. In a well-known passage, Justice Oliver Wendell Holmes said, "Three generations of imbeciles are enough." *Buck v. Bell*, 274 U.S. 200, 208, 47 S. Ct. 584, 585, 71 L. Ed. 1000 (1927). Since forced sterilization is rarely, if ever, practiced today, the courts have not had a chance to rule on the constitutionality of the practice under modern interpretations of the U.S. Constitution. If, however, the United States Supreme Court had such a case before it today, it would probably overrule *Buck v. Bell*.

ABORTION

In the early 1970s, abortion was a crime in every state. It was permitted only when the health of the woman necessitated it (usually to preserve her life) or when special circumstances warranted it, e.g., when the pregnancy was caused by rape or incest.

In 1973 the law was dramatically changed by the landmark case of *Roe v. Wade*, 410 U.S. 113, 93 S. Ct. 705, 35 L. Ed. 2d 147 (1973), in which the United States Supreme Court held that a pregnant woman's *right to privacy* included the right to terminate her pregnancy. The ruling in *Roe* was later modified by the 1992 case of *Planned Parenthood of Southeastern Pennsylvania v. Casey*. Before examining *Casey*, however, we need to look at what *Roe* said.

In *Roe v. Wade*, the Court did not conclude that the right to have an abortion was absolute. The extent of the right depended on the stage of a woman's pregnancy:

1. For the stage prior to approximately the end of the first trimester, the abortion decision and its effectuation must be left to the medical judgment of the pregnant woman's attending physician.

2. For the stage subsequent to approximately the end of the first trimester, the state, in promoting its interests in the health of the mother, may, if it chooses, regulate the abortion procedure in ways that are reasonably related to maternal health.

3. For the stage subsequent to viability, the state in promoting its interest in the potentiality of human life may, if it chooses, regulate, and even proscribe, abortion except where it is necessary, in appropriate medical judgment, for the preservation of the life or health of the mother.

Viability The stage of fetal development when the life of an unborn child may be continued indefinitely outside the womb by natural or artificial life-support systems.

A major theme of *Roe* was that the state should not be regulating abortions until **viability,** unless the regulations were clearly necessary to protect the health of the mother. If this necessity did not exist, the state could not prohibit a woman from obtaining an abortion during the first trimester when a fetus is not viable. *Roe* held that to deny her this right would infringe upon her constitutional right to privacy. Different considerations applied during the next twelve weeks—the second trimester. Between the end of the first trimester and the beginning of the child's viability (a child is usually considered viable after about six months), the state could regulate medical procedures to make sure that abortions are performed safely but could not prohibit abortions altogether. Once the child is viable—during the third trimester—abortions could be prohibited unless they were necessary to preserve the life or health of the mother.

The Court later reinforced *Roe* by holding that a wife may have an abortion without the consent of her husband.

Some limits, however, were upheld. For example, if a poor woman wanted an abortion for nonhealth reasons (i.e., a nontherapeutic abortion), the state was *not required* to pay for it, although a number of states decided to set aside funds for such abortions. Also, if a pregnant minor was living with and dependent on her parents, it was permissible for a state to require that the parents be notified of, and give their consent to, the child's desire to have an abortion— so long as the girl had the opportunity to go to court to try to convince a judge that she was a mature minor and that therefore parental notice and consent were not needed in her particular case.

These restrictions in *Roe*, however, did not significantly limit the number of abortions performed in America—approximately 1.5 million a year. The Supreme Court acknowledged that abortion continued to be "the most politically divisive domestic issue of our time." Some activities argued for a constitutional amendment that would return us to the pre-*Roe* days when states could extensively outlaw abortion. As it became clear that these efforts would not succeed, many wondered whether the appointment of conservatives to the Supreme Court by Presidents Reagan and Bush would lead to an overruling of *Roe* by the Court itself. The burning question of the day was whether there were now enough votes on the Court to abandon *Roe*. The answer came in the opinion of *Planned Parenthood of Southeastern Pennsylvania v. Casey,* 505 U.S. 833, 112 S. Ct. 2791, 120 L. Ed. 2d 674 (1992).

Casey did not overrule *Roe*. Though *Casey* made some important changes, the Court adhered to the essential features of *Roe:*

> It must be stated at the outset and with clarity that *Roe's* essential holding, the holding we reaffirm, has three parts. First is a recognition of the right of the woman to choose to have an abortion before viability and to obtain it without undue interference from the State. Before viability, the State's interests are not strong enough to support a prohibition of abortion or the imposition of a substantial obstacle to the woman's

effective right to elect the procedure. Second is a confirmation of the State's power to restrict abortions after fetal viability, if the law contains exceptions for pregnancies which endanger a woman's life or health. And third is the principle that the State has legitimate interests from the outset of the pregnancy in protecting the health of the woman and the life of the fetus that may become a child. These principles do not contradict one another; and we adhere to each. 112 S. Ct. at 2804.

The Due Process Clause of the Fourteenth Amendment declares that no state shall "deprive any person of life, liberty, or property, without due process of law." The basis of a woman's right to terminate her pregnancy is the protection of "liberty" in the Fourteenth Amendment. But every restriction on this liberty is not unconstitutional.

The key test continues to be viability. In *Roe*, the Court used a trimester analysis as a guide in the determination of viability. In *Casey*, the Court decided to reject this analysis as too rigid. In the future, the question of when a child was able to survive outside the womb would be determined by the facts of medicine and science rather than by rigid assumptions of what is possible during the trimesters of pregnancy.

After viability, a state can regulate, and even prohibit, abortion except where abortion is medically necessary to preserve the life of the mother. Before viability, however, a state cannot prohibit abortions. Nor can it place "undue burdens" on the right to seek an abortion. The state can pass laws designed to encourage women to choose childbirth over abortion and laws designed to further her health or safety so long as these laws do not present "substantial obstacles" in the path of her decision to abort a nonviable fetus.

Using these tests, the Court in *Casey* reached the following conclusions about specific laws enacted by the state of Pennsylvania:

☐ It is *not* an undue burden on the right to abortion for a state to require (except in a medical emergency) that at least 24 hours before performing an abortion a physician give a woman information about the nature of the procedure, the health risks of abortion and of childbirth, the probable gestational age of her unborn child, available medical assistance for childbirth, methods of obtaining child support from the father, and a list of agencies that provide adoption and other services as alternatives to abortion. Providing this information is not a substantial obstacle because the information allows women to give informed consent to whatever decision they make.

☐ It *is* an undue burden on the right to abortion for a state to require, except in a medical emergency, that no physician shall perform an abortion on a married woman without receiving a signed statement from the woman that she has notified her spouse that she is about to undergo an abortion. This is a substantial obstacle because many women may not seek an abortion due to a fear of psychological and physical abuse from their husband if they tell him about their plan to have an abortion. Furthermore, a woman does not need her husband's consent to undergo an abortion. Since he does not have a veto, notifying him about the planned abortion is not necessary.

The *Casey* opinion is not the final word on abortion. The justices in *Casey* did not all agree on how to decide the case. New facts will come before the Court in the future, which will lead to further clarification. As members of the Court are replaced by new justices, we should not be surprised to find more changes. It is still true that abortion is "the most politically divisive domestic issue of our time."

▰▰▰▰ THE BATTERED WIFE

Consider the following facts:

☐ Spousal violence occurs in close to one of every three marriages. Trent, *Wife Beating: A Psycho-Legal Analysis,* Case and Comment 14 (November-December 1979).

☐ Almost 2 million women are victims of severe assaults by their male partners each year. Over half of these men beat their wives or girlfriends at least three times a year.

☐ One-fifth to one-third of all women will be physically assaulted by a partner or ex-partner during their lifetime.

☐ One-third of murdered women are killed by their husbands or lovers.

☐ According to a recent poll, 20 percent of all Americans (and 25 percent of college-educated Americans) condone the use of physical violence in marriage. Strong and DeVault, *The Marriage and Family Experience,* 427 (4th ed. 1989); AMA, *Violence Against Women* 7 (1991).

These alarming figures are actually considered low, since partner violence is one of the most underreported crimes in the country. It would be more accurate to *double* the figures we have. Hence, researchers have concluded that the real number of women severely assaulted each year is closer to 4 million.

Historically, the wife was considered the property of her husband in many respects. Hence it is not surprising to find religious and legal approval of his use of physical force against her. Around 1475, for example, Friar Cherubino of Siena compiled the following *Rules of Marriage:*

> When you see your wife commit an offense, don't rush at her with insults and violent blows. . . . Scold her sharply and terrify her. And if this still doesn't work . . . take up a stick and beat her soundly, for it is better to punish the body and correct the soul than to damage the soul and spare the body. . . . Then readily beat her, not in rage but out of charity and concern for her soul, so that the beating will redound to your merit and her good. Quoted in T. Davidson, *Conjugal Crime,* 99 (1978).

Hence, wife beating was acceptable and indeed was considered a duty of the husband. Society even condoned a particular weapon for the deed: a "rod not thicker than his thumb," or a stick that was not too thick to pass through a wedding ring! United States Commission on Civil Rights, *Under the Rule of Thumb: Battered Women and the Administration of Justice* 2 (January 1982).

▰ CASE ▰

STATE V. BLACK

Supreme Court of North Carolina
60 N.C. 274 (1 Winst. 266) (1864)

Summary:

A husband cannot be convicted of battery on his wife, unless he inflicts a permanent injury, or uses such excessive violence or cruelty, as indicates malignity or vindictiveness: and it makes no difference that the husband and wife are living separate by agreement.

This was an indictment of assault and battery, tried before BAILEY, Judge, at—Term of Ashe Superior Court, 1864.

The defendant was indicted for an assault on Tamsey Black, his wife. The evidence showed, that the defendant and his wife lived separate from one another. The defendant was passing by the house of one Koonce, where his wife then resided, when she called to him in an angry manner and asked him, if he had patched Sal Daly's bonnet. (Sal Daly being a woman of ill-fame.)

She then went into the house, and defendant followed her and asked her what she wanted, when she repeated her question about the bonnet. Angry words then passed between them. He accused her of connection with a negro man, and she called him a hog thief, whereupon the defendant seized her by her hair, and pulled her down upon the floor, and held her there for sometime. He gave her no blows, but she stated on the trial, that her head was considerably hurt, and that her throat was injured, and continued sore for several months, but that he did not choke her, nor attempt to do so. At the trial she was entirely recovered. After she got up from the floor, she continued her abuse of him. A verdict of guilty was entered, subject to the opinion of the Court. The Judge, being of opinion with the State, gave judgment accordingly.

Winston, Sr., for the State

No counsel for the defendant in this Court.

PEARSON, C. J. A husband is responsible for the acts of his wife, and he is required to govern his household, and for that purpose, the law permits him to use towards his wife such a degree of force, as is necessary to control an unruly temper, and make her behave herself; and unless some permanent injury is inflicted, or there be an excess of violence, or such a degree of cruelty as shows that it is inflicted to gratify his own bad passions, the law will not invade the domestic forum, to go behind the curtain. It prefers to leave the parties to themselves, as the best mode of inducing them to make the matter up and live together as man and wife should.

Certainly, the exposure of a scene like that set out in this case, can do no good. In respect to the parties, a public exhibition in the Court House of such quarrels and fights between man and wife, widens the breach, makes a reconciliation almost impossible, and encourages insubordination; and in respect to the public, it has a pernicious tendency: so, *pro bono publico,* such matters are excluded from the Courts, unless there is a permanent injury or excessive violence or cruelty indicating malignity and vindictiveness.

In this case the wife commenced the quarrel. The husband, in a passion provoked by excessive abuse, pulled her upon the floor by the hair, but restrained himself, did not strike a blow, and she admits he did not choke her, and she continued to abuse him after she got up. Upon this state of facts the jury ought to have been charged in favor of the defendant. *State v. Pendergrass,* 18 N. C., 365; *Joyner v. Joyner,* 59 N. C., 322.

It was insisted by Mr. Winston that, admitting such to be the law when the husband and wife lived together, it did not apply when, as in the case, they were living apart. They may be so when there is a divorce "from bed and board," because the law then recognizes and allows the separation, but it can take no notice of a private agreement to live separate. The husband is still responsible for her acts, and the marriage relation and its incidents remain unaffected.

This decision must be certified to the Superior Court of law for Ashe County, that it may proceed according to law.

Eventually, laws were passed outlawing wife beating. Yet the crime continues at an alarming rate today. As indicated, women frequently do not report such violence, particularly when they are still living with their abuser/husband. Furthermore, when a woman does report the incident to the authorities, she often is not taken seriously. Many complain that the police handle violence in a "domestic quarrel" differently, that is, less seriously, from an assault on the street between strangers. Politically active women's groups have campaigned for a change in the attitude and policies of courts, legislatures, and law enforcement agencies. In addition, they have fought for the creation of shelters to which battered women can flee.

If a woman is persistent and desperate enough, her main remedy is to go to court to ask for an **injunction** (see Exhibit 16.2). In this situation, the injunction is to stop abusing the plaintiff and/or her children. Depending on the state, the injunction is called a *restraining order* or a *protective order*. For purposes of obtaining the injunction, **abuse** is often defined as attempting to cause bodily injury or intentionally, knowingly, or recklessly causing bodily injury, or by threat of force placing another person in fear of imminent serious physical harm.

Injunction A court order requiring a person to do or to refrain from doing a particular thing.

In addition to the civil remedy of an injunction, a woman can ask the state to prosecute the defendant for a crime, e.g., assault, aggravated assault, battery, aggravated battery, reckless conduct, disorderly conduct, harassment. Some states have special crimes that are limited to acts committed against a spouse.

☐ **EXHIBIT 16.2 Protective Order**

3-116.3

SUPERIOR COURT OF CALIFORNIA, COUNTY OF

STREET ADDRESS:

MAILING ADDRESS:

CITY AND ZIP CODE:

BRANCH NAME

FOR COURT USE ONLY

PROTECTED PERSON (NAME):

RESTRAINED PERSON (NAME):

EMERGENCY PROTECTIVE ORDER   COURT CASE NUMBER:

1. **THIS EMERGENCY PROTECTIVE ORDER WILL EXPIRE AT 5 P.M. ON:** _____
   (INSERT DATE OF NEXT COURT DAY)

2. Reasonable grounds appear that an immediate danger of domestic violence exists and this order should be issued
   a. AGAINST RESTRAINED PERSON *(name):* _____
   b. WHO must not contact, molest, attack, strike, threaten, sexually assault, batter, telephone, or otherwise harass or disturb the peace of the protected person
      (1) ☐ or the peace of the following family or household members *(names):* _____
      _____
      _____

   c. ☐ WHO must stay away from the protected person at least *(yards):* _____

   d. ☐ WHO must move out and not return to the residence at *(address):* _____

3. ☐ Temporary custody of the following minor children is given to the protected person:

   Children *(names and ages):* _____
   _____

4. ☐ The protected person has been given a copy of this order, the application, and instructions about how to get a more permanent order.

5. Date: [_____]

6. **Law Enforcement Officer:** .... ▶ _____
                        (PRINT NAME)   (SIGNATURE)

   a. Badge No.: _____   b. Incident Case No.: _____

   c. Agency: _____   d. Telephone No.: _____

7. **Service of this order and application on the restrained person was completed as follows:**

	Date	Time	Signature
a. ☐ I orally advised person of contents:	_____	_____	_____
b. ☐ I personally gave person copies:	_____	_____	_____

DESCRIPTION OF RESTRAINED PERSON (fill out what you know)

(1) approximate age: _____   (4) weight: _____   (7) vehicle make: _____

(2) race: _____   (5) hair color: _____   (8) vehicle model: _____

(3) height: _____   (6) eye color: _____   (9) vehicle license No.: _____

(10) other distinguishing features: _____

VIOLATION OF THIS ORDER IS A MISDEMEANOR PUNISHABLE BY A $1000 FINE, SIX MONTHS IN JAIL, OR BOTH. THIS ORDER SHALL BE ENFORCED BY ALL LAW ENFORCEMENT OFFICERS IN THE STATE OF CALIFORNIA.

(See reverse for important notices)

Form Adopted by Rule 1295.95
Judicial Council of California
1295.95 (New July 1, 1988)

Emergency Protective Order
(Domestic Violence Prevention)

Code of Civil Procedure, § 546(b)

WHITE copy to court, CANARY to restrained person, PINK to protected person

In 1994 Congress passed the Violence Against Women Act, which established a federal civil rights cause of action for victims of crimes of violence motivated by gender.[4] This could include wife beating, stalking, rape, and other sexual assaults. Under this Act, a victim can go into a federal court to seek compensatory and punitive damages, injunctive relief, and attorney fees. Later, in chapter 21, we will examine whether the victim of domestic violence can bring a traditional personal injury *tort* action against the abuser in a state court.

Unfortunately, these civil and criminal remedies have not been effective in substantially decreasing the incidence of domestic violence. In fact, many argue that the violence is on the rise.

Some women have taken the extreme step of killing the husband who has been abusing them. Does this killing constitute the crime of murder or manslaughter? In part, the answer depends on when the killing occurs. Compare the predicament of the women in the following two situations. Assume that both women had been physically abused by their husband or boyfriend for years:

> Carol is being physically attacked by her husband, who is coming at her with a knife. As he approaches, Carol shoots him.

> Hours after being beaten by her boyfriend, Helen takes a gun to his bedroom and shoots him while he is asleep.

It is highly unlikely that Carol has committed a crime. She is protected by the traditional defense of *self-defense*. Citizens can use deadly force that they reasonably believe is necessary to protect themselves from imminent death or serious bodily injury.

What about Helen? Unless she can prove temporary insanity, she must establish the elements of self-defense to avoid conviction. But she apparently was not in *imminent* danger at the time she shot her boyfriend. Arguably, for example, she could have left the home while he was sleeping if she felt that he might kill or maim her once he awoke. Women in Helen's situation have been prosecuted for crimes such as manslaughter and murder.

In these prosecutions, a novel argument that is often raised by the woman is the battered wife syndrome or, more broadly, the **battered woman syndrome.** She claims that she acted out of a *psychological paralysis.* A variety of circumstances combined to block all apparent avenues of escape: financial dependence, loneliness, guilt, shame, and fear of reprisal from her husband or boyfriend. Buda & Butler, *The Battered Wife Syndrome,* 23 Journal of Family Law 359 (1984–85). From this state of "learned helplessness," she kills him. This argument is not an independent defense; it is an argument designed to bolster the self-defense argument. More accurately, it is an attempt to broaden the definition of *imminent danger* in self-defense. To a woman subjected to the psychological terror and paralysis of long-term abuse, the danger from her husband or boyfriend is real and close at hand. At any moment his behavior might trigger a flashback in her mind to an earlier beating, causing her to honestly believe that she is in immediate danger.

Prosecutors are not sympathetic to the battered-woman-syndrome argument. They say it is too easy to exaggerate the extent of the abuse and, more importantly, the extent to which the abuse resulted in such a state of paralysis that the wife felt her only way to protect herself—immediately—was to kill her husband. Some courts, however, are at least willing to listen to testimony on

Battered Woman Syndrome Psychological helplessness because of a woman's financial dependence, loneliness, guilt, shame, and fear of reprisal from her husband or boyfriend who has repeatedly battered her in the past.

---

4. 42 U.S.C.A. § 13981.

the syndrome. This has been very helpful for the defendant because when jurors hear this testimony, they are often reluctant to return guilty verdicts even if the traditional elements of self-defense that the judge instructs them to apply do not warrant such a verdict.

ASSIGNMENT 16.5

For the following questions, see General Instructions for the State-Code Assignment in chapter 1.

a. In your state, if a wife is threatened with violence, what remedies does she have?

b. When, if ever, can an injunction or protective order be issued *ex parte,* meaning that the defendant is not present in court when the order is issued?

c. Without justification, a husband stabs his wife, but does not kill her. What are the possible crimes the husband can be charged with in your state?

ASSIGNMENT 16.6

Prepare a flowchart on obtaining an injunction (or restraining order) against violence threatened by a husband against his wife in your state. (See General Instructions for the Flowchart Assignment in chapter 1.)

ASSIGNMENT 16.7

a. Do you think that a court encourages killing when it allows evidence of the battered woman syndrome to be introduced in trials of women who kill their spouses or boyfriends? Explain why or why not.

b. Do you think it is possible for a battered *man* syndrome to exist? Explain why or why not.

■■■ MARITAL RAPE

The common law rule was that a husband cannot rape his wife. The "husband cannot be guilty of rape committed by himself upon his lawful wife, for by their mutual matrimonial consent and contract, the wife hath given up herself in this kind unto her husband which she cannot retract." 1 M. Hale, *The History of the Pleas of the Crown* 629 (1736). This view is still the law in some states. Most states, however, allow prosecution if the couple is living apart and a petition has been filed for divorce or separate maintenance. The reluctance of courts and legislatures to allow the criminal law of rape to apply to married couples is in part based on a fear that a wife will lie about whether she consented to sexual intercourse.

CASE

WARREN V. STATE
255 Ga. 151, 336 S.E.2d 221 (1985)
Supreme Court of Georgia.

Background: *Daniel Steven Warren was indicted for rape and sodomy of his wife while they were still living together. He moved to dismiss the indictment on the ground that a husband cannot be convicted of committing these crimes against his wife. The motion was denied. He then appealed to the Supreme Court of Georgia where he is the appellant.*

Decision on Appeal: Affirmed. There is no exception for husbands.
Opinion of the Court:

Justice Smith delivered the opinion of the court.

"When a woman says I do, does she give up her right to say I won't?"* This question does not pose

---

*Griffin, *In 44 States, It's Legal to Rape Your Wife,* 21 Student Lawyer. Another question posed is: "But if you can't rape your wife, who[m] can you rape?" Freeman, *"But If You Can't Rape Your Wife, Who[m] Can You Rape?": The Marital Rape Exemption Re-examined,* 15 Family Law Quarterly (1981).

the real question, because rape[†] and aggravated sodomy are not sexual acts of an ardent husband performed upon an initially apathetic wife, they are acts of violence that are accompanied with physical and mental abuse and often leave the victim with physical and psychological damage that is almost always long lasting. Thus we find the more appropriate question: When a woman says "I do" in Georgia does she give up her right to State protection from the violent acts of rape and aggravated sodomy performed by her husband. The answer is no. We affirm. . . .

The appellant asserts that there exists within the rape statute an implicit marital exclusion that makes it legally impossible for a husband to be guilty of raping his wife. Until the late 1970's there was no real examination of this apparently widely held belief. Within the last few years several jurisdictions have been faced with similar issues and they have decided that under certain circumstances a husband can be held criminally liable for raping his wife.

What is behind the theory and belief that a husband could not be guilty of raping his wife? There are various explanations for the rule and all of them flow from the common law attitude toward women, the status of women and marriage.

Perhaps the most often used basis for the marital rape exemption is the view set out by Lord Hale in 1 Hale P.C. 629. It is known as Lord Hale's contractual theory. The statement attributed to Lord Hale used to support the theory is: "but a husband cannot be guilty of a rape committed by himself upon his lawful wife, for by their mutual matrimonial consent and contract the wife hath given up herself in this kind unto her husband which she cannot retract."

There is some thought that the foundation of his theory might well have been the subsequent marriage doctrine of English law, wherein the perpetrator could, by marrying his victim, avoid rape charges. It was thus argued as a corollary, rape within the marital relationship would result in the same immunity. Another theory stemming from medieval times is that of a wife being the husband's chattel or property. Since a married woman was part of her husband's property, nothing more than a chattel, rape was nothing more than a man making use of his own property. A third theory is the unity in marriage or unity of person theory that held the very being or legal existence of a woman was suspended during marriage, or at least was incorporated and consolidated into that of her husband. In view of the fact that there was only one legal being, the husband, he could not be convicted of raping himself.

These three theories have been used to support the marital rape exemption. Others have tried to fill the chasm between these three theories with justifications for continuing the exemption in the face of changes in the recognition of women, their status, and the status of marriage. Some of the justifications include: Prevention of fabricated charges; Preventing wives from using rape charges for revenge; Preventing state intervention into marriage so that possible reconciliation will not be thwarted. A closer examination of the theories and justifications indicates that they are no longer valid, if they ever had any validity.

Hale's implied consent theory was created at a time when marriages were irrevocable and when all wives promised to "love, honor, and obey" and all husbands promised to "love, cherish, and protect until death do us part." Wives were subservient to their husbands, her identity was merged into his, her property became his property, and she took his name for her own.

There have been dramatic changes in women's rights and the status of women and marriage. Today our State Constitution provides that, "no person shall be deprived of life, *liberty*, or property except by due process," (Emphasis supplied.) Art. I, § I, Par. I, and "protection to *person* and property is the paramount duty of government and shall be impartial and complete. No person shall be denied the equal protection of the laws." (Emphasis supplied.) Art. I, § I, Par. II. Our state Constitution also provides that each spouse has a right to retain his or her own property. Art. I, § I, Par. XXVII. Our statutory laws provide that, "[t]he rights of citizens include, *without limitation*, the following: (1) The right of *personal security*, [and] (2) The right of personal liberty . . ." (Emphasis supplied.) OCGA § 1–2–6. Women in Georgia "are entitled to the privilege of the elective franchise and have the right to hold any civil office or perform any civil function as fully and completely as do male citizens." OCGA § 1–2–7. Couples who contemplate marriage today may choose either spouse's surname or a combination of both names for their married surname, OCGA § 19–3–33.1. No longer is a wife's domicile presumed

---

[†] "As one author has observed, people have 'trouble with rape' because: [T]he mention of rape makes us all uneasy—for different reasons depending on who we are. It makes men uneasiest of all perhaps, and usually brings forth an initial response of nervous laughter or guffaw-evoking jokes. After all, as far as the normal, but uninformed, man knows, rape is something he might suddenly do himself some night if life becomes too dull. It isn't, of course, but he knows too little about it to realize that. On the other hand, the thoughtful normal man, after hearing the details of a forcible rape, finds it difficult to believe. . . . He knows that all thoughts of sex—which he equates with fun, romance, and mutual admiration—would leave him if the woman were *really* struggling to get free. . . . He does not realize that, to the rapist, the act is not 'love,' nor ardor, and usually not even passion; it is a way of debasing and degrading a woman. . . ." (Emphasis in original.) Massaro, *Experts, Psychology, Credibility, and Rape: The Rape Trauma Syndrome Issue and Its Implications for Expert Psychological Testimony*, 69 Minn. Law Review 395, 399 n. 27 (1985).

to be that of her husband, OCGA § 19–2–3 and no longer is the husband head of the family with the wife subject to him. OCGA § 19–3–8. Marriages are revocable without fault by either party, OCGA § 19–5–3(13); either party, not just the husband, can be required to pay alimony upon divorce, OCGA § 19–6–1; and both parties have a joint and several duty to provide for the maintenance, protection, and education of their children, OCGA § 19–7–2. Couples may write antenuptial agreements in which they are able to decide, prior to marriage, future settlements, OCGA § 19–3–62; and our legislature has recognized that there can be violence in modern family life and it has enacted special laws to protect family members who live in the same household from one another's violent acts, Ga.L.1981, 880; OCGA § 19–13–1 et seq. . . .

One would be hard pressed to argue that a husband can rape his wife because she is his chattel. Even in the darkest days of slavery when slaves were also considered chattel, rape was defined as "the carnal knowledge of a female whether free or slave, forcibly and against her will." Georgia Code, § 4248 (1863). Both the chattel and unity of identity rationales have been cast aside. "Nowhere in the common law world—[or] in any modern society—is a woman regarded as chattel or demeaned—by denial of a separate legal identity and the dignity associated with recognition as a whole human being." *Trammel v. United States*, 445 U.S. 40, 52, 100 S. Ct. 906, 913 (1980).

We find that none of the theories have any validity. The justifications likewise are without efficacy. There is no other crime we can think of in which all of the victims are denied protection simply because someone might fabricate a charge; there is no evidence that wives have flooded the district attorneys with revenge filled trumped-up charges,‡ and once a marital relationship is at the point where a husband rapes his wife, state intervention is needed for the wife's protection.

There never has been an expressly stated marital exemption included in the Georgia rape statute. Furthermore, our statute never included the word "unlawful" which has been widely recognized as signifying the incorporation of the common law spousal exclusion. A reading of the statute indicates that there is no marital exclusion. "A person commits the offense of rape when he has carnal knowledge of a female forcibly and against her will." OCGA § 16–6–1. . . .

Judgment affirmed.

---

‡ " '[E]mbittered and vengeful wives are not rushing to their District Attorney to falsely claim rape in order to gain leverage on their husbands in a divorce. Victims are very reluctant to report the crime.' . . .'' *People v. De Stefano*, 467 N.Y.S.2d 506, 515 (Co. Ct. 1983). Furthermore, studies show that the average person finds alleged husband-wife rapes the lowest in credibility, 69 Minn. Law Review n. 63 at 408, and juries convict only 3 of 42 rape suspects in simple rapes, i.e., where there is only one assailant, he is known by the victim, and there is no evidence of extrinsic violence. 69 Minn. Law Review 395, n. 52 at 405.

ASSIGNMENT 16.8

a. The Georgia statute says: "A person commits the offense of rape when he has carnal knowledge of a female forcibly and against her will." OCGA § 16–6–1. The court in *Warren* suggests that there might be an argument that the statute excludes husbands if the word "unlawful" appeared in the statute. What is this argument? Assume the statute read, "A person commits the offense of rape when he has *unlawful* carnal knowledge of a female forcibly and against her will."

b. Under what circumstances, if any, can a husband be guilty of raping his wife in your state? (See General Instructions for the State-Code Assignment and the Court-Opinion Assignment in chapter 1.)

SUMMARY

Historically, a married woman had very few rights independent of her husband. Today her situation is very different. For example, her right to own and dispose of property and to enter contracts is now equal to that of her husband. There are some restrictions on contracts and conveyances between spouses, e.g., they cannot enter a contract to provide services and support if they are still living together, and they cannot transfer property to each other in order to defraud creditors. However, these restrictions apply equally to husbands and wives.

When a husband dies, his wife has a right of dower in his property. Many states have replaced this with a right to elect a forced share of his estate. In most states the wife is not required to take her husband's surname upon marriage, nor is she required to keep it upon divorce if she used it when married.

An applicant for credit cannot be discriminated against on the basis of sex or marital status. Sex discrimination in employment is illegal unless sex is a bona fide occupational qualification. Salaries cannot be determined on the basis of gender. Certain forms of pregnancy-related discrimination and sexual harassment are also prohibited. These laws are enforced by the federal Equal Employment Opportunity Commission and by state agencies that administer rules on fair employment practices.

In the area of sexuality and reproductive rights, neither men nor women can be denied access to contraceptives. But they can be subjected to forced sterilization if they are mentally retarded or insane.

A state cannot place undue burdens on a woman's right to an abortion before viability.

Wife beating is a major problem in our society in spite of the laws against it and the availability of restraining orders and protective orders to keep the offending husband or boyfriend away. A few women have taken the drastic step of killing their abuser. In such cases, the defense of the battered woman syndrome is sometimes raised within the context of self-defense.

Finally, marital rape is not a crime in every state, although most states allow prosecution if a petition has been filed for divorce or separate maintenance.

■■■■■ KEY CHAPTER TERMINOLOGY

Married Women's Property Acts
Conveyances
Dower
Curtesy
Forced Share

Right of Election
Intestate
Bona Fide Occupational Qualification (BFOQ)
Roe v. Wade

Viability
Injunction
Abuse
Battered Woman Syndrome

17 ILLEGITIMACY AND PATERNITY PROCEEDINGS

ILLEGITIMACY

"The status of illegitimacy has expressed through the ages society's condemnation of irresponsible liaisons beyond the bonds of marriage. But visiting this condemnation on the head of an infant is illogical and unjust. Moreover, imposing disabilities on the illegitimate child is contrary to the basic concept of our system that legal burdens should bear some relationship to individual responsibility or wrongdoing. Obviously, no child is responsible for his birth and penalizing the illegitimate child is an ineffectual—as well as an unjust—way of deterring the parent. Courts are powerless to prevent the social opprobrium suffered by these hapless children, but the Equal Protection Clause does enable us to strike down discriminatory laws relating to status of birth where . . . the classification is justified by no legitimate state interest, . . ." *Weber v. Casualty & Surety Co.,* 406 U.S. 164, 175, 92 S. Ct. 1400, 1406, 31 L. Ed. 2d 768 (1972).

Filius Nullius An illegitimate child—"the son [or child] of no one."

At common law, the illegitimate child (still referred to as a *bastard* in many legal texts) was **filius nullius,** the child of nobody. The central disability imposed by this status was that the child born out of wedlock had no right to inherit from either parent. In addition, the child had no right to be supported by the father. Fortunately, the pronounced discrimination that has existed for centuries between the legitimate and the illegitimate child is eroding. This is not to say, however, that the discrimination has completely ended.

INHERITANCE

Intestate Die without leaving a valid will.

Most states have passed statutes permitting an illegitimate child to inherit from its mother when the latter dies **intestate.** Some states have tried to prevent the child from inheriting from its father who dies intestate, but such laws have been declared unconstitutional. *Trimble v. Gordon,* 430 U.S. 762, 97 S. Ct. 1459, 52 L. Ed. 2d 31 (1977). Cf. *Labine v. Vincent,* 401 U.S. 532, 91 S. Ct. 1017, 28 L. Ed. 2d 288 (1971). Yet restrictions on inheritance do exist. For example, assume that an illegitimate child waits until after his or her father dies before declaring that a parent-child relationship existed. Some states would not allow such a

428

child to inherit, insisting that paternity must be determined by a court *before* death as a condition of inheriting from an intestate parent.

TESTATE DISTRIBUTION

Assume that the father of an illegitimate child dies **testate,** and that a clause in the will gives property "to my children" or "to my heirs." If the father has legitimate and illegitimate children living when he dies, the question sometimes arises as to whether he intended the word "children" or "heirs" to include his illegitimate children. To resolve this question of intent, the court must look at all of the circumstances, e.g., how much contact the illegitimate child had with the father at the time the father wrote the will and at the time he died. A surprisingly large number of cases exist in which the court concluded that the illegitimate child was *not* included in the word "children" or "heirs."

Testate Die leaving a valid will.

SUPPORT

There was a time when many state laws did not obligate a father to support his illegitimate children. Such laws have been invalidated as an improper discrimination between legitimate and illegitimate children. Hence, so long as paternity can be established, a father has an equal duty to support all his children.

WRONGFUL DEATH

When a parent dies due to the wrongful act of another, who can sue? Legitimate and illegitimate children have an equal right to bring wrongful death actions against defendants who have caused the death of one or both parents.

WORKER'S COMPENSATION

When a father dies from an injury on the job, the worker's compensation laws of the state permit the children of the deceased to recover benefits. If the state gives a preference to legitimate children over illegitimate children in claiming these benefits, the state is unconstitutionally denying equal protection of the law to the illegitimate children.

SOCIAL SECURITY

Social security laws discriminate against illegitimate children in various phases of the social security system. Some of these discriminatory provisions have been declared unconstitutional, yet others have been allowed to stand. While it is unconstitutional to deny social security survivorship benefits to a child solely because that child is illegitimate, it may be permissible to impose greater procedural burdens on illegitimate children than on legitimate children in applying for benefits. For example, if the law requires that a child be "dependent" on the deceased father as a condition of receiving survivorship benefits, an illegitimate child can be forced to *prove* that he or she was dependent on the father, whereas no such requirement will be imposed on the legitimate child—the law will *presume* that the legitimate child was dependent on the father without requiring specific proof of it.

ARTIFICIAL INSEMINATION

There are three main kinds of **artificial insemination:**

1. Artificial insemination with the semen of the husband (AIH)

Artificial Insemination The impregnation of a woman by a method other than sexual intercourse.

2. Artificial insemination with the semen of a third-party donor (AID)

3. Artificial insemination in which the semen of the husband is mixed (confused) with that of a third-party donor (AIC or CIA)

Children born through AIH are clearly legitimate; the natural father is the mother's husband. States differ as to the legitimacy of the children born through AID and AIC. In some states, such children are illegitimate. Most states, however, provide that the child is legitimate only if the insemination was with the consent of the husband of the mother. This consent also obligates the husband to support the child no matter how the insemination occurred.

ASSIGNMENT 17.1	Answer the following questions by examining your state code. (See General Instructions for the State-Code Assignment in chapter 1.)

a. What are the inheritance rights of an illegitimate child in your state? From whom can an illegitimate child inherit?

b. Who can inherit from an illegitimate child?

c. Is a child born through artificial insemination legitimate?

███ LEGITIMATION AND PATERNITY

Legitimation The steps that enable an illegitimate child to become a legitimate child.

Paternity Proceeding A formal process to determine whether a particular man is the biological father of a particular child.

Legitimation confers the status of legitimacy on an illegitimate child. A major reason parties go through legitimation is to clarify and assure rights of inheritance. A **paternity proceeding** is a process by which the fatherhood of a child is determined. In most states, a finding of paternity does not necessarily lead to the legitimation of the child.

LEGITIMATION

States have different methods by which illegitimate children can be legitimated:

☐ *Acknowledgment.* The father publicly recognizes or acknowledges the illegitimate child as his. States differ on how this acknowledgment must take place. In some states, it must be in writing and witnessed. In others, no writing is necessary if the man's activities strongly indicate that he is the father of the child, e.g., the father treats the child the same as the children who were born legitimate.

☐ *Marriage.* If the mother and father of the illegitimate child marry, the child is often automatically legitimated.

☐ *Combination of acknowledgment and marriage.* Some states require marriage of the parents and some form of acknowledgment by the father.

☐ *Legitimation proceeding.* A few states have special proceedings by which illegitimate children can be legitimated.

☐ *Paternity proceedings.* Although most paternity proceedings deal with fatherhood only, in a few states a finding of paternity also legitimates the child.

☐ *Legitimation by birth.* In a very few states, all children are legitimate whether or not their parents were married at the time of birth.

As indicated earlier, children of annulled marriages are considered legitimate according to special statutes, even though technically the parents were not validly married at the time the children were born (see chapter 9).

In what way(s) can an illegitimate child be legitimated in your state? (See General Instructions for the State-Code Assignment in chapter 1.)

PATERNITY

A major method by which a father is forced to support his illegitimate child is through a paternity proceeding, sometimes called a **filiation** proceeding or a bastardy proceeding. Once fatherhood is determined, the support obligation is imposed. Most paternity proceedings in the country today are instigated by the state to try to recover some of the welfare money paid to custodial parents. In fact, programs such as Aid to Families with Dependent Children require the custodial parent to cooperate in the paternity proceeding.

The starting point in establishing paternity is to obtain detailed facts from the mother. The questionnaire in Exhibit 17.1 has this objective.

The paternity proceeding itself looks a good deal like a criminal proceeding in some states. A warrant is issued for the arrest of the **putative** (i.e., alleged) father, the jury renders a guilty or not guilty verdict, etc. In most states, however, the proceeding is civil rather than criminal.

The mother (on her own or at the prompting of the welfare department) usually initiates the paternity proceeding, although the child is often also given standing to sue through a specially appointed representative, e.g., a **guardian ad litem.** (Exhibit 17.2 shows an example of a paternity petition.) When the mother brings the action, it is important to know whether the child was made a party to the proceeding and was represented. If not, then in some states, the child will not be bound by the judgment. For example:

> Mary, the mother of Sam, brings a paternity proceeding against Kevin, alleging he is the father of Sam. Sam is not made a party to the proceeding. A guardian ad litem is not appointed for him, and he is not otherwise represented in court. The court finds that Kevin is not the father of Sam. Ten years later, Sam brings his own action against Kevin for support, alleging that he is the son of Kevin.

Is Sam's support action ten years later barred by the defense of **res judicata?** That is, was the fatherhood issue already resolved in the paternity proceeding? States differ in their answer to this question. Many will bar the later suit of the child only if the latter was a party to the earlier case that decided the fatherhood issue. In such states, Sam *would* be able to relitigate the paternity issue against Kevin since he was not represented on his own or through a guardian ad litem in the proceeding ten years earlier.

A related question is whether the mother can enter a settlement with the putative father under which she agrees to drop the paternity proceeding in exchange for the defendant's agreement to pay a certain amount for the support of the child and for the mother's expenses in giving birth to the child. In some states, it is illegal to enter into such an agreement. In states where this type of settlement is permitted, the child must be represented and/or the settlement must be approved by the court.

The paternity proceeding requires **personal jurisdiction** over the defendant–putative father (see chapter 14). This generally means that service of process must be made on the defendant in person within the forum state, i.e., the state where the paternity proceeding is being brought. If the defendant is not a resident of the forum state, personal jurisdiction over him may be obtainable under the state's **long arm statute** on the basis of his not having supported his alleged

Filiation (1) A judicial determination of paternity. (2) The relation of child to father.

Putative Alleged or reputed.

Guardian ad Litem A special guardian appointed by the court to represent the interests of another.

Res Judicata When a judgment on the merits has been rendered, the parties cannot relitigate the same dispute; they have already had their day in court.

Personal Jurisdiction The power of a court to render a decision that binds an individual defendant.

Long Arm Statute A law that gives a state court personal jurisdiction over a nonresident based on his or her purposeful contact with the state.

☐ **EXHIBIT 17.1 Paternity Questionnaire**

1. Your full name _____
   Your Social Security number _____
   Your address _____
   Your home phone _____ Your work phone _____
   Your date of birth _____
   With whom are you living: _____

2. List two people who will always know where you live:
   Name _____ Name _____
   Address _____ Address _____
   _____ _____
   Phone _____ Phone _____

3. Give the following information regarding the father of your child:
   Full name _____
   Address _____
   Date of birth _____ Social Security number _____
   Home phone _____ Work phone _____
   Do you have a picture of the father: _____

4. Child's name _____ Child's date of birth _____ Child's sex _____

5. Do you have a picture of the child: _____

6. Does the child look like the father: _____

7. Does the child have the same coloring: _____

8. When and where did you meet the father: _____

9. When did you begin dating the father: _____

10. Did you ever live with the father: _____ If so, where and when: _____
    Landlord _____ Phone _____
    Address _____

11. Others who knew you were living together:
    Name _____ Name _____
    Relationship to you _____ Relationship to you _____
    Address _____ Address _____
    Phone _____ Phone _____

12. When did you first have sexual relations with the father: _____

13. When did you last have sexual relations with him: _____

14. Where was the child conceived? (Where did you get pregnant):
    City _____ County _____ State _____

15. Date father was told that you were pregnant: _____

16. Who told the father that you were pregnant: _____

17. What did he say when he was told you were pregnant: _____
    _____

18. Was a father listed on your child's birth certificate: _____ Did he sign it: _____

19. If no father was listed, explain why the father was not named on the birth certificate: _____

20. Write anything the father said suggesting to you that he is the child's father such as "Isn't our baby cute," or "I am glad you had my baby."
    _____
    _____

21. Did the father sign any papers or write any letters suggesting he is your baby's father: _____

22. What did he sign: _____ Where: _____

23. Did the father offer to help pay for an abortion? If so, briefly explain what he said, when, where, and if anyone else was present: _____
    _____

24. Did the father ever give or offer to give you money for the child? If so, how much and when: _____

25. Did the father ever buy the child gifts? If so, list the gifts and dates given: _____
    _____

Continued

☐ **EXHIBIT 17.1   Paternity Questionnaire—*Continued***

26. Did you ever tell anyone that the father of your child is someone other than the man you are naming on this form: _____ If so, whom did you tell: _____

27. What was said (include name of other man named): _____

28. Give the names, addresses, phone numbers of all witnesses who may be called to testify who have:
    a. Seen you and the father together during time of conception (8–10 months prior to birth).
    b. Seen you and the father kissing, necking, petting, or aware of or have knowledge of any intimate relations you had with the alleged father.
    c. Heard the father make a statement to anyone about you getting an abortion or helping pay for an abortion.
    d. Heard the father make a statement to anyone suggesting or admitting he was the father of the child. (Indicate for each witness briefly what his or her testimony would be.)
    Name _____ Phone _____
    Address _____
    Testimony _____
    Name _____ Phone _____
    Address _____
    Testimony _____

29. Answer these questions for the 8th month before the birth (one month pregnant):
    a. Month _____ Year _____
    b. Were you having sex with the father: _____
    c. How frequently did you have intercourse: _____
    d. Did you use birth control on any occasion: _____
    e. Did the father use birth control on any occasion: _____
    f. Did you have sex with any other men during that month: _____
    If so, list their names, addresses, or other information that may be helpful in locating them.
    Name _____ Address _____
    Phone _____
    Name _____ Address _____
    Phone _____

30. Answer these questions for the 7th month before the birth (two months pregnant):
    a. Month _____ Year _____
    b. Were you having sex with the father: _____
    c. How frequently did you have intercourse: _____
    d. Did you use birth control on any occasion: _____
    e. Did the father use birth control on any occasion: _____
    f. Did you have sex with any other men during that month: _____
    If so, list their names, addresses, or other information that may be helpful in locating them.
    Name _____ Address _____
    Phone _____
    Name _____ Address _____
    Phone _____

31. Answer these questions for the 11th month before the birth (two months before you became pregnant):
    a. Month _____ Year _____
    b. Were you having sex with the father: _____
    c. How frequently did you have intercourse: _____
    d. Did you use birth control on any occasion: _____
    e. Did the father use birth control on any occasion: _____
    f. Did you have sex with any other men during that month: _____
    If so, list their names, addresses, or other information that may be helpful in locating them.
    Name _____ Address _____
    Phone _____
    Name _____ Address _____
    Phone _____

32. Answer these questions for the 10th month before the birth (one month before you became pregnant):
    a. Month _____ Year _____
    b. Were you having sex with the father: _____
    c. How frequently did you have intercourse: _____
    d. Did you use birth control on any occasion: _____

Continued

☐ **EXHIBIT 17.1 Paternity Questionnaire—*Continued***

e. Did the father use birth control on any occasion: _____

f. Did you have sex with any other men during that month: _____
   If so, list their names and addresses, or other information that may be helpful in locating them.
   Name _____ Address _____
   Phone _____
   Name _____ Address _____
   Phone _____

33. Answer these questions for the 9th month before the birth (the month you became pregnant):
   a. Month _____ Year _____
   b. Were you having sex with the father: _____
   c. How frequently did you have intercourse: _____
   d. Did you use birth control on any occasion: _____
   e. Did the father use birth control on any occasion: _____
   f. Did you have sex with any other men during that month: _____
      If so, list their names, addresses, or other information that may be helpful in locating them.
      Name _____ Address _____
      Phone _____
      Name _____ Address _____
      Phone _____

34. Are you presently married: _____ If so, give name of husband. _____

35. Date of marriage _____ Place of marriage _____

36. Were you married at any time between one year before and one year after the birth of the child? _____
   If so, give name of each husband, date, and place of marriage, and, if applicable, the date and place of divorce or annulment:
   Name _____ Date of marriage _____
   Place _____ Date of divorce/annulment _____
   Name _____ Date of marriage _____
   Place _____ Date of divorce/annulment _____

37. On what date did your last menstrual flow begin before the birth of your child: _____

38. On what date did your last menstrual flow end before the birth of your child: _____

39. Do you have a calendar or other records showing these dates: _____

40. Do you have a diary or other written records of the dates you had intercourse with your child's father: _____

41. Name of doctor who cared for you before the child was born: _____

42. Name of doctor who cared for child after birth: _____

43. Address: _____

44. Circle one: Child premature, overdue, or normal term.

45. Exact due date _____ Birth weight _____

46. Who paid for the birth of the child:
   FHP _____ Medicaid _____ Other (please name) _____

47. Name of hospital in which child was born: _____

State of _____   )
) ss.
County of _____   )

_____ , being duly sworn states that she has read the above document and that the statements contained therein are true to the best of her knowledge.

_____
Signature

_____
Date

Subscribed and sworn to before me this _____ day of _____ , 19 _____ .

_____
Notary Public

Resides at: _____

My Commission Expires: _____

☐ **EXHIBIT 17.2   Paternity Petition**

FAMILY COURT OF
COUNTY OF

....

In the Matter of a Paternity Proceeding

_____ Petitioner,

—against—

_____ Respondent,

....

                                              Docket No.
                                        PATERNITY PETITION
                                             (Parent)

TO THE FAMILY COURT:
   The undersigned Petitioner respectfully shows that:
   1. Petitioner resides at _____
   2. Petitioner had sexual intercourse with the above named Respondent (on several occasions covering a period of time beginning on or about the _____ day of _____ , 19 ___ , and ending on or about the _____ day of _____ , 19 ___ , and as a result thereof (Petitioner) became pregnant.
   3. *(a) (Petitioner) gave birth to a (male) (female) child out of wedlock on the _____ day of _____ , 19 _____ , at _____ .
       *(b) (Petitioner) is now pregnant with a child who is likely to be born out of wedlock.
   4. (Respondent) who resides at _____ is the father of the child.
   5. (Respondent) (has acknowledged) (acknowledges) paternity of the child (in writing) (and) (by furnishing support).
   6. No previous application has been made to any court or judge for the relief sought herein (except _____ .)

WHEREFORE, Petitioner prays that this Court issue a summons or warrant requiring the Respondent to show cause why the Court should not enter a declaration of paternity, an order of support and such other and further relief as may be appropriate under the circumstances.

                                        _____
                                                  Petitioner

Dated: _____ , 19 _____ .

*Alternative allegations.

---

child in the forum state, or on the basis that his in-state acts of intercourse caused the mother's pregnancy.

Once the trial on the paternity issue begins, the defendant may be faced with a *presumption of legitimacy*. A child born to a married woman is presumed to be legitimate unless conclusively proven otherwise. This means that if the defendant is the husband of the mother and denies paternity, he must introduce very strong evidence that he is not the father, e.g., evidence that he is sterile. At one time, neither spouse could introduce evidence that he or she had no sexual intercourse around the time of conception (i.e., evidence of nonaccess) if such evidence would tend to "bastardize" or "illegitimize" the child. This was known as **Lord Mansfield's rule**. Hence, if a defendant had not had sexual intercourse with his wife in years, he could not introduce evidence to this effect if it would tend to bastardize the mother's recently born child.

The United States Supreme Court recently traced the origin of these rules in its opinion, *Michael H. v. Gerald D*, 109 S. Ct. 2333, 2342–43 (1989):

> The presumption of legitimacy was a fundamental principle of the common law. H. Nicholas, Adulturine Bastardy 1 (1836). Traditionally, that presumption could be rebutted only by proof that a husband was incapable of procreation or had had no access to his wife during the relevant period. *Id.*, at 9–10 (citing Bracton, De Legibus et Consuetudinibus Angliae, bk. i, ch. 9, p. 6; bk. ii, ch. 29, p. 63, ch. 32, p. 70 (1569)). As explained by Blackstone, nonaccess could only be proved "if the husband be out of the kingdom of England (or, as the law somewhat loosely phrases it, *extra quatuor*

maria [beyond the four seas]) for above nine months. . . ." 1 Blackstone's Commentaries 456 (Chitty ed. 1826). And, under the common law both in England and here, "neither husband nor wife [could] be a witness to prove access or nonaccess." J. Schouler, Law of the Domestic Relations § 225, p. 306 (3d ed. 1882); R. Graveson & F. Crane, A Century of Family Law: 1857–1957, p. 158 (1957). The primary policy rationale underlying the common law's severe restrictions on rebuttal of the presumption appears to have been an aversion to declaring children illegitimate, see Schouler, *supra,* § 225, at 306–307; M. Grossberg, Governing the Hearth 201 (1985), thereby depriving them of rights of inheritance and succession, 2 Kent's Commentaries 175 (1827), and likely making them wards of the state. A secondary policy concern was the interest in promoting the "peace and tranquillity of States and families," Schouler, *supra,* § 225, at 304, quoting Boullenois, Traité des Status, bk. 1, p. 62, a goal that is obviously impaired by facilitating suits against husband and wife asserting that their children are illegitimate. Even though, as bastardy laws became less harsh, "[j]udges in both [England and the United States] gradually widened the acceptable range of evidence that could be offered by spouses, and placed restraints on the 'four seas rule' . . . [,] the law retained a strong bias against ruling the children of married women illegitimate." Grossberg, *supra,* at 202.

It is obviously very difficult for a husband to deny that he is the father of his wife's child. The harshness of this rule has been criticized. A number of states have either eliminated or substantially limited Lord Mansfield's rule.

The discovery of human blood groups and types has been of great assistance in paternity cases because they:

☐ Can be determined at birth or shortly thereafter

☐ Remain constant throughout an individual's life

☐ Are inherited

In 1981, the United States Supreme Court commented on the operation and effectiveness of blood group tests as follows:

If the blood groups and types of the mother and child are known, the possible and *impossible* blood groups and types of the true father can be determined under the rules of inheritance. For example, a group AB child cannot have a group O parent, but can have a group A, B, or AB parent. Similarly, a child cannot be type M unless one or both parents are type M, and the factor rh' cannot appear in the blood of a child unless present in the blood of one or both parents. . . . Since millions of men belong to the possible groups and types, a blood grouping test cannot conclusively establish paternity. However, it can demonstrate *non-paternity,* such as where the alleged father belongs to group O and the child is group AB. It is a negative rather than an affirmative test with the potential to scientifically exclude the paternity of a falsely accused putative father.

The ability of blood grouping tests to exonerate innocent putative fathers was confirmed by a 1976 report developed jointly by the American Bar Association and the American Medical Association. Miale, Jennings, Rettberg, Sell & Krause, *Joint AMA–ABA Guidelines: Present Status of Serologic Testing in Problems of Disputed Parentage,* 10 Family L. Q. 247 (Fall 1976). The joint report recommended the use of seven blood test "systems"—ABO, Rh, MNS, Kell, Duffy, Kidd, and HLA—when investigating questions of paternity. . . . These systems were found to . . . provide a 91% cumulative probability of negating paternity for erroneously accused Negro men and 93% for white men. . . .

The effectiveness of the seven systems attests the probative value of blood test evidence in paternity cases. The importance of that scientific evidence is heightened because "[t]here are seldom accurate or reliable eye witnesses since the sexual activities usually take place in intimate and private surroundings, and the self-serving testimony of a party is of questionable reliability." Larson, *Blood Test Exclusion Procedures in Paternity Litigation: The Uniform Acts and Beyond,* 13 J. Family L. 713 [1974].

Little v. Streater, 101 S. Ct. 2202, 2206 (1981).

Since 1981 when the preceding commentary was written, the effectiveness of scientific testing has increased significantly. Today newly discovered serologic and statistical methods have made major changes in the law of evidence in this area. A "wider range of genetic tests have come to be admissible, and not merely to demonstrate that it is biologically impossible for a particular man to be the father, but also to show that it is highly probable that a specific man *is* the father." Kay & Kanwischer, *Admissibility of Genetic Testing in Paternity Litigation,* 22 Family L. Quarterly 109, 109–10 (1988). The tests are used to indicate the likelihood or **probability of paternity** of a man who is not excluded by the tests:

> The test results will establish whether your client is excluded as being the father of the child; or if not, what is the probability or likelihood of his being the actual father. If the client is excluded by the blood test, then the case has ended and the mother will have to accuse some other man as being the father. If your client is not excluded, the probability or likelihood of his paternity will be mathematically determined. The likelihood that he is the actual father is then compared statistically to that of a fictional man who is assumed to have had sexual intercourse with the mother and who is assumed not to be excluded by the test. These results are expressed in the form of a "paternity index" and in the form of a "probability of paternity." For example, the paternity index would be expressed as (53 to 1) fifty-three to one; that is, the putative father is fifty-three times more likely to have fathered the child than some other man who could have had intercourse with the mother and who would not be excluded by the blood test. The "probability of paternity" is generally expressed in a percentage figure; for example, 98.15%. Neubaum, *Defense of Paternity Cases,* Case & Comment, 38–39 (July–August 1987).

Special testing laboratories have been established to conduct these tests. An example of how one such laboratory operates appears in Exhibit 17.3.

A relatively recent development in the scientific determination of paternity is **DNA testing,** which is also used in criminal cases. Exhibit 17.4 and the following article present an overview of the DNA testing process.

DNA PROFILING

Establishing Paternity, 64–66, Office of Child Support Enforcement (3rd ed. 1990).

Use of DNA profiling—a fundamental breakthrough in the field of identification—has tremendous potential application and impact in parentage testing. This new way of identifying an individual involves a test on actual genetic material known as deoxyribonucleic acid, typically known by its abbreviation, DNA. Two discoverers of the structure of DNA, Dr. James Watson and Dr. Francis Crick, were awarded a Nobel Prize for their work.

DNA, a molecule that carries the body's genetic information, is contained in every living organism in every cell which has a nucleus (over 99 percent of the cells in the human body). Our chromosomes are made of DNA. DNA is the "blueprint of life" and is what determines each person's unique genetic individuality. Each person's characteristics are based upon the order in which the 3 billion building blocks in a person's DNA are linked together. DNA actually consists of two long strands which coil around each other to form a double helix. In many respects, DNA is like a long zipper. The strands are always in exact alignment as determined by the sequence of the constituent building blocks. The strands can be separated, and the sister strands will zip back together in flawless alignment because the building blocks fit together perfectly.

DNA testing is significant because the configuration of DNA is different in virtually every individual, with the exception of identical twins. Although DNA testing is a relatively new achievement, examination of DNA has wide applicability in forensic science and special value in the settlement of disputed paternity matters.

To perform the analysis, DNA is removed intact from the cells. In paternity testing, blood is used because it can easily be obtained in sufficient quantity. In forensic cases, human cells may be obtained from samples of blood, semen, hair roots, or from any other DNA carrying cell in the body. After DNA is removed and purified, it is cut apart at specific sequences in a carefully controlled way using specialized restriction enzymes which act as biological scissors. Electrophoresis is then used.

The DNA fragments are placed at one end of a sheet of gel and exposed to an electrical charge that allows them to move across the gel. The smaller fragments of DNA move more rapidly through the gel than larger fragments causing the DNA to separate into bands by size. Scientists transfer the bands of DNA fragments from the gel onto a nylon membrane. The nylon membrane is heated and gene probes that have been labeled with a small amount of radioactive material are added. A "gene probe" is a shorter section of DNA—perhaps several hundred or several thousand building blocks (or teeth) long from one strand—which will zip up without fail in the right spot on its partner strand.

Typically, several probes are used, each of which identify the alleles of a single DNA locus. The probes attach themselves to specific invisible bands of repetitive DNA. Technicians then place the membrane(s) on film that is sensitive to the radioactive probes allowing them to obtain an image of the repetitive DNA.

The resulting image obtained from the gene probe looks much like the striped bar code which, together with a computer, is used to scan millions of items every day, such as consumer items in a grocery store. Using the bar code analogy, each dark band visible on the bar code reflects where the gene probe has located its correct partner strand, among the millions of fragments generated by the restriction enzymes acting on the individual's DNA.

The chances that two unrelated persons will have the same DNA are 1 in a quadrillion. Even with siblings (except identical twins), the chances are one in 10 trillion. Every bar in the child's code can be attributed to either the mother or the father, with an even split in the number attributionable to each.

The first step in the analysis is to compare the child's code with the mother's and locate all the bars that match up. The remaining bars in the child's code are then compared with those of the alleged father. If the man is, in fact, the father, every remaining bar will match up with one of the father's code. If the man is not the father, very few bars will match.

As the body of scientific data develops, their use as a supplemental test continues, and as quality control procedures and accreditation guidelines are established, the DNA probes may emerge as the most useful approach to confirming or disproving parentage.

One consequence of the effectiveness of all of these tests is that most disputed paternity cases today are resolved on the basis of the tests rather than by trial. Testing can be expensive, however. If the putative father is indigent, the state must pay for the tests. If he refuses to undergo the tests, many states will either force him to be tested or allow the trial court to take his refusal into consideration in making the paternity decision. The strong implication of such a refusal is that he has something to hide. Many states provide state-appointed counsel for the putative father in these proceedings.

ASSIGNMENT 17.3	

a. In what way(s) can the fatherhood of a child be determined by a court in your state?

b. Select the main way that fatherhood is established in your state, e.g., a paternity proceeding, and prepare a flowchart of all the procedural steps of the process.

c. What is the statute of limitations for paternity actions in your state?

d. What is the standard of proof in paternity cases in your state? Does paternity have to be proven by a "preponderance of the evidence," by "clear and convincing evidence," "beyond a reasonable doubt," or by some other standard?

e. How, if at all, can blood grouping or similar tests be used in your state?

f. Can a polygraph test be used?

g. Does Lord Mansfield's rule apply in your state?

(See General Instructions for the State-Code Assignment, General Instructions for the Flowchart Assignment, and General Instructions for the Court-Opinion Assignment in chapter 1.)

□ **EXHIBIT 17.3   Paternity Testing Procedures**

PATERNITY TESTING
Parker Laboratories

Parker Laboratories, provides paternity testing for disputed paternity cases. The tests performed at Parker are ABO, HLA, Rh, MNSs, Duffy, Kidd and Kell. ABO, Rh, MNSs and HLA typing will be performed on all non-excluded cases. The cumulative probability of exclusion (CPE) for these four systems is 97% for Caucasians and 96% for Blacks. Duffy, Kidd and Kell typings are reserved for the non-excluded cases with low likelihoods of paternity. The addition of these three systems provides a CPE of 98% for Caucasians and 97% for Blacks.

If more markers are required, the blood will be sent to a reference laboratory for serum protein and red cell enzyme testing. When combined with the testing performed at the Parker Laboratories, this further testing yields a CPE greater than 99%.

Paternity cannot be proven with 100% certainty. Non-paternity can be proven by obtaining exclusions.

Testing will be performed in duplicate by separate technologists and reviewed by the medical director before mailing. A copy of the final results will be sent to the alleged father's attorney, the mother's attorney and the child's attorney, if any. An explanation of the results will accompany the final reports.

We recommend that the mother, alleged father and child's blood specimens be drawn at the same time and place, preferably at the Parker laboratory, in order that each can serve as witness to the event. At the time an appointment for paternity testing is made, the following information is required:

1. Name of alleged father
2. Name of mother
3. Name and age of child
4. Names, addresses and phone numbers of all attorneys involved

If it is not possible for the parties to come to the laboratory to have specimens drawn, a kit will be sent to the laboratory that will be drawing the blood. However, the Parker Laboratories does not take responsibility for any errors in identification of the blood samples if they are not drawn at our laboratory. The kit will contain all information necessary for the drawing and sending of the blood; e.g., instructions for drawing, identification and consent forms, tubes and labels. A witness must sign the identification and consent forms, check the driver's license of each party and ensure that the tubes are properly labelled. Photographs and fingerprints are required to be taken on all parties.

Specimens must reach Parker Laboratories within 24 hours after being drawn. Federal Express or some other similar air carrier service which delivers within 24 hours is recommended. Blood should arrive at our laboratory before 10:30 a.m. on the day of the scheduled appointment.

If testing is required from a reference laboratory, letters will be sent immediately to all involved attorneys concerning the further testing.

A written report of final test results will be mailed within a two week period in most cases. Phone reports will not be given.

---

a. In a paternity action a mother is asked to state with whom she has had sexual intercourse during the period of possible conception. Can she refuse to answer?

b. In a divorce action, the court concludes that Tom is the father of two children born during the marriage and is ordered to pay child support for them. Five years later, a criminal nonsupport case is brought against Tom who admits that he made only two of the child support payments in the five years. During the criminal trial, he contests paternity and asks the court to order blood tests for himself, his ex-wife, and the two children. Assume these tests were not available at the time of the divorce action. What result? (See General Instructions for the Legal-Analysis Assignment in chapter 1.)

ASSIGNMENT 17.4

Of course, not every father must be dragged into court in order to establish paternity. Some openly declare paternity even though they do not wish to marry the mother, or may not be able to because she is already married to someone else or because he is already married. In some states, a father in such cases can file a document declaring paternity. In New York, for example, there is a special office within the Department of Social Services where a father can "register" himself as the father by filing an *Instrument to Acknowledge Paternity of an Out of Wedlock Child* (see Exhibit 17.5). This document will ensure that he will receive legal notice of an attempt to adopt the child. Additionally, it will

☐ **EXHIBIT 17.4   The DNA Fingerprinting Process**

1. Blood sample.

2. DNA is extracted from blood cells.

3. DNA is cut into fragments by a restriction enzyme.

4. The DNA fragments are separated into bands during electrophoresis in an agarose gel.

5. The DNA band pattern in the gel is transferred to a nylon membrane by a technique known as Southern Blotting.

6. The radioactive DNA probe is prepared and introduced.

7. The DNA probe binds to specific DNA sequences on the membrane.

8. Excess DNA probe is washed off.

9. At this stage the radioactive probe is bound to the DNA pattern on the membrane.

10. X-ray film is placed next to the membrane to detect the radioactive pattern.

11. The X-ray film is developed to make visible the pattern of bands that is known as a **DNA Fingerprint.**

SOURCE: *Cellmark Diagnostics,* National L. J., 25 (December 18, 1989).

☐ **EXHIBIT 17.5   Form to Register Paternity**

The **Putative Father Registry** is a confidential file maintained in Albany to register fathers of children born out of wedlock.

PURPOSE

The Putative Father Registry was developed to ensure that, if an individual has registered (or has been registered by a court) as the father of a particular child, he will receive legal notice if that child is to be adopted. Additionally, registration provides such a child the right of inheritance in the event of the death of an out of wedlock father. A father may be registered for both purposes provided he follows the instructions in this leaflet.

REGISTRATION

The attached form, called "An Instrument to Acknowledge Paternity of An Out of Wedlock Child," must be filled out in the presence of a witness and signed and notarized before it is returned to the address indicated. Once it is received it will be filed in the Putative Father Registry. The New York State Department of Social Services shall, upon request from any court or authorized agency, provide the names and addresses of persons listed with the registry. The department will not divulge this information to any other party.

The mother and other legal guardian of the child, (if any) will be contacted by registered mail to notify her (them) that a registration has been received.

INSTRUMENT TO ACKNOWLEDGE PATERNITY OF AN OUT OF WEDLOCK CHILD
(pursuant to Section 4–1.2 of New York Estates, Powers and Trust Law)

I _____ , residing at _____
    NAME OF FATHER   ADDRESS

_____ hereby acknowledge that I am
  TOWN   STATE   ZIP CODE

the natural father of _____ born on _____ in
                  NAME OF CHILD   DATE OF BIRTH

_____ . The natural mother of the child
  TOWN   STATE   ZIP CODE

_____ is _____ who resides
  CHILD'S NAME   NAME OF NATURAL MOTHER

at _____

Witness _____   _____
           SIGNATURE   NATURAL FATHER (SIGNATURE)

_____
         ADDRESS

_____
   TOWN   STATE   ZIP CODE

COMPLETE THIS SECTION

STATE OF NEW YORK
COUNTY OF _____

On the _____ day of _____ _____ , before
         DAY   MONTH   YEAR

me came _____ to me known to be the individual described
           NATURAL FATHER

herein and who executed the foregoing instrument, and acknowledges to me that he executed same.

_____
         NOTARY PUBLIC

STATE OF NEW YORK
COUNTY OF _____

This instrument must be filed with the New York State Department of Social Services, Putative Father Register, 40 North Pearl Street, Albany, New York 12243, within sixty days after it is completed. The natural mother indicated on this instrument will be sent notification of this acknowledgement within seven days after its filing.

make clear that the child has a right to inherit from the father in the event that the latter dies without leaving a valid will.

Recently, it became even easier for a father to acknowledge paternity. Unmarried fathers are often present in the hospital during or soon after the birth of their child. The federal government now requires every state to establish a program allowing fathers while in the hospital to sign a simple form voluntarily acknowledging paternity. Before being asked to sign, the father will be given information on the child support duties of parents. This acknowledgment will be of considerable help months or years later if he becomes estranged from the mother and refuses to pay child support on the ground that he is not the father.

CASE

PETTINATO V. PETTINATO

582 A.2d 909 (1990)
Supreme Court of Rhode Island.

Background: *Gregory Pettinato sued Susanne Pettinato for divorce and custody of their son Gregory, Jr. During the litigation, she denied that he was the father. The Family Court granted the divorce and gave custody to the father. The case is now on appeal brought by Susanne before the Supreme Court of Rhode Island.*

Decision on Appeal: *Affirmed. Susanne is estopped from denying Gregory's paternity.*

Opinion of the Court:

Justice Shea delivered the opinion of the court. . . .

Although many of the facts were disputed, it appears that a relationship developed between Gregory and Susanne in the fall of 1984. The parties disagreed about the date when they began sexual relations. However, it is undisputed that the parties were engaging in sexual relations by February 1985. Susanne testified that she did not engage in sexual relations with Gregory between February 14, 1985, and April 7, 1985. During that period she traveled to Florida for two weeks. Moreover, Susanne testified, she did not speak with Gregory until after November 1985 when she returned to Rhode Island from her second trip to Florida.

Susanne gave birth to Gregory, Jr., on January 5, 1986. Despite the parties' discrepancies regarding events leading to the child's birth, Gregory was named as the child's father on the birth certificate filed on January 13, 1986.

Susanne testified that she told Gregory while in the hospital after giving birth that Gregory, Jr., was the child of the man she had stayed with while in Florida. Gregory disputed this testimony. He testified that Susanne telephoned him in April 1985, informed him of her pregnancy, and stated that he, Gregory, was the father. Gregory first became aware of Susanne's denial of his paternity at the time of this divorce action when she filed her answers to interrogatories.

The evidence established that the parties had a fairly nomadic existence after the birth of Gregory, Jr. For approximately one month after the child's birth, Susanne and the child lived at her parents' home.

Gregory was forbidden by her parents to visit Susanne or Gregory, Jr., although the parties would arrange to meet at a friend's house without the knowledge of Susanne's parents. Thereafter, Susanne and the child shared a rented apartment with a friend for approximately three months before moving into an apartment with Gregory.

Gregory, Susanne, and Gregory, Jr., lived in an apartment from May 1986 until October 1986. All three then moved into Gregory's parents' home in October 1986. Gregory and Susanne married on December 21, 1986. Gregory testified that he married Susanne because he "thought it would be the proper thing to do to make a family and be on our own together and bring up our child." The parties remained at his parents' home until Susanne moved out on April 26, 1987. Susanne initially left Gregory, Jr., with Gregory and his parents. Susanne testified, however, that the Cranston police retrieved Gregory, Jr., the next day and brought the child to her at a friend's home. . . .

Over the objections of Gregory, the court heard testimony from Marjorie Kimball, a medical technologist at the Rhode Island Blood Center. Kimball testified that she performed genetic blood testing on Gregory, Susanne, and Gregory, Jr. As a result of this genetic blood testing, Kimball concluded that it was not possible for Gregory to be the biological father of Gregory, Jr.

The trial justice issued an interlocutory decision pending entry of final judgment on October 11, 1988. He granted the petition of Gregory for an absolute divorce and awarded Gregory permanent custody of Gregory, Jr., subject to all reasonable rights of visitation for Susanne. . . .

On appeal Susanne argues that the trial justice improperly overlooked and/or misconceived the expert testimony regarding the genetic blood testing that excluded Gregory as the biological father of Gregory, Jr. Susanne contends that as the natural parent of Gregory, Jr., she is entitled to custody of the child absent a showing of unfitness. . . .

In this case we consider for the first time the rights of parents whose legal presumption of paternity is later challenged during a divorce proceeding. It is undisputed that Gregory is the presumptive natural father of Gregory, Jr. . . . § 15–8–3 Presumption of paternity:

(a) A man is presumed to be the natural father of a child if: . . . (3) After the child's birth, he and the child's natural mother have married, or attempted to marry, each other by a marriage solemnized in apparent compliance with law, although the attempted marriage could be declared invalid, and: (i) He has acknowledged his paternity of the child in writing filed with the clerk of the [F]amily [C]ourt; or (ii) With his consent, he is named as the child's father on the child's birth certificate; or, (iii) He is obligated to support the child under a written voluntary promise or by court order; (4) He acknowledges his paternity of the child in a writing filed with the clerk of the [F]amily [C]ourt, who shall promptly inform the mother of the filing of the acknowledgement, and she does not dispute the acknowledgement, within a reasonable time after being informed thereof, in a writing filed with the clerk of the [F]amily [C]ourt. If another man is presumed under this section to be the child's father, acknowledgement may be effected only with the written consent of the presumed father or after the presumption has been rebutted.

(b) A presumption under this section may be rebutted in an appropriate action only by clear and convincing evidence. If two (2) or more presumptions arise which conflict with each other, the presumption which on its facts is founded on the weightier considerations of policy and logic controls. The presumption is rebutted by a court decree establishing paternity of the child by another man.

Susanne admits that Gregory has met the requirements of § 15–8–3(a)(3)(ii). The parties married after Gregory, Jr.'s birth, and with his consent Gregory was named as the child's father on the birth certificate. Nevertheless, Susanne contends, the results of the genetic blood testing that excluded Gregory as the biological father provide the "clear and convincing" evidence required by § 15–8–3(b) to rebut the presumption of Gregory's paternity.

We are concerned about the situation before the court wherein a mother can tell a man that he is the father of her child, marry him and live together as a family, and then illegitimize the child during a divorce proceeding by attacking the legal presumption of paternity that she helped to bring about. The situation before us is a matter of first impression in this state. After reviewing the conclusions arrived at by other states that have considered this issue, we have reached the conclusion that Susanne may not defeat Gregory's legal presumption of paternity.

We are of the opinion that a mother should be equitably estopped from using the genetic blood testing permitted by § 15–8–11 to disestablish a child's paternity in connection with a routine divorce proceeding. The underlying rationale of the equitable-estoppel doctrine is that "under certain circumstances, a person might be estopped from challenging paternity where that person has by his or her conduct accepted a given person as father of the child." *John M. v. Paula T.*, 524 Pa. 306, 318, 571 A.2d 1380, 1386 (1990). Where the equitable-estoppel doctrine is operative, evidence of genetic blood tests is considered irrelevant in a divorce proceeding wherein the basic issue is the termination of the marriage bond—not the paternity of a child. "[T]he law will not permit a person in these situations to challenge the status which he or she has previously accepted [or created]." Id.

The circumstances of the case before us, in our opinion, compel the application of the equitable-estopped doctrine. Gregory has represented himself to be and has been accepted as Gregory, Jr.'s natural father. He married Susanne, believing her representation that the child was his child. He married her with the intention that the couple would raise their child in a family unit. Gregory consented to being named as the father on Gregory, Jr.'s birth certificate. The three lived together and represented themselves to the community as a family. Susanne never questioned Gregory's paternity until after he commenced divorce proceedings that followed her leaving him. At the time he filed for divorce, Susanne had become pregnant again but not by Gregory.

Taken together, this court's adherence to the statutory presumption of paternity in § 15–8–3(a)(3)(ii) and the court's application of the equitable-estoppel doctrine lead to the same point: the genetic blood test results offered into evidence were not relevant because legal paternity had been established and biological paternity was not at issue. *Scott v. Mershon*, 394 Pa. Super. 411, 417–418, 576 A.2d 67, 71 (1990). Therefore, the genetic blood test results disestablishing Gregory's paternity should not have been admitted. We reject Susanne's contention that the trial justice overlooked and/or misconceived the expert testimony regarding genetic blood testing. That testimony should have been excluded as irrelevant on Gregory's objection to its admission. . . .

For these reasons the defendant's appeal is denied and dismissed, the judgment appealed from is affirmed, and the papers of the case are remanded to the Family Court.

ASSIGNMENT 17.5

a. What is the difference between legal paternity and biological paternity? Why was the distinction important in *Pettinato?*

b. Assume that the paternity issue was not raised in the divorce case and that Susanne was granted custody of the son. Years later, Gregory refuses to pay child support. He wants to introduce evidence of the genetic blood tests that prove he is not the father. Can he introduce this evidence?

■ SUMMARY

At one time, an illegitimate child had very few rights. This situation has changed, although the discrimination has not been entirely eliminated. An illegitimate child can now fully inherit from his or her father who dies intestate. Some states insist, however, that paternity be established before the parent dies. If the parent dies testate, leaving property "to my children," or "to my heirs," the answer to the question of whether illegitimate children were included in these phrases depends on the intent of the parent.

Legitimate and illegitimate children have the same right to be supported, to bring wrongful-death actions because of the death of a parent, and to receive worker's compensation benefits if the parent dies on the job. To obtain social security benefits, however, an illegitimate child must prove he or she was dependent on a deceased father, whereas the law presumes the dependence of a legitimate child.

In most states, when a child is born through artificial insemination with the semen of a man other than the husband, the latter has a duty to support the child, and the child is considered legitimate if the husband consented to the insemination.

Legitimation can occur in a number of ways: acknowledgment of paternity, marriage of the mother and father, legitimation proceeding, paternity proceeding, etc. In some states, all children are legitimate regardless of whether the mother and father ever married.

A major function of a paternity proceeding is to establish a father's duty of support. For this purpose, the court must have personal jurisdiction over him. The child should be joined as a party in the proceeding to ensure that the judgment will be binding on the child. If the defendant is married to the mother, he may face a number of evidentiary obstacles at the trial, e.g., the presumption of legitimacy and Lord Mansfield's rule. Traditional blood group testing can help establish the nonpaternity, though not the paternity, of a particular defendant. More modern scientific techniques, however, claim the ability to establish the high probability of paternity.

All states allow a father to file a paternity acknowledgment in the hospital at the birth of his child.

■ KEY CHAPTER TERMINOLOGY

Filius Nullius	Paternity Proceeding	Personal Jurisdiction
Intestate	Filiation	Long Arm Statute
Testate	Putative	Lord Mansfield's Rule
Artificial Insemination	Guardian ad Litem	Probability of Paternity
Legitimation	Res Judicata	DNA Testing

THE LEGAL STATUS OF CHILDREN

CHAPTER OUTLINE

■■■■ AGE OF MAJORITY AND EMANCIPATION

In most states and for most purposes, an adult is an individual who is eighteen years of age or older. A **minor** is anyone under eighteen. (Note: a person reaches eighteen on the day *before* his or her eighteenth birthday.) At this age, *majority* is achieved. There was a time, however, when the age of majority was twenty-one, and in some states it still is. Furthermore, a person may be a minor for one purpose, but not for another. Hence, one cannot always rely on eighteen as the critical age to determine rights and obligations. Three questions must always be asked:

1. What is the individual trying to do, e.g., vote, drink alcohol, drive, enter a contract, avoid a contract?

2. Does the state set a specific age as the minimum for that task or objective?

3. Has the individual been emancipated? If so, does the emancipation mean that the person is no longer a minor for purposes of that particular task or objective?

Emancipation is the loss of a parent's legal control over a child. Children can be emancipated before the age of majority if certain events take place that clearly indicate they are living independently of their parents with the consent of the latter. Such events include marriage, entering military service, abandonment by the parents, an explicit agreement between the parents and the child that the latter can live independently, etc. In some states, a child can apply to a court for an order of emancipation when the consent of the parents cannot be obtained. As we discuss the various rights and obligations of minors, we will see that it is sometimes important to know whether emancipation has occurred.

Minor Someone under the age of majority, which is usually eighteen.

Emancipation Becoming legally independent of one's parent or legal guardian.

ASSIGNMENT 18.1

How does emancipation occur in your state? Find one opinion written by a court in your state in which the court held that emancipation had occurred. State the facts of the opinion. What specific events led the court to conclude that emancipation had occurred? (See General Instructions for the Court-Opinion Assignment in chapter 1.)

CONTRACTS

Disaffirm To repudiate.

As a general rule (to which there are exceptions), a minor does not have legal capacity to enter a binding contract. Consequently, a minor has no legal obligation to perform a contract if he or she **disaffirms** it at any time before reaching majority or within a reasonable time after reaching majority. In effect, such contracts are voidable.

> Tom is fifteen years of age—clearly a minor. He goes to the ABC Truck Co. and purchases a truck. The sales contract calls for a small down payment (which Tom pays) with the remainder to be paid in installments—on credit. Six months later, Tom changes his mind about the truck and decides to take it back to the dealer. The truck is still in good working order.

If Tom were an adult, he would be bound by his contract. Once an adult and a merchant enter into a contract, they both are bound by it. Neither party can rescind a contract simply because of a change of mind. The difference in our example is that Tom is a minor. Most states give minors the right to disaffirm their contracts so long as they do so while they are still minors or within a reasonable time (e.g., several months) after they have reached majority. In Tom's case, this would mean that he is not bound by the contract to buy the truck. He can take it back and perhaps even force the company to return whatever money he paid on it. In some states, however, the merchant can keep all or part of the purchase price paid thus far to cover depreciation resulting from the minor's use of the item.

Why are minors given this right to disaffirm? The objective of the law is to protect young people from their immaturity. Merchants are on notice that if they deal with minors, they do so at their own risk.

This does not mean that every contract of a minor is invalid. If the minor does not disaffirm, the contract is valid and can be enforced against the minor. Similarly, if a minor tries to disaffirm too late, the contract will be enforced. Suppose that Tom tried to disaffirm the truck contract when he was twenty years old in a state where the age of majority is eighteen. It won't work. He must disaffirm *before* he reaches majority or within a *reasonable* time thereafter.

Estop To be prevented from asserting a right or a defense because it would be unfair or inequitable to do so.

What happens if the minor commits fraud to induce the merchant to enter a contract, e.g., lies about his or her age through a forged birth certificate? Some courts take the position that such wrongdoing by the minor **estops** him or her from being able to disaffirm. Other courts, however, argue that the policy of protecting minors against their own immaturity is so strong that even their own fraud will not destroy their right to disaffirm.

Necessaries The basic items needed by family members to maintain a standard of living.

Guardian ad Litem A special guardian appointed by the court to represent the interests of another.

Special statutes have been passed in many states to limit the minor's right to disaffirm, particularly with respect to certain kinds of contracts. In several states, for example, some employment contracts, such as sports and show business contracts, are binding on minors. Similarly, contractual arrangements with banks and other lending institutions cannot be disaffirmed in many states. Finally, when a minor makes a contract with a merchant for **necessaries** such as food or clothing (see chapter 12), the contract can rarely be disaffirmed.

When a guardian has been appointed over a minor and the guardian enters a contract on behalf of that minor, the contract generally cannot be disaffirmed by the minor. Suppose, for example, that a minor is involved in litigation and an offer of settlement is made. A settlement is a contract. If a court appoints a **guardian ad litem** who negotiates a settlement contract on behalf of the minor, which the court finds is fair, the minor cannot later disaffirm the settlement.

Most states have enacted the Uniform Gifts to Minors Act pursuant to which gifts of certain kinds of property, e.g., securities, can be made to minors through custodians of the property. The custodian can sell the property on behalf of the minor. Contracts made by the custodian for this purpose cannot be disaffirmed by the minor.

Suppose that a minor has become emancipated before reaching the age of majority, e.g., by marrying or by being abandoned by the parents. Does this end the child's power to disaffirm? There is no absolute answer to this question. A minor so emancipated may be denied the power to disaffirm in some states, while in others, it will not affect the power.

ASSIGNMENT 18.2

Answer the following questions by examining the statutory code of your state or the opinions of the courts in your state. (See General Instructions for the State-Code Assignment and the Court-Opinion Assignment in chapter 1.)

a. What is the minimum age to enter a contract that cannot be disaffirmed in your state?

b. Are there specific kinds of contracts a minor cannot disaffirm in your state? If so, what are they?

c. Does lying about his or her age in entering a contract affect the minor's power to disaffirm the contract in your state? If so, how?

d. Is a minor required to return the goods purchased from a merchant as a condition of exercising the power to disaffirm?

e. Does your state have the Uniform Gifts to Minors Act? If so, give the citation and briefly explain how it works.

ASSIGNMENT 18.3

George is a wealthy thirteen-year-old who owns an expensive painting. He signs a contract to exchange the painting for a valuable horse owned by Helen, an equally wealthy twelve-year-old. Both George and Helen are represented by their separate attorneys during the negotiations on the contract. Once the contract is signed and the items are exchanged, what rights do George and Helen have? Assume that there are no problems with the quality and condition of the painting and the horse. (See General Instructions for the Legal-Analysis Assignment in chapter 1.)

▭▭▭ PROPERTY AND EARNINGS

A minor can own real property and most personal property in his or her own name. The parents of a minor do not own and cannot dispose of the minor's property. Earnings are an exception. A minor does *not* have a right to keep his or her own earnings. The parent with the duty to support the child has a right to keep the child's earnings. If, however, the child has not yet reached the age of majority but has been emancipated (e.g., by express agreement with the parents, by marriage, by abandonment by the parents), the parents would not be entitled to the child's earnings.

▭▭▭ DOMICILE

The **domicile** of a minor is the domicile of the parents—even in some instances when the minor lives in a different state from the parents. With parental consent, however, a minor can acquire his or her own separate domicile. Similarly, if a minor who has not yet reached the age of majority is emancipated, most states give that individual the power to acquire his or her own domicile.

Domicile For adults, domicile is the place where they have been physically present with the intent to make that place a permanent home.

ESTATES

States have specified a minimum age for a person to have the legal capacity to dispose of his or her property by a will. Some states have different minimum ages for the disposition of personal property (e.g., clothes, cash) and of real property (e.g., land). In a few states, the emancipation of the minor by his or her marriage will enable the minor to make a valid will before reaching the minimum age.

If the parent of a minor dies, the court will appoint a guardian over the person and/or estate of the minor. This person is called a general guardian, a guardian of the estate, or a guardian ad litem. It is this guardian's duty to:

☐ Manage the minor's property

☐ Collect funds due the minor

☐ Sell, lease, or mortgage the minor's property (with the approval of the court)

☐ Invest the minor's funds

☐ Pay the minor's debts

☐ Support the minor from the minor's funds

☐ Represent the minor in court when needed

Estate All the assets or property of a person that is available to satisfy that person's obligations.

For such services, the minor must pay the guardian a fee, which might be a percentage of the minor's **estate.** If the guardian is not an attorney and legal services are required, the guardian will hire an attorney on behalf of the minor.

ASSIGNMENT 18.4

Answer the following questions by examining the statutory code of your state and/or the opinions of the courts of your state. (See General Instructions for the State-Code Assignment and General Instructions for the Court-Opinion Assignment in chapter 1.)

a. What is the minimum age for an individual to execute a valid will in your state?

b. When a minor dies without leaving a valid will (i.e., dies intestate), what happens to his or her property?

c. What happens to the estate of a minor when his or her parents die? Is a guardian appointed? What are the duties of this person?

EDUCATION

School attendance is compulsory for children up to a designated age, usually sixteen. The school does not have to be public if an alternate private school meets minimum educational standards.

Children at home can be subject to corporal (i.e., physical) punishment by their parents so long as the punishment does not constitute abuse. Teachers are **in loco parentis,** which means that they stand in the place of parents. As such, teachers can also impose corporal punishment on children if reasonably necessary for proper education and discipline. Subjecting children to such punishment is *not* considered cruel and unusual punishment under the Constitution.

In Loco Parentis Standing in the place of (and able to exercise some of the rights of) parents.

A student cannot be expelled or given a long-term suspension from school without being accorded certain procedural rights. For example:

☐ The right to receive written notice of the charges against him or her

☐ The right to a hearing on the charges to determine whether they are valid

☐ The right to an impartial hearing officer. (The latter cannot be directly involved in the matter. For example, the teacher who brought the charges against the student cannot be the hearing officer.)

☐ The right to be represented by counsel at the hearing

☐ The right to present evidence and to confront the accuser at the hearing

If the student is faced with a less severe punishment, such as a short-term suspension, all of these procedural rights are not provided. The student has a right to know the basis of the charges and the right to respond to them, but not necessarily to a hearing with legal representation.

■■■■ NEGLECT AND ABUSE

Statutes exist to protect children who have been neglected or abused by their parents. **Neglect** is often defined as failing to give support, education, medical care, or other care necessary for the child's welfare, e.g., the refusal of a parent to give a child a needed operation, leaving a young child unattended at home for a long period of time. **Abuse** often involves physical harm inflicted by the parent on the child. (See Exhibit 18.1 for relevant statistics on maltreatment by parents and by others.)

Neglect The failure to provide support, medical care, education, moral example, or discipline.

Abuse Physically harming a person.

If a court finds that a child has been neglected or abused, a number of options are usually available. Criminal penalties might be imposed. The court may have the power to terminate the parent's parental rights (discussion in chapter 19), or the child may be placed in the custody of the state's child welfare agency for foster care placement.

Answer the following questions after examining your state statutory code. (See General Instructions for the State-Code Assignment in chapter 1.)

ASSIGNMENT 18.5

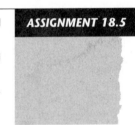

a. What is the state-code definition of a neglected, abandoned, dependent, or abused child in your state?

b. What court has subject matter jurisdiction to determine whether a child is neglected, abandoned, dependent, or abused?

c. What can the court do once it determines that such a child exists?

---

a. Prepare a checklist of questions you could use to help determine whether a child has been neglected, abandoned, etc. (See General Instructions for the Checklist-Formulation Assignment in chapter 1.)

ASSIGNMENT 18.6

b. Draft a flowchart of the procedural steps that are necessary in your state to determine whether a child has been neglected, abandoned, etc. (See General Instructions for the Flowchart Assignment in chapter 1.)

■■■■ DELINQUENCY

At common law, a minor below the age of seven was incapable of committing a crime—or so the law conclusively presumed. Evidence that such a child was in fact capable of committing a crime was inadmissible. A minor between the ages of seven and fourteen could be guilty of a crime if the prosecutor could show that the minor was mature enough to have formed the criminal intent necessary for the particular crime. A rebuttable presumption existed that a mi-

☐ **EXHIBIT 18.1 Child Abuse and Neglect Cases Reported and Investigated: 1991 and 1992**

[Based on reports alleging child abuse and neglect that were referred for investigation by the respective child protective services agency in each State.]

STATE	1991				1992			
	Population under 18 years old	Number of reports[1]	Number of children subject of a report	Investigation disposition, number of children substantiated[2]	Population under 18 years old	Number of reports[1]	Number of children subject of a report	Investigation disposition, number of children substantiated[2]
United States	65,142,000	1,767,674	2,689,193	860,261	66,166,000	1,898,911	2,855,691	991,758
Alabama	1,071,000	28,462	43,969	21,334	1,076,000	28,311	43,246	23,265
Alaska	180,000	[3]8,983	8,983	6,252	185,000	[3]9,892	9,892	8,544
Arizona	1,010,000	26,531	44,844	28,091	1,047,000	29,339	51,216	30,556
Arkansas	626,000	15,860	33,520	8,118	629,000	17,250	36,089	7,538
California	8,163,000	302,834	416,757	71,226	8,423,000	326,120	463,090	73,675
Colorado	883,000	31,796	50,874	8,688	909,000	34,409	55,740	9,237
Connecticut	764,000	14,369	22,080	15,957	771,000	14,369	22,080	15,957
Delaware	168,000	4,367	7,941	2,209	172,000	4,586	8,292	2,157
District of Columbia ..	121,000	5,119	9,444	4,046	117,000	5,596	12,093	3,718
Florida	2,998,000	117,887	184,720	82,386	3,106,000	116,403	180,285	88,563
Georgia	1,775,000	40,142	68,057	43,460	1,800,000	51,225	46,192	46,192
Hawaii	288,000	[3]5,017	5,017	2,191	293,000	[3]5,310	5,310	2,277
Idaho	318,000	9,477	19,507	7,103	324,000	12,230	24,020	6,395
Illinois	2,998,000	67,751	117,912	39,572	3,029,000	74,220	131,592	43,433
Indiana	1,465,000	41,954	63,192	33,329	1,461,000	39,233	58,970	30,283
Iowa	725,000	19,025	27,553	8,154	735,000	19,432	28,094	7,834
Kansas	[4]672,000	9,133	[4]19,280	(NA)	678,000	[3]22,079	22,079	11,585
Kentucky	959,000	33,505	52,912	24,469	964,000	35,997	56,438	24,437
Louisiana	1,233,000	25,579	44,612	14,997	1,238,000	26,087	47,893	16,050
Maine	310,000	4,080	9,503	4,373	306,000	4,826	10,177	4,927
Maryland	1,201,000	29,254	46,806	(NA)	1,226,000	30,062	48,699	(NA)
Massachusetts	1,374,000	35,614	58,218	28,048	1,384,000	32,286	52,581	24,601
Michigan	2,484,000	49,074	113,932	26,366	2,509,000	51,601	117,316	25,931

STATE	1991				1992			
	Population under 18 years old	Number of reports[1]	Number of children subject of a report	Investigation disposition, number of children substantiated[2]	Population under 18 years old	Number of reports[1]	Number of children subject of a report	Investigation disposition, number of children substantiated[2]
Minnesota	1,189,000	17,480	26,663	9,948	1,206,000	17,988	27,462	11,217
Mississippi	751,000	14,377	20,138	7,207	748,000	17,528	32,076	10,712
Missouri	1,340,000	46,343	76,249	22,235	1,350,000	49,286	79,493	24,339
Montana	224,000	7,236	[4]11,029	(NA)	226,000	9,691	14,760	5,328
Nebraska	435,000	7,993	17,087	5,841	439,000	7,961	17,029	5,262
Nevada	321,000	12,858	20,573	7,413	338,000	13,914	22,540	7,699
New Hampshire	280,000	6,550	10,480	2,872	280,000	6,755	10,943	917
New Jersey	1,842,000	[3]53,750	53,750	19,489	1,863,000	[3]50,443	50,443	17,499
New Mexico	458,000	[3]18,234	18,234	5,117	469,000	[3]26,969	26,969	6,716
New York	4,366,000	131,476	212,420	55,586	4,422,000	137,779	228,457	92,238
North Carolina	1,643,000	45,315	71,427	24,636	1,662,000	55,411	88,472	29,546
North Dakota	173,000	3,925	6,435	3,262	172,000	4,515	7,565	3,669
Ohio	2,819,000	88,255	144,218	57,934	2,820,000	95,376	148,101	61,327
Oklahoma	845,000	[3]21,328	21,328	8,287	858,000	[3]24,092	24,092	8,063
Oregon	748,000	23,530	37,648	7,961	766,000	25,622	41,506	8,705
Pennsylvania	2,830,000	[3]23,861	23,861	7,986	2,844,000	[3]25,891	25,891	8,419
Rhode Island	230,000	8,844	13,820	5,919	233,000	8,395	12,886	4,931
South Carolina	938,000	18,956	30,978	10,735	945,000	19,712	33,854	11,348
South Dakota	200,000	[3]11,205	11,205	3,826	204,000	10,486	10,486	2,903
Tennessee	1,230,000	[3]29,715	29,715	10,367	1,246,000	[3]31,231	31,231	11,469
Texas	4,969,000	97,676	153,753	58,199	5,072,000	110,937	174,255	62,342
Utah	642,000	14,534	23,254	10,179	654,000	15,910	27,047	10,875
Vermont	145,000	3,175	2,689	1,437	144,000	2,750	3,205	1,498
Virginia	1,539,000	34,067	50,732	13,702	1,562,000	35,880	55,680	14,472
Washington	1,315,000	39,067	59,311	(NA)	1,355,000	39,704	55,836	41,879
West Virginia	437,000	13,888	22,221	(NA)	438,000	12,932	20,949	(NA)
Wisconsin	1,311,000	[3]44,963	44,963	17,657	1,330,000	[3]47,622	47,622	19,213
Wyoming	136,000	3,260	5,379	2,097	138,000	3,268	5,458	2,017

NA Not available. [1]Except as noted, reports are on incident/family based basis or based on number of reported incidents regardless of the number of children involved in the incidents. [2]Type of investigation disposition that determines that there is sufficient evidence under State law to conclude that maltreatment occurred or that the child is at risk of maltreatment. [3]Child-based report that enumerates each child who is a subject of a report. [4]1990 data.

SOURCE: U.S. Department of Health and Human Services, National Center on Child Abuse and Neglect, National Child Abuse and Neglect Data System, Working Paper 2, 1991 Summary Data Component, May 1993; Child Maltreatment—1992, May 1994.

nor between these ages could *not* possess the requisite criminal intent. This simply meant that the court would assume the absence of this intent unless the prosecutor affirmatively proved otherwise. Minors over fourteen were treated and tried the same as adults.

In the early part of this century, a trend developed to remove the stigma of criminality from the misconduct of minors. Juvenile courts were created. Terms such as **juvenile delinquent,** PINS (Person In Need of Supervision), MINS (Minor In Need of Supervision), and CHIPS (Child In Need of Protection and Services) began to be widely used. A juvenile delinquent is a person under a certain age, e.g., sixteen, whose conduct would constitute a crime if performed by an adult. A PINS, MINS, or CHIPS is a person who has committed a so-called *status offense*, which in this context means noncriminal misconduct by a person under a certain age. Examples of such offenses include habitual truancy from school and incorrigibility at home. When a juvenile court decides that a child fits into one of these special categories, it has a number of options, including sending the child home with a warning, institutionalization in a juvenile facility, probation under the supervision of a youth counselor, and **foster home** placement.

While this system of special treatment is now widely used, it has been criticized as too lenient, particularly when the child commits a serious act such as homicide or sexual assault. Experts say that hundreds of children under age twelve commit homicides each year. Anderson, *Grown-up Crime, Boy Defendant,* 75 Amer. Bar Assoc. J. 26, 27 (November 1989). When a child of a specified age is accused of particularly heinous conduct of this kind, most states give a judge discretion in deciding whether the case should be handled in a juvenile court or whether the regular criminal adult courts should take over.

Juvenile Delinquent A young person under a designated age whose conduct would constitute a crime if committed by an adult.

Foster Home A temporary home for a child when his or her own family cannot provide care and when adoption is either not possible at the present time or is under consideration.

ASSIGNMENT 18.7

Most of the following questions can be answered by examining your state statutory code. (See General Instructions for the State-Code Assignment in chapter 1.)

a. What is a juvenile delinquent in your state?

b. What court has subject matter jurisdiction to determine juvenile delinquency?

c. Is any classification other than juvenile delinquent used in your state to describe a minor who has misbehaved, e.g., the classification of PINS? If so, define the classification.

d. Draft a flowchart of the procedural steps required in your state to process a juvenile delinquency case. (See General Instructions for the Flowchart Assignment in chapter 1.)

e. Once a minor has been found to be a juvenile delinquent, what disposition options are available to the court in your state?

f. Under what circumstances, if any, can a child be prosecuted in an adult criminal court?

☐ **Notes on the Legal Status of Children**

1. Twenty-one has been the traditional minimum voting age, although most states have recently lowered this to eighteen.

2. On the tort liability of a minor, see chapter 21.

3. On the abortion rights of minors, see chapter 16.

▪▪▪ SUMMARY

The age of majority is eighteen, but a state may impose different age requirements for performing different activities. Emancipation before the age of majority can make a minor eligible for some of these activities.

A number of special laws apply to minors. For example, they have the right to disaffirm contracts they have entered. They can own real and personal property in their own name, but unless they have been emancipated, their parents have a right to keep their earnings. Also, minors cannot acquire their own domicile without parental consent, and in most states, an unemancipated minor is ineligible to make a will. If the parents of a minor die, the court will appoint a guardian to oversee his or her affairs.

School is compulsory until a designated age. Teachers stand in the place of parents and, as such, can impose reasonable corporal punishment. However, students are entitled to certain procedural rights, e.g., a hearing, if the school wants to expel or suspend them long term.

When a parent neglects or abuses a child, the state has a number of options, e.g., criminal prosecution, foster home placement, and termination of parental rights. A child below the age of seven cannot commit a crime, but one between seven and fourteen can be prosecuted if the state can overcome the presumption that such a child is not old enough to form the necessary criminal intent. A modern tendency is to treat misbehaving children as juvenile delinquents or as persons in need of supervision rather than as defendants in criminal courts.

■ KEY CHAPTER TERMINOLOGY

Minor
Emancipation
Disaffirm
Estop
Necessaries

Guardian ad Litem
Domicile
Estate
In Loco Parentis
Neglect

Abuse
Juvenile Delinquent
Foster Home

19 ADOPTION

■■■■■ INTRODUCTION

A number of important terms should be defined and distinguished before discussing the subject of adoption.

☐ **Custody** The control and care of an individual.

☐ **Guardianship** The legal right to the custody of an individual.

☐ **Ward** An individual who is under guardianship.

☐ **Termination of Parental Rights** A judicial declaration that a parent shall no longer have any right to participate in decisions affecting the welfare of the child.

☐ **Adoption** The legal process by which an adoptive parent assumes the rights and duties of a natural (i.e., biological) parent.

☐ **Paternity** The fatherhood of a child.

☐ **Foster Care** A child welfare service that provides shelter and substitute family care when a child's own family cannot care for it. Foster care is designed to last for a temporary period during which adoption is neither desirable nor possible, or during the period when adoption is under consideration.

☐ **Stepparent** A person who marries the natural mother or father of a child, but is not one of the child's natural parents. For example, assume that Ted and Mary marry each other. It is the second marriage for both. Ted has a son, Bill, from his first marriage. Mary has a daughter, Alice, from her first marriage. Ted is the natural father of Bill and the stepfather of Alice. Mary is the natural mother of Alice and the stepmother of Bill. If Alice adopts Bill, she becomes his *adoptive parent;* she will no longer be his stepparent.

ASSIGNMENT 19.1

a. Find statutes or court opinions that define the words *custody* and *guardianship* in your state. For each word, try to find at least one statute or opinion that defines the word. If either or both words have more than one meaning in your state, give each meaning. (See General Instructions for the State-Code Assignment and General Instructions for the Court-Opinion Assignment in chapter 1.)

b. Prepare a flowchart of guardianship procedures in your state involving a minor child. If there is more than one kind of such guardianship in your state, select any one. (See General Instructions for the Flowchart Assignment in chapter 1.)

c. Draft a custody agreement under which your best friend agrees to care for your child while you are in the hospital for six months. (See General Instructions for the Agreement-Drafting Assignment in chapter 1.)

Adoption establishes a permanent, legal, parent-child relationship between the child and a person who is not the natural parent of the child. (Approximately 2 percent of children in the country today live with adoptive parents. See Exhibit 19.1.) In many states, an adoption leads to the reissuance of the child's birth certificate, listing the adoptive parent as the "mother" or "father" of the child. The relationship is permanent in that only the court can end the relationship by terminating the parental rights of the adoptive parent. Even the divorce or death of the adoptive parent does not end the relationship. Assume, for example, that Tom marries Linda and then adopts her son, Dave, by a previous marriage. If Tom subsequently divorces Linda, he does not cease to be Dave's parent. His obligation to support Dave, for example, continues after the divorce. Similarly, when Tom dies, Dave can inherit from Tom as if he were a natural child of Tom. In this sense, the parent-child relationship continues even after the death of the adoptive parent.

■■■■■ KINDS OF ADOPTION

The three main kinds of adoption are agency adoption, independent adoption, and black market adoption. A fourth, equitable adoption, will be considered later in the chapter.

AGENCY ADOPTION

In an **agency adoption,** the child is placed for adoption by a licensed private or public agency. There are two main circumstances in which such agencies become involved. First, the parent (usually the mother) voluntarily transfers the child to the agency by executing a formal surrender document that relinquishes all parental rights in the child. Second, a court terminates the parental rights of a parent because of abandonment, abuse, or neglect, and asks the agency to place the child for adoption.

INDEPENDENT/PRIVATE ADOPTION

In an **independent adoption** (also called a private adoption), a natural parent places the child for adoption with the adoptive parents, often with the help of an attorney, a doctor, or both. (See Exhibit 19.2 for sample adoption ads.) As with agency adoptions, a court must give its approval to the independent adoption. Furthermore, the state may require an agency to investigate the prospective adoption and file a report, which is considered by the court. It should be

□ **EXHIBIT 19.1**
Living Arrangements of Children in 1980 and 1990

CATEGORY	NUMBER IN 1980	NUMBER IN 1990
Children living with both natural parents	39,523,000	37,026,000
Children living with natural mother and stepfather	5,355,000	6,643,000
Children living with adoptive parents	1,350,000	974,000
Children living with natural father and stepmother	727,000	608,000
Unknown	293,000	197,000

SOURCE: *Statistical Abstract of the United States,* Table 79 (1994).

noted, however, that in an independent adoption, the level of involvement by the agency is far less extensive and intrusive than in a traditional agency adoption, where the agency supervises the entire process.

Most, but not all, independent adoptions are initiated by a stepparent or by someone who is otherwise already related to the child. Yet many independent adoptions occur when no such relationship exists.

Here is an example of how an independent adoption might occur:

> When Ralph and Nancy Smith discovered that they were infertile, they decided to adopt. Several visits to adoption agencies, however, were quite discouraging. One agency had a long waiting list of couples seeking to adopt healthy, white infants; it was not taking any new applications. Another accepted their application, but warned that the process might take up to five years, with no guarantee that a child would eventually become available. Nationally, hundreds of thousands of women are waiting to adopt a relatively small number of healthy, white infants. The small number of available children is due to the widespread use of abortion and the declining social stigma attached to the single-parent motherhood.
>
> Acting on the advice of a friend, the Smiths then tried the alternative of an independent adoption. They placed personal ads in newspapers and magazines seeking to contact an unwed pregnant woman who would be willing to relinquish her child for adoption. They also sent their résumé and letters of inquiry to doctors, members of

□ **EXHIBIT 19.2**
Sample ads used in adoption.

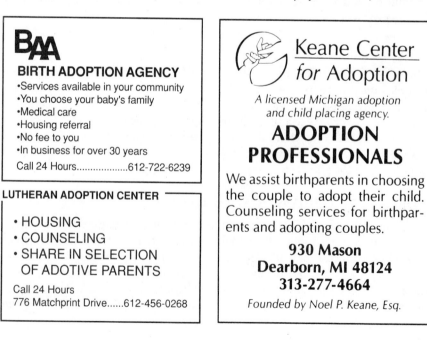

BAA
BIRTH ADOPTION AGENCY
• Services available in your community
• You choose your baby's family
• Medical care
• Housing referral
• No fee to you
• In business for over 30 years
Call 24 Hours.................612-722-6239

LUTHERAN ADOPTION CENTER
• HOUSING
• COUNSELING
• SHARE IN SELECTION OF ADOTIVE PARENTS
Call 24 Hours
776 Matchprint Drive......612-456-0268

Keane Center *for* **Adoption**
A licensed Michigan adoption and child placing agency.
ADOPTION PROFESSIONALS
We assist birthparents in choosing the couple to adopt their child. Counseling services for birthparents and adopting couples.
930 Mason Dearborn, MI 48124 313-277-4664
Founded by Noel P. Keane, Esq.

the clergy, and attorneys specializing in independent adoptions. In some cities, the yellow pages had listings for attorneys with this specialty. Their efforts were finally successful when an attorney led them to Diane Kline, a seventeen-year-old pregnant girl. The Smiths prepared a scrapbook on their life, which Diane reviewed. She then interviewed the Smiths and decided to allow them to adopt her child. The Smiths paid the attorney's fees, Diane's medical bills, the cost of her psychological counseling, travel expenses, and living expenses related to the delivery of the baby. Diane signed a consent form relinquishing her rights in the baby and agreeing to the adoption by the Smiths, who formally applied to the court for the adoption. A social worker at a local agency investigated the case and made a report to the court, which then issued an order authorizing the adoption.

In this example, the natural mother had personal contact with the adoptive parents. This is not always the case. Independent adoptions can also resemble agency adoptions, where anonymity is more common.

Note that the money paid by the Smiths covered medical, legal, and related expenses. Other payments would be illegal. Assume, for example, that Diane had hesitated about going through with the adoption and the Smiths had offered her $10,000 above expenses. This could constitute illegal *baby buying,* turning an independent adoption into a **black market adoption.** Such a payment to a birth parent, to an attorney, or to anyone is illegal. A person may pay those expenses that are naturally and reasonably connected with the adoption, so long as no cash or other consideration is given to induce someone to participate in the adoption. (The separate but related problems of surrogate motherhood will be considered in the next chapter.)

In some states, independent adoptions are more common than agency adoptions. Critics argue that illegal payments are frequent, and that the lack of safeguards in independent adoptions can lead to disastrous consequences. A dramatic example occurred in 1988 when a New York City attorney was convicted in the battery death of a six-year-old girl who had been placed in his care so that he might arrange an independent adoption. The attorney had kept the child—and then abused her—when prospective adoptive parents failed to pay his fee for the adoption. Proponents of independent adoptions view this case as an aberration and maintain that the vast majority of independent adoptions are legal and are adequately supervised.

BLACK MARKET ADOPTION

Frustration with agency adoptions leads to the alternative of independent adoptions. And frustration with both kinds of legal adoptions leads to *black market adoptions,* which involve a payment beyond reasonable expenses.

An adoption becomes baby buying when the payment is for the placement of the child rather than for reasonable expenses. (See Exhibit 19.6 at the end of this chapter.) The most blatant example is the *baby broker* who financially entices women to give up their children and then charges adoptive parents a large "fee" for arranging the adoption. In 1990, a typical black market adoption cost up to $50,000.

It is difficult to know how many independent adoptions turn into black market adoptions, since the participants have an interest in keeping quiet about the illegal payment. To discourage such payments, some states require the adoptive parent to file with the court a list of all expenditures pertaining to the adoption. This, however, has not stopped black market adoptions, and critics argue that the only way to do so is to eliminate independent adoptions so that all adoptions will be more adequately supervised by traditional public and private agencies.

ASSIGNMENT 19.2

Answer the following questions based on your state code. (See General Instructions for the State-Code Assignment in chapter 1.)

a. Are independent or private adoptions allowed in your state? If so, how do they differ from agency adoptions? In what ways does the state try to prevent "baby buying"?

b. Is it a crime to "buy" a baby? If so, how is this crime committed?

WHO MAY BE ADOPTED?

In the vast majority of cases, the person adopted (called the adoptee) is a child, usually an infant. Yet in most states it is possible for one adult to adopt another adult as well. The most common reason for this practice is that the adoptive parent wants to give the adopted adult rights of inheritance from the adoptive parent. In effect, the latter is designating an heir.

Suppose, however, that a homosexual wants to adopt his or her homosexual lover. A few courts have allowed it, but most courts would agree with New York in disallowing it. The "sexual intimacy" between such individuals "is utterly repugnant to the relationship between child and parent in our society, and . . . a patently incongruous application of our adoptive laws." *In the Matter of Robert Paul P.*, 63 N.Y.2d 233, 481 N.Y.S.2d 652, 653 (1984).

ASSIGNMENT 19.3

Can one adult adopt another adult in your state? If so, can one homosexual adult adopt another? (Check your state code and cases, interpreting its relevant provisions. See General Instructions for the State-Code Assignment and General Instructions for the Court-Opinion Assignment in chapter 1.)

WHO MAY ADOPT?

The petitioners (i.e., the persons seeking to become the adoptive parents) will be granted the adoption if it is in "the best interest of the child." Such a broad standard gives the judge a good deal of discretion. In addition to relying on the child welfare agency's investigation report, the judge will consider a number of factors, no one of which is usually controlling.

1. *Age of petitioner.* Most states require the petitioner to be an adult. The preference is for someone who is not unusually older than the child. A court would be reluctant, for example, to allow a seventy-five-year-old to adopt an infant, unless special circumstances warranted it.

2. *Marital status of petitioner.* While many states allow single persons to adopt, the preference is for someone who is married. His or her spouse is usually required to join in the petition.

3. *Health of petitioner.* Adoptive parents are not expected to be physically and emotionally perfect. If a particular handicap will not seriously interfere with the raising of the child, it will not by itself bar the adoption.

4. *Race.* Most judges and adoption agencies prefer that the race of the child be the same as that of the adoptive parents. Some states have time periods during which the search for adoptive parents must be limited to adoptive parents of the same race. This obviously limits the number of interracial or transracial adoptions that occur. The problem, however, is that there are not enough same-race adoptive parents available. In 1994 Congress passed the Multiethnic Placement Act, which prohibits states from delaying or denying the placement of a child solely on the basis of race, color, or national origin. If an agency receives federal assistance, it cannot "categorically deny to any person the opportunity to become an adoptive or a foster parent, solely on the basis of the race, color, or national origin of the adoptive or foster parent, or the child, involved; or delay or deny the placement of a child for adoption or into foster care, or otherwise discriminate in making a placement decision, solely on the basis of the race, color, or national origin of the adoptive or foster parent, or the child, involved." 42 U.S.C.A. § 5115a.

5. *Religion.* When possible or practicable, the religion of the adoptive parents should be the same as the religion of the natural parents. Interfaith adoptions, though allowed, are generally not encouraged.

6. *Wishes of the child.* The court will consider the opinion of the prospective adoptee if he or she is old enough to communicate a preference.

7. *Economic status.* The adoptive parents must have the financial means to care for the child. The court will examine their current financial status and prospects for the future in light of the child's support needs.

8. *Home environment and morality.* Everyone's goal is for the child to be brought up in a wholesome, loving home where values are important and where the child will be nutured to his or her potential. Illegal or conspicuously unorthodox lifestyles are frowned upon.

Earlier we saw that most states do not allow the adoption of a homosexual adult by another homosexual. The hesitancy is stronger against a homosexual adopting a child. Even in Denmark where same-sex marriages are now legal, the couple cannot adopt minor children. There are circumstances, however, when a gay *natural* parent will be given custody of his or her child following a divorce. This is usually because the child is old enough to have already established a healthy relationship with this parent, and because the heterosexual natural parent is either absent or unfit. Courts are more reluctant, however, to allow a homosexual to *adopt* a child with whom he or she does not already have a biological relationship. In **second-parent adoptions,** a few states have made an exception. For example, a lesbian applies to adopt the child of her partner who has just given birth via artificial insemination. Most second-parent adoptions, however, involve a heterosexual couple.

Second-Parent Adoption The adoption of a child by a partner (or cohabitant) of a natural parent who does not give up his or her own parental rights.

ASSIGNMENT 19.4

a. In your state, who is eligible to adopt children? Who is not eligible?

b. What standards exist to guide a judge's decision in your state on whether to approve a particular adoption?

c. Mary Jones is a Baptist. She wants to place her one-year-old child for adoption. Mr. and Mrs. Johnson want to adopt the child and file the appropriate petition to do so in your state. The Johnsons are Jewish. Mary Jones consents to the adoption. What effect, if any, will the religious differences between Mary Jones and the Johnsons have on the adoption? Assume that Mary has no objection to the child's being raised in the Jewish faith.

d. Same facts as in part (c) above except that the Johnsons are professed atheists. Mary Jones does not care. (See General Instructions for the State-Code Assignment in chapter

1. You may also need to check court opinions. See General Instructions for the Court-Opinion Assignment in chapter 1.)

e. Both Paul and Helen Smith are deaf and mute. They wish to adopt the infant daughter of Helen's best friend, a widow who just died. Prepare an investigation strategy to collect evidence relevant to whether the adoption should be permitted. (See General Instructions for the Investigation-Strategy Assignment in chapter 1.)

ASSIGNMENT 19.5

a. Contact a *private* agency in your state involved in adoption placement. Ask the agency what criteria it uses in recommending an adoption. Also, ask the agency to send you any available literature that lists such standards, e.g., pamphlets, applications. Compare these standards with your answers to the questions in the preceding assignment (19.4). Does the agency's practice conform with the standards of the law of your state?

b. Same question as in part (a) above except that this time a *public* agency should be contacted.

(Note: Let your teacher know in advance which private and public agency you propose to contact. The teacher may want to coordinate the contacts so that no single agency receives more than its share of contacts from the class.)

■■■■ ADOPTION PROCEDURE

A rather elaborate set of procedures exists for adoption; it is not easy to adopt a child. Courts are very concerned about protecting the interests of the child, the natural parents, and the adoptive parents. When the most sought-after babies (i.e.., healthy, white infants) are in short supply, the temptation to "buy" a baby on the black market is heightened. One way to try to control this is by increasing procedural safeguards in the process.

JURISDICTION AND VENUE

Subject Matter Jurisdiction The power of the court to hear a particular category or kind of case.

Choice of Venue The selection of the court to try the case when more than one court has subject-matter jurisdiction to hear that kind of case.

Subject matter jurisdiction refers to the power of the court to hear a particular kind of case. Not every court in a state has subject matter jurisdiction to issue adoption decrees. The state constitution or state statutes will designate one or perhaps two courts that have authority to hear adoption cases, e.g., the state family court or the state juvenile court. There are also specifications for selecting the county or district in which the adoption proceeding must be brought. The selection is referred to as the **choice of venue.** It will usually depend on the residence (or occasionally on the domicile) of one or more of the participants, usually the natural parents, the adoptive parents, or the child.

ASSIGNMENT 19.6

a. What court or courts in your state have the power to hear adoption cases?

b. In what county or section of your state must the adoption proceeding be initiated? Does your answer depend upon the residence or domicile of any of the participants? If so, what is the definition of residence or domicile?

(To answer the above questions, you may have to check your state constitution, state statutory code, and perhaps opinions of your state courts. See General Instructions for the State-Code Assignment in chapter 1.)

PETITION

States differ on the form and content of the adoption **petition** filed by the adoptive parents to begin the adoption proceeding. The petition will contain such data as the names of the petitioners; their ages; whether they are married and, if so, whether they are living together; the name, age, and religion of the child, etc. While the natural parents play a large role in the adoption proceeding, not all states require that they be mentioned in the petition itself. (For an example of the format of a petition, see Exhibit 19.3.)

ASSIGNMENT 19.7

a. What must a petition for adoption contain in your state? Must it name the natural parents? (See General Instructions for the State-Code Assignment in chapter 1.)

b. Draft an adoption petition. Assume that you are seeking to adopt the one-year-old baby of a woman who has recently been hospitalized. This friend has no other relatives. The natural father of the child is no longer alive. You can make up facts you need to draft the petition. (Although an adoption petition is not a complaint, you may find some of the suggestions on drafting complaints to be useful. See Exhibit 1.3 in chapter 1.)

NOTICE

Due process of law requires that both natural parents be given *notice* of the petition to adopt the child by the prospective adoptive parents. (Later when we study the Baby Richard and Baby Jessica cases, we will see the importance of this requirement.) The preferred method of providing notice is to personally serve the natural parents with process within the state where the adoption petition is brought. If this is not possible, the court may allow substituted service, e.g., registered mail.

There was a time when the father of an illegitimate child was not entitled to notice of the adoption proceeding; only the mother of such a child was given notice. The situation has changed, however, due to recent decisions of the United States Supreme Court. While the full scope of the rights of the father of an illegitimate child have not yet been fully defined by the courts, it is clear that he can no longer be ignored in the adoption process. As we shall see, however, there is a difference between a parent's right to notice of the adoption proceeding and the parent's right to prevent the adoption by refusing to consent to it.

ASSIGNMENT 19.8

a. In your state, who must receive notice of an adoption proceeding?

b. When can substituted service of process (e.g., mail, publication) be used in your state for persons who must receive notice of adoption proceedings?

(See General Instructions for the State-Code Assignment and General Instructions for the Court-Opinion Assignment in chapter 1.)

CONSENT

Adoption occurs in essentially two ways: with the consent of the natural parents or without their consent. When consent is necessary, the state's statute will usually specify the manner in which the consent must be given, e.g., whether it must be witnessed, whether it must be in writing, whether the formalities for consent differ for agency adoptions as opposed to independent adoptions, whether the consent form must mention the names of the parties seeking to adopt the child, etc. Some states say that the consent is not valid if it is obtained prior to the birth of the child. Many states say that it cannot be obtained until at least seventy-two hours after birth. Once the consent is validly

☐ **EXHIBIT 19.3 Adoption Petition**

FAMILY COURT OF THE STATE OF _____
COUNTY OF _____

<table>
<tr><td>In the Matter of the
Adoption by</td><td>Index No.</td></tr>
<tr><td>_____ of _____
a minor having the first
name of</td><td></td></tr>
<tr><td></td><td>PETITION
(Agency)</td></tr>
<tr><td>whose last name is contained
in the Schedule annexed to
the Petition herein.</td><td></td></tr>
</table>

TO THE FAMILY COURT:

1. (a) The name and place of residence of the petitioning adoptive mother is:
    Name:
    Address:
She is (of full age) (a minor), born on
She is (unmarried) (married to
and they are living together as husband and wife).
Her religious faith is
Her occupation is
and her approximate annual income is $

   (b) The name and place of residence of the petitioning adoptive father is:
    Name:
    Address:
He is (of full age) (a minor), born on
He is (unmarried) (married to
and they are living together as husband and wife).
His religious faith is
His occupation is
and his approximate annual income is $

2. As nearly as can be ascertained, the full name, date and place of birth of the (male) (female) adoptive child are set forth in the Schedule annexed to this Petition and verified by a duly constituted official of an authorized agency.

3. (a) As nearly as can be ascertained, the religious faith of the adoptive child is
   (b) As nearly as can be ascertained, the religious faith of the natural parents of the adoptive child is

4. The manner in which the adoptive parents obtained the adoptive child is as follows:

5. The adoptive child has resided continuously with the adoptive parents since

6. The name by which the adoptive child is to be known is

7. The consent of the above-mentioned authorized agency has been duly executed and is filed herewith. The consent of the natural parents of the adoptive child is not required because

8. No previous application has been made to any court or judge for the relief sought herein.

9. The adoptive child has not been previously adopted.

10. To the best of petitioners' information and belief, there are no persons other than those hereinbefore mentioned interested in this proceeding.

11. WHEREFORE, your petitioners pray for an order approving the adoption of the aforesaid adoptive child by the above named adoptive parents and directing that the said adoptive child shall be regarded and treated in all respects as the child of the said adoptive parents and directing that the name of the said adoptive child be changed as specified in paragraph 6 above and that henceforth (s)he shall be known by that name.

SOURCE: 1 GUIDE TO AMERICAN LAW, 103 (1983).

given, the mother has a period of time, e.g., ten days, during which she has the right to change her mind and revoke the consent. See Exhibit 19.4 for an example of a consent form.

Both natural parents must consent to the adoption unless the parental rights of one or both of them have been formally terminated because of unfitness. An **unfit** parent loses the power to veto the adoption. As indicated earlier, the father of an illegitimate child has a right to present his views on the propriety of the proposed adoption. He must be given notice of the adoption proceeding unless he has abandoned the child. If he has lived with his illegitimate child, supported him or her, or otherwise maintained close contacts with the child, a court will grant him the same rights as the mother. He *will* be allowed to veto the proposed adoption.

Unfit Demonstrating abuse or neglect that is substantially detrimental to a child.

Often a child welfare agency will place the child in a foster home. Foster parents cannot prevent the adoption of the child by someone else. The consent of foster parents to the adoption is not necessary. This does not mean that the foster parents can be ignored entirely. When an agency attempts to remove the child from the foster home, many states give the foster parents the right to object to the removal and to present their arguments against the removal. While foster parents may be given a right to be heard on the removal, they cannot veto the adoption of the child.

☐ **EXHIBIT 19.4 Consent Form**

CONSENT TO ADOPTION

We, the undersigned, being the father and mother, respectively, of _____ , who was born on _____ , 19___ , in _____ County, California, and being the persons entitled to the sole custody of said child do hereby give our full and free consent to the adoption of said child by _____ and _____ , his wife, and do hereby relinquish to said persons forever all of our rights to the care, custody, control, services, and earnings of said child.

Each of us hereby promises that, as soon as adoption proceedings are commenced in the state of _____ , we will properly execute any further instruments or papers necessary to effectuate the adoption of said child by said persons.

Each of us hereby authorizes said persons, or either of them, to procure and provide any and all medical, hospital, dental, and other care needed for said child, it being understood by us that said persons have agreed to, and will pay, such expenses without seeking reimbursement from us prior to the adoption of said child.

Each of us fully understand that, upon the signing of this instrument, we have irrevocably relinquished and waived all right to withdraw the consent and authority herein given.

DATED: _____ , 19___ .

_____
[*Name and Signature of Party*]

_____
[*Name and Signature of Party*]

Witnesses:

_____

_____

Notary Public: (SEAL)

_____

My commission expires _____

SOURCE: D. Adams, CALIFORNIA CODE FORM (1960).

ASSIGNMENT 19.9

a. Give the citation to the statute that contains the formalities necessary for consent to adoption in your state.

b. Who must give consent?

c. Is it necessary to obtain the consent of a natural parent who is mentally ill?

d. Is it necessary to obtain the consent of a natural parent who previously was *not* awarded custody of the child in a divorce proceeding?

e. Is there a minimum age for giving consent? Can a parent who is a minor consent or withhold consent to adoption of his or her child?

f. When, if ever, must the child consent to his or her own adoption?

g. In what form or with what formalities must the consent be given? Does your answer differ for a public agency adoption as opposed to an independent adoption? If so, explain the difference.

h. Does the consent form have to name the prospective adoptive parents?

(See General Instructions for the State-Code Assignment in chapter 1. You may also need to check court opinions for some of the above questions. See General Instructions for the Court-Opinion Assignment in chapter 1.)

ASSIGNMENT 19.10

In Assignment 19.7, part (b), you drafted an adoption petition based primarily on facts that you invented yourself. Using those facts, draft a consent form (to be signed by the mother) that complies with the statutory requirements for consent in your state.

Once a natural parent consents to the adoption, can the consent be changed, assuming that it was given according to the requisite formalities? When the adoptive decree has been entered, most states will *not* allow the consent to be revoked, but some states permit revocation beforehand if:

1. The court determines that the revocation would be in the best interest of the child.

2. The court determines that the consent was obtained by fraud, duress, or undue pressure.

See Exhibit 19.5 for an example of a notice of hearing on revocation.

ASSIGNMENT 19.11

When, if ever, can consent to adoption be revoked in your state? (See General Instructions for the State-Code Assignment in chapter 1. You may also have to check court opinions of your state if no statutes on revocation exist. See General Instructions for the Court-Opinion Assignment in chapter 1.)

INVOLUNTARY TERMINATION OF PARENTAL RIGHTS

It would be illogical to permit a natural parent to prevent the adoption of his or her child by withholding consent if that parent has abandoned the child. Many statutes, therefore, provide that abandonment as well as extreme cruelty, conviction of certain crimes, or willful neglect will mean that the consent of a parent engaged in such conduct is not necessary. The difficulty, however, is the absence of any clear definition of terms such as abandonment or extreme cruelty. Many courts have taken the position that a parent does not lose the right to withhold consent to an adoption unless the parent's conduct demonstrates *a clear intention to relinquish all parental duties.* Nonsupport in itself, for example, may not be enough if the parent has made some effort to see the child, at least occasionally.

☐ **EXHIBIT 19.5   Notice of Hearing on Issue of Revocation of Adoption**

STATE OF NEW YORK
_____ COURT
COUNTY OF _____
ADDRESS _____

In the Matter of the Adoption of
_____

Adoptive Child

NOTICE OF HEARING ON ISSUE OF REVOCATION
AND DISPOSITION AS TO CUSTODY, PRIVATE
PLACEMENT ADOPTION

PLEASE TAKE NOTICE that the _____ Court, _____ County, New York, on the _____ day of _____ , 19__ at _____ o'clock or as soon thereafter as counsel can be heard, will hear and determine whether the revocation of consent of the parent in the above entitled matter shall be permitted and, in any event, hear and determine what disposition should be made with respect to the custody of said child.

_____
Chief Clerk of the _____ Court

To: _____
Adoptive Parents

_____
Parents

_____ , Esq.
Attorney for Adoptive Parent(s)

_____ , Esq.
Attorney for Parent(s)

_____
Law Guardian

SOURCE: WEST'S MCKINNEY'S FORMS, NEW YORK § 22:24 (1986)

As demonstrated in the following checklist, many factors are relevant to the question of whether a parent had the *intention to abandon* or otherwise relinquish all rights in the child. A court will consider all of these factors in combination; no one factor is usually determinative.

▪▪▪ Interviewing and Investigation Checklist

Factors Relevant to Whether an Intent to Abandon the Child Existed

Legal Interviewing Questions

1. How old are you now?

2. With whom is your child living?

3. Is the person who is caring for the child your relative, a friend, a stranger?

4. How did the child get there?

5. How long has the child been there?

6. When is the last time you saw the child?

7. How often do you see your child per month?

8. How many times do you speak to your child on the phone per month?

9. How often do you write to your child?

10. Did you ever say to anyone that you did not want your child or that you wanted your child to find a home with someone else? If so, explain.

11. Did you ever say to anyone that you wanted your child to live with someone else temporarily until you got back on your feet again? If so, explain.

12. Have you ever placed your child in a public or private adoption agency? Have you ever discussed adoption with anyone? If so, explain.

13. Have you ever been charged with neglecting, abandoning, or failing to support your child? If so, explain.

—Continued

—Continued

14. Has your child ever been taken from you for any period of time? If so, explain.

15. Have you ever been found by a court to be mentally ill?

16. How much have you contributed to the support of your child while you were not living with the child?

17. Did you give the child any presents? If so, what were they and when did you give them?

18. While your child was not with you, did you ever speak to the child's teachers or doctors? If so, explain how often you did so.

19. Were you on public assistance while the child was not living with you? If so, what did you tell the public assistance workers about the child?

20. How well is the child being treated now?

21. Could anyone claim that the child lived under immoral or unhealthy circumstances while away from you and that you knew of these circumstances?

22. Has the child ever been charged with juvenile delinquency? Has the child ever been declared a person in need of supervision?

Possible Investigation Tasks

☐ Interview relatives, friends, and strangers who knew that the client visited the child.

☐ Interview anyone with whom the client may have discussed the reasons for leaving the child with someone else.

☐ Prepare an inventory of all the money and other property given by the client for the support of the child while the child was living with someone else.

☐ Collect receipts, e.g., canceled check stubs, for all funds given by the client for such support.

☐ Locate all relevant court records, if any, e.g., custody order in divorce proceeding, neglect or juvenile delinquency petitions and orders.

☐ Interview state agencies that have been involved with the child. Determine how responsive the client has been to the efforts of the agency to help the child and the client.

To take the drastic step of ordering an involuntary termination of parental rights, there must be clear and convincing evidence that the parent is unfit. It is not enough to show that the parent has psychological or financial problems, or that there are potential adoptive parents waiting in the wings who can provide the child with a superior home environment. There must be a specific demonstration of unfitness through abandonment, willful neglect, etc.

The parent can be represented by counsel at the termination proceeding. There is, however, no automatic right to state-appointed counsel if the parent cannot afford to pay one. A court must decide on a case-by-case basis whether an indigent parent needs free counsel because of the complexity of the case.

If parental rights are terminated and there are adoptive parents available, a separate adoption procedure will take place. Of course, the parent whose rights have been terminated is not asked to consent to the adoption.

ASSIGNMENT 19.12

a. When is the consent of a natural parent *not* necessary in your state for the adoption of his or her child?

b. Is there a proceeding to terminate the parental rights in your state that is separate from the adoption process? If so, explain.

c. When will parental rights be terminated in your state? What are the grounds? What standard of proof must be met? Clear and convincing evidence?

d. Who can initiate a petition to terminate parental rights in your state? (See General Instructions for the State-Code Assignment in chapter 1.)

e. Prepare a flowchart of all the procedural steps necessary to terminate parental rights in your state. (See General Instructions for the Flowchart Assignment in chapter 1.)

Mary is the mother of two children. She is convicted of murdering her husband, their father. What facts do you think need to be investigated in order to determine whether Mary's parental rights should be terminated? (See General Instructions for the Investigation-Strategy Assignment in chapter 1.)

PLACEMENT

Before ruling on a petition for adoption, the court, as indicated, will ask a public or private child welfare agency to investigate the case and make a recommendation to the court. The agency, in effect, assumes a role that is very similar to that of a social worker or a probation officer in many juvenile delinquency cases.

a. What is the role of child welfare agencies in your state after an adoption petition has been filed?

b. Once an agency files a report in your state containing the results of its investigation and its recommendation on the proposed adoption, who has access to the report? Can the prospective adoptive parents have access to it? Can they (through their attorney) question the person who wrote the report?

(See General Instructions for the State-Code Assignment in chapter 1. You may also need to check court opinions of your state. See General Instructions for the Court-Opinion Assignment in chapter 1.)

ASSIGNMENT 19.14

CAN CHILDREN DIVORCE THEIR PARENTS?

No. It is, of course, logically impossible to divorce someone to whom you are not married. The concept of parental divorce was created by the media in the Florida case of *Gregory K. v. Rachel K.* Gregory was an eleven-year-old, **unemancipated** child who asked a court to terminate the rights of his natural mother so that his foster parents could adopt him. Since he was the party who initiated the action, the media described him as a child who wanted to "divorce" his parents. The *trial* court allowed him to bring the action, terminated the parental rights of his mother, and granted the adoption.

The decision sparked considerable controversy. Some hailed it as the beginning of a major child's rights movement, comparing Gregory to the black woman who began the civil rights movement by refusing to sit in the back of the bus. "Gregory is the Rosa Parks of the youth rights movement," according to the chairperson of the National Child Rights Alliance. *Boy Wants "Divorce" from Parents,* American Bar Association Journal, 24 (July 1992). Others were deeply disturbed by the decision. They thought it would open a floodgate of litigation brought by disgruntled children against their parents. A presidential candidate lamented that "kids would be suing their parents for being told to do their homework or take out the trash." *Boy Wins "Divorce" from Mom,* American Bar Association Journal, 16 (December 1992).

On appeal, however, the Florida Court of Appeals ruled it was an error for the trial court to allow Gregory to initiate the termination action. A minor suffers the disability of **nonage** and hence does not have **standing** to ask a court to terminate the rights of his or her natural parents. Yet the court agreed that the parental rights of Gregory's mother should be terminated. When Gregory filed his petition, his foster parent simultaneously brought his own petition to terminate the rights of Gregory's natural mother on the ground that she had

Unemancipated
Legally dependent on one's parent or legal guardian.

Nonage Below the required minimum age to enter a desired relationship or perform a particular task.

Standing The right to bring a case and seek relief from a court.

abandoned him. Foster parents *do* have standing in Florida to bring such petitions, and in this case, the adult's termination petition had merit. Hence, although Gregory eventually got the result he wanted (termination of parental rights plus adoption), the court, in effect, shut the door to comparable actions initiated by children in the future. "Courts historically have recognized that unemancipated minors do not have the legal capacity to initiate legal proceedings in their own names." *Kingsley v. Kingsley,* 623 So. 2d 780, 783 (Fla. Dist. Ct. App. 1993).

CHALLENGES TO THE ADOPTION DECREE

Interlocutory Non final; interim.

In many states, an adoption decree does not become final immediately. An **interlocutory** (temporary) decree of adoption is first issued, which becomes final after a set period of time. During the interlocutory period, the child is placed with the adoptive parents. Since it would be very unhealthy for the child to be moved from place to place as legal battles continue to rage among any combination of adoptive parents, natural parents, and agencies, statutes place time limitations within which challenges to the adoption decree must be brought, e.g., two years.

ASSIGNMENT 19.15

a. Is there an interlocutory period in your state that must pass before the adoption can become final? If so, how long is it?

b. After the trial court in your state issues a final adoption decree, to what court can the decree be appealed?

c. If someone wants to challenge an adoption decree in your state, within what period of time must the challenge be brought? What happens if the challenge is not brought within this time?

(See General Instructions for the State-Code Assignment in chapter 1. You may also need to check the court rules of your state courts, and perhaps court opinions as well. See General Instructions for the Court-Opinion Assignment in chapter 1.)

d. Draft a flowchart of all the procedural steps involved in an adoption proceeding in your state. (See General Instructions for the Flowchart Assignment in chapter 1.)

"JOURNALISTIC TERRORISM"

We turn now to one of the most dramatic cases in the history of family law—the Illinois case of Baby Richard: *In re Petition of Doe.* Before the glare of cameras and national media, a four-year-old boy was taken from his adoptive parents and turned over to his natural father, Otakar Kirchner, whom the boy had never met. One newspaper account said the biological father "took physical custody of the sobbing child as he frantically reached for his adoptive mother in front of the house where the boy had lived since he was four days old."[1] The public's reaction was intense. Newspapers, newscasts, and talk shows gave the story extensive coverage. The case was called "nightmarish," "monstrous," "absolutely horrible," "state sanctioned child abuse." The governor of Illinois said that Baby Richard was being "brutally, tragically torn away from the only par-

---

1. *Unnecessary Cruelty,* The San Diego Union-Tribune, May 4, 1995, at B-12.

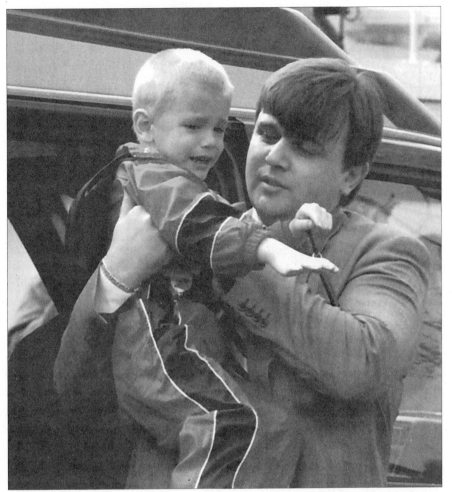

The day of reckoning. Baby Richard is carried away to a new home by his biological father, Otakar Kirchner, as the child cries and reaches for his adoptive mother.

ents he has ever known." The opinion in *In re Petition of Doe* was written by Justice Heiple. When it was published, he was denounced. One columnist, Bob Greene, was particularly critical. Justice Heiple took the highly unusual step of responding to this criticism in the supplemental opinion he wrote denying a rehearing of the case. He referred to the criticism as "journalistic terrorism." As we study *In re Petition of Doe*, you need to decide for yourself to what extent the case demonstrates a collapse of the legal system.

CASE

IN RE PETITION OF DOE & DOE TO ADOPT BABY BOY JANIKOVA

159 Ill. 2d 347, 638 N.E. 2d 181 (1994)
Supreme Court of Illinois
June 16, 1994.
Supplemental Opinion on Denial of Rehearing
July 12, 1994.

Background: *Baby Boy Janikova (known in the media as Baby Richard) lived for three years with John and Jane Doe,*
his adoptive parents. The Supreme Court of Illinois then ruled that he had been improperly adopted and ordered him returned. He was four years old by the time the order was finally carried out.

Daniella Janikova and Otakar Kirchner were not married when their son—also referred to as Baby Boy Janikova—was born. Otakar was out of the country at the time. Four days after the birth, Daniella consented to have the baby adopted by John and Jane Doe. Daniella did not tell Otakar about the adoption by the Does. In fact, she told him the baby was born dead. Fifty-seven days after the boy's birth, Otakar learned the truth. Within two weeks, he challenged the legality of the adoption on the ground that he did not consent to it. Lengthy litigation and media attention followed. The trial court found that Otakar was unfit because he did not show sufficient interest in the child during the first thirty days of the child's life, and therefore his consent to the adoption was not required. On appeal before the appellate court, Justice Rizzi affirmed, ruling that the adoption was in the best interest of the child. The case is now on appeal before the Supreme Court of Illinois. (During the litigation, Daniella married Otakar and, therefore, now joins him in seeking to revoke the adoption.)

Decision on Appeal: *Reversed. Justice Heiple of the Supreme Court held that the adoption was invalid because it violated the rights of the natural father. The use of the best-interest-of-the-child standard by Justice Rizzi in the appellate court "grossly misstated the law."*

Opinion of the Court:

Justice HEIPLE delivered the opinion of the court. . . .

Otakar and Daniella began living together in the fall of 1989, and Daniella became pregnant in June of 1990. For the first eight months of her pregnancy, Otakar provided for all of her expenses.

In late January 1991, Otakar went to his native Czechoslovakia to attend to his gravely ill grandmother for two weeks. During this time, Daniella received a phone call from Otakar's aunt saying that Otakar had resumed a former romantic relationship with another woman.

Because of this unsettling news, Daniella left their shared apartment, refused to talk with Otakar on his return, and gave birth to the child at a different hospital than where they had originally planned. She gave her consent to the adoption of the child by the Does, telling them and their attorney that she knew who the father was but would not furnish his name. Daniella and her uncle warded off Otakar's persistent inquiries about the child by telling him that the child had died shortly after birth.

Otakar found out that the child was alive and had been placed for adoption 57 days after the child was born. He then began the instant proceedings by filing an appearance contesting the Does' adoption of his son. . . . [T]he trial court ruled that Otakar was an unfit parent under section 1 of the Adoption Act (750 ILCS 50/1 (West 1992)) because he had not shown a reasonable degree of interest in the child within the first 30 days of his life. Therefore, the father's consent was unnecessary under section 8 of the Act (750 ILCS 50/8 (West 1992)).

The finding that the father had not shown a reasonable degree of interest in the child is not supported by the evidence. In fact, he made various attempts to locate the child, all of which were either frustrated or blocked by the actions of the mother. Further, the mother was aided by the attorney for the adoptive parents, who failed to make any effort to ascertain the name or address of the father despite the fact that the mother indicated she knew who he was. Under the circumstances, the father had no opportunity to discharge any familial duty.

In the opinion below, the appellate court, wholly missing the threshold issue in this case, dwelt on the best interests of the child. Since, however, the father's parental interest was improperly terminated, there was no occasion to reach the factor of the child's best interests. That point should never have been reached and need never have been discussed.

Unfortunately, over three years have elapsed since the birth of the baby who is the subject of these proceedings. To the extent that it is relevant to assign fault in this case, the fault here lies initially with the mother, who fraudulently tried to deprive the father of his rights, and secondly, with the adoptive parents and their attorney, who proceeded with the adoption when they knew that a real father was out there who had been denied knowledge of his baby's existence. When the father entered his appearance in the adoption proceedings 57 days after the baby's birth and demanded his rights as a father, the petitioners should have relinquished the baby at that time. It was their decision to prolong this litigation through a lengthy, and ultimately fruitless, appeal.

The adoption laws of Illinois are neither complex nor difficult of application. Those laws intentionally place the burden of proof on the adoptive parents in establishing both the relinquishment and/or unfitness of the natural parents and, coincidentally, the fitness and the right to adopt of the adoptive parents. In addition, Illinois law requires a good-faith effort to notify the natural parents of the adoption proceedings. These laws are designed to protect natural parents in their preemptive rights to their own children wholly apart from any consideration of the so-called best interests of the child. If it were otherwise, few parents would be secure in the custody of their own children. If best interests of the child were a sufficient qualification to determine child custody, anyone with superior income, intelligence, education, etc., might challenge and deprive the parents of their right to their own children. The law is otherwise and was not complied with in this case.

Accordingly, we reverse.

SUPPLEMENTAL OPINION UPON DENIAL OF REHEARING

Justice HEIPLE, writing in support of the denial of rehearing:

On Thursday, June 16, 1994, this court reversed a decision by a divided appellate court which had affirmed certain adoption proceedings in the circuit court of Cook County. Our reversal was the result of the failure of the courts below to correctly apply Illinois law in terminating the natural father's parental rights. This cause is now before the court on petitions for rehearing filed by the adoptive parents and the guardian ad litem for the child. The following is offered in support of today's order denying rehearing.

I have been a judge for over 23 years. In that time, I have seldom before worked on a case that involved the spread of so much misinformation, nor one which dealt with as straightforward an application of law to fact.

[A] . . . conspiracy was undertaken to deny the natural father any knowledge of his son's existence. It began when the biological mother, 8 1/2 months pregnant, was misinformed that the father, her fiance, had left her for another woman. She left their shared home and, at the encouragement of a social worker, agreed to give up her child. The social worker called her personal attorney, who contacted the adoptive mother (that attorney's friend and employee). At the behest of the adoptive parents and their attorney, the mother gave birth at a different hospital than she and the father had planned to avoid the father's intervention; the mother surrendered the baby to strangers four days after his birth; and then falsely told the father that the child had died. All of this occurred in the space of less than three weeks.

The father did not believe the mother, and he immediately began an intensive and persistent search and inquiry to learn the truth and locate the child. On the 57th day following the child's birth, the father learned of his son's existence and of the pending adoption. On that day, he hired a lawyer and contested the adoption of his son by strangers. One may reasonably ask, What more could he have done? What more should he have done? The answer is that he did all that he could and should do.

The . . . adoptive parents should have relinquished the baby at that time. That is to say, on the 57th day. Instead of that, however, they were able to procure an entirely erroneous ruling from a trial judge that allowed the adoption to go forward. The father's only remedy at that stage was a legal appeal which he took. He is not the cause of the delay in this case. It was the adoptive parents' decision to prolong this litigation through a long and ultimately fruitless appeal. Now, the view has been expressed that the passage of time warrants their retention of the child; that it would not be fair to the child to return him to his natural parents, now married to each other, after the adoptive parents have delayed justice past the child's third birthday.

For a fuller and more detailed account of the father's efforts and the underlying facts, one may refer to the dissenting opinion authored by Justice Tully in the appellate court decision rendered below. (254 Ill. App. 3d 405, 418, 627 N.E.2d 648 (Tully, P. J., dissenting).) As noted by Justice Tully, Justice Rizzi, writing the majority opinion for himself and Justice Cerda, "patently distorted and slanted the facts on a number of important points." I would further add that Justice Rizzi grossly misstated the law.

If, as stated by Justice Rizzi, the best interests of the child is to be the determining factor in child custody cases (254 Ill. App. 3d at 412), persons seeking babies to adopt might profitably frequent grocery stores and snatch babies from carts when the parent is looking the other way. Then, if custody proceedings can be delayed long enough, they can assert that they have a nicer home, a superior education, a better job or whatever, and that the best interests of the child are with the baby snatchers. Children of parents living in public housing or other conditions deemed less than affluent and children with single parents might be considered particularly fair game. The law, thankfully, is otherwise.

In 1972, the United States Supreme Court, in the case of *Stanley v. Illinois* (1972), 405 U.S. 645, 92 S. Ct. 1208, 31 L. Ed. 2d 551 ruled that unmarried fathers cannot be treated differently than unmarried mothers or married parents when determining their rights to the custody of their children. The courts of Illinois are bound by that decision. Subsequently, in 1990, a unanimous Illinois Supreme Court pointed out that when ruling on parental unfitness, a court is not to consider the child's best interests, since the child's welfare is not relevant in judging the fitness of the natural parent; that only after the parent is found by clear and convincing evidence to be unfit does the court proceed to consider the child's best interest and whether that interest would be served if the child were adopted by the petitioners. *In re Adoption of Syck* (1990), 138 Ill. 2d 255, 276–78, 562 N.E.2d 174.

Under Illinois law, a parent may be divested of his parental rights either voluntarily (e.g., consenting to an adoption (see Ill. Rev. Stat. 1991, ch. 40, par. 1513)) or involuntarily (e.g., finding of abuse, abandonment, neglect or lack of sufficient interest (see Ill. Rev. Stat. 1991, ch. 40, par. 1510)). . . . [T]he adoption laws of Illinois are neither complex nor difficult of application. These laws intentionally place the burden of proof on the adoptive parents. In addition, Illinois law requires a good-faith effort to notify the natural father of the adoption proceedings. (Ill. Rev. Stat. 1991, ch. 40, par. 1509.) We call this due process of law. In the case at hand, both the adoptive parents and their attorney knew that a real father existed whose name was known to the mother but who refused to disclose it. Under these circumstances, the adoptive parents proceeded at their peril.

The best interest of the child standard is not to be denigrated. It is real. However, it is not triggered until it has been validly determined that the child is available for adoption. And, a child is not available for adoption until the rights of his natural parents have been properly terminated. Any judge, lawyer, or guardian ad litem who has even the most cursory familiarity with adoption laws knows that. Justice Rizzi, if he is to be taken at face value, does not know that.

Columnist Bob Greene apparently does not care. Rather, columnist Greene has used this unfortunate controversy to stimulate readership and generate a series of syndicated newspaper columns in the Chicago Tribune and other papers that are both false and misleading. In so doing, he has wrongfully cried "fire" in a crowded theatre, and has needlessly alarmed other adoptive parents into ill-founded concerns that their own adoption proceedings may be in jeopardy. In support of his position, Greene has stirred up contempt against the Supreme Court as an institution, concluding one of his columns by referring to all of the Justices with the curse, "Damn them all." Chicago Tribune, June 19, 1994, page 1.

Greene's implicit objective is to secure justice for a child. With that ethical and moral imperative, of course, no one could disagree. Greene, however, elevates himself above the facts, above the law, and above the Supreme Court of Illinois. He arrogates to himself the right to decide the case.

In support of his objective, Greene brings to bear the tools of the demagogue, namely, incomplete information, falsity, half-truths, character assassination and spurious argumentation. He has conducted a steady assault on my abilities as a judge, headlining one of his columns "The Sloppiness of Justice Heiple." Another was entitled "Supreme Injustice for a Little Boy." He has shown my picture in his columns with bylines reading, respectively, "Justice Heiple: Ruling takes boy from home," and "James D. Heiple: No justice for a child."

Make no mistake about it. These are acts of journalistic terrorism. These columns are designed to discredit me as a judge and the Supreme Court as a dispenser of justice by stirring up disrespect and hatred among the general population.

Lest we forget the place from which he comes, let us remind ourselves that Greene is a journalist with a product to sell. He writes columns for a living. His income is dependent on writing and selling his columns to newspapers. He cannot secure either sales or earnings by writing on subjects that lack impact or drama. So, he must seek out subjects that are capable of generating wide public interest. An adoption case involving two sets of parents contesting for the custody of a three-year-old boy is a ready-made subject for this type of journalist. So far, so good.

The trouble with Greene's treatment of the subject, however, is that his columns have been biased, false and misleading. They have also been destructive to the cause of justice both in this case and in the wider perspective. Part of Greene's fury may be attributable to the fact that he staked out his views on this case in a published column that appeared on August 22, 1993. (Chicago Tribune, August 22, 1993, page 1.) Subsequently, on June 16, 1994, the Supreme Court had the audacity to base its decision on the law rather than on his newspaper column. So much for his self-possessed moralizing.

That Greene has succeeded to a limited degree cannot be denied. I have, indeed, received several pieces of hate mail with such epithets as idiot, jerk, etc. The Governor, in a crass political move, announced his attempt to intervene in the case. And the General Assembly, without meaningful debate of consideration, rushed into law a constitutionally infirm statute with the goal of changing the Supreme Court's decision.

Both the Governor and the members of the General Assembly who supported this bill might be well advised to return to the classroom and take up Civics 101. The Governor, for his part, has no understanding of this case and no interest either public or private in its outcome. The legislature is not given the authority to decide private disputes between litigants. Neither does it sit as a super court to review unpopular decisions of the Supreme Court. We have three branches of government in this land. They are designated as the legislative, the executive and the judicial. Legislative adjudication of private disputes went by the wayside generations ago. Moreover, this case cannot be decided by public clamor generated by an irresponsible journalist. Neither can it be decided by its popularity or lack thereof. This case can only be decided by a court of law. That is a judicial function pure and simple. For the Supreme Court to surrender to this assault would be to surrender its independence, its integrity and its reason for being. In so doing, neither justice to the litigants nor the public interest would be served. Under the circumstances, this case looms even larger than the child or the two sets of contesting parents.

Many law suits are painful matters. This case is no exception. Capital cases, for instance, demand the forfeiture of the life of the defendant. Damage suits take money away from some people and give it to others. No one ever claimed that both sides walk away from a law suit with smiles on their faces. No member of this court ever entertained any thought that the decision it rendered in this case would be easy to accept by the losing litigants. Such an event would be incredible.

As for the child, age three, it is to be expected that there would be an initial shock, even a longing for a time in the absence of the persons whom he had viewed as parents. This trauma will be overcome, however, as it is every day across this land by children who suddenly find their parents separated by divorce or lost to them through death. It will not be an insurmountable trauma for a three-year-old child to be returned, at last, to his natural parents who want to raise him as their own. It will work itself out in the fullness of time. As for the adoptive parents, they will have to live with their pain and the knowledge that they wrongfully deprived a father of his child past the child's third birthday. They and their lawyer brought it on themselves.

This much is clear. Adoptive parents who comply with the law may feel secure in their adoptions. Natural parents may feel secure in their right to raise their own children. If there is a tragedy in this case, as has been suggested, then that tragedy is the wrongful breakup of a natural family and the keeping of a child by strangers without right. We must remember that the purpose of an adoption is to provide a home for a child, not a child for a home.

ASSIGNMENT 19.16

a. Someone obviously made a major blunder in this case. From infancy, Baby Richard lived with one set of adults. Years later, he is forced to live with other adults. Who does Justice Heiple say is to blame? Why? Which of the following cast of characters do *you* think is to blame and why: the natural mother, her attorney, the relatives of the natural mother, her social worker, the natural father, his attorney, the adoptive parents, their attorney, Baby Richard's guardian at litem, the trial court (that granted the adoption), the appellate court (that said it was in the best interest of the child that he go with the Does), the Supreme Court of Illinois (that gave the child to his natural father)?

b. What do you think of the quality of the legal representation given to the Does by their attorney?

c. In chapter 11 we learned that custody decisions are based on the best interest of the child. Did this case say that the best interest of the child is irrelevant?

d. What do you think could have been done to avoid this tragedy?

e. Is it relevant that Daniella married Otakar and therefore agreed with him that the adoption should be set aside?

f. Do you think it was wise for Justice Heiple to attack Bob Greene as a journalistic terrorist?

g. Justice Heiple said, "It will not be an insurmountable trauma for a three-year-old child to be returned, at last, to his natural parents who want to raise him as their own." Do you agree? If Justice Heiple thought the trauma *would be* insurmountable, would he have ruled differently? Recall that he said the best interest of the child was irrelevant in this case.

h. Rich and Paula Davis are the natural parents of John. Following a divorce, Rich is granted custody of John. Rich illegally takes John to another state, where his girlfriend adopts him. During the adoption proceeding, Rich falsely tells the court that John's mother, Paula, is dead. Paula therefore never receives notice of the adoption proceeding. Years later, after the passing of the statute of limitations, Paula learns about the adoption for the first time. Can she still challenge the adoption? How would this case be decided in Illinois in view of *In re Petition of Doe?*

BABY JESSICA

The Baby Jessica case is another highly publicized example of a biological father successfully challenging an adoption on the basis of the biological mother's lies. Cara Clausen gave birth to Baby Jessica in Iowa. Within days of the birth, she put her up for adoption to Jan and Roberta DeBoer, who took her to Michigan. In the adoption proceedings, Cara lied about who the biological father was. Three weeks later, she had a change of heart and told the biological father, Dan Schmidt, what had happened. He then sought to get Baby Jessica back from the adoptive parents. He argued that he never consented to the adoption and was never found to be unfit. After two and a half years of litigation, the Iowa and Michigan courts nullified the adoption and ordered Baby Jessica returned. See *In re Baby Girl Clausen*, 502 N.W.2d 649 (Mich. 1993); and *In the Interest of B.G.C.*, 496 N.W.2d 239 (Iowa 1992). The federal courts refused to change this result. In *DeBoer v. DeBoer*, 114 S. Ct. 1, 2 (1993), the United States Supreme Court said, "Neither Iowa law, Michigan law, nor federal law au

thorizes unrelated persons to retain custody of a child whose natural parents have not been found to be unfit simply because they may be better able to provide for her future and her education. '[C]ourts are not free to take children from parents simply by deciding another home appears more advantageous.' "

▰▰▰▰ CONSEQUENCES OF ADOPTION

Once the adoption becomes final, the adopted child and the adoptive parents have almost all the rights and obligations toward each other that natural parents and children have toward each other. The major exception involves the death of a relative of the adoptive parent.

EXAMPLE Kevin is the adopted child of Paul. Paul's brother, Bill, dies intestate (i.e., without leaving a valid will). Can Kevin inherit from Bill?

In some states, the answer would be no: an adopted child cannot take an intestate share of a relative of its adoptive parents. Other states do not impose this limitation.

In most other respects, an adopted child is treated the same as a natural child:

☐ Adopted children can take the name of their adoptive parents.

☐ The birth certificate can be changed to reflect the new parents.

☐ Adopted children can inherit from their adoptive parents (and in a few states can continue to inherit from their natural parents).

☐ Adoptive parents have a right to the services and earnings of the adopted children.

☐ Adoptive parents must support adopted children.

☐ Adopted children are entitled to worker's compensation benefits due to an on-the-job injury of their adoptive parent.

☐ If an adoptive parent dies with a will leaving property to "my heirs" or to "my children" or to "my issue," without mentioning any individuals by name, most (but not all) courts are inclined to conclude that the intention of the deceased adoptive parent was to include adopted children as well as natural children within the designation of "heirs," "children," or "issue."

ASSIGNMENT 19.17

a. What rights and obligations are assumed by adoptive parents and children in your state?

b. In the example immediately above involving Kevin, Paul, and Bill, could Kevin inherit from Bill in your state?

c. Suppose that Kevin's natural parent (Paul) dies intestate. Can Kevin inherit from his natural parent in your state?

d. Helen is the natural child of George and Sally; Bob is their adopted child. Can Helen and Bob marry in your state?

(Check statutes and cases on the above questions. See General Instructions for the State-Code Assignment and General Instructions for the Court-Opinion Assignment in chapter 1.)

CONFIDENTIALITY

In recent years there has been great controversy over whether adopted children have a right to discover the identity of their natural parents. The traditional answer has been no. Once the adoption becomes final, the record is sealed. The data within it are confidential. Some states, however, have created limited exceptions to this rule. If *good cause* can be shown, access to part of the adoption records may be allowed. For example, an adopted child may need medical information on its natural parents to help treat diseases that might be hereditary. Similarly, the adopted child may need some information about the identity of its natural parents to avoid unknowingly marrying a natural brother or sister. Access to any information in the records is the exception, however. The need must be great. Many courts have held that it is not enough for the adopted child to prove that he or she is experiencing emotional distress due to not knowing the identity of his or her natural parents.

Some independent or private adoptions give the participants the option of maintaining limited contact between the natural parent and the child after the adoption. These are called **open adoptions,** involving face-to-face meetings or an exchange of identifying information. Some believe that such adoptions should be discouraged. Young women "are finding it harder to get on with their lives. . . ." "They start living for the photos that the adoptive parents send them every month." Adoptive parents sometimes "find themselves not only raising a new baby but providing counseling for the birth mother who often finds it difficult to break her bond with the child." The Council of State Governments, *Adoption,* State Government News 31 (September 1989). Not many adoptive parents, therefore, pursue open adoptions. A few states have established a register in which adopted children and natural parents can indicate a willingness to communicate with each other. If both do not register, however, the traditional rule of anonymity prevails. Exhibit 19.6 provides a state-by-state overview of adoption rules including confidentiality.

Open Adoption An adoption in which the natural parent maintains certain kinds of contact with his or her child after the adoption.

Under what circumstances, if any, can an adopted child gain access to adoption records? (See General Instructions for the State-Code Assignment in chapter 1. You may also have to check court opinions. See General Instructions for the Court-Opinion Assignment in chapter 1.)

ASSIGNMENT 19.18

EQUITABLE ADOPTION

Assume that John Smith enters a contract with Mary Jones to adopt Mary's child, Bill, but fails to perform the contract. Such contracts are occasionally in writing but more often are simply oral understandings between parties who know each other very well. Assume further that John takes custody of Bill, treats him as a member of his family, but never goes through formal adoption procedures as he had promised. John then dies intestate, i.e., without leaving a valid will. Technically, Bill cannot inherit from John because the adoption never took place. This argument will be used by John's natural children to prevent an unadopted child—Bill—from sharing in the estate.

☐ **EXHIBIT 19.6   Adoption in America**

	IS INDEPENDENT ADOPTION LEGAL?	CAN A PROFIT-MAKING OR-GANIZATION BE LICENSED TO PROVIDE CHILDREN?	WHAT IS THE LENGTH OF TIME BETWEEN FILING FOR AND FINALIZING AN ADOPTION?	HOW SOON AFTER BIRTH CAN A MOTHER CONSENT TO ADOPTION?	HOW LONG IS SHE GIVEN TO REVOKE HER CONSENT?*
Alabama	Yes‡	Yes	6 months	Anytime	Not specified
Alaska	Yes	Yes	Varies	Anytime	10 days
Arizona	Yes	Yes	6 months	72 hours	No time
Arkansas	Yes	Yes	6 months	24 hours	10 days
California	Yes‡	No	Usually 6–12 months	After hospital discharge‡	Until adoption is filed‡
Colorado	Yes‡	Yes	6 months	Anytime in court	Several days
Connecticut	No	No	1 year after placement	48 hours	20–30 days
Delaware	No	Yes	2–30 days	Anytime once drug-free	Until parental rights ended
D.C.	Yes	Yes	6–12 months	72 hours	10 days
Florida	Yes	No	At least 30 days	Anytime	Not specified
Georgia	Yes‡	No	At least 60 days	Anytime	10 days
Hawaii	Yes	No	Varies (131-day average)	3 days	Until placement
Idaho	Yes	Yes	30 days	Anytime	30 days
Illinois	Yes	Yes	6 months	72 hours	No time
Indiana	Yes	Yes	Varies	State policy: 48 hours	Until adoption is final
Iowa	Yes	Yes	6 months from placement	72 hours	Until parental rights ended
Kansas	Yes	Yes	At least 30 days	Anytime	Until adoption is final‡
Kentucky	Yes‡	Yes	Usually within 180 days	5 days, in court	No time
Louisiana	Yes	Yes	6–12 months	5 days	30 days
Maine	Yes	Yes	Varies, a week to several months	Anytime in probate court	Varies
Maryland	Yes	Yes	2–6 months	15 days	90 days
Massachusetts	No	No	Varies	4 days	No time
Michigan	No	Yes	1 year	Anytime	Until placement‡
Minnesota	No‡	No	At least 3 months	Anytime	10 working days
Mississippi	Yes	Yes	0–6 months	72 hours	No time
Missouri	Yes	Yes	9 months	48 hours	Until adoption hearing
Montana	Yes‡	No	No time set	Anytime	Until adoption is final
Nebraska	Yes‡	Yes	6 months	Varies	No time
Nevada	Yes	No	6 months	72 hours	No time
New Hampshire	Yes	No	At least 6 months	72 hours	Until adoption is final
New Jersey	Yes	No	At least 6 months	72 hours	Not specified
New Mexico	Yes	Yes	90–180 days from placement	72 hours	No time

Continued

□ **EXHIBIT 19.6   Adoption in America—*Continued***

	IS INDEPENDENT ADOPTION LEGAL?	CAN A PROFIT-MAKING OR-GANIZATION BE LICENSED TO PROVIDE CHILDREN?	WHAT IS THE LENGTH OF TIME BETWEEN FILING FOR AND FINALIZING AN ADOPTION?	HOW SOON AFTER BIRTH CAN A MOTHER CONSENT TO ADOPTION?	HOW LONG IS SHE GIVEN TO REVOKE HER CONSENT?*
New York	Yes	No	6 months	Anytime	0–45 days
North Carolina	Yes‡	Yes	1 year	Anytime	1–3 months
North Dakota	No	Yes	At least 6 months	72 hours	10 days
Ohio	Yes	Yes	6 months	72 hours	Until adoption is final
Oklahoma	Yes	No	6 months	Anytime	30 days
Oregon	Yes	Yes	About 90 days	Anytime	Until placement
Pennsylvania	Yes	Yes	No set time	72 hours	Until adoption is final
Rhode Island	Yes	No	At least 6 months	15 days	1 year
South Carolina	Yes	Yes	90–365 days	Anytime	No time
South Dakota	Yes	Yes	6 months, 10 days	5 days	30-day appeal period
Tennessee	Yes	No	6 months	Anytime	15 days
Texas	Yes	Yes‡	6 months	Anytime	0–60 days
Utah	Yes	Yes	At least 6 months	Anytime once drug-free	Until adoption is final
Vermont	Yes	No	6 months from placement	Anytime	10 days
Virginia	Yes‡	Yes	0–12 months	Anytime; effective in 10 days	Before placement or in court
Washington	Yes	Yes	No set time	Before birth‡	Until adoption is final‡
West Virginia	Yes	Yes	At least 6 months	72 hours	No time
Wisconsin	Yes‡	Yes	At least 6 months	Anytime in court	No time
Wyoming	Yes	Yes	6 months	Anytime	No time‡

	WHAT EXPENSES ARE PROSPECTIVE PARENTS ALLOWED TO PAY?**	WHAT ARE THE LEGAL PENALTIES FOR BABY SELLING AND FOR BABY BUYING?	ARE SEALED RECORDS AVAILABLE TO ADULT ADOPTEES?
Alabama	Not defined by law	Maximum 3 months in jail and/or $100 fine	Yes†
Alaska	Not defined by law; must report all payments to court	No defined penalties; judge decides	Yes
Arizona	Birthmother's medical, legal, and counseling costs; must report to court	6 months to 1.9 years in prison and/or $1,000 to $150,000 fine	No
Arkansas	Birthmother's medical, living, and other costs; must report to court	Felony: 3–10 years in prison	No†
California	Not defined by law; all payments must be reported to court	Misdemeanor: local D.A. decides penalty	No
Colorado	Reasonable expenses approved by court	Felony: 4–16 years in prison and/or up to $750,000 fine	No†

Continued

☐ **EXHIBIT 19.6 Adoption in America—*Continued***

	WHAT EXPENSES ARE PROSPECTIVE PARENTS ALLOWED TO PAY?**	WHAT ARE THE LEGAL PENALTIES FOR BABY SELLING AND FOR BABY BUYING?	ARE SEALED RECORDS AVAILABLE TO ADULT ADOPTEES?
Connecticut	Agency fees, birthmother's medical, living, counseling costs; must report to court	Felony: 1–5 years in prison and/or $5,000 fine	No†
Delaware	Agency fees, birthmother's legal costs; must report to court	No defined penalties; judge decides	No
D.C.	Not defined by law	90 days in jail and/or $300 fine	No
Florida	Not defined by law; must report all payments to court	Felony: maximum 5 years in prison	No
Georgia	Birthmother's medical costs; must report to court	Felony: maximum 10 years in prison and/or $1,000 fine	No
Hawaii	Not defined by law	No defined penalties; judge decides	No
Idaho	Not defined by law	Felony: maximum 14 years in prison and/or $5,000 fine	No†
Illinois	Birthmother's medical and legal costs; must report to court	Felony: 1–3 years in prison and/or $10,000 fine	No†
Indiana	Birthmother's medical, legal, and other court-approved costs	Felony: maximum 2 years in prison and/or $10,000 fine	No†
Iowa	Birthmother's medical and other costs; must report to court	30 days in jail and/or $100 fine	No
Kansas	Not defined by law; must report all payments to court	No defined penalties; judge decides	Yes
Kentucky	Not defined by law; must report all payments to court	6 months in prison and/or $500 to $2,000 fine	No†
Louisiana	Birthmother's medical, legal, and living costs‡; must report to court	Felony: maximum 5 years in prison and/or $5,000 fine	No†
Maine	Not defined by law	No defined penalties; judge decides	No†
Maryland	Birthmother's medical and legal costs	Maximum 3 months in jail and/or $100 fine	No†
Massachusetts	In identified adoption, all of birthparents' adoption-related costs	2½–5 years in jail and/or $5,000 to $30,000 fine	No
Michigan	Agency fees and other court-approved costs	Maximum 90 days in jail and/or $100 fine	No
Minnesota	Agency fees	Maximum 90 days in jail and/or $700 fine	No†
Mississippi	Birthmother's medical and legal costs	Maximum 5 years in prison and/or $5,000 fine	No
Missouri	Not defined by law	Felony: maximum 7 years in prison and/or $5,000 fine	No†
Montana	Not defined by law; must report all payments to court	Maximum fine: $1,000	No
Nebraska	Not defined by law	Maximum 3 months in jail and/or $500 fine	No†
Nevada	Birthmother's medical and necessary living costs; must report to court	1–6 years in prison and/or a maximum $5,000 fine	No†
New Hampshire	Not defined by law	No defined penalties; judge decides	No
New Jersey	Birthmother's medical and reasonable living costs; must report to court	3–5 years in prison and/or $7,500 fine	No†

Continued

☐ **EXHIBIT 19.6   Adoption in America—*Continued***

	WHAT EXPENSES ARE PROSPECTIVE PARENTS ALLOWED TO PAY?**	WHAT ARE THE LEGAL PENALTIES FOR BABY SELLING AND FOR BABY BUYING?	ARE SEALED RECORDS AVAILABLE TO ADULT ADOPTEES?
New Mexico	Not defined by law; must report all payments to court	Maximum fine: $500	No
New York	Birthmother's medical, legal, and other necessary costs	No defined penalties; judge decides	No†
North Carolina	Agency fees	Misdemeanor: court decides penalty	No
North Dakota	Not defined by law; must report all payments to court	Felony: maximum 5 years in prison and/or $5,000 fine	No†
Ohio	Birthmother's medical, legal, and other costs; must report to court	Maximum 6 months in jail and/or $500 to $1,000 fine	No
Oklahoma	Birthmother's medical, legal, and counseling costs; must be approved by court	Minimum 1 year in jail	No
Oregon	Not defined by law; must report all payments to court	No defined penalties; judge decides	No†
Pennsylvania	Birthmother's medical costs; must report to court	Maximum 5 years in prison and/or $10,000 fine	No†
Rhode Island	Not defined by law	No defined penalties; judge decides	Yes‡
South Carolina	Not defined by law; must report all payments to court	Felony: maximum 10 years in prison and/or $10,000 fine	No†
South Dakota	Not defined by law; must report all payments to court	Felony: maximum 2 years in prison and/or $2,000 fine	No†
Tennessee	Birthmother's medical and legal costs; must report to court	Felony: 1–10 years in prison	No†
Texas	Birthmother's medical and legal costs	Felony: 2–10 years in prison and/or $5,000 fine	No†
Utah	Birthmother's medical, legal, and other adoption-related costs	Must forfeit payment and pay $10,000 maximum fine	No†
Vermont	Law specifies only those "directly related to mother's support"; must report to court	No defined penalties; judge decides	No
Virginia	Not defined by law	No defined penalties; judge decides	No
Washington	Birthmother's medical and legal costs	Felony: maximum 5 years in prison and/or $10,000 fine	No
West Virginia	Birthmother's medical and legal costs; must report to court	No defined penalties; judge decides	No
Wisconsin	Birthmother's medical, legal, and counseling costs; must report to court	Felony: maximum 2 years in prison and/or $10,000 fine	No†
Wyoming	Not defined by law	No defined penalties; judge decides	No

SOURCE: © 1989 by the National Committee for Adoption, Inc. From *Adoption Factbook,* available from the Committee at P.O. Box 33366, Wash., D.C. 20033. Note: Adoptions of American Indians are governed by the federal Indian Child Welfare Act, which prevents a mother from signing consent papers until 10 days after birth and allows her to revoke her consent until an adoption is final.

*Assuming no fraud, duress, or coercion is proved. **Living expenses usually include medical, housing, food, travel, and clothing costs. †Information may be obtained through a voluntary state registry or adoption agency. ‡With restrictions or exceptions.

Many feel that it would be unfair to deny the child inheritance benefits simply because the deceased failed to abide by the agreement to adopt. To avoid the unfairness, some courts conclude that such a child was adopted under the doctrine of **equitable adoption** and hence is entitled to the inheritance rights of adopted children. The doctrine is also referred to as *adoption by estoppel;* challengers will be estopped (i.e., prevented) from denying that such a child has been adopted.

Some courts will reach the same result *even if there was no initial agreement to adopt.* If clear evidence exists that the deceased treated the child as his or her own in every way, a court might rule that a contract to adopt was *implied.* When the deceased dies intestate, equitable adoption status will be accorded the child so that he or she will have full inheritance rights from the deceased.

Equitable Adoption
For purposes of inheritance, a child will be considered the adopted child of a person who made a contract to adopt the child but failed to go through the formal adoption procedures.

ASSIGNMENT 19.19

To what extent, if at all, does your state recognize equitable adoption or adoption by estoppel? (See General Instructions for the Court-Opinion Assignment in chapter 1.)

ASSIGNMENT 19.20

Contact a paralegal, an attorney, or a legal secretary in your state who has worked on adoption cases in the past. Obtain answers to the following questions. (See General Instructions for the Systems Assignment in chapter 1.)

1. How many adoption cases have you worked on?

2. How many of them have been uncontested?

3. Approximately how long does it take to process an uncomplicated, uncontested adoption?

4. Is there a difference between working on an adoption case and working on another kind of case in the law office? If so, what is the difference?

5. What are the major steps for processing an adoption in this state? What documents must be filed? What court appearances must be made? Etc.

6. What formbook or other treatise do you use, if any, that is helpful?

7. Does your office have its own internal manual that covers any aspect of adoption practice?

8. In an adoption case, what is the division of labor among the attorney, the paralegal, and the legal secretary?

■ WRONGFUL ADOPTION

Wrongful Adoption A tort action seeking damages for wrongfully stating or failing to disclose to prospective adoptive parents available facts on the health or other condition of the adoptee that would be relevant to the decision on whether to adopt.

Suppose that an adoption agency misrepresents the mental or physical health of a child or the medical history of the child's birth family. For example, an agency fails to tell prospective adoptive parents that a child had been sexually abused or falsely tells them that the child does not have a genetic disorder. The adoption goes forward. The adoptive parents then discover that the child has severe medical problems. Can they sue the agency for damages covering the increased cost of child rearing? The period for challenging the adoption itself may have passed. Furthermore, the adoptive parents may have bonded with the child and hence do not want to "send him back" even if it were possible to annul or abrogate the adoption. In such cases, some states have allowed the adoptive parents to sue, particularly when they made clear to the agency that they did not want to adopt a problem child. Their argument is that they would not have adopted the child if they had been presented with all the facts. They cannot expect a guarantee that the child will be perfect. But they are entitled to available information that might indicate a significant likelihood of future medical problems. The failure to provide such information may constitute the tort of **wrongful adoption.**

■ SUMMARY

There are three main kinds of adoptions. First is an agency adoption, where a child is placed for adoption by a private or public agency. Second is an independent/private adoption, where a natural parent places a child for adoption with the adoptive parents, often through an intermediary such as an attorney and after an investigation by an adoption agency. In such an arrangement, any payment to the natural mother beyond covering her expenses constitutes illegal baby buying. Third is a black market adoption, where illegal payments are made to the natural mother beyond her expenses.

A court will allow an adoption if it is in the best interest of the child. In making this determination, a number of factors are considered: the petitioner's age, marital status, health, race, religion, economic status, home environment, and lifestyle. If the child is old enough, his or her preference will usually be considered.

An adoption must follow strict procedures. The court must have subject matter jurisdiction. Proper venue must be selected. The petition must contain the required information. The natural parents must be notified of the proceeding and must consent to the adoption unless their parental rights have been terminated because of conduct that clearly demonstrates an intention to relinquish parental duties.

(A child does not have standing to petition a court to terminate the parental rights of his or her parent.) Under certain circumstances, a parent will be given the right to revoke an earlier consent to the adoption. An agency investigates the prospective adoptive parents and reports back to the court. An interlocutory decree of adoption is then made by the court, which becomes final within a designated period of time.

Once the adoption becomes final, the adopted child is treated the same as a natural child with respect to inheritance rights, support rights, etc. In a traditional adoption, the records are sealed, and matters such as the identity of the natural parents are kept confidential except in relatively rare circumstances. In an open adoption, there may be varying degrees of contact between a natural parent and the child after the adoption becomes final.

An equitable adoption occurs when a person dies before fulfilling a contract to adopt a child, and when unfairness can be avoided only by treating the child as having been adopted for purposes of inheritance. The failure of an adoption agency to give available information about the health of the prospective adoptee might constitute the tort of wrongful adoption.

■ KEY CHAPTER TERMINOLOGY

Custody
Guardianship
Ward
Termination of Parental Rights
Adoption
Paternity
Foster Care
Stepparent

Agency Adoption
Independent Adoption
Black Market Adoption
Second-Parent Adoption
Subject-Matter Jurisdiction
Choice of Venue
Petition
Unfit

Unemancipated
Nonage
Standing
Interlocutory
Open Adoption
Equitable Adoption
Wrongful Adoption

20

SURROGACY AND THE NEW SCIENCE OF MOTHERHOOD

"Abram's wife Sarai had not borne him any children. But she had an Egyptian slave girl named Hagar, and so she said to Abram, 'The Lord has kept me from having children. Why don't you sleep with my slave girl? Perhaps she can have a child for me.' "
Genesis 16:1–2 (TEV)

"The reproductive capabilities available to assist infertile couples today are astonishing. Pioneering doctors can now remove eggs from a woman, fertilize them in a laboratory, and reinsert them into that same woman or into another woman; regulate the woman's hormone balance to enhance implantation; monitor the gestation of embryo and fetus, and perform surgery on the fetus in some cases. We now have the ability to separate a child's genetic, gestational, and legal parents so that it is possible to have five different individuals contributing to the birth of a single child: egg donor, sperm donor, womb donor or gestator, and the social parents who will raise the child."
Billig, *High Tech Earth Mothering*, 9 DISTRICT LAWYER, 57 (July/August 1985).

"Just as men have the right to sell their sperm and become surrogate fathers, so women should have the right to sell their reproductive services and become . . . surrogate mothers."
Gale, *The Right to Pregnancy by Contract*, NEW YORK TIMES BOOK REV. 12 (December 17, 1989).

One of the most dramatic family law issues to emerge in the last twenty years has been surrogate motherhood. An unpregnant woman enters a contract to become pregnant, to give birth to a child, and then to relinquish all parental rights upon birth through adoption. Due to spectacular scientific advances, a variety of methods of becoming pregnant are available (see Exhibit 20.1). Unfortunately, traditional legal principles do not always fit results made available by the innovations of medicine and biology.

When something goes wrong in a surrogacy contract, e.g., the surrogate mother changes her mind about giving up the child, someone inevitably sues.

□ **EXHIBIT 20.1   New Ways to Make Babies**

**Artificial Insemination
and Embryo Transfer**

1. Father is infertile. Mother is inseminated by
   donor and carries child.

2. Mother is infertile but able to carry child. Donor
   of ovum is inseminated by father; then embryo
   is transferred and mother carries child.

3. Mother is infertile and unable to carry child.
   Donor of ovum is inseminated by father and
   carries child.

4. Both parents are infertile, but mother is able to
   carry child. Donor of ovum is inseminated by
   sperm donor, then embryo is transferred and
   mother carries child.

Legend

Sperm from father	
Ovum from mother	
Baby born of mother	
Sperm from donor	
Ovum from donor	
Baby born of donor (Surrogate)	

In Vitro Fertilization

1. Mother is fertile but unable to conceive. Ovum
   from mother and sperm from father are
   combined in laboratory. Embryo is placed in
   mother's uterus.

2. Mother is infertile but able to carry child. Ovum
   from donor is combined with sperm from father.

3. Father is infertile and mother is fertile but unable
   to conceive. Ovum from mother is combined
   with sperm from donor.

4. Both parents are infertile, but mother is able to
   carry child. Ovum and sperm from donors are
   combined in laboratory.

5. Mother is infertile and unable to carry child.
   Ovum of donor is combined with sperm from
   father. Embryo is transferred to donor.

6. Both parents are fertile, but mother is unable to
   carry child. Ovum from mother and sperm from
   father are combined. Embryo is transferred to
   donor.

7. Father is infertile; mother is fertile but unable to
   carry child.

SOURCE: Strong & DeVault, The Marriage and Family Experience, 234 (4th Ed. 1989).

The courts then enter the picture. But what law does a court apply to such a
contract? The first instinct of the court is to look to the legislature to determine
whether any statutes apply. Until recently, no such statutes existed. Hence the
court is forced to write common law to resolve the controversy. (Common law
is judge-made law created in the absence of other controlling law such as statutes.) This approach has not been satisfactory. The development of common
law is painfully slow, and many feel that it is ill-suited to respond to the rapid
developments of science in this area.

Consequently, state legislatures have been under pressure to do something. But the legislatures are not sure what to do. Are new statutes needed? If so, what kind? The following report examines some of the options a legislature should consider.

SURROGATE PARENTING

D. Bennett, *Surrogate Parenting* (1988) (Background Paper 88-2 prepared for the Legislative Counsel Bureau of Nevada)

I. Introduction

In March 1987, the nation's attention focused on a breach of contract battle underway in New Jersey. The contract in question was between Elizabeth and William Stern and Mary Beth Whitehead (now Mary Beth Whitehead-Gould). The Sterns had contracted with Ms. Whitehead in 1985 to act as a surrogate mother. [Under the terms of the contract, Ms. Whitehead was to be artificially inseminated with Mr. Stern's sperm, become pregnant, give birth to a baby, turn it over to the Sterns, and cooperate in the termination of her parental rights. Mrs. Stern would then adopt the baby.] Upon the birth of the baby—known as Baby M in the case—Ms. Whitehead reconsidered and refused to relinquish her parental rights. The Sterns then sued in an attempt to hold Ms. Whitehead to the terms of the contract.

On March 31, 1987, a New Jersey trial court upheld the contract, granted permanent custody to the Sterns, permitted Mrs. Stern to adopt the child, and denied any rights to Ms. Whitehead. On February 3, 1988, the New Jersey Supreme Court approved only the custody portion of the lower court's decision, ruling that surrogate parenting contracts fall under the New Jersey "baby-selling" statutes and are therefore illegal.[1]

The publicity surrounding this case led to a flurry of activity in legislative bodies around the country as pro- and anti-surrogacy groups attempted to sway policymaking bodies to one side or the other. . . .

II. Definitions

Although the term **surrogate parenting** has become widely used since the Baby M case, it can refer to more than one method of achieving parenthood. In addition, the parties involved in a surrogacy contract may not necessarily be limited to a married couple contracting with a single woman. The parties could involve a married surrogate mother, a single father, or single-sex couples. However, for ease of discussion, . . . the terms "married couple," "husband," and "wife" will be used, keeping in mind that a broader definition may apply to these words.

A. Methods

Four general methods of surrogate parenting are recognized. These methods are:

1. *Artificial Insemination by Husband (AIH).* The AIH method is an arrangement in which the surrogate, a woman other than the wife of the sperm donor, is artificially inseminated with the sperm of the husband of a married couple.

2. *In Vitro Fertilization (IVF).* **In vitro fertilization** is a process by which a sperm and an egg are joined in a laboratory and the fertilized egg is implanted in the surrogate.

3. *Artificial Insemination by Donor (AID[1]).* The AID[1] method is a technique in which the surrogate is artificially inseminated with the sperm of a donor other than the contracting male. Such sperm is typically a specimen obtained from a sperm bank.*

4. *Natural Insemination (NI).* The NI method involves a situation where sexual intercourse occurs between the surrogate and the husband of a married couple.

Of the four methods, AIH is the most common and NI is the least. Sometimes, the IVF and AID[1] methods are chosen in surrogate parenting situations, but not as frequently as AIH. . . . Because AIH is the most common method chosen in surrogate parenting agreements, that definition will be applied to the term surrogate parenting in this [discussion].

B. Agreements

The agreement between the surrogate mother and the intended parents takes one of two forms: (1) commercial; or (2) noncommercial. Both agreements involve similar factors. A couple contracts with a woman to bear a child for them. The woman agrees to be artificially inseminated with the husband's sperm, carry the child to term and surrender her parental rights to the biological father upon the birth of the child.

Once the husband has full parental rights to the child [upon birth], the wife (technically the child's stepmother) begins adoption proceedings. Some . . . [states allow] the wife to forgo formal adoption procedures and obtain a substitute birth certificate from

---

1. *In the Matter of Baby M,* 109 N.J. 396, 537 A.2d 1227 (1988).

---

*AID[2] is a technique in which the *wife* is artificially inseminated with the sperm of a donor other than her husband. Such sperm is also typically a specimen obtained from a sperm bank.

a court of competent jurisdiction. In return, the couple agrees to pay all of the surrogate's medical expenses and other necessary expenses (e.g., maternity clothing).

The difference between a commercial and a noncommercial agreement centers on whether a fee is paid to the surrogate mother. If a fee—usually around $10,000—is paid, then the agreement is considered to be commercial. However, many surrogacy agreements are between family members or friends and do not involve the payment of a fee. These agreements are the noncommercial contracts.

A major argument in the courts and the legislatures involves the nature of this fee. Is it a fee for the surrogate mother's services or is it a fee in exchange for the surrender of her parental rights? . . .

Another factor in surrogacy contracts is the **broker.** Either a private agency or a lawyer, the broker is a third party who coordinates a surrogate parenting agreement. Although a broker receives a fee (in the $10,000–$20,000 range), a broker could be used in both commercial and noncommercial arrangements. However, most arrangements made through a broker include a fee paid to the surrogate mother.

III. Reasons for Choosing Surrogate Parenting Agreements

According to a study of surrogacy recently completed in Wisconsin, the demand for surrogate mothers stems primarily from female infertility. The National Center for Health Statistics estimates that 10 to 15 percent of all married couples are infertile (defined as partners who are sexually active, not using contraception, and unable to conceive after at least one year). The Center excludes the surgically sterile from its statistics. The Wisconsin study also cites evidence that suggests the number of infertile women is on the increase due to the use of intrauterine birth control devices, greater incidence of sexually transmitted diseases, previous abortions and the postponement of childbearing to establish careers. Studies indicate that women who delay having children have a greater risk of being infertile, bearing children with birth defects, and/or being physically impaired. The most common treatments for female infertility are drugs and surgery. Until recently, when these treatments failed, adoption of an unrelated child was the only alternative available.

Couples who want children, but cannot conceive, usually consider adoption. The Wisconsin study noted that, despite a marked increase in the number of live births to single women, fewer unrelated individuals are adopted. Adoption experts believe that the increasing willingness of single mothers to keep their children is a significant factor in limiting the number of infants available for adoption. The stigma once attached to single mothers has diminished. Peers and relatives often encourage single mothers to keep their babies. Medical personnel and social workers are less likely to encourage women to give babies up for adoption.

Laws have changed in recent years to allow single mothers more time to make or revoke a decision to allow adoption. Consequently, couples often cite long waiting periods and other obstacles to adoption (such as the age limit placed on prospective parents) as reasons for seeking surrogate mothers. [R. Roe, *Childbearing by Contract,* 4 (Wisconsin Legislative Bureau, March, 1988).]

Not all couples who contract with a surrogate have failed at adoption. Some couples would rather be childless than adopt an unrelated child. For such families, a genetic link to their child is of primary importance. For example, William Stern lost most of his family in Adolf Hitler's holocaust and wanted a child biologically linked to him. Newspaper interviews of intended fathers confirm the importance some of them place on a biological link when seeking surrogates. One father favored a surrogate birth because "that child will be biologically half-mine" while another father stated that "we believe strongly in heredity."

IV. Major Arguments for and against Surrogate Parenting

A review of the literature on surrogate parenting reveals several common policy positions on each side of this issue.

A. Supporting Arguments

Those who support surrogacy contracts and the regulation of them generally cite the following:

☐ A limitation placed on the fees charged by brokers and the licensing and regulation of brokers will ensure competency, honesty and legitimacy in this process.

☐ Due to the ever-decreasing number of babies available for adoption and the ever-increasing technology in the area of human reproduction, couples who desperately want children will continue to seek out surrogate mothers. Consequently, some form of protection must be provided for the couple, the surrogate mother, and the resulting child.

☐ Proper examination of both couple and surrogate as provided in state law would ensure:

1. That the couple is emotionally and financially ready to bear the responsibility of parenthood.

2. That the couple is truly in need of this service, such as when the wife is unable to carry a child to term.

3. That the woman who will bear the child is emotionally, physically, and psychologically able to carry the child and to give up her rights to the child at birth.

The majority of surrogate contracts are completed without [controversy]. Only a small percentage of surrogate mothers have refused to surrender the resulting babies. . . .

B. Opposing Arguments

Those people who advocate a ban on surrogacy contracts argue that:

☐ Children will be psychologically damaged when they discover that they were "bought."

☐ Surrogate parenting arrangements are in violation of the Thirteenth Amendment of the United States Constitution, which applies to slavery and can be interpreted to forbid the buying and selling of people.

☐ Surrogate parenting will become another form of economic exploitation of rich people over poor. As exemplified by the Baby M affair, the adoptive couples tend to have an economic and educational advantage over the surrogate. [A] study of potential and existing surrogate mothers also indicates that most of the women are unemployed or on some form of public assistance and only have a high school diploma. Thus, surrogate parenting arrangements will serve to create a class of "womb-sellers."

☐ There are plenty of nonwhite babies, older children, and special needs children available for adoption.

☐ Women will be forced—not because they choose, but because the contract requires—to abort fetuses upon demand or to become pregnant again in the case of a miscarriage.

V. Issues in State Law

According to the Wisconsin study of surrogacy, court decisions and discussions of surrogacy indicated that four existing areas of law affect surrogate parenting agreements. These areas are (1) adoption and termination of parental rights; (2) artificial insemination and legal paternity; (3) child custody; and (4) contracts. . . .

A. Adoption Laws

Two aspects of many state adoption laws may restrict or prevent surrogate parenting agreements. One forbids compensation in exchange for the consent to an adoption, and the other forbids consent to an adoption to be given prior to the birth of the child.

At least 24 states . . . prohibit the payment of compensation for adoptions. Often called **baby-selling** laws, these statutes range from those prohibiting all payments to those allowing payment of certain expenses. Nevada for example, forbids the payment of a fee in return for the mother's agreement to terminate her parental rights of the child.

While surrogacy opponents favor the use of adoption statutes to control it, proponents maintain that modern anti–baby-selling laws predate surrogate parenting and were designed to protect unwed mothers. Under a surrogacy agreement, the intended father is also the biological father; therefore, how can he buy his own child? Also, proponents argue, surrogates have voluntarily agreed to surrender the child. She is not doing so under pregnancy related stress. Finally, the fees are paid primarily to replace lost work time or pain and suffering.

All 50 states . . . have laws that prohibit a mother from granting consent to adoption before a child's birth or for some period of time after birth. Waiting periods range up to as much as 20 days (Pennsylvania). A mother's consent to surrender a newborn for adoption is not valid in Nevada until at least 72 hours after birth.

However, as with baby-selling laws, consent laws were designed to protect unwed mothers. The decisions facing an unwed mother are not like those facing the surrogate mother who has voluntarily chosen to bear children for another couple.

B. Paternity Laws

Paternity laws may also affect surrogate arrangements. Some states retain the common law rule that the husband of a woman who gives birth to a child is presumed to be the father. Courts in many of these states will not admit evidence to the contrary. A majority of states now allow a rebuttal to the presumption of paternity, but place a strict burden of proof on the contending party. . . .

Surrogate supporters argue that paternity laws were designed to protect the child, particularly the rights to inheritance, and were not drafted in anticipation of surrogate parenting arrangements. Rights and duties outlined in surrogate agreements fall on the natural father and would secure the child's rights. Critics point out that paternity determinations are made by courts and do not necessarily give custody to one party or the other.

Paternity laws could also affect surrogate arrangements based on the reliance on artificial insemination. Since most surrogate mothers are artificially inseminated, laws on that subject might be relevant. At least 30 states . . . have laws that presume that the husband of the woman being inseminated is the child's father and that relieves the sperm donor of any legal obligation.

Although some critics approve applying artificial insemination law to surrogate agreements, others find the analogy suspect and open to court challenge.

C. Custody Issues

The traditional basis for custody decisions is a determination of the best interest of the child. The standards for judging the suitability of intended parents include marital and family status, mental and physical health, income and property, any history of child abuse or neglect and other relevant facts. In the case of Baby M, custody of the child was awarded to the Sterns because the court felt it was in the best interest of the child. Ms. Whitehead's divorce after 13 years of marriage and subsequent marriage to the father of her unborn child 2 weeks after the divorce were key factors in the court's decision.

A spokesperson for the National Committee for Adoption objects to surrogate contracts because they are not required to take into account the best interest of the child. Unlike normal adoption proceedings, no one screens intended parents. Currently, surrogacy agreements require nothing more than the financial ability to hire a lawyer and pay the surrogate mother.

Supporters of surrogate agreements argue that intended parents should receive the same treatment as ordinary parents, since the only qualification they lack is the physical ability to have children. Supporters also maintain that surrogate agreements are inherently in the best interest of the child because the intended parents have given much thought to their actions and decided that they truly want a child. Adoption proceedings, on the other hand, were devised to provide a permanent home for a child who otherwise would not have one. In a surrogate agreement, the child's home is provided by contract.

D. Contractual Duties

Existing federal and state contract laws do not address the issues of the surrogate's liability or acceptable remedies in case of breach of contract, nor do they address the responsibilities of the intended parents.

Contracts impose a number of duties on one or both of the intended parents. These duties include the payment of expenses and fees and the assumption of responsibility for the child at birth. If the birth mother performs as agreed, does she have recourse if the other party refuses to pay all or part of the expenses and fees? What happens if the intended parents refuse to take the child? Can the surrogate mother sue the natural father for child support?

Some of these issues are already facing state courts. For example, in Texas, a 24-year-old surrogate mother died of heart failure in her eighth month of pregnancy; and in Washington, D.C., a baby born through a surrogate agreement was diagnosed as having acquired immune deficiency syndrome (AIDS). Now, neither the surrogate mother nor contracting parents want the AIDS baby. These issues were not previously addressed in the contracts.

Enforcement of a surrogate mother's duties are even more difficult. She agrees to be inseminated, bear a child and surrender all parental rights. She is also to refrain from sexual intercourse during the insemi-

nation period and has the duty to refrain from activities that may harm the fetus. If medical clauses are included in the contract, what recourse do the intended parents have if the surrogate refuses to follow them? If she refuses the insemination, are any expenses refunded to the intended parents? If the surrogate chooses to have an abortion in the first trimester, which is legally her right, can the intended parents sue for expenses? Can they sue for damages if the surrogate decides to keep the child?

Even if the surrogate agreement clears all other legal hurdles, many questions remain about the responsibilities of each party to the contract.

VI. State Regulation

States differ on how to handle surrogacy contracts:

□ Some states are silent on the subject. No statutes exist, and no cases have yet been litigated in the courts.

□ A few states have outright bans on all commercial and noncommercial surrogacy contracts.

□ Some states prohibit commercial surrogacy contracts.

□ Some states prohibit fees to the surrogate beyond the expenses involved.

□ Some states prohibit fees to an **intermediary,** the person who facilitates the surrogacy arrangement such as by bringing the surrogate and couple together.

□ Some states allow surrogacy contracts, but closely regulate the process including medical and psychological screening, home studies, the payment of fees, time periods within which the surrogate can change her mind, the identification of the legal parents, etc.

In August 1988, the National Conference of Commissioners on Uniform State Laws drafted and approved for use in all state legislatures the **Uniform Status of Children of Assisted Conception Act.** The model act provides two alternatives for consideration by state legislatures: one to regulate surrogate parenting agreements (Alternative A), and the other to ban the agreements (Alternative B).

Alternative A would allow surrogate parenting contracts and provides a regulatory framework. A court hearing would be held at which both parties would be required to submit medical evidence to prove that the would-be mother cannot bear her own child and that the surrogate mother is mentally and physically fit to bear the child. The proposal also would allow the surrogate mother to pull out of the agreement up to 180 days into her pregnancy.

The opposing language in the act (Alternative B) simply bans all surrogate parenting agreements. It does not make any distinction between commercial and noncommercial contracts; all such contracts are void.

Uniform Status of Children of Assisted Conception Act

National Conference of Commissioners on Uniform States Laws (1988)

Section 1. Definitions

In this [Act]:

(1) "**Assisted conception**" means a pregnancy resulting from (i) fertilizing an egg of a woman with sperm of a man by means other than sexual intercourse or (ii) implanting an embryo, but the term does not include the pregnancy of a wife resulting from fertilizing her egg with sperm of her husband.

(2) "**Donor**" means an individual [other than a surrogate] who produces egg or sperm used for assisted conception, whether or not payment is made for the egg or sperm used, but does not include a woman who gives birth to a resulting child.

[(3) "**Intended parents**" means a man and woman, married to each other, who enter into an agreement under this [Act] providing that they will be the parents of a child born to a surrogate through assisted conception using egg or sperm of one or both of the intended parents.]

(4) "**Surrogate**" means an adult woman who enters into an agreement to bear a child conceived through assisted conception for intended parents. . . .

Section 2. Maternity

[Except as provided in Sections 5 through 9,] a woman who gives birth to a child is the child's mother. . . .

Section 3. Assisted Conception by Married Woman

[Except as provided in Sections 5 through 9,] the husband of a woman who bears a child through assisted conception is the father of the child, notwithstanding a declaration of invalidity or annulment of the marriage obtained after the assisted conception, unless within two years after learning of the child's birth he commences an action in which the mother and child are parties and in which it is determined that he did not consent to the assisted conception.

Section 4. Parental Status of Donors and Deceased Individuals

[Except as otherwise provided in Sections 5 through 9:]

(a) A donor is not a parent of a child conceived through assisted conception.
(b) An individual who dies before implantation of an embryo, or before a child is conceived other than through sexual intercourse, using the individual's egg sperm, is not a parent of the resulting child. . . .

Alternative A

Comment

A state that chooses Alternative A should also consider Section 1(3) and the bracketed language in Sections 1(2), 2, 3, and 4.

[Section 5. Surrogacy Agreement

(a) A surrogate, her husband, if she is married, and intended parents may enter into a written agreement whereby the surrogate relinquishes all her rights and duties as a parent of a child to be conceived through assisted conception, and the intended parents may become the parents of the child pursuant to Section 8.

(b) If the agreement is not approved by the court under Section 6 before conception, the agreement is void and the surrogate is the mother of a resulting child and the surrogate's husband, if a party to the agreement, is the father of the child. If the surrogate's husband is not a party to the agreement or the surrogate is unmarried, paternity of the child is governed by [the Uniform Parentage Act]. . . .

Continued

Uniform Status of Children
of Assisted Conception Act—*Continued*

Section 6. Petition and Hearing for Approval of Surrogacy Agreement

(a) The intended parents and the surrogate may file a petition in the [appropriate court] to approve a surrogacy agreement if one of them is a resident of this State. The surrogate's husband, if she is married, must join in the petition. A copy of the agreement must be attached to the petition. The court shall name a [guardian ad litem] to represent the interests of a child to be conceived by the surrogate through assisted conception and [shall] [may] appoint counsel to represent the surrogate.

[(b) The court shall hold a hearing on the petition and shall enter an order approving the surrogacy agreement, authorizing assisted conception for a period of 12 months after the date of the order, declaring the intended parents to be the parents of a child to be conceived through assisted conception pursuant to the agreement and discharging the guardian ad litem and attorney for the surrogate, upon finding that:

(1) the court has jurisdiction and all parties have submitted to its jurisdiction under subsection (e) and have agreed that the law of this State governs all matters arising under this [Act] and the agreement;

(2) the intended mother is unable to bear a child or is unable to do so without unreasonable risk to an unborn child or to the physical or mental health of the intended mother or child, and the finding is supported by medical evidence;

(3) The [relevant child-welfare agency] has made a home study of the intended parents and the surrogate and a copy of the report of the home study has been filed with the court;

(4) the intended parents, the surrogate, and the surrogate's husband, if she is married, meet the standards of fitness applicable to adoptive parents in this State;

(5) all parties have voluntarily entered into the agreement and understand its terms, nature, and meaning, and the effect of the proceeding;

(6) the surrogate has had at least one pregnancy and delivery and bearing another child will not pose an unreasonable risk to the unborn child or to the physical or mental health of the surrogate or the child, and this finding is supported by medical evidence;

(7) all parties have received counseling concerning the effect of the surrogacy by [a qualified health-care professional or social worker] and a report containing conclusions about the capacity of the parties to enter into and fulfill the agreement has been filed with the court;

(8) a report of the results of any medical or psychological examination or genetic screening agreed to by the parties or required by law has been filed with the court and made available to the parties;

(9) adequate provision has been made for all reasonable health-care costs associated with the surrogacy until the child's birth including responsibility for those costs if the agreement is terminated pursuant to Section 7; and

(10) the agreement will not be substantially detrimental to the interest of any of the affected individuals.

(c) Unless otherwise provided in the surrogacy agreement, all court costs, attorney's fees, and other costs and expenses associated with the proceeding must be assessed against the intended parents.

(d) Notwithstanding any other law concerning judicial proceedings or vital statistics, the court shall conduct all hearings and proceedings under this section in camera. The court shall keep all records of the proceedings confidential and subject to inspection under the same standards applicable to adoptions. At the request of any party, the court shall take steps necessary to ensure that the identities of the parties are not disclosed.

Continued

Uniform Status of Children
of Assisted Conception Act—*Continued*

(e) The court conducting the proceedings has exclusive and continuing jurisdiction of all matters arising out of the surrogacy until a child born after entry of an order under this section is 180 days old. . . .

Section 7. Termination of Surrogacy Agreement

(a) After entry of an order under Section 6, but before the surrogate becomes pregnant through assisted conception, the court for cause, or the surrogate, her husband, or the intended parents may terminate the surrogacy agreement by giving written notice of termination to all other parties and filing notice of the termination with the court. Thereupon, the court shall vacate the order entered under Section 6.

(b) A surrogate who has provided an egg for the assisted conception pursuant to an agreement approved under Section 6 may terminate the agreement by filing written notice with the court within 180 days after the last insemination pursuant to the agreement. Upon finding, after notice to the parties to the agreement and hearing, that the surrogate has voluntarily terminated the agreement and understands the nature, meaning, and effect of the termination, the court shall vacate the order entered under Section 6.

(c) The surrogate is not liable to the intended parents for terminating the agreement pursuant to this section. . . .

Section 8. Parentage under Approved Surrogacy Agreement

(a) The following rules of parentage apply to surrogacy agreements approved under Section 6:

   (1) Upon birth of a child to the surrogate, the intended parents are the parents of the child and the surrogate and her husband, if she is married, are not parents of the child unless the court vacates the order pursuant to Section 7(b).
   (2) If, after notice of termination by the surrogate, the court vacates the order under Section 7(b) the surrogate is the mother of a resulting child, and her husband, if a party to the agreement, is the father. If the surrogate's husband is not a party to the agreement or the surrogate is unmarried, paternity of the child is governed by [the Uniform Parentage Act].

(b) Upon birth of the child, the intended parents shall file a written notice with the court that a child has been born to the surrogate within 300 days after assisted conception. Thereupon, the court shall enter an order directing the [Department of Vital Statistics] to issue a new birth certificate naming the intended parents as parents and to seal the original birth certificate in the records of the [Department of Vital Statistics]. . . .

Section 9. Surrogacy: Miscellaneous Provisions

(a) A surrogacy agreement that is the basis of an order under Section 6 may provide for the payment of consideration.

(b) A surrogacy agreement may not limit the right of the surrogate to make decisions regarding her health care or that of the embryo or fetus.

(c) After the entry of an order under Section 6, marriage of the surrogate does not affect the validity of the order, and her husband's consent to the surrogacy agreement is not required, nor is he the father of a resulting child.

(d) A child born to a surrogate within 300 days after assisted conception pursuant to an order under Section 6 is presumed to result from the assisted conception. The presumption is conclusive as to all persons who have notice of the birth and who do not commence within 180 days after notice, an action to assert the contrary in which the child and the parties to the agreement are named as parties. The action must be commenced in the court that issued the order under Section 6.

Continued

Uniform Status of Children
of Assisted Conception Act—*Continued*

(e) A health-care provider is not liable for recognizing the surrogate as the mother before receipt of a copy of the order entered under Section 6 or for recognizing the intended parents as parents after receipt of an order entered under Section 6. . . .]

[End of Alternative A]

Alternative B

Surrogate Agreements

An agreement in which a woman agrees to become a surrogate or to relinquish her rights and duties as parent of a child thereafter conceived through assisted conception is void. However, she is the mother of a resulting child, and her husband, if a party to the agreement, is the father of the child. If her husband is not a party to the agreement or the surrogate is unmarried, paternity of the child is governed by [the Uniform Parentage Act].] . . .

[End of Alternative B]

---

a. Should surrogacy contracts be banned? If not, what kind of regulation is needed?

b. Do you approve of an advertisement such as the following one placed in the want ad section of the newspaper along with ads for accountants and truck drivers:

> "CASH AVAILABLE NOW. Married or single women needed as surrogate mothers for couples unable to have children. Conception to be by artificial insemination. We pay well! Contact the Infertility Clinic today."

c. Do you favor Alternative A or B in the Uniform Status of Children of Assisted Conception Act? Why?

d. What is the current law in your state on the validity of surrogacy contracts? (See General Instructions for the State-Code Assignment and General Instructions for the Court-Opinion Assignment in chapter 1.)

ASSIGNMENT 20.1

CASE

JOHNSON V. CALVERT

5 Cal. 4th 84, 851 P.2d 776, 19 Cal. Rptr. 2d 494 1993
Supreme Court of California.

Background: *This is a case of* **gestational surrogacy** *in which the sperm and egg of a couple are combined in vitro in a laboratory and the resulting embryo is then implanted in a surrogate mother who carries the child to term. The surrogate mother gives birth to a child with whom she has no genetic relationship.*

Anna Johnson, a licensed vocational nurse, agreed to became a gestational surrogate. An embryo created by the sperm and egg of Mark and Crispina Calvert was implanted in Johnson. The agreement, however, fell apart while Johnson was still pregnant. Crispina Calvert and Anna Johnson filed separate actions to be declared the

mother of the child who was eventually born. (Anna named the child Matthew; the Calverts named him Christopher.) The cases were consolidated. The trial court ruled that Mark and Crispina were the child's "genetic, biological and natural" father and mother. It called Anna a "genetic stranger" to the child. The Court of Appeal affirmed. The case is now on appeal before the Supreme Court of California.

Decision on Appeal: Judgment affirmed. In a gestational surrogacy contract, the natural mother of the child is the woman whose intent was to raise the child as her own. Only Crispina had this intent.

Opinion of the Court:

Justice PANELLI delivered the opinion of the court.

In this case we address several of the legal questions raised by recent advances in reproductive technology. When, pursuant to a surrogacy agreement, a zygote* formed of the gametes† of a husband and wife is implanted in the uterus of another woman, who carries the resulting fetus to term and gives birth to a child not genetically related to her, who is the child's "natural mother" under California law? . . . And is such an agreement barred by any public policy of this state? We conclude that the husband and wife are the child's natural parents, and that this result does not offend . . . public policy.

Mark and Crispina Calvert are a married couple who desired to have a child. Crispina was forced to undergo a hysterectomy in 1984. Her ovaries remained capable of producing eggs, however, and the couple eventually considered surrogacy. In 1989 Anna Johnson heard about Crispina's plight from a coworker and offered to serve as a surrogate for the Calverts.

On January 15, 1990, Mark, Crispina, and Anna signed a contract providing that an embryo created by the sperm of Mark and the egg of Crispina would be implanted in Anna and the child born would be taken into Mark and Crispina's home "as their child." Anna agreed she would relinquish "all parental rights" to the child in favor of Mark and Crispina. In return, Mark and Crispina would pay Anna $10,000 in a series of installments, the last to be paid six weeks after the child's birth. Mark and Crispina were also to pay for a $200,000 life insurance policy on Anna's life. The zygote was implanted on January 19, 1990. Less than a month later, an ultrasound test confirmed Anna was pregnant.

Unfortunately, relations deteriorated between the two sides. Mark learned that Anna had not disclosed she had suffered several stillbirths and miscarriages. Anna felt Mark and Crispina did not do enough to obtain the required insurance policy. She also felt abandoned during an onset of premature labor in June. In July 1990, Anna sent Mark and Crispina a letter demanding the balance of the payments due her or else she would refuse to give up the child. The following month, Mark and Crispina responded with a lawsuit, seeking a declaration they were the legal parents of the unborn child. Anna filed her own action to be declared the mother of the child, and the two cases were eventually consolidated. . . .

The child was born on September 19, 1990, and blood samples were obtained from both Anna and the child

for analysis. The blood test results excluded Anna as the genetic mother. The parties agreed to a court order providing that the child would remain with Mark and Crispina on a temporary basis with visits by Anna.

At trial in October 1990, the parties stipulated that Mark and Crispina were the child's genetic parents. After hearing evidence and arguments, the trial court ruled that Mark and Crispina were the child's "genetic, biological and natural" father and mother, that Anna had no "parental" rights to the child, and that the surrogacy contract was legal and enforceable against Anna's claims. The court also terminated the order allowing visitation. Anna appealed from the trial court's judgment. The Court of Appeal for the Fourth District, Division Three, affirmed. We granted review. . . .

[In California, there are two kinds of evidence that can be used to establish the existence of a parent-child relationship: evidence on who gave birth to the child, and genetic evidence derived from blood testing. Our statutes do not say what a court must do when the two kinds of evidence lead to conflicting results. There is] . . . undisputed evidence that Anna, not Crispina, gave birth to the child and that Crispina, not Anna, is genetically related to him. Both women thus have adduced evidence of a mother and child relationship. . . . Yet for any child California law recognizes only one natural mother, despite advances in reproductive technology rendering a different outcome biologically possible.** . . .

Because two women each have presented acceptable proof of maternity, we do not believe this case can be decided without enquiring into the parties' intentions as manifested in the surrogacy agreement. Mark and Crispina are a couple who desired to have a child of their own genetic stock but are physically unable to do so without the help of reproductive technology. They affirmatively intended the birth of the child, and took the steps necessary to effect in vitro fertilization. But for their acted-on intention, the child would not exist. Anna agreed to facilitate the procreation of Mark's and Crispina's child. The parties' aim was to bring Mark's and Crispina's child into the world, not for Mark and Crispina to donate a zygote to Anna. Crispina from the outset intended to be the child's mother. Although the gestative function Anna

---

*An organism produced by the union of two gametes. (McGraw-Hill Dict. of Scientific and Technical Terms (4th ed. 1989) p. 783.)

†A cell that participates in fertilization and development of a new organism, also known as a germ cell or sex cell. (McGraw-Hill Dict. of Scientific and Technical Terms, supra, p. 2087.)

**We decline to accept the contention of amicus curiae the American Civil Liberties Union (ACLU) that we should find the child has two mothers. Even though rising divorce rates have made multiple parent arrangements common in our society, we see no compelling reason to recognize such a situation here. The Calverts are the genetic and intending parents of their son and have provided him, by all accounts, with a stable, intact, and nurturing home. To recognize parental rights in a third party with whom the Calvert family has had little contact since shortly after the child's birth would diminish Crispina's role as mother.

performed was necessary to bring about the child's birth, it is safe to say that Anna would not have been given the opportunity to gestate or deliver the child had she, prior to implantation of the zygote, manifested her own intent to be the child's mother. No reason appears why Anna's later change of heart should vitiate the determination that Crispina is the child's natural mother.

We conclude that although [California law] recognizes both genetic consanguinity and giving birth as means of establishing a mother and child relationship, when the two means do not coincide in one woman, she who intended to procreate the child— that is, she who intended to bring about the birth of a child that she intended to raise as her own—is the natural mother under California law.[††] . . .

Our conclusion finds support in the writings of several legal commentators. . . . (See Shultz, *Reproductive Technology and Intent-Based Parenthood: An Opportunity for Gender Neutrality* (1990) Wis. L. Rev. 297 [Schultz].) "Within the context of artificial reproductive techniques," Professor Schultz argues, "intentions that are voluntarily chosen, deliberate, express and bargained-for ought presumptively to determine legal parenthood." (Id., at p. 323.) . . . Moreover, as Professor Schultz recognizes, the interests of children, particularly at the outset of their lives, are "[un]likely to run contrary to those of adults who choose to bring them into being." (Id., at p. 397.) Thus, "[h]onoring the plans and expectations of adults who will be responsible for a child's welfare is likely to correlate significantly with positive outcomes for parents and children alike." (Ibid.)

Under Anna [Johnson's view,] a woman who agreed to gestate a fetus genetically related to the intending parents would, contrary to her expectations, be held to be the child's natural mother, with all the responsibilities that ruling would entail, if the intending mother declined to accept the child after its birth. In what we must hope will be the extremely rare situation in which neither the gestator nor the woman who provided the ovum for fertilization is willing to assume custody of the child after birth, a rule recognizing the intending parents as the child's legal, natural parents should best promote certainty and stability for the child.

In deciding the issue of maternity . . . we have felt free to take into account the parties' intentions, as expressed in the surrogacy contract, because in our view the agreement is not, on its face, inconsistent with public policy. . . .

Anna urges that surrogacy contracts violate several social policies. Relying on her contention that she is the child's legal, natural mother, she cites the public policy embodied in Penal Code section 273, prohibiting the payment for consent to adoptions of a child.[***] She argues further that the policies underlying the adoption laws of this state are violated by the surrogacy contract because it in effect constitutes a prebirth waiver of her parental rights.

We disagree. Gestational surrogacy differs in crucial respects from adoption and so is not subject to the adoption statutes. The parties voluntarily agreed to participate in in vitro fertilization and related medical procedures before the child was conceived; at the time when Anna entered into the contract, therefore, she was not vulnerable to financial inducements to part with her own expected offspring. As discussed above, Anna was not the genetic mother of the child. The payments to Anna under the contract were meant to compensate her for her services in gestating the fetus and undergoing labor, rather than for giving up "parental" rights to the child. Payments were due both during the pregnancy and after the child's birth. We are, accordingly, unpersuaded that the contract used in this case violates the public policies embodied in Penal Code section 273 and the adoption statutes. For the same reasons, we conclude these contracts do not implicate the policies underlying the statutes governing termination of parental rights. . . .

It has been suggested that gestational surrogacy may run afoul of prohibitions on involuntary servitude. (See U.S. Const., Amend. XIII; Cal. Const., art. I,

---

[††]Thus, under our analysis, in a true "egg donation" situation, where a woman gestates and gives birth to a child formed from the egg of another woman with the intent to raise the child as her own, the birth mother is the natural mother under California law. . . .

[***]Penal Code section 273 provides, in pertinent part, as follows: "(a) It is a misdemeanor for any person or agency to offer to pay money or anything of value, or to pay money or anything of value, to a parent for the placement for adoption, for the consent to an adoption, or for cooperation in the completion of an adoption of his or her child. (b) This section does not make it unlawful to pay the maternity-connected medical or hospital and necessary living expenses of the mother preceding and during confinement as an act of charity, as long as the payment is not contingent upon placement of the child for adoption, consent to the adoption, or cooperation in the completion of the adoption." See also Penal Code section 181, which provides: "Every person who holds, or attempts to hold, any person in involuntary servitude, or assumes, or attempts to assume, rights of ownership over any person, or who sells, or attempts to sell, any person to another, or receives money or anything of value, in consideration of placing any person in the custody, or under the power or control of another, or who buys, or attempts to buy, any person, or pays money, or delivers anything of value, to another, in consideration of having any person placed in his custody, or under his power or control, or who knowingly aids or assists in any manner anyone thus offending, is punishable by imprisonment in the state prison for two, three, or four years."

§ 6; Pen. Code, § 181.) Involuntary servitude has been recognized in cases of criminal punishment for refusal to work. (*Pollack v. Williams* (1944) 322 U.S 4, 18; see, generally, 7 Witkin, *Summary of Cal. Law* (9th ed. 1988) Constitutional Law, §§ 411–414, pp. 591–596.) We see no potential for that evil in the contract at issue here, and extrinsic evidence of coercion or duress is utterly lacking. We note that although at one point the contract purports to give Mark and Crispina the sole right to determine whether to abort the pregnancy, at another point it acknowledges: "All parties understand that a pregnant woman has the absolute right to abort or not abort any fetus she is carrying. Any promise to the contrary is unenforceable." We therefore need not determine the validity of a surrogacy contract purporting to deprive the gestator of her freedom to terminate the pregnancy.

Finally, Anna and some commentators have expressed concern that surrogacy contracts tend to exploit or dehumanize women, especially women of lower economic status. Anna's objections center around the psychological harm she asserts may result from the gestator's relinquishing the child to whom she has given birth. Some have also cautioned that the practice of surrogacy may encourage society to view children as commodities, subject to trade at their parents' will.

We are all too aware that the proper forum for resolution of this issue is the Legislature, where empirical data, largely lacking from this record, can be studied and rules of general applicability developed. However, in light of our responsibility to decide this case, we have considered as best we can its possible consequences.

We are unpersuaded that gestational surrogacy arrangements are so likely to cause the untoward results Anna cites as to demand their invalidation on public policy grounds. Although common sense suggests that women of lesser means serve as surrogate mothers more often than do wealthy women, there has been no proof that surrogacy contracts exploit poor women to any greater degree than economic necessity in general exploits them by inducing them to accept lower-paid or otherwise undesirable employment. We are likewise unpersuaded by the claim that surrogacy will foster the attitude that children are mere commodities; no evidence is offered to support it. The limited data available seem to reflect an absence of significant adverse effects of surrogacy on all participants.

The argument that a woman cannot knowingly and intelligently agree to gestate and deliver a baby for intending parents carries overtones of the reasoning that for centuries prevented women from attaining equal economic rights and professional status under the law. To resurrect this view is both to foreclose a personal and economic choice on the part of the surrogate mother, and to deny intending parents what may be their only means of procreating a child of their own genetic stock. Certainly in the present case it cannot seriously be argued that Anna, a licensed vocational nurse who had done well in school and who had previously borne a child, lacked the intellectual wherewithal or life experience necessary to make an informed decision to enter into the surrogacy contract. . . .

The judgment of the Court of Appeal is affirmed.

---

a. Isn't it true that the child in the *Johnson* case has three biological parents, two of whom are mothers? Why couldn't there be a three-parent solution to this case?

b. Do you think a gestational mother can bond with her child prenatally? If so, would this be relevant to Anna Johnson's claim to be declared the natural/legal mother?

c. Do you think that a gestational mother makes a substantial or significant contribution to the birth of a child? If so, why not determine who the legal/natural parent is on the basis of whether it would be in the best interest of the child to be with the gestational mother or with the intended genetic mother? Since both have serious claims, why shouldn't the test be: Who would make the better parent?

d. Assume that California had adopted the Uniform Status of Children of Assisted Conception Act (Alternative A). How would the *Johnson* case have been decided under this Act?

ASSIGNMENT 20.2

▮▮ SUMMARY

The main methods of achieving surrogate motherhood are artificial insemination and in vitro fertilization. Married couples seek the services of surrogates because of female infertility and the relatively small number of babies available through adoption.

Those who argue that surrogate contracts should be legalized point out that since society cannot stop the practice of surrogacy, it would be better to regulate it to ensure competency and honesty in the process. Those who would ban surrogate contracts denounce the very notion of "buying and selling babies" in an atmosphere of exploitation.

Numerous questions arise as the topic of surrogacy comes before the legislatures of the country. For example, if a surrogate mother is paid as she goes through adoption, has there been a violation of the law that prohibits paying someone to consent to an adoption? Under current paternity laws, is the husband of the surrogate mother presumed to be the father of the child that she is under contract to allow another man to adopt? On the ultimate question of custody, what assurances exist that giving the child to the couple that hires the surrogate mother will always be in the best interest of the child? Also, numerous enforcement questions must be addressed when it becomes clear that one of the parties to the surrogate contract refuses to go along with its terms, or when something happens that is not covered in the terms of the contract, e.g., the surrogate mother gives birth to a baby with AIDS.

State legislatures have handled such questions in different ways, including the following: doing nothing; prohibiting surrogate contracts; permitting such contracts, but regulating them; and finally, giving serious consideration to a new model act called the *Uniform Status of Children of Assisted Conception Act* proposed by the National Conference of Commissioners on Uniform State Laws.

◾◾◾ KEY CHAPTER TERMINOLOGY

Surrogate Parenting	Intermediary	Donor
In Vitro Fertilization	Uniform Status of Children of	Intended Parents
Broker	Assisted Conception Act	Surrogate
Baby Selling	Assisted Conception	Gestational Surrogacy

TORTS

CLASSIFICATION OF TORTS

Tort A civil wrong that has caused harm to person or property for which a court will provide a remedy.

Torts can be classified as follows:

INTENTIONAL TORTS AGAINST PROPERTY

☐ **Trespass** A wrongful entry on the property of another.

☐ **Conversion** The exercise of dominion or control over someone's property without authorization.

☐ **Nuisance** The use of one's property in such a way as to interfere with someone else's enjoyment of his or her property.

INTENTIONAL TORTS AGAINST THE PERSON

☐ **Assault** The attempt to inflict harmful or offensive contact on a person, placing that person in fear or apprehension of the contact.

☐ **Battery** Harmful or offensive contact with a person.

☐ **False Imprisonment** The detention or restraint of a person without authorization (this tort does not necessarily involve prisons, jails, police, etc.; a person, for example, can falsely imprison his or her neighbor in a garage).

☐ **Malicious Prosecution** Bringing a civil or criminal action against someone for malicious reasons when no reasonable basis or probable cause exists for the action.

☐ **Slander** Oral statements that are false and that injure the reputation of another.

☐ **Libel** Written statements that are false and that injure the reputation of another.

Immunity A defense that prevents someone from being sued for what would otherwise be wrongful conduct.

UNINTENTIONAL TORT: NEGLIGENCE

☐ **Negligence** Injury to person or property caused by a failure to act with reasonable care.

Intrafamily Torts A tort committed by one family member against another.

INTRAFAMILY TORTS

Historically, an **immunity** existed for most **intrafamily torts.** This had the effect of rendering tortious conduct nontortious. Courts have always been reluctant to permit tort actions among any combination of husband, wife, and une-mancipated child (children are **emancipated** when they are legally independent of their parents or legal guardians). This reluctance is based on the theory that family harmony will be threatened if members know that they can sue each other in tort. If the family carries **liability insurance,** there is also fear that family members will fraudulently try to collect under the policy by fabricating tort actions against each other. Furthermore, courts simply did not want to get involved. According to an 1877 opinion, "it is better to draw the curtain, shut out the public gaze, and leave the parties to forgive and forget." *Abbott v. Abbott*, 67 Me. 304, 307 (1877). At common law, a more technical reason was given for why husbands and wives could not sue each other. The husband and wife were considered to be one person, and that one person was the husband! Hence, to allow a suit between spouses would theoretically amount to one person suing himself. With the passage of the Married Women's Property Acts (see chapter 16) and the enforcement of the laws against sex discrimination, a wife now has her separate identity so that she can sue and be sued like anyone else.

Reform in the law, however, has not meant that intrafamily tort immunity no longer exists. A distinction must be made between suits against the person (such as battery) and a suit against property (such as conversion). For torts *against property*, most states allow suits between spouses and between parent and child. Most states, however, retain the immunity in some form when the suit involves a tort *against the person*. The state of law is outlined in Exhibit 21.1.

☐ **EXHIBIT 21.1**
Intrafamily Torts

SPOUSE AGAINST SPOUSE

1. In most states, spouses can sue each other for intentional or negligent injury to their property, e.g., negligence, trespass, conversion.
2. In some states, spouses cannot sue each other for intentional or negligent injury to their person—a personal tort action, e.g., negligence, assault, battery.
3. Some states permit personal tort actions if the man and woman are divorced or if the tort is covered by liability insurance.
4. Some states permit intentional tort actions against the person to be brought by spouses against each other, but continue to forbid negligence actions for injury to the person.

CHILD AGAINST PARENT(S)

1. In all states, a child can sue the parent for intentional or negligent injury caused by the parent to the child's property, e.g., negligence, trespass, conversion.
2. In many states, a child cannot sue a parent for intentional or negligent injury caused by the parent to the child's person—a personal tort action, e.g., negligence, assault, battery.
3. If the child is emancipated (e.g., married, member of the armed forces, self-supporting), the child in all states can sue the parent for intentional or negligent injury caused by the parent to the child's person, e.g., negligence, assault, battery.
4. Some states will permit any child (emancipated or not) to sue the parent for intentional torts causing injury to the person, but continue to forbid actions for negligence causing injury to the person.
5. A few states allow the child to sue the parent for all intentional torts causing injury to the person, except where a tort arises out of the parent's exercise of discipline over the child.

OTHER RELATED PERSONS

Brothers and sisters, aunts and uncles, grandparents and grandchildren, and other relatives can sue each other in tort. The restrictions imposed on spouse suits and child suits do not apply to tort actions involving other relatives.

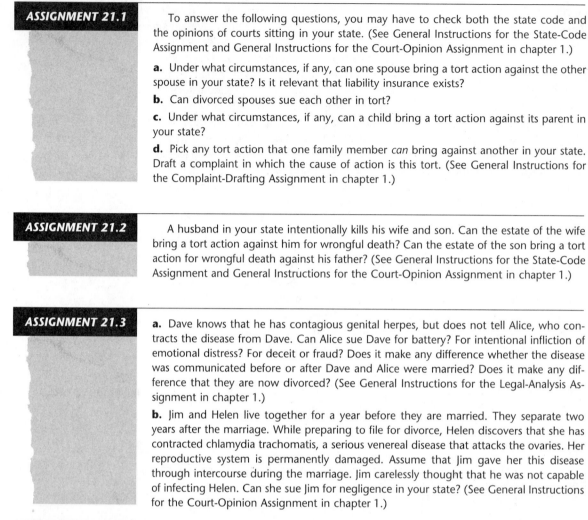

ASSIGNMENT 21.1

To answer the following questions, you may have to check both the state code and the opinions of courts sitting in your state. (See General Instructions for the State-Code Assignment and General Instructions for the Court-Opinion Assignment in chapter 1.)

a. Under what circumstances, if any, can one spouse bring a tort action against the other spouse in your state? Is it relevant that liability insurance exists?

b. Can divorced spouses sue each other in tort?

c. Under what circumstances, if any, can a child bring a tort action against its parent in your state?

d. Pick any tort action that one family member *can* bring against another in your state. Draft a complaint in which the cause of action is this tort. (See General Instructions for the Complaint-Drafting Assignment in chapter 1.)

ASSIGNMENT 21.2

A husband in your state intentionally kills his wife and son. Can the estate of the wife bring a tort action against him for wrongful death? Can the estate of the son bring a tort action for wrongful death against his father? (See General Instructions for the State-Code Assignment and General Instructions for the Court-Opinion Assignment in chapter 1.)

ASSIGNMENT 21.3

a. Dave knows that he has contagious genital herpes, but does not tell Alice, who contracts the disease from Dave. Can Alice sue Dave for battery? For intentional infliction of emotional distress? For deceit or fraud? Does it make any difference whether the disease was communicated before or after Dave and Alice were married? Does it make any difference that they are now divorced? (See General Instructions for the Legal-Analysis Assignment in chapter 1.)

b. Jim and Helen live together for a year before they are married. They separate two years after the marriage. While preparing to file for divorce, Helen discovers that she has contracted chlamydia trachomatis, a serious venereal disease that attacks the ovaries. Her reproductive system is permanently damaged. Assume that Jim gave her this disease through intercourse during the marriage. Jim carelessly thought that he was not capable of infecting Helen. Can she sue Jim for negligence in your state? (See General Instructions for the Court-Opinion Assignment in chapter 1.)

CASE

HAKKILA V. HAKKILA

112 N.M. 172, 812 P.2d 1320 (1991)
Court of Appeals of New Mexico.

Background: Arnold Hakkila sued Peggy Hakkila for divorce. Peggy counterclaimed for divorce on the ground of cruel and inhuman treatment and also sought damages for the tort of intentional infliction of emotional distress based upon conduct occurring during the marriage. The district court granted the divorce and awarded Peggy $141,000 in damages for the tort. The case is now on appeal before the Court of Appeals of New Mexico.

Decision on Appeal: Reversed. The husband's insults and outbursts during the ten-year marriage were insufficiently outrageous to establish liability for intentional infliction of emotional distress.

Opinion of the Court:

Justice HARTZ delivered the opinion of the court.
. . .

Husband and wife were married on October 29, 1975. Each had been married before. They permanently separated in February 1985. Husband filed his petition for dissolution of marriage the following month. Husband, who holds a Ph.D. in chemistry, had been employed at Los Alamos National Laboratory throughout the marriage. Wife, a high school graduate with credit hours toward a baccalaureate degree in chemistry and a vocational degree as a chemical technician, had been employed at the laboratory as a secretary for seven years and as a chemical technician for about seven and one-half years. She voluntarily terminated her employment in December 1979.

The district court found that "[wife's] emotional and mental health, especially since the parties' separation, has been shown to have been characterized by acute depression and one psychotic episode." The district court's findings noted conflicting testimony concerning wife's past and current mental condition. The district court summarized one psychologist's testimony as diagnosing wife "as subject to a borderline personality disorder pre-dating the parties' marriage," and summarized another's as diagnosing her as "an intellectualizing personality in the early years of her marriage and as suffering from acute depression since approximately 1981." Apparently all the experts agreed that wife was temporarily emotionally disabled at the time of the hearing.

Finding No. 22 summarized husband's intentional misconduct: The manner in which [husband] treated [wife] during the marriage and which resulted in her disability and impairment is as follows. [Husband] on occasions throughout the marriage and continuing until the separation[:] **a.** assaulted and battered [wife], **b.** insulted [wife] in the presence of guests, friends, relatives, and foreign dignitaries, **c.** screamed at [wife] at home and in the presence of others, **d.** on one occasion locked [wife] out of the residence over night in the dead of winter while she had nothing on but a robe, **e.** made repeated demeaning remarks regarding [wife's] sexuality, **f.** continuously stated to [wife] that she was crazy, insane, and incompetent, **g.** refused to allow [wife] to pursue schooling and hobbies, **h.** refused to participate in normal marital relationship with [wife] which ultimately resulted in only having sexual relations with [wife] on four occasions in the last three years of the marriage, **i.** blamed his sexual inadequacies upon [wife]. Finding No. 26 stated: [Husband's] acts in intentionally inflicting severe emotional distress upon [wife] was so outrageous in character and so extreme in degree as to be beyond all possible bounds of decency and were atrocious and utterly intolerable. . . . With respect to each of the matters listed by the district court in Finding No. 22, the record shows:

a. There was evidence of several incidents of assault and battery. In late 1984 when wife was pushing her finger in husband's chest, he grabbed her wrist and twisted it severely. In 1981 during an argument in their home husband grabbed wife and threw her face down across the room, into a pot full of dirt. In 1978 when wife was putting groceries in the camper, husband slammed part of the camper shell down on her head and the trunk lid on her hands. In 1976 and "sometimes thereafter" during consensual sexual intercourse husband would use excessive force in attempting to stimulate wife with his hands.

b. The one incident in which husband insulted wife in the presence of others was at a friend's Christmas party. At about 11:00 p.m. wife approached husband, who was "weaving back and forth with his hands in his pockets," and suggested that they go home. Husband began screaming,

"You f _____ bitch, leave me alone." Wife excused herself and walked home alone.

c. Wife also testified that when she and husband were home alone he would go into rages and scream at her. There was no evidence of his screaming at her in the presence of others except for the incident described in "b."

d. The locking-out incident occurred after husband returned from a trip. Wife had been at a friend's home where she had eaten dinner and had some wine. During an argument that had ensued when he returned, she grabbed his shirt and popped all the buttons off. She went downstairs and stepped outside. He closed and locked the door. She went across the street to a home of neighbors, who let her in. He then threw his clothes into a camper and drove off for the night. When he returned the next morning, they made up and made love.

e. On several occasions husband told wife that "you prefer women to men." He did not use the word "lesbian." He testified that he meant only that wife preferred the company of other women to his company. She did not testify that his remarks had sexual connotations.

f. Throughout the marriage husband made remarks such as, "You're just plain sick, you're just stupid, you're just insane."

g. With respect to the finding that husband "refused to allow [wife] to pursue schooling and hobbies," husband's brief-in-chief contends that no evidence supports the finding. Wife's answer brief does not respond to the contention, so we will not consider that finding as support for the judgment.

h., i. With respect to the final two items in the finding, husband acknowledges that their sexual relationship atrophied and that wife testified that (1) it was his decision not to engage in sexual relations more frequently, and (2) he blamed her for their poor sexual relationship.

SHOULD WE RECOGNIZE THE TORT OF INTENTIONAL INFLICTION OF EMOTIONAL DISTRESS IN THE MARITAL CONTEXT?

Husband argues that as a matter of public policy one spouse should have no cause of action against the other spouse for intentional infliction of emotional distress. . . . We reject, at least for the time being, husband's suggestion. Nevertheless, the policy grounds opposing recognition of the tort in this context counsel caution in permitting lawsuits of this nature. . . .

The tort (also known as the tort of "outrage") is described in *Restatement (Second) of Torts* Section 46 (1965) (the *Restatement*): Outrageous Conduct Causing Severe Emotional Distress. (1) One who by extreme and outrageous conduct intentionally or recklessly causes severe emotional distress to another is subject to liability for such emotional distress, and if bodily harm to the other results from it, for such bodily harm. (2) Where such conduct is directed at a third person, the actor is subject to liability if he intentionally or recklessly causes severe emotional distress (a) to a member of such person's immediate family who is present at the time, whether or not such distress results in bodily harm, or (b) to any other person who is present at the time, if such distress results in bodily harm.

Wife contends that we must recognize the tort when committed by one spouse against the other because New Mexico has abandoned immunity for interspousal torts. See *Maestas v. Overton*, 87 N.M. 213, 531 P.2d 947 (1975) (wrongful death—airplane crash); *Flores v. Flores*, 84 N.M. 601, 506 P.2d 345 (Ct. App. 1973) (intentional stabbing). Yet the abolition of immunity does not mean that the existence of the marriage must be ignored in determining the scope of liability. After explaining the reasons for abolition of interspousal immunity, the commentary to *Restatement* Section 895F points out: The intimacy of the family relationship may . . . involve some relaxation in the application of the concept of reasonable care, particularly in the confines of the home. Thus, if one spouse in undressing leaves shoes out where the other stumbles over them in the dark, or if one spouse spills coffee on the other while they are both still sleepy, this may well be treated as not negligence. Id., comment h. The comment refers to Section 895G comment k, which explains that despite abolition of parental immunity: The intimacies of family life also involve intended physical contacts that would be actionable between strangers but may be commonplace and expected within the family. Family romping, even roughhouse play and momentary flares of temper not producing serious hurt, may be normal in many households, to the point that the privilege arising from consent becomes analogous.

Thus, the family relationship can be an important consideration in analyzing intrafamilial torts, both negligent and intentional. Despite the abolition of interspousal immunity, we must still evaluate wife's claims in light of the marital context in which they arose. Cf. *Restatement* § 46(2) (liability for outrage when conduct is directed at third person may depend on family relationship of plaintiff and third person).

To appreciate the importance of the marital context to the tort of outrage, one must examine the policy considerations underlying restrictions on the scope of the tort. Perhaps the most striking aspect of the tort is that liability does not flow from every act that intends to cause, and does cause, emotional distress.

One restriction on the tort is the limitation that the conduct be "extreme and outrageous." Why this limitation? Why should not anyone who "intentionally or recklessly causes severe emotional distress to another" be subject to liability?

Several explanations have been offered. As Professor Magruder stated, "[I]t would be unfortunate if the law closed all the safety valves through which irascible tempers might legally blow off steam." Magruder, *Mental and Emotional Disturbance in the Law of Torts*, 49 Harv. L. Rev. 1033, 1053 (1936). Courts must recognize that we are not yet as civilized as we might wish. Many, if not all, of us need some freedom to vent emotions in order to maintain our mental health. The law should not require a degree of civility beyond our capacity. Indeed, it has been suggested that because of pervasive incivility in our society, judicial resources would be taxed if a cause of action were permitted for every intentional infliction of emotional distress. Givelber, *The Right to Minimum Social Decency and the Limits of Evenhandedness: Intentional Infliction of Emotional Distress by Outrageous Conduct*, 82 Colum. L. Rev. 42, 57 (1982).

Intentionally making another person unhappy or upset may also serve useful purposes besides simply preserving the mental health of the perpetrator. As Professor Givelber notes, such conduct may be "justified either in pursuit of one's legal rights (e.g., debt collection) or in service of a greater social good (e.g., cross-examination at trial) or for the [recipient's] 'own good' (e.g., basic training)." Id. (footnote omitted). See *Hustler Magazine, Inc. v. Falwell*, 485 U.S. 46, 54, 108 S. Ct. 876, 881, 99 L. Ed. 2d 41 (1988) (noting virtues of some intentionally injurious political cartoons).

An additional reason for restricting the scope of the tort is that there may be a protected liberty interest in conduct that would otherwise be tortious. As Dean Prosser wrote, "There is still, in this country, such a thing as liberty to express an unflattering opinion of another, however wounding it may be to his feelings * * * *" Prosser, *Insult and Outrage*, 44 Cal. L. Rev. 40, 44 (1956). Similarly, the interest in personal autonomy apparently has led courts to reject a cause of action when a person intentionally causes emotional distress by engaging in an extramarital relationship, as in *Browning v. Browning*, 584 S.W.2d 406 (Ky. Ct. App. 1979).

Finally, the requirement that the conduct be extreme and outrageous provides reliable confirmation of two other elements of the tort—injury and causation—thereby reducing the possibility of unfounded, or even fraudulent, lawsuits. See id.; Prosser, supra, at 44–45. When conduct is extreme and outrageous, it is more likely that the victim has actually suffered severe emotional distress, and it is more likely that the severe emotional distress suffered by the victim was actually caused by the perpetrator's misconduct rather than by another source.

Considerations that justify limiting liability for intentional infliction of emotional distress to only outrageous conduct also suggest a very limited scope for the tort in the marital context.

Conduct intentionally or recklessly causing emotional distress to one's spouse is prevalent in our society. This is unfortunate but perhaps not surprising, given the length and intensity of the marital relationship. Yet even when the conduct of feuding spouses is not particularly unusual, high emotions can readily cause an offended spouse to view the other's misconduct as "extreme and outrageous." Thus, if the tort of outrage is construed loosely or broadly, claims of outrage may be tacked on in typical marital disputes, taxing judicial resources.

In addition, a spouse's most distressing conduct is likely to be privileged. Partners who are pledged to live together for a lifetime have a right to criticize each other's behavior. Cf. Cole, *Intentional Infliction of Emotional Distress Among Family Members,* 61 Den. U. L. Rev. 553, 574 (1984) ("Because the family's functioning depends on open and free communication, even negative give and take is necessary."). Even though one may question the utility of such comments, spouses are also free to express negative opinions of one another. "You look awful" or even "I don't love you" can be very wounding, but these statements cannot justify liability. See *Restatement* § 46 illustration 13 (you look "like a hippopotamus").

Not only should intramarital activity ordinarily not be the basis for tort liability, it should also be protected against disclosure in tort litigation. Although the spouse who raises a claim of outrage has no right to complain of the exposure of matters relevant to the claim, courts must be sensitive to the privacy interests of the defending spouse. Any litigation of a claim is certain to require exposure of the intimacies of married life. This feature of the tort distinguishes it from intramarital torts already recognized in New Mexico. For example, a suit by one spouse against another arising out of an automobile accident poses no such risk. Nor does one ordinarily think of exposure of an incident of battery as implicating legitimate privacy interests. In contrast, in this case the judge found that it was extreme and outrageous conduct for husband to refuse sexual relations with wife. Should we really use this tort as a basis for inquiry into a matter of such intimacy? Cf. *Thompson v. Chapman,* 93 N.M. 356, 600 P.2d 302 (Ct. App. 1979) (actions for alienation of affections engender more harm than good.). In determining the scope of the tort of outrage in the marital context, it is necessary to consider the privacy interests of the accused spouse.

Moreover, largely because so much interspousal communication is privileged (not in the evidentiary sense, but in the sense that it cannot be the basis for liability), a reliable determination of causation is difficult if not impossible when outrage is alleged in this context. The connection between the outrageousness of the conduct of one spouse and the severe emotional distress of the other will likely be obscure. Although the victim spouse may well be suffering severe emotional distress, was it caused by the outrageousness of the conduct or by the implied (and privileged) message of antipathy? What could be more devastating to one's spouse than to say, "I don't love you any more"—a statement that could not form the basis for a cause of action? Rejection alone can create severe emotional distress. Suicides by jilted lovers are legion. Every adult knows individuals who have sunk into disabling depression when a spouse seeks divorce. As a result, litigation of an interspousal claim of outrage could easily degenerate into a battle of self-proclaimed experts performing psychological autopsies to "discover" whether the cause of the emotional distress was some particular despicable conduct or simply rejection by a loved one. Of course, no such problem arises in the context of previously recognized intramarital torts. If one spouse commits battery on another or causes an accident by driving negligently, the injuries to the other spouse can readily be tied to the tortious conduct.

In summary, concerns that necessitate limiting the tort of intentional infliction of emotional distress to "extreme and outrageous" conduct—(1) preventing burdensome litigation of the commonplace, (2) protecting privileged conduct and (3) avoiding groundless allegations of causation—argue strongly in favor of extreme care in recognizing intramarital claims of outrage.

A cautious approach to the tort of intramarital outrage also finds support in the public policy of New Mexico to avoid inquiry into what went wrong in a marriage. New Mexico was the first state to provide for no-fault divorce on the ground of incompatibility. See NMSA 1978, § 40–4–1(A) (Repl. Pamp. 1989). New Mexico apportions community property without regard to fault, and grants alimony without consideration of punishment to either spouse.

In addition, although the tort has not been formally abolished, our courts have expressed dissatisfaction with the tort of alienation of affection, which has features similar to the tort of outrage in the marital context. See *Thompson v. Chapman,* 93 N.M. at 358, 600 P.2d at 304 (" '[T]he interests which the action seeks to protect are not protected by its existence, and the harm it engenders far outweighs any reason for its continuance.' ").

Consequently, in determining when the tort of outrage should be recognized in the marital setting, the threshold of outrageousness should be set high enough—or the circumstances in which the tort is recognized should be described precisely enough, e.g., child snatching,—that the social good from recognizing the tort will not be outweighed by unseemly and invasive litigation of meritless claims.

Some jurisdictions have apparently set the threshold of outrageousness so high in the marital context as to bar all suits. See *Whittington v. Whittington,* 766 S.W.2d 73 (Ky. Ct. App. 1989) (no tort of outrage for adultery and fraud by spouse); *Pickering v. Pickering,* 434 N.W.2d 758 (S.D. 1989) (barring tort of intentional infliction of emotional distress if predicated on conduct which leads to dissolution of marriage). Cf. *Harris v. McDavid,* 553 So.2d 567 (Ala. 1989) (no tort of outrage in termination of affair of unmarried couple); *Chiles v. Chiles,* 779 S.W.2d 127 (Tex. Ct. App. 1989) (tort of intentional infliction of emotional distress not recognized in divorce proceeding). But see *Simmons v. Simmons,* 773 P.2d 602 (Colo. Ct. App. 1988) (marriage does not preclude wife's action for damages for outrage). . . .

Thus far, however, New Mexico has not witnessed an onslaught of claims of outrage by one spouse against the other. There is no need at this time to adopt husband's recommendation that all such claims be barred.

We now move to the specifics of the case before us. The merits of wife's claim can be disposed of summarily. Husband's insults and outbursts fail to meet the legal standard of outrageousness. See, e.g., *Sanders v. Lutz,* 109 N.M. 193, 196, 784 P.2d 12, 15 (1989) (to recover, must show conduct was " 'beyond all possible bounds of decency * * * and utterly intolerable' "). He was privileged to refrain from intercourse. There was no evidence that the other conduct caused severe emotional distress, as opposed to transient pain or discomfort. See *Restatement* § 46 emotional distress.)

Indeed, this case illustrates the risk of opening the door too wide to claims of this nature. Despite the claim's lack of merit, husband was subjected to a six-day trial, to say nothing of discovery and other preparation, surveying the rights and wrongs of a ten-year marriage. Motions for summary judgment should be viewed sympathetically in similar cases. If the potential harms from this kind of litigation are too frequently realized, it may be necessary to reconsider husband's suggestion that the tort of outrage be denied in the interspousal context.

We reverse the decision in favor of wife on her claim of intentional infliction of emotional distress.

ASSIGNMENT 21.4

If you were the judge, how would you have decided *Hakkila v. Hakkila?* In the second to last paragraph of the opinion, the court suggests that the *husband* was a victim. Do you think he was?

☐ Notes on Intrafamily Crimes and Contracts

1. The state can always *criminally* prosecute one family member for crimes committed against another family member's person or property. There is no intrafamily criminal immunity.

2. To a large extent, it is possible for family members to enter into contracts with each other, e.g., a husband and wife can enter a business partnership with each other, or a father who owns a department store can hire his daughter as president. Since such contracts are legal and enforceable, it follows that the parties can bring *breach-of-contract* actions against each other for alleged violations of these contracts. There is no intrafamily breach-of-contract immunity. Not all contracts among family members, however, are legal. In general, a party cannot enter into a contract to do what the law already requires that party to do. When two parties are happily married, for example, they cannot enter a contract to support each other. They already have this obligation under the law of marriage. Such a contract is said to be "without consideration," and hence unenforceable. On the other hand, business contracts among family members are treated differently. They are almost always enforceable in intrafamily contract actions.

a. Can one spouse rape another in your state? (See also Assignment 16.8 in chapter 16.)

b. Can parents be prosecuted in your state for murder, manslaughter, or some other charge for the death of their child because they refuse to allow medical treatment on the basis of a religious belief that such treatment is against the will of God?

(See General Instructions for the State-Code Assignment and the General Instructions for the Court-Opinion Assignment in chapter 1.)

▆▆▆▆ WRONGFUL LIFE, WRONGFUL BIRTH, WRONGFUL PREGNANCY

Doctors have been sued in three different kinds of cases for causing the birth of an unwanted child due to negligence, e.g., the doctor made a careless mistake performing a sterilization operation or an abortion.

☐ **Wrongful Life** An action by or on behalf of an unwanted deformed or impaired child for its own damages.

☐ **Wrongful Birth** An action by parents of an unwanted deformed or impaired child for their own damages.

☐ **Wrongful Pregnancy** An action by parents of a healthy child they did not want.

Most states deny a child the right to bring a **wrongful life** case for the anguish of being born deformed. A major reason for this decision is the enormous difficulty of calculating the damages that should be awarded in such a case. According to one court, "The infant plaintiff would have us measure the difference between his life with defects against the utter void of nonexistence, but it is impossible to make such a determination." *Gleitman v. Cosgrove*, 49 N.J. 22, 25, 227 A.2d 689, 692 (1967). Another court was worried that allowing this infant to sue might encourage other infants to sue for being "born into the world under conditions they might regard as adverse. One might seek damages for inheriting unfortunate family conditions; one for being born into a large and destitute family, another because a parent has an unsavory reputation." *Zepeda v. Zepeda*, 190 N.E.2d 849, 858 (Ill. App. 1963).

Wrongful **birth** cases by parents, on the other hand, have been more successful.

Example A woman contracts German measles early in her pregnancy. Her doctor negligently advises her that the disease will not affect the health of the child. In fact, the child is born with severe defects caused by the disease. If she had known the risks, the woman would have aborted the pregnancy.

States disagree on whether parents can bring a wrongful birth action in such a case. Those that allow it are not reluctant to try to assess the financial and emotional damages of the parents in giving birth to the deformed or impaired child. They can recover their monetary losses attributed to the child's condition and damages for emotional distress.

When the unwanted child is born healthy, a **wrongful pregnancy** action (also called a **wrongful conception** action) by the parents is often allowed. The damages, however, are often limited to the costs of prenatal care and delivery; they rarely extend to the costs of raising the healthy child. The healthy child is usually not allowed to bring the same kind of action in his or her own right.

a. A pregnant woman in your state has a genetic disease that could lead to the birth of a deformed child. Her doctor negligently fails to diagnose this disease and inform the woman. The child is born deformed with this disease. If she had known of the disease, she would have aborted the pregnancy. Who can bring an action in your state against the doctor for negligence and for what damages? (See General Instructions for the Court-Opinion Assignment in chapter 1.)

b. A pharmacist in your state sells an unmarried couple birth control pills that are negligently defective. A healthy, illegitimate child is born to this couple. Who can bring an action in your state against the pharmacist for negligence and for what damages? (See General Instructions for the Court-Opinion Assignment in chapter 1.)

■■■■ DERIVATIVE ACTIONS

Actions are **derivative** if they are dependent on an underlying wrongful act to someone else. Otherwise, they are nonderivative. The two main derivative actions are loss of consortium and loss of services.

LOSS OF CONSORTIUM

Consortium is the companionship, love, affection, sexual relationship, and services (e.g., cooking, making repairs around the house) that one spouse provides another. There can be a recovery for a wrongful injury to consortium. At one time, only the husband could recover for such a **loss of consortium.** In every state, this view has been changed by statute or has been ruled unconstitutional. Either spouse can now recover for loss of consortium.

The loss-of-consortium action works as follows:

☐ Rich and Ann are married.

☐ Paul, a stranger, injures Ann by negligently hitting her with his car (or by one of the intentional torts such as battery).

☐ Ann sues Paul for negligence. She receives damages to cover her medical bills, lost wages, if any, pain and suffering, punitive damages, if any.

☐ Rich then brings a *separate* suit against Paul for loss of his wife's consortium. He receives damages to compensate him for loss or impairment he can prove to the companionship he had with Ann before the accident—to the love, affection, sexual intercourse, and services that she gave him as his wife before the accident.

In his action against Paul, Rich cannot recover for injuries sustained by Ann. Ann must recover for such injuries in her own action against Paul. Paul's liability to Rich is limited to the specific injuries sustained by Rich—loss or impairment of his wife's consortium. If Ann loses her suit against Paul, e.g., because she was contributorily negligent, Rich will *not* be able to bring his consortium suit. To recover for loss of consortium, there must be an underlying successfully litigated tort.

Parties do not have to be married for consortium in one form or another to exist between them. For example:

☐ Jim and Rachel are engaged to be married. The defendant negligently injures Rachel before the wedding. Can Jim sue the defendant for loss of consortium?

☐ Barbara and Paul are living together; they are not married. The defendant negligently injures Paul. Can Barbara sue the defendant for loss of consortium?

□ Gabe is the son of Bill. The defendant negligently injures Bill. Can Gabe sue the defendant for loss of parental society (*partial consortium*, sometimes called **parental consortium**)?

In the vast majority of states, the answer is *no* to each of these questions. A marriage license is a precondition to a suit for loss of consortium. This conclusion has been criticized. Since the essence of consortium is the emotional commitment and devotion between two people and not the formality of the relationship, a serious interference with this commitment and devotion should be the basis of recovery, according to the critics. The loss suffered by Jim, Barbara, and Gabe is just as real as the loss suffered by a person whose spouse has been injured. Recovery is denied in most states, though.

LOSS OF SERVICES

Suppose that it is the unemancipated child who is injured by the defendant. A parent has a right to services and earnings from the child. In most states, the parent can recover separate damages from the defendant for interference with this right, i.e., for **loss of services.** If, for example, a minor child is crippled by a battery committed by the defendant, the child will be able to recover for the injuries sustained as a result of the battery. The parent can receive *separate* damages due to the fact that the child is no longer able to provide the same services to the home that were possible prior to the accident, e.g., cutting the grass and running errands.

The spouse's claim for damages for loss of consortium rights in the other spouse is *derivative* in that it depends upon the existence of an underlying tort committed by the defendant. The same is true of the parent's claim for damages for loss of services of the child. If the underlying injury was not wrongful or tortious, the parent cannot recover.

---

a. Describe the loss of consortium action that can be brought in your state by a person whose spouse has been negligently injured.

b. Under what circumstances, if any, can a loss of consortium action be brought in your state by an unmarried person whose lover was negligently injured? Assume that they lived together and held themselves out as husband and wife for twenty years, had children together, but never married.

c. Can a child sue a third party for loss of parental consortium in your state?

d. Can a parent bring an action for loss of child services and earnings in your state?

(See General Instructions for the State-Code Assignment and General Instructions for the Court-Opinion Assignment in chapter 1.)

ASSIGNMENT 21.7

■■■■ NONDERIVATIVE ACTIONS

In many states, a series of nonderivative actions can be brought by one family member because of what the defendant did with or to another family member. These actions consist of the following torts:

□ Alienation of affections

□ Criminal conversation

□ Enticement of spouse

□ Abduction or enticement of a child

□ Seduction

To establish any of these causes of action, there is no need to prove an underlying tort; they are torts in their own right. They are nonderivative.

A number of states have passed statutes (sometimes called **heart-balm statutes**) that have abolished some or all of the above tort actions. The actions are not looked upon with favor and are seldom used today even where they have not been abolished.

ALIENATION OF AFFECTIONS

Elements of Alienation of Affections

1. Defendant (e.g., a lover, an in-law) intended to diminish the marital relationship between the plaintiff and the latter's spouse.

2. Affirmative conduct of the defendant in carrying out this intent.

3. Affections between plaintiff and spouse were in fact alienated.

4. Defendant caused the alienation ("but for" the defendant, the alienation would not have occurred, or defendant was a substantial factor in producing the alienation).

CRIMINAL CONVERSATION

Element of Criminal Conversation

Defendant had sex with the plaintiff's spouse (adultery).

ENTICEMENT OF SPOUSE

Elements of Enticement of Spouse

1. Defendant intended to diminish the marital relationship between the plaintiff and the latter's spouse.

2. Affirmative conduct by defendant:
   a. to entice or encourage the spouse to leave the plaintiff's home, *or*
   b. to harbor the spouse and encourage the latter to stay away from the plaintiff's home

3. Plaintiff's spouse left home.

4. Defendant caused the plaintiff to leave home or to stay away ("but for" what defendant did, the plaintiff would not have left or stayed away, or the defendant was a substantial factor in the spouse's leaving or staying away).

ABDUCTION OR ENTICEMENT OF A CHILD

Elements of Abduction or Enticement of Child

1. Defendant intended to interfere with the parent's custody of the child.

2. Affirmative conduct by the defendant:
   a. to abduct or force the child from the parent's custody, *or*
   b. to entice or encourage the child to leave the parent, *or*
   c. to harbor the child and encourage the latter to stay away from the parent's custody.

3. The child left the custody of the parent.

4. Defendant caused the child to leave or to stay away ("but for" what the defendant did, the child would not have left or stayed away, or the defendant was a substantial factor in the child's leaving or staying away).

SEDUCTION

Element of Seduction

The defendant has sex with the plaintiff's minor daughter by force or with the consent of the daughter.

ASSIGNMENT 21.8

Can any of the above five causes of actions be brought in your state? Check your state code and opinions written by courts in your state. If you find older cases that have permitted any of these actions, shepardize these cases to be sure that they still represent good law in your state. (See General Instructions for the State-Code Assignment and General Instructions for the Court-Opinion Assignment in chapter 1.)

▓▓▓ VICARIOUS LIABILITY OF FAMILY MEMBERS

Vicarious liability means that one person is liable solely because of what someone else does. For example, if a trucker negligently hits a pedestrian while making a delivery, the trucker's boss, the *employer*, is liable. The liability is vicarious since it is based on what someone else—the employee—has done.

The person injured could also sue the employee who is directly responsible for the injury. We are all personally liable for our own torts even if someone else is vicariously liable. Often, however, the one directly responsible has minimal resources out of which to satisfy a judgment. The person who is vicariously liable is usually the **deep pocket** who does have such resources.

In general, vicarious liability cannot exist among family members. While there are exceptions, the basic principle is that one family member is not liable for the torts of another family member. Thus, a spouse is not liable for the torts committed by the other spouse. Children are not liable for the torts of their parents, and vice versa. For example:

Mary is the ten-year-old daughter of Diane. Mary throws a brick through the window of Jim's hardware store.

Jim must sue *Mary* for the damage done to the store. Her mother is *not* vicariously liable for the tort of her daughter.

The first exception to this rule is fairly limited. A number of states have passed statutes that make parents vicariously liable for the torts of their children, but only up to a relatively modest amount, e.g., $1,000.

In the above example involving Diane and her daughter, note that there was no indication that Diane did anything wrong or improper herself. Suppose, however, that Diane knew that her daughter, Mary, had a habit of throwing bricks into windows. Or assume that Diane was with Mary when she threw the brick at Jim's window. If Diane failed to use reasonable care to control Mary in these circumstances, Diane *would* be liable to Jim. But this would not be a case of vicarious liability. When parents act unreasonably in failing to use available opportunities to control their children, the parents are *independently* liable for **negligence** in a suit brought by the person injured by the child. Since, however, parents are rarely with their children when the latter act mischievously, and rarely know when their children are about to commit specific acts of mischief, it is usually very difficult to prove that the parents negligently failed to control and supervise their children.

Vicarious Liability
Being liable because of what someone else has done. Standing in the place of someone else who is the one who actually committed the wrong.

Deep Pocket The person or organization that probably has sufficient resources to pay damages if a judgment is awarded by the court.

Negligence
Unreasonable conduct that causes injury or damage to someone to whom you owe a duty of reasonable care.

Jim is the thirteen-year-old son of Harry. Jim takes Harry's car on a joy ride and negligently injures George. Whom can George sue? (See General Instructions for the State-Code Assignment and General Instructions for the Court-Opinion Assignment in chapter 1.)

The second exception to the rule of no intrafamily vicarious liability is the **family-purpose doctrine,** according to which a defendant will be liable for torts committed by a driver of the defendant's car who is a member of the defendant's family. Not all states have the doctrine, and those that have it do not all agree on its elements. Generally, the elements of the doctrine are as follows:

Elements of Family-Purpose Doctrine

1. Defendant must own the car, or have an ownership interest in it (e.g., co-owner), or control the use of the car.

2. Defendant must make the car available for family use rather than for the defendant's business (in some states, the defendant must make it available for general family use rather than for a particular occasion only).

3. The driver must be a member of the defendant's immediate household.

4. The driver must be using the car for a family purpose at the time of the accident.

5. The driver must have had the defendant's express or implied consent to be using the car at the time of the accident.

The defendant does not have to be the traditional head of the household and does not have to be in the car at the time of the accident. Again, individual states, by case law or by statute, may impose different elements to the doctrine or may reject it entirely.

a. Is there a family-purpose doctrine in your state? If so, what are its components or elements? (See General Instructions for the State-Code Assignment and General Instructions for the Court-Opinion Assignment in chapter 1.)

b. Fred has just bought a used car, but it will not be ready for a week. During the week he is waiting, he rents a car, paying a per-mile charge on it. He tells his family that the car is to be used only to drive to work. One day while the car is at home and Fred is at the supermarket, his child becomes sick. Fred's mother, who is staying with Fred until an opening comes up in a local nursing home, drives the child to the hospital. On the way, she has an accident, injuring the plaintiff. The plaintiff sues Fred for negligence. Apply the five elements of the family-purpose doctrine to determine whether it would apply. (See General Instructions for the Legal-Analysis Assignment in chapter 1.) How would this case be handled in your state? (Refer to your answer to part [a] above.)

SUMMARY

There is an immunity for some intrafamily torts, which means that the injured party cannot sue. Courts traditionally have been reluctant to allow suits for intrafamily torts since the courtroom is hardly the best place to resolve family conflicts. But immunity is not the rule in every case. It depends on who the parties are and on what tort has been committed.

Intrafamily torts that damage property (e.g., trespass) are treated differently from torts that in-

jure the person (e.g., battery). Generally, spouses can sue each other for negligent or intentional damage to property. The same is true for such damage caused by the parent to a child's property. There is no immunity for property torts. For torts against the person, in many states, one spouse cannot sue another, and a child cannot sue a parent; immunity does apply to these torts in such states. There are some exceptions to these rules. For example, many states grant immunity only for negligent injury to the person; thus, any family member can sue another for intentional injury to the person in such states.

If a doctor makes a negligent mistake that results in the birth of a deformed child when the parents had tried to avoid that birth by abortion or sterilization, the parents can bring a wrongful-birth action. If the child is born healthy, the parents may be able to bring an action for wrongful pregnancy or for wrongful conception, but the damages are limited. The courts, however, usually do not allow the child to bring his or own separate wrongful-life action.

The two main derivative actions are loss of consortium (covering injury to the companionship, love, affection, sexual relationship, and services that one spouse provides another) and loss of services (covering an interference with the right of parents to the services of their unemancipated child). The main nonderivative actions are alienation of affections, criminal conversation, enticement of a spouse, abduction or enticement of a child, and seduction.

Vicarious liability exists when one person is liable for someone else's tort. Vicarious liability cannot exist among family members, with two major exceptions. First, some states have statutes that impose limited vicarious liability on parents for the torts committed by their children. Second, under the family-purpose doctrine, the owner of a car can be liable for a tort committed by a family member driving the car for a "family purpose."

■■■■■ KEY CHAPTER TERMINOLOGY

Tort	Immunity	Loss of Services
Trespass	Intrafamily Torts	Heart-Balm Statute
Conversion	Emancipated	Alienation of Affections
Nuisance	Liability Insurance	Criminal Conversation
Assault	Wrongful Life	Enticement of Spouse
False Imprisonment	Wrongful Birth	Abduction
Battery	Wrongful Pregnancy	Seduction
Malicious Prosecution	Wrongful Conception	Vicarious Liability
Slander	Derivative	Deep Pocket
Libel	Loss of Consortium	Family-Purpose Doctrine
Negligence	Parental Consortium	

FAMILY LAW
PARALEGAL JOB
DESCRIPTIONS

██████ LEGAL ASSISTANT JOB DESCRIPTION
FAMILY LAW

SOURCE: *Attorneys' Guide to Practicing with Legal Assistants* (State Bar of Texas, 1986).

GENERAL RESPONSIBILITIES

Assist attorney through all phases of divorce and custody proceedings, including drafting pleadings, investigating financial affairs of the parties, assisting in discovery and at trial, and maintaining close relationship with client, all as illustrated by the following examples.

All job functions must be performed under the *direct supervision of a lawyer*. The words "draft," "drafting," and "prepare" mean a preliminary writing to be approved by the attorney.

SPECIFIC DUTIES

Initial Client Interview (After attorney has talked with client)

1. Establish rapport with client and gather facts pertaining to preparation of initial pleadings.

2. Have client sign ancillary forms necessary for initial discovery, such as authorizations for medical records, income tax returns, employment records, etc.

3. Instruct client how to prepare the financial information statement and other forms to aid in discovery of the parties' assets and liabilities.

4. Prepare memorandum to the file.

Initial Pleadings

1. Draft pleadings.

2. After attorney approval, arrange for client's signature if applicable, see that pleadings are filed, get hearing set if necessary, and arrange for service if necessary.

3. Put hearing date on calendar and notify client of the date.

Preparation for Temporary Hearing and Post-Hearing Procedure

1. Arrange for client to meet with attorney for briefing as to what to expect at the hearing and to discuss the client's financial information statement.

2. Draft temporary orders for attorney approval.

3. Transmit temporary orders to opposing counsel for approval, and upon receipt of executed orders, return to attorney for review and filing.

4. Keep in close contact with client to ensure compliance with temporary orders.

5. Set up child support payment account for client if he/she receives an award of child support.

Discovery

1. Monitor deadlines set by the court, such as filing of sworn inventory and appraisement, production of tax returns and other documents, appraisals, etc.

2. Work with client in obtaining all information necessary to prepare an inventory and appraisement, submit to attorney for approval, obtain client's signature, file with the court, and submit copy to opposing counsel.

3. Review inventory received from opposing counsel, compare with client's inventory, and prepare a memorandum for attorney evaluating both.

4. If separate property is involved, work with client on tracing.

5. Draft written interrogatories and requests for admissions.

6. Assist client in answering interrogatories and requests for admissions; then submit proposed answers to attorney.

7. Schedule, attend with attorney, and index depositions.

8. Act as intermediary between the attorney and accountants, appraisers, private investigators, and other agents.

Trial and Post-Trial

1. Prepare trial notebook.

2. Organize and index necessary exhibits.

3. Prepare, file, and follow up on service of subpoenas.

4. Schedule and notify witnesses as instructed by attorney.

5. Attend trial with attorney.

6. Draft decree.

7. Follow up on entry of decree or order, and draft all necessary closing documents, such as deeds, title transfers, stock transfers, etc.

■■■■■ FAMILY LAW LEGAL ASSISTANT

SOURCE: Colorado Bar Association Legal Assistant Committee.[1]

Family law legal assistants may perform all or part of the following tasks:

A. Screen Prospective Clients by Telephone Interviews

B. Commencement of Action

1. Initial interview with client to obtain information for pleadings.

2. Prepare initial pleadings, including petition, summons and waiver of service, affidavit as to children, and response.

---

1. This list of tasks has been approved by the Legal Assistant Committee of the Colorado Bar, not by the Board of Governors of the Bar.

3. Draft correspondence with clients, courts, and other attorneys.

4. Arrange for service of process.

C. *Temporary Orders*

1. Prepare motions for temporary orders or temporary injunctions.

2. Notice and set hearings.

3. Assist in settlement negotiations.

4. Draft stipulations for temporary orders after negotiations.

D. *Financial Affidavits*

1. Work with clients in gathering and compiling financial information.

2. Analyze income and expense information provided by client.

3. Work with accountants, financial advisers, brokers, and other financial experts retained by client.

4. Retain appraisers for real estate, business and personal property.

5. Prepare financial affidavits.

E. *Discovery*

1. Prepare discovery requests

2. Assist clients in gathering documents and data to respond to discovery requests.

3. Prepare responses to discovery requests.

4. Organize, index, and summarize discovered materials.

F. *Settlement Negotiations*

1. Assist attorney in analysis of proposed settlements.

2. Research legal questions and assist in drafting briefs and memoranda.

3. Assist in drafting separation agreements.

G. *Hearings*

1. Notice and set final orders hearing.

2. Research legal questions and assist in drafting briefs and memoranda.

3. Assist in preparation of trial exhibits and trial notebook.

4. Arrange for expert witnesses and assist in preparing witnesses and clients for trial.

5. Attend hearings.

6. Prepare decree.

H. *Post Decree*

1. Prepare documents for transfers of assets.

2. Arrange for filing and recording of transfer documents.

3. Review bills for tax-deductible fees and prepare opinion letters to client.

4. Draft pleadings for withdrawal from case.

I. *Special Projects*

1. Develop forms for gathering information from client.

2. Maintain files on the following: separation-agreement provisions, current case law, resource materials for clients, and experts in various fields (e.g., custody, evaluation, business appraisals, etc.).

FAMILY LAW FOR PARALEGALS

Y. Spiegel, *Family Law for Paralegals* 6 THE JOURNAL 7 (Sacramento Association of Legal Assistants, June 1986).

The role of a legal assistant in a family law practice is exciting and varied. Whereas all areas of law can be interesting, the opportunities for client contact, full involvement and case responsibility in family law make it a truly satisfying area of specialty. Family law affords tremendous scope for helping people in a very basic change in their lives. With the divorce rate at roughly 50 percent, there are few families who haven't been touched in some way by the problems and trauma of a court action. Our job as legal assistants can be to smooth the way through this difficult time for the client, making the experience kinder, easier to understand, more efficient, and hopefully, less expensive. Divorce is not the only area covered in family law. Adoption, grandparent visitation issues, and emancipation of minors also come under this topic. . . .

The teamwork between attorney and legal assistant is crucial to the success of a paralegal working in the family law area. Your skills and interests, as well as the degree of trust and communication between you and your boss will determine the tasks that you will be assigned. If there is good communication and rapport between you as team members, the clients will come to rely on both of you in handling the case, and your participation will be invaluable.

In my office the attorney conducts the initial interview with the client. This is primarily done to establish the attorney/client bond, which is crucial to the successful processing of the case. Any general questions which the client has about the dissolution process, as well as discussing strategy, fees and expectations are all done at this stage. If there is an immediate need for temporary orders, such as restraining orders or temporary custody or support, the attorney will begin the information gathering process by taking detailed notes of the client's situation. The initial interview is usually concluded by inviting me into the office to be introduced as the "paralegal who will be assisting me with your case." This gives me the authority to contact the client on behalf of the attorney to gather more detailed information, and to answer the client's questions as to general procedure. I find that the clients are, for the most part, pleased to know that a paralegal will be working on their case. I am usually more accessible than the attorney to answer their questions, or to convey information, and they are billed at a lower rate for my time.

It is usually my responsibility to draft the opening documents. These include the summons, petition, and the income and expense forms. With the recent adoption of the Agnos income and expense forms, this job has become quite critical. The Agnos forms are complicated and in some instances intimidating, and clients often need a lot of assistance in filling them out. I find that often our women clients don't understand that the forms are meant to demonstrate "need" for support. They spend all their time trying to make their income on the form come out even with their expenses, and that is usually impossible. It is often my job to tell them that if they don't show the court any evidence of the need for support, the judge won't order any. I am also responsible for drafting mediation counseling stipulations, property declarations and even orders to show cause and motions for pendente lite relief. I rely on notes from the attorney, as well as my own interviews with the client to obtain facts necessary to create the pleadings. The attorney then reviews the documents for accuracy and obtains the signature of the client. When the documents are filed, I see that the papers are served on the client's spouse and keep the client informed of subsequent developments.

Discovery plays an important role in family law. Over the years my office has developed a set of family law interrogatories on our word processor, which can be modified and used to flush out the details of the community, quasi-community, and separate property. Any real property or pension plans must be appraised for their value as community property, and this is also the responsibility of the legal assistant. Building a strong working relationship with the various legal support personnel, such as appraisers, actuaries, deposition reporters, mediation and rehabilitation counselors, process servers, and photocopy services is essential. These people trust and respect my role as professional and as a representative of my office, and often go out of their way to assist us in emergencies because of the relationship which we have built over the years.

Preparing and arranging the service of deposition notices is another important part of family law practice which falls within the scope of the paralegal's responsibility. After the transcript of the deposition has come back from the reporter, it is my job to index and summarize it for the attorney's use in trial preparation. Comparing the bank account dates, numbers, balances and other descriptions of property with the opposing party's previous descriptions is an important part of establishing the full extent of community or separate property interest and achieving an equal division.

Child custody and visitation is often the most traumatic aspect of a family law case. Parents who are separating are often terrified of what the effect will be on their children, and are frequently afraid that dividing their households will result in loss of closeness and opportunities for quality parenting time. Fortunately, California courts lean heavily in favor of joint custody whenever feasible. Mediation counseling programs have been set up in Sacramento, Yolo, and Solano counties and elsewhere to assist parents in working out arrangements for custody and visitation with the assistance of trained facilitators. The agreements they work out are then presented as stipulations to the court. Wherever possible, a judge will not hear a motion for custody or visitation until the parties have been to mediation. This is practical and beneficial, since the mediation session is often the first time that the parties have been able to sit down and actually *listen* to each other since their problems began. It also provides a beginning for the future cooperation that they will have to achieve to be separated parents with children in common. It is my job as legal assistant to prepare the mediation counseling stipulation, to see that it is signed by all parties and attorneys, to make sure that it is filed with the court, and then arrange contact between the mediator and the parties.

If the parties are unable to settle their disputes (and we try very hard to settle every family law case without the necessity of a trial) then I draft a trial brief setting out the facts, the history of the case, the contested and uncontested issues, our proposal for an equal division of property, and a memorandum setting forth the applicable law. Updated income and expense and property declarations must be filed along with the trial brief, and any appraisals or actuarial analyses of pension funds must also be updated as of the time of trial.

Before the day of the trial, I contact the client to make sure that he or she is psychologically prepared to go, and make arrangements with the client for last minute prepping by the attorney. I organize the file to make all exhibits and necessary documents fingertip-accessible to the attorney trying the case, and I subpoena any witnesses who may be needed. It is very hard to get a firm court date because of case congestion, and the client must be assisted in dealing with the resulting anxiety and inconvenience. If the case does go to trial, I often go along to help my boss keep organized with respect to the documents, take notes as to areas of inquiry to be explored, run emergency errands, and keep the witnesses organized.

When the judgment is prepared, either by stipulation in the form of a marital settlement agreement, or by reducing a decision by the trial court to judgment form, I often draft the first document for review by the attorney and client. Keeping track of dates, such as deadlines for appeal, and eligibility for final judgment is also my responsibility. Preparing transfer deeds and noticing pension plans of the divorced spouse's interest are some of the wrap-up details.

As the family law case progresses, a paralegal becomes intimately familiar with the client's life and affairs. You are in a unique position to offer comfort and guidance to people in deep transition. While the legal professional's role should never be confused with that of a therapist or psychiatrist, your positive attitude and sensitivity to the client's situation can make a big difference in how they experience the adjustment to what amounts to an entirely new life. Over the past six years in a practice which is predominantly devoted to family law, I have watched hundreds of clients pass through this difficult change in their lives, heal their wounds, and create more successful and satisfying lifestyles. This is a very rewarding part of my job.

While I have had to skip over many areas of a legal assistant's responsibilities in the area of family law, I have tried to give you a sense of some of the duties that a paralegal may have. Your particular tasks will be assigned by the attorney. Short of giving the client legal advice and appearing as their representative in court, there is tremendous scope for the utilization of paralegals in a family law practice.

UNIFORM CHILD CUSTODY JURISDICTION ACT

§ 1. Purposes of Act; Construction of Provisions.—

(a) The general purposes of this Act are to:

(1) avoid jurisdictional competition and conflict with courts of other states in matters of child custody which have in the past resulted in the shifting of children from state to state with harmful effects on their well-being;

(2) promote cooperation with the courts of other states to the end that a custody decree is rendered in that state which can best decide the case in the interest of the child;

(3) assure that litigation concerning the custody of a child take place ordinarily in the state with which the child and his family have the closest connection and where significant evidence concerning his care, protection, training, and personal relationships is most readily available, and that courts of this state decline the exercise of jurisdiction when the child and his family have a closer connection with another state;

(4) discourage continuing controversies over child custody in the interest of greater stability of home environment and of secure family relationships for the child;

(5) deter abductions and other unilateral removals of children undertaken to obtain custody awards;

(6) avoid re-litigation of custody decisions of other states in this state insofar as feasible;

(7) facilitate the enforcement of custody decrees of other states;

(8) promote and expand the exchange of information and other forms of mutual assistance between the courts of this state and those of other states concerned with the same child; and

(9) make uniform the law of those states which enact it.

(b) This Act shall be construed to promote the general purposes stated in this section.

§ 2. Definitions—As used in this Act:

(1) "contestant" means a person, including a parent, who claims a right to custody or visitation rights with respect to a child;

(2) "custody determination" means a court decision and court orders and instructions providing for the custody of a child, including visitation rights; it does not include a decision relating to child support or any other monetary obligation of any person;

(3) "custody proceeding" includes proceedings in which a custody determination is one of several issues, such as an action for divorce or separation, and includes child neglect and dependency proceedings;

(4) "decree" or "custody decree" means a custody determination contained in a judicial decree or order made in a custody proceeding, and includes an initial decree and a modification decree;

(5) "home state" means the state in which the child immediately preceding the time involved lived with his parents, a parent, or a person acting as parent, for at least 6 consecutive months, and in the case of a child less than 6 months old the state in which the child lived from birth with any of the persons mentioned. Periods of temporary absence of any of the named persons are counted as part of the 6-month or other period;

(6) "initial decree" means the first custody decree concerning a particular child;

(7) "modification decree" means a custody decree which modifies or replaces a prior decree, whether made by the court which rendered the prior decree or by another court.

(8) "physical custody" means actual possession and control of a child;

(9) "person acting as parent" means a person, other than a parent, who has physical custody of a child and who has either been awarded custody by a court or claims a right to custody; and

(10) "state" means any state, territory, or possession of the United States, the Commonwealth of Puerto Rico, and the District of Columbia.

§ 3. Jurisdiction.—

(a) A court of this State which is competent to decide child custody matters has jurisdiction to make a child custody determination by initial or modification decree if:

(1) this State (i) is the home state of the child at

515

the time of commencement of the proceeding, or (ii) had been the child's home state within 6 months before commencement of the proceeding and the child is absent from this State because of his removal or retention by a person claiming his custody or for other reasons, and a parent or person acting as parent continues to live in this State; or

(2) it is in the best interest of the child that a court of this State assume jurisdiction because (i) the child and his parents, or the child and at least one contestant, have a significant connection with this State, and (ii) there is available in this State substantial evidence concerning the child's present or future care, protection, training, and personal relationships; or

(3) the child is physically present in this State and (i) the child has been abandoned or (ii) it is necessary in an emergency to protect the child because he has been subjected to or threatened with mistreatment or abuse or is otherwise neglected [or dependent] or

(4)(i) it appears that no other state would have jurisdiction under prerequisites substantially in accordance with paragraphs (1), (2), or (3), or another state has declined to exercise jurisdiction on the ground that this State is the more appropriate forum to determine the custody of the child, and (ii) it is in the best interest of the child that this court assume jurisdiction.

(b) Except under paragraphs (3) and (4) of subsection (a), physical presence in this State of the child, or of the child and one of the contestants, is not alone sufficient to confer jurisdiction on a court of this State to make a child custody determination.

(c) Physical presence of the child, while desirable, is not a prerequisite for jurisdiction to determine his custody.

§ 4. Notice and Opportunity to Be Heard.—Before making a decree under this Act, reasonable notice and opportunity to be heard shall be given to the contestants, any parent whose parental rights have not been previously terminated, and any person who has physical custody of the child. If any of these persons is outside this State, notice and opportunity to be heard shall be given pursuant to Section 5.

§ 5. Notice to Persons Outside this State; Submission to Jurisdiction.—

(a) Notice required for the exercise of jurisdiction over a person outside this State shall be given in a manner reasonably calculated to give actual notice, and may be:

(1) by personal delivery outside this State in the manner prescribed for service of process within this State;

(2) in the manner prescribed by the law of the place in which the service is made for service of process in that place in an action in any of its courts of general jurisdiction;

(3) by any form of mail addressed to the person to be served and requesting a receipt; or

(4) as directed by the court [including publication, if other means of notification are ineffective].

(b) Notice under this section shall be served, mailed, or delivered, [or last published] at least [10, 20] days before any hearing in this State.

(c) Proof of service outside this State may be made by affidavit of the individual who made the service, or in the manner prescribed by the law of this State, the order pursuant to which the service is made, or the law of the place in which the service is made. If service is made by mail, proof may be a receipt signed by the addressee or other evidence of delivery to the addressee.

(d) Notice is not required if a person submits to the jurisdiction of the court.

§ 6. Simultaneous Proceedings in Other States.—

(a) A court of this State shall not exercise its jurisdiction under this Act if at the time of filing the petition a proceeding concerning the custody of the child was pending in a court of another state exercising jurisdiction substantially in conformity with this Act, unless the proceeding is stayed by the court of the other state because this State is a more appropriate forum or for other reasons.

(b) Before hearing the petition in a custody proceeding the court shall examine the pleadings and other information supplied by the parties under section 9 and shall consult the child custody registry established under section 16 concerning the pendency of proceedings with respect to the child in other states. If the court has reason to believe that proceedings may be pending in another state it shall direct an inquiry to the state court administrator or other appropriate official of the other state.

(c) If the court is informed during the course of the proceeding that a proceeding concerning the custody of the child was pending in another state before the court assumed jurisdiction it shall stay the proceeding and communicate with the court in which the other proceeding is pending to the end that the issue may be litigated in the more appropriate forum and that information be exchanged in accordance with sections 19 through 22. If a court of this State has made a custody decree before being informed of a pending proceeding in a court of another state it shall immediately inform that court of the fact. If the court is informed that a proceeding was commenced in another state after it assumed jurisdiction it shall likewise inform the other court to the end that the issues may be litigated in the more appropriate forum.

§ 7. Inconvenient Forum.—

(a) A court which has jurisdiction under this Act to make an initial or modification decree may decline to exercise its jurisdiction any time before making a decree if it finds that it is an inconvenient forum to make a custody determination under the circumstances of the case and that a court of another state is a more appropriate forum.

(b) A finding of inconvenient forum may be made upon the court's own motion or upon motion of a party or a guardian ad litem or other representative of the child.

(c) In determining if it is an inconvenient forum, the court shall consider if it is in the interest of the child that another state assume jurisdiction. For this purpose it may take into account the following factors, among others:

(1) if another state is or recently was the child's home state;

(2) if another state has a closer connection with the child and his family or with the child and one or more of the contestants;

(3) if substantial evidence concerning the child's present or future care, protection, training, and personal relationships is more readily available in another state;

(4) if the parties have agreed on another forum which is no less appropriate; and

(5) if the exercise of jurisdiction by a court of this State would contravene any of the purposes stated in section 1.

(d) Before determining whether to decline or retain jurisdiction the court may communicate with a court of another state and exchange information pertinent to the assumption of jurisdiction by either court with a view to assuring that jurisdiction will be exercised by the more appropriate court and that a forum will be available to the parties.

(e) If the court finds that it is an inconvenient forum and that a court of another state is a more appropriate forum, it may dismiss the proceedings, or it may stay the proceedings upon condition that a custody proceeding be promptly commenced in another named state or upon any other conditions which may be just and proper, including the condition that a moving party stipulate his consent and submission to the jurisdiction of the other forum.

(f) The court may decline to exercise its jurisdiction under this Act if a custody determination is incidental to an action for divorce or another proceeding while retaining jurisdiction over the divorce or other proceeding.

(g) If it appears to the court that it is clearly an inappropriate forum it may require the party who commenced the proceedings to pay, in addition to the costs of the proceedings in this State, necessary travel and other expenses, including attorneys' fees, incurred by other parties or their witnesses. Payment is to be made to the clerk of the court for remittance to the proper party.

(h) Upon dismissal or stay of proceedings under this section the court shall inform the court found to be the more appropriate forum of this fact, or if the court which would have jurisdiction in the other state is not certainly known, shall transmit the information to the court administrator or other appropriate official for forwarding to the appropriate court.

(i) Any communication received from another state informing this State of a finding of inconvenient forum because a court of this State is the more appropriate forum shall be filed in the custody registry of the appropriate court. Upon assuming jurisdiction the court of this State shall inform the original court of this fact.

§ 8. Jurisdiction Declined by Reason of Conduct.—

(a) If the petitioner for an initial decree has wrongfully taken the child from another state or has engaged in similar reprehensible conduct the court may decline to exercise jurisdiction if this is just and proper under the circumstances.

(b) Unless required in the interest of the child, the court shall not exercise its jurisdiction to modify a custody decree of another state if the petitioner, without consent of the person entitled to custody, has improperly removed the child from the physical custody of the person entitled to custody or has improperly retained the child after a visit or other temporary relinquishment of physical custody. If the petitioner has violated any other provision of a custody decree of another state the court may decline to exercise its jurisdiction if this is just and proper under the circumstances.

(c) In appropriate cases a court dismissing a petition under this section may charge the petitioner with necessary travel and other expenses, including attorneys' fees, incurred by other parties or their witnesses.

§ 9. Information under Oath to Be Submitted to the Court.—

(a) Every party in a custody proceeding in his first pleading or in an affidavit attached to that pleading shall give information under oath as to the child's present address, the places where the child has lived within the last 5 years, and the names and present addresses of the persons with whom the child has lived during that period. In this pleading or affidavit every party shall further declare under oath whether:

(1) he has participated (as a party, witness, or in any other capacity) in any other litigation concerning the custody of the same child in this or any other state;

(2) he has information of any custody proceed-

ing concerning the child pending in a court of this or any other state; and

(3) he knows of any person not a party to the proceedings who has physical custody of the child or claims to have custody or visitation rights with respect to the child.

(b) If the declaration as to any of the above items is in the affirmative the declarant shall give additional information under oath as required by the court. The court may examine the parties under oath as to details of the information furnished and as to other matters pertinent to the court's jurisdiction and the disposition of the case.

(c) Each party has a continuing duty to inform the court of any custody proceeding concerning the child in this or any other state of which he obtained information during this proceeding.

§ 10. Additional Parties.—If the court learns from information furnished by the parties pursuant to section 9 or from other sources that a person not a party to the custody proceeding has physical custody of the child or claims to have custody or visitation rights with respect to the child, it shall order that person to be joined as a party and to be duly notified of the pendency of the proceeding and of his joinder as a party. If the person joined as a party is outside this State he shall be served with process or otherwise notified in accordance with section 5.

§ 11. Appearance of Parties and the Child.—

[(a) The court may order any party to the proceeding who is in this State to appear personally before the court. If that party has physical custody of the child the court may order that he appear personally with the child.]

(b) If a party to the proceeding whose presence is desired by the court is outside this State with or without the child the court may order that the notice given under section 5 include a statement directing that party to appear personally with or without the child and declaring that failure to appear may result in a decision adverse to that party.

(c) If a party to the proceeding who is outside this State is directed to appear under subsection (b) or desires to appear personally before the court with or without the child, the court may require another party to pay to the clerk of the court travel and other necessary expenses of the party so appearing and of the child if this is just and proper and under the circumstances.

§ 12. Binding Force and Res Judicata Effect of Custody Decree.—A custody decree rendered by a court of this State which had jurisdiction under section 3 binds all parties who have been served in this State or notified in accordance with section 5 or who have submitted to the jurisdiction of the court, and who have been given an opportunity to be heard. As to these parties the custody decree is conclusive as to all issues of law and fact decided and as to the custody determination made unless and until that determination is modified pursuant to law, including the provisions of this Act.

§ 13. Recognition of Out-of-State Custody Decrees.—The courts of this State shall recognize and enforce an initial or modification decree of a court of another state which had assumed jurisdiction under statutory provisions substantially in accordance with this Act or which was made under factual circumstances meeting the jurisdictional standards of the Act, so long as this decree has not been modified in accordance with jurisdictional standards substantially similar to those of this Act.

§ 14. Modification of Custody Decree of Another State.—

(a) If a court of another state has made a custody decree, a court of this State shall not modify that decree unless (1) it appears to the court of this State that the court which rendered the decree does not now have jurisdiction under jurisdictional prerequisites substantially in accordance with this Act or has declined to assume jurisdiction to modify the decree and (2) the court of this State has jurisdiction.

(b) If a court of this State is authorized under subsection (a) and section 8 to modify a custody decree of another state it shall give due consideration to the transcript of the record and other documents of all previous proceedings submitted to it in accordance with section 22.

§ 15. Filing and Enforcement of Custody Decree of Another State.—

(a) A certified copy of a custody decree of another state may be filed in the office of the clerk of any [District Court, Family Court] of this State. The clerk shall treat the decree in the same manner as a custody decree of the [District Court, Family Court] of this State. A custody decree so filed has the same effect and shall be enforced in like manner as a custody decree rendered by a court of this State.

(b) A person violating a custody decree of another state which makes it necessary to enforce the decree in this State may be required to pay necessary travel and other expenses, including attorneys' fees, incurred by the party entitled to the custody or his witnesses.

§ 16. Registry of Out-of-State Custody Decrees and Proceedings.—The clerk of each [District Court, Family Court] shall maintain a registry in which he shall enter the following:

(1) certified copies of custody decrees of other states received for filing;

(2) communications as to the pendency of custody proceedings in other states;

(3) communications concerning a finding of inconvenient forum by a court of another state; and

(4) other communications or documents concerning custody proceedings in another state which may affect the jurisdiction of a court of this State or the disposition to be made by it in a custody proceeding.

§ 17. Certified Copies of Custody Decree.—The Clerk of the [District Court, Family Court] of this State, at the request of the court of another state or at the request of any person who is affected by or has a legitimate interest in a custody decree, shall certify and forward a copy of the decree to that court or person.

§ 18. Taking Testimony in Another State.—In addition to other procedural devices available to a party, any party to the proceeding or a guardian ad litem or other representative of the child may adduce testimony of witnesses, including parties and the child, by deposition or otherwise in another state. The court on its own motion may direct that the testimony of a person be taken in another state and may prescribe the manner in which and the terms upon which the testimony shall be taken.

§ 19. Hearings and Studies in Another State; Orders to Appear.—

(a) A court of this State may request the appropriate court of another state to hold a hearing to adduce evidence, to order a party to produce or give evidence under other procedures of that state, or to have social studies made with respect to the custody of a child involved in proceedings pending in the court of this State; and to forward to the court of this State certified copies of the transcript of the record of the hearing, the evidence otherwise adduced, or any social studies prepared in compliance with the request. The cost of the services may be assessed against the parties or, if necessary, ordered paid by the [County, State].

(b) A court of this State may request the appropriate court of another state to order a party to custody proceedings pending in the court of this State to appear in the proceedings, and if that party has physical custody of the child, to appear with the child. The request may state that travel and other necessary expenses of the party and of the child whose appearance is desired will be assessed against another party or will otherwise be paid.

§ 20. Assistance to Courts of Other States.—

(a) Upon request of the court of another state the courts of this State which are competent to hear custody matters may order a person in this State to appear at a hearing to adduce evidence or to produce or give evidence under other procedures available in this State [or may order social studies to be made for use in a custody proceeding in another state]. A certified copy of the transcript of the record of the hearing or the evidence otherwise adduced [and any social studies prepared] shall be forwarded by the clerk of the court to the requesting court.

(b) A person within this State may voluntarily give his testimony or statement in this State for use in a custody proceeding outside this State.

(c) Upon request of the court of another state a competent court of this State may order a person in this State to appear alone or with the child in a custody proceeding in another state. The court may condition compliance with the request upon assurance by the other state that state travel and other necessary expenses will be advanced or reimbursed.

§ 21. Preservation of Documents for Use in Other States.—In any custody proceeding in this State the court shall preserve the pleadings, orders and decrees, any record that has been made of its hearings, social studies, and other pertinent documents until the child reaches [18, 21] years of age. Upon appropriate request of the court of another state the court shall forward to the other court certified copies of any or all such documents.

§ 22. Request for Court Records of Another State.—If a custody decree has been rendered in another state concerning a child involved in a custody proceeding pending in a court of this State, the court of this State upon taking jurisdiction of the case shall request of the court of the other state a certified copy of the transcript of any court record and other documents mentioned in section 21.

§ 23. International Application.—The general policies of this Act extend to the international area. The provisions of this Act relating to the recognition and enforcement of custody decrees of other states apply to custody decrees and decrees involving legal institutions similar in nature to custody institutions rendered by appropriate authorities of other nations if reasonable notice and opportunity to be heard were given to all affected persons.

[§ 24. Priority.—Upon the request of a party to a custody proceeding which raises a question of existence or exercise of jurisdiction under this Act the case shall be given calendar priority and handled expeditiously.]

§ 25. Severability.—If any provision of this Act or the application thereof to any person or circumstance is held invalid, its invalidity does not affect other provisions or applications of the Act which can be given effect without the invalid provision or application, and to this end the provisions of this Act are severable.

C PARENTAL KIDNAPING PREVENTION ACT OF 1980

(28 U.S.C.A. 1738A)

§ 1738A. Full faith and credit given to child custody determinations

(a) The appropriate authorities of every State shall enforce according to its terms, and shall not modify except as provided in subsection (f) of this section, any child custody determination made consistently with the provisions of this section by a court of another State.

(b) As used in this section, the term—

(1) "child" means a person under the age of eighteen;

(2) "contestant" means a person, including a parent, who claims a right to custody or visitation of a child;

(3) "custody determination" means a judgment, decree, or other order of a court providing for the custody or visitation of a child, and includes permanent and temporary orders, and initial orders and modifications;

(4) "home State" means the State in which, immediately preceding the time involved, the child lived with his parents, a parent, or a person acting as parent, for at least six consecutive months, and in the case of a child less than six months old, the State in which the child lived from birth with any of such persons. Periods of temporary absence of any such person are counted as part of the six-month or other period;

(5) "modification" and "modify" refer to a custody determination which modifies, replaces, supersedes, or otherwise is made subsequent to, a prior custody determination concerning the same child, whether made by the same court or not;

(6) "person acting as a parent" means a person, other than a parent, who has physical custody of a child and who has either been awarded custody by a court or claims a right to custody;

(7) "physical custody" means actual possession and control of a child; and

(8) "State" means a State of the United States, the District of Columbia, the Commonwealth of Puerto Rico, or a territory or possession of the United States.

(c) A child custody determination made by a court of a state is consistent with the provisions of this section only if

(1) such court has jurisdiction under the law of such State; and

(2) one of the following conditions is met:

(A) such State (i) is the home State of the child on the date of the commencement of the proceeding, or (ii) had been the child's home State within six months before the date of the commencement of the proceeding and the child is absent from such State because of his removal or retention by a contestant or for other reasons, and a contestant continues to live in such State;

(B)(i) it appears that no other State would have jurisdiction under subparagraph (A), and (ii) it is in the best interest of the child that a court of such State assume jurisdiction because (I) the child and his parents, or the child and at least one contestant, have a significant connection with such State other than mere physical presence in such State, and (II) there is available in such State substantial evidence concerning the child's present or future care, protection, training, and personal relationships;

(C) the child is physically present in such State and (i) the child has been abandoned, or (ii) it is necessary in an emergency to protect the child because he has been subjected to or threatened with mistreatment or abuse;

(D)(i) it appears that no other State would have jurisdiction under subparagraph (A), (B), (C), or (E), or another State has declined to exercise jurisdiction on the ground that the State whose jurisdiction is in issue is the more appropriate forum to determine the custody of the child, and (ii) it is in the best interest of the child that such court assume jurisdiction; or

(E) the court has continuing jurisdiction pursuant to subsection (d) of this section.

(d) The jurisdiction of a court of a State which has made a child custody determination consistently with the provisions of this section continues as long as the requirement of subsection (c)(1) of this section continues to be met and such State remains the residence of the child or of any contestant.

(e) Before a child custody determination is made, reasonable notice and opportunity to be heard shall be given to the contestants, any parent whose parental rights have not been previously terminated and any person who has physical custody of a child.

(f) A court of a State may modify a determination of the custody of the same child made by a court of another State, if—

(1) it has jurisdiction to make such a child custody determination; and

(2) the court of the other State no longer has jurisdiction, or it has declined to exercise such jurisdiction to modify such determination.

(g) A court of a State shall not exercise jurisdiction in any proceeding for a custody determination commenced during the pendency of a proceeding in a court of another State where such court of that other State is exercising jurisdiction consistently with the provisions of this section to make a custody determination.

D FEDERAL INTERNATIONAL CHILD ABDUCTION ACT

(42 U.S.C.A. 11601)

§ 11601. Findings and declarations

(a) Findings. The Congress makes the following findings:

(1) The international abduction or wrongful retention of children is harmful to their well-being.

(2) Persons should not be permitted to obtain custody of children by virtue of their wrongful removal or retention.

(3) International abductions and retentions of children are increasing, and only concerted cooperation pursuant to an international agreement can effectively combat this problem.

(4) The Convention on the Civil Aspects of International Child Abduction, done at The Hague on October 25, 1980, establishes legal rights and procedures for the prompt return of children who have been wrongfully removed or retained, as well as for securing the exercise of visitation rights. Children who are wrongfully removed or retained within the meaning of the Convention are to be promptly returned unless one of the narrow exceptions set forth in the Convention applies. The Convention provides a sound treaty framework to help resolve the problem of international abduction and retention of children and will deter such wrongful removals and retentions.

(b) Declarations. The Congress makes the following declarations:

(1) It is the purpose of this Act to establish procedures for the implementation of the Convention in the United States.

(2) The provisions of this Act are in addition to and not in lieu of the provisions of the Convention.

(3) In enacting this Act the Congress recognizes—

(A) the international character of the Convention; and

(B) the need for uniform international interpretation of the Convention.

(4) The Convention and this Act empower courts in the United States to determine only rights under the Convention and not the merits of any underlying child custody claims.

§ 11602. Definitions.

For the purposes of this Act—

(1) the term "applicant" means any person who, pursuant to the Convention, files an application with the United States Central Authority or a Central Authority of any other party to the Convention for the return of a child alleged to have been wrongfully removed or retained or for arrangements for organizing or securing the effective exercise of rights of access pursuant to the Convention;

(2) the term "Convention" means the Convention on the Civil Aspects of International Child Abduction, done at The Hague on October 25, 1980;

(3) the term "Parent Locator Service" means the service established by the Secretary of Health and Human Services under section 453 of the Social Security Act (42 U.S.C. 653);

(4) the term "petitioner" means any person who, in accordance with this Act, files a petition in court seeking relief under the Convention;

(5) the term "person" includes any individual, institution, or other legal entity or body;

(6) the term "respondent" means any person against whose interests a petition is filed in court, in accordance with this Act, which seeks relief under the Convention;

(7) the term "rights of access" means visitation rights;

(8) the term "State" means any of the several States, the District of Columbia, and any commonwealth, territory, or possession of the United States; and

(9) the term "United States Central Authority" means the agency of the Federal Government designated by the President under section 7(a) [42 USCS § 11606(a)].

§ 11603. Judicial remedies

(a) Jurisdiction of the courts. The courts of the States and the United States district courts shall have concurrent original jurisdiction of actions arising under the Convention.

(b) Petitions. Any person seeking to initiate judicial proceedings under the Convention for the return of a child or for arrangements for organizing or securing the effective exercise of rights of access to a child may do so by commencing a civil action by filing a petition for the relief sought in any court which has jurisdiction of such action and which is authorized to exercise its jurisdiction in the place where the child is located at the time the petition is filed.

(c) Notice. Notice of an action brought under subsection (b) shall be given in accordance with the applicable law governing notice in interstate child custody proceedings.

(d) Determination of case. The court in which an action is brought under subsection (b) shall decide the case in accordance with the Convention.

(e) Burdens of proof. (1) A petitioner in an action brought under subsection (b) shall establish by a preponderance of the evidence—

(A) in the case of an action for the return of a child, that the child has been wrongfully removed or retained within the meaning of the Convention; and

(B) in the case of an action for arrangements for organizing or securing the effective exercise of rights of access, that the petitioner has such rights.

(2) In the case of an action for the return of a child, a respondent who opposes the return of the child has the burden of establishing—

(A) by clear and convincing evidence that one of the exceptions set forth in article 13b or 20 of the Convention applies; and

(B) by a preponderance of the evidence that any other exception set forth in article 12 or 13 of the Convention applies.

(f) Application of the Convention. For purposes of any action brought under this Act—

(1) the term "authorities", as used in article 15 of the Convention to refer to the authorities of the state of the habitual residence of a child, includes courts and appropriate government agencies;

(2) the terms "wrongful removal or retention" and "wrongfully removed or retained", as used in the Convention, include a removal or retention of a child before the entry of a custody order regarding that child; and

(3) the term "commencement of proceedings", as used in article 12 of the Convention, means, with respect to the return of a child located in the United States, the filing of the petition in accordance with subsection (b) of this section.

(g) Full faith and credit. Full faith and credit shall be accorded by the courts of the States and the courts of the United States to the judgment of any other such court ordering or denying the return of the child, pursuant to the Convention, in an action brought under this Act.

(h) Remedies under the Convention not exclusive. The remedies established by the Convention and this Act shall be in addition to remedies available under other laws or international agreements.

§ 11604. Provisional remedies

(a) Authority of courts. In furtherance of the objectives of article 7(b) and other provisions of the Conventions, and subject to the provisions of subsection (b) of this section, any court exercising jurisdiction of an action brought under section 4(b) of this Act [42 USCS § 11630(b)] may take or cause to be taken measures under Federal or State law, as appropriate, to protect the well-being of the child involved or to prevent the child's further removal or concealment before the final disposition of the petition.

(b) Limitation on authority. No court exercising jurisdiction of an action brought under section 4(b) [42 USCS § 11603(b)] may, under subsection (a) of this section, order a child removed from a person having physical control of the child unless the applicable requirements of State law are satisfied.

§ 11605. Admissibility of documents

With respect to any application to the United States Central Authority, or any petition to a court under section 4 [42 USCS § 11603], which seeks relief under the Convention, or any other documents or information included with such application or petition or provided after such submission which relates to the application or petition, as the case may be, no authentication of such application, petition, document, or information shall be required in order for the application, petition, document, or information to be admissible in court.

§ 11606. United States Central Authority

(a) Designation. The President shall designate a Federal agency to serve as the Central Authority for the United States under the Convention.

(b) Functions. The functions of the United States Central Authority are those ascribed to the Central Authority by the Convention and this Act.

(c) Regulatory authority. The United States Central Authority is authorized to issue such regulations as may be necessary to carry out its functions under the Convention and this Act.

(d) Obtaining information from Parent Locator Service. The United States Central Authority may, to the extent authorized by the Social Security Act [42 USCS §§ 301 et seq.], obtain information from the Parent Locator Service.

§ 11607.   Costs and fees

(a) Administrative costs. No department, agency, or instrumentality of the Federal Government or of any State or local government may impose on an applicant any fee in relation to the administrative processing of applications submitted under the Convention.

(b) Costs incurred in civil actions. (1) Petitioners may be required to bear the costs of legal counsel or advisors, court costs incurred in connection with their petitions, and travel costs for the return of the child involved and any accompanying persons, except as provided in paragraphs (2) and (3).

(2) Subject to paragraph (3), legal fees or court costs incurred in connection with an action brought under section 4 [42 USCS § 11603] shall be borne by the petitioner unless they are covered by payments from Federal, State, or local legal assistance or other programs.

(3) Any court ordering the return of a child pursuant to an action brought under section 4 [42 USCS § 11603] shall order the respondent to pay necessary expenses incurred by or on behalf of the petitioner, including court costs, legal fees, foster home or other care during the course of proceedings in the action, and transportation costs related to the return of the child, unless the respondent establishes that such order would be clearly inappropriate.

§ 11608.   Collection, maintenance, and dissemination of information

(a) In general. In performing its functions under the Convention, the United States Central Authority may, under such conditions as the Central Authority prescribes by regulation, but subject to subsection (c), receive from or transmit to any department, agency, or instrumentality of the Federal Government or of any State or foreign government, and receive from or transmit to any applicant, petitioner, or respondent, information necessary to locate a child or for the purpose of otherwise implementing the Convention with respect to a child, except that the United States Central Authority—

(1) may receive such information from a Federal or State department, agency, or instrumentality

only pursuant to applicable Federal and State statutes; and

(2) may transmit any information received under this subsection notwithstanding any provisions of law other than this Act.

(b) Requests for information. Requests for information under this section shall be submitted in such manner and form as the United States Central Authority may prescribe by regulation and shall be accompanied or supported by such documents as the United States Central Authority may require.

(c) Responsibility of government entities. Whenever any department agency, or instrumentality of the United States or of any State receives a request from the United States Central Authority for information authorized to be provided to such Central Authority under subsection (a), the head of such department, agency, or instrumentality shall promptly cause a search to be made of the files and records maintained by such department, agency, or instrumentality in order to determine whether the information requested is contained in any such files or records. If such search discloses the information requested, the head of such department, agency, or instrumentality shall immediately transmit such information to the United States Central Authority, except that any such information the disclosure of which—

(1) would adversely affect the national security interests of the United States or the law enforcement interests of the United States or of any State; or

(2) would be prohibited by section 9 of title 13, United States Code;

shall not be transmitted to the Central Authority. The head of such department, agency, or instrumentality shall, immediately upon completion of the requested search, notify the Central Authority of the results of the search, and whether an exception set forth in the paragraph (1) or (2) applies. In the event that the United States Central Authority receives information and the appropriate Federal or State department, agency, or instrumentality thereafter notifies the Central Authority that an exception set forth in paragraph (1) or (2) applies to that information, the Central Authority may not disclose that information under subsection (a).

(d) Information available from Parent Locator Service. To the extent that information which the United States Central Authority is authorized to obtain under the provisions of subsection (c) can be obtained through the Parent Locator Service, the United States Central Authority shall first seek to obtain such information from the Parent Locator Service, before requesting such information directly under the provisions of subsection (c) of this section.

(e) Recordkeeping. The United States Central Authority shall maintain appropriate records concerning its activities and the disposition of cases brought to its attention.

§ 11609. Interagency coordinating group.

The Secretary of State, the Secretary of Health and Human Services, and the Attorney General shall designate Federal employees and may, from time to time, designate private citizens to serve on an interagency coordinating group to monitor the operation of the Convention and to provide advice on its implementation to the United States Central Authority and other Federal agencies. This group shall meet from time to time at the request of the United States Central Authority. The agency in which the United States Central Authority is located is authorized to reimburse such private citizens for travel and other expenses incurred in participating at meetings of the interagency coordinating group at rates not to exceed those authorized under subchapter I of chapter 57 of title 5, United States Code [5 USCS §§ 5701 et seq.], for employees of agencies.

§ 11610. Authorization of appropriations.

There are authorized to be appropriated for each fiscal year such sums as may be necessary to carry out the purposes of the Convention and this Act.

E REVISED UNIFORM RECIPROCAL ENFORCEMENT OF SUPPORT ACT

Part I: General Provisions

§ 1. Purposes

The purposes of this Act are to improve and extend by reciprocal legislation the enforcement of duties of support.

§ 2. Definitions

(a) "Court" means the [here insert name] court of this State and when the context requires means the court of any other state as defined in a substantially similar reciprocal law.

(b) "Duty of support" means a duty of support whether imposed or imposable by law or by order, decree, or judgment of any court, whether interlocutory or final or whether incidental to an action for divorce, separation, separate maintenance, or otherwise and includes the duty to pay arrearages of support past due and unpaid.

(c) "Governor" includes any person performing the functions of Governor or the executive authority of any state covered by this Act.

(d) "Initiating state" means a state in which a proceeding pursuant to this or a substantially similar reciprocal law is commenced. "Initiating court" means the court in which a proceeding is commenced.

(e) "Law" includes both common and statutory law.

(f) "Obligee" means a person including a state or political subdivision to whom a duty of support is owed or a person including a state or political subdivision that has commenced a proceeding for enforcement of an alleged duty of support or for registration of a support order. It is immaterial if the person to whom a duty of support is owed is a recipient of public assistance.

(g) "Obligor" means any person owing a duty of support or against whom a proceeding for the enforcement of a duty of support or registration of a support order is commenced.

(h) "Prosecuting attorney" means the public official in the appropriate place who has the duty to enforce criminal laws relating to the failure to provide for the support of any person.

(i) "Register" means to [record] [file] in the Registry of Foreign Support Orders.

(j) "Registering court" means any court of this State in which a support order of a rendering state is registered.

(k) "Rendering state" means a state in which the court has issued a support order for which registration is sought or granted in the court of another state.

(l) "Responding state" means a state in which any responsive proceeding pursuant to the proceeding in the initiating state is commenced. "Responding court" means the court in which the responsive proceeding is commenced.

(m) "State" includes a state, territory, or possession of the United States, the District of Columbia, the Commonwealth of Puerto Rico, and any foreign jurisdiction in which this or a substantially similar reciprocal law is in effect.

(n) "Support order" means any judgment, decree, or order of support in favor of an obligee whether temporary or final, or subject to modification, revocation, or remission, regardless of the kind of action or proceeding in which it is entered.

§ 3. Remedies Additional to Those Now Existing

The remedies herein provided are in addition to and not in substitution for any other remedies.

§ 4. Extent of Duties of Support

Duties of support arising under the law of this State, when applicable under section 7, bind the obligor present in this State regardless of the presence or residence of the obligee.

Part II: Criminal Enforcement

§ 5. Interstate Rendition

The Governor of this State may

(1) demand of the Governor of another state the surrender of a person found in that state who is charged criminally in this State with failing to provide for the support of any person; or

(2) surrender on demand by the Governor of another state a person found in this State who is charged criminally in that state with failing to provide for the support of any person. Provisions for extradition of criminals not inconsistent with this Act apply to the demand even if the person whose surrender is demanded was not in the demanding state at the time of the commission of the crime and has not fled therefrom. The demand, the oath, and any proceedings for extradition pursuant to this section need not state or show that the person whose surrender is demanded has fled from justice or at the time of the commission of the crime was in the demanding state.

§ 6. Conditions of Interstate Rendition

(a) Before making the demand upon the Governor of another state for the surrender of a person charged criminally in this State with failing to provide for the support of a person, the Governor of this State may require any prosecuting attorney of this State to satisfy him that at least [60] days prior thereto the obligee initiated proceedings for support under this Act or that any proceeding would be of no avail.

(b) If, under a substantially similar Act, the Governor of another state makes a demand upon the Governor of this State for the surrender of a person charged criminally in that state with failure to provide for the support of a person, the Governor may require any prosecuting attorney to investigate the demand and to report to him whether proceedings for support have been initiated or would be effective. If it appears to the Governor that a proceeding would be effective but has not been initiated he may delay honoring the demand for a reasonable time to permit the initiation of a proceeding.

(c) If proceedings have been initiated and the person demanded has prevailed therein the Governor may decline to honor the demand. If the obligee prevailed and the person demanded is subject to a support order, the Governor may decline to honor the demand if the person demanded is complying with the support order.

Part III: Civil Enforcement

§ 7. Choice of Law

Duties of support applicable under this Act are those imposed under the laws of any state where the obligor was present for the period during which support is sought. The obligor is presumed to have been present in the responding state during the period for which support is sought until otherwise shown.

§ 8. Remedies of State or Political Subdivision Furnishing Support

If a state or a political subdivision furnishes support to an individual obligee it has the same right to initiate a proceeding under this Act as the individual obligee for the purpose of securing reimbursement for support furnished and of obtaining continuing support.

§ 9. How Duties of Support Enforced

All duties of support, including the duty to pay arrearages, are enforceable by a proceeding under this Act including a proceeding for civil contempt. The defense that the parties are immune to suit because of their relationship as husband and wife or parent and child is not available to the obligor.

§ 10. Jurisdiction

Jurisdiction of any proceeding under this Act is vested in the [here insert title of court desired].

§ 11. Contents and Filing of [Petition] for Support; Venue

(a) The [petition] shall be verified and shall state the name and, so far as known to the obligee, the address and circumstances of the obligor and the persons for whom support is sought, and all other pertinent information. The obligee may include in or attach to the [petition] any information which may help in locating or identifying the obligor including a photograph of the obligor, a description of any distinguishing marks on his person, other names and aliases by which he has been or is known, the name of his employer, his fingerprints, and his Social Security number.

(b) The [petition] may be filed in the appropriate court of any state in which the obligee resides. The court shall not decline or refuse to accept and forward the [petition] on the ground that it should be filed with some other court of this or any other state where there is pending another action for divorce, separation, annulment, dissolution, habeas corpus, adoption, or custody between the same parties or where another court has already issued a support order in some other proceeding and has retained jurisdiction for its enforcement.

§ 12. Officials to Represent Obligee

If this State is acting as an initiating state the prosecuting attorney upon the request of the court [a state department of welfare, a county commissioner, an overseer of the poor, or other local welfare officer] shall represent the obligee in any proceeding under this Act. [If the prosecuting attorney neglects or refuses to represent the obligee the [Attorney General] may order him to comply with the request of the court or may undertake the representation.] [If the prosecuting attorney neglects or refuses to represent the obligee, the [Attorney General] [State Director of Public Welfare] may undertake the representation.]

§ 13. Petition for a Minor

A [petition] on behalf of a minor obligee may be executed and filed by a person having legal custody of the minor without appointment as guardian ad litem.

§ 14. Duty of Initiating Court

If the initiating court finds that the [petition] sets forth facts from which it may be determined that the obligor owes a duty of support and that a court of the responding state may obtain jurisdiction of the obligor or his property it shall so certify and cause 3 copies of the [petition] and its certificate and one copy of this Act to be sent to the responding court. Certification shall be in accordance with the requirements of the initiating state. If the name and address of the responding court is unknown and the responding state has an information agency comparable to that established in the initiating state it shall cause the copies to be sent to the state information agency or other proper official of the responding state, with a request that the agency or official forward them to the proper court and that the court of the responding state acknowledge their receipt to the initiating court.

§ 15. Costs and Fees

An initiating court shall not require payment of either a filing fee or other costs from the obligee but may request the responding court to collect fees and costs from the obligor. A responding court shall not require payment of a filing fee or other costs from the obligee but it may direct that all fees and costs requested by the initiating court and incurred in this State when acting as a responding state, including fees for filing of pleadings, service of process, seizure of property, stenographic or duplication service, or other service supplied to the obligor, be paid in whole or in part by the obligor or by the [state or political subdivision thereof]. These costs or fees do not have priority over amounts due to the obligee.

§ 16. Jurisdiction by Arrest

If the court of this state believes that the obligor may flee it may

(1) as an initiating court, request in its certificate that the responding court obtain the body of the obligor by appropriate process; or

(2) as a responding court, obtain the body of the obligor by appropriate process. Thereupon it may release him upon his own recognizance or upon his giving a bond in an amount set by the court to assure his appearance at the hearing.

§ 17. State Information Agency

(a) The [Attorney General's Office, State Attorney's Office, Welfare Department or other Information Agency] is designated as the state information agency under this Act. It shall

(1) compile a list of the courts and their addresses in this State having jurisdiction under this Act and transmit it to the state information agency of every other state which has adopted this or a substantially similar Act. Upon the adjournment of each session of the [legislature] the agency shall distribute copies of any amendments to the Act and a statement of their effective date to all other state information agencies;

(2) maintain a register of lists of courts received from other states and transmit copies thereof promptly to every court in this state having jurisdiction under this Act; and

(3) forward to the court in this State which has jurisdiction over the obligor or his property petitions, certificates, and copies of the Act it receives from courts or information agencies of other states.

(b) If the state information agency does not know the location of the obligor or his property in the state and no state location service is available it shall use all means at its disposal to obtain this information, including the examination of official records in the state and other sources such as telephone directories, real property records, vital statistics records, police records, requests for the name and address from employers who are able or willing to cooperate, records of motor vehicle license offices, requests made to the tax offices both state and federal where such offices are able to cooperate, and requests made to the Social Security Administration as permitted by the Social Security Act as amended.

(c) After the deposit of 3 copies of the [petition] and certificate and one copy of the Act of the initiating state with the clerk of the appropriate court, if the state information agency knows or believes that the prosecuting attorney is not prosecuting the case diligently it shall inform the [Attorney General] [State Director of Public Welfare] who may undertake the representation.

§ 18. Duty of the Court and Officials of This State as Responding State

(a) After the responding court receives copies of the [petition], certificate, and Act from the initiating court the clerk of the court shall docket the case and notify the prosecuting attorney of his action.

(b) The prosecuting attorney shall prosecute the case diligently. He shall take all action necessary in accordance with the laws of this State to enable the court to obtain jurisdiction over the obligor or his property and shall request the court [clerk of the court] to set a time and place for a hearing and give notice thereof to the obligor in accordance with law.

(c) [If the prosecuting attorney neglects or refuses to represent the obligee the [Attorney General] may order him to comply with the request of the court or may undertake the representation.] [If the prosecuting attorney neglects or refuses to represent the obligee, the [Attorney General] [State Director of Public Welfare] may undertake the representation]

§ 19. Further Duties of Court and Officials in the Responding State

(a) The prosecuting attorney on his own initiative shall use all means at his disposal to locate the obligor or his property, and if because of inaccuracies in the [petition] or otherwise the court cannot obtain jurisdiction the prosecuting attorney shall inform the court of what he has done and request the court to continue the case pending receipt of more accurate information or an amended [petition] from the initiating court.

(b) If the obligor or his property is not found in the [county], and the prosecuting attorney discovers that the obligor or his property may be found in another [county] of this State or in another state he shall so inform the court. Thereupon the clerk of the court shall forward the documents received from the court in the initiating state to a court in the other [county] or to a court in the other state or to the information agency or other proper official of the other state with a request that the documents be forwarded to the proper court. All powers and duties provided by this Act apply to the recipient of the documents so forwarded. If the clerk of a court of this State forwards documents to another court he shall forthwith notify the initiating court.

(c) If the prosecuting attorney has no information as to the location of the obligor or his property he shall so inform the initiating court.

§ 20. Hearing and Continuance

If the obligee is not present at the hearing and the obligor denies owing the duty of support alleged in the petition or offers evidence constituting a defense the court, upon request of either party, shall continue the hearing to permit evidence relative to the duty to be adduced by either party by deposition or by appearing in person before the court. The court may designate the judge of the initiating court as a person before whom a deposition may be taken.

§ 21. Immunity from Criminal Prosecution

If at the hearing the obligor is called for examination as an adverse party and he declines to answer upon the ground that his testimony may tend to incriminate him, the court may require him to answer, in which event he is immune from criminal prosecution with respect to matters revealed by his testimony, except for perjury committed in this testimony.

§ 22. Evidence of Husband and Wife

Laws attaching a privilege against the disclosure of communications between husband and wife are inapplicable to proceedings under this Act. Husband and wife are competent witnesses [and may be compelled] to testify to any relevant matter, including marriage and parentage.

§ 23. Rules of Evidence

In any hearing for the civil enforcement of this Act the court is governed by the rules of evidence applicable in a civil court action in the _____ Court. If the action is based on a support order issued by another court a certified copy of the order shall be received as evidence of the duty of support, subject only to any defenses available to an obligor with respect to paternity (Section 27) or to a defendant in an action or a proceeding to enforce a foreign money judgment. The determination or enforcement of a duty of support owed to one obligee is unaffected by any interference by another obligee with rights of custody or visitation granted by a court.

§ 24. Order of Support

If the responding court finds a duty of support it may order the obligor to furnish support or reimbursement therefor and subject the property of the obligor to the order. Support orders made pursuant to this Act shall require that payments be made to the [clerk] [bureau] [probation department] of the court of the responding state. [The court and prosecuting attorney of any [county] in which the obligor is present or has property have the same powers and duties to enforce the order as have those of the [county] in which it was first issued. If enforcement is impossible or cannot be completed in the [county] in which the order was issued, the prosecuting attorney shall send a certified copy of the order to the prosecuting attorney of any [county] in which it appears that proceedings to enforce the order would be effective. The prosecuting attorney to whom the certified copy of the order is forwarded shall proceed with enforcement and report the results of the proceedings to the court first issuing the order.]

§ 25. Responding Court to Transmit Copies to Initiating Court

The responding court shall cause a copy of all support orders to be sent to the initiating court.

§ 26. Additional Powers of Responding Court

In addition to the foregoing powers a responding court may subject the obligor to any terms and conditions proper to assure compliance with its orders and in particular to:

(1) require the obligor to furnish a cash deposit or a bond of a character and amount to assure payment of any amount due;

(2) require the obligor to report personally and to make payments at specified intervals to the [clerk] [bureau] [probation department] of the court; and

(3) punish under the power of contempt the obligor who violates any order of the court.

§ 27. Paternity

If the obligor asserts as a defense that he is not the father of the child for whom support is sought and it appears to the court that the defense is not frivolous, and if both of the parties are present at the hearing or the proof required in the case indicates that the presence of either or both of the parties is not necessary, the court may adjudicate the paternity issue. Otherwise the court may adjourn the hearing until the paternity issue has been adjudicated.

§ 28. Additional Duties of Responding Court

A responding court has the following duties which may be carried out through the [clerk] [bureau] [probation department] of the court:

(1) to transmit to the initiating court any payment made by the obligor pursuant to any order of the court or otherwise; and

(2) to furnish to the initiating court upon request a certified statement of all payments made by the obligor.

§ 29. Additional Duty of Initiating Court

An initiating court shall receive and disburse forthwith all payments made by the obligor or sent by the responding court. This duty may be carried out through the [clerk] [bureau] [probation department] of the court.

§ 30. Proceedings Not to Be Stayed

A responding court shall not stay the proceeding or refuse a hearing under this Act because of any pending or prior action or proceeding for divorce, separation, annulment, dissolution, habeas corpus, adoption, or custody in this or any other state. The court shall hold a hearing and may issue a support order pendente lite. In aid thereof it may require the obligor to give a bond for the prompt prosecution of the pending proceeding. If the other action or proceeding is concluded before the hearing in the instant proceeding and the judgment therein provides for the support demanded in the [petition] being heard the court must conform its support order to the amount allowed in the other action or proceeding. Thereafter the court shall not stay enforcement of its support order because of the retention of jurisdiction for enforcement purposes by the court in the other action or proceeding.

§ 31. Application of Payments

A support order made by a court of this State pursuant to this Act does not nullify and is not nullified by a support order made by a court of this State pursuant to any other law or by a support order made by a court of any other state pursuant to a substantially similar act or any other law, regardless of priority of issuance, unless otherwise specifically provided by the court. Amounts paid for a particular period pursuant to any support order made by the court of another state shall be credited against the amounts accruing or accrued for the same period under any support order made by the court of this State.

§ 32. Effect of Participation in Proceeding

Participation in any proceeding under this Act does not confer jurisdiction upon any court over any of the parties thereto in any other proceeding.

§ 33. Intrastate Application

This Act applies if both the obligee and the obligor are in this State but in different [counties]. If the court of the [county] in which the [petition] is filed finds that the [petition] sets forth facts from which it may be determined that the obligor owes a duty of support and finds that a court of another [county] in this State may obtain jurisdiction over the obligor or his property, the clerk of the court shall send the [petition] and a certification of the findings to the court of the [county] in which the obligor or his property is found. The clerk of the court of the [county] receiving these documents shall notify the prosecuting attorney of their receipt. The prosecuting attorney and the court in the [county] to which the copies are forwarded then shall have duties corresponding to those imposed upon them when acting for this State as a responding state.

§ 34. Appeals

If the [Attorney General] [State Director of Public Welfare] is of the opinion that a support order is erroneous and presents a question of law warranting an appeal in the public interest, he may

(a) perfect an appeal to the proper appellate court if the support order was issued by a court of this State, or

(b) if the support order was issued in another state, cause the appeal to be taken in the other state. In either case expenses of appeal may be paid on his order from funds appropriated for his office.

Part IV: Registration of Foreign Support Orders

§ 35. Additional Remedies

If the duty of support is based on a foreign support order, the obligee has the additional remedies provided in the following sections.

§ 36. Registration

The obligee may register the foreign support order in a court of this State in the manner, with the effect, and for the purposes herein provided.

§ 37. Registry of Foreign Support Orders

The clerk of the court shall maintain a Registry of Foreign Support Orders in which he shall [file] foreign support orders.

§ 38. Official to Represent Obligee

If this State is acting either as a rendering or a registering state the prosecuting attorney upon the request of the court [a state department of welfare, a county commissioner, an overseer of the poor, or other local welfare official] shall represent the obligee in proceedings under this Part.

[If the prosecuting attorney neglects or refuses to represent the obligee, the [Attorney General] may order him to comply with the request of the court or may undertake the representation.] [If the prosecuting attorney neglects or refuses to represent the obligee, the [Attorney General] [State Director of Public Welfare] may undertake the representation.]

§ 39. Registration Procedure; Notice

(a) An obligee seeking to register a foreign support order in a court of this State shall transmit to the clerk of the court (1) three certified copies of the order with all modifications thereof, (2) one copy of the reciprocal enforcement of support act of the state in which the order was made, and (3) a statement verified and signed by the obligee, showing the post office address of the obligee, the last known place of residence and post office address of the obligor, the amount of support remaining unpaid, a description and the location of any property of the obligor available upon execution, and a list of the states in which the order is registered. Upon receipt of these documents the clerk of the court, without payment of a filing fee or other cost to the obligee, shall file them in the Registry of Foreign Support Orders. The filing constitutes registration under this Act.

(b) Promptly upon registration the clerk of the court shall send by certified or registered mail to the obligor at the address given a notice of the registration with a copy of the registered support order and the post office address of the obligee. He shall also docket the case and notify the prosecuting attorney of his action. The prosecuting attorney shall proceed diligently to enforce the order.

§ 40. Effect of Registration; Enforcement Procedure

(a) Upon registration the registered foreign support order shall be treated in the same manner as a support order issued by a court of this State. It has the same effect and is subject to the same procedures, defenses, and proceedings for reopening, vacating, or staying as a support order of this State and may be enforced and satisfied in like manner.

(b) The obligor has [20] days after the mailing of notice of the registration in which to petition the court to vacate the registration or for other relief. If he does not so petition the registered support order is confirmed.

(c) At the hearing to enforce the registered support order the obligor may present only matters that would be available to him as defenses in an action to enforce a foreign money judgment. If he shows to the court that an appeal from the order is pending or will be taken or that a stay of execution has been granted the court shall stay enforcement of the order until the appeal is concluded, the time for appeal has expired, or the order is vacated, upon satisfactory proof that the obligor has furnished security for payment of the support ordered as required by the rendering state. If he shows to the court any ground upon which enforcement of a support order of this State may be stayed the court shall stay enforcement of the order for an appropriate period if the obligor furnishes the same security for payment of the support ordered that is required for a support order of this State.

§ 41. Uniformity of Interpretation

This Act shall be so construed as to effectuate its general purpose to make uniform the law of those states which enact it.

§ 42. Short Title

This Act may be cited as the Revised Uniform Reciprocal Enforcement of Support Act (1968).

§ 43. Severability

If any provision of this Act or the application thereof to any person or circumstance is held invalid, the invalidity does not affect other provisions or applications of the Act which can be given effect without the invalid provision or application, and to this end the provisions of this Act are severable.

The following pages contain sample URESA forms that are often used throughout the country.

COURT/ADMINISTRATIVE AGENCY IDENTIFICATION AND CASE NUMBER

PLAINTIFF/PETITIONER

ADDRESS

VS

DEFENDANT/RESPONDENT

ADDRESS

The Uniform Support Petition is a standard form for URESA cases. The petition is a legal pleading as opposed to an administrative form, and its purpose is to show how the court has jurisdiction, to show enough facts to notify the defendant/respondent of the claim being made, and to provide plaintiff/petitioner with a means to request specific court ordered action or relief. The Uniform Support Petition is simple and straightforward, yet provides some flexibility. Properly prepared it should be legally sufficient to initiate URESA cases and respond to URESA request in all states.

☐ IV-D   ☐ NON IV-D

OTHER REFERENCE NUMBER

UNIFORM SUPPORT PETITION

This petition of plaintiff/petitioner respectfully shows the court that:

1. This is a petition for:

   ☐ ESTABLISHMENT OF PATERNITY   ☐ SUPPORT   ☐ MEDICAL COVERAGE   ☐ ARREARAGE

   ☐ REIMBURSEMENT   ☐ OTHER _____

   ☐ The General Testimony for URESA is attached and incorporated by reference.   ☐ A Paternity Affidavit is attached and incorporated by reference.

2. _____ resides in   CITY, COUNTY, STATE
   and has custody of the following dependents of defendant/respondent:

DEPENDENTS' NAMES (First MI Last)	DATE OF BIRTH (Month, Day, Year)

   ☐ Additional Names on attached sheet.

3. _____ and defendant/respondent were:

   ☐ Never married to each other

   ☐ Married on . . . .   DATE

   ☐ Divorce pending

   ☐ Divorced on . . . .   DATE   in   COUNTY AND STATE

Form OS **550** (3/87)

UNIFORM SUPPORT PETITION
PAGE 1 OF 3 PAGES

UNIFORM SUPPORT PETITION

CASE NUMBER

4. Defendant/respondent resides in:

CITY, COUNTY, STATE

Defendant/respondent's last known employer is:

NAME, ADDRESS

5. The dependents are entitled to support and/or medical coverage from the defendant/respondent, who has a legal obligation to pay support pursuant to the laws of the initiating jurisdiction, which is enforceable under the reciprocal support statute which is:

REFERENCE

The responding state may obtain jurisdiction of defendant/respondent and/or his property.

6. Since on or about

DATE

defendant/respondent has refused or neglected to provide reasonable support for the above named dependents.

7. Defendant/respondent:

☐ a. is under a court order to provide support pursuant to:

☐ original Divorce decree . . . .

DATED

NOTE: A CERTIFIED COPY OF THE CURRENT ORDER IS ATTACHED AND INCORPORATED BY REFERENCE.

☐ other support order or agreement

☐ failure to comply with the support order has resulted in an arrearage of: . . . .

ARREARAGE AMOUNT
$ as of

DATE

☐ b. is not under a court order to provide support however
(name) _____

☐ PRINCIPAL ONLY   ☐ INCLUDES INTEREST

is entitled to reimbursement as stated in the testimony attached and incorporated by reference, in the amount of: . . . .

REIMBURSEMENT AMOUNT
$ as of

DATE

☐ c. should pay a reasonable amount of ongoing support for the dependents which is: . . . . or greater amount as permitted by the law of the responding state.

AMOUNT (CHILD SUPPORT)
$ per

MONTH, WEEK

AMOUNT (SPOUSAL)
$ per

MONTH, WEEK

☐ d. Other special pleading:

8. (name) _____

NAME & ADDRESS OF AGENCY

☐ has made an assignment of rights; and/or

☐ has given authority to the following agency to collect support for the above named dependents.

UNIFORM SUPPORT PETITION

CASE NUMBER

Wherefore, plaintiff/petitioner requests an order for the following:

☐ Establishment of paternity

☐ Child support in the amount of: . . . .

AMOUNT (CHILD SUPPORT)		MONTH, WEEK
$	per	

☐ Spousal support in the amount of: . . . .

AMOUNT (SPOUSAL)		MONTH, WEEK
$	per	

☐ Registration and enforcement of the current support order

☐ Medical coverage

☐ Arrearage in the amount of: . . . .

ARREARAGE AMOUNT		DATE
$	as of	

☐ Reimbursement in the amount of: . . . .

REIMBURSEMENT AMOUNT		DATE
$	as of	

☐ Payment of costs and attorneys' fees by the defendant/respondent. (see instructions)

☐ Other:

Under penalties of perjury, all information and facts stated in this petition are true to the best of my knowledge and belief.

DATE	SIGNATURE OF PLAINTIFF/PETITIONER OR REPRESENTATIVE

SWORN TO AND SIGNED BEFORE ME THIS DATE	NOTARY PUBLIC	COMMISSION EXPIRES

Form OS 550 (3/87)

UNIFORM SUPPORT PETITION
PAGE 3 OF 3 PAGES

RESPONDING JURISDICTION COURT/ADM. AGENCY COPY

COURT/ADMINISTRATIVE AGENCY IDENTIFICATION AND CASE NUMBER

| PLAINTIFF/PETITIONER | This document provides a framework for stating the detailed information necessary to support the action requested in the petition, as relevant to the particular case. |

VS

DEFENDANT/RESPONDENT

☐ IV-D   ☐ NON IV-D

OTHER REFERENCE NUMBER

GENERAL TESTIMONY FOR URESA

_____ being duly sworn, under penalties of perjury, testifies as follows:
(Name)

I. PERSONAL INFORMATION

1. NAME AND COMPLETE HOME ADDRESS	2. HOME/MESSAGE PHONE	3. WORK PHONE
	4. SOCIAL SEC. NO.	5. DATE OF BIRTH
6. RELATIONSHIP TO DEFENDANT/RESPONDENT:	DATE OF MARRIAGE	PLACE OF MARRIAGE (STATE)
☐ NEVER MARRIED ☐ MARRIED	STATE (COMMON LAW MARRIAGE)	DATES (FROM - TO)
☐ COMMON LAW MARRIAGE ☐ DIVORCED		
☐ OTHER: _____	DATE OF DIVORCE	DATE OF SUPPORT ORDER
☐ SUPPORT ORDER ENTERED ☐ NO SUPPORT ORDER	DATE OF SEPARATION	COURT AND LOCATION (DIVORCE AND SEPARATION)
NOTE: ATTACH A CERTIFIED COPY OF THE DIVORCE DECREE OR SEPARATION AGREEMENT AND THE CURRENT SUPPORT ORDER.		
7. PRESENT MARITAL STATUS:	NAME OF NEW SPOUSE OR NON MARITAL PARTNER	
☐ MARRIED TO DEFENDANT/RESPONDENT		
☐ MARRIED TO NEW SPOUSE		
☐ LIVING WITH NON-MARITAL PARTNER		
☐ SINGLE		

GENERAL TESTIMONY FOR URESA   CASE NUMBER

II. DEPENDENTS' HOUSEHOLD INFORMATION

1. The following are the dependents for whom support is sought from the defendant/respondent:

FULL NAME	DATE OF BIRTH	IS PATERNITY AN ISSUE YES OR NO	SUPPORT ORDER ESTABLISHED YES OR NO	LIVING WITH PETITIONER? YES OR NO

NOTE; A PATERNITY AFFIDAVIT IS REQUIRED FOR EACH CHILD NOT OF THE MARRIAGE WHOSE PATERNITY IS AT ISSUE.

2. Did the dependents reside with the custodian during the entire period for which support is sought?   ☐ YES ☐ NO (if no, explain)

2. Does anyone else not of the marriage, live in custodian's household?   ☐ YES ☐ NO (if yes, provide information)

FULL NAME	DATE OF BIRTH	RELATIONSHIP	SOURCE OF INCOME OR SUPPORT	AMOUNT/MONTH GROSS	NET

III. DEFENDANT/RESPONDENT INFORMATION

1. FULL NAME (INCLUDE NICKNAME, ALIAS, ETC.)

2. RESIDENCE ADDRESS

SOCIAL SECURITY NO.   DATE OF BIRTH

HOME/MESSAGE PHONE   WORK PHONE

3. EMPLOYER NAME AND ADDRESS

OCCUPATION, TRADE OR PROFESSION

ESTIMATED GROSS MONTHLY INCOME   OTHER INCOME

4. REAL OR PERSONAL PROPERTY

Form OS 548 (3/87)

GENERAL TESTIMONY FOR URESA

GENERAL TESTIMONY FOR URESA

CASE NUMBER

5. PHYSICAL DESCRIPTION OF DEFENDANT/RESPONDENT

RACE	HEIGHT	WEIGHT	HAIR COLOR	EYE COLOR

SCARS, MARKS OR OTHER DISTINGUISHING FEATURES

6. PRESENT MARITAL STATUS

☐ MARRIED

☐ LIVING WITH NON-MARITAL PARTNER

☐ SINGLE

☐ UNKNOWN

NAME OF NEW SPOUSE OR NON-MARITAL PARTNER

IS CURRENT SPOUSE/PARTNER EMPLOYED? ☐ YES ☐ NO

ESTIMATED GROSS MONTHLY EARNINGS

NAME AND ADDRESS OF CURRENT SPOUSE'S EMPLOYER

7. Is defendant/respondent responsible for dependents that are not living in the petitioner's household?   ☐ YES ☐ NO   ☐ UNKNOWN

FULL NAME (OF OTHER DEPENDENTS)	DATE OF BIRTH	RELATIONSHIP	LIVING WITH

This information is used to determine if medical coverage is currently provided for the dependents. If coverage is not provided additional information in this section is a basis for adding medical coverage to any new orders.

IV. MEDICAL INSURANCE

1. Are dependents for whom support is sought presently covered by medical insurance?   ☐ YES ☐ NO

2. MEDICAL COVERAGE IS PROVIDED FOR DEPENDENT CHILDREN:

☐ CUSTODIAN

☐ STATE MEDICAID

☐ CUSTODIAN'S EMPLOYMENT

☐ RESPONDENT'S EMPLOYMENT

☐ _____

INSURANCE COMPANY OF CUSTODIAN'S EMPLOYER

POLICY NUMBER

INSURANCE COMPANY OF RESPONDENT'S EMPLOYER

POLICY NUMBER

THE MONTHLY COST PAID BY THE CUSTODIAN FOR MEDICAL INSURANCE FOR THE RESPONDENT'S CHILDREN ONLY IS: $ _____

3. The petitioner can purchase needed medical insurance at a monthly cost of: $ _____

4. Were the children ever covered by medical insurance provided by the defendant/respondent's current employer?   ☐ YES ☐ NO

5. Do any of the respondent's children have special needs or extra-ordinary medical expenses not covered by insurance?   ☐ YES ☐ NO (if yes, explain)

Form OS 548 (3/87)

GENERAL TESTIMONY FOR URESA

RESPONDING JURISDICTION COURT/ADM. AGENCY COPY

GENERAL TESTIMONY FOR URESA

CASE NUMBER

V. SUPPORT ORDER AND PAYMENT INFORMATION

1. Describe current ordered support:
   (Include the original order and all modifications)

NOTE: PLEASE ATTACH A CERTIFIED COPY OF ALL CURRENT
ORDERS THAT RELATE TO SUPPORT

DATE OF ORDER	ORDERED SUPPORT AMOUNTS			
	CURRENT AMOUNT	PER MO, WK, ETC.	TOWARD ARREARAGE	PER MO, WK, ETC.
	NAME AND ADDRESS OF COURT OR ADMINISTRATIVE AGENCY			
	NAME AND ADDRESS OF COURT OR ADMINISTRATIVE AGENCY			

2. Summary of defendant/respondent arrearage

☐ Adjudicated arrearage . . . .

DATE OF ORDER	AMOUNT	FROM (DATE) TO (DATE)
	$	

☐ By order

Issued by

COURT OR ADMINISTRATIVE AGENCY	

☐ By operation of law . . . .

AMOUNT	FROM (DATE) TO (DATE)
$	

☐ Unadjudicated arrearage
(Amount not included in adjudicated arrearage)

AMOUNT	FROM (DATE) TO (DATE)
$	

Total Arrearage

☐ Principal only . . . .

AMOUNT	AS OF (DATE)
$	

☐ Includes interest, explain:

3. Defendant/respondent made the last support
   payment of: . . . .

AMOUNT	DATE OF PAYMENT
$	

4. Defendant/respondent's support payment history: ☐ A certified copy of Audit/Payment history is attached.

FROM (YEAR)	TO (YEAR)	AGENCY WHICH PREPARED AUDIT/PAYMENT HISTORY

Form OS 548 (3/87)

RESPONDING JURISDICTION COURT/ADM. AGENCY COPY

GENERAL TESTIMONY FOR URESA

The Order and Judgment form is for use by the judge/hearing officer who decides the case in the responding jurisdiction. This form includes a statement of the relevant findings, the order as issued by the trier of fact, sets up a payment schedule for the defendant/respondent. In any case which establishes an order for support, this form provides for wage withholding.

COURT/ADMINISTRATIVE AGENCY IDENTIFICATION AND CASE NUMBER

PLAINTIFF/PETITIONER

VS

DEFENDANT/RESPONDENT

☐ IV-D   ☐ NON IV-D

OTHER REFERENCE NUMBER

ORDER AND JUDGMENT

This matter was heard on (date) _____ before _____
with the following persons present:

Petitioner: ☐ present   ☐ not present Represented by: _____

Respondent: ☐ present   ☐ not present Represented by: _____

After considering all of the evidence, the Court/Administrative Agency FINDS:

1. ☐ That the defendant/respondent could not be located for service of process.

2. ☐ That the Court/Administrative Agency has jurisdiction of the parties and subject matter of this case.

3. ☐ That the defendant/respondent is not obligated to pay support on the following grounds:

4. ☐ That the defendant/respondent is the parent of the following child(ren):

NAME	DATE OF BIRTH

5. ☐ That the defendant/respondent owes a duty of support to the following dependents:

NAME	DATE OF BIRTH	RELATIONSHIP TO DEFENDANT/RESPONDENT

6. ☐ That $ _____ per _____ is a reasonable amount of support for defendant/respondent to pay.

7. ☐ That the defendant/respondent is in arrears in the amount of $ _____ as of _____.

8. ☐ That the defendant/respondent owes reimbursement in the amount of $ _____ as of _____.

Form OS 551 (3/87)

ORDER AND JUDGMENT
PAGE 1 OF 3 PAGES

RESPONDING JURISDICTION COURT/ADM. AGENCY

ORDER AND JUDGMENT

CASE NUMBER

Findings (continued)

9. ☐ That the defendant/respondent's income is: ....

INCOME	AMOUNT	PER
GROSS		
NET		

10. ☐ The Court/Administrative Agency further finds that:

THEREFORE, It is hereby ordered that:

1. ☐ This petition and supporting documents be returned to the initiating jurisdiction for location of the defendant/respondent.

2. ☐ This case be dismissed.

3. ☐ The defendant/respondent is the parent of the following child(ren):

NAME	DATE OF BIRTH

4. ☐ Judgment is entered in favor of plaintiff/petitioner, _____
and against defendant/respondent in the amount of $ _____ for arrearages.

5. ☐ Judgment is entered in favor of plaintiff/petitioner, _____
and against defendant/respondent in the amount of $ _____ for reimbursement.

6. ☐ The defendant/respondent shall pay $ _____ per _____
beginning _____ , to be paid as follows:

A.

PAYEE #1 (NAME AND ADDRESS)	FOR	AMOUNT
	CHILD SUPPORT	
	CHILD SUPPORT ARREARAGE	
	REIMBURSEMENT	
	SPOUSAL SUPPORT	
	SPOUSAL SUPPORT ARREARAGE	
	PAYEE #1 TOTAL	$

B.

PAYEE #2 (NAME AND ADDRESS)	FOR	AMOUNT
	CHILD SUPPORT	
	CHILD SUPPORT ARREARAGE	
	REIMBURSEMENT	
	SPOUSAL SUPPORT	
	SPOUSAL SUPPORT ARREARAGE	
	PAYEE #2 TOTAL	$

7. ☐ The defendant/respondent shall provide health insurance coverage for the child(ren) and provide assistance in obtaining payment for insured services.

ORDER AND JUDGMENT	CASE NUMBER

Order/Judgment (continued)

8. ☐ The defendant/respondent shall pay medical expenses, including dental and ophthalmological services for the child(ren) as follows:

9. ☐ The defendant/respondent shall pay and judgment is entered in favor of:

PAYEE (NAME AND ADDRESS)	FOR	AMOUNT
	COURT COSTS	
	COST OF PATERNITY TESTS	
	PLAINTIFF/PETITIONER'S ATTORNEY'S FEES	
	OTHER: (BOND)	
	TOTAL JUDGMENT	$

(NAME OF BONDSMAN IF APPLICABLE)

10. ☐ The defendant/respondent shall notify the Court/Administrative Agency of any change of address/employment within 10 days.

11. ☐ It is further ordered that:

12. ☒ NOTICE: This is an income withholding order. Support payments in arrears by _____ days may be withheld from income without further order of any court or further application for services.

DATE	PRESIDING OFFICER
DATE	JUDGE

RESPONDING JURISDICTION COURT/ADM. AGENCY

COURT/ADMINISTRATIVE AGENCY IDENTIFICATION AND CASE NUMBER

PLAINTIFF/ PETITIONER

VS

DEFENDANT/ RESPONDENT

☐ IV-D   ☐ NON IV-D

OTHER REFERENCE NUMBER

CERTIFICATE AND ORDER

The undersigned, _____ _____ ,
Judge/ Presiding Officer of the above named Court/ Administrative Agency, hereby certifies as follows:

1.   On (date) _____ a petition was filed by the plaintiff/petitioner in this Court/Administrative Agency in a proceeding against the defendant/respondent under the provisions of the reciprocal support statute seeking support of the dependents named in the attached petition.

2.   The defendant/respondent is believed to be residing in your jurisdiction at:

3.   In the opinion of the undersigned Judge/ Presiding Officer, the enclosed petition and testimony set forth facts from which it may be determined that the defendant/respondent owes a duty of support to the named dependents and that such petition should be dealt with according to law.

4.   All payments should be made payable to and sent to:

WHEREFORE, it is ORDERED that three copies of this Certificate, with the petition, testimony, and the required copies of this state's reciprocal support statute, be transmitted to:

DATE

SIGNATURE (JUDGE/ PRESIDING OFFICER)

Form OS 552 (3/87)

RESPONDING FILE COPY

CERTIFICATE AND ORDER
PAGE 1 OF 1 PAGE

CHILD SUPPORT ENFORCEMENT AGENCIES

TITLE IV-D AGENCIES

ALABAMA
Department of Human Resources
Division of Child Support
50 Ripley St.
Montgomery, AL 36130-1801
(205) 242-9300

ALASKA
Child Support Enforcement
Division
Department of Revenue
550 W. 7th Ave., Suite 310
Anchorage, AK 99501-3556
(907) 269-6270

ARIZONA
Division of Child Support
Enforcement
P.O. Box 40458
Phoenix, AZ 85067
Street Address: 3443 N. Central
Ave. 4th Floor
Phoenix, AZ 85012
(602) 274-7646

ARKANSAS
Department of Finance and
Administration
Division of Revenue
Child Support Enforcement Unit
P.O. Box 8133
Little Rock, AR 72203
Street Address: Donaghey
Building
7th and Main
(501) 682-8417

CALIFORNIA
Child Support Program Branch
Department of Social Services
744 P St., Mail Stop 9-010
Sacramento, CA 95814
(916) 654-1556

COLORADO
Division of Child Support
Enforcement
Department of Social Services
1575 Sherman St., 2nd Floor
Denver, CO 80203-1714
(303) 866-5994

CONNECTICUT
Child Support Division
Department of Human Resources
1049 Asylum Ave.
Hartford, CT 06105
(203) 566-3053, 566-4429 or
566-2522

DELAWARE
Division of Child Support
Enforcement
Department of Health & Social
Services
Biggs Building, DHHS Campus
P.O. Box 904
New Castle, DE 19720
(302) 577-4863

DISTRICT OF COLUMBIA
Department of Human Services
Bureau of Paternity and Child
Support Enforcement
613 G St., NW, Suite 1100
Washington, DC 20001
(202) 724-5610

FLORIDA
Office of Child Support
Enforcement
Department of Health &
Rehabilitative Services
1317 Winewood Blvd.
Tallahassee, FL 32399-0700
(904) 488-9900

GEORGIA
Child Support Enforcement
15 Floor

2 Peachtree St., NW
Atlanta, GA 30357
(404) 657-3856

GUAM
Child Support Enforcement Unit
Family Division
238 Archbishop F.C. Flores St.
Suite 701, Pacific News Building
Agana, GU 96910
(671) 475-3360-63

HAWAII
Child Support Enforcement
Agency
Department of Attorney General
P.O. Box 1860
Honolulu, HI 96805-1860
(808) 587-3698

IDAHO
Bureau of Child Support
Enforcement
Department of Health and Welfare
Statehouse Mail, 5th Floor
Boise, ID 83720
(208) 334-5711

ILLINOIS
Child Support Enforcement
Division
Illinois Department of Public Aid
201 S. Grand Ave. East
Springfield, IL 62762-0001
(217) 524-4602

INDIANA
Child Support Enforcement
Division
402 W. Washington St., Rm W360
Indianapolis, IN 46204
(317) 232-4894

IOWA
Child Support Recovery Unit
Department of Human Services
Hoover Building—5th Floor

Des Moines, IA 50319
(515) 281-5580

KANSAS
Child Support Enforcement
Program
Department of Social &
Rehabilitation Services
300 SW Oakley St., Biddle
Building
Topeka, KS 66606
(913) 296-3237

KENTUCKY
Division of Child Support
Enforcement
Cabinet for Human Resources
275 E. Main St., 6th Floor East
Frankfort, KY 40621
(800) 248-1163

LOUISIANA
Support Enforcement Services
Office of Eligibility
Determinations
P.O. Box 94065
Baton Rouge, LA 70804-4065
Street Address: 618 Main St.
(504) 342-7397

MAINE
Division of Support Enforcement
and Recovery
Bureau of Income Maintenance
Department of Human Services
State House, Station 11
Augusta, ME 04333
(207) 289-2886

MARYLAND
Child Support Enforcement
Administration
311 W. Saratoga St.
Baltimore, MD 21201
(301) 333-3981

MASSACHUSETTS
Child Support Enforcement Unit
Department of Revenue
141 Portland St.
Cambridge, MA 02139-1937
(617) 727-4200, ext. 482

MICHIGAN
Office of Child Support
Department of Social Services
P.O. Box 30037
Lansing, MI 48909
Street Address: 235 S. Grand Ave.
Suite 1406

Lansing, MI 48933
(517) 373-7570

MINNESOTA
Office of Child Support
Department of Human Services
444 Lafayette Rd., 4th Floor
St. Paul, MN 55155-3846
(612) 296-2499

MISSISSIPPI
Division of Child Support
Enforcement
Department of Human Services
P.O. Box 352
Jackson, MS 39205
Street Address: 750 N. State St.
Jackson, MS 39202
(601) 359-4863

MISSOURI
Department of Social Services
Division of Child Support
Enforcement
227 Metro Drive
P.O. Box 1527
Jefferson City, MO 65102-1527
(314) 751-4301

MONTANA
Child Support Enforcement
Division
Department of Social and
Rehabilitation Services
P.O. Box 202943
Helena, MT 59620
Street Address: 3075 N. Montana
Ave., Suite 112
(406) 444-4614

NEBRASKA
Child Support Enforcement
Office
Department of Social Services
P.O. Box 95026
Lincoln, NE 68509
Street Address: 301 Centennial
Mall South
5th Floor
(402) 471-9390

NEVADA
Child Support Enforcement
Program
Nevada State Welfare Division
2527 N. Carson St., Capitol
Complex
Carson City, NV 89710
(702) 687-4082

NEW HAMPSHIRE
Child Support Enforcement
Services
Division of Human Services
Health and Human Services
Building
6 Hazen Drive
Concord, NH 03301
(603) 271-4427

NEW JERSEY
Department of Human Services
Bureau of Child Support and
Paternity Programs
CN 716
Trenton, NJ 08625
(800) 621-5437

NEW MEXICO
Child Support Enforcement
Bureau
Department of Human Services
P.O. Box 25109
Santa Fe, NM 87504
Street Address: 2025 S. Pacheo
(505) 827-7200

NEW YORK
Office of Child Support
Enforcement
Department of Social Services
P.O. Box 14
Albany, NY 12260
Street Address: One Commerce
Plaza
(518) 474-9081

NORTH CAROLINA
Child Support Enforcement
Section
Division of Social Services
Department of Human Resources
100 E. Six Forks Rd.
Raleigh, NC 27603-1393
(919) 571-4120

NORTH DAKOTA
Department of Human Services
Child Support Enforcement
Agency
P.O. Box 7190
Bismarck, ND 58507
(701) 224-3582

OHIO
Office of Child Support
Department of Human Services
30 E. Broad St., 27th Floor
Columbus, OH 43266-0423
(614) 752-6561

OKLAHOMA
Child Support Enforcement Unit
Department of Human Services
P.O. Box 53552
Oklahoma City, OK 73125
Street Address: 2409 N. Kelley
Ave.
Annex Building
(405) 522-5871, ext. 2874

OREGON
Recovery Services Section
Adult and Family Services
Division
Department of Human Resources
P.O. Box 14506
Salem, OR 97310
Street Address: 260 Liberty St. NE
(503) 378-5439

PENNSYLVANIA
Bureau of Child Support
Enforcement
Department of Public Welfare
P.O. Box 8018
Harrisburg, PA 17105
(717) 787-3672

PUERTO RICO
Child Support Enforcement
Program
Department of Social Services
P.O. Box 3349
San Juan, PR 00902-3349
(809) 722-4731

RHODE ISLAND
Bureau of Family Support
Department of Human Services
77 Dorance St.
Providence, RI 02903
(401) 277-2847

SOUTH CAROLINA
Department of Social Services
Child Support Enforcement
Division
P.O. Box 1469
Columbia, SC 29202-1469
Street Address: 3150 Harden St.
(803) 737-5870

SOUTH DAKOTA
Office of Child Support
Enforcement
Department of Social Services
700 Governor's Drive
Pierre, SD 57501-2291
(605) 773-3641

TENNESSEE
Child Support Services
Department of Human Services
Citizens Plaza Building—12th
Floor
400 Deadrick St.
Nashville, TN 37248-7400
(615) 741-1820

TEXAS
Child Support Enforcement
Division
Office of the Attorney General
P.O. Box 12548
Austin, TX 78711-2017
Street Address: 300 W. 15th St.,
Suite 1401 M
Austin, TX 78704
(512) 463-9888

UTAH
Office of Recovery Services
Department of Social Services
120 North 200 West, 4th Floor
Salt Lake City, UT 84145-0011
(801) 538-4401

VERMONT
Office of Child Support Services
103 South Main St.
Waterbury, VT 05671-1901
(802) 241-2319

VIRGIN ISLANDS
Paternity and Child Support
Division
Department of Justice
GERS Building, 2nd Floor
48B-50C Krondprans Gade
St. Thomas, VI 00802
(809) 774-5666

VIRGINIA
Division of Support Enforcement
Department of Social Services
730 E. Broad St.
Richmond, VA 23219
(804) 692-1501

WASHINGTON
Office of Support Enforcement
DSHS Revenue Division
P.O. Box 9162
Olympia, WA 98507-9162
(206) 586-3520
Street Address: 712 Pear St. SE
Olympia, WA 98507

WEST VIRGINIA
Child Advocate Office

Division of Health & Human
Services
Building 6, Room 817
State Capitol Complex
Charleston, WV 25305
(304) 558-3780

WISCONSIN
Division of Economic Support
P.O. Box 7935
Madison, WI 53707-7935
Street Address: 1 W. Wilson St.
Room 382
(608) 266-9909

WYOMING
Child Support Enforcement
Section
Division of Public Assistance and
Social Services
Department of Family Services
Hathaway Building, 2300 Capital
Ave.
Cheyenne, WY 82002-0490
(307) 777-6948

MILITARY AGENCIES
(When seeking to *collect* child support from members of the armed services)

ARMY
Defense Finance
and Accounting Service
Indianapolis Center
DFAS-I-GG
Indianapolis, IN 46249-0160
(317) 542-2155

MARINE CORPS
Commanding Officer,
Defense Finance
and Accounting Service
Kansas City Center
Kansas City, MO 64197-0001
(816) 926-7103

NAVY
Director, Navy Family Allowance
Activity
Anthony J. Celebrezze Federal
Building
Cleveland, OH 44199-2087
(216) 522-5301

AIR FORCE
Defense Finance
and Accounting Service
Denver Center
DFAS-DE

Denver, CO 80279-5000
(303) 676-7524

COAST GUARD
Commanding Officer (LGL)
U.S. Coast Guard PPC
Federal Building
444 S.E. Quincy Street
Topeka, KS 66683-3591
(913) 295-2984

MILITARY AGENCIES
(When seeking to *locate* parents in the military)

ARMY
Army Worldwide Locator
Commander, USAEREC
Fort Harrison, IN 46249-5301
(317) 542-4211

MARINE CORPS
CMC MMRB-10
Headquarters, USMC
Building 2008 Suite 201
Quantico, VA 22134-0001
(703) 640-3942

COAST GUARD
Commander (MPC-S-3)
Military Personnel Command Rm 4613
2100 2nd Street, SW
Washington, DC 20593-0001
(202) 267-1663

AIR FORCE
Headquarters
AFMPC/RMIQL
550 C Street West, Suite 50

Randolph AFB, TX
(512) 652-5774

NAVY (for locate w/o support orders)
Bureau of Naval Personnel
P-324D
2 Navy Annex
Washington, DC 20370-0210
(703) 614-3155

NAVY (when there is a support order)
Defense Financing Accounting Service
Att. Dependency Claims
1240 E. 9th Street
Cleveland Center
Cleveland, OH 44199

Divorce, Marriage, Birth, and Death Records

Where to Write for Vital Records (DHHS Publication No. (PHS) 93-1142)

■■■■■ Where to Write for Vital Records

An official certificate of every birth, death, marriage, and divorce should be on file in the locality where the event occurred. The Federal Government does not maintain files or indexes of these records. These records are filed permanently either in a State vital statistics office or in a city, county, or other local office.

To obtain a certified copy of any of the certificates, write or go to the vital statistics office in the State or area where the event occurred. Addresses and fees are given below for each event in the State or area concerned.

To ensure that you receive an accurate record for your requests and that your request is filled with all due speed, please follow the steps outlined below for the information in which you are interested:

☐ Write to the appropriate office to have your request filled.

☐ Under the appropriate office, information has been included for birth and death records concerning whether the State will accept checks or money orders and to whom they should be made payable. This same information would apply when marriage and divorce records are available from the State office. However, it is impossible for us to list fees and addresses for all county offices where marriage and divorce records may be obtained.

☐ For all certified copies requested, make check or money order payable for the correct amount for the number of copies you wish to obtain. Cash is not recommended because the office cannot refund cash lost in transit.

☐ Because all fees are subject to change, a telephone number has been included in the information for each State for use in verifying the current fee.

☐ Type or print all names and addresses in the letter.

☐ Give the following facts when writing for **birth or death records:**

    1. Full name of person whose record is being requested.

    2. Sex.

    3. Parents' names, including maiden name of mother.

    4. Month, day, and year of birth or death.

    5. Place of birth or death (city or town, county, and State; and name of hospital, if known).

    6. Purpose for which copy is needed.

    7. Relationship to person whose record is being requested.

□ Give the following facts when writing for **marriage records:**

    1. Full names of bride and groom.

    2. Month, day, and year of marriage.

    3. Place of marriage (city or town, county, and State).

    4. Purpose for which copy is needed.

    5. Relationship to persons whose record is being requested.

□ Give the following facts when writing for **divorce records:**

    1. Full names of husband and wife.

    2. Date of divorce or annulment.

    3. Place of divorce or annulment.

    4. Type of final decree.

    5. Purpose for which copy is needed.

    6. Relationship to persons whose record is being requested.

The state-by-state addresses begin on page 551.

■■■■ FOREIGN OR HIGH-SEAS BIRTHS AND DEATHS AND CERTIFICATES OF CITIZENSHIP

BIRTH RECORDS OF PERSONS BORN IN FOREIGN COUNTRIES WHO ARE U.S. CITIZENS AT BIRTH

The birth of a child abroad to U.S. citizen parent(s) should be reported to the nearest U.S. Consulate or Embassy as soon after the birth as possible. To do this, the child's parent or legal guardian should file an Application for Consular Report of Birth Abroad of a Citizen of the United States of America (Form FS-579/SS-5). This form may also be used to apply for a social security number for the child. A $10.00 fee is charged for reporting the birth.

The application must be supported by evidence to establish the child's U.S. citizenship. Usually, the following documents are needed:

1. the child's foreign birth certificate;

2. evidence of the U.S. citizenship of the parent(s) such as a certified copy of a birth certificate, U.S. passport, or Certificate of Naturalization or Citizenship;

3. evidence of the parents' marriage, if applicable; and

4. affidavit(s) of the physical presence of the parent(s) in the United States.

Each document should be certified as a true copy of the original by the registrar of the office that issued the document. Other documents may be needed in some cases. Contact the nearest U.S. Embassy or Consulate for details on what evidence is needed.

When the application is approved, a Consular Report of Birth Abroad of a Citizen of the United States of America (Form FS-240) is given to the applicant. This document, known as the Consular Report of Birth, has the same value as proof of citizenship as the Certificate of Citizenship issued by the Immigration and Naturalization Service.

A Consular Report of Birth can be prepared only at a U.S. Embassy or Consulate overseas, and only if the person who is the subject of the report is under 18 years of age when the application is made. A person residing abroad who is now 18 years of age or over, and whose claim to U.S. citizenship has never been documented, should contact the nearest U.S. Embassy or Consulate for assistance in registering as a U.S. citizen.

As of November 1, 1990, the U.S. Department of State no longer issues multiple copies of the Consular Report of Birth. However, a replacement Consular Report of Birth may be issued if the original document is lost or mutilated. The U.S. Department of State also issues certified copies of the Certification of Report of Birth (DS-1350), which contains the same information as on the Consular Report of Birth. The DS-1350 serves most needs and can be issued in multiple copies. Documents are issued only to the subject of the Consular Report of Birth, the subject's parents or legal guardian, or a person who submits written authorization from the subject.

To request copies of the DS-1350 or a replacement FS-240, write to Passport Services, Correspondence Branch, U.S. Department of State, 1425 K St. NW, Room 386, Washington, DC 20522-1705. Please include the following items:

1. the full name of the child at birth (and any adoptive name);

2. the date and place of birth;

3. the names of the parents;

4. the serial number of the FS-240 (if the FS-240 was issued after November 1, 1990);

5. any available passport information;

6. the signature of the requestor and the requestor's relationship to the subject;

7. a check or money order for $10.00 per document requested, made payable to the U.S. Department of State; and

8. if applying for a replacement FS-240, a notarized affidavit by the subject, parent, or legal representative that states the name, date, and place of birth of the subject, and the whereabouts of the original FS-240.

To obtain a Consular Report of Birth in a new name, send a written request and fees as noted above, the original (or replacement) Consular Report of Birth, or if not available, a notarized affidavit about its whereabouts. Also, send a certified copy of the court order or final adoption decree which identifies the child and shows the change of name with the request. If the name has been changed informally, submit public records and affidavits that show the change of name.

BIRTH RECORDS OF ALIEN CHILDREN ADOPTED BY U.S. CITIZENS

Birth certifications for alien children adopted by U.S. citizens and lawfully admitted to the United States may be obtained from the Immigration and Naturalization Service (INS) if the birth information is on file.

Certification may be issued for children under 21 years of age who were born in a foreign country. Requests must be submitted on INS Form G-641, which can be obtained from any INS office. (Address can be found in a telephone directory.) For Certification of Birth Data (INS Form G-350), a $15.00 search fee, paid by check or money order, should accompany INS Form G-641.

Certification can be issued in the new name of an adopted or legitimated child after proof of an adoption or legitimation is submitted to INS. Because it may be issued for a child who has not yet become a U.S. citizen, this certification (Form G-350) is not proof of U.S. nationality.

CERTIFICATE OF CITIZENSHIP

Persons who were born abroad and later naturalized as U.S. citizens or who were born in a foreign country to a U.S. citizen (parent or parents) may apply for a certificate of citizenship pursuant to the provisions of Section 341 of the Immigration and Nationality Act. Application can be made for this document in the United States at the nearest office of the Immigration and Naturalization Service (INS). The INS will issue a certification of citizenship for the person if proof of citizenship is submitted and the person is within the United States. The decision whether to apply for a certificate of citizenship is optional; its possession is not mandatory because a valid U.S. passport or a Form FS-240 has the same evidentiary status.

DEATH RECORDS OF U.S. CITIZENS WHO DIE IN FOREIGN COUNTRIES

The death of a U.S. citizen in a foreign country may be reported to the nearest U.S. consular office. If reported, and a copy of the local death certificate and evidence of U.S. citizenship are presented, the consul prepares the official "Report of the Death of an American Citizen Abroad" (Form OF-180). A copy of the Report of Death is then filed permanently in the U.S. Department of State (see exceptions below).

To obtain a copy of a report filed in 1960 or after, write to Passport Services, Correspondence Branch, U.S. Department of State, Washington, DC 20522-1705. The fee for a copy is $10.00. Fee may be subject to change.

Reports of Death filed before 1960 are maintained by the National Archives and Records Service, Diplomatic Records Branch, Washington, DC 20408. Requests for such records should be sent directly to that office.

Reports of deaths of persons serving in the Armed Forces of the United States (Army, Navy, Marines, Air Force, or Coast Guard) or civilian employees of the Department of Defense are not maintained by the U.S. Department of State. In these cases, requests for copies of records should be sent to the National Personnel Records Center (Military Personnel Records), 9700 Page Ave., St. Louis, Missouri 63132-5100.

RECORDS OF BIRTH AND DEATH OCCURRING ON VESSELS OR AIRCRAFT ON THE HIGH SEAS

When a birth or death occurs on the high seas, whether in an aircraft or on a vessel, the record is usually filed at the next port of call.

1. If the vessel or aircraft docked or landed at a foreign port, requests for copies of the record may be made to the U.S. Department of State, Washington, DC 20522-1705.

2. If the first port of entry was in the United States, write to the registration authority in the city where the vessel or aircraft docked or landed in the United States.

3. If the vessel was of U.S. registry, contact the local authorities at the port of entry and/or search the vessel logs at the U.S. Coast Guard Facility at the vessel's final port of call for that voyage.

RECORDS MAINTAINED BY FOREIGN COUNTRIES

Most, but not all, foreign countries record births and deaths. It is not possible to list in this publication all foreign vital records offices, the charges they make for copies of records, or the information they may require to locate a record. However, most foreign countries will provide certifications of births and deaths occurring within their boundaries.

Persons who need a copy of a foreign birth or death record should contact the Embassy or the nearest Consulate in the United States of the country in which the death occurred. Addresses and telephone numbers for these offices are listed in the U.S. Department of State Publication 7846, "Foreign Consular Offices in the United States," which is available in many local libraries. Copies of this publication may also be purchased from the U.S. Government Printing Office, Washington, DC 20402.

If the Embassy or Consulate is unable to provide assistance, U.S. citizens may obtain assistance by writing to the Office of Overseas Citizens Services, U.S. Department of State, Washington, DC 20520-4818. Aliens residing in the United States may be able to obtain assistance through the Embassy or Consulate of their country of nationality.

OBTAINING VITAL RECORDS IN AMERICA: A STATE-BY-STATE SURVEY

PLACE OF EVENT	COST OF COPY	ADDRESS	REMARKS
ALABAMA			
Birth or Death	$12.00	Center for Health Statistics State Department of Public Health P.O. Box 5625 Montgomery, AL 36103-5625	State office has had records since January 1908. Additional copies at same time are $4.00 each. Fee for special searches is $10.00 per hour. Money order or check should be made payable to **Center for Health Statistics.** Personal checks are accepted. To verify current fees, the telephone number is **(205) 242-5033.**
Marriage	$12.00	Same as Birth or Death	State office has had records since August 1936.
	Varies	See remarks	Probate Judge in county where license was issued.
Divorce	$12.00	Same as Birth or Death	State office has had records since January 1950.
	Varies	See remarks	Clerk or Register of Court of Equity in county where divorce was granted.
ALASKA			
Birth or Death	$7.00	Department of Health and Social Services Bureau of Vital Statistics P.O. Box H-02G Juneau, AK 99811-0675	State office has had records since January 1913. Money order should be made payable to **Bureau of Vital Statistics.** Personal checks are *not* accepted. To verify current fees, the telephone number is **(907) 465-3391.** This will be a **recorded** message.

Continued

—Continued

PLACE OF EVENT	COST OF COPY	ADDRESS	REMARKS
ALASKA, Continued			
Marriage	$7.00	Same as Birth or Death	State office has had records since 1913.
Divorce	$7.00	Same as Birth or Death	State office has had records since 1950.
	Varies	See remarks	Clerk of Superior Court in judicial district where divorce was granted. Juneau and Ketchikan (First District), Nome (Second District), Anchorage (Third District), Fairbanks (Fourth District).
AMERICAN SAMOA			
Birth or Death	$2.00	Registrar of Vital Statistics Vital Statistics Section Government of American Samoa Pago Pago, AS 96799	Registrar has had records since 1900. Money order should be made payable to **ASG Treasurer.** Personal checks are *not* accepted. To verify current fees, the telephone number is **(684) 633-1222, ext. 214.** Personal identification required before record will be sent.
Marriage	$2.00	Same as Birth or Death	
Divorce	$1.00	High Court of American Samoa Tutuila, AS 96799	
ARIZONA			
Birth (long form)	$8.00	Vital Records Section	State office has had records since July 1909 and abstracts of records filed in counties before then.
Birth (short form)	$5.00	Arizona Department of Health Services P.O. Box 3887	
Death	$5.00	Phoenix, AZ 85030	Check or money order should be made payable to **Office of Vital Records.** Personal checks are accepted. To verify current fees, the telephone number is **(602) 255-3260.** This will be a **recorded** message. Applicants must submit a copy of picture identification or have their request notarized.
Marriage	Varies	See remarks	Clerk of Superior Court in county where license was issued.
Divorce	Varies	See remarks	Clerk of Superior Court in county where divorce was granted.
ARKANSAS			
Birth	$5.00	Division of Vital Records	State office has had records since February 1914 and some original Little Rock and Fort Smith records from 1881. Additional copies of death record, when requested at the same time, are $1.00 each.
Death	$4.00	Arkansas Department of Health 4815 West Markham Street Little Rock, AR 72201	
			Check or money order should be made payable to **Arkansas Department of Health.** Personal checks are accepted. To verify current fees, the telephone number is **(501) 661-2336.** This will be a **recorded** message.

Continued

—Continued

PLACE OF EVENT	COST OF COPY	ADDRESS	REMARKS
ARKANSAS, *Continued*			
Marriage	$5.00	Same as Birth or Death	Coupons since 1917.
	Varies	See remarks	Full certified copy may be obtained from County Clerk in county where license was issued.
Divorce	$5.00	Same as Birth or Death	Coupons since 1923.
	Varies	See remarks	Full certified copy may be obtained from Circuit or Chancery Clerk in county where divorce was granted.
CALIFORNIA			
Birth	$12.00	Vital Statistics Section	State office has had records since July 1905. For earlier records, write to County Recorder in county where event occurred.
Death	$8.00	Department of Health Services P.O. Box 730241 Sacramento, CA 94244-0241	
			Check or money order should be made payable to **State Registrar, Department of Health Services** or **Vital Statistics.** Personal checks are accepted. To verify current fees, the telephone number is **(916) 445-2684.**
Heirloom Birth	$31.00	Not available until further notice	Decorative birth certificate (11" × 14") suitable for framing.
Marriage	$12.00	Same as Birth or Death	State office has had records since July 1905. For earlier records, write to County Recorder in county where event occurred.
Divorce	$12.00	Same as Birth or Death	Fee is for search and identification of county where certified copy can be obtained. Certified copies are not available from State Health Department.
	Varies	See remarks	Clerk of Superior Court in county where divorce was granted.
CANAL ZONE			
Birth or Death	$2.00	Panama Canal Commission Vital Statistics Clerk APOAA 34011	Records available from May 1904 to September 1979.
Marriage	$1.00	Same as Birth or Death	Records available from May 1904 to September 1979.
Divorce	$0.50	Same as Birth or Death	Records available from May 1904 to September 1979.
COLORADO			
Birth or Death	$12.00	Vital Records Section Colorado Department of Health 4300 Cherry Creek Drive South Denver, CO 80222-1530	State office has had death records since 1900 and birth records since 1910. State office also has birth records for some counties for years before 1910. Additional copies of the same record ordered at the same time are $6.00.

Continued

—*Continued*

PLACE OF EVENT	COST OF COPY	ADDRESS	REMARKS
COLORADO, *Continued*			Check or money order should be made payable to **Colorado Department of Health.** Personal checks are accepted. To verify current fees, the telephone number is **(303) 756-4464.** This will be a **recorded** message.
Marriage	See remarks	Same as Birth or Death	Certified copies are not available from State Health Department. Statewide index of records for 1900–39 and 1975 to present. Fee for verification is $12.00
	Varies	See remarks	Copies available from County Clerk in county where license was issued.
Divorce	See remarks	Same as Birth or Death	Certified copies are not available from State Health Department. Statewide index of records for 1900–39 and 1968 to present. Fee for verification is $12.00.
	Varies	See remarks	Copies available from Clerk of District Court in county where divorce was granted.
CONNECTICUT			
Birth or Death	$5.00	Vital Records Department of Health Services 150 Washington Street Hartford, CT 06106	State office has had records since July 1897. For earlier records, write to Registrar of Vital Statistics in town or city where event occurred.
			Check or money order should be made payable to **Department of Health Services.** Personal checks are accepted. FAX requests are not accepted. Must have original signature on request. To verify current fees, the telephone number is **(203) 566-2334.** This will be a **recorded** message.
Marriage	$5.00	Same as Birth or Death	Records since July 1879 at State Registry.
		See remarks	For older records, contact the Registrar of Vital Statistics in town where marriage occurred.
Divorce		See remarks	Applicant must contact Clerk of Superior Court where divorce was granted. State office does not have divorce decrees and cannot issue certified copies.
DELAWARE			
Birth or death	$5.00	Office of Vital Statistics Division of Public Health P.O. Box 637 Dover, DE 19903	State office has death records since 1930 and birth records since 1920. Additional copies of the same record requested at the same time are $3.00 each.
			Check or money order should be made payable to **Office of Vital Statistics.** Personal checks are accepted. To verify current fees, the telephone number is **(302) 739-4721.**

Continued

—Continued

PLACE OF EVENT	COST OF COPY	ADDRESS	REMARKS
DELAWARE, **Continued**			
Marriage	$5.00	Same as Birth or Death	Records since 1930. Additional copies of the same record requested at the same time are $3.00 each.
Divorce	See remarks	Same as Birth or Death	Records since 1935. Inquiries will be forwarded to appropriate office. Fee for search and verification of essential facts of divorce is $5.00 for each 5-year period searched. Certified copies are not available from State office.
	$2.00	See remarks	Prothonotary in county where divorce was granted up to 1975. For divorces granted after 1975, the parties concerned should contact Family Court in county where divorce was granted.
DISTRICT OF COLUMBIA			
Birth or Death	$12.00	Vital Records Branch Room 3009 425 I Street, NW Washington, DC 20001	Office has had death records since 1855 and birth records since 1874, but no death records were filed during the Civil War. Cashiers check or money order should be made payable to **DC Treasurer.** To verify current fees, the telephone number is **(202) 727-9281.**
Marriage	$5.00	Marriage Bureau 515 5th Street, NW Washington, DC 20001	
Divorce	$2.00	Clerk, Superior court for the District of Columbia, Family Division 500 Indiana Avenue, NW Washington, DC 20001	Records since September 16, 1956.
	Varies	Clerk, U.S. District Court for the District of Columbia Washington, DC 20001	Records before September 16, 1956.
FLORIDA			
Birth Death	$9.00 $5.00	Department of Health and Rehabilitative Services Office of Vital Statistics P.O. Box 210 1217 Pearl Street Jacksonville, FL 32231	State office has some birth records dating back to April 1865 and some death records dating back to August 1877. The majority of records date from January 1917. (If the exact date is unknown, the fee is $9.00 (births) or $5.00 (deaths) for the first year searched and $2.00 for each additional years up to a maximum of $50.00. Fee includes one certification of record if found or certified statement stating record not on file.) Additional copies are $4.00 each when requested at the same time.

Continued

—Continued

PLACE OF EVENT	COST OF COPY	ADDRESS	REMARKS
FLORIDA, *Continued*			Check or money order should be made payable to **Office of Vital Statistics.** Personal checks are accepted. To verify current fees, the telephone number is **(904) 359-6900.** This will be a **recorded** message.
Marriage	$5.00	Same as Birth or Death	Records since June 6, 1927. (If the exact date is unknown, the fee is $5.00 for the first year searched and $2.00 for each additional year up to a maximum of $50.00. Fee includes one copy of record if found or certified statement stating record not on file.) Additional copies are $4.00 each when requested at the same time.
Divorce	$5.00	Same as Birth or Death	Records since June 6, 1927. (If the exact date is unknown, the fee is $5.00 for the first year searched and $2.00 for each additional year up to a maximum of $50.00. Fee includes one copy of record if found or certified statement stating record not on file.) Additional copies are $4.00 each when requested at the same time.
GEORGIA			
Birth or Death	$10.00	Georgia Department of Human Resources Vital Records Unit Room 217-H 47 Trinity Avenue, SW Atlanta, GA 30334	State office has had records since January 1919. For earlier records in Atlanta or Savannah, write to County Health Department in county where event occurred. Additional copies of same record ordered at same time are $5.00 each except birth cards, which are $10.00 each.
			Money order should be made payable to **Vital Records, GA. DHR.** Personal checks are *not* accepted. To verify current fees, the telephone number is **(404) 656-4900.** This is a **recorded** message.
Marriage	$10.00	Same as Birth or Death	Centralized State records since June 9, 1952. Certified copies are issued at State office. Inquiries about marriages occurring before June 9, 1952, will be forwarded to appropriate Probate Judge in county where license was issued.
	Varies	See remarks	Probate Judge in county where license issued.
Divorce	$2.00 for certification plus $0.50 per page	See remarks	Centralized State records since June 9, 1952. Certified copies are not issued at State office. Inquiries will be forwarded to appropriate Clerk of Superior Court in county where divorce was granted.
		See remarks	Clerk of Superior Court in county where divorce was granted.

Continued

—Continued

PLACE OF EVENT	COST OF COPY	ADDRESS	REMARKS
GUAM			
Birth or Death	$5.00	Office of Vital Statistics Department of Public Health and Social Services Government of Guam P.O. Box 2816 Agana, GU, M.I. 96910	Office has had records since October 16, 1901. Money order should be made payable to **Treasurer of Guam.** Personal checks are *not* accepted. To verify current fees, the telephone number is **(671) 734-4589.**
Marriage	$5.00	Same as Birth or Death	
Divorce	Varies	Clerk, Superior Court of Guam Agana, GU, M.I. 96910	
HAWAII			
Birth or Death	$2.00	Office of Health Status Monitoring State Department of Health P.O. Box 3378 Honolulu, HI 96801	State office has had records since 1853. Check or money order should be made payable to **State Department of Health.** Personal checks are accepted for the correct amount only. To verify current fees, the telephone number is **(808) 586-4533.** This is a **recorded** message.
Marriage	$2.00	Same as Birth or Death	
Divorce	$2.00	Same as Birth or Death	Records since July 1951.
	Varies	See remarks	Circuit Court in county where divorce was granted.
IDAHO			
Birth	$8.00	Vital Statistics Unit Idaho Department of Health and Welfare 450 West State Street Statehouse Mail Boise, ID 83720-9990	State office has had records since July 1911. For records from 1907 to 1911, write to County Recorder in county where event occurred.
Wallet card	$8.00		
Death	$8.00		
Heirloom Birth	$30.00	Same as Birth or Death	Decorative birth certificates (8½" × 11" and 5" × 7") are suitable for framing. Check or money order should be made payable to **Idaho Vital Statistics.** Personal checks are accepted. To verify current fees, the telephone number is **(208) 334-5988.** This is a **recorded** message.
Marriage	$8.00	Same as Birth or Death	Records since May 1947. Earlier records are with County Recorder in county where license was issued.
	Varies	See remarks	County Recorder in county where license was issued.
Divorce	$8.00	Same as Birth or Death	Records since May 1947. Earlier records are with County Recorder in county where divorce was granted.
	Varies	See remarks	County records in county where divorce was granted.

Continued

—Continued

PLACE OF EVENT	COST OF COPY	ADDRESS	REMARKS
ILLINOIS			
Birth or Death	$15.00 certified copy $10.00 certification	Division of Vital Records Illinois Department of Public Health 605 West Jefferson Street Springfield, IL 62702-5097	State office has had records since January 1916. For earlier records and for copies of State records since January 1916, write to County Clerk in county where event occurred (county fees vary). The fee for a search of the State files is $10.00. If the record is found, one certification is issued at no additional charge. Additional certifications of the same record ordered at the same time are $2.00 each. The fee for a full certified copy is $15.00. Additional certified copies of the same record ordered at the same time are $2.00 each.
			Money orders, certified checks, or personal checks should be made payable to **Illinois Department of Public Health.** To verify current fees, the telephone number is **(217) 782-6553.** This will be a **recorded** message.
Marriage	$5.00	Same as Birth or Death	Marriage Index since January 1962. Selected items may be verified (fee $5.00). Certified copies are NOT available from State office.
			For certified copies, write to the County Clerk in county where license was issued.
Divorce	$5.00	Same as Birth or Death	Divorce Index since January 1962. Selected items may be verified (fee $5.00). Certified copies are NOT available from State office.
			For certified copies, write to the Clerk of Circuit Court in county where divorce was granted.
INDIANA			
Birth Death	$6.00 $4.00	Vital Records Section State Department of Health 1330 West Michigan Street P.O. Box 1964 Indianapolis, IN 46206-1964	State office has had birth records since October 1907 and death records since 1900. Additional copies of the same record ordered at the same time are $1.00 each. For earlier records, write to Health Officer in city or county where event occurred.
			Check or money order should be made payable to **Indiana State Department of Health.** Personal checks are accepted. To verify current fees, the telephone number is **(317) 633-0274.**
Marriage	See remarks	Same as Birth or Death	Marriage index since 1958. Certified copies are not available from State Health Department.
	Varies	See remarks	Clerk of Circuit County or Clerk of Superior Court in county where license was issued.

Continued

—Continued

PLACE OF EVENT	COST OF COPY	ADDRESS	REMARKS
INDIANA, Continued			
Divorce	Varies	See remarks	County Clerk in county where divorce was granted.
IOWA			
Birth or Death	$6.00	Iowa Department of Public Health Vital Records Section Lucas Office Building 321 East 12th Street Des Moines, IA 50319-0075	State office has had records since July 1880. Check or money order should be made payable to **Iowa Department of Public Health.** To verify current fees, the telephone number is **(515) 281-4944.** This will be a **recorded** message.
Marriage	$6.00	Same as Birth or Death	State office has had records since July 1880.
Divorce	See remarks	Same as Birth or Death	Brief statistical record only since 1906. Inquiries will be forwarded to appropriate office. Certified copies are not available from State Health Department.
	$6.00	See remarks	Clerk of District Court in county where divorce was granted.
KANSAS			
Birth Death	$10.00 $7.00	Office of Vital Statistics Kansas State Department of Health and Environment 900 Jackson Street Topeka, KS 66612-1290	State office has had records since July 1911. For earlier records, write to county Clerk in county where event occurred. Additional copies of same record ordered at same time are $5.00 each. Check or money order should be made payable to **State Registrar of Vital Statistics.** Personal checks are accepted. To verify current fees, the telephone number is **(913) 296-1400.** This will be a **recorded** message.
Marriage	$7.00	Same as Birth or Death	State office has had records since May 1913.
	Varies	See remarks	District Judge in county where license was issued.
Divorce	$7.00	Same as Birth or Death	State office has had records since July 1951.
	Varies	See remarks	Clerk of District Court in county where divorce was granted.
KENTUCKY			
Birth Death	$7.00 $6.00	Office of Vital Statistics Department for Health Services 275 East Main Street Frankfort, KY 40621	State office has had records since January 1911 and some records for the cities of Louisville, Lexington, Covington, and Newport before then. Check or money order should be made payable to **Kentucky State Treasurer.** Personal checks are accepted. To verify current fees, the telephone number is **(502) 564-4212.**

Continued

—Continued

PLACE OF EVENT	COST OF COPY	ADDRESS	REMARKS
KENTUCKY, *Continued*			
Marriage	$6.00	Same as Birth or Death	Records since June 1958.
	Varies	See remarks	Clerk of County Court in county where license was issued.
Divorce	$6.00	Same as Birth or Death	Records since June 1958.
	Varies	See remarks	Clerk of Circuit Court in county where decree was issued.
LOUISIANA			
Birth (long form) Birth (short form) Death	$10.00 $7.00 $5.00	Vital Records Registry Office of Public Health 325 Loyola Avenue New Orleans, LA 70112	State office has had records since July 1914. Birth records for City of New Orleans are available from 1892. Death records are available since 1942. Older birth, death, and marriage records are available through the Louisiana State Archives, P.O. Box 94125, Baton Rouge, LA 70804.
			Check or money order should be made payable to **Vital Records.** Personal checks are accepted. To verify current fees, the telephone number is **(504) 568-5152.**
Marriage Orleans Parish	$5.00	Same as Birth or Death	
Other Parishes	Varies	See remarks	Certified copies are issued by Clerk of Court in parish where license was issued.
Divorce	Varies	See remarks	Clerk of Court in parish where divorce was granted.
MAINE			
Birth or Death	$10.00	Office of Vital Statistics Maine Department of Human Services State House Station 11 Augusta, ME 04333-0011	State office has had records since 1892. Records for 1892–1922 are available at the Maine State Archives. For earlier records, write to the municipality where the event occurred. Additional copies of same record ordered at same time are $4.00 each.
			Check or money order should be made payable to **Treasurer, State of Maine.** Personal checks are accepted. To verify current fees, he telephone number is **(207) 289-3184.**
Marriage	$10.00	Same as Birth or Death	Same as Birth or Death
Divorce	$10.00	Same as Birth or Death	Same as Birth or Death
	Varies	See remarks	Clerk of District Court in judicial division where divorce was granted.

Continued

—Continued

PLACE OF EVENT	COST OF COPY	ADDRESS	REMARKS
MARYLAND			
Birth or Death	$4.00	Division of Vital Records Department of Health and Mental Hygiene Metro Executive Building 4201 Patterson Avenue P.O. Box 68760 Baltimore, MD 21215-0020	State office has had records since August 1898. Records for City of Baltimore are available from January 1875. Will not do research for genealogical studies. Must apply to State of Maryland Archives, 350 Rowe Blvd., Annapolis, MD 21401, (301) 974-3914. Check or money order should be made payable to **Division of Vital Records.** Personal checks are accepted. To verify current fees, the telephone number is **(301) 225-5988.** This will be a **recorded** message.
Marriage	$4.00	Same as Birth or Death	Records since June 1951.
	Varies	See remarks	Clerk of Circuit Court in county where license was issued or Clerk of Court of Common Pleas of Baltimore City (for licenses issued in City of Baltimore).
Divorce Verification only	No fee	Same as Birth or Death	Records since January 1961. Certified copies are not available from State office. Some items may be verified.
	Varies	See remarks	Clerk of Circuit Court in county where divorce was granted.
MASSACHUSETTS			
Birth or Death	$6.00 (In person) $11.00 (Mail request) $3.00 (State Archives)	Registry of Vital Records and Statistics 150 Tremont Street, Room B-3 Boston, MA 02111	State office has records since 1901. For earlier records, write to The Massachusetts Archives at Columbia Point, 220 Morrissey Boulevard, Boston, MA 02125 (617) 727-2816. Check or money order should be made payable to **Commonwealth of Massachusetts.** Personal checks are accepted. To verify current fees, the telephone number is **(617) 727-7388.** This will be a **recorded** message.
Marriage	Same as Birth or Death	Same as Birth or Death	Records since 1901.
Divorce	See remarks	Same as Birth or Death	Index only since 1952. Inquirer will be directed where to send request. Certified copies are not available from State office.
	$3.00	See remarks	Registrar of Probate Court in county where divorce was granted.
MICHIGAN			
Birth or Death	$13.00	Office of the State Registrar and Center for Health Statistics Michigan Department of Public Health 3423 North Logan Street Lansing, MI 48909	State office has had records since 1867. Copies of most records since 1867 may also be obtained from County Clerk in county where event occurred. Fees vary from county to county. Detroit records may be obtained from the City of Detroit Health Department for births occurring since 1893 and for deaths since 1897.

Continued

—Continued

PLACE OF EVENT	COST OF COPY	ADDRESS	REMARKS
MICHIGAN, *Continued*			Check or money order should be made payable to **State of Michigan.** Personal checks are accepted. To verify current fees, the telephone number is **(517) 335-8655.** This will be a **recorded** message.
Marriage	$13.00	Same as Birth or Death	Records since April 1867.
	Varies	See remarks	County Clerk in county where license was issued.
Divorce	$13.00	Same as Birth or Death	Records since 1897.
	Varies	See remarks	County Clerk in county where divorce was granted.
MINNESOTA			
Birth Death	$11.00 $8.00	Minnesota Department of Health Section of Vital Statistics 717 Delaware Street, SE P.O. Box 9441 Minneapolis, MN 55440	State office has had records since January 1908. Copies of earlier records may be obtained from Local Registrar in county where event occurred or from the St. Paul City Health Department if the event occurred in St. Paul. Additional copies of the birth record when ordered at the same time are $5.00 each. Additional copies of the death record when ordered at the same time are $2.00 each.
			Check or money order should be made payable to **Treasurer, State of Minnesota.** Personal checks are accepted. To verify current fees, the telephone number is **(612) 623-5121.**
Marriage	See remarks	Same as Birth or Death	Statewide index since January 1958. Inquiries will be forwarded to appropriate office. Certified copies are not available from State Department of Health.
	$8.00	See remarks	Local Registrar in county where license was issued. Additional copies of the marriage record when ordered at the same time are $2.00 each.
Divorce	See remarks	Same as Birth or Death	Index since January 1970. Certified copies are not available from State office.
	Varies	See remarks	Local Registrar in county where divorce was granted.
MISSISSIPPI			
Birth Birth (short form) Death	$12.00 $7.00 $10.00	Vital Records State Department of Health 2423 North State Street Jackson, MS 39216	State office has had records since 1912. Full copies of birth certificates obtained within 1 year after the event are $7.00. Additional copies of same record ordered at same time are $3.00 each for birth; $2.00 each for death and marriage.

Continued

—Continued

PLACE OF EVENT	COST OF COPY	ADDRESS	REMARKS
MISSISSIPPI, *Continued*			For out-of-State requests, only bank or postal money orders are accepted and should be made payable to **Mississippi State Department of Health.** Personal checks are accepted *only* for in-State requests. To verify current fees, the telephone number is **(601) 960-7981.** A **recorded** message may be reached on **(601) 960-7450.**
Marriage	$10.00	Same as Birth or Death	Statistical records only from January 1926 to July 1, 1938, and since January 1942.
	$3.00	See remarks	Circuit Clerk in county where license was issued.
Divorce	See remarks	Same as Birth or Death	Records since January 1926. Certified copies are not available from State office. Index search only available at $6.00 for each 5-year increment. Book and page number for county record provided.
	Varies	See remarks	Chancery Clerk in county where divorce was granted.
MISSOURI Birth or Death	$10.00	Missouri Department of Health Bureau of Vital Records 1730 East Elm P.O. Box 570 Jefferson City, MO 65102-0570	State office has had records since January 1910. If event occurred in St. Louis (City), St. Louis County, or Kansas City before 1910, write to the City or County Health Department. Copies of these records are $3.00 each in St. Louis City and $5.00 each in St. Louis County. In Kansas City, $6.00 for first copy and $3.00 for each additional copy ordered at same time.
			Check or money order should be made payable to **Missouri Department of Health.** Personal checks are accepted. To verify current fees on birth and death records, the telephone number is **(314) 751-6400.**
Marriage	No fee	Same as Birth or Death	Indexes since July 1948. Correspondent will be referred to appropriate Recorder of Deeds in county where license was issued.
	Varies	See remarks	Recorder of Deeds in county where license was issued.
Divorce	No fee	Same as Birth or Death	Indexes since July 1948. Certified copies are not available from State Health Department. Inquiries will be forwarded to appropriate office.
	Varies	See remarks	Clerk of Circuit Court in county where divorce was granted.

Continued

—Continued

PLACE OF EVENT	COST OF COPY	ADDRESS	REMARKS
MONTANA			
Birth or Death	$10.00	Bureau of Records and Statistics State Department of Health and Environmental Sciences Helena, MT 59620	State office has had records since late 1907. Check or money order should be made payable to **Montana Department of Health and Environmental Sciences.** Personal checks are accepted. To verify current fees, the telephone number is **(406) 444-2614.**
Marriage	See remarks	Same as Birth or Death	Records since July 1943. Some items may be verified. Inquiries will be forwarded to appropriate office. Apply to county where license was issued if known. Certified copies are not available from State office.
	Varies	See remarks	Clerk of District Court in county where license was issued.
Divorce	See remarks	Same as Birth or Death	Records since July 1943. Some items may be verified. Inquiries will be forwarded to appropriate office. Apply to court where divorce was granted if known. Certified copies are not available from State office.
	Varies	See remarks	Clerk of District Court in county where divorce was granted.
NEBRASKA			
Birth Death	$8.00 $7.00	Birth of Vital Statistics State Department of Health 301 Centennial Mall South P.O. Box 95007 Lincoln, NE 68509-5007	State office has had records since late 1904. If birth occurred before then, write the State office for information. Check or money order should be made payable to **Bureau of Vital Statistics.** Personal checks are accepted. To verify current fees, the telephone number is **(402) 471-2871.** This is a **recorded** message.
Marriage	$7.00 Varies	Same as Birth or Death See remarks	Records since January 1909. County Court in county where license was issued.
Divorce	$7.00 Varies	Same as Birth or Death See remarks	Records since January 1909. Clerk of District Court in county where divorce was granted.
NEVADA			
Birth Death	$11.00 $8.00	Division of Health—Vital Statistics Capitol Complex 505 East King Street #102 Carson City, NV 89710	State office has records since July 1911. For earlier records, write to County Recorder in county where event occurred. Check or money order should be made payable to **Section of Vital Statistics.** Personal checks are accepted. To verify current fees, the telephone number is **(702) 687-4480.**

Continued

—Continued

PLACE OF EVENT	COST OF COPY	ADDRESS	REMARKS
NEVADA, Continued			
Marriage	See remarks	Same as Birth or Death	Indexes since January 1968. Certified copies are not available from State Health Department. Inquiries will be forwarded to appropriate office.
	Varies	See remarks	County Recorder in county where license was issued.
Divorce	See remarks	Same as Birth or Death	Indexes since January 1968. Certified copies are not available from State Health Department. Inquiries will be forwarded to appropriate office.
	Varies	See remarks	County Clerk in county where divorce was granted.
NEW HAMPSHIRE			
Birth or Death	$10.00	Bureau of Vital Records Health and Welfare Building 6 Hazen Drive Concord, NH 03301	State office has had records since 1640. Copies of records may be obtained from State office or from City or Town Clerk in place where event occurred. Additional copies ordered at the same time are $6.00 each.
			Check or money order should be made payable to **Treasurer, State of New Hampshire.** Personal checks are accepted. To verify current fees, the telephone number is **(603) 271-4654.** This will be a **recorded** message.
Marriage	$10.00	Same as Birth or Death	Records since 1640.
	$10.00	See remarks	Town Clerk in town where license was issued.
Divorce	$10.00	Same as Birth or Death	Records since 1808.
	Varies	See remarks	Clerk of Superior Court where divorce was granted.
NEW JERSEY			
Birth or Death	$4.00	State Department of Health Bureau of Vital Statistics South Warren and Market Streets CN 370 Trenton, NJ 08625	State office has had records since June 1878. Additional copies of same record ordered at same time are $2.00 each. If the exact date is unknown, the fee is an additional $1.00 per year searched.
		Archives and History Bureau State Library Division State Department of Education Trenton, NJ 08625	For records from May 1848 to May 1878. Check or money order should be made payable to **New Jersey State Department of Health.** Personal checks are accepted. To verify current fees, the telephone number is **(609) 292-4087.** This will be a **recorded** message.
Marriage	$4.00	Same as Birth or Death	If the exact date is unknown, the fee is an additional $1.00 per year searched.
	$2.00	Archives and History Bureau State Library Division State Department of Education Trenton, NJ 08625	For records from May 1848 to May 1878.

Continued

—Continued

PLACE OF EVENT	COST OF COPY	ADDRESS	REMARKS
NEW JERSEY, **Continued**			
Divorce	$10.00	Public Information Center CN 967 Trenton, NJ 08625	The fee is for a certified Blue Seal copy. Make check payable to **Clerk of the Superior Court.**
NEW MEXICO			
Birth Death	$10.00 $5.00	Vital Statistics New Mexico Health Services Division P.O. Box 26110 Santa Fe, NM 87502	State office has had records since 1920 and delayed records since 1880. Check or money order should be made payable to **Vital Statistics.** Personal checks are accepted. To verify current fees, the telephone number is **(505) 827-2338.** This will be a **recorded** message.
Marriage	Varies	See remarks	County Clerk in county where license was issued.
Divorce	Varies	See remarks	Clerk of Superior Court where divorce was granted.
NEW YORK (except New York City)			
Birth or Death	$15.00	Vital Records Section State Department of Health Empire State Plaza Tower Building Albany, NY 12237-0023	State office has had records since 1880. For records before 1914 in Albany, Buffalo, and Yonkers, or before 1880 in any other city, write to Registrar of Vital Statistics in city where event occurred. For the rest of the State, except New York City, write to State office. Check or money order should be made payable to **New York State Department of Health.** Personal checks are accepted. To verify current fees, the telephone number is **(518) 474-3075.** This will be a **recorded** message.
Marriage	$5.00 $5.00	Same as Birth or Death See remarks	Records from 1880 to present. For records from 1880–1907 and licenses issued in the cities of Albany, Buffalo, or Yonkers, apply to—Albany: City Clerk, City Hall, Albany, NY 12207; Buffalo: City Clerk, City Hall, Buffalo, NY 14202; Yonkers: Registrar of Vital Statistics, Health Center Building, Yonkers, NY 10701.
Divorce	$15.00 Varies	Same as Birth or Death See remarks	Records since January 1963. County Clerk in county where divorce was granted.
NEW YORK CITY			
Birth or Death	$15.00	Division of Vital Records New York City Department of Health P.O. Box 3776 New York, NY 10007	Office has birth records since 1910 and death records since 1949 for those occurring in the Boroughs of Manhattan, Brooklyn, Bronx, Queens, and Staten Island. For birth records prior to 1910 and death records prior to 1949, write to Archives Division, Department of Records and Information Services, 31 Chambers Street, New York, NY 10007.

Continued

—Continued

PLACE OF EVENT	COST OF COPY	ADDRESS	REMARKS
NEW YORK CITY, Continued			Certified check or money order should be made payable to **New York City Department of Health.** To verify current fees, the telephone numbers are **(212) 619-4530** or **(212) 693-4637.** These are **recorded** messages.
Marriage Bronx Borough	$10.00	City Clerk's Office 1780 Grand Concourse Bronx, NY 10457	Records from 1847 to 1865. Archives Division, Department of Records and Information Services, 31 Chambers Street, New York NY 10007, except
Brooklyn Borough	$10.00	City Clerk's Office Municipal Building Brooklyn, NY 11201	Brooklyn records for this period which are filed with County Clerk's Office, Kings County, Supreme Court Building,
Manhattan Borough	$10.00	City Clerk's Office Municipal Building New York, NY 10007	Brooklyn, NY 11201. Additional copies of same record ordered at same time are $5.00 each. Records from 1866 to 1907.
Queens Borough	$10.00	City Clerk's Office 120-55 Queens Boulevard Kew Gardens, NY 11424	City Clerk's Office in borough where marriage was performed. Records from 1908 to May 12, 1943. New York City
Staten Island Borough (no longer called Richmond)	$10.00	City Clerk's Office Staten Island Borough Hall Staten Island, NY 10301	residents write to City Clerk's Office in the borough of bride's residence; nonresidents write to City Clerk's Office in borough where license was obtained. Records since May 13, 1943. City Clerk's Office in borough where license was issued.
Divorce			See New York State
NORTH CAROLINA Birth or Death	$10.00	Department of Environment, Health, and Natural Resources Division of Epidemiology Vital Records Section 225 North McDowell Street P.O. Box 29537 Raleigh, NC 27626-0537	State office has had birth records since October 1913 and death records since January 1, 1946. Death records from 1913 through 1945 are available from Archives and Records Section, 109 East Jones Street, Raleigh, NC 27611. Additional copies of the same record ordered at the same time are $5.00 each. Check or money order should be made payable to **Vital Records Section.** Personal checks are accepted. To verify current fees, the telephone number is **(919) 733-3526.**
Marriage	$10.00 $3.00	Same as Birth or Death See remarks	Records since January 1962. Registrar of Deeds in county where marriage was performed.
Divorce	$10.00 Varies	Same as Birth or Death See remarks	Records since January 1958. Clerk of Superior Court where divorce was granted.

Continued

—Continued

PLACE OF EVENT	COST OF COPY	ADDRESS	REMARKS
NORTH DAKOTA			
Birth	$7.00	Division of Vital Records	State office has had some records since
Death	$5.00	State Capitol	July 1893. Years from 1894 to 1920 are
		600 East Boulevard Avenue	incomplete. Additional copies of birth
		Bismarck, ND 58505	records are $4.00 each; death records are $2.00 each.
			Money order should be made payable to **Division of Vital Records.** To verify current fees, the telephone number is **(701) 224-2360.**
Marriage	$5.00	Same as Birth or Death	Records since July 1925. Requests for earlier records will be forwarded to appropriate office. Additional copies are $2.00 each.
	Varies	See remarks	County Judge in county where license was issued.
Divorce	See remarks	Same as Birth or Death	Index of records since July 1949. Some items may be verified. Certified copies are not available from State Health Department. Inquiries will be forwarded to appropriate office.
	Varies	See remarks	Clerk of District Court in county where divorce was granted.
NORTHERN MARIANA ISLANDS			
Birth or Death	$3.00	Superior Court	Office has had records for birth and
		Vital Records Section	death since 1945 and records for
		P.O. Box 307	marriage since 1954. Years from 1945 to
		Saipan, MP 96950	1950 are incomplete.
Marriage	$3.00	Same as Birth or Death	Money order or Bank Cashiers Check should be made payable to **Superior Court.** Personal checks are *not* accepted. To verify current fees, the telephone number is **(670) 234-6401**, ext. **15.**
Divorce	$0.50 per page for Divorce Decree plus $2.50 for certification	Same as Birth or Death	Office has had records for divorce since 1960.
OHIO			
Birth or Death	$7.00	Bureau of Vital Statistics Ohio Department of Health P.O. Box 15098 Columbus, OH 43215-0098	State office has had birth records since December 20, 1908. For earlier birth and death records, write to the Probate Court in the county where the event occurred. The State Office has death records for deaths that occurred after December 31, 1936. Death records for deaths that occurred December 20, 1908–December 31, 1936, can be obtained from the Ohio Historical Society, Archives Library Division, 1985 Velma Avenue, Columbus, OH 43211-2497.

Continued

—*Continued*

PLACE OF EVENT	COST OF COPY	ADDRESS	REMARKS
OHIO, *Continued*			Check or money order should be made payable to **State Treasury.** Personal checks are accepted. To verify current fees, the telephone number is **(614) 466-2531.** This will be a **recorded** message.
Marriage	See remarks	Same as Birth or Death	Records since September 1949. All items may be verified. Certified copies are not available from State Health Department. Inquiries will be referred to appropriate office.
	Varies	See remarks	Probate Judge in county where license was issued.
Divorce	See remarks	Same as Birth or Death	Records since September 1949. All items may be verified. Certified copies are not available from State Health Department. Inquiries will be forwarded to appropriate office.
	Varies	See remarks	Clerk of Court of Common Pleas in county where divorce was granted.
OKLAHOMA Birth or Death	$5.00	Vital Records Section State Department of Health 1000 Northeast 10th Street P.O. Box 53551 Oklahoma City, OK 73152	State office has had records since October 1908. Check or money order should be made payable to **Oklahoma State Department of Health.** Personal checks are accepted. To verify current fees, the telephone number is **(405) 271-4040.**
Marriage	Varies	See remarks	Clerk of Court in county where license was issued.
Divorce	Varies	See remarks	Clerk of Court in county where divorce was granted.
OREGON Birth or Death	$13.00	Oregon Health Division Vital Statistics Section P.O. Box 14050 Portland, OR 97214-0050	State office has had records since January 1903. Some earlier records for the City of Portland since approximately 1880 are available from the Oregon State Archives, 1005 Broadway, NE, Salem, OR 97310.
Heirloom Birth	$28.00	Same as Birth or Death	Presentation style calligraphy certificate suitable for framing. Money order should be made payable to **Oregon Health Division.** To verify current fees, the telephone number is **(503) 731-4095.** This will be a **recorded** message.
Marriage	$13.00	Same as Birth or Death	Records since January 1906.
	Varies	See remarks	County Clerk in county where license was issued. County Clerks also have some records before 1906.
Divorce	$13.00	Same as Birth or Death	Records since 1925.
	Varies	See remarks	County Circuit Court Clerk in county where divorce was granted. County Clerks also have some records before 1925.

Continued

—Continued

PLACE OF EVENT	COST OF COPY	ADDRESS	REMARKS
PENNSYLVANIA			
Birth	$4.00	Division of Vital Records	State office has had records since
Wallet card	$5.00	State Department of Health	January 1906.
Death	$3.00	Central Building	For earlier records, write to Register of Wills, Orphans Court, in county seat of county where event occurred. Persons born in Pittsburgh from 1870 to 1905 or in Allegheny City, now part of Pittsburgh, from 1882 to 1905 should write to Office of Biostatistics, Pittsburgh Health Department, City-County Building, Pittsburgh, PA 15219. For events occurring in City of Philadelphia from 1860 to 1915, write to Vital Statistics, Philadelphia Department of Public Health, 401 North Broad Street, Room 942, Philadelphia, PA 19108.
		101 South Mercer Street	
		P.O. Box 1528	
		New Castle, PA 16103	
			Check or money order should be made payable to **Division of Vital Records.** Personal checks are accepted. To verify current fees, the telephone number is **(412) 656-3100.**
Marriage	Varies	See remarks	Make application to the Marriage License Clerks, County Court House, in county where license was issued.
Divorce	Varies	See remarks	Make application to the Prothonotary, Court House, in county seat of county where divorce was granted.
PUERTO RICO			
Birth or Death	$2.00	Department of Health Demographic Registry P.O. Box 11854 Fernández Juncos Station San Juan, PR 00910	Central office has had records since July 22, 1931. Copies of earlier records may be obtained by writing to local Registrar (Registrador Demografico) in municipality where event occurred or by writing to central office for information.
			Money order should be made payable to **Secretary of the Treasury.** Personal checks are *not* accepted. To verify current fees, the telephone number is **(809) 728-7980.**
Marriage	$2.00	Same as Birth or Death	
Divorce	$2.00	Same as Birth or Death	
		See remarks	Superior Court where divorce was granted.
RHODE ISLAND			
Birth or Death	$10.00	Division of Vital Records Rhode Island Department of Health Room 101, Cannon Building 3 Capitol Hill Providence, RI 02908-5097	State office has had records since 1853. For earlier records, write to Town Clerk in town where event occurred. Additional copies of the same record ordered at the same time are $5.00 each.

Continued

—Continued

PLACE OF EVENT	COST OF COPY	ADDRESS	REMARKS
RHODE ISLAND, Continued			Money order should be made payable to **General Treasurer, State of Rhode Island.** To verify current fees, the telephone number is **(401) 277-2811.** This will be a **recorded** message.
Marriage	$10.00	Same as Birth or Death	Records since January 1853. Additional copies of the same record ordered at the same time are $5.00 each.
Divorce	$1.00	Clerk of Family Court 1 Dorrance Plaza Providence, RI 02903	
SOUTH CAROLINA Birth or Death	$8.00	Office of Vital Records and Public Health Statistics South Carolina Department of Health and Environmental Control 2600 Bull Street Columbia, SC 29201	State office has had records since January 1915. City of Charleston births from 1877 and deaths from 1821 are on file at Charleston County Health Department. Ledger entries of Florence City births and deaths from 1895 to 1914 are on file at Florence County Health Department. Ledger entries of Newberry City births and deaths from the late 1800's are on file at Newberry County Health Department. These are the only early records obtainable. Additional copies of the same birth records ordered at the same time of certification are $3.00.
			Check or money order should be made payable to **Department of Health and Environmental Control.** Personal checks are accepted. To verify current fees, the telephone number is **(803) 734-4830.**
Marriage	$8.00 Varies	Same as Birth or Death See remarks	Records since July 1950. Records since July 1911. Probate Judge in county where license was issued.
Divorce	$8.00 Varies	Same as Birth or Death See remarks	Records since July 1962. Records since April 1949. Clerk of county where petition was filed.
SOUTH DAKOTA Birth or Death	$5.00	State Department of Health Center for Health Policy and Statistics Vital Records 523 E. Capitol Pierre, SD 57501	State office has had records since July 1905 and access to other records for some events that occurred before then. Money order should be made payable to **South Dakota Department of Health.** Personal checks are accepted. To verify current fees, the telephone number is **(605) 773-3355.** This will be a **recorded** message.
Marriage	$5.00	Same as Birth or Death See remarks	Records since July 1905. County Treasury in county where license was issued.

Continued

—Continued

PLACE OF EVENT	COST OF COPY	ADDRESS	REMARKS
SOUTH DAKOTA, **Continued**			
Divorce	$5.00	Same as Birth or Death	Records since July 1905.
	Varies	See remarks	Clerk of Court in county where divorce was granted.
TENNESSEE			
Birth (long form) Birth (short form) Death	$10.00 $5.00 $5.00	Tennessee Vital Records Department of Health Cordell Hull Building Nashville, TN 37247-0350	State office has had birth records for entire State since January 1914, for Nashville since June 1881, for Knoxville since July 1881, and for Chattanooga since January 1882. State office has had death records for entire State since January 1914, for Nashville since July 1874, for Knoxville since July 1887, and for Chattanooga since March 6, 1872. Birth and death enumeration records by school district are available for July 1908 through June 1912. Vital Records Office keeps death records for 50 years; older records are maintained by Tennessee Library and Archives, Archives Division, Nashville, TN 37243-0312. For Memphis birth records from April 1874 through December 1887 and November 1898 to January 1, 1914, and for Memphis death records from May 1848 to January 1, 1914, write to Memphis–Shelby County Health Department, Division of Vital Records, Memphis, TN 38105. Additional copies of the same birth, marriage, or divorce record, requested at the same time, are $2.00 each.
			Check or money order should be made payable to **Tennessee Vital Records.** Personal checks are accepted. To verify current fees, the telephone number is **(615) 741-1763.**
Marriage	$10.00	Same as Birth or Death	Records since July 1945.
	Varies	See remarks	County Clerk in county where license was issued.
Divorce	$10.00	Same as Birth or Death	Records since July 1945.
	Varies	See remarks	Clerk of Court in county where divorce was granted.
TEXAS			
Birth Death	$11.00 $9.00	Bureau of Vital Statistics Texas Department of Health 1100 West 49th Street Austin, TX 78756-3191	State office has had records since 1903. Additional copies of same death record ordered at same time are $3.00 each.
			Check or money order should be made payable to **Texas Department of Health.** Personal checks are accepted. To verify current fees, the telephone number is **(512) 458-7111.** This is a **recorded** message.

Continued

—Continued

PLACE OF EVENT	COST OF COPY	ADDRESS	REMARKS
TEXAS, Continued			
Marriage	See remarks		Records since January 1966. Certified copies are not available from State office. Fee for search and verification of essential facts of marriage is $9.00 each.
	Varies	See remarks	County Clerk in county where license was issued.
Divorce	See remarks		Records since January 1968. Certified copies are not available from State office. Fee for search and verification of essential facts of divorce is $9.00 each.
	Varies	See remarks	Clerk of District Court in county where divorce was granted.
UTAH			
Birth	$12.00	Bureau of Vital Records	State office has had records since 1905. If event occurred from 1890 to 1904 in Salt Lake City or Ogden, write to City Board of Health. For records elsewhere in the State from 1898 to 1904, write to County Clerk in county where event occurred. Additional copies, when requested at the same time, are $5.00 each.
Death	$9.00	Utah Department of Health 288 North 1460 West P.O. Box 16700 Salt Lake City, UT 84116-0700	
			Check or money order should be made payable to **Utah Department of Health.** Personal checks are accepted. To verify current fees, the telephone number is **(801) 538-6105.** This is a **recorded** message.
Marriage	$9.00	Same as Birth or Death	State office has had records since 1978. Only short-form certified copies are available.
	Varies	See remarks	County Clerk in county where license was issued.
Divorce	$9.00	Same as Birth or Death	State office has had records since 1978. Only short-form certified copies are available.
	Varies	See remarks	County Clerk in county where divorce was granted.
VERMONT			
Birth or Death	$5.00	Vermont Department of Health Vital Records Section Box 70 60 Main Street Burlington, VT 05402	State office has had records since 1981. Check or money order should be made payable to **Vermont Department of Health.** Personal checks are accepted. To verify current fees, the telephone number is **(802) 863-7275.**
Birth, Death, or Marriage	$5.00	Division of Public Records US Route 2—Middlesex 133 State Street Montpelier, VT 05633	Records prior to 1981. To verify current fees, the telephone number is **(802) 828-3286.**
	$5.00	See remarks	Town or City Clerk of town where birth or death occurred.

Continued

—Continued

PLACE OF EVENT	COST OF COPY	ADDRESS	REMARKS
VERMONT, Continued			
Marriage	$5.00	Same as Birth or Death	State office has had records since 1981.
	$5.00	See remarks	Town Clerk in town where license was issued.
Divorce	$5.00	Same as Birth or Death	State office has had records since 1981.
	$5.00	See remarks	Town Clerk in town where divorce was granted.
VIRGINIA			
Birth or Death	$5.00	Division of Vital Records State Health Department P.O. Box 1000 Richmond, VA 23208-1000	State office has had records from January 1853 to December 1896 and since June 14, 1912. Only the cities of Hampton, Newport News, Norfolk, and Richmond have records between 1896 and June 14, 1912.
			Check or money order should be made payable to **State Health Department.** Personal checks are accepted. To verify current fees, the telephone number is **(804) 786-6228.** This is a **recorded** message.
Marriage	$5.00	Same as Birth or Death	Records since January 1853.
	Varies	See remarks	Clerk of Court in county or city where license was issued.
Divorce	$5.00	Same as Birth or Death	Records since January 1918.
	Varies	See remarks	Clerk of Court in county or city where divorce was granted.
VIRGIN ISLANDS			
Birth or Death St. Croix	$10.00	Registrar of Vital Statistics Charles Harwood Memorial Hospital Christiansted St. Croix, VI 00820	Registrar has had birth and death records on file since 1840.
St. Thomas and St. John	$10.00	Registrar of Vital Statistics Knud Hansen Complex Hospital Ground Charlotte Amalie St. Thomas, VI 00802	Registrar has had birth records on file since July 1906 and death records since January 1906.
			Money order for birth and death records should be made payable to **Bureau of Vital Statistics.** Personal checks are *not* accepted. To verify current fees, the telephone number is **(809) 774-9000 ext. 4621 or 4623.**
Marriage	See remarks	Bureau of Vital Records and Statistical Services Virgin Islands Dept. of Health Charlotte Amalie St. Thomas, VI 00801	Certified copies are not available. Inquiries will be forwarded to the appropriate office.
St. Croix	$2.00	Chief Deputy Clerk Family Division Territorial Court of the Virgin Islands P.O. Box 929 Christiansted St. Croix, VI 00820	

Continued

—Continued

PLACE OF EVENT	COST OF COPY	ADDRESS	REMARKS
VIRGIN ISLANDS, Continued			
St. Thomas and St. John	$2.00	Clerk of the Territorial Court of the Virgin Islands Family Division P.O. Box 70 Charlotte Amalie St. Croix, VI 00801	
Divorce	See remarks	Same as Marriage	Certified copies are not available. Inquiries will be forwarded to appropriate office.
St. Croix	$5.00	Same as Marriage	Money order for marriage and divorce records should be made payable to **Territorial Court of the Virgin Islands.** Personal checks are *not* accepted.
St. Thomas and St. John	$5.00	Same as Marriage	
WASHINGTON			
Birth or Death	$11.00	Department of Health Center for Health Statistics P.O. Box 9709 Olympia, WA 98507-9709	State office has had records since July 1907. For King, Pierce, and Spokane counties, copies may also be obtained from county health departments. County Auditor of county of birth has registered births prior to July 1907.
			Check or money order should be made payable to **Department of Health.** To verify current fees, the telephone number is **(206) 753-5936.**
Marriage	$11.00	Same as Birth or Death	State office has had records since January 1968.
	$2.00	See remarks	County Auditor in county where license was issued.
Divorce	$11.00	Same as Birth or Death	State office has had records since January 1968.
	Varies	See remarks	County Clerk in county where divorce was granted.
WEST VIRGINIA			
Birth or Death	$5.00	Vital Registration Office Division of Health State Capital Complex Bldg. 3 Charleston, WV 25305	State office has had records since January 1917. For earlier records, write to Clerk of County Court in county where event occurred.
			Check or money order should be made payable to **Vital Registration.** Personal checks are accepted. To verify current fees, the telephone number is **(304) 558-2931.**
Marriage	$5.00	Same as Birth or Death	Records since 1921. Certified copies available from 1964.
	Varies	See remarks	County Clerk in county where license was issued.

Continued

—Continued

PLACE OF EVENT	COST OF COPY	ADDRESS	REMARKS
WEST VIRGINIA, **Continued**			
Divorce	See remarks	Same as Birth or Death	Index since 1968. Some items may be verified (fee $5.00). Certified copies are not available from State office.
	Varies	See remarks	Clerk of Circuit Court, Chancery Side, in county where divorce was granted.
WISCONSIN			
Birth	$10.00	Vital Records	State Office has scattered records earlier
Death	$7.00	1 West Wilson Street P.O. Box 309 Madison, WI 53701	than 1857. Records before October 1, 1907, are very incomplete. Additional copies of the same record ordered at the same time are $2.00 each.
			Check or money order should be made payable to **Center for Health Statistics.** Personal checks are accepted. To verify current fees, the telephone number is **(608) 266-1371.** This will be a **recorded** message.
Marriage	$7.00	Same as Birth or Death	Records since April 1836. Records before October 1, 1907, are incomplete. Additional copies of the same record ordered at the same time are $2.00 each.
Divorce	$7.00	Same as Birth or Death	Records since October 1907. Additional copies of the same record ordered at the same time are $2.00 each.
WYOMING			
Birth	$8.00	Vital Records Services	State office has had records since July
Death	$6.00	Hathaway Building Cheyenne, WY 82002	1909.
			Money order should be made payable to **Vital Records Services.** To verify current fees, the telephone number is **(307) 777-7591.**
Marriage	$8.00	Same as Birth or Death	Records since May 1941.
	Varies	See remarks	County Clerk in county where license was issued.
Divorce	$8.00	Same as Birth or Death	Records since May 1941.
	Varies	See remarks	Clerk of District Court where divorce took place.

ORGANIZATIONS AND RESOURCES

Academy of Family Mediators
355 Tyrol W.
1500 South Hwy 100
Golden Valley, MN 55416
(612) 525-8670

Adoptees' Liberty Movement
Association
P.O. Box 154
Washington Bridge Station
New York, NY 10033
(212) 581-1568
(assists adoptees in finding birth
parents)

Adoptive Families of America,
Inc.
3333 Hwy 100 North
Minneapolis, MN 55422
(612) 535 4829

Al-Anon Family Groups
1372 Broadway
New York, NY 10018
(800) 356-9996

Alcoholics Anonymous
P.O. Box 459, Grand Central
Station
New York, NY 10163
(212) 686-1100

American Academy of Adoption
Attorneys
P.O. Box 33053
Washington, DC 20033-0053
(202) 331-1955

American Academy of
Matrimonial Lawyers
20 N. Michigan Ave., Suite 540
Chicago, IL 60602
(312) 263-6477

American Arbitration Association
140 W. 51st St.
New York, NY 10020
(212) 484-4000

American Association for
Marriage and Family Therapy
1100 17th St. NW, 10th Floor

Washington, DC 20036-1609
(800) 374-2638

American Association for
Protecting Children
9725 East Hampden Ave.
Denver, CO 80231-4919
(303) 695-0811

American Association of Retired
Persons
1909 K St. NW
Washington, DC 20049
(202) 872-4700

American Association for Sex
Educators, Counselors, and
Therapists
435 N. Michigan Ave., Suite 1717
Chicago, IL 60611
(312) 644-8557

American Bar Association
Center for Children and the Law
1800 M St. NW
Washington, DC 20036
(202) 331-2250

American Bar Association
Family Law Section
750 N. Lake Shore Dr.
Chicago, IL 60611
(312) 988-5584

American Civil Liberties Union
132 W. 43rd St.
New York, NY 10036
(212) 944-9800

American College of Nurse-
Midwives
1522 K St. NW, Suite 1000
Washington, DC 20005
(202) 289-0171

American Divorce Association for
Men (ADAM)
1519 S. Arlington Heights Rd
Arlington Heights, IL 60005
(708) 364-1555

American Fertility Society
1209 Montgomery Hwy

Montgomery, AL 35216-2809
(205) 933-8494

American Men's Studies
Association
22 East St.
Northampton, MA 01060

American Society of Separated
and Divorced Men
575 Keep Ave.
Elgin, IL 60120
(708) 695-2200

Association for Couples in
Marriage Enrichment
P.O. Box 10596
Winston-Salem, NC 26108
(800) 634-8325

Association for Voluntary
Sterilization, Inc.
122 E. 42nd St.
New York, NY 10017
(212) 573-8322

Association of Family and
Conciliation Courts
329 W. Wilson St.
Madison, WI 53703
(608) 251-0604

AZT Hotline
(800) 843-9388

Birthright
686 N. Broad St.
Woodbury, NJ 08096
(800) 848-5683
(counseling services for pregnant
women)

Center for Dispute Settlement
1666 Connecticut Ave. NW,
Suite 501
Washington, DC 20009
(202) 265-9572

Center for Surrogate Parenting,
Inc.
8383 Wilshire Blvd., Suite 750
Beverly Hills, CA 90211
(213) 655-1974

Center for Women Policy Studies
2000 P St. NW, #508
Washington, DC 20036
(202) 872-1770

Centers for Disease Control
Technical Information Services
Atlanta, GA 30333
(404) 329-3311

Child Find of America
7 Innis Ave.
New Paltz, NY 12561
(914) 255-1848
(800) I-AM-LOST

Children's Defense Fund
122 C St. NW
Washington, DC 20001
(202) 628-8787

Children's Rights Council
220 I St. NE
Washington, DC 20002
(202) 547-6227

Child Welfare League of America
440 1st St. NW
Washington, DC 20001
(202) 638-2952

Committee for Mother & Child
Rights, Inc.
Rt. 1, Box 256A
Clear Brook, VA 22624
(703) 722-3652

Community Dispute Services
140 W. 51st St.
New York, NY 10020
(212) 484-4000

Divorce Mediation Services
Association of Family and
Conciliation Courts
1227 Spruce St.
Boulder, CO
(303) 447-8116

Equal Rights Advocates
1370 Mission St.
San Francisco, CA 94103
(415) 621-0505

Family Law Council
P.O. Box 217
Fair Lawn, NJ 07410
(promotes alternatives to divorce
litigation)

Family Mediation Association
2380 SW 34th Way
Fort Lauderdale, FL 33312

Father's Advocacy, Information,
and Referral Corp.
(800) 722-FAIR

Fathers for Equal Rights, Inc.
3623 Douglas Ave.
Des Moines, IA 50310
(515) 277-8789

Federal Parent Locator Service
Department of Health and
Human Services
Office of Child Support
Enforcement
Washington, DC 20201
(202) 245-1647

Good Samaritan Project Teen
Hotline
Kansas City, MO
(800) 234-TEEN
(AIDS/HIV hotline)

Grandparents'/Children's Rights
5728 Ban Ave.
Hassled, MI 48840
(517) 339-8663

Help Abolish Legal Tyranny
(HALT)
1319 F St. NW
Washington, DC 20004
(202) 347-9600

Herpes Resource Center
P.O. Box 13827
RTT Park, NC 27709
(919) 361-8488

Howard and Georgeanna Jones
Institute for Reproductive
Medicine
601 College Ave.
Norfolk, VA 23507-1912
(804) 446-8948

Incest Survivors Anonymous
P.O. Box 5613
Long Beach, CA 90805-0613

Institute for Mediation and
Conflict Resolution
99 Hudson St.
New York, NY 10013
(212) 966-3660

Institute for Reproductive
Medicine
Eastern Virginia Medical School
Norfolk General Hospital
825 Fairfax Ave.
Norfolk, VA 23507
(804) 446-8948

Interace
P.O. Box 582
Forest Hills, NY 11375-9998
(718) 657-2271
(support for interracial couples
and adoptive families)

Justice for Children
18418 Snowwood
Spring, TX 77388
(713) 225-HELP

Joint Custody Association
10606 Wilkens Ave.
Los Angeles, CA 90024
(213) 475-5352

Lawyers for Children
1100 Lafayette St.
New York, NY 10013
(212) 966-6420

Medicaid/Medicare
Department of Health and
Human Services
Washington, DC 20013
(202) 245-7000

Men's Rights Association
Route 6
Forest Lake, MN 55025
(612) 464-7887

Mothers Against Drunk Driving
(MADD)
669 Airport Fwy, Suite 310
Hurst, TX 76053
(817) 268-6233

Mothers without Custody
P.O. Box 56762
Houston, TX 77256
(301) 552-2319

National Abortion Rights Action
League
156 15th St. NW, Suite 700
Washington, DC 20005
(202) 371-0779

National Adoption Center
1500 Walnut St., Suite 701
Philadelphia, PA 19107
(800) TO-ADOPT

National Academy of
Conciliators
5530 Wisconsin Ave., Suite 1130
Chevy Chase, MD 20815
(301) 654-6515

National AIDS Hotline
(800) 342-AIDS

National Association of Counsel for Children
1205 Oneida St.
Denver, CO 80220
(303) 321-3963
(800) 525-0246

National Association of Social Workers
7981 Eastern Ave.
Silver Spring, MD 20910
(800) 638-8799

National Center for Mediation Education
2083 West St., Suite 3C
Annapolis, MD 21401
(301) 261-8445

National Center for Missing & Exploited Children
2101 Wilson Blvd., Suite 550
Arlington, VA 22201
(703) 235-3900
(800) 826-7653

National Center for the Prevention and Control of Rape
5000 Fishers Lane, Room 6C-12
Rockville, MD 20857

National Center for Youth Law
1663 Mission St.
San Francisco, CA 94103
(415) 543-3307

National Center on Child Abuse and Neglect
Department of Health and Human Services
P.O. Box 1182
Washington, DC 20013
(202) 245-0586

National Center on Women & Family Law, Inc.
799 Broadway, Rm. 402
New York, NY 10003
(212) 674-8200

National Child Abuse Hotline
(800) 422-4453

National Child Rights Alliance
P.O. Box 422
Ellenville, NY 12428
(914) 647-3670

National Child Support Enforcement Association
444 N. Capitol, NW, Suite 613
Washington, DC 20001
(202) 624-8180

National Clearinghouse for Alcohol and Drug Information
P.O. Box 2345
Rockville, MD 20852
(800) 729-6689

National Clearinghouse on Child Abuse and Neglect Information
P.O. Box 1182
Washington, DC 20013
(703) 821-2086

National Clearinghouse on Marital and Date Rape
2325 Oak
Berkeley, CA 94708
(415) 548-1770

National Coalition Against Domestic Violence
P.O. Box 15127
Washington, DC 20003
(202) 293-8860
(800) 333-SAFE

National Committee for Adoption
1930 17th St. NW
Washington, DC 20009
(202) 328-1200

National Committee for Fair Divorce and Alimony Laws
11 Park Pl.
New York, NY 10007
(212) 766-4030

National Committee for Prevention of Child Abuse
332 S. Michigan Ave., Suite 1600
Chicago, IL 60604-4357
(312) 663-3520
(800) 422-4453

National Congress of Men and Children
2020 Pennsylvania Ave. NW
Washington, DC 20006
(313) 354-3080

National Council for Adoption
1930 17th St. NW
Washington, DC 20009
(202) 328-1200

National Council of Juvenile and Family Court Judges
University of Nevada
P.O. Box 8970
Reno, NV 89507
(702) 784-6012

National Council on Family Relations

1910 W. County Rd. B, Suite 147
St. Paul, MN 55113
(612) 633-6933

National Domestic Violence Hotline
(800) 333-SAFE

National Federation of Parents and Friends of Lesbians and Gays
P.O. Box 27605
Washington, DC 20038
(202) 638-4200

National Gay and Lesbian Task Force
1734 14th St. NW
Washington, DC 20009
(202) 332-6483
(800) 221-7044

National Gay and Lesbian Crisis Line
(800) 221-7044

National Gay Rights Advocates
540 Castro St.
San Francisco, CA 94114
(415) 863-3624

National Health Information Center
P.O. Box 1133
Washington, DC 20013-1133
(301) 565-4167
(800) 336-4797

National Herpes Hotline
(919) 361-8488

National Information Center for Children and Youth with Disabilities
P.O. Box 1492
Washington, DC 20013
(800) 999-5599

National Institute for Dispute Resolution
1901 L St., Suite 600
Washington, DC 20036
(202) 466-4764

National Juvenile Court Services Association
P.O. Box 8970
Reno, NV 89507
(702) 784-4859

National Lesbian and Gay Lifeline
(800) 543-3661

National Network of Runaway and Youth Services

1400 I St. NW
Washington, DC 20005
(202) 682-4114

National Organization for
Changing Men
P.O. Box 451
Watseka, IL 60970
(815) 347-2279

National Organization for Men
11 Park Pl.
New York, NY 10007
(212) 686-MALE
(212) 766-4030
(718) 494-1719 (computer bulletin
board)

National Organization for Women
1000 16th St. NW, Suite 700
Washington, DC 20036
(202) 331-0066

National Pro-Family Coalition
721 2nd St. NE
Washington, DC 20002
(202) 546-3003

National Resource Center for
Child Advocacy and Protection
American Bar Association
1800 M St. NW
Washington, DC 20036
(202) 331-2250

National Resource Center on
Child Abuse and Neglect
9725 East Hampden Ave.
Denver, CO 80231
(303) 695-0811

National Right to Life Committee
419 7th St. NW
Washington, DC 20045
(202) 626-8800

National Runaway Switchboard
3080 N. Lincoln Ave.
Chicago, IL 60657
(800) 621-4000
(800) 621-3230

National STD Hotline
(800) 227-8922
(information on sexually
transmitted diseases)

National Task Force for
Children's Constitutional Rights
P.O. Box 1620
Litchfield, CT 06759
(203) 567-KIDS

National VD Hotline
(800) 227-8922
(800) 982-5883 (CA)

National Women's Law Center
1616 P St. NW
Washington, DC 20036
(202) 328-5160

North American Council on
Adoptable Children
1821 University Ave., Suite N-498
St. Paul, MN 55104
(612) 644-3036

Office of Citizens Consular
Services
Department of State
2201 C St. NW, Rm. 4817
Washington, DC 20520
(202) 647-3666

Overseas Citizen Services
Department of State
Washington, DC 20520
(202) 647-3666
(202) 647-5225

Parents and Friends of Lesbians
and Gays
P.O. Box 24565
Los Angeles, CA 90024
(213) 472-8952

Parents Anonymous
7120 Franklin Ave.
Los Angeles, CA 90046
(800) 421-0353
(800) 882-1250
(support group for parents who
abuse their children)

Parents United
P.O. Box 952
San Jose, CA 95108
(408) 453-7616
(800) 422-4453
(referral and counseling on child
abuse)

Parents without Partners
8807 Colesville Rd.
Silver Spring, MD 20910
(301) 588-9354
(800) 637-7974

Pension Rights Center
1346 Connecticut Ave. NW, Rm.
1019
Washington, DC 20036
(202) 296-3776

Planned Parenthood Federation of
America
810 Seventh Ave.
New York, NY 10019
(212) 541-7800

Rabbinical Council of America
275 7th Ave.
New York, NY 10001

Religious Coalition for Abortion
Rights
100 Maryland Ave. NE, Suite 307
Washington, DC 20002
(202) 543-7032

Resolve, Inc.
5 Water St.
Arlington, MA 02174
(617) 643-2424
(information on infertility)

San Francisco AIDS Foundation
25 Van Ness Ave.
San Francisco, CA 94103
(800) 367-2437

Select Committee on Children,
Youth, and Families
U.S. House of Representatives
House Office Building Annex 2,
Room H2-385
Washington, DC 20515

Sex Information and Education
Council of the United States
32 Washington Plaza, 5th Floor
New York, NY 10003
(212) 673-3850

Single Mothers by Choice
P.O. Box 1642
New York, NY 10028
(212) 988-0993

Single Parent Resource Center
141 West 28th St.
New York, NY 10001
(212) 947-0221

Stepfamily Association of
America
215 Centennial Mall South,
Suite 212
Lincoln, NE 68508-1834
(402) 477-7837

Step Family Foundation
333 West End Ave.
New York, NY 10023
(212) 877-3244
(212) 744-6924 (hotline)

Teratogen Registry
(800) 532-3749
(information on the effects of
drugs and medication on unborn
babies)

Tough Love
Box 1069
Doylestown, PA 18901
(215) 348-7090

Vanished Childrens Alliance
(800) 235-3535
(to report sighting missing
children)

Victims of Incest Can Emerge
Survivors

P.O. Box 148309
Chicago, IL 60614
(800) 7-VOICE-8

Women's Bureau
Work and Family Clearinghouse
Department of Labor
Division of Information and
Publications
Washington, DC 20210
(202) 523-6652

Women's Equity Action League
1250 I St. NW, Suite 305
Washington, DC 20005
(202) 898-1588

Women's Legal Defense Fund
1875 Connecticut Ave. NW
Washington, DC 20009
(202) 986-2600

Women Organized Against Sexual
Harassment
2437 Edwards St.
Berkeley, CA 94702

Worldwide Marriage Encounter
1908 E. Highland Ave., #A
San Bernadino, CA 92404
(714) 881-3456
(retreats for Catholic couples)

GLOSSARY

Abandonment See Desertion.

Abduction The unlawful taking away of another.

Absolute Divorce See Divorce.

Abuse Physically harming a person.

Abuse of Process A tort with the following elements: (1) a use of civil or criminal proceedings, (2) for an improper or ulterior purpose, (3) resulting in actual damage. For example, you have someone arrested in order to pressure him to marry your daughter, whom he impregnated. Encouraging marriage is not the purpose of the criminal law.

Acceptance An assent or acquiescence to an offer.

Accounting A statement or report on the financial condition or status of a person, company, estate, transaction, enterprise, etc.

Account Receivable A regular business debt not yet collected.

Acknowledgment A formal recognition or affirmation that something is genuine.

Actuarial Pertaining to the calculation of statistical risks, premiums, estate values, etc.

Actuary A statistician. A person skilled in mathematical calculations to determine insurance risks.

Adjudicate To decide by judicial process; to judge.

Adjusted Basis See Tax Basis.

Adjusted Gross Income The total amount received after making allowed deductions.

Administration The management and settlement of the estate of a decedent.

Administrative Agency A part of the executive branch of government whose function is to execute or carry out the law.

Administrator A person appointed by a court to manage or administer the estate of a deceased, often when no valid will exists. See also Personal Representative.

Adoption The legal process by which an adoptive parent assumes the rights and duties of the natural (i.e., biological) parent. The latter's parental rights are terminated.

Adoption by Estoppel See Equitable Adoption, Estopped.

Adultery Sexual relations between a married person and someone other than his or her spouse.

Adversarial Proceeding A proceeding in court or at an agency where both parties to a dispute can appear and argue their opposing positions.

Adversary (1) Involving a dispute between opposing sides who argue their case before a neutral official such as a judge. (2) An opponent.

AFDC Aid to Families with Dependent Children, a public assistance program.

Affidavit A written statement of facts given under oath or affirmation.

Affinity Relationship by marriage rather than by blood.

Affirmative Defense A defense that raises new facts not in the plaintiff's complaint.

Agency A relationship in which one person acts for another or represents another by the latter's express or implied authority. See also Administrative Agency.

Aggravated Damages Money paid to cover special circumstances that justify an increase in the amount paid, e.g., the presence of malice.

Aggrieved (1) Injured or wronged. (2) The person injured or wronged.

Alienation The act of transferring property, or title to property.

Alienation of Affections A tort that is committed when the defendant diminishes the marital relationship between the plaintiff and the latter's spouse.

Alimony Money or other property paid in fulfillment of a duty to support one's spouse after a separation or divorce. Note, however, that the Internal Revenue Service uses a broader definition of alimony for purposes of determining whether it is *deductible*. See also Rehabilitative Alimony.

Alimony in Gross Lump-sum alimony.

Allele One member of a pair or series of genes.

Alternate Payee A nonemployee entitled to receive pension benefits of an employee or former employee pursuant to a Qualified Domestic Relations Order.

A Mensa et Thoro See Legal Separation.

American Bar Association A voluntary, national organization of attorneys.

American Digest System See Digest. The American Digest System is the most comprehensive digest in existence. It covers almost every court in the country.

American Jurisprudence, 2d   A national legal encyclopedia.

American Law Reports   A set of reporters that contain selected opinions from many different courts. In addition, the ALR volumes contain a research paper—called an *annotation*—that gives a survey of the law on a particular issue found in the opinion.

Amicus Curiae   Friend of the court. A nonparty to litigation who gives advice or suggestions to a court on resolving a dispute before it.

Amnesty   Forgiveness; a general pardon from the state.

Ancillary   Subordinate; auxiliary, aiding.

Annotated   Organized by subject matter with research references or other commentary.

Annotation   A set of notes or commentaries on something. The most widely used annotations are those printed in *American Law Reports.*

Annuity   A fixed sum payable to an individual at specified intervals for a limited period of time or for life.

Annulment   A declaration by a court that a valid marriage never existed.

Answer   The pleading filed by the defendant that responds to the complaint of the plaintiff.

Antenuptial Agreement   A contract made by two individuals who are about to be married that covers support, property division, and related matters in the event of the death of one of the parties or the dissolution of the marriage by divorce or death. Also called Premarital Agreement and Prenuptial Agreement. The Uniform Premarital Agreement Act defines a premarital agreement as an agreement between prospective spouses made in contemplation of marriage and to be effective upon marriage.

Appearance   Formally going before a court.

Appellant   The party bringing an appeal because of disagreement with the decision of a lower tribunal.

Appellee   The party against whom an appeal is brought.

Appreciation   An increase in the value of property.

Arbitration   The process of submitting a dispute to a third party outside the judicial system who will resolve the dispute for the parties.

Arm's Length, At   As between two strangers who are looking out for their own self-interests. At a distance; without trusting the other's fairness; free of personal bias or control.

Arraignment   Bringing the accused before a court to hear the criminal charges and to enter a plea thereto.

Arrears, Arrearages   Payments that are due but have not been made.

Artificial Insemination   The impregnation of a woman by a method other than sexual intercourse.

Assign   To transfer rights or property to someone. The noun is *assignment.* The person who makes the transfer is called the *assignor.* The person who receives the transfer is called the *assignee* or one of the *assigns.*

Assignee   The person to whom ownership or rights are transferred. See also Assigns.

Assignment   The transfer of ownership or other rights.

Assignor   The person who transfers ownership or rights to another.

Assigns   As a noun, it is a synonym for *assignees,* who are the persons to whom ownership or other rights have been or will be transferred. As a verb, it means to transfer ownership or other rights.

Assisted Conception   A pregnancy resulting from (1) fertilizing an egg of a woman with sperm of a man by means other than sexual intercourse, or (2) implanting an embryo. The sperm is not that of her husband.

At Arm's Length   See Arm's Length.

Attachment   A court authorization of the seizure of the defendant's property so that it can be used to satisfy a judgment against him or her.

Attorney-Client Privilege   The right of a client to refuse to answer questions that would disclose communications between the client and his or her attorney. The purpose of the communication must be the facilitation of legal services from the attorney to the client. The client can also prevent the attorney from making such disclosures.

Attorney Work Product   The following material is protected from discovery: (1) the private memoranda of an attorney, and (2) mental impressions or personal recollections prepared or formed by an attorney in anticipation of litigation or for trial.

A Vinculo Matrimonii   See Divorce.

Banns of Marriage   A public announcement of a proposed marriage.

Basis   See Tax Basis.

Bastardy   Pertaining to a child born before his or her parents were married, or born to parents who never married.

Battered Woman Syndrome   Psychological helplessness because of a woman's financial dependence, loneliness, guilt, shame, and fear of reprisal from her husband or boyfriend who has repeatedly battered her in the past.

Beneficiary   The person named in a document such as a will or insurance policy to receive property or other benefit.

Bequest   A gift of personal property in a will.

Betrothal   A mutual promise to marry.

BFOQ   See Bona Fide Occupational Qualification.

Bias   A predisposition to act in a certain way. A preconceived idea of how something should be decided.

Bigamy   Entering or attempting to enter a marriage when a prior marriage is still valid.

Bilateral Divorce   A divorce granted by a court when both the husband and the wife are present before the court.

Bill   A proposed statute offered for passage by the legislature.

Bill for Divorce   Petition or complaint for a dissolution of the marriage.

Biological Parent   One's natural parent; a parent by blood.

Bird's Nest Custody   Joint custody where the child remains in one home and each parent moves in and out during alternating periods of time.

Black Market Adoptions   An adoption that involves a payment beyond reasonable expenses in order to facilitate the adoption.

Blue Book   See Uniform System of Citation.

Boilerplate   Language that is commonly used in a document. It sometimes refers to nonessential language often found in the same kind of document.

Bona Fide Occupational Qualification (BFOQ)   Sex discrimination that is reasonably necessary for the operation of a particular business or enterprise.

Book value   The value at which an asset is carried on the balance sheet.

Canon   (1) A rule of behavior. (2) A maxim or guideline.

Canon Law   Church or ecclesiastical law.

Canons of Ethics   Rules that embody standards of conduct. In the legal profession, the canons of ethics are often referred to as a Code of Ethics or as a Code of Professional Responsibility that governs attorneys. The current canons of ethics of the American Bar Association are found within the Model Rules of Professional Responsibility.

Capacity   (1) The legal power to do something. (2) The ability to understand the nature and effects of one's actions or inaction.

Capital Improvements   Structural improvements on property, as opposed to ordinary maintenance work.

Capitalization   The total amount of the various securities issued by a corporation.

Caption of Complaint   The heading or beginning of the complaint that contains the name of the court, the names of the parties, their litigation status, and the name of the document, e.g., Complaint for Divorce.

CARTWHEEL   A research technique designed to increase the effectiveness of your use of an index in a reference book. The technique helps you identify a large variety of word or phrase substitutes to check in an index.

Case Law   The body of law found in court opinions. See Court Opinion.

Cash Surrender Value   The amount of money that an insurance policy would yield if cashed in with the insurance company. The amount an insurer will pay upon cancellation of the policy before death.

Cause of Action   An allegation of facts that, if proved, would give a party a right to judicial relief. A cause of action is a legally acceptable reason for suing; it is a theory of recovery.

Ceremonial Marriage   A marriage that is entered in compliance with the statutory requirements, e.g., obtaining a marriage license, having the marriage performed (i.e., solemnized) by an authorized person.

Challenge for Cause   The elimination of a prospective juror during *voir dire*, which is the jury selection process, for a specific reason such as bias.

Chambers   A judge's private office.

Chattel   See Personal Property.

Chinese Wall   Steps taken in an office to prevent a tainted employee from having any contact with a particular case in order to avoid the disqualification of the office from the case. The employee is tainted because he or she has a conflict of interest in the case.

Choice of Venue   See Venue.

Chose in Action   The right to recover something through a lawsuit.

Citation   A reference to any material printed on paper or stored in a computer database. It is the "address" where you can locate and read the material.

Civil Contempt   See Contempt of Court.

Civil Fraud   See Fraud.

Civil Procedure   The body of law governing the methods and practices of civil litigation.

Closed Case File   The file of a client whose case is no longer being worked on.

Code A book or set of books that contains rules or laws organized by subject matter. The state code, also called the *state statutory code,* is a collection of statutes written by the state legislature organized by subject matter.

Code of Ethics See Canons of Ethics.

Code of Regulations Laws written by administrative agencies organized by subject matter.

Cohabitants Two unmarried people living together in the way that husbands and wives live together.

Cohabitation Living together as husband and wife whether or not the parties are married.

Cohabitation Agreement A contract made by two individuals who intend to stay unmarried indefinitely that covers financial and related matters while living together, upon separation, or upon death.

Collateral Attack A nondirect attack or challenge to the validity of a judgment. An attack brought in a different proceeding.

Collusion (1) An agreement to commit fraud. (2) An agreement between a husband and wife in a divorce proceeding that one or both will lie to the court to facilitate the obtaining of the divorce.

Comity The court's decision to give effect to the laws and judicial decisions of another state as a matter of deference and mutual respect even if no obligation exists to do so.

Commingling of Funds Mixing general law firm funds with client funds in a single account. More broadly, it means combining one's own funds with those to whom a fiduciary duty is owed. See also Fiduciary.

Common Law Judge-made law created in the absence of other controlling law such as statutory law.

Common Law Marriage The marriage of two people who have not gone through a ceremonial marriage. They have agreed to be husband and wife, lived together as husband and wife, and held themselves out to the public as husband and wife.

Common Law Property Property acquired during the marriage in a state other than a community property state. Upon divorce, the parties are given an equitable, but not necessarily equal, division of such property. At one time, however, common law property was usually given to the party who had legal title to the property.

Common Representation See Multiple Representation.

Community Estate The community property of a husband and wife.

Community Property Property in which each spouse has a one-half interest because it was acquired during the marriage, regardless of who earned it or who has title to it. (It does not include property acquired by gift or inheritance, which is the separate property of the spouse who receives it.) *Common law property,* on the other hand, is property owned by the spouse who earned it.

Compensatory Damages Money that will restore the injured party to the position he or she was in before the injury or loss; money that will make the aggrieved party whole.

Competent Using the knowledge, skill, thoroughness, and preparation reasonably needed to represent a particular client.

Complaint A pretrial document filed in court by one party against another that states a grievance, called a cause of action.

Conciliation The resolution or settlement of a dispute in an amicable manner. A Conciliation Service is a court-authorized process whereby a counselor attempts to determine if parties filing for divorce can be reconciled, and if not, whether they can agree on the resolution of support, custody, and property division issues.

Concurrent Jurisdiction When two or more courts have the power to hear the same kind of case, each court has concurrent jurisdiction over such a case.

Condonation An express or implied forgiveness by the innocent spouse of the marital fault committed by the other spouse.

Conducive to Divorce Tending to encourage or contribute to divorce.

Confidence A confidence is any information protected by the attorney-client privilege. A *secret* is any information gained in the professional relationship if the client has requested that it be held secret or if its disclosure would embarrass or be detrimental to the client.

Confidentiality The ethical obligation not to disclose information relating to the representation of a client.

Conflict of Interest You have a divided loyalty that actually or potentially places a person at a disadvantage even though you owe that person undivided loyalty.

Conflict of Law An inconsistency between the laws of different legal systems such as two states or two countries.

Conjugal Pertaining to marriage; appropriate for married persons.

Connivance A willingness or a consent by one spouse that a marital wrong be done by the other spouse.

Consanguinity   Relationship by blood.

Conservator   A person appointed by the court to manage the affairs of an adult who is not competent to do so on his or her own.

Consideration   Something of value that is exchanged between the parties, e.g., an exchange of money for services; an exchange of promises to do something or to refrain from doing something.

Consortium   Companionship, love, affection, sexual relationship, and services that a person enjoys with and from his or her spouse. See Loss of Consortium.

Constitution   The basic legal document of a government that allocates power among the three branches of the government, and that may also enumerate fundamental rights of individuals.

Constructive Desertion   The conduct of the spouse who stayed home justified the other spouse's departure; or the spouse who stayed home refuses a sincere offer of reconciliation from the other spouse who initially left.

Constructive Trust   A trust created by operation of law against one who has improperly obtained legal possession of or legal rights to property through fraud, duress, abuse of confidence, or other unconscionable conduct. See also Trust.

Consumer Price Index   A monthly report by the U.S. Bureau of Labor Statistics that tracks the price level of a group of goods and services purchased by the average consumer.

Consummation   Sexual intercourse for the first time between spouses.

Contempt of Court   Obstructing or assailing the authority or dignity of the court such as by intentionally violating a court order. The purpose of a *civil* contempt proceeding is to compel future compliance with a court order. The purpose of a *criminal* contempt proceeding is to punish the offender.

Contested   Disputed; challenged.

Contingency   An event that may or may not occur.

Contingent   Conditional; dependent on something that may not happen.

Contingent Fee   A fee is contingent if the amount of the fee is dependent on the outcome of the case. A fixed fee is paid regardless of outcome.

Continuance   The postponement or adjournment of a proceeding to a later date.

Contract   An agreement that a court will enforce. The elements of a contract are offer, acceptance, and consideration. The parties must have the legal capacity to enter a contract. Some contracts must be in writing. See also Antenuptial Agreement, Cohabitation Agreement, Implied Contract, Separation Agreement.

Contract Cohabitation   See Cohabitation Agreement.

Conversion   (1) The unauthorized exercise of dominion and control over someone's personal property. (2) Once a judicial separation has been in place for a designated period of time, the parties can ask a court for a divorce on that basis alone. The latter is called a *convertible divorce*.

Conveyance   The transfer of an interest in land.

Co-parenting   Two individuals who share the task of raising a child. Usually, at least one of the individuals is not a biological parent of the child. Sometimes, however, co-parenting refers to two biological parents who have joint custody of the child.

Copulate   To engage in sexual intercourse.

Co-respondent   The person who allegedly had sexual intercourse with a defendant charged with adultery.

Corpus   The body of something; the aggregate of something.

Corpus Juris Secundum   A national legal encyclopedia.

Corroboration   Additional evidence of a point beyond that offered by the person asserting the point.

Count   A separate and independent claim or charge in a pleading such as a complaint.

Counterclaim   A claim made by the defendant against the plaintiff.

Court Opinion   The written explanation by a court of why it reached a certain conclusion or holding.

Court Rules   Rules of procedure that govern the mechanics of litigation before a particular court.

Covenant   A promise or agreement.

Coverture   The status of being a married woman.

Credit Clouding   To notify a creditor or credit bureau that a debtor is delinquent on certain debts.

Criminal Contempt   See Contempt of Court.

Criminal Conversation   A tort committed by having sex with the plaintiff's spouse.

Criminal Fraud   See Fraud.

Criminal Law   The body of law covering acts declared to be crimes by the legislature for statutory crimes, or by the courts for common law crimes.

Curtesy   The right of a husband to the lifetime use of all the land his deceased wife owned during the marriage (if issue were born of the marriage).

Custodial Parent The parent with whom the child is living. The parent with physical custody of the child.

Damages Money paid because of a wrongful injury or loss to person or property. See also Aggravated Damages, Compensatory Damages, Mitigation of Damages, and Punitive Damages.

Decedent The person who has died, the deceased.

Deep Pocket The person or organization that probably has sufficient resources to pay damages if a judgment is awarded by the court.

Default Judgment A judgment rendered when the other side failed to appear.

Defendant The party against whom a claim is brought at the commencement of litigation.

Defense Allegations of fact or legal theories offered to offset or defeat claims or demands.

Defined-Benefit Plan A pension plan where the amount of the benefit is fixed but not the amount of the contribution.

Defined-Contribution Plan A pension plan where the amount of the contribution is generally fixed but the amount of the benefit is not.

Deposition A pretrial discovery device, usually conducted outside the courtroom, during which one party questions the other party or a witness for the other party.

Depository The party or place where something is stored.

Depository Library, Federal A library that receives certain law books from the federal government free (e.g., the United States Code), in exchange for which the library must allow the public to have access to those books.

Depreciation A decrease in value.

Derivative Actions A suit whose success is dependent on the success of a separate suit.

Descent Acquiring property by inheritance rather than by will; acquiring property from a decedent who died intestate.

Desertion One spouse voluntarily but without justification leaves another (who does not consent to the departure) for an uninterrupted period of time with the intent not to return to resume cohabitation. Also called *abandonment*. See Constructive Desertion.

Devise Land acquired by will. The person to whom land is given by will is the devisee.

Digest (1) Sets of books containing small paragraph summaries of court opinions. (2) A summary of a document or a series of documents.

Direct Attack A challenge to the validity of a judgment made in a proceeding brought specifically for that purpose, e.g., an appeal of a judgment brought immediately after it was rendered by the trial court.

Dirty Hands Wrongdoing or other inappropriate behavior that would make it unfair or inequitable to allow a person to assert a right or a defense he or she would normally have.

Disaffirm Contracts The right of a minor to repudiate and refuse to perform a contract he or she has entered.

Disbursement Payment.

Discharged Released; forgiven so that the debt is no longer owed.

Discipline Imposing correction or punishment.

Discovery Steps that a party can take before trial to obtain information from the other side in order to prepare for trial.

Disinterested Impartial; having no desire or interest in either side winning. See also Bias.

Dissipate Waste, destroy, or squander.

Distributive Share The portion of an estate that a person receives from a person who dies intestate, i.e., without leaving a valid will.

Divided Custody See Split Custody.

Divided Loyalty Representing a client when a conflict of interest exists. See Conflict of Interest.

Divisible Divorce A divorce decree that is enforceable in another state only in part. That part of a divorce decree that dissolves the marriage is enforceable (if the plaintiff was domiciled in the state), but that part of the divorce that ordered alimony, child support, or a property division is not (if the court did not have personal jurisdiction over the defendant).

Divorce A declaration by a court that a marriage has been dissolved so that the parties are no longer married to each other.

Divorce Kits A package of do-it-yourself materials containing standard forms and written instructions on how to obtain a divorce without an attorney.

DNA Deoxyribonucleic acid. A constituent of living cell nuclei.

Docket Number A docket is a list or calendar of cases to be tried or heard at a specific term of the court. Cases on this list are assigned a number.

Doctor-Patient Privilege The right of a patient to refuse to disclose any confidential (private) communications with his or her doctor that relate to the medical care. The patient can also prevent the doctor from making such disclosures.

Domestic Partners   Two persons of the same sex who live together in an intimate relationship, who register with the government as domestic partners, and who thereby acquire limited rights enjoyed by a traditional married couple.

Domicile   The place where a person has been physically present with the intent to make that place a permanent home; the place to which one intends to return when away. A residence, on the other hand, is simply the place where you are living at a particular time. A person can have more than one residence, but generally can have only one domicile.

Domicile by Choice   A domicile chosen by a person with the legal capacity to choose.

Domiciliary   One who is domiciled in a particular state.

Donee   The person who receives a gift.

Donor   The person who gives a gift.

Dower   The right of a widow to the lifetime use of one-third of the land her deceased husband owned during the marriage.

Draft   (1) As a verb, draft means to write a document, e.g., a letter, contract, or memorandum. (2) As a noun, it means a version of a document that is not yet final or ready for distribution.

Dual Divorce   A divorce granted to both the husband and the wife.

Durational Maintenance   See Rehabilitative Alimony.

Duress   Coercion; acting under the pressure of an unlawful act or threat.

Election against Will   Obtaining a designated share of a deceased spouse's estate in spite of what the latter provided or failed to provide for the surviving spouse in a will. A forced share of a decedent's estate.

Element   A portion of a rule that is a precondition to the applicability of the entire rule.

Element in Contention   The portion of a rule (i.e., the element) that forms the basis of a legal issue because the parties disagree on the interpretation or application of that element to the facts of the case.

Emancipated   Legally independent of one's parent or legal guardian.

Emolument   Compensation for services.

Encumber   To impose a burden, claim, lien, or charge on property.

Encumbrance   A claim, lien, or other charge against property.

Enoch Arden Doctrine   The presumption that a spouse is dead after being missing for a designated number of years.

Equitable Adoption   For purposes of inheritance, a child will be considered the adopted child of a person who made a contract to adopt the child but failed to go through the formal adoption procedures.

Equitable Distribution   The fair, but not necessarily equal, division between former spouses of property acquired during the marriage.

Equitable Estoppel   See Estopped.

Escalation Clause   A provision in a contract or other document that provides for an increase or decrease in the amount to be paid based upon a factor over which the parties do not have complete control.

Escrow   Property (e.g., money, stock, deed) delivered by one person (called the *grantor, promisor,* or *obligor*) to another (e.g., a bank, an escrow agent) to be held by the latter until a designated condition or contingency occurs, at which time the property is to be delivered to the person for whose benefit the escrow was established (called the *grantee, promisee, obligee,* or *beneficiary*).

Estate   (1) All the property left by the deceased. After being used to pay debts, this property is distributed to those entitled under the will or the laws of intestacy. (2) The amount or extent of one's interest in property.

Estopped   Prevented from asserting a right or a defense because it would be unfair or inequitable to do so.

Ethics   Standards or rules of behavior to which members of an occupation, profession, or other organization are expected to conform.

Et Ux   And wife.

Evidence   Anything offered to establish the existence or nonexistence of a fact in dispute.

Ex Parte Divorce   A divorce rendered by a court when only one of the spouses was present in the state. The court did not have personal jurisdiction over the defendant.

Exclusive Jurisdiction   A court has exclusive jurisdiction when only that court has the power to hear a certain kind of case.

Executed   Carried out according to its terms.

Execution of Judgment   The process of carrying out or satisfying the judgment of a court. Using a writ of execution, a court officer (e.g., a sheriff) is commanded to seize the property of the losing litigant, sell it, and pay the winning litigant out of the proceeds.

Executor   A person designated in a will to carry out the terms of the will and handle related matters. If a female, this person is sometimes called an *executrix*. See also Personal Representative.

Executory   Unperformed as yet.

Executrix   See Executor.

Exemplary Damages   See Punitive Damages.

Extradition   The process by which a state or country turns over an individual who has been accused or convicted of a crime to another state or country.

Facilitation of Divorce   That which makes a divorce easier to obtain.

Fact Particularization   A fact-gathering technique designed to help you identify a large variety of questions you can try to answer through interviewing and investigation.

Fair Market Value   The amount that a willing buyer would pay a willing seller for property, neither being under any compulsion to buy or sell and both having reasonable knowledge of or access to the relevant facts.

False Arrest   An arrest of an individual without a privilege to do so.

False Imprisonment   A tort with the following elements: (1) the defendant performs an act that completely confines the plaintiff within fixed boundaries set by the defendant; (2) the defendant intends the confinement; (3) the defendant causes the confinement; and (4) the plaintiff is either conscious of the confinement or is harmed by it.

Family Purpose Doctrine   The owner of a car who makes it available for family use will be liable for injuries caused while a member of the immediate family is using the car with the owner's consent for a family purpose at the time of the accident.

Fault Grounds   Marital wrongs that will justify the granting of a divorce, e.g., adultery.

Federal Parent Locator Service (FPLS)   See Parent Locator Service.

Fee Splitting   (1) A single bill to a client covering the fee of two or more lawyers who are not in the same firm. (2) Giving a nonlawyer part of the fee of a particular client. The latter is often done as payment for making a referral of the client.

Fiduciary   (1) As an adjective, pertaining to good faith, loyalty, trust, and candor; pertaining to the obligation to protect another's interest and to provide fair treatment. (2) As a noun, a person who owes another good faith, loyalty, trust, candor; a person who owes another an obligation to protect his or her interest and to provide fair treatment.

Filiation   A judicial determination of paternity. The relation of child to father.

Filius Nullius   The status of an illegitimate child at common law ("the son [or child] of no one").

Fixed Fee   See Contingent Fee.

Flowchart   An overview of the step-by-step process by which something is done.

Forced Share   See Election against Will.

Foreign Divorce   A divorce obtained in another state or country.

Forensic   Pertaining to use in courts.

Formbook   A practical treatise or manual containing standard forms along with checklists, summaries of the law, etc. See also Treatise.

Fornication   Sexual relations between unmarried persons or between persons who are not married to each other.

Forum   (1) The place where the parties are presently litigating their dispute. (2) A court or tribunal hearing a case.

Forum Non Conveniens   The discretionary power of a court to decline the exercise of its jurisdiction when it would be more convenient and the ends of justice would be better served if the action were tried in another court.

Forum Shopping   Seeking a court that will be favorable to you. Traveling from court to court until you find one that will provide a favorable ruling.

Forum State   The state in which the parties are now litigating a case.

Foster Home   A temporary home for a child when his or her own family cannot provide care and when adoption is either not possible at the present time or is under consideration.

Fraud   Knowingly making a false statement of present fact with the intention that the plaintiff rely on the statement. The plaintiff's reasonable reliance on the statement harms him or her. See also Statute of Frauds.

Friendly Divorce   A divorce proceeding in which the husband and wife are not contesting the dissolution of the marriage, nor anything related thereto. An uncontested divorce.

Front Loading   Making substantial "alimony" payments shortly after the separation or divorce in an attempt to disguise a property division as deductible alimony.

Full Faith and Credit Clause   "Full Faith and Credit shall be given in each State to the public Acts, Records, and judicial Proceedings of every other State." Article IV of the *United States Constitution.*

Garnishment A proceeding whereby a debtor's money or other property under the control of another is given to a third person to whom the debtor owes a debt.

Genetic Testing The analysis of inherited factors (usually blood) of mother, child, and alleged father to help prove or disprove that a particular man fathered a particular child.

Gestational Surrogacy The sperm and egg of a couple are fertilized in vitro in a laboratory, and the resulting embryo is then implanted in a surrogate mother who gives birth to a child with whom she has no genetic relationship.

Get A bill of divorcement in a Jewish divorce.

Gift The voluntary delivery of something with the present intent to transfer title and control, for which no payment or consideration is made. Once the item is accepted, the gift is irrevocable. The person making the gift is the *donor*. The person receiving it is the *donee*.

Goodwill The reputation of a business that causes it to generate additional customers.

Grantor A transferor; a person who makes a grant.

Gross Income The total amount received or earned before deductions.

Grounds (1) Acceptable reasons for seeking a particular result. (2) Foundation or basis for one's belief or conduct.

Guarantee A warranty or assurance that a particular result will be achieved.

Guardian ad Litem A special guardian appointed by the court to represent the interests of another.

Guardianship The legal right to the custody of an individual.

Harmless Without injury or damage.

Hearsay Testimony in court of a statement made by another out of court when the statement is being offered to assert the truth of the matter in the statement.

Heart Balm Action An action based on a broken heart, e.g., breach of promise to marry, alienation of affections, and seduction.

Heart Balm Statute A statute that abolishes heart balm actions.

Heir One who receives property by inheritance rather than by will.

Hold Harmless In the event of trouble, to relieve someone of responsibility or liability.

Holographic Wholly in the handwriting of a person.

Home State The state where the child has lived for at least six consecutive months or since birth if the child is less than six months old.

Homestead One's dwelling house along with adjoining land and buildings.

Hornbook A text that summarizes an area of the law, usually with commentary and extensive footnotes. See also Legal Treatise.

Hornbook Law Elementary principles of law often summarized in law books called hornbooks.

Husband-Wife Privilege See Marital Communications.

Illegitimate Child A child born when his or her parents are not married to each other.

Illicit Cohabitation Sexual intercourse between unmarried persons who are living together. See also Cohabitation.

Imminent Near at hand; coming soon; about to happen; immediate

Immunity A defense that prevents someone from being sued for what would otherwise be wrongful conduct.

Impediment A legal obstacle that prevents the formation of a valid marriage or other contract.

Implied Contract A contract that is not created by an express agreement between the parties but is inferred as a matter of reason and justice from their conduct and the surrounding circumstances. A contract that is manifested by conduct and circumstances rather than words of agreement. A contract that a reasonable person would infer exists, even though there is no express agreement. Also called an Implied in Fact Contract.

Imputed Disqualification Something is imputed when it is forced upon or attributed to someone or something else. If, for example, a lawyer or paralegal causes a law firm to be disqualified, we have an imputed disqualification.

In Camera In the judge's private chambers.

Incest Sexual intercourse between two people who are too closely related to each other as defined by court cases or statute.

Inchoate Partial; not yet complete.

Incident to Closely connected to something else.

Incompatibility A no-fault ground for divorce that exists when there is such discord between the husband and wife that it is impossible for them to live together in a normal marital relationship.

Incorrigible Habitually disobedient and disruptive.

Indemnify To compensate another for any loss of expense incurred.

Indemnity The right to have another person pay you the amount you were forced to pay.

Independent Professional Judgment Advice given by an attorney who is not subject to a conflict of interest. See Conflict of Interest.

Indigent Poor; without means to afford something.

In Forma Pauperis As a poor person. As such, certain filing fees are waived.

Inheritance Property received from someone who dies without leaving a valid will. The state determines who receives such property.

Injunction A court order requiring a person to do or to refrain from doing a particular thing.

In Loco Parentis Standing in the place of (and able to exercise some of the rights of) parents.

In Personam Jurisdiction See Personal Jurisdiction.

In Rem Jurisdiction The power of the court to make a decision affecting a particular *res*, which is a thing or status.

Instrument A formal document such as a will, deed, mortgage, or contract.

Intake Memorandum A written report that summarizes an interview with a new client of the office. It normally contains basic facts on the client and on his or her legal problems. See also Interoffice Memorandum; Memorandum of Law.

Intentional Infliction of Emotional Distress Intentionally causing severe emotional distress by extreme or outrageous conduct.

Intentional Torts Torts other than negligence and strict liability, e.g., assault, battery.

Intercept Program A procedure by which the government seizes designated benefits owed to a parent in order to cover the latter's delinquent child support payments.

Interlocutory Not final; interim.

Interoffice Memorandum A written report addressed to someone in the office where you work, usually a supervisor.

Interrogatories A written set of factual questions sent by one party to another before the trial begins.

Interspousal Between or pertaining to a husband and wife.

Intestate Dying without leaving a valid will.

Intestate Succession Obtaining property from a deceased who died without leaving a valid will. The persons entitled to this property are identified in the statute on intestate distribution.

Intrafamily Torts Torts committed by one family member on another.

In Vitro Fertilization The surgical removal of a woman's eggs and their fertilization with a man's sperm in the laboratory.

Irreconcilable Differences A no-fault ground for divorce that exists when there is such discord between the husband and wife that there has been an irremediable breakdown of the marriage.

Irremediable Breakdown See Irreconcilable Differences.

Irrevocable That which cannot be revoked or recalled.

Issue (1) Everyone who has descended from a common ancestor. (2) A legal question. See also Legal Periodical.

Joint and Several Liability More than one person is legally responsible. They are responsible together and/or individually for the entire amount.

Joint Custody Each parent shares legal custody and/or shares physical custody, often over alternating, but not necessarily equal, periods of time. Also called *shared custody.*

Joint Representation See Multiple Representation.

Joint Tenancy Property that is owned equally by two or more persons with the right of survivorship.

Joint Venture An express or implied agreement to participate in a common enterprise in which the parties have a mutual right of control.

Judgment Debtor/Judgment Creditor The person who loses and therefore must pay a money judgment is the judgment debtor. The winner is the judgment creditor.

Judicial Separation See Legal Separation.

Jurisdiction (1) The power of a court to act in a particular case. (2) The geographic area over which a particular court has authority. See also Concurrent Jurisdiction, Exclusive Jurisdiction, In Rem Jurisdiction, Personal Jurisdiction, and Subject-Matter Jurisdiction.

Juvenile Delinquent A young person under a designated age whose conduct would constitute a crime if committed by an adult.

Law Review/Law Journal A law review is a legal periodical published by a law school. Also called a law journal. See Legal Periodical.

Legal Advice Telling a specific person how the law applies to the facts of that person's legal problem or concern.

Legal Analysis   The application of rules of law to facts in order to answer a legal question or issue.

Legal Capacity   See Capacity.

Legal Custody   The right and duty to make decisions about raising a child.

Legal Encyclopedia   A legal encyclopedia is a multivolume set of books that summarizes almost every major legal topic.

Legal Issue   A question of law. See also Legal Analysis.

Legal Malpractice   See Malpractice.

Legal Periodical   An ongoing publication (e.g., published quarterly) that contains articles, studies, reports, or other information on legal topics.

Legal Separation   A declaration by a court that parties can live separate and apart even though they are still married to each other. Also called a *judicial separation*, a *limited divorce*, a *divorce a mensa et thoro*, and a *separation from bed and board*.

Legal Treatise   A legal treatise is a book written by a private individual (or by a public official writing as a private citizen) that provides an overview, summary, or commentary on a legal topic.

Legatee   A person to whom property (usually personal property) is given by will.

Legitimacy   The status or condition of being born in wedlock.

Legitimation   The steps that enable an illegitimate child to become a legitimate child.

Legitimize   To formally declare that children born out of wedlock are legitimate.

Letter of Authorization   A letter that tells the recipient that the office represents the client and that the client consents to the release of any information about the client to the office.

Letter of Nonengagement   A letter sent by a lawyer to a prospective client explicitly stating that the lawyer will not be representing this person.

Levy   To seize in order to satisfy a claim.

LEXIS   A legal database for computer research.

Liabilities   That which one owes; debts.

Lien   A security or encumbrance on property; a claim or charge on property for the payment of a debt. The property cannot be sold until the debt is satisfied.

Limited Divorce   See Legal Separation.

Living Apart   A no-fault ground for divorce that exists when a husband and wife have lived separately for a designated period of consecutive time.

Long Arm Jurisdiction   The power that a court obtains over a nonresident defendant who has such sufficient purposeful contact with the state that it is fair and reasonable for the state to adjudicate a dispute involving the defendant.

Loose-Leaf Service   A law book published as a three-ring binder containing pages that can be inserted and removed with relative ease.

Lord Mansfield's Rule   The testimony of either spouse is inadmissible on the question of whether the husband had access to the wife at the time of conception since such evidence would tend to bastardize (i.e., declare illegitimate) the child.

Loss of Consortium   A tort action for the loss of or the interference with the companionship, love, affection, sexual relationship, and services that the plaintiff enjoyed with his or her spouse before the latter was wrongfully injured by the defendant.

Loss of Services   A tort action for the loss of or the interference with the right of a parent to the services and earnings of his or her child because of the wrongful injury inflicted on the child by the defendant.

Lucid Interval   A period of time during which a person has the mental capacity to understand what he or she is doing.

Maintenance   Food, clothing, shelter, and other necessaries of life.

Majority   A designated age of legal adulthood in the state, usually eighteen.

Malice   Animosity; the intent to inflict injury.

Malicious Prosecution   A tort with the following elements: (1) to initiate or procure the initiation of legal proceedings—civil or criminal, (2) without probable cause, (3) with malice, and (4) the proceedings terminate in favor of the person against whom they were brought.

Malpractice   Professional wrongdoing. Legal malpractice normally refers to negligence by an attorney.

Manual   A practical treatise often containing standard forms along with checklists, summaries of the law, etc. Sometimes called a *Practice Manual*. See also Treatise.

Marital Communications   Those communications between a husband and wife while cohabiting. According to the privilege for marital communications, or the husband-wife privilege, one spouse cannot disclose in court any confidential communications that occurred between the spouses during the marriage.

Market Value   See Fair Market Value.

Married Women's Property Acts   Statutes removing

all or most of the legal disabilities imposed on women as to the disposition of their property.

Marriage   See Ceremonial Marriage, Common Law Marriage.

Martindale-Hubbell   The *Martindale-Hubbell Law Directory* contains a listing of the names and addresses of many of the practicing lawyers in the country. It also has a feature called the "Martindale-Hubbell Law Digest" that contains brief summaries of the law of every state.

Mediation   The process of submitting a dispute to a third party (other than a judge) who will help the parties reach their own resolution of the dispute.

Memorandum   A memorandum is any writing or notation sent to a person or to a file. It can be a highly formal and lengthy document or a simple one-line note. The plural of memorandum is *memoranda*.

Memorandum of Law   A written explanation of how the law applies to a given set of facts. See also Intake Memorandum.

Meretricious   Pertaining to unlawful sexual relations; vulgar or tawdry.

Meritorious   Having merit; having a reasonable basis to believe that a person's claim or defense will succeed.

Microfilm   Reels or cassettes that contain images or photographs that have been greatly reduced in size. Many law books and periodicals have been placed on microfilm.

Migratory Divorce   A divorce obtained in a state to which one or both of the spouses traveled before returning to their original state.

Minimum Fee Schedule   A list of fees announced by the bar association that an attorney *must* charge, at a minimum, for designated services rendered. Charging lower than the minimum would be unethical. (Today, however, minimum fee schedules are illegal.)

Minor   Someone under the age of majority in the state, which is usually eighteen.

Miscegenation   Mixing the races. The marriage or cohabitation of persons of different races.

Mitigating Circumstances   Facts that in fairness justify a reduction in damages because of the conduct of the aggrieved party.

Mitigation of Damages   Steps the aggrieved party could have taken to lessen the amount of injury or harm caused by the wrongdoer.

Model Rules of Professional Responsibility   See Canons of Ethics.

Mortgage   An interest in land that provides security

for the performance of a duty or the payment of a debt.

Multiple Representation   Representing more than one side in a legal matter or controversy. Also called joint representation and common representation.

National Conference of Commissioners on Uniform State Laws   See Uniform Laws.

Necessaries   The basic items needed by family members to maintain a standard of living. These items can be purchased and charged to the spouse who has failed to provide them.

Neglect   The failure to provide support, medical care, education, moral example, discipline, and other necessaries.

Negligence   Unreasonable conduct that causes injury or damage to someone to whom you owe a duty of reasonable care.

Nisi   Not final; interim.

No-Fault Grounds   Reasons for granting a divorce that do not require proof that either spouse committed marital wrongs.

Nonage   Below the required minimum age to enter a desired relationship or perform a particular task.

Noncustodial Parent   The parent with whom a child is not living.

Nonengagement   See Letter of Nonengagement.

Nonmolestation Clause   A clause in an agreement that the parties will not bother each other.

Notes to Decisions   Small paragraph summaries of court opinions that have interpreted a particular statute. These paragraphs are printed after the text of the statute within annotated codes.

Nuisance   An unreasonable interference with the use and enjoyment of land.

Obligor/Obligee   The person who has an obligation is the obligor. The person to whom this obligation is owed is the obligee.

Offer   To present something that can be accepted or rejected.

Open Adoption   An adoption in which the natural parent maintains certain kinds of contact with his or her child after the latter is adopted.

Operation of Law   Automatically because of the law. A result occurs by operation of law when it happens because the law mandates the result, not because a party agrees to produce the result.

Opinion   See Court Opinion.

Order to Show Cause (OSC)   An order telling a person to appear in court and explain why a certain order should not be entered.

Outstanding Unpaid.

Palimony A nonlegal term for payments made by one nonmarried party to another after they cease living together, usually because they entered an express or implied contract to do so while they were living together or cohabiting.

Paralegal A person with legal skills who works under the supervision of an attorney or who is otherwise authorized to use those skills.

Parens Patriae Parent of the country, referring to the state's role in protecting children and those under disability.

Parental Alienation Syndrome A disorder suffered by some children at the center of a custody dispute. They idealize one parent while expressing hatred for the other, even though the relationship with both parents was relatively positive before the dispute.

Parent Locator Service, State A state government agency that helps locate parents who are delinquent in child support payments. If the search involves more than one state, the Federal Parent Locator Service (FPLS) can help. The FPLS also helps in parental kidnapping cases.

Partition The dividing of land held by joint tenants and tenants in common. The division results in individual ownership.

Partnership A voluntary contract between two (or more) persons to use their resources in a business or other venture, with the understanding that they will proportionately share losses and profits.

Paternity Fatherhood.

Payee One to whom money is paid or is to be paid.

Payor One who makes a payment of money or who is obligated to do so.

Pecuniary Pertaining to or consisting of money.

Pendente Lite While the litigation is going on.

Per Curiam By the court. A court opinion that does not name the particular judge who wrote it.

Peremptory Challenges The elimination of a prospective juror during *voir dire*, which is the jury selection process. No reason need be given.

Periodic Payments A payment of a fixed amount for an indefinite period, or the payment of an indefinite amount for a fixed or indefinite period.

Personal Jurisdiction The power that a court obtains over an individual after proper service of process on him or her. The court's power to render a

decision that binds the individual defendant. Also called *in personam jurisdiction.*

Personal Property Movable property; any property other than real property. Also called chattels.

Personal Representative An executor or administrator of the estate of the deceased. Someone who formally acts on behalf of the estate of the deceased.

Petition A formal request that the court take some action. A complaint.

Physical Custody The parent with whom the child actually lives has physical custody.

Plaintiff The party bringing a claim against another.

Pleadings Formal documents that contain allegations and responses of the parties in litigation. The major pleadings are the complaint and answer.

Pocket Part A pocket in the inside back cover of some bound volumes. In this pocket you will find pamphlets that update the bound volume.

Polygamy The practice of having more than one spouse at the same time, usually more than two.

Post-Nuptial After marriage. See Separation Agreement.

Practice Manuals See Manual.

Practice of Law Assisting another to secure his or her legal rights. See Unauthorized Practice of Law.

Prayer A formal request.

Premarital Agreement See Antenuptial Agreement.

Premises (1) Lands and buildings. (2) The foregoing statements; matters stated earlier (in consideration of the premises).

Prenuptial Before marriage. See Antenuptial Agreement.

Preponderance of Evidence A standard of proof that is met if the evidence shows it is more likely than not that an alleged fact is true or false as alleged.

Present Value The amount of money an individual would have to be given now in order to produce or generate a certain amount of money in a designated period of time.

Presents, These This legal document.

Presumption An assumption of fact that can be drawn when another fact or set of facts is established. The presumption is *rebuttable* if a party can introduce evidence to show that the assumption is false.

Presumptive Created or arising out of a presumption; based on inference.

Primary Authority Any *law* that a court could rely on in reaching its conclusion, e.g., a constitutional provision, statute, regulation, ordinance, other court opinion.

Primary Caregiver Presumption The primary person who has taken care of the child should have custody.

Privilege A benefit, advantage, or right enjoyed by an individual.

Privilege against Self-Incrimination The right to refuse to answer questions that directly or indirectly connect the individual to a crime.

Privilege for Marital Communication See Marital Communications.

Probate A court proceeding at which a will is proved to be valid or invalid.

Probation Restricted and supervised living in the community in lieu of institutionalization.

Procedural Law Laws that pertain to the technical steps for bringing or defending actions in litigation before a court or an administrative agency. An example would be the number of days within which a party can request a jury trial in a divorce case after the complaint has been filed.

Proctor A person appointed for a particular purpose, e.g., protect the interests of a child.

Professional Responsibility See Canons of Ethics.

Pro Hac Vice For this particular occasion.

Proof of Service A statement that service of process on the defendant has been made.

Property Division The distribution of property accumulated by spouses as a result of their joint efforts during the marriage. Sometimes referred to as a property settlement.

Pro Se On one's own behalf; not using an attorney.

Pro Se Divorce A divorce obtained when a party represents himself or herself.

Prosecute To commence and proceed with a lawsuit.

Protective Order A court order directing a person to refrain from harming or harassing another.

Provocation The plaintiff incited the acts constituting the marital wrong by the other spouse.

Proxy Marriage The performance of a valid marriage ceremony through agents because one or both of the prospective spouses are absent.

Psychological Parent An adult who is not legally responsible for the care of a child, but who has formed a substantial emotional bond with the child.

Public Assistance Welfare or other forms of financial help from the government to the poor.

Public Policy The principle inherent in the customs, morals, and notions of justice that prevail in a state. The foundation of public laws. The principles that are naturally and inherently right and just.

Punitive Damages Money that is paid to punish the wrongdoer and to deter others from similar wrongdoing. Also called Exemplary Damages.

Putative Alleged or reputed.

Putative Spouse A person who reasonably believed he or she entered a valid marriage even though there was a legal impediment that made the marriage unlawful.

QDRO See Qualified Domestic Relations Order.

QMCSO See Qualified Medical Child Support Order.

Qualified Domestic Relations Order (QDRO) A court order that allows a nonemployee to reach pension benefits of an employee or former employee in order to satisfy a support or other marital obligation to the nonemployee.

Qualified Medical Child Support Order An order, decree, or judgment issued by a court that orders medical support or health benefits for the child of a parent covered under a group health insurance plan.

Quantum Meruit "As much as he deserves." Valuable services are rendered or materials are furnished by the plaintiff, and accepted, used, or enjoyed by the defendant under such circumstances that the plaintiff reasonably expected to be paid.

Quasi Community Property Property acquired by the spouses when they lived in a non-community property state before moving to a community property state. If they had acquired it in a community property state, it would have been community property.

Quasi Contract A contract created by the law to avoid unjust enrichment.

Quasi Marital Property Property that will be treated as having been acquired or improved while the parties were married even though the marriage was never valid.

Quitclaim A release or giving up of whatever claim or title you have in property. You are turning over whatever you have, without guaranteeing anything.

Real Property/Real Estate Land and anything permanently attached to the land.

Realize To obtain something actually, rather than on paper only.

Reasonable See Unreasonable.

Rebuttable Presumption See Presumption.

Recapture Rule The recalculation of a tax liability when the parties have improperly attempted to disguise a property division as alimony through front loading. See Front Loading.

Receivership The court appointment of someone to control and manage the defendant's property in order to ensure compliance with a court order.

Reconciliation The full resumption of the marital relationship.

Recrimination The party seeking the divorce (the plaintiff) has also committed a serious marital wrong.

Regional Digest See Digest. A regional digest contains summaries of opinions written by courts in a designated cluster of states. The full text of the opinions is found in the corresponding regional reporter for the digest.

Regional Reporter The volumes that contain the full text of opinions from courts within a designated cluster of states.

Regulation A law enacted by an administrative agency.

Rehabilitative Alimony Alimony for a limited time until the payee can get back on his or her feet and become financially self-sufficient. It is also known as *durational maintenance.*

Remand To send back for further proceedings.

Remedy The method or means by which a court or other body will enforce a right or compensate someone for a violation of a right.

Remise To give up or release.

Reporters The volumes that contain the full text of court opinions.

Reprimand A form of public discipline by which an attorney's conduct is declared to have been improper, but that does not limit his or her right to practice law.

Request for Admissions A request from one party to another that it agree that a certain fact is true or that a specified document is genuine so that there will be no need to present proof on such matters during the trial.

Res A thing or object; a status.

Rescission The cancellation of something.

Residence The place where someone is living at a particular time. See also domicile.

Res Judicata When a judgment on its merits has been rendered, the parties cannot relitigate the same dispute.

Respondeat Superior An employer is responsible for the conduct of employees while they are acting within the scope of employment.

Respondent The party responding to a position or claim of another party; the defendant. See also Appellee.

Restatement of Torts A treatise written by the American Law Institute that articulates or restates the law of torts.

Restitution An equitable remedy in which a person is restored to his or her original position prior to the loss or injury. Restoring to the plaintiff the value of what he or she parted with.

Restraining Order A form of injunction initially issued ex parte to restrain the defendant from doing a threatened act.

Resulting Trust A trust implied in law from the intention of the parties. A trust that arises when a person transfers property under circumstances that raise the inference that he or she did not intend the transferee to actually receive any interest in the property. See also Trust.

Retainer (1) The contract of employment between lawyer and client. (2) Money paid by a client to ensure that a lawyer will be available to work for the client. (3) Prepayment or deposit against future fees and costs of representation.

Right of Survivorship When one owner dies, his or her share goes to the other owners; it does not go through the estate of the deceased owner.

Rules of Professional Responsibility See Canons of Ethics.

Sanctions Penalties or punishments of some kind. (The word *sanction* can also mean approval or authorization.)

Secondary Authority Any *nonlaw* that a court could rely on in reaching its conclusion, e.g., an article in a legal periodical, a treatise.

Second-Parent Adoption The adoption of a child by a partner (or cohabitant) of a natural parent who does not give up his or her own parental rights.

Secret See Confidence.

Security Interest An interest in property that provides that the property may be sold on default in order to satisfy a debt for which the security interest was given.

Self-Incrimination See Privilege against Self-Incrimination.

Separate Maintenance Court-ordered spousal support while the spouses are separated.

Separate Property Property totally owned by one spouse; noncommunity property.

Separation See Legal Separation, Separation Agreement.

Separation Agreement A contract between spouses who have separated or who are about to separate in which the terms of their separation are spelled out, e.g., support obligations, child custody, division of property accumulated during the marriage. The agreement may or may not be later incorporated and merged in a divorce decree. Also called a post-nuptial contract.

Sequester To remove or hold until legal proceedings or legal claims are resolved. The noun is sequestration.

Service of Process Providing a formal notice to the defendant that orders him or her to appear in court in order to answer the allegations in the claims made by the plaintiff.

Settlor See Trust.

Severable Removable without destroying what remains. Something is severable when what remains after it is taken away can survive without it. The opposite of severable is essential or indispensable.

Severally Individually, separately.

Sham Pretended, false, empty.

Shared Custody See Joint Custody.

Shepardize To use the set of law books called *Shepard's Citations* to obtain specific information about a document, e.g., whether an opinion has been overruled, or whether a statute has been repealed.

Sole Custody One parent has physical and legal custody.

Solemnization The performance of a formal ceremony in public.

Solemnize The verb for solemnization.

Sole Proprietorship A form of business in which one person owns all the assets.

Solicitation Asking or urging someone to do something.

Specialization The development of experience and expertise in a particular area of practice.

Specific Performance A remedy for breach of contract that forces the wrongdoing party to complete the contract as promised.

Split Custody (1) One parent has legal custody, with physical custody going to each parent during alternating periods when the child lives with him or her. (2) Each parent receives sole custody of at least one

sibling with visitation rights as to the other siblings. The latter definition is also referred to as *divided custody.*

Standard Form A frequently used format for a document such as a contract, complaint, or tax return. The form is designed to be used by many individuals, often by filling in blanks that call for specific information commonly needed for such documents.

Standing The right to bring a case and seek relief from a court.

State Parent Locator Service (SPLS) See Parent Locator Service.

Statute An act of the legislature declaring, commanding, or prohibiting something.

Statute of Frauds The requirement that certain kinds of contracts be in writing in order to be enforceable, e.g., a contract for the sale of land; a contact that by its terms cannot be performed within a year.

Statute of Limitations The time within which a suit must be brought. If it is brought after this time, it is barred.

Statutory Code See Code.

Stepparent A person who marries the natural mother or father of a child, but who is not one of the child's natural parents.

Sterility Inability to have children; infertile.

Stipulation An agreement between the parties on a matter so that evidence on the matter does not have to be introduced at the trial.

Sua Sponte On its own motion.

Subject-Matter Jurisdiction The power of the court to hear a particular category or kind of case; its authority to make rulings on certain subject matters.

Subpoena A command to appear in court.

Subscribe To sign at the end of the document.

Substantive Law Laws that pertain to rights and obligations other than purely procedural matters. An example would be the right to a divorce on the ground of irreconcilable differences.

Substituted Service Service of process other than by handing the process documents to the defendant in person, e.g., service by mail.

Succession Obtaining property of the deceased, usually when there is no will.

Summary Dissolution A divorce obtained in an expedited manner because of the lack of controversy between the husband and wife.

Summons A formal notice from the court served on the defendant ordering him or her to appear and answer the allegations of the plaintiff.

Supervised Visitation Visitation by a parent with his or her child while another adult (other than the custodial parent) is present.

Surety Bond The obligation of a guarantor to pay a second party upon default by a third party in the performance the third party owes the second party.

Surrogate Mothers A woman who is artificially inseminated with the semen of a man who is not her husband, with the understanding that she will surrender the baby at birth to the father and his wife.

Survivorship See Right of Survivorship.

System An organized method of accomplishing a task that seeks to be more effective or efficient than alternative methods.

Talak "I divorce you." Words spoken by a husband to his wife in a Moslem divorce.

Tangible Having a physical form.

Tax Basis One's initial capital investment in property. An adjusted basis is calculated after making allowed adjustments and deductions to the initial capital investment, e.g., an increase in the basis because of a capital improvement.

Tenancy by the Entirety A joint tenancy held by a husband and wife. See also Joint Tenancy.

Tenancy in Common Property owned by two or more persons in shares that may or may not be equal, with no right of survivorship. Each tenant in common has a right to possession of the property. See also Right of Survivorship.

Tender Years Presumption Young children are better off living with their mother than with their father.

Termination of Parental Rights A judicial declaration that a parent shall no longer have a right to participate in decisions affecting the welfare of the child.

Testament A will.

Testate Dying with a valid will.

Testator The person who has died leaving a valid will.

Tort A civil wrong that has caused harm to a person or property for which a court will provide a remedy. Conduct that consists of a breach of contract or a crime may also constitute a tort.

Tort Immunity One who enjoys a tort immunity cannot be sued for what would otherwise be a tort.

Transferor/Transferee The person who transfers property is the transferor; the person to whom property is transferred is the transferee.

Transitory Divorce A divorce granted in a state where neither spouse was domiciled at the time.

Treatise Any book written by a private individual (or by a public official writing in a nonofficial capacity) that provides an overview of and commentary on an area of the law. Hornbooks, manuals, and formbooks are treatises.

Trespass Wrongfully intruding on land in possession of another.

Trimester Three months.

Trust When property is in trust, its legal title is held by one party (the trustee) for the benefit of another (the beneficiary). The creator of the trust is called the settlor.

Unauthorized Practice of Law Performing functions that only attorneys are allowed to perform. Violating the state statute on who can practice law. Engaging in legal tasks without attorney supervision and/or without special authorization to engage in such tasks.

Unconscionable Shocking to the conscience; substantially unfair.

Uncontested Not disputed; not challenged. See also Friendly Divorce.

Undertaking A promise, engagement, or enterprise.

Unemancipated Legally dependent on one's parent or legal guardian.

Unethical Conduct See Ethics, Canons of Ethics.

Unfit Demonstrating abuse or neglect that is substantially detrimental to a child.

Uniform Laws Proposed statutes written by the National Conference of Commissioners on Uniform State Laws. The proposals are submitted to state legislatures for consideration.

Uniform System of Citation The bible of citation form—also called the *blue book*. See Citation.

Unjust Enrichment Receiving property or benefit from another when in fairness and equity the recipient should make restitution of the property or provide compensation for the benefit even though there was no express or implied promise to do so.

Unreasonable That which is contrary to the behavior of an ordinary, prudent person under the same circumstances.

URESA Uniform Reciprocal Enforcement of Support Act.

Venue The place of the trial. When more than one court has subject-matter jurisdiction to hear a particular kind of case, the selection of the court is called *choice of venue*.

Verification of Complaint A sworn statement that the contents of the complaint are true.

Vested Fixed so that it cannot be taken away by future events or conditions; accrued so that you now have a right to present or future possession or enjoyment.

Viability The stage of fetal development when the life of an unborn child may be continued indefinitely outside the womb by natural or artificial support systems.

Vicariously Liable Being liable because of what someone else has done. Standing in the place of someone else who is the one who actually committed the wrong.

Visitation The right of a noncustodial parent to visit and spend time with his or her children.

Void Invalid whether or not a court declares it so.

Void ab Initio Invalid from the time it started.

Voidable Invalid only if a court declares it so.

Voir Dire Jury selection.

Waiver The relinquishment or giving up of a right or privilege because of an explicit rejection of it or because of a failure to take appropriate steps to claim it at the proper time.

Ward An individual, often a minor, under the care of a court-appointed guardian.

Welfare See Public Assistance.

WESTLAW A legal database for computer research.

Will A document that specifies the disposition of one's property and provides related instructions upon death.

Words and Phrases A multivolume legal dictionary published by West. Most of its definitions come from court opinions.

Work Product, Attorney See Attorney Work Product.

Writ of Execution See Execution of Judgment.

Wrongful Adoption A tort seeking damages for wrongfully stating or failing to disclose to prospective adoptive parents available facts on the health or other condition of the adoptee that would be relevant to the decision on whether to adopt.

Wrongful Birth An action by parents of an unwanted deformed child for their own damages. The defendant wrongfully caused the birth.

Wrongful Life An action by or on behalf of an unwanted deformed child for its own damages. The defendant wrongfully caused the birth.

Wrongful Pregnancy An action by parents of a healthy child that they did not want. The defendant wrongfully caused the birth. Also called *wrongful conception*.

Zygote A cell produced by the union of two gametes before cleavage.

INDEX

The Bifurcated Divorce Game
A Game for Adults

START

THE BIG FIGHT

Wife sees lawyer

Wife's lawyer won't begin without $
Go back to START

Wife sees another lawyer

Husband won't leave the home
SEE ADVERSE INSTRUCTION

Wife seeks injunction

Wife asks for everything

Husband represents himself
SEE SPECIAL INSTRUCTION

INJUNCTIVE RELIEF

Husband wants to reconcile
Go back to START

Husband gets lawyer
SEE SPECIAL INSTRUCTIONS

Husband's lawyer gets venue change

Husband files a response

Parties exchange financial data

Husband denies paternity
Go back to START

Wife does not tell truth on affidavit
SEE ADVERSE INSTRUCTIONS

TEMPORARY ORDERS

Depositions

Interrogatories

Husband won't pay
Back to INJUNCTIVE RELIEF

Disposition of real estate

Division of personal property

Paternity set for Trial
Go back to START

Requests for admission

PROPERTY DIVISION

GAL appointed for children
SEE SPECIAL INSTRUCTIONS

Custody mediated
Advance to DECREE

Children want to live with relatives
Go back to START

Home studies conducted

CUSTODY DETERMINATION

Visitation arranged

Husband kidnaps children
Go back to START

FINAL DECREE

Wife won't convey real property
Back to PROPERTY DIVISION

Wife can't collect support
Back to PROPERTY DIVISION

Parties convey personal property

Both parties move to modify
Back to DECREE

Husband moves for change of custody
Back to CUSTODY DETERMINATION

Parties have nervous breakdown

Wage assignment done
SEE SPECIAL INSTRUCTIONS

FINISH(ED)

For 2-10 players:
Two spouses, plus, if available, 1-5 children, 2-3 lawyers.

Dice (one each)

Playing Board

Each player rolls his/her dice in turn, moving playing piece the number of spaces on the board corresponding to the number on the dice

SPECIAL INSTRUCTIONS: Player landing on this space advances two—all other players lose two spaces

ADVERSE INSTRUCTION: Player landing on this space loses two—all other players advance two spaces

Game created by Susan Wendall Whicher
Designed by Robert Woolley

4 Family Advocate 32 (Summer, 1981)
Family Law Section, American Bar Association